ESSAYS IN EARLY CHRISTIANITY

CHILIASM PROPHECY MODEL AND NON-ELECT SALVATION POSSIBILITY

JONATHAN RAMACHANDRAN

ESSAYS IN EARLY CHRISTIANITY

Chiliasm Prophecy Model and Non-Elect Salvation Possibility

Jonathan Ramachandran

Christian Publishing House
Cambridge, Ohio

Copyright © 2025 Jonathan Ramachandran

All rights reserved. Except for brief quotations in articles, other publications, book reviews, and blogs, no part of this book may be reproduced in any manner without prior written permission from the publishers. For information, write, support@christianpublishers.org

ESSAYS IN EARLY CHRISTIANITY: Chiliasm Prophecy Model and Non-Elect Salvation Possibility by Jonathan Ramachandran

ISBN-13: **978-1-949586-42-8**

Table of Contents

Preface 7
ACKNOWLEDGEMENTS 9
INTRODUCTION 10
Essay 1: Non-Elect Salvation Possibility (NESP) 15
Essay 2: Thousand Year Gap for Prophecy in 1 Thessalonians 4:17 and 1 Corinthians 15:52 with Chiliasm Church Fathers 59
Essay 3: Two Water of Life References Separated by 1000 Years? 95
Essay 4: Shadow of Death Possibly Describing Non-Elect Salvation 134
Essay 5: Does Thief in the Night Phrase refer to Secret Coming of Christ?.. 156
Essay 6: Non-Elect Salvation Possibility via Saved by Fire 176
Essay 7: Prophecy of 5 Wise and 5 Foolish Virgins in Chiliasm 186
Essay 8: Did Christ Imply Non-Elect Salvation in Matthew 19:16-22? 224
Essay 9: Other Church Fathers or Quotes for Non-Elect Salvation 245
Essay 10: Baptism by Fire 320
Appendix I: An Important Note on Methodology..................... 344
Appendix II: Author Photos 348
Appendix III: About the Author 351
Appendix IV: Why I wrote this Book 353
Appendix V: My Stance Regarding the Pentecostal Claim of Speaking in Tongues 354
Appendix VI: The Abrahamic Promise in Chiliasm Prophecy . 355
Appendix VII: Garden of Eden in Chiliasm Framework 357
Appendix VIII: Antichrist Prophecy in Chiliasm Model 359

Appendix IX: Chiliasm Description of the 1000 Years Wedding of the Lamb 370

Appendix X: Will all Christians be in the First Resurrection? .. 383

Appendix XI: Are All Christians Kings and Priests during the Millennium? 394

Appendix XII: Chiliasm Prophecy Extension – An Example of My Interpolation 403

Appendix XIII: Non-Elect Salvation Possibility for Servant Rank in Chiliasm 409

Appendix XIV: Christian Apologetics Answers – Why believe in Christ? 414

Appendix XV: Typos 429

Bibliography 430

Preface

In every generation, believers have wrestled with questions about the final destiny of mankind, the nature of judgment, and the hope found in Christ. *Hope Beyond the Elect* is not written for theologians alone, but for every sincere Christian who wants to understand the Bible more deeply in light of the earliest preserved teachings of the Church. This work reflects years of study and reflection on the writings of early Christian leaders—many of whom believed and taught Chiliasm, or the literal Millennial Reign of Christ.

Though the original version of this book was written as a scholarly volume, this new edition has been simplified without compromising the biblical doctrine, interpretive method, or convictions held throughout. It is now structured and presented for the average churchgoer who desires clarity without losing theological depth. While some chapters explore deep prophetic themes, all are anchored in the plain teachings of Scripture and supported with direct quotations from the earliest Christian writers whose voices remain preserved in history.

One of the key themes throughout this work is the possibility of what I call **Non-Elect Salvation**—the idea that some may be saved outside the Elect Bride of Christ, but only through a path of divine judgment and cleansing. Though this view is not commonly taught today, several early Christian voices—men like Justin Martyr, Irenaeus, Clement of Alexandria, and others—hinted at a more layered view of salvation than modern systems often acknowledge. By comparing their words with Scripture, I present this idea as a **possibility**, not a dogma, encouraging readers to test all things carefully.

I've chosen to rely only on literal Bible translation philosophy and the **historical-grammatical method** of interpretation. No allegorizing or speculative typology is used. Everything here is based either on the **plain meaning of the Bible** or **quotes from the early Church Fathers** themselves, avoiding modern denominational overlays and theological systems foreign to the ancient texts.

This edition is not exhaustive but faithful. I do not claim perfection. Some interpretations presented here may be right, others may not be. Yet, everything is offered in sincerity, with reverence for the truth of God's Word and the witness of early Christian history. My aim is not to speculate, but to lay out the evidence and draw reasoned conclusions from it—always aware that the Lord alone will reveal all truth in the Day of His judgment.

To those reading this with a heart to seek Jehovah and follow Christ more faithfully, may these pages serve as a tool for deeper understanding, firmer conviction, and enduring hope. Whether one accepts the possibility of **hope beyond the Elect** or not, the ultimate message remains the same: **Believe in the Lord Jesus Christ and you will be saved** (Acts 16:31). May that truth guide all who read this work.

Jonathan Ramachandran

ACKNOWLEDGEMENTS

I would like to thank God the Father, God the Son (our Lord Jesus Christ), and God the Holy Spirit—our most blessed Trinity—for his unfailing mercy in our errors and for all the good things he has done for us. I thank my family: my father (Ramachandran), my late mother (Grace Selwak Kumari), my uncle (JPS—John Perera Sugumaran), and my brothers (Shankar Timothy and Siralan Joshua) for their support throughout my life. I also express my gratitude to other family members, as well as to both Christian and non-Christian friends (too many to name here), for their visible and invisible support.

Special thanks go to Dr. John W. (Jack) Carter, editor of the distinguished pastoral journal *The American Journal of Biblical Theology* (AJBT), for editing my first journal publication (Essay 1 in this book) and for offering insightful comments on the standards of academic writing.

Last but not least, this work could not have been completed without the skilled hand and brilliance of Mr. Edward D. Andrews, CEO and President of Christian Publishing House, who contributed tremendously to the editing process and the publication of this book.

Jonathan Ramachandran

INTRODUCTION

Introduction

If the writings in this book are proven correct on Judgment Day, then all glory belongs to God. If they are found to be incorrect on any point—or on many—the error is entirely my own. In the former case, it would show that truth can sometimes stand in stark contrast to the prevailing theological opinions of the day. In the latter, it may serve as a rival hypothesis, illustrating the capacity of the human mind to err. Either way, it underscores how challenging it is to interpret Scripture accurately—and how easily one can fall into error.

The Bible is a product of divine genius, composed in such a way that it allows for multiple levels of meaning. This is evident in the wide range of interpretations—both exegetical and eisegetical—produced by Christians throughout history, all from the same sacred text.

I once responded to an academic journal editor who questioned the presupposition of biblical inerrancy upheld by pastoral journals with the following statement:

"Pastoral journals are correct in their commitment to Scriptural inerrancy, a view I hold as well. Where manuscript variants exist, one reading must be correct, while others may reflect human interference. I have little interest in textual criticism unless the meaning of the passage changes depending on the variant. My concern lies only where the message itself is altered."

I subsequently posed a question to that journal, to which I never received a reply (my own opinion is written in italics):

1. In the entire history of its theological publications, has JournalX ever produced a genuinely *new* doctrinal contribution not already stated by another journal? If so, which article? May I see a copy—or at least an abstract or link?

Journal articles that merely reaffirm the theological stances of ancient Christian leaders—whether church fathers or reformers—through manuscript analysis do not yield new doctrines or possibilities of faith. In contrast, if the interpretations proposed in this book are correct, they represent new discoveries in theological understanding, as summarized in the conclusion.

We can define a theological discovery as "new" when no prior scholarly publication or denomination has stated it as a doctrinal position or even as a possibility.

The writings of the early church fathers and Scripture itself have long been available. Yet many have read these same texts without recognizing the interpretations proposed here. This indicates that the interpretive insight—if correct—is the new element, and that is the ultimate aim of biblical study.

2. What is the most-viewed article in *JournalX*?

This is a rhetorical question. Popularity does not establish truth. Among Protestants, it is well understood that the majority of professing Christians in history—and even today—are Roman Catholics or Eastern Orthodox believers, both of whom venerate the Virgin Mary and practice various extra-biblical traditions.[1] Despite their continuous participation in the Great Commission over nearly 2,000 years, this merely proves that God allows human free will to operate even in matters of doctrine. According to Scripture, greater doctrinal precision leads to higher eternal reward, as the essays in this volume will further demonstrate.

3. What is the most-cited article in *JournalX*?

Again, the purpose of this question is to prompt reflection. The frequency with which something is quoted does not determine its truth. Doctrinal accuracy is not established by consensus, nor by the approval or admiration of the majority—even within the Christian community.

4. What article in *JournalX* has introduced a completely new interpretation of Scripture not found in any denomination or reformer?

By "new interpretation," I mean discoveries consistent with the **Chiliasm** model—such as the proposal that 1 Thessalonians 4:17 and 1 Corinthians 15:52 describe events separated by a literal 1,000 years. If correct, this interpretation exposes a gap that has gone unrecognized by generations of readers who consulted the same early sources but failed to discern this possibility.

---

[1] Christian population statistics: Catholics 1,278,009,000; Protestants 625,606,000; Independents 421,689,000; Orthodox 293,158,000; Total Christians 2,508,432,000. See Todd M. Johnson and Gina A. Zurlo, eds., *World Christian Database* (Leiden/Boston: Brill, 2024). www.worldchristiandatabase.org

The point is this: while linguistic analysis and related disciplines are valuable, they must not overshadow the task of **Scriptural interpretation**, for it is here that theological rightness or error is ultimately determined.

Though the final judgment of doctrinal truth rests with God, it is appropriate—and necessary—for believers to engage in careful and enthusiastic debate on such matters. Journals, whether academic or pastoral, should be evaluated not by their conformity to tradition or technical rigor alone, but by how many new insights they bring to theological understanding.

As a historical precedent, Clement of Rome affirmed that doctrinal accuracy may not always reside with the majority. He asserted that a person who separates from a church over error—if proven correct—would receive great honor and glory from the Lord. This tradition is affirmed by Irenaeus of Lyons as having apostolic origin.[2]

This is a clear demonstration of the free will God permits, even in matters of doctrinal accuracy within a church that outwardly agrees with Christ.[3] Clement of Rome writes:

"Who then among you is noble-minded? Who compassionate? Who full of love? Let him declare, If on my account sedition and disagreement and schisms have arisen, I will depart, I will go away wherever ye desire, and I will do whatever the majority commands; only let the flock of Christ live on terms of peace with the presbyters set over it. He that acts thus shall procure to himself great glory in the Lord; and every place will welcome him. For the earth is the Lord's, and the fullness thereof. These things they who live a godly life that is never to be repented of, both have done and always will do."[4]

---

[2] Irenaeus of Lyons writes concerning Clement of Rome, "For there were many still remaining who had received instructions from the apostles. In the time of this Clement, no small dissension having occurred among the brethren at Corinth, the Church in Rome dispatched a most powerful letter to the Corinthians, exhorting them to peace, renewing their faith, and declaring the tradition which it had lately received from the apostles." *Against Heresies*, Book 3, Chapter 3, Point 3. www.newadvent.org/fathers/0103303.htm

[3] Luke 6:22–23 reads, "Blessed are you when men hate you, and when they exclude you, and revile you, and cast out your name as evil, for the Son of Man's sake. Rejoice in that day and leap for joy! For indeed your reward is great in heaven, for in like manner their fathers did to the prophets" (NKJV).

[4] Clement of Rome, *1 Clement*, Chapter 54. Translated by John Keith. In *Ante-Nicene Fathers*, Vol. 9, edited by Allan Menzies (Buffalo, NY: Christian Literature Publishing Co., 1896). www.newadvent.org/fathers/1010.htm

We know that apostles and prophets were without error in prophecy, as stated in Deuteronomy 18:20–22.[5] However, Jeremiah 23:36[6] permits errors in prophetic interpretation if the speaker identifies the prophecy as a personal effort (such as an academic analysis). But when one claims to speak directly on behalf of Jehovah and the prophecy proves false, the consequences are severe and potentially eternal, as outlined in Jeremiah 23:38–40.[7] Therefore, one must avoid careless or presumptuous prophetic declarations. A prophet is not required to understand every prophecy—as Daniel himself admitted[8]—but **no true prophet of God ever falsely prophesied in Jehovah's name**.

Consider this practical example: many today have encountered self-proclaimed prophet "Z" who declares that "God told me" you must marry person A, accept a job with company B, appoint person C to full-time ministry, or hire person D into your business or government agency.

The problem arises if this same prophet "Z" does not even recognize that 1 Thessalonians 4:17 and 1 Corinthians 15:50–52 describe two distinct prophetic events separated by 1,000 years (as argued in this volume). If he has consistently misrepresented them as describing a single "rapture" event, how then can one honestly believe the Most Blessed Holy Spirit is speaking through him—when He makes no error?

All of this points again to the operation of human free will under God's sovereign allowance, ensuring each person faces a fair and personal test of accountability. Each one will answer for their own doctrine and actions—including myself. For instance, if the evangelistic success and large numbers

---

[5] Deuteronomy 18:20–22: "But the prophet who presumes to speak a word in My name, which I have not commanded him to speak, or who speaks in the name of other gods, that prophet shall die. And if you say in your heart, 'How shall we know the word which the Lord has not spoken?'—when a prophet speaks in the name of the Lord, if the thing does not happen or come to pass, that is the thing which the Lord has not spoken; the prophet has spoken it presumptuously; you shall not be afraid of him" (NKJV).

[6] Jeremiah 23:36: "And the oracle of the LORD you shall mention no more. For every man's word will be his oracle, for you have perverted the words of the living God, the LORD of hosts, our God" (NKJV).

[7] Jeremiah 23:38–40: "'But since you say, "The oracle of the Lord!" therefore thus says the Lord: "Because you say this word, 'The oracle of the Lord!' and I have sent to you, saying, 'Do not say, "The oracle of the Lord!"' therefore behold, I, even I, will utterly forget you and forsake you, and the city that I gave you and your fathers, and will cast you out of My presence. And I will bring an everlasting reproach upon you, and a perpetual shame, which shall not be forgotten'"'" (NKJV).

[8] Daniel 12:8: "Although I heard, I did not understand. Then I said, 'My lord, what shall be the end of these things?'" (NKJV).

of Catholics and Orthodox (who venerate the Virgin Mary—comprising about 60% of Christianity today and historically[9]) are less valued by God due to doctrinal errors, then within Protestantism it may likewise be true that those holding more accurate theology will be fewer in number. The implications of this are weighty, for heavenly reward is not based merely on profession, but on depth of obedience. Christ declared:

"Whoever therefore breaks one of the least of these commandments, and teaches men so, shall be called least in the kingdom of heaven; but whoever does and teaches them, he shall be called great in the kingdom of heaven. For I say to you, that unless your righteousness exceeds the righteousness of the scribes and Pharisees, you will by no means enter the kingdom of heaven."[10]

And again:

"But others save with fear, pulling them out of the fire, hating even the garment defiled by the flesh."[11]

---

[9] Todd M. Johnson and Gina A. Zurlo, eds., *World Christian Database* (Leiden/Boston: Brill, 2024). www.worldchristiandatabase.org

[10] Matthew 5:19–20: "Whoever therefore breaks one of the least of these commandments, and teaches men so, shall be called least in the kingdom of heaven; but whoever does and teaches them, he shall be called great in the kingdom of heaven. For I say to you, that unless your righteousness exceeds the righteousness of the scribes and Pharisees, you will by no means enter the kingdom of heaven" (NKJV)

[11] Jude 1:23: "But others save with fear, pulling them out of the fire, hating even the garment defiled by the flesh" (NKJV).

Essay 1: Non-Elect Salvation Possibility (NESP)

Reflection

It is a divine gift to recognize when something is seriously wrong, even if no one else in the church perceives it—just as Martin Luther did. The next necessity is courage: the willingness to speak out and stand firmly upon the authority of God's Word, even if doing so puts one's life at risk. Luther could scarcely have imagined that his convictions would give rise to what we now know as the Protestant Reformation, encompassing approximately two in five Christians today—roughly 40%—who continue to fulfill the Great Commission. God's providential hand upon Luther's life reveals that, despite human weakness, Jehovah is able to save and use individuals mightily. His example confirms the **wideness of divine mercy** available through salvation in Christ for all who believe in the Lord Jesus.

Introduction

Martin Luther famously published his Ninety-Five Theses in protest against the Roman Catholic Church's extra-biblical practices.[12] This bold act initiated the Protestant Reformation, which continues today as a movement striving toward biblical fidelity, though marked by denominational variety. While there is some degree of unity, Protestantism remains divided in both theology and practice. Yet, such divisions may serve a divine purpose, for Scripture itself states that they help to reveal who is approved in God's sight.[13]

The Gospel is not merely a proclamation about Christ—it is also a call to obey His words. Christ warned that many would say, "Lord, Lord," claiming to have prophesied, cast out demons, and performed miracles in His name, only to hear Him declare, "I never knew you." The way to avoid such condemnation is clearly stated: "Whoever hears these sayings of Mine, and does them."[14]

It is in this context that I propose a single reform I believe should be emphasized or recovered in the Christian faith.

---

[12] Stephen J. Nichols, *Martin Luther's 95 Theses*. Presbyterian & Reformed Pub Co, USA, 2002.

[13] 1 Corinthians 11:18–19.

[14] Matthew 7:21–24.

Sola Unity in Diversity

The parable of the sower reveals three categories of harvest—**thirtyfold, sixtyfold,** and **hundredfold**—which reflect differing levels of obedience to God's Word, and by extension, varying degrees of reward.[15] These distinctions indicate that even among Christians, there can be varying levels of doctrinal or practical accuracy, according to the **measure of faith** each one has received from God.[16]

1.1 Balance Between Tolerance and Doctrinal Friction

Since the **measure of faith** is apportioned by God, there is little value in attempting to force or compel another believer to accept a doctrinal view that he or she may never fully grasp—regardless of whether that view ultimately proves correct. Recognizing this can foster greater patience and reduce unnecessary conflict among Christians.

Each step toward greater doctrinal accuracy reflects a closer walk with God. He allows free will so that those who **diligently seek Him** may be duly rewarded. While strong theological expression is permissible, I do not advocate for practices of **theological shaming**. Judgment must be left to God. We ought to strive for **Christian unity**, showing love and cooperation in the areas where we agree. Sadly, it is not uncommon for Christians to be excluded from ministry or employment opportunities simply because they differ in doctrine or practice. Such exclusion is often unjust. A framework of doctrinal liberty is crucial, so that our personal convictions do not become a stumbling block for others. God alone will judge and reward each believer accordingly.[17]

True unity is demonstrated when believers are able to fellowship with others who differ in non-essential doctrines. Christians may abstain from participating in practices that contradict their conscience, yet still work together in areas of mutual agreement. This approach preserves each individual's theological integrity while promoting collective service in ministry. Doctrinal differences that fall within acceptable boundaries may affect one's final **reward**, but should not jeopardize salvation itself. Heretical doctrines, however, must be excluded from the conversation, as Scripture calls us to be holy in both word and thought.

---

[15] Matthew 13:8; Matthew 19:29, which calls the hundredfold level a final reward context.

[16] Romans 12:3, 6.

[17] Romans 14:4.

1.2 The Lord Jesus' Parable of the Wheat and the Tares

In the parable of the wheat and the tares, Christ teaches an even greater level of tolerance within His Church. He instructs that both the wheat and the tares should be permitted to grow together until the end of the age.[18] This model—ordained by God Himself—implies that Church governance is not to be executed with a heavy hand, but with patience and foresight. The Lord warns that prematurely uprooting the tares may result in uprooting the wheat as well. In other words, zealous but misguided efforts to purge perceived error could result in the exclusion of sincere and capable Christians. Leaders who act in such haste will be held accountable for the spiritual harm they cause.

This principle may also reflect the role of **free will** in spiritual transformation. A person who appears to be a tare today might become wheat tomorrow through genuine repentance. The Church must therefore function as a **cradle of repentance**, preserving space for restoration. St. Irenaeus of Lyons (c. 130–202 C.E.) articulates this concept clearly when he writes, *"But man, being endowed with reason, and in this respect like to God, having been made free in his will, and with power over himself, is himself the cause to himself, that sometimes he becomes wheat, and sometimes chaff."* [19]

If God permitted the broader institutional Church to remain in doctrinal error for nearly a thousand years—approximately from 500 to 1500 C.E.—then we must humbly acknowledge the possibility that any particular church or interpretation today could also be mistaken in certain areas. Let God be the Judge of which individuals or denominations are ultimately correct. Meanwhile, we are free to present our scriptural studies and early patristic references in defense of our position.

One doctrinal boundary generally agreed upon across Protestant, Catholic, and Orthodox traditions is found in the **Apostles' Creed** and more prominently, the **Nicene Creed** (325 C.E.).[20] These historical formulations help guard the Church from outright heresy while preserving some level of interpretive liberty within that boundary.

1.3 Non-Elect Salvation Possibility

---

[18] Matthew 13:28–29, the Parable of the Wheat and the Tares.

[19] Philip Schaff, *Ante-Nicene Fathers*, Vol. I, Christian Literature Publishing Co., 1885. St. Irenaeus of Lyons, *Against Heresies*, Book 4, Chapter 4.

www.ccel.org/ccel/schaff/anf01.ix.vi.v.html

[20] Philip Schaff, *Nicene and Post-Nicene Fathers: Second Series*, Vol. 14, *The Seven Ecumenical Councils*, Christian Literature Publishing Co., 1885. www.ccel.org/ccel/schaff/npnf214.html

St. Gregory Nazianzus (c. 329–390 C.E.) offers an important statement regarding the diversity of theological inquiry, especially concerning matters such as judgment and salvation. He writes:

> "Then here too I will provide thee with broad paths. Philosophize about the world or worlds; about matter; about soul; about natures endowed with reason, good or bad; about resurrection, about judgment, about reward, or the Sufferings of Christ. For in these subjects to hit the mark is not useless, and to miss it is not dangerous. But with God we shall have converse, in this life only in a small degree; but a little later, it may be, more perfectly, in the Same, our Lord Jesus Christ, to Whom be glory for ever. Amen."[21]

This statement appears to allow for doctrinal variation in subjects such as **judgment**, where historically there have been three principal theological views regarding the fate of the damned: **eternal hell**,[22] **annihilation**,[23] and **Christ-centered universalism**.[24]

St. Gregory's phrasing implies that one's position on judgment is not salvific in itself; that is, speculation in this area will neither save nor condemn. However, it may affect one's **eternal reward**. His position serves as a reminder that majority opinion—even when sustained for a thousand years and accompanied by widespread evangelistic success—can still be theologically mistaken, as Martin Luther's example clearly demonstrated.

In order not to misrepresent St. Gregory's meaning regarding "judgment," it is necessary to consider his other writings. These appear to point either toward universalism or, more precisely, toward a form of **non-elect salvation**.[25] For instance, he writes:

---

[21] St. Gregory Nazianzus, *First Theological Oration (Oration 27)*, Point IX. www.newadvent.org/fathers/310227.htm

[22] Paul Helm, *The Last Things: Death, Judgment, Heaven and Hell*. Carlisle, PA: Banner of Truth, 1989.

[23] LeRoy Edwin Froom, *The Conditionalist Faith of Our Fathers*, 2 vols. Washington, DC: Review and Herald, 1965.

[24] Richard Bauckham, *Universalism: A Historical Survey*. Themelios 4, no. 2, January 1979.

[25] *"Non-elect salvation"* is a term coined to classify those Church Father quotations that seem to refer to individuals being saved after death, often following a judgment of fire in hell. This view falls short of full universalism, as many of these same writers also affirm eternal hell or annihilation. Thus, the term is used to describe those who are "saved from hell" yet are not part of the elect.

> "Let these men then if they will, follow our way, which is Christ's way; but if they will not, let them go their own. Perhaps in it they will be baptized with Fire, in that last Baptism which is more painful and longer, which devours wood like grass, and consumes the stubble of every evil."[26]

This passage refers to **1 Corinthians 3:12–19** and envisions a fiery purification, possibly extended to those outside the Church—those not following Christ's path. It suggests a postmortem judgment that results in eventual salvation for some, even if through a more painful process. Such language supports the idea of a class of people who are **saved through fire**, without being part of the elect who are saved in the first resurrection or who are fully joined to the Church in this life.

2.0 Detailed Exploration of Non-Elect Salvation Possibility Example

This topic warrants careful consideration because it pertains directly to **prophecy** and the divergent interpretations throughout Church history concerning the fate of non-Christians. The earlier citation from St. Gregory Nazianzus appears to reference the context of **1 Corinthians 3:15**, describing a person being *"saved by fire."* This, however, does not seem to refer to faithful Christians, but rather to individuals such as the **Novatian heretics**—those who do not follow the path of Christ but walk in their own ways. For this reason, the passage may suggest a form of **non-elect salvation**.[27]

To extend this interpretation, let us consider the parable of the sower. In that parable, the seed sown on "good ground" symbolizes believers, yielding thirtyfold, sixtyfold, and hundredfold fruit—each level representing increasing obedience and corresponding reward. These **rewarded Christians** appear to align more closely with the description in **1 Corinthians 3:14**, where one's enduring works lead to receiving a reward.[28] In contrast, the person in **1 Corinthians 3:15**, whose works are burned entirely yet who is *"saved, yet so as through fire,"* receives **no reward**. Even the lowest level of reward—the thirtyfold—still implies some form of honor or recognition. Therefore, it may be more accurate to associate the "saved by

---

[26] St. Gregory Nazianzus, *Oration 39*, Chapter XIX, *Oration on the Holy Lights*. www.newadvent.org/fathers/310239.htm (Accessed August 2, 2024).

[27] 1 Corinthians 3:15: "If anyone's work is burned, he will suffer loss; but he himself will be saved, yet so as through fire" (NKJV).

[28] 1 Corinthians 3:14: "If anyone's work which he has built on it endures, he will receive a reward" (NKJV).

fire" individual with a different category altogether—possibly someone **outside the elect**, experiencing a lesser form of salvation.

A common objection arises from **1 Corinthians 3:11**, which states that the only foundation is **Jesus Christ**, leading some to insist that this passage refers exclusively to Christians.[29] However, this interpretation can be broadened by considering **Romans 2:6–11**, which speaks of God rendering judgment to each person according to his deeds. The passage describes a group who, without conscious knowledge of the Gospel, pursue righteousness and receive **glory, honor, and immortality**.[30] This concept is expanded in **Romans 2:14–16**, where Gentiles, who lack the Law, nevertheless act in accordance with it by nature, demonstrating that the **work of the Law is written on their hearts**. These individuals are judged by their conscience and may be **excused** on the Day of Judgment.[31]

Should these be considered **saved by works** simply because they never believed in Christ during their earthly lives? Not necessarily. Their salvation, if granted, would still be grounded in **Christ's perfect blood and atonement**, applied posthumously in the **spirit world**. Such individuals would not have rejected Christ; rather, they never had the opportunity to hear the Gospel and believe in Him. This may offer a theological framework for understanding how salvation can extend beyond the elect, while still being entirely dependent upon Christ's redemptive work.

This interpretive model explains why some early Church Fathers, such as St. Gregory, may have taught differently when discussing **1 Corinthians 3:15**. The complexity of the verse allows for multiple layers of meaning, and its **difficult interpretive nature** accounts for the diversity of opinions among patristic writers.

2.1 Unlearnt and Learnt Cases

In contrast to the earlier "unlearnt" case in **Romans 2:14–16**, **Romans 2:12–13** refers to those who have received and understood divine revelation. This "learnt" group is described as the **hearers of the Law**, who are only

---

[29] 1 Corinthians 3:11: "For no other foundation can anyone lay than that which is laid, which is Jesus Christ" (NKJV).

[30] Romans 2:6–11: "He will render to each one according to his deeds: eternal life to those who by patient continuance in doing good seek for glory, honor, and immortality; but to those who are self-seeking and do not obey the truth… tribulation and anguish… glory, honor, and peace… for there is no partiality with God" (NKJV).

[31] Romans 2:14–16: "When Gentiles, who do not have the law, by nature do the things in the law… these show the work of the law written in their hearts… in the day when God will judge the secrets of men by Jesus Christ" (NKJV).

justified if they also become **doers of the Law**—that is, if they obey the commands of the Gospel.[32] These may correspond to the category referenced in **1 Corinthians 3:15**, the so-called *"saved by fire"* group.

However, if a person truly has **faith in Christ**, it would follow that he should receive at least a **minimum reward**, placing him in the category of **1 Corinthians 3:14**, where enduring works result in divine commendation.[33] It is difficult to imagine a believer with genuine faith receiving no reward and being saved only by fire, since Scripture teaches that faith itself is a profound gift. Furthermore, as James affirms, **faith without works is dead**—hence, any person whose faith is alive must also have fruit, making them fit for reward.[34]

These interpretive distinctions are not intended to confuse, but to express the legitimate exegetical tension present when harmonizing these texts. Just as the unlearned are granted an opportunity to believe upon **seeing Christ** in the spirit world, so too might those described in **1 Corinthians 3:15** belong to a group who only come to faith **after seeing**, as described in **John 6:29, 36, and 40**.[35] In those passages, Christ rebukes those who saw Him and yet still refused to believe. The pattern of post-resurrection faith is further supported by the example of the Apostle Thomas, who came to believe only after seeing the risen Lord.[36]

Whether this interpretation is correct or speculative remains open to debate. The concept of **non-elect salvation** is drawn from careful reflection on early patristic sources and Scriptural connections. Yet a key question remains: If faith is possible after death through seeing the risen Christ, how is it fair to Christians who believed on earth without seeing?

2.2 Chiliasm Church Fathers

---

[32] Romans 2:12–13: "For as many as have sinned without law will also perish without law, and as many as have sinned in the law will be judged by the law (for not the hearers of the law are just in the sight of God, but the doers of the law will be justified)" (NKJV).

[33] 1 Corinthians 3:14: "If anyone's work which he has built on it endures, he will receive a reward" (NKJV).

[34] James 2:26: "For as the body without the spirit is dead, so faith without works is dead also" (NKJV).

[35] John 6:29, 36, 40: "This is the work of God, that you believe in Him whom He sent… But I said to you that you have seen Me and yet do not believe… that everyone who sees the Son and believes in Him may have everlasting life" (NKJV).

[36] John 20:29: "Jesus said to him, 'Thomas, because you have seen Me, you have believed. Blessed are those who have not seen and yet have believed'" (NKJV).

Certain early Church Fathers—whom I refer to as the **Chiliasm Church Fathers**—taught that Christians will participate in the **first resurrection**, reigning with Christ as **kings and priests** for a thousand years in **sinless human bodies** on the old earth and under the old heavens.[37] According to these sources, this reign is not the final state. At the conclusion of the Millennial Kingdom, at the **last trumpet**, believers undergo a transformation: their human, though sinless, bodies are changed into **celestial or angelic** bodies—no longer composed of flesh and blood—fit to inherit the **new heaven**.[38]

This eschatological view is striking in light of **2 Peter 1:20**, which declares that **no prophecy of Scripture is of any private interpretation**.[39] In harmony with this, Chiliasm Fathers interpreted **1 Corinthians 15:52**, which speaks of a sudden transformation *"at the last trumpet,"* not as a reference to the rapture at the beginning of the millennium, but as describing the final transformation at its conclusion.[40] This transformation is closely associated with the great mystery of Christ becoming **one flesh with His Bride**, the Church.[41]

This interpretation indirectly supports the **non-elect salvation** possibility. In the final chapters of Scripture, the **Bride** (the Church) is clearly distinguished from the **nations who are saved**.[42] The Bride is seen descending from heaven, having already undergone the full glorification process. In contrast, the saved nations exist in the **new earth** in **terrestrial (earthly) resurrection bodies**, not in celestial form.[43] Not all who are saved in this final order enter the heavenly city, suggesting a division in post-judgment destinies based not merely on salvation, but on degree and nature of resurrection glory.

It is not my purpose here to develop the full eschatological framework of Chiliasm, but these points illustrate how such a model provides coherent

---

[37] Revelation 1:6; 5:10; 20:4–6.

[38] Revelation 21:1: "Now I saw a new heaven and a new earth, for the first heaven and the first earth had passed away..." (NKJV).

[39] 2 Peter 1:20: "Knowing this first, that no prophecy of Scripture is of any private interpretation" (NKJV).

[40] 1 Corinthians 15:52: "In a moment, in the twinkling of an eye, at the last trumpet... and we shall be changed" (NKJV).

[41] Ephesians 5:31–32: "The two shall become one flesh... but I speak concerning Christ and the church" (NKJV).

[42] Revelation 21:9–10; 24–27.

[43] 1 Corinthians 15:40–42.

theological space for the idea of **non-elect salvation** alongside a gradation of glory in the resurrection.

2.3 Chiliasm Prophecy Regarding the Change from Human to Angelic

In the final chapter of Scripture, the **Bride**—that is, the Church—extends an invitation to others to receive salvation, saying, *"Come!... let him take the water of life freely"* (**Revelation 22:17**).[44] This indicates that others, beyond the Bride herself, are still being called to partake of eternal life. According to the teachings of the **Chiliasm Church Fathers**, Christians are resurrected into **sinless human bodies** and reign with Christ during the **millennial kingdom**, which occurs on the **old earth and under the old heavens**, where they had previously suffered.[45] After this millennial period, they are transformed from fleshly human form into an **angelic or heavenly state**, becoming *no longer flesh and blood*.

Thus, it can be inferred that during the millennial reign, believers—still in sinless human bodies—continue to receive life through the **"water of life,"** which proceeds from the throne of God and the Lamb.[46] However, once they undergo the final transformation and are *"changed"*—no longer human or composed of flesh and blood—they no longer require the **water of life** as a source of sustenance.[47] This is because, in their glorified state as the **one flesh** of Christ, they partake of divine life **directly from Him**, no longer mediated through an external source. If this understanding is correct, then it follows that the **nations who are saved** (as described in Revelation) continue to receive life in the final **new earth** by drinking from this **river of the water of life**, as they remain in **terrestrial (earthly)** resurrection bodies.

The change from **human** to **no longer flesh and blood**, as described by the Chiliasm Fathers, stands in marked contrast to nearly all modern interpretations of prophecy, whether Protestant, Catholic, or Orthodox.[48]

---

[44] Revelation 22:17: *"And the Spirit and the bride say, 'Come!' And let him who hears say, 'Come!' And let him who thirsts come. Whoever desires, let him take the water of life freely"* (NKJV).

[45] St. Irenaeus of Lyons, *Against Heresies*, Book 5, Chapter 32; Tertullian, *Against Marcion*, Book III, Chapter 25; online at www.newadvent.org.

[46] Revelation 7:9–17: *"These are the ones who come out of the great tribulation... for the Lamb who is in the midst of the throne will shepherd them and lead them to living fountains of waters"* (NKJV).

[47] Revelation 22:1: *"And he showed me a pure river of water of life, clear as crystal, proceeding from the throne of God and of the Lamb"* (NKJV).

[48] St. Justin Martyr (Dialogue with Trypho, Chapter 124), St. Irenaeus (Against Heresies, Book 4, Chapter 38), Tertullian (*Against Marcion*, Book 3, Chapter 25; Book 5, Chapter 10), St. Victorinus of Pettau (*Commentary on the Apocalypse*, ch. 18), and St. Methodius of Olympus (*Banquet of the Ten Virgins*, Discourse 9, Chapter 5), all describe the transition from human

One may rightly ask: could this prophetic understanding have been known to the early Church but later lost, only now being recovered through closer textual and historical analysis? Considering the weight of patristic testimony in favor of this view, one might reasonably conclude that this interpretation bears a high degree of probability. Nevertheless, as with all unfulfilled prophecy, its full meaning will remain **a mystery** until the time of its fulfillment.

Remarkably, even **St. Augustine of Hippo**, though not a Chiliast, appears to have preserved this prophetic expectation—that believers would eventually undergo a change from human nature into **angelic being** after their resurrection.[49] This indicates that the doctrine may have endured longer and more widely than often assumed.

2.4 Chiliasm Prophecy for the Timeline of the Last Trumpet

In my view, the early **Chiliasm Church Fathers** offer a more trustworthy framework for interpreting prophecy, particularly in light of the biblical affirmation that *"no prophecy of Scripture is of any private interpretation"* (2 Peter 1:20). Their proximity to the apostolic era and consistency with Scripture provide a compelling basis for considering their views as more likely to reflect the truth.

The only verse in the Bible that explicitly uses the phrase **"last trumpet"** is **1 Corinthians 15:52**. According to **St. Victorinus of Pettau**, this last trumpet occurs at the *end* of the **1,000-year Millennial Reign**, not at its beginning. His interpretation aligns closely with that of **St. Irenaeus of Lyons**, who seems to describe a **second group of righteous individuals** being raised in **identical human bodies**—which corresponds to **terrestrial glory** as described in **1 Corinthians 15:40**.[50] This appears to imply a form of **non-elect salvation**, especially since Irenaeus references this resurrection in

---

resurrection bodies to angelic or celestial forms after the Millennial Reign. These testimonies indicate a consistent early teaching that "flesh and blood" cannot inherit the final Kingdom, aligning with **1 Corinthians 15:50–52**.

[49] St. Augustine, *Catena Aurea*, Commentary on Matthew 25:1–13: *"When they have been taken in who have been changed into angelic being, all entrance into the kingdom of heaven is closed..."*; online source: ccel.org.

[50] 1 Corinthians 15:40: *"There are also celestial bodies and terrestrial bodies; but the glory of the celestial is one, and the glory of the terrestrial is another"* (NKJV).

the context of his **opponents**, suggesting that even some who had resisted the truth might ultimately be raised to life.[51]

This interpretation could correspond to the **"surprised sheep"** among the nations at the Final Judgment, who do not appear to know the Lord personally, yet are known by Him because of their acts of charity toward His people.[52] They are called "righteous" on the basis of having done good to **"His brethren"**—that is, to Christians themselves.[53]

Within the **Chiliasm Prophetic Timeline**, believers are already resurrected and reigning with Christ during the millennium. They are **glorified**, not merely in spirit but bodily, and live in **sinless human form** throughout that period. At the Final Judgment—after the millennial reign—they are transformed from **flesh and blood** into a **heavenly, incorruptible state**. In contrast, these *newly judged righteous* ones, the "surprised sheep," are only now receiving salvation. It would be improper, therefore, to conflate them with the Church, as they are being saved at the *end* of the 1,000 years.

This understanding provides a theological rationale for encouraging **non-Christians** to do **acts of charity** toward Christians. Such actions may result in mercy at the Final Judgment. We do not discourage faith or repentance, but we also acknowledge the **possibility** of **non-elect salvation** through such merciful judgment. At the same time, we must remain faithful in proclaiming the warning of **eternal hell** for those who reject Christ during this present life.

In the end, when both the possibility of **eternal punishment** and the **hope of postmortem mercy** are weighed, each person must decide whether to believe in Christ now—or face the consequences of their choice.

2.5 Evidence in the Book of 1 Enoch

Further corroboration for this doctrine of **transformation at Judgment Day** and the **non-elect salvation possibility** may be found in the Book of 1 Enoch, particularly **chapter 50**, which presents a sequence consistent with both themes. Although this book is **not recognized as**

---

[51] St. Irenaeus of Lyons, *Against Heresies*, Book 5, Chapter 13: *"At the end, when the Lord utters His voice by the last trumpet... the dead shall be raised... those that have done good to the resurrection of life..."* Online: www.newadvent.org/fathers/0103513.htm.

[52] Matthew 25:37–40: *"Then the righteous will answer Him, saying, 'Lord, when did we see You hungry and feed You...?'... The King will answer... 'inasmuch as you did it to one of the least of these My brethren, you did it to Me'"* (NKJV).

[53] Matthew 12:50: *"For whoever does the will of My Father in heaven is My brother and sister and mother"* (NKJV).

canonical by most Christian traditions, it is regarded as **Scripture** by the **Ethiopian Orthodox Tewahido Church**, which has preserved a unique and early canon from antiquity.[54]

According to **1 Enoch 50**, a **"change"** is said to occur to the **"elect"**—a term commonly interpreted as referring to **Christians or the righteous**—at the time of **Judgment Day**. The passage begins by describing this transformation in radiant terms: *"the light of days shall abide upon them"*, and they are clothed with *"glory"* and *"honour."*[55] This matches the **heavenly transformation** described in **1 Corinthians 15:52** and reinforces the Chiliasm Church Fathers' teaching that Christians are ultimately changed from **terrestrial** to **celestial glory** at the end of the 1,000 years.

What is especially noteworthy in this passage is the clear **juxtaposition** of the elect being glorified with another group of individuals—presumably **non-elect sinners**—who **witness this glorification, repent,** and are **saved**, though it is clearly stated that they **"shall have no honour through the name of the Lord of Spirits, yet through His name shall they be saved"**. This appears to affirm the possibility of **repentance after witnessing Judgment,** or what may be referred to as a **"believing after seeing"** salvation experience. Such a view would align with the concept of **non-elect salvation**, as the passage does not assign these individuals to the elect or

---

[54] Ethiopian Orthodox Tewahido Church Holy Synod. *A Short History, Faith and Order of the Ethiopian Orthodox Tewahido Church, Canonical Books*, Addis Ababa, 1983. www.ethiopianorthodox.org/english/canonical/books.html

[55] R.H. Charles, *The Apocrypha and Pseudepigrapha of the Old Testament*, Oxford: Clarendon Press, UK, 1913. Book of 1 Enoch, Chapter 50:

"1 And in those days a change shall take place for the holy and elect,
And the light of days shall abide upon them,
2 On the day of affliction on which evil shall have been treasured up against the sinners.
And the righteous shall be victorious in the name of the Lord of Spirits:
And He will cause the others to witness (this)
That they may repent
And forgo the works of their hands.
3 They shall have no honour through the name of the Lord of Spirits,
Yet through His name shall they be saved,
And the Lord of Spirits will have compassion on them,
For His compassion is great.
4 And He is righteous also in His judgement,
And in the presence of His glory unrighteousness also shall not maintain itself:
At His judgment the unrepentant shall perish before Him.
5 And from henceforth I will have no mercy on them, saith the Lord of Spirits."
Online source: www.ccel.org/c/charles/otpseudepig/enoch/ENOCH_2.HTM

reward-bearing class, but acknowledges their repentance and salvation as the result of **divine compassion**.

At the same time, **1 Enoch 50** makes a distinction between those who repent upon seeing and those who **refuse to repent**. The latter are described as **perishing eternally**, having **no further access to mercy**, reinforcing the finality of judgment for the unrepentant. This dichotomy closely parallels the biblical warnings in passages such as **Hebrews 10:26–27** and **Revelation 21:8**, while leaving room for the view that **some may still be redeemed**, even if only on the edge of final judgment.

Although **1 Enoch** is not an inspired text within the dominant Christian canon, its **alignment with early apostolic-era themes** and the **doctrinal insights it offers**—especially when it is consistent with Scripture—warrants serious consideration. Its eschatological language and its division between the **glorified elect**, the **repentant saved**, and the **irredeemably wicked** offers a framework that strongly supports the **Chiliasm prophetic model** and the **possibility of non-elect salvation**, without contradicting the biblical teaching of final judgment.

2.6 Earliest Chiliasm Quotes

One of the earliest extra-biblical testimonies of **Chiliasm**—the belief in a literal 1,000-year earthly reign of Christ—is found in the writings of **St. Papias**, Bishop of Hierapolis (c. 60 C.E. – c. 163 C.E.). He is described by **St. Irenaeus of Lyons** as *"an ancient man who was a hearer of John and a companion of Polycarp"*, a pedigree that strongly affirms his credibility as a transmitter of apostolic doctrine. **Eusebius** also acknowledges this connection, preserving his witness in the historical record.[56]

Given St. Papias' proximity to the apostles and their direct disciples, it is highly unlikely that he would err on so central a prophetic matter. His testimony harmonizes with Christ's parable of the Sower, which outlines **three reward levels—thirtyfold, sixtyfold, and hundredfold—** corresponding to varying degrees of fruitfulness among believers.[57] St. Papias taught that all who attain to these levels will be part of the **Wedding of the Lamb** and will ultimately dwell in the **heavenly Jerusalem**.[58]

---

[56] St. Irenaeus of Lyons, *Against Heresies*, Book 5, Chapter 33, (Schaff, *NPNF*, Vol. 1, Christian Literature Publishing Co., 1885), www.ccel.org/ccel/schaff/anf01.ix.vii.xxxiv.html; Eusebius, *Ecclesiastical History*, Book 3, Chapter 36, www.newadvent.org/fathers/250103.htm

[57] Mark 4:20, "But these are the ones sown on good ground, those who hear the word, accept it, and bear fruit: some thirtyfold, some sixty, and some a hundred" (NKJV).

[58] Revelation 19:7–9. Revelation 21:1–3.

Before examining his quote in detail, it is useful to review what the Bible says regarding the **stratification of heaven**. The clearest biblical evidence is found in **2 Corinthians 12:2–4**, where the Apostle Paul speaks of being *"caught up to the third heaven"*, which he also calls *"Paradise."* [59] While the Bible does not explicitly outline multiple layers of heaven beyond this passage, several Jewish traditions offer speculative models that may reflect early Christian thought. For instance, a legend recorded in *The Legends of the Jews* relates that Adam was taken to the *"Paradise of the third heaven"*, possibly alluding to the same cosmological understanding Paul held.[60] Other apocalyptic texts, like the Ascension of Levi, describe a **progressive ascent through the heavens**, each more glorious than the last.[61]

St. Papias' preserved statement reflects a sophisticated eschatology in which the final inheritance of the saved is **graded according to their fruitfulness**. He writes:

> "As the presbyters say, then those who are deemed worthy of an abode in heaven shall go there, others shall enjoy the delights of Paradise, and others shall possess the splendour of the city; for everywhere the Saviour will be seen, according as they shall be worthy who see Him. But that there is this distinction between the habitation of those who produce an hundredfold, and that of those who produce sixty-fold, and that of those who produce thirty-fold; for the first will be taken up into the heavens, the second class will dwell in Paradise, and the last will inhabit the city; and that on this account the Lord said, 'In my Father's house are many mansions': for all things belong to God, who supplies all with a suitable dwelling-place, even as His word says, that a share is given to all by the Father, according as each one is or shall be worthy. And this is the couch in which they shall recline who feast, being invited to the wedding. The presbyters, the disciples of the apostles, say that this is the gradation and arrangement of those who are saved." [62]

---

[59] 2 Corinthians 12:2–3, "God knows—such a one was caught up to the third heaven. 3And I know such a man—whether in the body or out of the body I do not know, God knows—4how he was caught up into Paradise and heard inexpressible words, which it is not lawful for a man to utter" (NKJV).

[60] Louis Ginzberg, *Legends of the Jews*, Vol. 1, *The Death of Adam*, The Jewish Publication Society, Philadelphia, 2003, 96.

bibleresourcespart2.wordpress.com/wp-content/uploads/2015/10/legends-of-the-jews-complete-in-2-volumes.pdf

[61] Ibid., *The Ascension of Levi*, 437.

[62] St. Papias, *Fragment V*, www.newadvent.org/fathers/0125.htm

This hierarchical view of eternal dwelling places is not only attributed to St. Papias but is also affirmed by **St. Irenaeus**, who regards it as authoritative and consistent with apostolic tradition.[63] According to this vision, the **heavenly Jerusalem** functions as the **lowest tier** in the heavenly order—the final abode for the thirtyfold class—yet it is also a **shared gathering place** for all the elect, consistent with **Hebrews 12:22–24**.[64]

This city descends and connects to the **new earth** described in **Revelation 21**, signifying the interface between the heavenly and earthly domains in the eternal state.[65] Some **Jewish traditions** even place the **heavenly Jerusalem** in the **fourth or seventh heaven**, depending on the source.[66] These traditions often pair the **heavenly Temple** with the **heavenly Jerusalem**, indicating a unified location for divine worship and dwelling.[67]

St. Papias' detailed eschatological framework is striking in its clarity and fidelity to Scriptural imagery. When read alongside similar early Jewish and Christian traditions, his writings provide invaluable insight into how the **earliest generation of post-apostolic Christians understood salvation, reward, and the architecture of the age to come.**

This means that **St. Papias' quote** implies a descending motion of the **heavenly Jerusalem**, likely originating from the **fourth or seventh heaven** according to Jewish tradition, and eventually becoming the **lowest heaven** that connects to the **final new earth**. According to his description, Christians who produce **sixtyfold fruit** receive their final abode in **Paradise**, which aligns with the **third heaven** as referenced by the Apostle Paul. Those who attain the **hundredfold fruit level** inherit even higher mansions in the heavens, above both Paradise and the city.

While all Christians—whether they produce thirtyfold, sixtyfold, or hundredfold—may have access to any part of these heavenly realms, their **final dwelling place**, or "mansion," corresponds to their level of

---

[63] St. Irenaeus of Lyons, *Against Heresies*, Book 5, Chapter 36, www.newadvent.org/fathers/0103536.htm

[64] Hebrews 12:22–24.

[65] Revelation 21:9.

[66] Ginzberg, *Legends of the Jews*, Vol. 1, *The First Day*, 9. "As to the fourth heaven in which the heavenly temple is situated, comp. Zebahim 62a; Menahot 110a... PR 20, 98b, seems to locate the heavenly temple in the seventh heaven."

[67] Ibid., *The Contest of the Mountains*, 595. "In the time to come God will cause the heavenly Jerusalem to descend upon these four mountains... the heavenly Jerusalem is substituted, as is often the case, by the Temple..."

fruitfulness, as affirmed by St. Papias. This concept finds its closest biblical parallel in the promise to the overcomers in **Revelation 3**, where Christ says:

> "Behold, I am coming quickly! Hold fast what you have, that no one may take your crown. He who overcomes, I will make him a pillar in the temple of My God, and he shall go out no more. I will write on him the name of My God and the name of the city of My God, the New Jerusalem, which comes down out of heaven from My God. And I will write on him My new name." [68]

This passage affirms both the **descending nature of the New Jerusalem** and the **personal inheritance** promised to those who persevere in faith and obedience.

When we consider this in light of **St. Papias' earlier quote**, the implications of Revelation 3 become even more significant.

First, this heavenly inheritance clearly applies **only to the elect—the Church, the Christians**—as affirmed in **verse 13**.[69] Each Christian is said to dwell from the **heavenly Jerusalem** onward, never to go out again (**verse 12**), which implies that their permanent, glorified abode is in the heavens and not on the earth. This strongly suggests that any righteous individuals whose final dwelling remains on the **new earth**, and not in heaven, could represent **non-elect salvation**—those who are saved, but are not members of the elect Bride.

Additionally, every Christian is said to **receive a crown (verse 11)**,[70] further distinguishing the **elect** as kings and priests. In contrast, the presence of **gates in the New Jerusalem** and the explicit restriction of access (**Revelation 21:24, 27**) implies that not all saved individuals from the nations will have free entry. If all saved persons were admitted equally into heaven, **there would be no need for such gates**. Thus, those who do not possess crowns or priestly status may be saved but remain outside the heavenly city, dwelling instead on the renewed earth.

Importantly, these events occur **after** the opening of the **Book of Life**,[71] within the **new heavens and new earth**,[72] and **not** during the **Millennial**

---

[68] Revelation 3:11–13 (NKJV).
[69] Revelation 3:13 (NKJV)
[70] Revelation 1:6 (NKJV)
[71] Revelation 20:11–15 (NKJV)
[72] Revelation 21:1–3 (NKJV)

Reign on the old earth and heavens.[73] According to the **Chiliasm Church Fathers**, the elect are resurrected in **perfect human bodies** during the Millennium. After this period, they undergo a transformation into **angelic, celestial forms**, fitting them for eternal dwelling in the heavens. Conversely, those among the nations who are saved at the **Great White Throne Judgment** possess **terrestrial glory** only[74]—suitable for the new earth, but not for entry into the heavens. This means no one can pass through the gates deceptively, for even the **physical nature** of the body defines where one can go.

Further, when combining the prophecies of **Tertullian, St. Victorinus**, and **St. Irenaeus of Lyons** concerning the **last trumpet**, a striking distinction appears. The **elect** are changed into heavenly glory **at the end** of the 1000 years, while a **second group of righteous individuals** are just then being raised and saved—indicating **non-elect salvation**. The **first resurrection** takes place **before** the 1000 years,[75] while the **second resurrection** occurs **after** it has ended.[76]

This fits a **literal reading** of Christ's prophecy[77] and the vision of **Daniel the prophet**,[78] which both describe a resurrection at the end where **both the wicked and the righteous** are raised simultaneously. Under this reading, the first resurrection is distinct and separate from this final event.

Additionally, in the **Gospel of John**, the phrase **"last day"** refers to the **Millennial Reign**,[79] the final epoch of this current world order. The phrases **"the hour now is"** and **"the hour is coming"** seem to denote two different moments within this "last day"—the beginning (first resurrection) and the end (second resurrection).[80]

This distinction appears again in John 5:25, where Christ says: *"Most assuredly, I say to you, the hour is coming, and now is, when the dead will hear the voice of the Son of God..."*[81] The first clause—"hour now is"—aligns with the **elect's resurrection** at the start of the 1000 years, while the second clause—"hour

---

[73] Revelation 20:4–6 (NKJV)
[74] 1 Corinthians 15:40 (NKJV)
[75] Revelation 20:4–6 (NKJV)
[76] Revelation 20:5 (NKJV)
[77] John 5:28–29 (NKJV)
[78] Daniel 12:2–3 (NKJV)
[79] John 6:40 (NKJV)
[80] Hebrews 4:6, 8–9 (NKJV)
[81] John 5:25 (NKJV)

is coming"—points to the **non-elect's resurrection** at the end, if this interpretation is valid.

St. Irenaeus of Lyons also confirms this reading. He describes the resurrection of **both the wicked and a second group of righteous individuals** occurring **simultaneously**, in association with the **last trumpet** and the phrase **"the hour shall come"**—omitting any reference to "hour now is".[82] This supports the notion that two distinct resurrection events are described in Scripture.

Turning again to **Daniel's prophecy**, it is evident that Christians, already resurrected during the Millennium, undergo their transformation into **celestial glory** at the time of this second resurrection. Daniel states, *"Those who are wise shall shine like the brightness of the firmament, and those who turn many to righteousness like the stars forever and ever"*[83]—a fitting image of glorified, angelic splendor.

It is no small matter that **St. Irenaeus** asserts that **every Christian is a priest**.[84] Therefore, any saved individuals in the final earth who are not priests must be **non-elect**, since priesthood is an essential mark of the elect.

As additional support, **St. Gregory Nazianzus** refers to a **"cleansing fire"** by which some are saved, and to another **unquenchable fire** by which others are condemned. He writes:

> "For I know a cleansing fire which Christ came to send upon the earth... I know also a fire which is not cleansing, but avenging... and one even more fearful still than these, the unquenchable fire... For all these belong to the destroying power; though some may prefer even in this place to take a more merciful view of this fire, worthily of Him That chastises."[85]

In a later passage, he distinguishes **three classes among the saved—slaves, hired servants, and sons**.[86] Since all who are elect are called **sons of God**,[87] and since the **Marriage of the Lamb** includes **only the elect** during the first resurrection,[88] it follows that the **hired servants** may represent

---

[82] St. Irenaeus of Lyons, *Against Heresies*, Book 5, Chapter 13
[83] Daniel 12:3 (NKJV)
[84] St. Irenaeus of Lyons, *Against Heresies*, Book 5, Chapter 34
[85] St. Gregory Nazianzus, *Oration 40*, Chapter 36
[86] St. Gregory Nazianzus, *Oration 40*, Chapter 13
[87] Galatians 3:26 (NKJV)
[88] Matthew 25:1–13

Israel's non-elect saved, and the **slaves** the **Gentile non-elect saved**—perhaps those described as the "surprised sheep" of the nations,[89] in the final judgment scene that summarizes the **entire Millennial Reign**.[90]

2.7 Does Error in Eschatology Make One a Heretic?

St. Justin of Rome (also known as **St. Justin Martyr**, c. 100–160 C.E.) affirms that **Chiliasm** is true prophecy,[91] yet he distinguishes between two categories of those who differ in eschatology: some who **err in interpretation yet remain pious and godly Christians**, and others who are **outright heretics**.[92]

It must be clearly stated that the interpretations offered in the earlier sections of this work—particularly regarding the possibility of **non-elect salvation** in relation to the **Chiliasm prophetic model**—are not presented as infallible conclusions but as **reasoned possibilities** based on extant early writings. The hope is that **other scholars**, using the **same primary sources**—namely, the writings of the **Chiliasm church fathers**—might construct alternative eschatological frameworks that either affirm or challenge these proposals. If other scholars or denominations (including Protestant groups) cannot build their eschatology upon these early witnesses, **is that not a precarious position**, especially in light of the verse that warns, **"no prophecy of Scripture is of any private interpretation"?**[93]

---

[89] Matthew 25:31–46

[90] Matthew 25:14–30

[91] St. Justin of Rome writes, "But I and others, who are right-minded Christians on all points, are assured that there will be a resurrection of the dead, and a thousand years in Jerusalem, which will then be built, adorned, and enlarged, [as] the prophets Ezekiel and Isaiah and others declare. ... And further, there was a certain man with us, whose name was John, one of the apostles of Christ, who prophesied, by a revelation that was made to him, that those who believed in our Christ would dwell a thousand years in Jerusalem; and that thereafter the general, and, in short, the eternal resurrection and judgment of all men would likewise take place. Just as our Lord also said, 'They shall neither marry nor be given in marriage, but shall be equal to the angels, the children of the God of the resurrection.' Luke 20:35" (*Dialogue with Trypho*, Chapters 80–81), www.newadvent.org/fathers/01286.htm.

[92] St. Justin of Rome writes, "I admitted to you formerly, that I and many others are of this opinion, and [believe] that such will take place, as you assuredly are aware; but, on the other hand, I signified to you that many who belong to the pure and pious faith, and are true Christians, think otherwise. Moreover, I pointed out to you that some who are called Christians, but are godless, impious heretics, teach doctrines that are in every way blasphemous, atheistical, and foolish." (*Dialogue with Trypho*, Chapter 80), www.newadvent.org/fathers/01286.htm.

[93] 2 Peter 1:20, "knowing this first, that no prophecy of Scripture is of any private interpretation" (NKJV).

If Jehovah declared through the apostles that prophecy is not open to private interpretation, then it follows that **in His providence**, He would have preserved **some degree of right interpretation** in the writings of the earliest and most faithful Christians. Whether the quotations and interpretations of the **Chiliasm church fathers** presented here are precisely accurate is open to discussion; however, **the burden of proof is not mine alone**. Every Christian group has the responsibility to examine these earliest testimonies and demonstrate that their own eschatology can be supported by them—**if truth is to be upheld consistently**.

Where these early writers differ, it is clear that **not all views can be correct**. This is precisely why I treat their teachings as **possibilities**, rather than dogma. To handle these writings honestly means to acknowledge **our limitations** and present interpretations that are **evidence-based**, even if open to revision. Jehovah understands the limits of human knowledge, and I believe that presenting well-grounded possibilities—especially from early **Chiliasm writers**—is a responsible approach to eschatological study.

I have chosen to prioritize the writings of **Chiliasm church fathers** because they are **the earliest surviving sources** in Christian history to explicitly address prophetic and eschatological matters. Where discrepancies arise, I usually defer to the **earlier voices**, particularly those of **St. Justin Martyr** and **St. Irenaeus of Lyons**, as the most reliable guides.

The common objection among some Protestant scholars—that these quotes were corrupted by **Roman Catholic or Eastern Orthodox transmission**—remains **unproven**. In fact, the **Catholic Church** later rejected Chiliasm under the influence of **St. Augustine of Hippo**, who was himself influenced by **Origen of Alexandria**.[94] Yet, **the same Catholic Church preserved the Chiliasm quotes**, which is a strong indication of their authenticity. Historically, Jehovah used **unbelieving Jews** to preserve the **Old Testament**. From a Protestant standpoint, is it unreasonable to suppose that **He could similarly use the Catholic Church** to preserve the **Chiliasm tradition**, even if they ultimately rejected its teachings?

2.8 St. Augustine of Hippo and his view on Eschatological Heresy

St. Augustine of Hippo (354 C.E. – 430 C.E.) is a giant of faith not just for Roman Catholics but also for the Orthodox and Protestants. However, not many know that the one who converted St. Augustine and even baptized

---

[94] *Catholic Encyclopedia*, "Millennium and Millenarianism," an article which explains the fundamental idea of millenarianism, as understood by Christian writers, published between 1907 and 1912, www.catholic.com/encyclopedia/millennium-and-millenarianism.

him around 386 C.E. was none other than **St. Ambrose of Milan**.[95] It is noteworthy that St. Ambrose (c. 340 C.E. – c. 397 C.E.) expressed what appears to be a form of **non-elect salvation** in his writings, as seen in the following quote: *"For now, since all do not believe, all do not seem to be in subjection. But when all have believed and done the will of God, then Christ will be all and in all. And when Christ is all and in all, then will God be all and in all."*[96] This idea has so permeated Roman Catholic theology that the **post–Vatican II Catechism** includes the line: *"In hope, the Church prays for 'all men to be saved.'"[97]

St. Augustine of Hippo does not consider even **Christian Universalists**—those who reject eternal hell but believe in a purgatorial hell that lasts only "to the ages"—to be heretics. This is significant because the Church Fathers were well known for openly labeling heresies. In fact, Augustine even suggested the possibility that a form of salvation **outside the kingdom of God** (what might be described as **non-elect salvation** on the **final new earth**) could be conceivable, even in the smallest degree.[98]

This allows us to follow his faith as well.[99] His openness to the **possibility** of non-elect salvation—when he writes of those who *"may wish to think about gradations of punishment, or the relief or intermission of their misery"*— shows that such a position was not treated as damnable. If St. Augustine and his own spiritual father St. Ambrose were not heretics for holding these views, then the position itself cannot be automatically condemned either.

2.9 Possible Scripture-Level Vision – Shepherd of Hermas

---

[95] TeSelle, Eugene. *Augustine the Theologian.* Wipf and Stock, USA, 2002. ISBN 978-1-57910-918-9, p. 343.

[96] St. Ambrose of Milan, *Exposition of the Christian Faith*, Book 5, Chapter 15. Available at: www.newadvent.org/fathers/34045.htm

[97] *Catechism of the Catholic Church*, CCC 1821. Available at: http://www.catholic-catechism.com/ccc_1.74.618.851.956.1256.1261.1349.1821.1900.2240.2574.2634.2822.htm

[98] St. Augustine of Hippo writes: *"112. It is quite in vain, then, that some—indeed very many—yield to merely human feelings and deplore the notion of the eternal punishment of the damned and their interminable and perpetual misery... Now, if this wrath were all there is in man's damnation, and even if it were present only in the slightest degree conceivable—still, to be lost out of the Kingdom of God, to be an exile from the City of God, to be estranged from the life of God... this would be a punishment so great that, if it be eternal, no torments that we know could be compared to it, no matter how many ages they continued. 113. The eternal death of the damned... will therefore abide without end... no matter what some people... may wish to think about gradations of punishment, or the relief or intermission of their misery."* (Enchiridion, "The Last Things", Chapter 29). Available at:

www.tertullian.org/fathers/augustine_enchiridion_02_trans.htm

[99] Hebrews 13:7, "Remember those who rule over you, who have spoken the word of God to you, whose faith follow, considering the outcome of their conduct."

The *Shepherd of Hermas* (also called *The Pastor*) was regarded by several early Church Fathers—including **Chiliasm proponents** such as **St. Irenaeus of Lyons** and even **Tertullian**—as Scripture. It was also included in some of the **earliest known biblical collections**, such as the Roman Canon (Muratorian Fragment) in the West and **Codex Sinaiticus** in the East.[100]

Tertullian, writing as a Montanist, admitted, *"But I would yield my ground to you, if the scripture of the Shepherd, which is the only one which favours adulterers, had deserved to find a place in the Divine canon; if it had not been habitually judged by every council of Churches (even of your own) among apocryphal and false (writings); ... I, however, imbibe the Scriptures of that Shepherd who cannot be broken."*[101] Though he ultimately rejected it as canonical, his description still reflects the esteem the work held.

Of greater weight is the witness of **St. Irenaeus of Lyons**, who explicitly refers to *The Shepherd* as Scripture, writing, *"Truly, then, the Scripture declared, which says, First of all believe that there is one God, who has established all things, and completed them..."*[102] This parallels a preserved passage from *The Shepherd*, which states: *"First of all, believe that there is one God who created and finished all things, and made all things out of nothing."*[103]

The **Muratorian Fragment** (c. 170 C.E.), the oldest surviving canonical list, also mentions *The Shepherd of Hermas*, stating: *"But Hermas wrote The Shepherd very recently, in our times... and therefore, it ought indeed to be read; but it cannot be read publicly to the people in church... for it is after their time."*[104] This indicates that while *The Shepherd* was not included among the apostolic writings, it was still held in high regard.

St. Athanasius of Alexandria, in his **39th Festal Letter**, did not place *The Shepherd* within the New Testament canon. Yet he allowed it for edifying instruction, placing it alongside works like *Esther*, which is accepted as

---

[100] Codex Sinaiticus. Available at: codexsinaiticus.org

[101] Tertullian (c. 155–240 C.E.), *On Modesty (De pudicitia)*, Chapter 10. Available at: newadvent.org/fathers/0407.htm

[102] St. Irenaeus of Lyons, *Against Heresies*, Book 4, Chapter 20. Available at: newadvent.org/fathers/0103420.htm

[103] *The Shepherd of Hermas*, Book 2, Commandment 1. Available at: newadvent.org/fathers/02012.htm

[104] G. M. Hahneman, "The Muratorian Fragment and the Origins of the New Testament Canon," in *The Canon Debate*, ed. L. M. McDonald and J. A. Sanders (Massachusetts: Hendrickson, 2002), 405–415.

canonical by Protestants today.[105] Though he made a distinction between canonical Scripture and ecclesiastical reading, his inclusion of *The Shepherd* in this latter category leaves room for consideration, especially since **no ecumenical council ever condemned the work**. Its exclusion from later usage seems due more to practical obscurity than doctrinal error.

The Shepherd of Hermas uses symbolic language to present its vision of salvation. It describes **the elect** as those within the "Tower of Repentance"—a parabolic reference to the **Church**.[106] This very imagery was also quoted by **St. Irenaeus**, who referenced the "beautiful elect tower" in his eschatological writings.[107]

Significantly, *The Shepherd* also introduces the concept of **non-elect salvation**. It refers to rejected stones—symbolic of people—who are not fit for inclusion in the Tower, yet are not utterly lost. Some of these stones had heard the Gospel and desired baptism but fell away into sin.[108]

This **non-elect salvation** is contingent upon repentance during **fiery punishment** and a past association with righteousness, likely through obedience to moral commands (holiness and charity). The text insists that they can no longer be added to the Tower—representing the Church—implying that their salvation is of a **different category**, one not associated with priesthood or kingship.

In this framework, we may equate the Tower (Church) with the **final New Heavens**, while the rejected but salvaged stones may correspond to the **final New Earth**—consistent with the earlier distinction between elect and non-elect destinations. Notably, this view also contradicts **Roman Catholic purgatory**, which asserts that souls are ultimately restored into the Church (i.e., the Tower) after purification. *The Shepherd*, by contrast, denies such reintegration, suggesting a **permanent exclusion from the Tower** while still allowing salvation in a **lesser realm**.

These individuals are not portrayed as ignorant of the Gospel; rather, they **knew the truth**, desired baptism, but fell back into sinful living. Thus,

---

[105] St. Athanasius, *39th Festal Letter* (c. 367 C.E.). Available at: ntcanon.org/Athanasius.shtml

[106] *The Shepherd of Hermas*, Book 1, Vision 3, Chapter 3. Available at: newadvent.org/fathers/02011.htm

[107] St. Irenaeus, *Against Heresies*, Book 4, Chapter 36. Available at: newadvent.org/fathers/0103436.htm

[108] *The Shepherd of Hermas*, Book 1, Vision 3, Chapter 7. Available at: newadvent.org/fathers/02011.htm

their repentance does not occur during earthly life, further confirming that this is not a case of unlearned ignorance but of **posthumous repentance** under divine discipline.

2.10 Rabbinical Judaism and its Two Types of Proselytes

In rabbinical Judaism, Gentile converts were generally classified into two distinct categories: the **"full proselyte"** (*ger tzedek*, or devout proselyte) and the **"half proselyte"** (*ger toshav*, or limited proselyte). The former was expected to observe the entire Torah, while the latter was only required to keep the **seven Noahide laws** in order to attain a place in the world to come. These seven include the prohibitions against **idolatry, blasphemy, murder, fornication** (immoral sexual acts), **theft, cruelty to animals** (e.g., tearing a limb from a living creature), and the command to **establish a system of justice**. This traditional enumeration is preserved in the **Babylonian Talmud (Sanhedrin 56a–b)** and **Tosefta Avodah Zarah 9:4**.[109]

A key area of debate among the rabbis regarding the *ger toshav* involves the definition and extent of **idolatry**, particularly how strictly or loosely it is to be interpreted.[110] This ambiguity may offer some theological space for considering Christ's **Parable of the Good Samaritan**[111] as an illustration of **non-elect salvation**. Though Christ plainly declared that the Samaritans "do not know God,"[112] He nevertheless commended the Samaritan who extended mercy and compassion—even toward an enemy Jew. This can be seen as an analogy for a non-Christian who practices the **Charity Doctrine** toward a Christian.

Such an interpretation aligns with the scenario of the **surprised sheep** in **Matthew 25**, who do not recognize Christ and ask, *"Lord, when did we see You hungry, thirsty, a stranger, naked, sick, or in prison?"* Yet, He receives them

---

[109] Berlin, Meyer; Zevin, Shlomo Yosef. "BEN NOAH." *Encyclopedia Talmudica: A Digest of Halachic Literature and Jewish Law from the Tannaitic Period to the Present Time, Alphabetically Arranged*, Vol. IV. Jerusalem: Yad Harav Herzog (Emet, 1992 [1969]), 360–380.

[110] See Klein, Reuven Chaim, "World Religions and the Noahide Prohibition of Idolatry," *Journal of Halacha and Contemporary Society* 79 (2022): 109–167. [hcommons.org/deposits/download/hc:50798/CONTENT/shituf-article.pdf]

[111] Luke 10:25, 27, 30, 33–37: A Samaritan, whom Jews regarded as religiously corrupt, is shown to fulfill the law's demand to love one's neighbor, even surpassing the conduct of the priest and Levite.

[112] John 4:22, "You worship what you do not know; we know what we worship, for salvation is of the Jews" (NKJV).

based on their charitable deeds done unto **His brethren**—that is, Christians.[113] In doing so, He declares them to be **righteous**.[114]

Note that within the **Chiliasm prophecy timeline**, this scene involving the "surprised sheep" unfolds at the **"last trumpet"**—at the **end of the 1,000 years**—not at Christ's Second Coming. This implies that **Christians would have been saved 1,000 years earlier**, and by that point, they undergo transformation from human beings to **those no longer composed of flesh and blood**, likely having an angelic or celestial nature. Accordingly, they would not be counted among those surprised or newly saved at that time, correct?

Indeed, **St. Irenaeus of Lyons** affirms that **elect salvation** occurs at the **beginning** of the 1,000 years—at Christ's Second Coming—an event he explicitly associates with the period he calls the "times of the kingdom."[115] However, he also makes clear that a **second group of righteous individuals** will be saved only at the **Great White Throne Judgment** following the close of the 1,000 years. He terms this later moment **"after the times of the kingdom"** and connects it to the "General Resurrection."[116] According to

---

[113] Matthew 12:50.

[114] Matthew 25:31–46.

[115] *St. Irenaeus of Lyons writes:* "But when this Antichrist shall have devastated all things in this world, he will reign for three years and six months, and sit in the temple at Jerusalem; and then the Lord will come from heaven in the clouds, in the glory of the Father, sending this man and those who follow him into the lake of fire; but bringing in for the righteous the times of the kingdom, that is, the rest, the hallowed seventh day; and restoring to Abraham the promised inheritance, in which kingdom the Lord declared, that many coming from the east and from the west should sit down with Abraham, Isaac, and Jacob. Matthew 8:11" (*Against Heresies*, Book 5, Chapter 30), www.newadvent.org/fathers/0103530.htm

St. Irenaeus of Lyons writes: "For in the times of the kingdom, the righteous man who is upon the earth shall then forget to die.... John, therefore, did distinctly foresee the first resurrection of the just, Luke 14:14, and the inheritance in the kingdom of the earth.... The apostle, too, has confessed that the creation shall be free from the bondage of corruption, [so as to pass] into the liberty of the sons of God.... subsequently bestowing in a paternal manner those things which neither the eye has seen, nor the ear has heard...." (*Against Heresies*, Book 5, Chapter 36), www.newadvent.org/fathers/0103536.htm

St. Irenaeus of Lyons writes: "These [hundredfold rewards] are to take place in the times of the kingdom, that is, upon the seventh day.... The predicted blessing, therefore, belongs unquestionably to the times of the kingdom, when the righteous shall bear rule upon their rising from the dead.... as the elders who saw John, the disciple of the Lord, related that they had heard from him how the Lord used to teach in regard to these times" (*Against Heresies*, Book 5, Chapter 33), www.newadvent.org/fathers/0103533.htm

[116] *St. Irenaeus of Lyons writes:* "But in the times of the kingdom, the earth has been called again by Christ... and Jerusalem rebuilt.... For after the times of the kingdom... he sets forth, too, the things connected with the general resurrection and the judgment.... The sea... gave

his interpretation of **Matthew 25:31–46**, this moment involves **the whole human race** being divided for judgment.[117]

Recall that **St. Irenaeus of Lyons** quotes the "**last trumpet**" context[118] to refer to this final resurrection at the *end of the 1,000 years*, which he identifies as taking place **after the times of the kingdom**—the moment of the **general resurrection**. He describes this event as including both the wicked and others among his theological opponents who, despite their errors, may have performed acts of goodness. This allows for the possibility of **non-elect salvation** at this later stage.[119]

Interestingly, **St. Justin of Rome** (also known as **St. Justin Martyr**) is recorded as having written that "**the flesh indeed dies**" in the context of entering the "**kingdom of heaven**."[120] This suggests that he viewed the transformation of the righteous from *flesh and blood* into a different, glorified form as a prerequisite for inheriting heaven—an idea consistent with **1 Corinthians 15:50**. This statement is quoted by **St. Methodius of Olympus**, who expands upon the concept elsewhere[121] in a vivid description of the bodily change from human to angelic form following the Millennial Reign. It

---

up the dead... and the books were opened.... this is what is called Gehenna...." (*Against Heresies*, Book 5, Chapter 35), www.newadvent.org/fathers/0103535.htm

[117] *St. Irenaeus of Lyons writes:* "But inasmuch as one and the same Lord has pointed out that the whole human race shall be divided at the judgment, as a shepherd divides the sheep from the goats...." (*Against Heresies*, Book 4, Chapter 40),
www.newadvent.org/fathers/0103440.htm

[118] 1 Corinthians 15:52—"at the last trumpet ... the dead will be raised incorruptible" (NKJV)

[119] *St. Irenaeus of Lyons writes:* "Let our opponents—that is, they who speak against their own salvation—inform us... The dead shall be raised, as He Himself declares: The hour shall come, in which all the dead which are in the tombs shall hear the voice of the Son of man, and shall come forth; those that have done good to the resurrection of life, and those that have done evil to the resurrection of judgment" (*Against Heresies*, Book 5, Chapter 13), www.newadvent.org/fathers/0103513.htm

[120] *St. Methodius quotes St. Justin:* "Justin of Neapolis... says that that which is mortal is inherited, but that which is immortal inherits; and that the flesh indeed dies, but the kingdom of heaven lives." (Fragments of St. Justin Martyr, Fragment 5), www.newadvent.org/fathers/0132.htm or in *St. Methodius of Olympus*, Part 3, "Discourse on the Resurrection," point VI: www.newadvent.org/fathers/0625.htm

[121] *St. Methodius of Olympus writes:* "After the space of a thousand years, [the body is] changed from a human and corruptible form into angelic size and beauty, where at last we virgins, when the festival of the resurrection is consummated, shall pass from the wonderful place of the tabernacle to greater and better things" (*Banquet of the Ten Virgins*, Discourse 9, Chapter 5), www.newadvent.org/fathers/062309.htm

is possible that Methodius's elaboration was based on a now-lost text by St. Justin.

Furthermore, St. Justin explicitly outlines the same **Chiliasm prophecy timeline**[122] as found in the writings of St. Irenaeus, who affirms their agreement. St. Irenaeus confirms that he had read Justin's writings and believed that both held to the same prophetic framework.[123]

With this background, and the acknowledgment of a second group of righteous individuals saved only after the Millennium, we may revisit the earlier Jewish proselyte categories and consider how New Testament doctrine might reframe their meanings:

i) Full proselyte (ger Tzedek, devout proselyte)

A **devout proselyte**, whether Jew or Gentile, is one who has converted to Christianity and is bound to **all** the doctrines and precepts of the Christian faith. This is the **elect salvation**. Such individuals are the **bride of Christ**, participating in the **first resurrection** to reign as **kings and priests** with Him. They inherit the **new heavens**, with varying degrees of reward corresponding to the **thirtyfold, sixtyfold, or hundredfold** fruit levels. They are granted all things, but with unique distinctions in reward. Their **celestial resurrection bodies**—no longer composed of flesh and blood—are given at the **last trumpet** when they are united with Christ in the consummation of the **marriage of the Lamb**. This union involves a mysterious sharing of **"one flesh"** with Christ and the inheritance of bodily glory.[124]

ii) **Half proselyte (ger toshav, limited proselyte)**

A **limited proselyte**, whether Jew or Gentile, is one who has **not converted to Christianity**, yet may still practice the **holiness and charity doctrine commands of Christ** to some degree. This can be inferred from the example of the **Good Samaritan** in **Luke 10:25–37** and the **Surprised Sheep of the Nations** in **Matthew 25:31–46**. Such individuals might

---

[122] *St. Justin of Rome writes:* "There will be a resurrection of the dead, and a thousand years in Jerusalem.... Afterward the general and eternal resurrection and judgment of all men will likewise take place" (*Dialogue with Trypho*, Chapters 80–81),
www.newadvent.org/fathers/01286.htm

[123] *St. Irenaeus of Lyons writes:* "In his book against Marcion, Justin does well say: I would not have believed the Lord Himself, if He had announced any other than He who is our framer... my faith toward Him is steadfast" (*Against Heresies*, Book 4, Chapter 6), www.newadvent.org/fathers/0103406.htm

[124] Matthew 28:19–20—"Go therefore and make disciples of all the nations... teaching them to observe all things that I have commanded you... I am with you always, even to the end of the age" (NKJV).

eventually come to **believe in Christ after seeing**, in fulfillment of **John 6:40**, and thus may attain **non-elect salvation**.

Their final reward would be a **terrestrial (earthly) resurrection body**, attained during the **second resurrection**, not the first. They would dwell among the **nations who are saved** on the **new earth**, subject to the **kings of the earth** who reign over them (cf. Revelation 21:24–26). Though the **heavenly New Jerusalem** descends to connect with the new earth, most of these non-elect saved individuals **would not be able to enter** the city itself, which remains the domain of the **bride of Christ**, the elect.[125]

2.11 Sheep of the Other Fold

The common interpretation that the **"sheep of the other fold"** refers to *Gentile believers*—in contrast to the "sheep of the house of Israel"—is found in later church fathers. However, this definition is surprisingly **absent** in the writings of **Chiliasm church fathers** such as **St. Justin of Rome** and **St. Irenaeus of Lyons**, whom we regard as more reliable in eschatological matters. When we examine the **Chiliasm quotations** of St. Irenaeus, there appears to be **two distinct groups of sheep** who are saved, yet separated by **1,000 years**. This seems to align with the idea of:

- **Elect salvation sheep**, saved during the **"times of the kingdom"**, that is, in the **first resurrection**,[126] and

- **Non-elect salvation sheep**, saved **after the times of the kingdom**, during the **general resurrection**.[127]

---

[125] Geoffrey W. Bromiley writes, "Some scholars have claimed that the term *'those who fear God' (yir'ei Elohim/Shamayim)* was used in rabbinic literature to denote Gentiles who were on the fringe of the synagogue. They were not converts to Judaism, although they were attracted to the Jewish religion and observed part of the law" (*The International Standard Bible Encyclopedia*, Fully Revised Edition, Vol. 3, Eerdmans, Grand Rapids: Michigan, ISBN 0-8028-3783-2, 1986), 1010.

[126] St. Irenaeus of Lyons writes, "But when this Antichrist shall have devastated all things in this world ... then the Lord will come ... bringing in for the righteous the times of the kingdom ... many coming from the east and from the west should sit down with Abraham, Isaac, and Jacob" (Against Heresies, Book 5, Chapter 30); "For in the times of the kingdom ... John, therefore, did distinctly foresee the first resurrection of the just ..." (Book 5, Chapter 36); "The predicted blessing ... belongs unquestionably to the times of the kingdom, when the righteous shall bear rule upon their rising from the dead ..." (Book 5, Chapter 33), www.newadvent.org/fathers/0103530.htm, /0103536.htm, /0103533.htm.

[127] St. Irenaeus of Lyons writes, "And in the Apocalypse John saw this new [Jerusalem] descending upon the new earth ... after the times of the kingdom ... connected with the general resurrection and the judgment ..." (Against Heresies, Book 5, Chapter 35); also, "the

This general resurrection is scheduled to occur at the **"last trumpet"**,[128] and since **only two trumpets** correspond to **two resurrections**,[129] the second group may represent the **sheep of the other fold**.[130]

Both **St. Justin**[131] and **St. Irenaeus**[132] referred to the "gentile sheep" as **"spotted or coloured sheep"** rather than using the "sheep of the other fold" terminology. This is important because "spotted" or "coloured" speaks of a **physical variation on the sheep's body** (which can symbolize ethnic diversity), while the Koine Greek word translated as "fold" is αὐλῆς (*aulēs*),[133] which refers to something external—namely, the **"house for the sheep"** or **sheep pen**. It does not indicate any internal quality or visible mark on the sheep itself. Therefore, the **elect salvation sheepfold (Fold 1)** can be understood as belonging to the **"house in the final new heavens,"** whereas the **non-elect salvation sheepfold (Fold 2)** corresponds to a **"house in the final new earth."** This interpretation aligns precisely with the earlier discussion regarding the two abodes of salvation.

---

whole human race shall be divided at the judgment ..." (Book 4, Chapter 40), www.newadvent.org/fathers/0103535.htm, /0103440.htm.

[128] St. Irenaeus of Lyons writes, "... so also at the end, when the Lord utters His voice by the last trumpet, 1 Corinthians 15:52 ... the dead shall be raised ... those that have done good to the resurrection of life, and those that have done evil to the resurrection of judgment. John 5:28" (Against Heresies, Book 5, Chapter 13), www.newadvent.org/fathers/0103513.htm.

[129] Revelation 20:5 reads, "But the rest of the dead did not live again until the thousand years were finished. This is the first resurrection" (NKJV).

[130] John 10:16 reads, "And other sheep I have which are not of this fold; them also I must bring, and they will hear My voice; and there will be one flock and one shepherd" (NKJV).

[131] St. Justin of Rome writes, "And it was foretold what each should be according to rank and according to foreknowledge. Jacob served Laban for speckled and many-spotted sheep; and Christ served, even to the slavery of the cross, for the various and many-formed races of mankind, acquiring them by the blood and mystery of the cross." *Dialogue with Trypho*, Chapter 134, www.newadvent.org/fathers/01289.htm.

[132] St. Irenaeus of Lyons writes, "In a foreign country were the twelve tribes born, the race of Israel, inasmuch as Christ was also, in a strange country, to generate the twelve-pillared foundation of the Church. Various colored sheep were allotted to this Jacob as his wages; and the wages of Christ are human beings, who from various and diverse nations come together into one cohort of faith." *Against Heresies*, Book 4, Chapter 21, www.newadvent.org/fathers/0103421.htm.

[133] Strong's Concordance: 833 αὐλή (*aulē*) – "from the same as 109; a yard (as open to the wind); by implication, a mansion:—court, (sheep-)fold, hall, palace." (Strong, James. *Strong's Exhaustive Concordance*, 1890, public domain), p. 61.

Around this time, **Clement of Alexandria**[134] interpreted the "sheep of the other fold" to refer to individuals who undergo afterlife judgment and are eventually placed in a **lesser eternal mansion**, which Roman Catholic doctrine later appeals to in support of purgatory—although in this context, the text implies a **permanent separation**, not reintegration with the glorified.

The most compelling reference to the "sheep of the other fold" comes from **St. Irenaeus of Lyons.**[135] His wording is difficult to decipher, as he seems to acknowledge a **partial truth held by the Gnostic heretics**—namely, that the Savior came to retrieve the "lost sheep" in order to **transfer it to the right hand**, that is, to the ninety-nine sheep that were secure and remained in the fold, though originally on the **left side**. However, he promptly refutes their conclusion, rejecting their numerological approach. He criticizes them for suggesting that salvation depends on symbolic **labels** and numerical totals. He argues that since their mystical system fails to reach a sum of **one hundred**, those associated with the left hand remain in corruption. His concluding remark—that "the enjoyment of rest did not imply salvation"—implies a **judicial separation**, not mere rest.

This notion of a **"transfer from left hand to right hand"** aligns remarkably well with **Matthew 25:31–46**, where Christ divides the sheep and goats during the **Judgment Day**. The sheep are placed on His right, and the goats on His left. This separation occurs at their resurrection—when the

---

[134] St. Clement of Alexandria writes, "And other sheep there are also, says the Lord, which are not of this fold (John 10:16)—deemed worthy of another fold and mansion, in proportion to their faith.... but though he quit the flesh, he must put off the passions, so as to be capable of reaching his own mansion.... the greatest torments, indeed, are assigned to the believer. For God's righteousness is good, and His goodness is righteous. And though the punishments cease in the course of the completion of the expiation and purification of each one, yet those have very great and permanent grief who are found worthy of the other fold, on account of not being along with those that have been glorified through righteousness." *The Stromata*, Book 6, Chapter 14, www.newadvent.org/fathers/02106.htm.

[135] St. Irenaeus of Lyons writes, "6. But further, as to their calling material substances on the left hand, and maintaining that those things which are thus on the left hand of necessity fall into corruption, while they also affirm that the Saviour came to the lost sheep, in order to transfer it to the right hand, that is, to the ninety and nine sheep which were in safety, and perished not, but continued within the fold, yet were of the left hand, it follows that they must acknowledge that the enjoyment of rest did not imply salvation. And that which has not in like manner the same number, they will be compelled to acknowledge as belonging to the left hand, that is, to corruption. ... And thus, in fine, they will be compelled to acknowledge that all those sacred names which do not reach a numerical value of one hundred, but only contain the numbers summed by the left hand, are corruptible and material." *Against Heresies*, Book 2, Chapter 24, www.newadvent.org/fathers/0103224.htm.

sheep and goats are raised simultaneously. Thus, this passage most likely refers to the **second resurrection**, not the first. The timing of this transfer makes it unlikely that these sheep are elect, who were already raised 1,000 years earlier. It more logically implies **non-elect salvation** occurring after Judgment Day.

Interestingly, this concept is echoed in a **non-canonical Jewish text**, the *Apocalypse of Abraham*, which depicts a division between people on the right and left, some of whom are **restored after judgment**.[136] Though not part of the Bible, such literature shows that the idea of **post-judgment restoration** was not considered impossible in Second Temple or early Christian thought. This is especially relevant when similar images appear in Irenaeus' own language.

Given this, one might ask: *Does Irenaeus describe salvation for some sheep in the spirit world context?* The answer appears to be yes. In one passage, **St. Irenaeus** compares the **saved sheep of Israel** (elect salvation) to the "lost sheep of Israel which has perished,"[137] suggesting that the **sheep of the other fold** may refer to those **not saved during earthly life**. This is reinforced in another passage where he uses the phrase **"seeking the sheep which had perished"** in the context of **Christ descending to the lower regions of the earth**, a clear allusion to the **spirit world**.[138] There, salvation comes **only after judgment**, as he writes, "when the time is fulfilled of that

---

[136] *Apocalypse of Abraham* reads: "And I saw there the Garden of Eden... and those who behaved righteously... half of them on the right side of the picture and half of them on the left... And He said to me: 'These which are on the left side... some for judgment and restoration, and others for vengeance and destruction at the end of the world... but these which are on the right side... are the people set apart for me.'" Chapters 21–22, trans. G.H. Box, *The Apocalypse of Abraham*, London: Macmillan Company, 1919, pp. 42–44; www.marquette.edu/maqom/box.pdf.

[137] St. Irenaeus of Lyons writes, "8. But as many as feared God, and were anxious about His law, these ran to Christ, and were all saved. For He said to His disciples: Go to the sheep of the house of Israel, Matthew 10:6 which have perished." *Against Heresies*, Book 4, Chapter 2, www.newadvent.org/fathers/0103402.htm.

[138] St. Irenaeus of Lyons writes, "and descend to those things which are of the earth beneath, seeking the sheep which had perished, which was indeed His own peculiar handiwork ... as the Head rose from the dead, so also the remaining part of the body — [namely, the body] of everyman who is found in life — when the time is fulfilled of that condemnation which existed by reason of disobedience, may arise ... each of the members having its own proper and fit position in the body. For there are many mansions in the Father's house, John 14:2 inasmuch as there are also many members in the body." *Against Heresies*, Book 3, Chapter 19, www.newadvent.org/fathers/0103319.htm.

condemnation which existed by reason of disobedience, [they] may arise."[139] This suggests that **some among the lost sheep may rise only after their appointed period of judgment**, highlighting the **possibility of non-elect salvation** from the realm of the dead.

2.12 Indian Evidence – Sadhu Sundar Singh and DGS Dhinakaran

Dr. D.G.S. Dhinakaran (1935–2008) was the founder of the *Jesus Calls* ministry and a renowned evangelical preacher in India. **Sadhu Sundar Singh** (1889–1929) was a well-known Indian Christian whose testimony and writings influenced many. He famously converted to Christianity after a dramatic personal encounter in which Christ appeared to him, following a period of hostility toward Christianity. At that time, he had burned a Bible and planned to take his own life on a railway line.[140]

Sundar Singh affirmed belief in **non-elect salvation**[141] and claimed to have received visions of such events occurring in the spirit world. In one vision, he saw a relatively moral atheist being saved after enduring a period of judgment in the afterlife.[142] In another, he witnessed a sincere Hindu

---

[139] Ephesians 4:9–10 reads, "9 (Now this, 'He ascended'—what does it mean but that He also first descended into the lower parts of the earth? 10 He who descended is also the One who ascended far above all the heavens, that He might fill all things)" (NKJV).

[140] Cyril J. Davey, *The Story of Sadhu Sundar Singh* (Chicago: Moody Press, 1963), 32–33.

[141] Sadhu Sundar Singh said, "I was also told that the love of God operates even in Hell. God does not shine in His full light, because those there could not bear it, but He gradually shows them more and more light, and by and by brings them on and moves their conscience towards something better, although they think that the desire is entirely their own. Thus God works on their minds from within, something in the same way, though in the opposite direction, as that in which Satan suggests temptation to us here. Thus, what with God's work within and the Light without, almost all those in Hell will ultimately be brought to Christ's feet. It will perhaps take millions of ages, but when it is attained they will be full of joy and thankfulness toward God; though they will still be less happy than those who have accepted Christ on earth. ... At least, that is the case with the majority, but there are some few personalities, Satan for instance, in regard to whom I was told, 'Don't ask about them.' And so I didn't like to ask, but I hoped that for them also there was some hope. ... Very few will be lost but many will be saved." (Streeter, Burnett and A. J. Appasamy, *The Sadhu: A Study in Mysticism and Practical Religion* [London: Macmillan, 1923], 100–102; online: pp. 128–130, endtimemanna.org/magnusson/Data/Sundar/The_Sadhu-Streeter_and_Appasamy.pdf).

[142] Sadhu Sundar Singh wrote (in Urdu), "DEATH OF A PHILOSOPHER ... The soul of a German philosopher entered into the world of spirits ... I asked one of the angels what the end of this man would be, and he replied, 'If this man's life had been altogether bad, then he would at once have joined the spirits of darkness, but he is not without a moral sense, so for a very long time he will wander blindly round in the dim light of the lower parts of the intermediate state, and keep on bumping his philosophical head, until tired of his foolishness, he repents. Then he will be ready to receive the necessary instruction from the angels appointed for that purpose, and, when instructed, will he be fit to enter into the fuller light of

idolater repenting and receiving salvation in the spirit world.[143] Despite these unorthodox beliefs, **Dr. D.G.S. Dhinakaran** reported that he had seen Sadhu Sundar Singh in Heaven.[144]

During his spiritual visions, **Sundar Singh** claimed to have conversed with **Emanuel Swedenborg**, and they discussed the eventual salvation of all spirits, including those initially lost.[145] Swedenborg (1688–1772) was a Christian mystic and writer who, in his own visions, claimed to have spoken with **St. Augustine of Hippo**[146] and similarly maintained belief in non-elect salvation even during his lifetime.[147]

God in the higher sphere.'" (*Visions of the Spiritual World*, trans. T. E. Riddle, Macmillan Co., 1926), 4–5;

endtimemanna.org/magnusson/Data/Sundar/Visions_of_the_Spiritual_World_by_S adhu_Sundar_Singh.pdf.

[143] Sadhu Sundar Singh wrote (in Urdu), "THE MANIFESTATION OF CHRIST ... I saw in a vision the spirit of an idolater on reaching the world of spirits begin at once to search for his god. Then the saints said to him, 'There is no god here save the One True God, and Christ, who is His manifestation.' At this, the man was a good deal astonished, but being a sincere seeker after truth, he frankly admitted that he had been in error. ... So, when these spirits saw Christ in this dim but attractive light, they were filled with joy and peace ... Then with all their hearts, they acknowledged Him as the Truth, and found healing, and, bowing in lowly adoration before Him, thanked and praised Him. And the saints, who had been appointed for their instruction, also rejoiced over them." (*Visions of the Spiritual World*, Macmillan Co., 1926), 6;

endtimemanna.org/magnusson/Data/Sundar/Visions_of_the_Spiritual_World_by_S adhu_Sundar_Singh.pdf.

[144] Dr. D.G.S. Dhinakaran writes, "There were occasions when the Lord enabled me to have some time in the Second Heaven with Sadhu Sundar Singh, the great and acclaimed Saint of India. The divine joy that was reflected on his face is beyond any description." (*An Insight Into Heaven*, True Friend Management Support Service Pvt. Ltd., 2007), 101.

[145] Sadhu Sundar Singh writes, "Yes, I have talked with the venerable Swedenborg and some other saints and angels about the hells, although I am unable to explain adequately all that they told me. But it is somewhat like this; No spirit can exist forever, if separated from God by sin or evil. It must either cease to exist or return to God who is the source of life. There is no spirit which will ever cease to exist; therefore every spirit finally must return to God, even though it may be after ages of ages." (A. J. Appasamy, *Sundar Singh* [Cambridge: Lutterworth, 1958], 216]; archive.org/stream/in.ernet.dli.2015.51820/2015.51820.Sundar-Singh-A-Biography-1958_djvu.txt.

[146] Emanuel Swedenborg wrote, "I have several times talked with Augustine, who was bishop of Hippo in Africa, in the third century. He said that he is there at this time, inspiring them with the worship of the Lord ... because through it there is being opened to them a communication with the human rational, hitherto closed up by the universal dogma that the understanding must be kept in obedience to the faith of the ministers of the church." (*True Christian Religion*, [1771], tr. John C. Ager [1906]), §840; sacred-texts.com/swd/tcr/tcr17.htm.

[147] Emanuel Swedenborg wrote, "The Mohammedans, like all nations who acknowledge one God, love justice and do good from religion, have their own heaven, but it is outside of

Conclusion

Many Pentecostal Christians sincerely believe **Dr. D.G.S. Dhinakaran's** testimony that he was taken to Heaven and saw even **Sadhu Sundar Singh** there. If this testimony is true, then **Sadhu Sundar Singh's** teachings on **non-elect salvation** may also be valid. If his views are mistaken, then they evidently do not affect one's salvation—since, by Dhinakaran's account, Sundar Singh was still seen in Heaven. In either case, Sundar Singh's views on non-elect salvation have influenced many, including both Christians and non-Christians, as documented in earlier sections.

As for me, though I have presented the evidence strongly and personally hope that **non-elect salvation** proves to be true, I must remain **neutral** regarding matters that cannot be known for certain until death—when one meets the Lord face to face.

This **neutral stance** is the position I often take on matters of prophecy: I present the strongest possible evidence for what seems most probable while clearly distinguishing that it is not a guarantee. This is so that I do not unintentionally mislead anyone. In doing so, I have made all relevant facts known in advance.

St. Justin of Rome firmly taught that no Christian enters Heaven until after the resurrection.[148] This is because a transformation must first take place—the change from our current human condition, which still consists of "flesh and blood," to the **celestial body** described in Scripture. This corresponds with Apostle Paul's teaching about the resurrection body: a transition from a **natural body** to a **spiritual body**.[149]

This is only accurately understood when we take all the **Chiliasm church father quotes** as a whole, discerning what may not have been written explicitly but is implied through consistency. **St. Justin of Rome** is not

---

the Christian heaven. ... Only those who give up their concubines and acknowledge the Lord our Savior ... are raised up from this into their higher heaven. ... It is because of their holding this belief that it is granted them by the Lord to ascend into the higher heaven." (*True Christian Religion*, §817, 832); sacred-texts.com/swd/tcr/tcr17.htm.

[148] **St. Justin of Rome** writes, "For if you have fallen in with some who are called Christians, but who do not admit this [truth], and venture to blaspheme the God of Abraham, and the God of Isaac, and the God of Jacob; who say there is no resurrection of the dead, and that their souls, when they die, are taken to heaven; do not imagine that they are Christians" (*Dialogue with Trypho*, Chapter 80), www.newadvent.org/fathers/01286.htm.

[149] 1 Corinthians 15:44, 46, 49 reads, "It is sown a natural body, it is raised a spiritual body. There is a natural body, and there is a spiritual body. However, the spiritual is not first, but the natural, and afterward the spiritual. And as we have borne the image of the man of dust, we shall also bear the image of the heavenly Man."

denying that some can receive visions of heaven if **God permits it** (as in 2 Corinthians 12:2). Rather, he was arguing against those who **deny the bodily resurrection**—that is, those who claim Christians can **live eternally in heaven** in a **purely disembodied spirit state**, bypassing the need for **bodily resurrection** first.

This is confirmed by the example of **Christ's own Resurrection**. After He rose, our Lord still said that He had **not yet ascended to the Father**.[150] This means that, even as a "Spirit," Christ **did not go to Heaven** immediately after death.[151] Only after the **Bodily Resurrection** and the **ascension forty days later** did He enter into Heaven.

The **Resurrection Body** of Christ is more than flesh and blood—it is glorified. Similarly, when the elect are raised from the dead, we do **not instantly receive** the full glory of that transformation. According to Chiliasm theology, our bodies are **not fully conformed** to Christ's until after the **marriage of the Lamb is complete**, at the end of the **1,000 years**. At that point, our bodies are transformed "to His glorious body."[152]

Now, Roman Catholics often cite both **St. Irenaeus of Lyons**[153] and **Tertullian**[154] for their emphasis on apostolic succession and doctrinal unity.

---

[150] John 20:17 reads, "Jesus said to her, 'Do not cling to Me, for I have not yet ascended to My Father; but go to My brethren and say to them, "I am ascending to My Father and your Father, and to My God and your God."'" (NKJV).

[151] Acts 1:9–11 reads, "Now when He had spoken these things, while they watched, He was taken up, and a cloud received Him out of their sight. And while they looked steadfastly toward heaven as He went up, behold, two men stood by them in white apparel, who also said, 'Men of Galilee, why do you stand gazing up into heaven? This same Jesus, who was taken up from you into heaven, will so come in like manner as you saw Him go into heaven.'" (NKJV).

[152] Philippians 3:21 reads, "who will transform our lowly body that it may be conformed to His glorious body," (NKJV).

[153] **St. Irenaeus of Lyons** writes, "Now all these [heretics] are of much later date than the bishops to whom the apostles committed the Churches; which fact I have in the third book taken all pains to demonstrate. It follows, then, as a matter of course, that these heretics aforementioned, since they are blind to the truth, and deviate from the [right] way, will walk in various roads; and therefore the footsteps of their doctrine are scattered here and there without agreement or connection. But the path of those belonging to the Church circumscribes the whole world, as possessing the sure tradition from the apostles, and gives unto us to see that the faith of all is one and the same," (*Against Heresies*, Book 5, Chapter 20), www.newadvent.org/fathers/0103520.htm.

[154] **Tertullian** writes, "But if there be any (heresies) which are bold enough to plant themselves in the midst of the apostolic age, that they may thereby seem to have been handed down by the apostles, because they existed in the time of the apostles, we can say: Let them produce the original records of their churches; let them unfold the roll of their bishops, running down in due succession from the beginning in such a manner that [that first bishop

They argue that their institution descends directly from the apostles. The problem with this claim, however, is that the **original Catholic churches** during the time of **St. Irenaeus** and **Tertullian** also **affirmed Chiliasm**. If even **one quote** from these men disagrees with the present-day Catholic doctrine, then it demonstrates that **either doctrinal diversity was permitted** in those early churches, or that **some interpretations eventually became dominant** through human free will—thus confirming the possibility of doctrinal shifts.

The same spiritual principle is evident in **Judaism** itself. The Jews preserved the **Old Testament Scriptures**, upheld the **Levitical priesthood**, and even converted Gentiles into Judaism for centuries. Yet by the time of Christ, **many were doctrinally in error**, with some even denying the Messiah Himself. Therefore, **prevalence of tradition** or **numerical dominance** does not necessarily imply **doctrinal truth**.

For me, the **earliest surviving writings** of Christianity—particularly from **St. Irenaeus of Lyons, St. Justin of Rome**, and **Tertullian**—preserve the ancient faith most accurately. Where they differ, those variations can be viewed as **possibilities**, but I place greater weight on the writings of **St. Irenaeus** and **St. Justin**. Even Roman Catholic historians admit **Tertullian made some errors**, and this is one reason why he was **not canonized as a saint**.

This same **St. Clement of Rome** (c. 35 C.E. – c. 99 C.E.), also known as **Pope Clement I** to Roman Catholics, was a direct disciple of the apostle **St. Peter**. He wrote a letter that is known today as *1 Clement*, which was considered **Scripture** in some segments of early Christianity. It was even included in the **5th-century Codex Alexandrinus**[155] and cited by **St. Irenaeus of Lyons** as a reliable expression of apostolic tradition.[156]

---

of theirs] bishop shall be able to show for his ordainer and predecessor some one of the apostles or of apostolic men,—a man, moreover, who continued steadfast with the apostles. For this is the manner in which the apostolic churches transmit their registers: as the church of Smyrna, which records that Polycarp was placed therein by John; as also the church of Rome, which makes Clement to have been ordained in like manner by Peter." (*Prescription Against Heretics*, Chapter 32), www.newadvent.org/fathers/0311.htm.

[155] *The Text of the New Testament: An Introduction to the Critical Editions and to the Theory and Practice of Modern Textual Criticism*, Kurt Aland & Barbara Aland, trans. Erroll F. Rhodes (Grand Rapids: William B. Eerdmans Publishing Company, 1995), 107, 109.

[156] St. Irenaeus of Lyons writes, "For there were many still remaining who had received instructions from the apostles. In the time of this Clement, no small dissension having occurred among the brethren at Corinth, the Church in Rome dispatched a most powerful letter to the Corinthians, exhorting them to peace, renewing their faith, and declaring the

In one striking passage, St. Clement makes a statement that almost sounds like a **prophetic warning**[157]—indicating that in rare instances, the person who departs from a church congregation may actually uphold **doctrinal accuracy** more than the majority. This is a powerful testimony to the **role of free will** in how doctrinal truth can be preserved or neglected within the church.

Put plainly, St. Clement of Rome asserts that **doctrinal accuracy may not always reside with the majority**. A person who leaves a church due to doctrinal corruption—if his reasons are correct—may attain **great honour and glory** in the eyes of the Lord.[158] This truth should encourage believers to hold firm to the **Scriptures and sound doctrine**, even when doing so may mean losing the approval of the masses. This principle applies not only to church practice, but also to **the interpretation of prophecy**.

How, then, does **God's Will** relate to the **number of converts** in a particular denomination? I believe God allows us to have the **leaders we deserve**. When believers are **zealous for truth and practice**, like **St. Irenaeus of Lyons**, then God may raise up teachers and shepherds who share that same zeal. Conversely, when Christians are complacent, **leaders of equal weakness** may rise.[159]

The prophet **Daniel** shows that while **leading others to righteousness** is a noble calling, it results in a lesser **glory**—like the stars—whereas possessing **prophetic insight** and doctrinal precision leads to a

---

tradition which it had lately received from the apostles." (*Against Heresies*, Book 3, Chapter 3), www.newadvent.org/fathers/0103303.htm.

[157] St. Clement of Rome writes, "Who then among you is noble-minded? Who compassionate? Who full of love? Let him declare, If on my account sedition and disagreement and schisms have arisen, I will depart, I will go away wherever ye desire, and I will do whatever the majority commands; only let the flock of Christ live on terms of peace with the presbyters set over it. He that acts thus shall procure to himself great glory in the Lord; and every place will welcome him. For the earth is the Lord's, and the fullness thereof. These things they who live a godly life that is never to be repented of, both have done and always will do." (*1 Clement*, Chapter 54), www.newadvent.org/fathers/1010.htm.

[158] Luke 6:22–23 reads, "Blessed are you when men hate you, and when they exclude you, and revile you, and cast out your name as evil, for the Son of Man's sake. Rejoice in that day and leap for joy! For indeed your reward is great in heaven, for in like manner their fathers did to the prophets" (NKJV).

[159] Romans 10:2 reads, "For I bear them witness that they have a zeal for God, but not according to knowledge" (NKJV).

greater glory, like the brightness of the heavens.[160] Even **St. Irenaeus of Lyons** interprets **Daniel 12:3** as referring to the **final resurrection body** and the **eternal glory** given to those with greater understanding.[161] So we should strive, not merely to be leaders or to influence the masses, but to **attain accuracy in truth**, whether doctrinal or prophetic, and let **God reward accordingly**.

Jehovah also gave a stern warning through **the prophet Jeremiah**. If someone speaks **a prophecy as their own idea**, even if it turns out wrong, no lasting judgment is declared because they did **not invoke the Name of God**.[162] But if someone says, "Jehovah has said," and yet it is not so, that person is **under divine judgment**, suffering **everlasting reproach** and **perpetual shame**—a punishment stressed by the use of the Hebrew word **olam** (eternity) repeated twice.[163] This shows the extreme seriousness of claiming divine authority falsely.

If **non-elect salvation** turns out to be true, then the **"few"** who are saved refer to the **Elect Salvation** group[164] who become **His Bride**[165] and

---

[160] Daniel 12:3 reads, "And those who have insight will shine like the glow of the expanse of heaven, and those who lead the many to righteousness, like the stars forever and ever" (NASB).

[161] St. Irenaeus of Lyons writes, "Preaching by anticipation the inheritance of the holy Jerusalem, and proclaiming beforehand that the man who loves God shall arrive at such excellency as even to see God, and hear His word, and from the hearing of His discourse be glorified to such an extent, that others cannot behold the glory of his countenance, as was said by Daniel: 'Those who do understand, shall shine as the brightness of the firmament, and many of the righteous as the stars forever and ever' (Daniel 12:3). Thus, then, I have shown it to be, if any one read the Scriptures." (*Against Heresies*, Book 4, Chapter 26), www.newadvent.org/fathers/0103426.htm.

[162] Jeremiah 23:36 reads, "And the oracle of the LORD you shall mention no more. For every man's word will be his oracle, for you have perverted the words of the living God, the LORD of hosts, our God" (NKJV).

[163] Jeremiah 23:38–40 reads, "But since you say, 'The oracle of the LORD!' therefore thus says the LORD: 'Because you say this word, "The oracle of the LORD!" and I have sent to you, saying, "Do not say, 'The oracle of the LORD!'" therefore behold, I, even I, will utterly forget you and forsake you, and the city that I gave you and your fathers, and will cast you out of My presence. And I will bring an everlasting reproach upon you, and a perpetual shame, which shall not be forgotten.'" (NKJV).

[164] Matthew 7:14 reads, "Because narrow is the gate and difficult is the way which leads to life, and there are few who find it" (NKJV).

[165] Revelation 21:9 reads partly, "Come, I will show you the bride, the Lamb's wife" (NKJV).

are granted access to heaven.[166] Meanwhile, Christ's Ransom for "many"[167] could include those of the **non-elect salvation** category, who receive their final abode on the **new earth** only.[168] In the final vision of the book of Revelation, these are the ones who are **invited by the Bride** to "take the water of life freely."[169] This **water of life** flows into the **new earth**, and the "healing from the leaves of the tree of life," whose Source is Christ,[170] appears to be intended for **the nations**—those who perhaps are **saved by fire**.[171]

This interpretation aligns with the **Chiliasm timeline**, where the Christians (Elect) are already resurrected and glorified for a **thousand years** before this final scene. Therefore, the idea that the **Elect Bride** would need healing from the **leaves of the tree of life** in the **eternal state** seems unlikely. Instead, the nations mentioned are possibly the **non-elect** who have gone through purification and are entering into the everlasting kingdom. This may be what **Daniel the prophet** meant when he wrote that "many shall be purified"[172]—suggesting a **refinement process**, possibly even postmortem, which some interpret as **"saved by fire."**

This possibility helps make sense of certain **broad-scope verses** in the Bible that seem to speak of a **larger group** being saved.[173] In such verses, **believers** are a **subset** of the saved, and not the entirety of it.[174] Even **St.**

---

[166] Matthew 7:21 reads, "Not everyone who says to Me, 'Lord, Lord,' shall enter the kingdom of heaven, but he who does the will of My Father in heaven" (NKJV).

[167] Matthew 26:28 reads, "For this is My blood of the new covenant, which is shed for many for the remission of sins" (NKJV).

[168] Revelation 21:24, 27 reads, "And the nations of those who are saved shall walk in its light, and the kings of the earth bring their glory and honor into it. ... But there shall by no means enter it anything that defiles ... but only those who are written in the Lamb's Book of Life" (NKJV).

[169] Revelation 22:17 reads, "And the Spirit and the bride say, 'Come!' ... Whoever desires, let him take the water of life freely" (NKJV).

[170] Revelation 22:1–2 reads, "He showed me a pure river of water of life, ... proceeding from the throne of God and of the Lamb. ... The leaves of the tree were for the healing of the nations" (NKJV).

[171] 1 Corinthians 3:15 reads, "If anyone's work is burned, he will suffer loss; but he himself will be saved, yet so as through fire" (NKJV).

[172] Daniel 12:10 reads, "Many shall be purified, made white, and refined, but the wicked shall do wickedly; and none of the wicked shall understand; but the wise shall understand" (NKJV).

[173] 1 Timothy 2:4 reads, "Who will have all men to be saved, and to come unto the knowledge of the truth" (KJV).

[174] 1 Timothy 4:10 reads, "The living God, who is the Saviour of all men, specially of those that believe" (KJV).

Jerome, translator of the **Latin Vulgate**, underscores the importance of **doctrinal accuracy**, applying it specifically in the context of **Daniel 12:3**, where he discusses the **different levels of glory** awarded based on spiritual understanding and the instruction of others.[175]

To close this discussion, the **Septuagint (LXX)** rendering of **Daniel 12** is quoted below, showing slight but theologically meaningful variations compared to the **Masoretic Text**, which may further support this nuanced reading.[176]

"**2** And many of them that sleep in the dust of the earth shall awake, some to everlasting life, and some to reproach and everlasting shame. **3** And the wise shall shine as the brightness of the firmament, and some of the many righteous as the stars for ever and ever.

10 Many must be tested, and thoroughly whitened, and tried with fire, and sanctified; but the transgressors shall transgress and none of the transgressors shall understand; but the wise shall understand."

(Daniel 12:2–3, 10, Brenton Septuagint Translation).[177]

Disclaimer

This article, titled *"Non-Elect Salvation Possibility"* (NESP), was recently published in *The American Journal of Biblical Theology*, Volume 26(6), February 9, 2025. This is my **first and only journal publication** (52 pages) so far. It can be accessed under the "Theological Research" section at:

www.biblicaltheology.com/Research/RamachandranJ01.pdf (from **www.biblicaltheology.com**)

The journal permits republication, as clearly stated in its copyright notice:

---

[175] St. Jerome of the Vulgate writes, "... Many people often ask whether a learned saint and an ordinary saint shall both enjoy the same reward and one and the same dwelling-place in heaven. ... The statement is made here, according to Theodotion's rendering, that the learned will resemble the very heavens, whereas the righteous who are without learning are only compared to the brightness of the stars." (*Commentary on Daniel*, Chapter 12, trans. Gleason L. Archer, 1958), 155–157. www.tertullian.org/fathers/jerome_daniel_02_text.htm

[176] Daniel 12:2–3, 10 (Masoretic) reads: "2And many of those who sleep in the dust of the earth shall awake, some to everlasting life, some to shame and everlasting contempt. 3Those who are wise shall shine like the brightness of the firmament, and those who turn many to righteousness like the stars forever and ever. ... 10Many shall be purified, made white, and refined, but the wicked shall do wickedly; and none of the wicked shall understand, but the wise shall understand." (NKJV)

[177] Daniel 12 (Brenton Septuagint Translation), biblehub.com/sep/daniel/12.htm

"The copyright of all published articles is retained by the author under Title 17 US Code 506. The Journal retains a 'fair use' agreement to edit, format to the journal specifications, and reproduce the author's work in any media that the Journal may publish in the future. The author is also free to republish the original manuscript in other journals once the work is published."

Source: **www.biblicaltheology.com/submit.html**

Sources

Internet links throughout this article were accessed August, 2024

Aland, Kurt; Aland, Barbara. *The Text of the New Testament: An Introduction to the Critical Editions and to the Theory and Practice of Modern Textual Criticism.* Erroll F. Rhodes (trans.). Grand Rapids: William B. Eerdmans Publishing Company, ISBN 978-0-8028-4098-1, 1995).

Appasamy, A. J. *Sundar Singh.* Cambridge: Lutterworth, 1958. archive.org/stream/in.ernet.dli.2015.51820/2015.51820.Sundar-Singh-A-Biography-1958_djvu.txt

Berlin, Meyer; Zevin, Shlomo Yosef. *Encyclopedia Talmudica: A Digest of Halachic Literature and Jewish Law from the Tannaitic Period to the Present Time, Alphabetically Arranged.* Vol. IV. Jerusalem: Yad Harav Herzog (Emet, ISBN 0873067142, eds. (1992) [1969]).

Bible Canon: *Codex Sinaiticus.* codexsinaiticus.org/en/codex/content.aspx

Bible. Unless noted, all Scripture is taken from the *New King James Version* (NKJV). Nashville: Published by Thomas Nelson, 1996, c1982. NKJV and other translations used are biblehub.com

Brenton. *Septuagint.* Daniel 12 (LXX). biblehub.com/sep/daniel/12.htm

Catechism of the Catholic Church. *CCC 1821.* http://www.catholic-catechism.com/ccc_1.74.618.851.956.1256.1261.1349.1821.1900.2240.2574.2634.2822.htm

Catholic Encyclopaedia, *Hermas.* www.catholic.com/encyclopedia/hermas

Catholic Encyclopaedia, *Millennium and Millenarianism.* Published between 1907 and 1912. www.catholic.com/encyclopedia/millennium-and-millenarianism

Cyril J. Davey. *The Story of Sadhu Sundar Singh* (Chicago: Moody Press, 1963).

Dhinakaran, D.G.S. *An Insight Into Heaven*. True Friend Management Support Service Pvt. Ltd. 2007.

Ethiopian Orthodox Tewahido Church Holy Synod. *A short history, faith and order of the Ethiopian Orthodox Tewahido Church*, Canonical Books, Addis Ababa 1983, www.ethiopianorthodox.org/english/canonical/books.html

Eusebius. *Ecclesiastical History*, Book 3, Chapter 36. www.newadvent.org/fathers/250103.htm

Geoffrey W. Bromiley. *The International Standard Bible Encyclopedia*. Fully Revised Edition, Vol. 3, Eerdmans, Grand Rapids: Michigan, ISBN 0-8028-3783-2, 1986.

G.H. Box. *Apocalypse of Abraham*. Society for promoting Christian Knowledge. London, Macmillan Company, 1919. www.marquette.edu/maqom/box.pdf

G.M. Hahneman. *The Muratorian Fragment and the Origins of the New Testament Canon in "The Canon Debate"* (ed. L. M. McDonald and J. A. Sanders, Massachusetts: Hendrickson, 2002), 405–415.

Klein, Reuven Chaim. "*World Religions and the Noahide Prohibition of Idolatry*" (PDF, 2022). Journal of Halacha and Contemporary Society. 79: 109–167. hcommons.org/deposits/download/hc:50798/CONTENT/shituf-article.pdf

LeRoy Edwin Froom. *The Conditionalist Faith of Our Fathers*, 2 vols. Washington, DC: Review and Herald, 1965.

Louis Ginzberg, *Legends of the Jews*, Volume 1. The Jewish Publication Society, Philadelphia, 2003. bibleresourcespart2.wordpress.com/wp-content/uploads/2015/10/legends-of-the-jews-complete-in-2-volumes.pdf

Paul Helm, *The Last Things: Death, Judgment, Heaven and Hell*. Carlisle, PA: Banner of Truth, 1989.

R.H. Charles. *The Apocrypha and Pseudepigrapha of the Old Testament*. Oxford: The Clarendon Press, UK, 1913. www.ccel.org/c/charles/otpseudepig/enoch/ENOCH_2.HTM

Richard Bauckham. *Universalism: A Historical Survey.* Themelios 4, no. 2, January 1979.

Sadhu Sundar Singh. *Visions of the Spiritual World.* Translated by Rev. T. E. Riddle of the New Zealand Presbyterian Mission, Kharar, Punjab, from Urdu into English, Macmillan Co., 1926. endtimemanna.org/magnusson/Data/Sundar/Visions_of_the_Spiritual_World_by_Sadhu_Sundar_Singh.pdf

Schaff, Philip. Ante-Nicene Fathers: NPNF2-14, Christian Literature Publishing Co, USA, 1885. *The Seven Ecumenical Councils*, 34. www.ccel.org/ccel/schaff/npnf214.html (2 August 2024).

Schaff, Philip. Ante-Nicene Fathers: Volume I, Christian Literature Publishing Co, USA, 1885. (St. Irenaeus of Lyons, *Against Heresies*, Book 4, Chapter 4). www.ccel.org/ccel/schaff/anf01.ix.vi.v.html

Shepherd of Hermas. Book 1, Vision 3. www.newadvent.org/fathers/02011.htm

Shepherd of Hermas. Book 2, Commandment 1. www.newadvent.org/fathers/02012.htm

St. Ambrose of Milan. *Exposition of the Christian Faith.* Book 5, Chapter 15. www.newadvent.org/fathers/34045.htm

St. Athanasius the Great. *39th Festal Letter* (c. 367 AD). http://www.ntcanon.org/Athanasius.shtml

St. Augustine of Hippo. *Catena Aurea*, Commentary on Matthew 25:1 – 13's Parable of the Five Wise/Foolish Virgins. ccel.org/ccel/aquinas/catena1/catena1.ii.xxv.html

St. Augustine of Hippo. *Enchiridion.* "The Last Things", Chapter 29. www.tertullian.org/fathers/augustine_enchiridion_02_trans.htm

St. Clement of Alexandria. *The Stromata*, Book 6. www.newadvent.org/fathers/02106.htm (6 August 2024).

St. Clement of Rome. *1 Clement.* www.newadvent.org/fathers/1010.htm

St. Gregory Nazianzus. *First Theological Oration* (Oration 27), Point IX. www.newadvent.org/fathers/310227.htm

St. Gregory Nazianzus. *Oration 39,* Chapter XIX, Oration on the Holy Lights. www.newadvent.org/fathers/310239.htm

St. Gregory Nazianzus. *Oration 40,* Chapter 13. www.newadvent.org/fathers/310240.htm

St. Gregory Nazianzus. *Oration 40,* Chapter 36.
www.ewtn.com/catholicism/library/select-orations-334-3741-11647

St. Irenaeus of Lyons. *Against Heresies,*
www.newadvent.org/fathers/0103224.htm

St. Jerome of the Vulgate. *Commentary on Daniel.* Translated by Gleason L. Archer, 1958. www.tertullian.org/fathers/jerome_daniel_02_text.htm

St. Justin of Rome (Justin Martyr). *Dialogue with Trypho,*
www.newadvent.org/fathers/01286.htm

St. Methodius of Olympus. *Banquet of the Ten Virgins,* Discourse 9, Chapter 5. www.newadvent.org/fathers/062309.htm

St. Methodius of Olympus. *From the Discourse on the Resurrection.*
www.newadvent.org/fathers/0625.htm

St. Papias of Hierapolis, *Fragment V.*
www.newadvent.org/fathers/0125.htm (3

St. Victorinus of Pettau. *Commentary on the Apocalypse.*
earlychurchrevival.wordpress.com/wp-content/uploads/2013/11/st-victorinus-of-poetovio-translated-by-kevin-edgecomb.pdf

Stephen J. Nichols. *Martin Luther's 95 Theses.* Presbyterian & Reformed Pub Co, USA, 2002.

Streeter, Burnett and A. J. Appasamy. *The Sadhu: a Study in Mysticism and Practical Religion.* London: Macmillan, 1923. endtimemanna.org/magnusson/Data/Sundar/The_Sadhu-Streeter_and_Appasamy.pdf

Strong, James. *Strong's Exhaustive Concordance.* 1890, public domain. library.hugenote.com/Data/pdf/Strongs.pdf

Swedenborg, Emanuel. *True Christian Religion.* [1771], tr. by John C. Ager [1906]). sacred-texts.com/swd/tcr/tcr17.htm

Tertullian. *Against Marcion,* www.newadvent.org/fathers/03123.htm

Tertullian. *On Modesty* ("De pudicitia").
www.newadvent.org/fathers/0407.htm

Tertullian. *Prescription against Heretics.* www.newadvent.org/fathers/0311.htm

TeSelle, Eugene. *Augustine the Theologian.* Wipf and Stock (USA, ISBN 978-1-57910-918-9, 2002).

Essay 2: Thousand Year Gap for Prophecy in 1 Thessalonians 4:17 and 1 Corinthians 15:52 with Chiliasm Church Fathers

KEYWORDS

Rapture, Pre-trib, Post-trib, Mid-trib, Pre-tribulation Rapture, Mid-tribulation Rapture, Post-tribulation Rapture, 1 Thessalonians, 1 Corinthians, 1 Thessalonians 4:17, 1 Corinthians 15:52, 1 Thess. 4:17, 1 Cor. 15:52, Change, Transformation, Human, Angelic, Terrestrial, Celestial, Resurrection, Irenaeus, Justin Martyr, Tertullian, Methodius, Victorinus, Church Fathers, Augustine, New Discovery, Theology, End Times, Daniel Prophecy, Christ, Body, Parables, Second Coming of Christ, Bride, Wife of the Lamb, Elect Salvation, Wedding of the Lamb, Prophecy, Eschatology, Chiliasm

ABSTRACT

This paper proposes that the verses found in **1 Thessalonians 4:17** and **1 Corinthians 15:52** describe two distinct prophetic events that are separated by a thousand-year period. The interpretation is not built merely on surface-level readings of the texts, but rather draws from the consistent implications within the writings of the earliest Church fathers—particularly those aligned with the **Chiliasm** model. These writings are compared with modern interpretations to identify points of doctrinal continuity and divergence. Each Church father quotation is examined closely, with attention given to the context and detail of their statements. Common objections to Chiliasm are addressed directly.

The framework for this interpretation rests on the prophetic model of **Chiliasm**, which affirms a literal one-thousand-year reign of Christ on earth prior to the final state. The roles and distinctions of these two verses are made clearer through patristic evidence, and interpolations are offered to explain why such a gap must exist. If valid, this study may serve as a **rediscovery of a lost interpretive tradition**—what one might call **prophetic archaeology** in analogy to traditional archaeology.

INTRODUCTION

This work presents an original line of research, as I have not encountered any scholar who has proposed that **1 Thessalonians 4:17** and **1 Corinthians 15:52** refer to two separate prophetic events. These verses are as follows:

> "Then we who are alive and remain shall be caught up together with them in the clouds to meet the Lord in the air. And thus we shall always be with the Lord."[178]

> "Now this I say, brethren, that flesh and blood cannot inherit the kingdom of God; nor does corruption inherit incorruption. Behold, I tell you a mystery: We shall not all sleep, but we shall all be changed—*in a moment, in the twinkling of an eye, at the last trumpet.* For the trumpet will sound, and the dead will be raised incorruptible, and we shall be changed."[179]

It is not sufficient to assume, based on a superficial reading, that these two passages refer to the same event. Nor is it appropriate to insert a thousand-year interval arbitrarily without justification. The method adopted here will demonstrate that a consistent thread appears in the writings of **Chiliasm**[180] **Church fathers**, who implicitly or explicitly treat these verses as referring to different stages in prophetic fulfillment.

These ancient voices—whose doctrinal positions were often rooted in the teachings handed down by their immediate predecessors—offer strong support for the view that a thousand-year gap separates these events. Their writings may thus preserve an early interpretive tradition that has been largely forgotten or neglected in later theological development.

Justin of Rome

Let us begin with **Justin of Rome** (c. 100–160 C.E.). Also known as **Justin Martyr** or **Justin of Neapolis**, he was a leading early Christian apologist, priest, and martyr. He stands as one of the foremost defenders of the divine Logos and exerted profound influence upon the development of later Christian philosophy and theology, particularly within Catholic and Protestant traditions. He is a recognized **Chiliasm Church Father**, and he is cited with approval in the **Lutheran Book of Concord**. He is also

---

[178] 1 Thessalonians 4-17 (NKJV).
[179] 1 Corinthians 15:50-52 (NKJV).
[180] J.P. Kirsch, "Millennium and Millenarianism", in *The Catholic Encyclopedia*, (New York: Robert Appleton Company, 1911). www.newadvent.org/cathen/10307a.htm

venerated in the Catholic Church, Eastern Orthodox Church, Oriental Orthodox Church, Anglican Communion, and Lutheran Church.

Justin appears to acknowledge only **two public comings of Christ**: the first in the past (His suffering and crucifixion), and the second in the future—after the appearance of the final Antichrist, the "man of apostasy"—who persecutes the saints. This second coming includes the context of **1 Thessalonians 4:17**, yet Justin offers no indication of a **secret coming** of Christ before the Great Tribulation, as postulated by pre-tribulation rapture theorists.

> "O unreasoning men! understanding not what has been proved by all these passages, that **two advents of Christ have been announced**: the one, in which He is set forth as suffering, inglorious, dishonoured, and crucified; but the other, in which He shall come from heaven with glory, when the man of apostasy, who speaks strange things against the Most High, shall venture to do unlawful deeds on the earth against us the Christians, who, having learned the true worship of God from the law, and the word which went forth from Jerusalem by means of the apostles of Jesus, have fled for safety to the God of Jacob and God of Israel; and we who were filled with war, and mutual slaughter, and every wickedness, have each through the whole earth changed our warlike weapons — our swords into ploughshares, and our spears into implements of tillage — and we cultivate piety, righteousness, philanthropy, faith, and hope, which we have from the Father Himself through Him who was crucified..."[181]

> "For the prophets have proclaimed **two advents** of His: the one, that which is already past, when He came as a dishonoured and suffering Man; but the second, when, according to prophecy, He shall come from heaven with glory, accompanied by His angelic host, when also He shall raise the bodies of all men who have lived, and shall clothe those of the worthy with immortality, and shall send those of the wicked, endued with eternal sensibility, into everlasting fire with the wicked devils. And that these things also have been foretold as yet to be, we will prove."[182]

---

[181] Justin of Rome, "Chapter 110," *Dialogue with Trypho*, www.newadvent.org/fathers/01288.htm
[182] Justin of Rome, "Chapter 52," *The First Apology*, www.newadvent.org/fathers/0126.htm

Justin's description of Christ's second coming here is a summarizing statement and does not contradict the **Chiliasm prophecy timeline**, particularly when he speaks of the wicked being raised and judged. His more detailed exposition, found in his **Dialogue with Trypho**, plainly states that there is a **1000-year separation** between the **first resurrection** of the righteous and the **general resurrection** for judgment:

> "But I and others, who are right-minded Christians on all points, are assured that there will be a **resurrection of the dead**, and a **thousand years in Jerusalem**, which will then be built, adorned, and enlarged, [as] the prophets Ezekiel and Isaiah and others declare... And further, there was a certain man with us, whose name was **John**, one of the apostles of Christ, who prophesied, by a revelation that was made to him, that those who believed in our Christ would dwell a thousand years in Jerusalem; and that thereafter the **general**, and, in short, the **eternal resurrection and judgment of all men** would likewise take place. Just as our Lord also said, 'They shall neither marry nor be given in marriage, but shall be equal to the angels, the children of the God of the resurrection.'" (Luke 20:35)[183]

Thus, in Justin's understanding, believers are changed to be **like angels** during the final resurrection and judgment. This aligns well with **1 Corinthians 15:50–52**, in which the change from mortal to immortal occurs "at the last trumpet," corresponding with the general resurrection. For Justin, this **change** represents a **transformation from human to angelic**, i.e., to a glorified, incorruptible state. His explanation is consistent with other Chiliasm Church Fathers, whose testimony will be presented later.

> "Listen, sirs, how the Holy Ghost speaks of this people, saying that they are all **sons of the Highest**; and how this very Christ will be present in their assembly, rendering judgment to all men. The words are spoken by David, and are, according to your version of them, thus: 'God stands in the congregation of gods; He judges among the gods. How long do you judge unjustly, and accept the persons of the wicked? Judge for the orphan and the poor, and do justice to the humble and needy. Deliver the needy, and save the poor out of the hand of the wicked. They know not, neither have they understood; they walk on in darkness: all the foundations of the earth shall be shaken. I said, You are gods, and

---

[183] Revelation 20:5, "But the rest of the dead did not live again until the thousand years were finished. This is the first resurrection" (NKJV).

are all children of the Most High. But you die like men, and fall like one of the princes. Arise, O God! judge the earth, for You shall inherit all nations.' But in the version of the Seventy it is written, 'Behold, you die like men, and fall like one of the princes,' in order to manifest the disobedience of men — I mean of Adam and Eve — and the fall of one of the princes, i.e., of him who was called the serpent, who fell with a great overthrow, because he deceived Eve..."[184]

"...But as my discourse is not intended to touch on this point, but to prove to you that the Holy Ghost reproaches men because they were made like God, free from suffering and death, provided that they kept His commandments, and were deemed deserving of the name of His sons, and yet they, becoming like Adam and Eve, work out death for themselves; let the interpretation of the Psalm be held just as you wish, yet thereby it is demonstrated that **all men are deemed worthy of becoming gods**, and of having power to become **sons of the Highest**; and shall be each by himself judged and condemned like Adam and Eve. Now I have proved at length that **Christ is called God**."[185]

Justin does not quote **1 Thessalonians 4:17** or **1 Corinthians 15:50–52** directly. However, his theological reasoning—especially his reference to the first and second resurrections, the 1000-year reign, and the transformation of the saints—strongly implies that he interpreted these passages as referring to **two distinct prophetic events**, separated by **a thousand years**.

Irenaeus of Lyons

Who was he? **Irenaeus of Lyons** (c. 130–202 C.E.) was the earliest post-apostolic theologian of substantial influence. He is called the **first Doctor of the Church** in order of time, the **father of Catholic theology**, and a **Chiliasm Church Father**. He was a **hearer of Polycarp**, who himself was a direct disciple of **the Apostle John**, the writer of the Book of Revelation. Irenaeus is also cited favorably in the **first Lutheran Fathers' Book of Concord** and is venerated by the **Catholic Church**, the **Eastern Orthodox Church**, **Oriental Orthodoxy**, the **Anglican Communion**, and the **Lutheran Church**.

---

[184] Justin of Rome, "Chapters 80–81," *Dialogue with Trypho*, www.newadvent.org/fathers/01286.htm

[185] Justin of Rome, "Chapter 124," *Dialogue with Trypho*, www.newadvent.org/fathers/01288.htm

Irenaeus of Lyons' interpretation of 1 Thessalonians 4:17 and 1 Corinthians 15:52 offers a unique insight into early Christian eschatology. He connects the distinctive rapture term in **1 Thessalonians 4:17**—namely, "caught up"—with an event that takes place **just before the inauguration of the millennial reign of Christ**. Irenaeus refers to this reign as **"the times of the kingdom,"** and he places this catching away of the Church **after the Beast (final Antichrist) persecutes the saints.**

> "And they shall lay Babylon waste, and burn her with fire, and shall give their kingdom to the beast, and put the Church to flight..."[186]

> "...so far useful and serviceable to the just, as stubble conduces towards the growth of the wheat, and its straw, by means of combustion, serves for working gold. And therefore, when in the end the Church shall be **suddenly caught up from this**, it is said, there shall be tribulation such as has not been since the beginning, neither shall be. (Matthew 24:21) For this is the last contest of the righteous, in which, when they overcome, they are crowned with incorruption."[187]

Irenaeus thus places the Church's sudden removal **after** the Great Tribulation, and he explicitly links this event to the **last contest** of the saints—not an escape from it. He does not speak of a secret rapture, but of a visible event following great persecution. This harmonizes with the literal wording of **Matthew 24:21**, which Christ Himself declared to occur **after** the "abomination of desolation."

In fact, **Irenaeus of Lyons** clearly writes that there are only **two advents of Christ**—the first, which is past, and the second, which is yet future. Therefore, **1 Thessalonians 4:17** must belong to this second advent in his view, since he never mentions any *secret coming of Christ*, as taught by **pre-tribulation rapture** proponents who attach **1 Thess. 4:17** to it:

> "And do not recognise the advent of Christ, which He accomplished for the salvation of men, nor are willing to understand that all the prophets announced His **two advents**: the one, indeed, in which He became a man subject to stripes, and knowing what it is to bear infirmity (Isaiah 53:3), and sat upon the

---

[186] Irenaeus of Lyons, *Book 5. Chapter 26. Point 1*, *Against Heresies*, www.newadvent.org/fathers/0103526.htm

[187] Irenaeus of Lyons, *Book 5. Chapter 29. Point 1*, *Against Heresies*, www.newadvent.org/fathers/0103529.htm

foal of an ass (Zechariah 9:9), and was a stone rejected by the builders, and was led as a sheep to the slaughter (Isaiah 53:7), and by the stretching forth of His hands destroyed Amalek (Exodus 17:11); while He gathered from the ends of the earth into His Father's fold the children who were scattered abroad (Isaiah 11:12), and remembered His own dead ones who had formerly fallen asleep, and came down to them that He might deliver them: but the second, in which He will come on the clouds (Daniel 7:13), bringing on the day which burns as a furnace (Malachi 4:1), and smiting the earth with the word of His mouth (Isaiah 11:4), and slaying the impious with the breath of His lips, and having a fan in His hands, and cleansing His floor, and gathering the wheat indeed into His barn, but burning the chaff with unquenchable fire (Matthew 3:12; Luke 3:17)."[188]

1 Corinthians 15:52's change from human to no longer flesh and blood—or what is elsewhere called becoming "gods"—occurs **at the end of the 1,000 years**, that is, **after the times of the kingdom**, during the **last trumpet**, when **all the remaining dead** in the tombs are judged. This is not the context of the first resurrection:

> "And in the Apocalypse John saw this new [Jerusalem] descending upon the new earth (Revelation 21:2). For after the times of the kingdom, he says, I saw a great white throne, and Him who sat upon it, from whose face the earth fled away, and the heavens ... (Revelation 20:11). And he sets forth, too, the things connected with the **general resurrection and the judgment**, mentioning the dead, great and small."[189]

> "1. Let our opponents—that is, they who speak against their own salvation—inform us [as to this point] ... that His words concerning its [future] resurrection may also be believed; so also at the end, when the Lord utters His voice **by the last trumpet** (1 Corinthians 15:52), **the dead shall be raised**, as He Himself declares: 'The hour shall come, in which **all the dead which are in the tombs shall hear the voice of the Son of man**, and shall come forth; those that have done good to the resurrection of life,

---

[188] Irenaeus of Lyons, *Book 4. Chapter 33. Point 1*, *Against Heresies*, www.newadvent.org/fathers/0103433.htm
[189] Irenaeus of Lyons, *Book 5. Chapter 35. Point 2*, *Against Heresies*, www.newadvent.org/fathers/0103535.htm

and those that have done evil to the resurrection of judgment' (John 5:28)."[190]

Please observe carefully how **Irenaeus of Lyons** explicitly connects **1 Corinthians 15:52**'s mention of **"the dead"** and the **"last trumpet"**—a unique phrase found only in that verse—to the **second resurrection**. This is further affirmed when these statements are read alongside his reference to the **"times of the kingdom"** and the **"general resurrection and judgment."** Note also that **no wicked are judged** during the first resurrection timeline, as **Justin Martyr** affirmed earlier.

A further striking implication is that **a second group of righteous individuals** seems to be **saved during the second resurrection**. Irenaeus quotes **John 5:28** plainly in support of this, implying a **literal interpretation**. These righteous ones—saved at that later time—rise **together with the wicked**, just as **Matthew 25:31–46** portrays: **only at the judgment itself** are the **sheep separated from the goats**. If taken literally, this supports the view that these "sheep of another fold" are saved **1,000 years after** the elect sheep, which fits the **non-elect salvation possibility** model.

This transformation from human to angelic, or to being called "gods," is recognized in **Orthodox theology** as *theosis*, and in broader Christian theology as **divinization**. Irenaeus of Lyons writes concerning the Bride or Church by quoting **Psalm 82**, similar to **Justin of Rome's** earlier exposition:

> "For we cast blame upon Him, because we have not been made **gods** from the beginning, but at first merely men, then at length gods; although God has adopted this course out of His pure benevolence, that no one may impute to Him invidiousness or grudgingness. He declares, *I have said, You are gods; and you are all sons of the Highest.* But since we could not sustain the power of divinity, He adds, *But you shall die like men*, setting forth both truths—the kindness of His free gift, and our weakness, and also that we were possessed of power over ourselves. For after His great kindness He graciously conferred good [upon us], and made men like to Himself, [that is] in their own power; while at the same time by His prescience He knew the infirmity of human beings, and the consequences which would flow from it; but through [His] love and [His] power, **He shall overcome the substance of created nature**. For it was necessary, at first, that **nature should be**

---

[190] Irenaeus of Lyons, *Book 5. Chapter 13. Point 1, Against Heresies*, www.newadvent.org/fathers/0103513.htm

exhibited; then, after that, that what was mortal should be conquered and swallowed up by immortality, and the corruptible by incorruptibility, and that man should be made after the image and likeness of God, having received the knowledge of good and evil."[191]

In his quote next, **Irenaeus of Lyons** uses the phrase **"translated into the kingdom of heaven"** to describe the inheritance of the body by the Spirit. This language aligns closely with the **chiliasm prophecy** interpretation of **1 Corinthians 15:52**, where the **"change in the twinkling of an eye"** refers to the transformation from **sinless human** (natural body) to **"no more flesh and blood"**, into a **celestial (heavenly) spiritual body.**[192] Perhaps this is also why **Revelation 21:9** describes the **bride descending from Heaven**, having been **"translated"** there at that time.[193]

> "For a living person inherits the goods of the deceased; and it is one thing to inherit, another to be inherited. ... What, therefore, is it that lives? The Spirit of God, doubtless. What, again, are the possessions of the deceased? The various parts of the man, surely, which rot in the earth. But these are inherited by the Spirit **when they are translated into the kingdom of heaven**. For this cause, too, did Christ die, that the Gospel covenant being manifested and known to the whole world, might in the first place set free His slaves; and then afterwards, as I have already shown, might constitute them heirs of His property, when the Spirit possesses them by inheritance. For he who lives inherits, but the flesh is inherited. In order that we may not lose life by losing that Spirit which possesses us, the apostle, exhorting us to the communion of the Spirit, has said, according to reason, in those words already quoted, that **flesh and blood cannot inherit the kingdom of God**. Just as if he were to say, Do not err; for unless the Word of God dwell with, and the Spirit of the Father be in you, and if you shall live frivolously and carelessly as if you were this

---

[191] Irenaeus of Lyons, *Book 4. Chapter 38. Point 4, Against Heresies,* www.newadvent.org/fathers/0103438.htm

[192] 1 Corinthians 15:40–42, "40There are also celestial bodies and terrestrial bodies; but the glory of the celestial is one, and the glory of the terrestrial is another. 41There is one glory of the sun, another glory of the moon, and another glory of the stars; for one star differs from another star in glory. 42So also is the resurrection of the dead" (NKJV).

[193] Revelation 21:9–10, "Come, I will show you the bride, the Lamb's wife ... and showed me the great city, the holy Jerusalem, descending out of heaven from God" (NKJV).

only, viz., mere flesh and blood, **you cannot inherit the kingdom of God.**"[194]

Tertullian of Carthage

Who was he? **Tertullian** (c. 155–240) is a **chiliasm Church Father**, honored as the **father of Latin Christianity** and regarded as the **founder of Western theological scholarship** for his prolific writings and enduring influence on Christianity in the Latin West.

The earliest surviving writings of Christian theology in significant detail chiefly involve these **chiliasm Church Fathers: Irenaeus of Lyons, Justin of Rome**, and **Tertullian**, who appear to preserve the ancient faith most accurately. Where they differ, the variance may reflect differing interpretive possibilities. However, I personally prefer **Irenaeus of Lyons** and **Justin of Rome** over **Tertullian**, since even the Roman Catholic tradition has acknowledged errors in Tertullian's later theology, such as his alignment with **Montanism**, and so he was not canonized.

Tertullian also only seems to recognize **two comings of Christ**—one in the past, and a future **public** second coming **in full glory**, as stated:

> "Chapter 21. ... For two comings of Christ having been revealed to us: a first, which has been fulfilled in the lowliness of a human lot; a second, which impends over the world, now near its close, in all the majesty of Deity unveiled; and, by misunderstanding the first, they have concluded that the second — which, as matter of more manifest prediction, they set their hopes on — is the only one."[195]

Tertullian understands that **1 Thessalonians 4:17** refers to a **post-tribulation rapture** occurring at the **start of the 1000-year reign** (millennial timeline), **after the time of the final Antichrist** (or **"beast"**):

> "Now the privilege of this favour awaits those who shall at the coming of the Lord be found in the flesh, and who shall, owing to the oppressions of the time of Antichrist, deserve by an instantaneous death, which is accomplished by a sudden change, to become qualified to join the rising saints; as he writes to the Thessalonians: 'For this we say unto you by the word of the Lord, that we which are alive and remain unto the coming of the Lord

---

[194] Irenaeus of Lyons, *Book 5. Chapter 9. Point 4, Against Heresies.* www.newadvent.org/fathers/0103509.htm

[195] Tertullian, *Chapter 21, Apology.* www.newadvent.org/fathers/0301.htm

shall not prevent them which are asleep. For the Lord Himself shall descend from heaven with a shout, with the voice of the archangel, and with the trump of God: and the dead in Christ shall rise first: then we too shall ourselves be caught up together with them in the clouds, to meet the Lord in the air: and so shall we ever be with the Lord.'"196

Tertullian views **1 Corinthians 15:52** as describing the **change from the sinless human body to the celestial body**—that is, "no more flesh and blood"—at the **end of the 1000 years**, and he gives perhaps the clearest explanation of this doctrine:

> "Of the heavenly kingdom this is the process. After its thousand years are over, within which period is completed the resurrection of the saints, who rise sooner or later according to their deserts, there will ensue the destruction of the world and the conflagration of all things at the judgment: **we shall then be changed in a moment into the substance of angels**, even by the investiture of an incorruptible nature, and so be removed to that kingdom in heaven.197 ... But the resurrection is one thing, and the kingdom is another. The resurrection is first, and afterwards the kingdom. We say, therefore, that the flesh rises again, but that when changed it obtains the kingdom. ... and **we shall be changed, in a moment, in the twinkling of an eye ... in order, indeed, that it may be rendered a fit substance for the kingdom of God.** "For we shall be like the angels." This will be the perfect change of our flesh—only after its resurrection. ... Having then become something else by its change, it will obtain the kingdom of God, **no longer the (old) flesh and blood**, but the body which God shall have given it. Rightly then does the apostle declare, **"Flesh and blood cannot inherit the kingdom of God;"** for this (honour) does he ascribe to the changed condition which ensues on the resurrection."198

Victorinus of Pettau

---

[196] Tertullian, *Chapter 41, On the Resurrection of the Flesh.*
www.newadvent.org/fathers/0316.htm
[197] Tertullian, *Book 3. Chapter 25, Against Marcion.*
www.newadvent.org/fathers/03123.htm
[198] Tertullian, *Book 5. Chapter 10, Against Marcion.*
www.newadvent.org/fathers/03125.htm

Who was he? **Victorinus of Pettau** (c. 303 C.E.) was a **chiliasm Church Father** and **bishop of Pettau**, remembered for producing the **earliest known Christian verse-by-verse commentary** on the Apocalypse of John (the Book of Revelation). He died as a **martyr for Christ**, sealing his testimony with his blood during the Diocletian persecution.

Victorinus clearly affirms that **1 Thessalonians 4:17** refers to the **rapture** when Christ returns during the **first resurrection** at the beginning of the **1,000-year reign of Christ**. He then distinguishes this from **1 Corinthians 15:52**, which he understands to speak of the **glorification of Christians at the end** of the millennial reign, coinciding with the **second resurrection**:

> "2 At this same first resurrection ... the dead in Christ will stand first, then we who are living, as we will be taken up with Him in the clouds to meet the Lord in the air; and thus we will always be with the Lord [1 Thessalonians 4:17].
>
> A We have heard the trumpet spoken of; it is observed that in another place the Apostle names another trumpet. Therefore he says to the Corinthians: At the last trumpet, the dead will rise, will become immortal, and we will be changed.
>
> B He says the dead will be raised immortal for bearing punishments, but it is shown that we are to be changed and to be covered in glory [1 Corinthians 15:52].
>
> Therefore where we hear 'the last trumpet,' we must understand also a first, for these are two resurrections. Therefore, however many were not previously to rise in the first resurrection and to reign with Christ over the world [Revelation 20:4–6], over all nations, will rise at the last trumpet, after the thousand years, that is, in the last resurrection, among the impious and sinners and perpetrators of various kinds [Revelation 20:11–15]."[199]

Victorinus thus affirms the **Chiliasm framework**: a **first resurrection** with Christ to reign on earth, followed by a **second resurrection** for judgment, in which some are glorified and others condemned. He distinguishes the glorification of the righteous after the millennium from the initial rapture of the elect at Christ's return.

---

[199] Victorinus of Pettau, *Chapter 20, Commentary on Revelation.* (2014): 18.
earlychurchrevival.files.wordpress.com/2013/11/st-victorinus-of-poetovio-translated-by-kevin-edgecomb.pdf

Methodius of Olympus

Who was he? Methodius (died c. 311 C.E.) was a **Chiliasm Church Father**, first bishop of Olympus and later of Tyre. Although biographical details about him are scarce, it is known that he died a martyr under the Diocletianic persecution. Only a portion of his extensive writings has survived. Among his extant works, *The Banquet of the Ten Virgins* extols the virtue of virginity, while *On the Resurrection* directly challenges several teachings of Origen. Methodius is also credited with a treatise on free will, defending the liberty of man against the fatalistic doctrines of the Gnostics.

Methodius taught that 1 Thessalonians 4:17 describes the rapture at the beginning of the 1,000 years, marking the commencement of the festival of the first resurrection. He explicitly connects this passage to the bodily resurrection of the righteous and their glorified celebration with Christ:

> "VII. [Now the passage, *The dead in Christ shall rise first: then we which are alive*, Methodius thus explains]: Those are our bodies; for the souls are we ourselves, who, rising, resume that which is dead from the earth; so that being caught up with them to meet the Lord, we may gloriously celebrate the splendid festival of the resurrection, because we have received our everlasting tabernacles, which shall no longer die nor be dissolved."[200]

In contrast, **he taught that 1 Corinthians 15:52's "change" occurs at the end of the 1,000 years**, after the completion of the first resurrection and just before the beginning of the second. This "change" transforms the already resurrected sinless human body into a higher, angelic or heavenly nature:[201]

> "For I also, taking my journey, and going forth from the Egypt of this life, came first to the resurrection, which is the true Feast of the Tabernacles, and there having set up my tabernacle, adorned with the fruits of virtue, on the first day of the resurrection, which is the day of judgment, celebrate with Christ the millennium of rest, which is called the seventh day, even the

---

[200] Methodius of Olympus, "Part 3. II. A Synopsis of Some Apostolic Words from the Same Discourse. Point 7," in *From the Discourse on the Resurrection*, www.newadvent.org/fathers/0625.htm

[201] Luke 20:34–36 — "Jesus answered and said to them, 'The sons of this age marry and are given in marriage. But those who are counted worthy to attain that age, and the resurrection from the dead, neither marry nor are given in marriage; nor can they die anymore, for they are equal to the angels and are sons of God, being sons of the resurrection.'"

true Sabbath. Then again from thence I, a follower of Jesus, who has entered into the heavens, Hebrews 4:14 as they also, after the rest of the Feast of Tabernacles, came into the land of promise, come into the heavens, not continuing to remain in tabernacles — that is, my body not remaining as it was before, but, after the space of a thousand years, changed from a human and corruptible form into angelic size and beauty, where at last we virgins, when the festival of the resurrection is consummated, shall pass from the wonderful place of the tabernacle to greater and better things."[202]

Justin of Rome (also called Justin Martyr), who lived in the generation after the apostles, is cited by Methodius in support of this doctrine. Justin affirmed a transitional phase in resurrection glory, writing:

"The flesh indeed dies, but the kingdom of heaven lives."[203]

Methodius seems to quote this to reinforce the idea that entrance into the heavenly kingdom requires a transformation beyond mere bodily resurrection. Given the vivid harmony between Methodius' own commentary and Justin's statement, it is possible that this quote reflects one of **Justin's lost works**, preserved through Methodius.

Why Must Christians First Be Resurrected in Sinless Human Bodies for 1,000 Years Before Being Changed into a Heavenly State?

According to the early **Chiliasm Church Fathers**, believers must first participate in the **1,000-year reign of Christ in sinless human resurrection bodies** before being transformed into an angelic or heavenly substance. This teaching is not arbitrary but deeply rooted in the justice of God and His covenantal dealings with man. The glorified change described in **1 Corinthians 15:52**—the moment in which "flesh and blood cannot inherit the kingdom of God"—is reserved for the conclusion of the millennium. Prior to that, the righteous are **resurrected in incorruptible, sinless human form** to be rewarded within the very creation in which they suffered.

Irenaeus of Lyons, in his monumental *Against Heresies*, gives the clearest theological explanation for this. He writes that the **earthly kingdom**

---

[202] Methodius of Olympus, "Discourse 9. Chapter 5," in *Banquet of the Ten Virgins*, www.newadvent.org/fathers/062309.htm

[203] "Fragment 5," in *Fragments of St. Justin Martyr*, www.newadvent.org/fathers/0132.htm; also cited in Methodius of Olympus, "Part 3. II. A Synopsis of Some Apostolic Words from the Same Discourse. Point VI," in *From the Discourse on the Resurrection*, www.newadvent.org/fathers/0625.htm

is the beginning of incorruption, and only **after** the saints reign in this renovated creation does the final judgment and change occur:

> "1. Inasmuch, therefore, as the opinions of certain [orthodox persons] are derived from heretical discourses, they are both ignorant of God's dispensations, and of the mystery of the resurrection of the just, and of the [earthly] kingdom which is the commencement of incorruption, by means of which kingdom those who shall be worthy are accustomed gradually to partake of the divine nature (*capere Deum*); and it is necessary to tell them respecting those things, that it behooves the righteous first to receive the promise of the inheritance which God promised to the fathers, and to reign in it, when they rise again to behold God in this creation which is renovated, and that the judgment should take place afterwards. For it is just that in that very creation in which they toiled or were afflicted, being proved in every way by suffering, they should receive the reward of their suffering; and that in the creation in which they were slain because of their love to God, in that they should be revived again; and that in the creation in which they endured servitude, in that they should reign. For God is rich in all things, and all things are His. It is fitting, therefore, that the creation itself, being restored to its primeval condition, should without restraint be under the dominion of the righteous; and the apostle has made this plain in the Epistle to the Romans."[204]

Tertullian also affirms this progression. He explicitly teaches that the city of God, prepared for the saints, is to refresh them with spiritual blessings as a **recompense** for what they sacrificed in the present world. This divine justice is fulfilled during the **millennial reign**, not immediately at death or transformation. The final glorification comes **after** the thousand years are completed:

> "Chapter 25. ... We say that this city has been provided by God for receiving the saints on their resurrection, and refreshing them with the abundance of all really spiritual blessings, as a recompense for those which in the world we have either despised or lost; since it is both just and God-worthy that His servants should have their joy in the place where they have also suffered affliction for His name's sake. Of the heavenly kingdom this is the

---

[204] Irenaeus of Lyons, *Against Heresies*, Book 5, Chapter 32, Point 1. www.newadvent.org/fathers/0103532.htm

process. After its thousand years are over, within which period is completed the resurrection of the saints, who rise sooner or later according to their deserts, there will ensue the destruction of the world and the conflagration of all things at the judgment: … when Abraham's seed, after the primal promise of being like the sand of the sea for multitude, is destined likewise to an equality with the stars of heaven — are not these the indications both of an earthly and a heavenly dispensation?"[205]

This transition from **earthly incorruptibility to heavenly glory** also aligns with the biblical concept of **spirit, soul, and body**—the complete man. The **Apostle Paul** prays for this triune preservation in view of the Lord's return (1 Thessalonians 5:23).[206] **Irenaeus of Lyons** elaborates on this structure:

> "They do not take this fact into consideration, that there are three things out of which, as I have shown, the complete man is composed —flesh, soul, and spirit. One of these does indeed preserve and fashion [the man]—this is the spirit; while as to another it is united and formed—that is the flesh; then [comes] that which is between these two—that is the soul, which sometimes indeed, when it follows the spirit, is raised up by it, but sometimes it sympathizes with the flesh, and falls into carnal lusts."[207]

Justin of Rome likewise acknowledges this threefold nature, reinforcing the idea that salvation includes not only the spirit but the **complete man**, and that **the body serves as the house for the soul**, just as the soul houses the spirit. Without the body, man is incomplete:

> "For the body is the house of the soul; and the soul the house of the spirit. These three, in all those who cherish a sincere hope and unquestioning faith in God, will be saved."[208]

---

[205] Tertullian, *Against Marcion*, Book 3, Chapter 25.
www.newadvent.org/fathers/03123.htm

[206] 1 Thessalonians 5:23 — "Now may the God of peace Himself sanctify you completely; and may your whole spirit, soul, and body be preserved blameless at the coming of our Lord Jesus Christ" (NKJV).

[207] Irenaeus of Lyons, *Against Heresies*, Book 5, Chapter 9, Point 1.
www.newadvent.org/fathers/0103509.htm

[208] Justin of Rome, *On the Resurrection*, Chapter 10.
www.newadvent.org/fathers/0131.htm

In summary, the **1,000-year reign in sinless human bodies is necessary** to fulfill God's promise of reward within the very world where His saints suffered. This earthly reign precedes the final glorification in heaven, in harmony with the complete structure of man and the just nature of Jehovah.

HOW DOES THIS COMPARE WITH OTHER BELIEFS AND RESEARCH?

In historical papers regarding **chiliasm**, it's often said that "other patriarchs excluded Chiliasm."[209] However, what is **unsaid** is that these same other patriarchs did not write about an allegorical view of the book of Revelation either, and so, their position on the doctrine is **unknown**.

In fact, these same papers demonstrate clearly that the **chiliasm quotes presented are from the earliest church fathers**, and claims such as these beliefs are held individually[210] and not by the church as a whole contradict recent discoveries such as the **Didache**,[211] which ends with these words:

> "And then shall appear the signs of the truth; first, the sign of an outspreading in heaven; then the sign of the sound of the trumpet; and the third, the resurrection of the dead; yet not of all, but as it is said: The Lord shall come and all His saints with Him. Then shall the world see the Lord coming upon the clouds of heaven."[212]

In this **church doctrinal stance** of the Didache, which is commonly dated to the **first century**,[213] the resurrection mentioned here which is "not of all" is clearly a **chiliasm confession** of the **first resurrection**, since the rest will be resurrected at the **end of 1000 years**. This is **intrinsically**

---

[209] J. C. De Smidt, "Chiliasm: An Escape from the Present into an Extra-Biblical Apocalyptic Imagination.", *Scriptura*, 45 (1993): 84.
scriptura.journals.ac.za/pub/article/view/1647/1508

[210] Ibid. 84.

[211] The Didache was rediscovered in 1875 with an old Latin translation in 1900. (Chapman, J., "Didache", in *The Catholic Encyclopedia*, (New York: Robert Appleton Company, 1908)). www.newadvent.org/cathen/04779a.htm

[212] M.B. Riddle, "Chapter 16", in *Didache, Ante-Nicene Fathers*, Vol. 7, edited by Alexander Roberts, James Donaldson, and A. Cleveland Coxe, (Buffalo, NY: Christian Literature Publishing Co., 1886). www.newadvent.org/fathers/0714.htm

[213] Frank Leslie Cross & Elizabeth A. Livingstone, *The Oxford Dictionary of the Christian Church*, 3rd ed. (Oxford: University Press, 2005): 482.

implied, since all other known allegorical views consider the existence of **only one resurrection** for both the righteous and wicked at the same time.

The **allegorists** view the second resurrection to happen at the **second coming of Christ**.[214] This "one resurrection" involving both the righteous and unrighteous to happen at the same time is a **common belief to almost all reformers** and can be seen in the **Augsburg Confession** even though it contradicts the **Didache**, compare:

> "1 Also they teach that at the Consummation of the World Christ will appear for judgment, and 2 will raise up all the dead; He will give to the godly and elect eternal life and everlasting joys, 3 but ungodly men and the devils He will condemn to be tormented without end."[215]

Notice also that the **allegorical view** is totally absent even in individual Church Father writings from this same earliest time period. It is first found in the writings of **Origen of Alexandria** (c. 185–253) in the East and **Augustine of Hippo** (c. 354–430) in the West.[216] Despite this, and strangely, the allegorical view is often claimed to be the doctrinal stance from antiquity. However, it clearly lacks any earlier historical quotes in time.

A general rule of thumb would be this: **views not rooted in any patristic quote ought to be cautiously considered.** For example, **John Wesley** (1703–1791), the key founder of the Methodist churches, held one of the strangest eschatological opinions—he believed in **two consecutive millenniums** for a total of **2000 years after the Second Coming of Christ**.[217] This is clearly a **private interpretation**, since no Church Father

---

[214] Francois P. Möller, "A Hermeneutical Commentary on Revelation 20:1–10", in *In die Skriflig/In Luce Verbi*, 53(1) (2019): 7. doi.org/10.4102/ids.v53i1.2459

[215] Francis Monseth, *Millennialism in American Lutheranism in Light of Augsburg Confession, Article XVII*, Doctor of Theology Dissertation, 137, (Concordia Seminary, St. Louis, Missouri 63105, USA, 1986). scholar.csl.edu/thd/137

[216] J. C. De Smidt, "Chiliasm: An Escape from the Present into an Extra-Biblical Apocalyptic Imagination," *Scriptura*, 45 (1993): 84–85.
scriptura.journals.ac.za/pub/article/view/1647/1508

[217] Robert B. Brown, *Joy of Heaven to Earth Come Down: Perfection and Millennium in the Eschatology of John Wesley*, Master of Philosophy thesis (University of Manchester [Nazarene Theological College], UK, 2011): 4, 32, 63, 69.
pure.manchester.ac.uk/ws/portalfiles/portal/54511356/FULL_TEXT.PDF

ever taught such a view, and therefore it has the **least likely chance to be true**.[218]

John Calvin (1509–1564), founder of the Reformed churches and Calvinism, **rejected Chiliasm's literal 1000 years** under the following chief argument:

> "But Satan has not only befuddled men's senses to make them bury with the corpses the memory of resurrection; he has also attempted to corrupt this part of the doctrine with various falsifications that he might at length destroy it... but a little later there followed the chiliasts, who limited the kingdom to a thousand years.... For if they do not put on immortality, then Christ himself, to whose glory they shall be transformed, has not been received into undying glory."[219]

The error in Calvin's reasoning is his failure to distinguish that the **1000 years is not a limitation but a distinct dispensation**—a designated timeframe in which the saints are in **sinless human resurrection bodies** before the final transformation into the **non-fleshly, heavenly form**.

This is evident in Calvin's commentary, which **lacks the concept of change from human to angelic**. He writes:

> "Paul's intention is to explain what he had said—that we will be conformed to Christ, because flesh and blood cannot inherit the kingdom of God.... His answer is, that although all will not die, yet they will be renewed, that mortality and corruption may be done away."[220]

Calvin's framework **skips over the millennial reward in human form** taught by the early chiliast Fathers and instead jumps directly to glorification without reconciling Revelation 20 or the sequential resurrections described by Methodius, Irenaeus, and Tertullian.

---

[218] John Wesley, *Wesley's Notes on the Bible* (Grand Rapids: Francis Asbury, 1987): 772–778 (CCEL version). ccel.org/ccel/w/wesley/notes/cache/notes.pdf

[219] John Calvin, *The Institutes of the Christian Religion*, Vol. 2, John T. McNeill ed., trans. Ford Lewis Battles; *The Library of Christian Classics*, Vol. 21 (Philadelphia: Westminster Press, 1960): 995

[220] John Calvin, *Commentary on Corinthians*, Vol. 2, via Tim Perrine, CCEL Staff Writer (Grand Rapids, MI: Christian Classics Ethereal Library, 2009): 48. www.ccel.org/ccel/calvin/calcom40.i.vi.html (ccel.org/ccel/c/calvin/calcom40/cache/calcom40.pdf)

Calvin views the **1 Corinthians 15** change as merely a renewal into immortality, conforming to Christ. In his understanding, the phrase "**flesh and blood**" refers to the **mortal, sinful flesh** of the natural life. This has influenced many theologians up to the present day, most of whom interpret **1 Thessalonians 4** and **1 Corinthians 15** as referring to the **same event**. By doing so, however, they may have **overlooked the distinctive Chiliasm prophecy details** presented throughout this writing.

For example:

> "Rooted in biblical passages such as 1 Thessalonians 4:16–17 and 1 Corinthians 15:51–52, the Rapture envisions a sudden gathering of believers to meet Christ in the air."[221]

Some scholars, such as **Jeffrey R. Asher**, argue that Paul, in 1 Corinthians 15, is merely **negating pre-conceived impossibilities**—namely, that a **terrestrial resurrected body cannot dwell in celestial realms.**[222] Others, like **Elton L. Hollon**, suggest Paul is describing a **merged body** with both terrestrial and celestial properties.[223]

The difficulty with these interpretations is that they **dilute the absolute force** of Paul's statement: "**flesh and blood cannot inherit the kingdom of God**" (1 Corinthians 15:50, NKJV). If the proposed resurrected body still retains **terrestrial or fleshly attributes**, then the verse is no longer being interpreted literally.

By contrast, **chiliasm fathers** maintain that there will be an **absolute change**—from human flesh to an **angelic or celestial form**—in order to inherit the final heavens, which is also called the **kingdom of God** in Scripture.[224] This provides a consistent understanding across dispensations: the **earthly millennium** requires a **terrestrial (sinless human) body**, while

---

[221] Douglas C. Youvan, "The Evolution and Divergence of Rapture Theology: Historical Development and Denominational Perspectives," *ResearchGate* (July 2024): 2. DOI:10.13140/RG.2.2.19515.43044

[222] Jeffrey R. Asher, "Polarity and Change in 1 Corinthians 15," in *Hermeneutische Untersuchungen zur Theologie*, 42 (Tübingen: Mohr Siebeck, 2000): 250

[223] Elton L. Hollon, "Paul's Account of Change at the Resurrection in 1 Corinthians 15:42-44a," *The Heythrop Journal* (3 December 2024).
onlinelibrary.wiley.com/doi/10.1111/heyj.14585

[224] Matthew 19:23–24, "Then Jesus said to His disciples, 'Assuredly, I say to you that it is hard for a rich man to enter the kingdom of heaven. And again I say to you, it is easier for a camel to go through the eye of a needle than for a rich man to enter the kingdom of God.'" (NKJV)

the **final kingdom of the heavens**, which begins **after the 1000 years**, requires a **celestial transformation**.[225]

Christ's resurrection body alone is perfect from the beginning, as Philippians 3:21 states: "who will transform our lowly body that it may be conformed to His glorious body."[226] In contrast, our own conformity to Christ's **glorious body** is **gradual**. This transformation does not occur all at once but unfolds **throughout the 1000-year reign**, which is the period of the **marriage of the Lamb**. It reaches its culmination at the end of the millennium. **Irenaeus of Lyons** supports this understanding, writing:

> "…they are both ignorant of God's dispensations, and of the mystery of the resurrection of the just, and of the [earthly] kingdom which is the commencement of incorruption, by means of which kingdom those who shall be worthy are accustomed gradually to partake of the divine nature (*capere Deum*)."[227]

Modern believers in **chiliasm** still tend to **interpret 1 Thessalonians 4:17 (the rapture)** and **1 Corinthians 15:52 (the change)** as the **same event**, primarily because of the assumption that both refer to the **same trumpet**. This leads to two broad camps: **pre-tribulation** and **post-tribulation** rapture advocates.

The **pre-tribulation position** suggests that the rapture will occur **before** a period of tribulation (typically 3.5 to 7 years), which will be followed by Christ's second coming and the start of the **millennial reign**.[228] According to this view, the **"last trumpet"** of 1 Corinthians 15:52 is not the same as the **seventh trumpet** of Revelation 11:15.[229]

---

[225] Revelation 21:1, "Now I saw a new heaven and a new earth, for the first heaven and the first earth had passed away. Also there was no more sea." (NKJV)

[226] Philippians 3:21, "who will transform our lowly body that it may be conformed to His glorious body," (NKJV).

[227] Irenaeus of Lyons, *Against Heresies*, Book 5, Chapter 32, Point 1. www.newadvent.org/fathers/0103532.htm

[228] Sri Binar, Harman Laia, & Widi Prasetyo, "Exegesis of Revelation 20:1–10 about 'The Millennial Kingdom,'" *Journal Kerugma* (2019): 37.
www.researchgate.net/publication/341791082_EXEGESIS_OF_REVELATION_20 1-10_ABOUT_THE_MILLENNIAL_KINGDOM

[229] Thomas D. Ice, "The Last Trumpet," *Article Archives*, 86 (Liberty University, USA, May 2009). digitalcommons.liberty.edu/pretrib_arch/86

By contrast, the **post-tribulation view** holds that these two trumpet passages **do refer to the same trumpet**, sounded at Christ's visible return at the end of the tribulation.[230]

However, the **Chiliasm church fathers**, as cited in this work, **introduce a radically different perspective**: that **1 Thessalonians 4:17** and **1 Corinthians 15:52** are separated by **a full 1000 years**. If correct, this is a **distinctly ancient prophetic interpretation** that challenges most modern models. According to this reading, the **seventh trumpet** of Revelation 11:15[231] marks the **start** of the 1000-year reign, possibly identifying it with 1 Thessalonians 4:17, while the **last trumpet** of 1 Corinthians 15:52 signifies a later event—namely, the **change at the end** of the millennium, just before the **new heavens and new earth** begin.

CONCLUSION

Why are all these details important? **Doctrinal accuracy** is rewarded more greatly in the heavenly order than lesser accuracy. This is seen in Daniel 12:3, where those who "turn many to righteousness" are said to shine like **stars**, while the **wise** (who presumably teach more exact doctrine) will shine like **the brightness of the firmament**.[232] Likewise, the **"testimony of Jesus is the spirit of prophecy"** (Revelation 19:10),[233] so a mistaken view of prophecy may lead to a distorted testimony of Christ. Consequently, theological works—even if correct in other areas—may be diminished in value if the prophetic foundation is flawed. This is implied in 1 Timothy 5:17, where "double honor" is attributed to those who labor in **word and doctrine**,[234] suggesting a greater reward for greater accuracy.

To understand the **literal 1000 years** of **Chiliasm**, let us consider **Tertullian**. Based on his earlier citations, he plainly teaches three key elements:

---

[230] Jim McKeever, *Christians Will Go Through the Tribulation: And How to Prepare for It* (Medford, OR: Omega Publications, 1978): 45–46

[231] Revelation 11:15, "Then the seventh angel sounded: And there were loud voices in heaven, saying, 'The kingdoms of this world have become the kingdoms of our Lord and of His Christ, and He shall reign forever and ever!'" (NKJV)

[232] Daniel 12:3, "Those who are wise shall shine Like the brightness of the firmament, And those who turn many to righteousness Like the stars forever and ever" (NKJV).

[233] Revelation 19:10, "The testimony of Jesus is the spirit of prophecy" (NKJV). biblehub.com/revelation/19-10.htm

[234] 1 Timothy 5:17, "Let the elders who rule well be counted worthy of double honor, especially those who labor in the word and doctrine." (NKJV).

Christ has two comings.

The Second Coming corresponds with **1 Thessalonians 4**. After the 1000 years, the **change** into an **angelic**, non-flesh-and-blood body occurs, as described in **1 Corinthians 15**.

These quotes are drawn from different books, but that presents no problem. When read together, Tertullian clearly places the **coming of Christ** (1 Thessalonians 4:17) at the **start of the millennium**, and the **change** (1 Corinthians 15:52) **only after** the 1000 years. This proves a real **time gap** between the two events. It is not speculation—it is plainly stated in his own words.

Tertullian never says that we go to the final heavens at the moment of the rapture in 1 Thessalonians 4:17, but only that we meet the Lord "in the air." Even if this means a journey into heaven, it is still the **present heaven**, not the **final new heavens** and **new earth** described in Revelation 21:1.[235] Entry into that **incorruptible realm** requires the transformation described in 1 Corinthians 15:52—from "human" (flesh and blood) to "angelic" (no longer flesh and blood).

Why must Christians first be raised in **sinless human bodies** for 1000 years? **Tertullian** explains that the **earthly dispensation** is a time for **reward and repayment**. The saints are compensated for the **non-sinful joys denied** in this present life. Some will rise later within the millennium, according to their faithfulness—**"according to their deserts."** This corresponds with **Irenaeus'** statement that the **renewed creation** in which believers suffered is also the arena in which they are repaid.

After the 1000 years, we are changed into beings **no longer flesh and blood**, fit to enter the **final heavens**. At this point, the **current earth and heavens** are destroyed, and the **new heavens and new earth** emerge. The reason for this change is clarified by **Irenaeus**, who contrasts the temporary and corruptible nature of the current creation with the incorruptible nature of the new:

> "For neither is the substance nor the essence of the creation annihilated...but the fashion of the world passes away; that is, those

---

[235] Revelation 21:1, "Now I saw a new heaven and a new earth, for the first heaven and the first earth had passed away. Also there was no more sea." (NKJV).

things among which transgression has occurred, since man has grown old in them."[236]

He continues:

> "But when this [present] fashion [of things] passes away, and man has been renewed... then there shall be the new heaven and the new earth... And as the presbyters say, then those who are deemed worthy of an abode in heaven shall go there, others shall enjoy the delights of paradise, and others shall possess the splendour of the city; for everywhere the Saviour shall be seen according as they who see Him shall be worthy."[237]

Both **Victorinus** and **Methodius** confirm this sequence. Even if details vary, the **general framework** remains intact and supportable. Disagreements in detail merely reflect that some individual explanations may be **partially right**, while others are **fully correct** if they can be harmonized with Scripture and earlier testimony.

Other **Chiliasm fathers**[238] writings also seem to affirm a **1000-year gap** between the events described in **1 Thessalonians 4:17** and **1 Corinthians 15:52**, even when such a gap must be discerned **intrinsically** rather than through direct statements. The interpretations below are based on **quotes already presented** in earlier sections for each Church father:

Justin of Rome

Justin's first quotation affirms only **two advents of Christ**: one past (the Incarnation) and one future, the **public Second Coming**. Thus, the reference in **1 Thessalonians 4** must be placed at **Christ's future return**,

---

[236] Irenaeus of Lyons, *Against Heresies*, Book 5, Chapter 36, Point 1. www.newadvent.org/fathers/0103536.htm

[237] Irenaeus of Lyons, *Against Heresies*, Book 5, Chapter 36, Point 1. www.newadvent.org/fathers/0103536.htm

[238] Irenaeus of Lyons writes, "But when this Antichrist shall have devastated all things in this world... the Lord will come from heaven in the clouds... bringing in for the righteous the times of the kingdom... in which kingdom the Lord declared, that many coming from the east and from the west should sit down with Abraham, Isaac, and Jacob" (*Against Heresies*, Book 5, Chapter 30, Point 4). www.newadvent.org/fathers/0103530.htm

Further, "John, therefore, did distinctly foresee the first resurrection of the just... and what the prophets have prophesied concerning it harmonize [with his vision]" (*Book 5, Chapter 36, Points 2–3*). www.newadvent.org/fathers/0103536.htm

And also, "These are [to take place] in the times of the kingdom... when the righteous shall bear rule upon their rising from the dead" (*Book 5, Chapter 33, Points 2–3*). www.newadvent.org/fathers/0103533.htm

corresponding with the **First Resurrection** before the **Second Resurrection**, which occurs after the 1000 years. Since the **1 Corinthians 15** passage uses the phrase **"last trumpet"** and states that **"the dead shall be raised"**, it more naturally aligns with the **general resurrection** at the end of the 1000 years. Justin's statement that Christians will become like **"gods"** at the **end of this 1000 years**, when they render judgment to all men, supports the notion of a **bodily transformation** and **judgment** at that time. His distinction between "gods" (Christians) and "all men" mirrors the chiliasm model which places the **first resurrection** at the start of the 1000 years and the **general resurrection** with judgment at its end. This makes it unlikely that Justin is associating **1 Corinthians 15** with the first resurrection.

Irenaeus of Lyons

Irenaeus, in his first citation for this section, refers to the Church being **"suddenly caught up"**—a direct reference to the language of **1 Thessalonians 4:17** ("caught up")—placing this at **Christ's public Second Coming**, which destroys the Antichrist and inaugurates the **millennial reign**. Other quotes confirm that he believed in **only two comings** of Christ: one fulfilled, and the other still future and public. This further supports the idea that **1 Thessalonians 4** is aligned with the Second Coming and the **start of the millennium**.

Subsequent quotes from Irenaeus clearly place the **general resurrection** (i.e., the **second resurrection**) at the **end of the 1000 years**. He explicitly refers to the **"last trumpet"**, found only in **1 Corinthians 15:52**, in connection with the **bodily resurrection of both the righteous and the wicked**—a general resurrection. He even applies this as an **evangelistic hope** toward his **opponents**, implying a universal resurrection at the final judgment.

This **last trumpet** also includes the transformation of the righteous from **flesh and blood** to a **glorified, incorruptible form**. Since this bodily change is needed to enter the **eternal kingdom** (cf. 1 Corinthians 15:50), and since Irenaeus ties this event to the **general resurrection and final judgment**, it must occur **after** the millennial reign. Therefore, this proves a **clear 1000-year gap** between **1 Thessalonians 4** and **1 Corinthians 15**, consistent with **Chiliasm**.

Irenaeus also identifies the **"times of the kingdom"** with the **First Resurrection**, which takes place at **Christ's return** and marks the beginning of the millennium.[1] His references to the **Second Resurrection** use the phrase **"after the times of the kingdom"**,[239] and he connects this explicitly with the **last trumpet**.[240] This second resurrection involves **the whole human race**, as shown in his application of **Matthew 25:31–46**,[241] thus confirming its universal scope and its placement at the **end of the millennium**.

This harmonizes with **Revelation 20:5–6**, which also teaches a resurrection of the rest of the dead only **after** the 1000 years:

> "But the rest of the dead did not live again until the thousand years were finished. This is the first resurrection. Blessed and holy is he who has part in the first resurrection. Over such the second death has no power, but they shall be priests of God and of Christ, and shall reign with Him a thousand years."[242]

Victorinus of Pettau

Victorinus' exposition is also **crystal clear** in affirming a **1000-year gap** between **1 Thessalonians 4:17** and **1 Corinthians 15:52**. He explicitly cites the **"caught up"** phrase from **1 Thessalonians 4:17** as referring to the **Second Coming of Christ**, the moment when the righteous are gathered to meet the Lord in the air. In the **same passage**, he distinguishes this trumpet from the **"last trumpet"** of **1 Corinthians 15:52**, making it evident that these are **not the same trumpet**. He plainly says that since **1 Corinthians** refers to a "last trumpet," there must be a **first**—implying that the **1 Thessalonians trumpet** is earlier in sequence.

Victorinus then provides a decisive conclusion: the **last trumpet** occurs **after the thousand years**, at which point believers are **changed** and "covered in glory." This matches the event Paul speaks of in **1 Corinthians 15:52**, where "we shall be changed." The implication is unavoidable— Victorinus places **1 Thessalonians 4:17** at the **start of the millennium** (the First Resurrection), and **1 Corinthians 15:52** at the **end of the millennium**

---

[239] "For after the times of the kingdom... [John] sets forth... the general resurrection and the judgment, mentioning the dead, great and small" (*Book 5, Chapter 35, Point 2*). www.newadvent.org/fathers/0103535.htm

[240] "When the Lord utters His voice by the last trumpet... the dead shall be raised... those that have done good to the resurrection of life, and those that have done evil to the resurrection of judgment" (*Book 5, Chapter 13, Point 1*). www.newadvent.org/fathers/0103513.htm

[241] "The whole human race shall be divided at the judgment... some He will say, Come... receive the kingdom... others... Depart... into everlasting fire" (*Book 4, Chapter 40, Point 2*). www.newadvent.org/fathers/0103440.htm

[242] Revelation 20:5–6 (NKJV)

(the Second Resurrection), thereby affirming a **literal 1000-year gap** between the two prophetic events.

This **change into glory** harmonizes with the transformation described by both **Tertullian** and **Methodius**, who interpret the change as from **human** to **angelic** nature. Such glorification is also consistent with the prophetic imagery of **Daniel 12:3**, which states that the wise "shall shine like the brightness of the firmament," while "those who turn many to righteousness [shall shine] like the stars forever and ever." Christ similarly affirms this in **Matthew 13:43**, saying, "Then the righteous will shine forth as the sun in the kingdom of their Father."[243]

Methodius of Olympus

Methodius also quotes directly from **1 Thessalonians 4:17**, clearly applying it to the **public Second Coming of Christ**. He affirms that this event occurs at the **commencement of the 1000 years**, which he describes as the beginning of the **festival of the resurrection**. For Methodius, this "festival" is no metaphor; it is **literal**, lasting the full thousand years. He never quotes **1 Corinthians 15:52** in reference to this beginning moment. Rather, he reserves Paul's phrase—"we shall be changed"—for the **end** of the 1000-year millennial reign, aligning with the transformation described by **Tertullian** and **Victorinus**. Linguistically and theologically, he uses identical concepts: the change is from **human** to **angelic** or **glorious**, and it takes place at the **close of the millennium**. Thus, once again, the **1000-year gap** between **1 Thessalonians 4:17** and **1 Corinthians 15:52** is affirmed.

This transformation may also find a unique witness in the **Book of 1 Enoch**, which—though non-canonical for most churches—was historically held as Scripture in the **Ethiopian Orthodox Tewahido Church**. In **Chapter 50**, the text describes the **elect** (interpreted as Christians) undergoing a transformation: "the light of days shall abide upon them" and they will be filled with "glory and honour" on the **day of affliction**, when **sinners are judged**. This context aligns not with the **start** of the 1000 years, but with its **end**, at the **Second Resurrection**—which again places the change at the same timing as **1 Corinthians 15:52**.[244]

---

[243] 1 Matthew 13:43 (NKJV)

[244] Ethiopian Orthodox Tewahido Church Holy Synod, "Canonical Books," in *A Short History, Faith and Order of the Ethiopian Orthodox Tewahido Church* (Addis Ababa, 1983). www.ethiopianorthodox.org/english/canonical/books.html

R.H. Charles, *Book of 1 Enoch*. Chapter 50, in *The Apocrypha and Pseudepigrapha of the Old Testament* (Oxford: The Clarendon Press, 1913).

In further support of this timeline, **Lactantius** (c. 250–325 C.E.), a well-respected scholar and advisor to **Emperor Constantine I**, affirms the same understanding. He interprets the change described in **1 Corinthians 15:52**—the moment "in the twinkling of an eye"—as a **transformation from human to angelic** at the **end of the 1000 years**, not at its start. He describes the **Second Coming of Christ** with unmistakable apocalyptic detail, linking **1 Thessalonians 4:16–17** to the **First Resurrection** and the beginning of the millennial reign. His concluding emphasis is powerful: he testifies that these details have been **faithfully followed by the holy prophets and Christians**, indicating that this was **not a marginal belief**, but one rooted in the consistent faith of the early church.[245]

After the description of the second coming of Christ above, **Lactantius** writes **chronologically** in order of time, describing the judgments which are to happen during the millennium—this includes the first resurrection as well:

> "But He, when He shall have destroyed unrighteousness, and executed His great judgment, and shall have recalled to life the righteous, who have lived from the beginning, will be engaged among men a thousand years, and will rule them with most just command. ... Then they who shall be alive in their bodies shall not die, but during those thousand years shall produce an infinite multitude, and their offspring shall be holy, and beloved by God; but they who shall be raised from the dead shall preside over the living as judges. But the nations shall not be entirely extinguished, but some shall be left as a victory for God, that they may be the occasion of triumph to the righteous, and may be subjected to perpetual slavery. About the same time also the prince of the devils, who is the contriver of all evils, shall be bound with chains, and shall be imprisoned during the thousand years of the heavenly rule in which righteousness shall reign in the world, so that he may contrive no evil against the people of God."[246]

---

www.ccel.org/c/charles/otpseudepig/enoch/ENOCH_2.HTM

[245] 1 Thessalonians 4:16–17, "For the Lord Himself will descend from heaven with a shout, with the voice of an archangel, and with the trumpet of God. And the dead in Christ will rise first. Then we who are alive and remain shall be caught up together with them in the clouds to meet the Lord in the air. And thus we shall always be with the Lord." (NKJV)

Lactantius, "Book 7 (VII, Of a Happy Life). Chapter 19," in *Divine Institutes*. www.newadvent.org/fathers/07017.htm

[246] Lactantius, *Divine Institutes*, Book 7, Chapter 24.

Notice that the **immortals of the first resurrection** exist alongside the **mortals of the millennial reign** in this quote. Next, **Lactantius** highlights that **Satan will be bound for 1000 years** during this millennium, agreeing with a literal reading of the timeline of events listed in the Book of Revelation, chapters 19–21:

> "We have said, a little before, that it will come to pass at the commencement of the sacred reign, that the prince of the devils will be bound by God. But he also, when the thousand years of the kingdom, that is, seven thousand of the world, shall begin to be ended, will be loosed afresh, and being sent forth from prison, will go forth and assemble all the nations, which shall then be under the dominion of the righteous, that they may make war against the holy city; and there shall be collected together from all the world an innumerable company of the nations, and shall besiege and surround the city. Then the last anger of God shall come upon the nations, and shall utterly destroy them; and first He shall shake the earth most violently, and by its motion the mountains of Syria shall be rent, and the hills shall sink down precipitously, and the walls of all cities shall fall, and God shall cause the sun to stand, so that he set not for three days, and shall set it on fire."[247]

Some who attack **Chiliasm** argue that the literal **7000 years timespan** for the history of the earth is incompatible with empirical historical measurements. This problem only exists if we assume these 7000 years occur consecutively.

However, this difficulty can be resolved by viewing the 7000 years **analogously** with the well-known **Daniel 70 weeks prophecy**, where **69 weeks were consecutive**, but the **last week** (i.e. final 7 years) is **separated** and placed at the end of the age. This final week refers to the time of the **Antichrist**, which has not yet been fulfilled and is future.[248]

A proposed interpolation here is that **6000 years** may have elapsed **continuously** toward the fulfillment of Scripture regarding God's redemptive plan, particularly regarding the Jewish people, but the **last 1000 years** (Chiliasm's millennium) is **set apart**, to follow **non-consecutively** after the second coming of Christ. In Daniel's prophecy, the use of **"7 days"**

---

[247] Lactantius, *Divine Institutes*, Book 7, Chapter 26.
[248] Nathan Jarrett, "The Prophecy of Prophecies: Correcting Harold Hoehner's Interpretation of Daniel's 70 Weeks", in *Eleutheria: John W. Rawlings School of Divinity Academic Journal*, 5(2), (USA, 2021): 289, 290, 305. doi.org/10.70623/QNLJ6499.

represents **7 years**, and likewise, **"1000 years"** in Revelation 20:5 ought to be taken literally and not spiritualized.

Next, **Lactantius** clearly teaches that the **change** described in **1 Corinthians 15:52**—the transformation from **human to angelic nature**—occurs **after** the 1000-year millennial reign. This change is experienced by those who were raised in the **first resurrection** and possibly by righteous mortals who survive to the end of that period:

> "But when the thousand years shall be completed, the world shall be renewed by God, and the heavens shall be folded together, and the earth shall be changed, and God shall transform men into the similitude of angels, and they shall be white as snow; and they shall always be employed in the sight of the Almighty, and shall make offerings to their Lord, and serve Him forever. At the same time shall take place that second and public resurrection of all, in which the unrighteous shall be raised to everlasting punishments. … But their lord with his servants shall be seized and condemned to punishment, together with whom all the band of the wicked, in accordance with their deeds, shall be burnt for ever with perpetual fire in the sight of angels and the righteous. This is the doctrine of the holy prophets which we Christians follow;"[249]

Like **Lactantius**, some **chiliasts**[250] believe that the second resurrection is exclusively for the **wicked**, who are raised to eternal condemnation. However, **Irenaeus'** quote regarding the **last trumpet** hints at the possibility of a **second badge of righteous** being raised at that time alongside the wicked. This was addressed previously. The distinction here is that **Lactantius** does not support **non-elect salvation**, whereas **Irenaeus'** wording leaves the door open for it depending on how one understands the general resurrection.

A note on the translations used: The use of **primary materials** translated into English is already a scholarly practice. Whether one reads the original manuscript, or a translation sourced online, in print, or from academic journals, the standard of credibility lies in whether **another qualified scholar** can contest the translation with better access to the originals. If that occurs, the fault does not lie with us, as we are relying on

---

[249] Lactantius, *Divine Institutes*, Book 7, Chapter 26.

[250] Matt Waymeyer, "The First Resurrection in Revelation 20," *The Master's Seminary Journal* [MSJ], Vol. 27, No. 1 (Sun Valley, CA, Spring 2016): 5, 8. tms.edu/wp-content/uploads/2021/09/TMSJ-Volume-27-Number-1.pdf.

established translations provided by earlier scholars. Therefore, the **Chiliasm claims** presented here stand firm upon the basis of the translations cited.

To claim that the **Holy Spirit did not intend the 1000 years in Revelation to be literal** is a **dangerous and speculative assertion**. This interpretation is primarily promoted by the **Roman Catholic Church** and **Eastern Orthodoxy**, both of which also advocate extra-biblical practices such as **prayers to the virgin Mary**. They assert that the **Holy Spirit guided** the dominance of these beliefs within the institutional church for centuries, but this is not persuasive from a **Protestant standpoint**. Many **modern theologians** inherit these allegorical views, not because of their strength, but due to unfamiliarity with the **primary source writings of the Chiliasm Church Fathers** presented in this work. With exposure to these texts, it becomes evident that a **literal 1000 years** after the Second Coming of Christ is indeed a serious and historically grounded possibility.

These observations are significant for several reasons.

First, to assert that the **Holy Spirit allowed Tertullian or other Chiliasm fathers to err** in their understanding is an open-ended claim. If permitted in their case, it implies that any modern denomination could also fall into interpretive error regarding these verses. Instead of engaging in speculative finger-pointing, our aim here is to **present possibilities and interpolations** based on the assumption that these historical quotes are **accurately preserved**. In doing so, we offer an **honest presentation** of the evidence found within the writings of early Christian Chiliasts.

Reading the **primary source materials** is of paramount importance. Only then can they be meaningfully compared against **later interpretations**—especially those that stand in **opposition to Chiliasm**. The rejection of Chiliasm often begins with the familiar refrain, *"We cannot assume the 1000 years is literal..."*. This assertion is problematic because the **earliest Church Fathers took the 1000 years literally**, until figures like **Origen** and **Eusebius** began interpreting these passages allegorically.

The **Roman Catholic Church**, heavily influenced by **Augustine**, followed Origen's path. This **allegorical reinterpretation of the 1000 years** conveniently resolved interpretive difficulties, because allegory allows nearly anything to be claimed while minimizing contradictions. For instance, once the Catholic Church extended beyond 1000 years in continuous existence, they used that fact to assert their **institutional continuity as proof** of their exclusive authority to fulfill the Great Commission. This would be incompatible with the view that the **literal 1000 years reign of Christ** is still future. Consequently, admitting to a **literal 1000-year reign** would potentially undermine other Catholic doctrines. Therefore, the literal reading is ignored in favor of an allegorical one.

Yet **God would not have included an explicit reference to 1000 years** (e.g., Revelation 20:5) if it were merely symbolic. In such a case, **non-numerical, figurative terms** like "day" or "hour" would have sufficed. Thus, the explicit numerical declaration strongly supports a **literal 1000-year interpretation**.

Further support comes from **Daniel 12:3**, which contains a prophecy about **greater understanding** and **doctrinal accuracy**, referring to "those who are wise" who will "shine like the brightness of the firmament." This seems to imply a **"double honor"** for those who labor faithfully in the Word, as **1 Timothy 5:17** mentions. The implication, as understood by some Church Fathers such as **Jerome**, is that a more accurate theology—especially in doctrine or prophecy—may result in **a greater glory in the resurrection** for the faithful. Those who convert many into righteousness may still be rewarded, but perhaps not to the same extent as those who labor in **teaching sound doctrine**.[251]

The proper scholarly posture is to **avoid presumptuous claims** about prophetic or doctrinal certainty. Instead, evidence should be presented with

---

[251] Daniel 12:2–3, 10, translated based on the Masoretic Text: "2And many of those who sleep in the dust of the earth shall awake, some to everlasting life, some to shame and everlasting contempt. 3Those who are wise shall shine like the brightness of the firmament, and those who turn many to righteousness like the stars forever and ever. ... 10Many shall be purified, made white, and refined, but the wicked shall do wickedly; and none of the wicked shall understand, but the wise shall understand." (NKJV).

1 Timothy 5:17, "Let the elders that rule well be counted worthy of double honour, especially they who labour in the word and doctrine." (KJV).

Jerome of the Vulgate writes: "But the teachers shall resemble the very heavens, and those who have instructed others shall be compared to the brightness of the stars. For it is not enough to know wisdom unless one also instructs others; and the tongue of instruction which remains silent and edifies no one else can receive no reward for labor accomplished. This passage is expressed by Theodotion and the Vulgate edition [of the Septuagint] in the following fashion: 'And those who understand shall shine forth like the radiance of the firmament, and many of the righteous like the stars forever and ever.' Many people often ask whether a learned saint and an ordinary saint shall both enjoy the same reward and one and the same dwelling-place in heaven. Well then, the statement is made here, according to Theodotion's rendering, that the learned will resemble the very heavens, whereas the righteous who are without learning are only compared to the brightness of the stars. And so the difference between learned godliness and mere godly rusticity shall be the difference between heaven and the stars." (Gleason L. Archer Jr., "Chapter 12. Points 146–147," in *Jerome's Commentary on Daniel*, Grand Rapids: Baker Book House, 1958),
www.tertullian.org/fathers/jerome_daniel_02_text.htm.

care, allowing the Church at large to consider it. God will reward those who pursued accuracy on that Day. Christian scholars bear a responsibility to **elevate these earliest writings of Chiliasm**, precisely because they are the **first recorded interpretations**, and therefore most accountable to the original apostolic traditions.

As Christians, we must always **seek Jehovah** in prayer and study, but we must also **refrain from claiming divine endorsement** of our views, lest we mislead others if proven wrong. May He pardon our errors and honor what we have faithfully discerned to be true.

BIBLIOGRAPHY

Archer, Gleason L., Jr. *Jerome's Commentary on Daniel*. (Grand Rapids: Baker Book House, 1958).

Asher, Jeffrey R., "Polarity and Change in 1 Corinthians 15", in *Hermeneutische Unter-suchngen zur Theologie*, 42, (Tubingen: Mohr Siebeck, DM 168, 2000).

Bible. biblehub.com

Binar, Sri & Laia, Harman & Prasetyo, Widi., "Exegesis of Revelation 20:1-10 about "The Millennial Kingdom", in *Journal Kerugma*, (2019). www.researchgate.net/publication/341791082_EXEGESIS_OF_REVELATION_201-10_ABOUT_THE_MILLENNIAL_KINGDOM

Brown, Robert B. *Joy of Heaven to Earth Come Down: Perfection and Millennium in the Eschatology of John Wesley*. Master of Philosophy thesis. (University of Manchester [Nazarene Theological College], UK, 2011).

Calvin, John. *Commentary on Corinthians*. Vol. 2 (Grand Rapids, MI: Christian Classics Ethereal Library, 2009).

Calvin, John. *The Institutes of the Christian Religion*. Vol. 2, John T. McNeill ed., translated by Ford Lewis Battles; The Library of Christian Classics, Vol. 21 (Philadelphia: The Westminster Press, 1960).

Charles, R.H.. *The Apocrypha and Pseudepigrapha of the Old Testament*, (Oxford: The Clarendon Press, UK, 1913).

Cross, Frank Leslie; Livingstone, Elizabeth A. *The Oxford dictionary of the Christian Church*. 3rd ed., (Oxford: University Press. eds., 2005).

De Smidt, J. C., "Chiliasm: An Escape from the Present into an Extra-Biblical Apocalyptic Imagination.", *Scriptura*, 45, (1993). scriptura.journals.ac.za/pub/article/view/1647/1508

Ethiopian Orthodox Tewahido Church Holy Synod. *A short history, faith and order of the Ethiopian Orthodox Tewahido Church*, (Addis Ababa 1983). www.ethiopianorthodox.org/english/canonical/books.html

Hollon, Elton L. "Paul's Account of Change at the Resurrection in 1 Corinthians 15:42-44a", in *The Heythrop Journal*, (3 December 2024). onlinelibrary.wiley.com/doi/10.1111/heyj.14385

Ice, Thomas D., "The Last Trumpet", in *Article Archives*, 86, (Liberty University, USA, May 2009). digitalcommons.liberty.edu/pretrib_arch/86

Irenaeus of Lyons. *Against Heresies*. Translated by Alexander Roberts and William Rambaut. From Ante-Nicene Fathers, Vol. 1. Edited by Alexander Roberts, James Donaldson, and A. Cleveland Coxe. (Buffalo, NY: Christian Literature Publishing Co., 1885).

J. Chapman. "Didache". In *The Catholic Encyclopedia*. (New York: Robert Appleton Company, 1908).

Jarrett, Nathan., "The Prophecy of Prophecies: Correcting Harold Hoehner's Interpretation of Daniel's 70 Weeks.", in *Eleutheria: John W. Rawlings School of Divinity Academic Journal*, 5(2), (USA, 2021). doi.org/10.70623/QNLJ6499

Justin of Rome (Justin Martyr). *Dialogue with Trypho*. Translated by Marcus Dods and George Reith. From Ante-Nicene Fathers, Vol. 1. Edited by Alexander Roberts, James Donaldson, and A. Cleveland Coxe. (Buffalo, NY: Christian Literature Publishing Co., 1885).

Justin of Rome (Justin Martyr). *Fragments of St. Justin Martyr*. Translated by Alexander Roberts. From Ante-Nicene Fathers, Vol. 1. Edited by Alexander Roberts, James Donaldson, and A. Cleveland Coxe. (Buffalo, NY: Christian Literature Publishing Co., 1885).

Justin of Rome (Justin Martyr). *On the Resurrection*. Translated by Marcus Dods. From Ante-Nicene Fathers, Vol. 1. Edited by Alexander Roberts, James Donaldson, and A. Cleveland Coxe. (Buffalo, NY: Christian Literature Publishing Co., 1885).

Justin of Rome (Justin Martyr). *The First Apology*. Translated by Marcus Dods and George Reith. From Ante-Nicene Fathers, Vol. 1. Edited by Alexander Roberts, James Donaldson, and A. Cleveland Coxe. (Buffalo, NY: Christian Literature Publishing Co., 1885).

Kirsch, J.P.. *Catholic Encyclopedia*. (New York: Robert Appleton Company, 1911).

Lactantius. *Divine Institutes*. Translated by William Fletcher. From Ante-Nicene Fathers, Vol. 7. Edited by Alexander Roberts, James Donaldson, and A. Cleveland Coxe. (Buffalo, NY: Christian Literature Publishing Co., 1886).

McKeever, Jim. *Christians Will Go through the Tribulation: And How to Prepare for It*. (Medford, OR: Omega Publications, 1978).

Methodius of Olympus. *Banquet of the Ten Virgins*. Translated by William R. Clark. From Ante-Nicene Fathers, Vol. 6. Edited by Alexander Roberts, James Donaldson, and A. Cleveland Coxe. (Buffalo, NY: Christian Literature Publishing Co., 1886).

Methodius of Olympus. *From the Discourse on the Resurrection*. Translated by William R. Clark. From Ante-Nicene Fathers, Vol. 6. Edited by Alexander Roberts, James Donaldson, and A. Cleveland Coxe. (Buffalo, NY: Christian Literature Publishing Co., 1886).

Möller, Francois P., "A hermeneutical commentary on Revelation 20:1-10", in *In die Skriflig/In Luce Verbi*, 53(1), (2019): 1-11. doi.org/10.4102/ids.v53i1.2459

Monseth, Francis. *Millennialism in American Lutheranism in Light of Augsburg Confession, Article XVII*. Doctor of Theology Dissertation. 137. (Concordia Seminary, St. Louis, Missouri 63105, USA, 1986). scholar.csl.edu/thd/137

Ramachandran, Jonathan. "Thousand Year Gap for Prophecy in 1 Thessalonians 4:17 and 1 Corinthians 15:52 with Chiliasm Church Fathers." *Journal of Biblical Theology* (JBT) Vol 8, no. 3 (1 June 2025): 185-208. https://www.biblicaltheology.com/research.html

Ramachandran, Jonathan. "Thousand Year Gap for Prophecy in 1 Thessalonians 4:17 and 1 Corinthians 15:52 with Chiliasm Church Fathers." The *American Journal of Biblical Theology* (AJBT) Vol 26, no. 22 (1 June 2025). www.biblicaltheology.com/Research/RamachandranJ02.pdf

Riddle, M.B.. *Didache*. Ante-Nicene Fathers, Vol. 7. Edited by Alexander Roberts, James Donaldson, and A. Cleveland Coxe. (Buffalo, NY: Christian Literature Publishing Co., 1886).

Tertullian. *Against Marcion*. Translated by Peter Holmes. From Ante-Nicene Fathers, Vol. 3. Edited by Alexander Roberts, James Donaldson, and A. Cleveland Coxe. (Buffalo, NY: Christian Literature Publishing Co., 1885).

Tertullian. *Apology*. Translated by S. Thelwall. From Ante-Nicene Fathers, Vol. 3. Edited by Alexander Roberts, James Donaldson, and A. Cleveland Coxe. (Buffalo, NY: Christian Literature Publishing Co., 1885).

Tertullian. *On the Resurrection of the Flesh*. Translated by Peter Holmes. From Ante-Nicene Fathers, Vol. 3. Edited by Alexander Roberts, James Donaldson, and A. Cleveland Coxe. (Buffalo, NY: Christian Literature Publishing Co., 1885).

Victorinus of Pettau. *Ancient Bible Commentaries in English - Victorinus on Revelation Commentary on Revelation by St. Victorinus*. By John Litteral, Kevin P. Edgecomb. (Createspace Independent Publishing Platform, 2014).

Waymeyer, Matt., "The First Resurrection in Revelation 20.", *The Master's Seminary Journal [MSJ]*, Vol. 27 (No.1), (Sun Valley, CA 91352, USA, Spring 2016): 5, 8. tms.edu/wp-content/uploads/2021/09/TMSJ-Volume-27-Number-1.pdf

Wesley, John. *Wesley's Notes on the Bible*. (Grand Rapids: Francis Asbury, 1987).

Youvan, Douglas C., "The Evolution and Divergence of Rapture Theology: Historical Development and Denominational Perspectives", in *Research Gate*, (July 2024). DOI:10.13140/RG.2.2.19515.43044

Essay 3: Two Water of Life References Separated by 1000 Years?

KEYWORDS

Water of Life, Millennial Reign of Christ, Non-Elect Salvation, Book of Revelation Prophecy, Eschatology, Chiliasm

ABSTRACT

The "water of life" prophecy plays a critical role in interpreting key chapters within the Book of Revelation. This study approaches the subject from a **Chiliasm** framework. Chiliasm teaches that Christians who partake in the Marriage of the Lamb are raised first during the **Second Coming of Christ** and reign with Him over the earth for **1000 years**, alongside mortal humans. After this millennial reign, the general resurrection of all the dead—both just and unjust—follows.

This essay proposes that the two prominent references to the **water of life** in Revelation—**Revelation 7:9–17** and **Revelation 22:17**—are separated by this 1000-year period. The first passage appears to refer exclusively to the elect, while the second seems to portray the Bride (i.e., the elect) inviting **others** (possibly non-elect) to partake of the water of life. If interpreted literally, this distinction may suggest a post-millennial opportunity for salvation for others.

This paper seeks to demonstrate a literal **millennial gap** between these two references, using quotes from early **Chiliasm church fathers** and additional theological interpolations to support this proposition.

INTRODUCTION

Scripture appears to refer to the **water of life** in two distinct contexts, separated by a 1000-year gap according to the **Chiliasm** timeline. Christians, when resurrected in **sinless human bodies**, are granted access to the water of life at the **beginning** of Christ's millennial reign. This event coincides with His **Second Coming** and the **first resurrection**, which takes place on this current (restored) **old earth** and **old heavens**.[252] Revelation 7:9–17 is widely regarded as referring to the multitude of Christians saved at Christ's return.[253]

Mortals (sinners) will continue to live alongside resurrected **Christian immortals** during this **millennial reign**, which necessitates that it takes place on the **current old earth**, since it remains touchable by sin. By contrast, the **final new earth** cannot be defiled by sin. But some may ask: doesn't Isaiah 65:17 refer to a "new heavens and new earth," suggesting this reign occurs in a new realm?

The answer lies in the **context**. The passage in Isaiah describes a **renewed** form of the present world, not the final state of Revelation 21:1–3.[254] Justin Martyr affirms this view in his citation of Isaiah 65:17:

> "But I and others, who are right-minded Christians on all points, are assured that there will be a resurrection of the dead, and a thousand years in Jerusalem, which will then be built, adorned, and enlarged, the prophets Ezekiel and Isaiah and others declare. For Isaiah spake thus concerning this space of a thousand years: 'For there shall be the new heaven and the new earth, and the former shall not be remembered, or come into their heart; but they shall find joy and gladness in it, which things I create'."[255]

This **renewed millennial earth** still has a **sea** (cf. Ezekiel 47:7–12), but the **final new earth** described in Revelation **has no sea** (Revelation 21:1), marking a clear distinction.

Furthermore, the **tree of life** also seems to function in a two-stage pattern—first **allegorically** during the millennial reign, and then **literally** in the eternal new creation. Such differences, evident when carefully comparing passages, suggest that the **two "water of life" events** refer to distinct moments separated by the 1000 years of Chiliasm. A comparative table outlining these differences will be provided later in the essay.

At the **end of the 1000 years**, after the second resurrection and final judgment, **some non-Christians** may be invited to partake of the **water of life**, as they are **welcomed** at that future time by **"the bride"**—the glorified

---

[252] Revelation 7:9–17 (NKJV). biblehub.com/nkjv/revelation/7.htm

[253] Luke A. Powery, "Revelation 7:9–17," *Interpretation* 79, no. 1 (2025): 75–77. https://doi.org/10.1177/00209643241285801

[254] Revelation 21:1–3, "Now I saw a new heaven and a new earth, for the first heaven and the first earth had passed away" (NKJV). biblehub.com/nkjv/revelation/21.htm

[255] Justin of Rome (Justin Martyr), *Dialogue with Trypho*, Chapter 81. www.newadvent.org/fathers/01286.htm

elect, or overcomers, who already participated in the **first resurrection** and **marriage of the Lamb**. This scene takes place on the **final new earth** and **new heavens**, where no sin remains and the **Book of Life's contents have already been revealed**. This culminating moment, described in the closing chapter of the Bible,[256] appears to distinguish between different categories of salvation, each consistent with the **Chiliasm framework**:

i) **Elect salvation** — Those called the **Bride**, having already participated in the **first resurrection** and entered the **marriage of the Lamb** (cf. Matthew 25:1–13). They are clearly the ones who reign with Christ and now, in perfected glory, extend the invitation to others:

> "And the Spirit and the bride say, 'Come!'"[257]

ii) **Non-elect salvation for Israel** — These are referred to as **"servants"**, even in this final scene, never as the Bride. This aligns with the language of Matthew 25:14–30, where the faithful servants enter into the joy of their master but are distinct from the bridal company:

> "And there shall be no more curse, but the throne of God and of the Lamb shall be in it, and His servants shall serve Him. They shall see His face, and His name shall be on their foreheads."[258]

iii) **Non-elect salvation for Gentiles** — Described as **"the thirsty"** ones who now desire the water of life. This connects with the group in Matthew 25:31–46, the "sheep" who showed kindness to Christ's brethren and are granted entrance into the Kingdom. Though never called the Bride or servants, they are still invited to partake:

> "And the Spirit and the bride say, 'Come!' And let him who hears say, 'Come!' And let him who thirsts come. Whoever desires, let him take the water of life freely."[259]

Such language, when taken **literally**, provides a consistent prophetic framework where the elect, Israel, and righteous Gentiles each experience different **roles** and **rewards** in the eternal state, all in alignment with the prophetic Chiliasm model.

---

[256] Revelation 21:1 (NKJV), biblehub.com/nkjv/revelation/21.htm; Revelation 22:1–5, 17 (NKJV), biblehub.com/nkjv/revelation/22.htm
[257] Revelation 22:17 (NKJV), biblehub.com/revelation/22-17.htm
[258] Revelation 22:3–4 (NKJV), biblehub.com/nkjv/revelation/22.htm
[259] Revelation 22:17 (NKJV), biblehub.com/revelation/22-17.htm

WATER OF LIFE

Under this arrangement of verses, let's consider those Scriptures which may describe the **second occurrence** of the **water of life** in prophetic context. According to the **Chiliasm framework**,[260] Christians have already been transformed—**no longer human**, having put off "flesh and blood"—into something **angelic**, having shared "one flesh"[261] with Christ during the **Marriage of the Lamb**.[262] At this stage, they may no longer require the **water of life**, since with their **glorious bodies** they are able to partake of life **directly from Christ**. It is reasonable to infer that the **sinless resurrected human body** could only partake of divine life through this **water of life** during the 1000 years, as earlier described in Revelation 7.

Interestingly, even **Augustine of Hippo**, though later abandoning Chiliasm, seemed to maintain that entering the Kingdom of Heaven requires a **change from human to angelic** nature.[263] Allegorical interpretations of the **water of life** are evident in post-Nicene fathers. **Augustine** himself equates it with the **Holy Spirit**,[264] a view continued later by **Thomas Aquinas**,[265] and foundational to the Roman Catholic interpretation of these

---

[260] Justin of Rome (Justin Martyr, c. 100–160 C.E.) calls Christians "gods rendering judgment to all men" (*Dialogue with Trypho*, Chapter 124),
www.newadvent.org/fathers/01288.htm. See also Irenaeus of Lyons (c. 130–202 C.E.), *Against Heresies*, Book 4, Chapter 38, www.newadvent.org/fathers/0103438.htm; Tertullian, *Against Marcion*, Book 3, Chapter 25, www.newadvent.org/fathers/03123.htm and Book 5, Chapter 10, ccel.org/ccel/schaff/anf03.v.iv.vi.x.html; Victorinus of Pettau (c. 303 C.E.), *Commentary on the Apocalypse*, 18, earlychurchrevival.wordpress.com/wp-content/uploads/2013/11/st-victorinus-of-poetovio-translated-by-kevin-edgecomb.pdf; Methodius of Olympus (died c. 311 C.E.), *Banquet of the Ten Virgins*, Discourse 9, Chapter 5, www.newadvent.org/fathers/062309.htm.

[261] Revelation 19:9, "Write: 'Blessed are those who are called to the marriage supper of the Lamb!'" (NKJV), biblehub.com/revelation/19-9.htm.

[262] Ephesians 5:31–32, "'For this reason a man shall leave his father and mother and be joined to his wife, and the two shall become one flesh.' This is a great mystery, but I speak concerning Christ and the church." (NKJV), biblehub.com/nkjv/ephesians/5.htm.

[263] Augustine of Hippo (c. 354–430 C.E.) writes, "When they have been taken in who have been changed into angelic being, all entrance into the kingdom of heaven is closed; after the judgment, there is no more place for prayers or merit. [marg. note: 1 Cor 15:51]." (*Catena Aurea*, Commentary on Matthew 25:1–13),
ccel.org/ccel/aquinas/catena1/catena1.ii.xxv.html.

[264] Saint Augustine and Edmund Hill, *Homilies on the Gospel of John 1–40* (Works of Saint Augustine: A Translation for the 21st Century), New City Press, 2009, p. 284.

[265] Saint Augustine, Thomas Aquinas, Daniel Keating, Matthew Levering, *Commentary on the Gospel of John, Chapters 1–5*, Books 1–5 (CUA Press, 2010), p. 91.

verses.[266] Some liturgical sources suggest the Holy Spirit **imparts the water's regenerative power** during **baptismal consecration.**[267] However, this spiritualized reading was not universally held.

In contrast, **Tertullian** firmly grounded the meaning in Christ Himself, writing that those who do not receive Christ, **"the fount of water of life,"** are without hope.[268] **Irenaeus** expands on this by linking the water of life to the **knowledge of truth**:

> "Since therefore we have such proofs, it is not necessary to seek the truth among others which it is easy to obtain from the Church; since the apostles, like a rich man [depositing his money] in a bank, lodged in her hands most copiously all things pertaining to the truth: so that every man, whosoever will, can draw from her the water of life. Revelation 22:17. For she is the entrance to life; all others are thieves and robbers."[269]

This aligns with Christ's own statement:

> "And this is eternal life, that they may know You, the only true God, and Jesus Christ whom You have sent."[270]

In another passage, Irenaeus directly associates this **living water** with the **Holy Spirit**,[271] which also agrees with **Ignatius of Antioch**, who spoke of an **inward living water** drawing him to the Father.[272] Thus, the phrase **"water of life"** may simultaneously bear **multiple legitimate meanings**, from **Christ**, to **the Holy Spirit**, to **the knowledge of God**, and even **the sacramental context**, depending on Scriptural and patristic usage.

Next, we investigate the language found in the conclusion of the Apocalypse, where the **Spirit** (Holy Spirit) Himself invites others to partake

---

[266] Congregation for the Doctrine of the Faith (CDF), "Catechism 1137 of the Catholic Church," *Instruction Pastoralis Actio* (AAS 72, 1980), 1137–1156,
www.catholicculture.org/culture/library/catechism/index.cfm?recnum=3646.

[267] Johnson E. Maxwell, *The Rites of Christian Initiation: Their Evolution and Interpretation*, Liturgical Press, 2007, p. 288.

[268] Tertullian, *An Answer to the Jews*, Chapter 13.

[269] Irenaeus of Lyons, *Against Heresies*, Book 3, Chapter 4,
www.newadvent.org/fathers/0103304.htm.

[270] John 17:3 (NKJV), biblehub.com/john/17-3.htm.

[271] Irenaeus of Lyons, *Against Heresies*, Book 5, Chapter 18,
www.newadvent.org/fathers/0103518.htm.

[272] Ignatius of Antioch, *Epistle to the Romans*, Chapter 7,
www.newadvent.org/fathers/0107.htm.

of the **water of life** freely, together with the **Bride**[273] (i.e., the Church). A **literal** reading of this verse suggests that those being invited are distinct from the elect, likely those who are **"thirsty"**—a term which may imply they are **without the Holy Spirit**. Those who partake of life by means of the **water of life** at this future time are probably **non-elect**, since the **Bride** has already received life during the millennial reign and therefore is no longer in need of this sustenance.[274]

The dual nature of Scripture—**literal and allegorical**, both equally valid—allows us to interpret the **water of life** in several complementary ways. Revelation speaks of a **literal "pure river of water of life, clear as crystal,"** flowing from the throne of God and of the Lamb.[275] Though its source is Christ, it is described as a distinct **intermediary object** through which divine life is conveyed to those who drink of it.

Justin of Rome and **Irenaeus of Lyons** both quote **tree of life** passages in connection to the **millennial reign** and the **first resurrection**, possibly implying **two distinct occurrences** of this tree, separated by 1000 years—one on the renewed old earth and the other on the final new earth.[276] Since the **tree of life** and **water of life** appear together in these prophetic texts, the distinction may also apply to both symbols.

By contrast, **non-Chiliast** interpretations such as those of **Augustine**,[277] **John Calvin**,[278] and **Martin Luther**[279] view the tree of life **symbolically** or **sacramentally**, rather than as a physical element of an earthly dispensation. In these systems, there is no literal resurrection of the righteous in sinless **human** bodies for 1000 years prior to a final transformation into angelic glory. However, both **Irenaeus**[280] and

---

[273] Revelation 22:17, "And the Spirit and the bride say, 'Come!' And let him who hears say, 'Come!' And let him who thirsts come. Whoever desires, let him take the water of life freely" (NKJV). biblehub.com/revelation/22-17.htm.

[274] John 6:35, "Jesus said ... 'he who believes in Me shall never thirst'" (NKJV). biblehub.com/john/6-35.htm.

[275] Revelation 22:1 (NKJV). biblehub.com/revelation/22-1.htm.

[276] Revelation 21:1 and Revelation 22:1–5.

[277] Augustine of Hippo, *The City of God*, Book 13, Chapters 20–23. www.newadvent.org/fathers/120113.htm.

[278] John Calvin, "Genesis 2:9," in *Commentary on Genesis*, trans. John King (Baker, 2009), pp. 116–117.

[279] Theo M. M. A. C. Bel, "Man is a Microcosmos: Adam and Eve in Luther's Lectures on Genesis (1535–1545)," *Concordia Theological Quarterly*, Vol. 69, No. 2 (April 2005): 170–171, 175–176. ctsfw.net/media/pdfs/BellManMicrocosmos.pdf.

[280] Irenaeus of Lyons, *Against Heresies*, Book 5, Chapter 32.

Tertullian[281] affirm that such a bodily **resurrection** and **rewarding in the flesh** must precede the transformation into something no longer human.

Consider also that the **human body** is capable of receiving nourishment from a literal tree of life. This is precisely why Jehovah cast man from Eden—to prevent him from eating of the tree and living forever in a sinful condition.[282] The **Tree of Life** is therefore not merely symbolic; it implies **literal sustenance** in a sinless human resurrection body.

Irenaeus tells us that **Papias of Hierapolis**, a direct hearer of the apostles, taught a **literal Chiliasm** where the resurrected Christians inhabit a **renewed old earth** full of miraculous agricultural abundance. He also wrote that the animals will cease being carnivorous in that day—again, literally—yet acknowledged that allegorical interpretations such as **taming Gentile passions** also hold true.[283] In other words, the **literal and allegorical meanings** of these passages operate simultaneously.

The **only person** in these early records who is noted to have **doubted** the literal fulfillment of this Chiliastic prophecy was **Judas**, the traitor. In response to Judas's disbelief, the Lord replied:

> "When the traitor Judas did not give credit to them, and put the question, 'How then can things about to bring forth so abundantly be wrought by the Lord?' the Lord declared, 'They who shall come to these [times] shall see.'"[284]

After Christ returns and destroys the Antichrist and the Beast, the **first resurrection** of the righteous occurs, followed by the **millennial reign**.

---

www.newadvent.org/fathers/0103532.htm.

[281] Tertullian, *Against Marcion*, Book 3, Chapter 25.

www.newadvent.org/fathers/03123.htm.

[282] Genesis 3:22, "Then the LORD God said, 'Behold, the man has become like one of Us, to know good and evil. And now, lest he put out his hand and take also of the tree of life, and eat, and live forever'" (NKJV). biblehub.com/genesis/3-22.htm.

[283] Irenaeus of Lyons, *Against Heresies*, Book 5, Chapter 33.

www.newadvent.org/fathers/0103533.htm.

[284] Ibid., Chapter 33.

During this period, an **earthly Jerusalem temple** will be rebuilt[285] for **mortal Israelites** who still dwell upon the earth.[286]

Justin of Rome describes the long life enjoyed even by **mortals** during the **1000-year millennial reign of Christ**, explicitly citing **Isaiah 65:20** as referring to that time. He further notes that the phrase, *"the days of the tree [of life] shall be the days of My people; the works of their toil shall abound,"* **obscurely predicts a thousand years.**[287]

Similarly, **Irenaeus of Lyons** also references **Isaiah 65:20** in the same **millennial context**—the time of the **first resurrection**. He identifies **all Christians**, as **disciples of the Lord**, to be **Levites and priests**, that is, the **Bride or Church from heaven.**[288] This distinction allows for the possibility that **non-priests**—those among the "nations who are saved"[289]—are a **separate category**, potentially representing **non-elect salvation**, based on Irenaeus's quote below:

> "Now, in the preceding book I have shown that all the disciples of the Lord are Levites and priests, they who used in the temple to profane the Sabbath, but are blameless (Matthew 12:5). Promises of such a nature, therefore, do indicate in the clearest manner the feasting of that creation in the kingdom of the righteous, which God promises that He will Himself serve."[290]

WATER OF LIFE BIBLE VERSES COMPARISON TABLE

A comparison of **water of life** and **tree of life** characteristics within the **Chiliasm prophecy timeline** follows next. This table will outline the

---

[285] Irenaeus of Lyons, *Against Heresies*, Book 5, Chapter 35.
www.newadvent.org/fathers/0103535.htm.

[286] Isaiah 65:20, "There shall be no more thence an infant of days, nor an old man that hath not filled his days: for the child shall die an hundred years old; but the sinner being an hundred years old shall be accursed" (KJV). biblehub.com/isaiah/65-20.htm.

[287] Justin of Rome (Justin Martyr), *Dialogue with Trypho*, Chapter 81.
www.newadvent.org/fathers/01286.htm.

[288] Revelation 21:9–10, "Come, I will show you the bride, the Lamb's wife … and showed me the great city, the holy Jerusalem, descending out of heaven from God" (NKJV).

[289] Revelation 21:24–27, "24And the nations of those who are saved shall walk in its light, and the kings of the earth bring their glory and honor into it. 25Its gates shall not be shut at all by day (there shall be no night there). 26And they shall bring the glory and the honor of the nations into it. 27But there shall by no means enter it anything that defiles, or causes an abomination or a lie, but only those who are written in the Lamb's Book of Life" (NKJV).

[290] Irenaeus of Lyons, *Against Heresies*, Book 5, Chapter 34.
www.newadvent.org/fathers/0103534.htm.

distinctions between the **two prophetic occurrences**—one during the **millennial reign** and the other on the **final new earth**—demonstrating how these passages may imply **elect vs non-elect salvation**, based on their differing descriptions. This interpolation seeks to faithfully align the traits found in the Scriptures to the previously discussed framework.

Water/Tree of life Bible Verses at start of 1000 years Millennial Reign for Christians in human sinless resurrection body (Elect Salvation) during First Resurrection but changed to no more human into angelic at end of this 1000 years when Marriage of Lamb is completed in Old Earth/Heavens.	Water/Tree of life Bible Verses at end of 1000 years Millennial Reign for non-Christians including fallen Christians in human sinless resurrection body (non-Elect Salvation) during the Second Resurrection in New earth/Heavens (if this interpretation is true).
i) Christians partake of the Water of life immediately after the final great tribulation and first resurrection on the old earth. "5Therefore they are before the throne of God, and serve Him day and night in His temple. And He who sits on the throne will dwell among them. 16They shall neither hunger anymore nor thirst anymore; the sun shall not strike them, nor any heat; 17for the Lamb who is in the midst of the throne will shepherd them and lead them to [c]living fountains of waters. And God will wipe away every tear from their eyes." (Revelation 7:15 – 17, NKJV) ii) River of Life allegorical fulfilment during the Millennial reign includes usage by mere mortals and so cannot be referring to the final one.	i) The recipients of for the Water of life here are after book of life results are revealed and on the final new earth and heavens. "1Now I saw a new heaven and a new earth, for the first heaven and the first earth had passed away. Also there was no more sea … 5Then He who sat on the throne said, "Behold, I make all things new." And He said [b]to me, "Write, for these words are true and faithful." 6And He said to me, "It[c] is done! I am the Alpha and the Omega, the Beginning and the End. I will give of the fountain of the water of life freely to him who thirsts. 7He who overcomes [d]shall inherit all things, and I will be his God and he shall be My son. 8But the cowardly,

"12Along the bank of the river, on this side and that, will grow all kinds of trees used for food; their leaves will not wither, and their fruit will not fail. They will bear fruit every month, because their water flows from the sanctuary. Their fruit will be for food, and their leaves for medicine." (Ezekiel 47:12, NKJV)

iii) There is a literal sea with fishes in it when this allegorical fulfilment of the Water of life happens during the millennium.

"When it reaches the sea, its waters are healed. 9And it shall be that every living thing that moves, wherever [c]the rivers go, will live. There will be a very great multitude of fish, because these waters go there; for they will be healed, and everything will live wherever the river goes. 10It shall be that fishermen will stand by it from En Gedi to En Eglaim; they will be places for spreading their nets. Their fish will be of the same kinds as the fish of the Great Sea, exceedingly many. 11But its swamps and marshes will not be healed; they will be given over to salt." (Ezekiel 47:8 – 11, NKJV)

iv) A literal moon and sun still exists during the millennial reign of Christ.

"Then the moon shall be confounded, and the sun ashamed, when the LORD of hosts shall reign in mount Zion, and in Jerusalem, and

[e]unbelieving, abominable, murderers, sexually immoral, sorcerers, idolaters, and all liars shall have their part in the lake which burns with fire and brimstone, which is the second death." ... 10And he carried me away in the Spirit to a great and high mountain, and showed me the [h]great city, the [i]holy Jerusalem, descending out of heaven from God, ... 22But I saw no temple in it, for the Lord God Almighty and the Lamb are its temple. 23The city had no need of the sun or of the moon to shine [l]in it, for the [m]glory of God illuminated it. The Lamb is its light. 24And the nations [n]of those who are saved shall walk in its light, and the kings of the earth bring their glory and honor [o]into it. 25Its gates shall not be shut at all by day (there shall be no night there). 26And they shall bring the glory and the honor of the nations into [p]it." (Revelation 21:1, 5 – 8, 10, 22 – 26, NKJV)

ii) Even Christians (the "Bride") seem to call to some "others" to partake of the "Water of life" freely toward the "Thirsty" at that final time and via the "freewill" choice of "Whoever desires, let him take the water of life freely" and the "leaves of the Tree of life" are used for final "healing" of "nations who are saved" (possibly due to being "saved by

before his ancients gloriously." (Isaiah 24:23, KJV)

v) Sinners/Mortals exists during the millennium meaning it is still affected by sin and so it is before great white throne judgment day.

"There shall be no more thence an infant of days, nor an old man that hath not filled his days: for the child shall die an hundred years old; but the sinner being an hundred years old shall be accursed. ..." (Isaiah 65:20, KJV)

"4And in that day His feet will stand on the Mount of Olives, which faces Jerusalem on the east. And the Mount of Olives shall be split in two, From east to west, Making a very large valley; Half of the mountain shall move toward the north And half of it toward the south. ... 8And in that day it shall be That living waters shall flow from Jerusalem, Half of them toward [e]the eastern sea And half of them toward [f]the western sea; In both summer and winter it shall occur. 9And the Lord shall be King over all the earth. In that day it shall be— "The Lord is one," And His name one. ... 16And it shall come to pass that everyone who is left of all the nations which came against Jerusalem shall go up from year to year to worship the King, the Lord of hosts, and to keep the Feast of Tabernacles. 17And it shall be that whichever of the families of the earth do not come up to Jerusalem to worship the King, the Lord of hosts, on them there will be no rain."

fire" of 1 Corinthians 3:15 case) while the rest are damned.

"1And he showed me a [a]pure river of water of life, clear as crystal, proceeding from the throne of God and of the Lamb. 2In the middle of its street, and on either side of the river, was the tree of life, which bore twelve fruits, each tree yielding its fruit every month. The leaves of the tree were for the healing of the nations. 3And there shall be no more curse, but the throne of God and of the Lamb shall be in it, and His servants shall serve Him. ... 17And the Spirit and the bride say, "Come!" And let him who hears say, "Come!" And let him who thirsts come. Whoever desires, let him take the water of life freely." (Revelation 22:1 – 3, 17, NKJV)

iii) Second resurrection only happens at the end of 1000 years Millennial Reign of Christ. No final judgment of any sinners or wicked occurs earlier since they need to be in their final resurrection bodies first.

"4And I saw thrones, and they sat on them, and judgment was committed to them. Then I saw the souls of those who had been beheaded for their witness to Jesus and for the word of God, who had not worshiped the beast or his image, and had not received his mark on their

(Zechariah 14: 4, 8 - 9, 16 - 18, NKJV) vi) One last rebellion of mortals/sinners is at end of this 1000 years who are destroyed by heavenly fire (Revelation 20:7 – 10) and after that "Lake of Fire" Judgment Day begins. "7Now when the thousand years have expired, Satan will be released from his prison 8and will go out to deceive the nations which are in the four corners of the earth, Gog and Magog, to gather them together to battle, whose number is as the sand of the sea. 9They went up on the breadth of the earth and surrounded the camp of the saints and the beloved city. And fire came down from God out of heaven and devoured them. 10The devil, who deceived them, was cast into the lake of fire and brimstone where[b] the beast and the false prophet are. And they will be tormented day and night forever and ever." (Revelation 20:7 – 10, NKJV)	foreheads or on their hands. And they lived and reigned with Christ for [a]a thousand years. 5But the rest of the dead did not live again until the thousand years were finished. This is the first resurrection. 6Blessed and holy is he who has part in the first resurrection. Over such the second death has no power, but they shall be priests of God and of Christ, and shall reign with Him a thousand years." (Revelation 20:4 – 6, NKJV)
Further comparison details.	
1) "… When it reaches the sea, its waters are healed … very great multitude of fish, because these waters go there; …" (Ezekiel 47:8 – 9, NKJV) = Literal sea still existing on old earth.	1) "… 1Now I saw a new heaven and a new earth, for the first heaven and the first earth had passed away. Also there was no more sea …." (Revelation 21:1, NKJV) = The final new earth has no more sea.

2) "… 15Therefore they are before the throne of God, and serve Him day and night in His temple …" (Revelation 7:15, NKJV) = Temple still existing in this Old Earth/Old heavens.	2) "… 22But I saw no temple in it, …" (Revelation 21:22, NKJV) = No temple in the final New earth/New heavens nor in the final new heavenly Jerusalem city.
3) "… and serve Him day and night in His temple. …" (Revelation 7:15, NKJV) = Night exists in this earthly Jerusalem city.	3) "… 5There shall be no night there …" (Revelation 21:5, NKJV) = No night in the final new heavenly Jerusalem city.
4) "… Moon shall be confounded, and the sun ashamed …" (Isaiah 24:23, KJV) = Sun and moon still existing during the millennium.	4) "… 23The city had no need of the sun or of the moon to shine …" (Revelation 21:23, NKJV) = No sun nor moon in the final new heavenly Jerusalem city.
5) "… LORD of hosts shall reign in mount Zion, and in Jerusalem …" (Isaiah 24:23, KJV) = Heavenly mount Zion contrasted against earthly Jerusalem during the millennial reign.	5) "… showed me the [h]great city, the [i]holy Jerusalem, descending out of heaven from God, …" (Revelation 21:10, NKJV) = Final new heavenly Jerusalem city context.
6) "… bank of the river, on this side and that, will grow all kinds of trees used for food …Their fruit will be for food, and their leaves for medicine …" (Ezekiel 47:12, NKJV) = Earthly Tree/Water of life used by mortals of millennial reign (allegory, not the real one).	6) "… The leaves of the tree were for the healing of the nations. … And let him who thirsts come. Whoever desires, let him take the water of life freely. …" (Revelation 22:2, 17, NKJV) = Heavenly Tree/Water of life only to be applied to final sinless resurrection body.

7) "He who has an ear, let him hear what the Spirit says to the churches. To him who overcomes I will give to eat from the tree of life, which is in the midst of the Paradise of God." (Revelation 2:7, NKJV) = Only Christians (the "Churches/Overcomers") can eat of the "fruit" of the Tree of life probably because they have celestial heavenly body so can partake of it in the Paradise of God (heaven zone).	7) "… nations of those who are saved … The leaves of the tree were for the healing of the nations. …" (Revelation 21:24, 22:2, NKJV) = The saved nations seem to only be able to partake of the "leaves" (not fruit) of the Tree of life for "healing" probably due to having only an earthly or terrestrial final resurrection body in comparison.
8) "14Blessed are those who [g]do His commandments, that they may have the right to the tree of life, and may enter through the gates into the city. 15[h]But outside are dogs and sorcerers and sexually immoral and murderers and idolaters, and whoever loves and practices a lie.16"I, Jesus, have sent My angel to testify to you these things in the churches. I am the Root and the Offspring of David, the Bright and Morning Star." (Revelation 22:14 – 16, NKJV)

Notice that only those who do His Commandments get the right to go past the "gates" into the "city" referring to the final new Jerusalem (lowest heaven which descends and connects to the final earth in the final scene) while those outside can refer to sinners where some could be saved by fire and require the healing of the leaves of the tree of life. | 8) "Then the LORD God said, "Behold, the man has become like one of Us, to know good and evil. And now, lest he put out his hand and take also of the tree of life, and eat, and live forever"—" (Genesis 3:22, NKJV)

Notice that the Tree of life cannot be applied to any sinful human body but only to a final sinless resurrection body meaning those "saved nations" partaking the "leaves of the Tree of life" for "healing" earlier cannot be referring to the Millennial reign timeline of "sinners/mortals" but those of the final scene after book of life results are revealed too and these could be "saved by fire" (1 Corinthians 3:15 with Daniel 12:10) and hence require "healing" post-Judgment to be "saved". |

9) "11For no other foundation can anyone lay than that which is laid, which is Jesus Christ. 12Now if anyone builds on this foundation with gold, silver, precious stones, wood, hay, straw, 13each one's work will become clear; for the Day will declare it, because it will be revealed by fire; and the fire will test each one's work, of what sort it is. 14If anyone's work which he has built on it endures, he will receive a reward." (1 Corinthians 3:11 – 14, NKJV) 1 Corinthians 3:14 reveals the case with reward so seems to match Revelation 22:14 here for those entering heaven.	9) "15If anyone's work is burned, he will suffer loss; but he himself will be saved, yet so as through fire." (1 Corinthians 3:15, NKJV) 1 Corinthians 3:15 seems to be a case with no reward but just "saved by fire" in comparison so could be one of the sinners mentioned to be "outside" in Revelation 22:15 and require "healing" from "leaves" of Tree of life as Revelation 22:2 means to be part of "nations who are saved" but do not enter heaven on that final earth (Revelation 21:24 – 27) and could not go pass its gates.
10) "… That living waters shall flow from Jerusalem, … 16And it shall come to pass that everyone who is left of all the nations …17And it shall be that whichever of the families of the earth do not come up to Jerusalem to worship the King, the Lord of hosts, on them there will be no rain …" (Zechariah 14: 8, 16, 17, NKJV) = Mortal (Sinners) exist on earth during Millennial reign "Water of life" timeline and notice that the Lake of Fire Judgment has not happened yet (indicating which timeline). Notice that the mortals partake of the allegorical water of life while Christians partake of the real Water of life during the millennium because only those of first resurrection (His	10) "… I will give of the fountain of the water of life freely to him who thirsts. 7He who overcomes [d]shall inherit all things, and I will be his God and he shall be My son. 8But the cowardly, [e]unbelieving, abominable, murderers, sexually immoral, sorcerers, idolaters, and all liars shall have their part in the lake which burns with fire and brimstone, which is the second death." (Revelation 21:1, 6 – 8, NKJV) = Nor mortal nor sinners mentioned among the partakers of the actual Water/Tree of life on the final new earth timeline when the Lake of Fire results have been revealed. Notice that the source of the Water/Tree of life is

Bride) are in sinless human resurrection body at that time.	Christ in Revelation 22:1 – 2 and that's how probably a newly saved resurrected sinless human body can partake of His Resurrection and Life via that medium.
11) Second Coming of Christ "11Now I saw heaven opened, and behold, a white horse. And He who sat on him was called Faithful and True, and in righteousness He judges and makes war. … 19And I saw the beast, the kings of the earth, and their armies, gathered together to make war against Him who sat on the horse and against His army. 20Then the beast was captured, and with him the false prophet who worked signs in his presence, by which he deceived those who received the mark of the beast and those who worshiped his image. These two were cast alive into the lake of fire burning with brimstone. 21And the rest were killed with the sword which proceeded from the mouth of Him who sat on the horse. And all the birds were filled with their flesh." (Revelation 19:11, 19 – 21, NKJV) = Notice that the "Beast" (Last Antichrist) and "false prophet" are cast "alive" into the Lake of Fire after Christ's Second Coming and immediately after this the 1000 years Millennial Reign of Christ begins with the First Resurrection as the next chapter in Revelation 20:1 - 6 shows.	11) First Resurrection and Chiliasm's Millennium "1Then I saw an angel coming down from heaven, having the key to the bottomless pit and a great chain in his hand. 2He laid hold of the dragon, that serpent of old, who is the Devil and Satan, and bound him for a thousand years; 3and he cast him into the bottomless pit, and shut him up, and set a seal on him, so that he should deceive the nations no more till the thousand years were finished. But after these things he must be released for a little while." (Revelation 20:1 – 3, NKJV) = Notice that during the "1000 years Millennial Reign of Christ, Satan is locked in the bottomless pit" meaning it cannot be now (as non-Chiliasm positions err allegorically) and this only happens after the Second Coming of Christ has occurred with only the "Beast" (Antichrist) and "False Prophet" cast into the Lake of Fire first. Satan is not cast into the Lake of Fire during the 1000 years Millennium itself contradicts many modern positions which claim that Judgment Day occurs

	immediately after the Second Coming of Christ.
12) Second Resurrection and General Resurrection "11Then I saw a great white throne and Him who sat on it, from whose face the earth and the heaven fled away. And there was found no place for them. 12And I saw the dead, small and great, standing before [c]God, and books were opened. And another book was opened, which is the Book of Life. And the dead were judged according to their works, by the things which were written in the books. 13The sea gave up the dead who were in it, and Death and Hades delivered up the dead who were in them. And they were judged, each one according to his works. 14Then Death and Hades were cast into the lake of fire. This is the second [d]death. 15And anyone not found written in the Book of Life was cast into the lake of fire." (Revelation 20:11 – 15, NKJV) = When compared with Verses in Revelation 20:1 – 6 and Revelation 20:7 – 10, we see clearly that great white throne Judgment Day only occurs at the end of this 1000 years Millennial Reign of Christ which is the *Chiliasm* Timeline Prophecy position.	12) End of the Millennium "7Now when the thousand years have expired, Satan will be released from his prison 8and will go out to deceive the nations which are in the four corners of the earth, Gog and Magog, to gather them together to battle, whose number is as the sand of the sea. 9They went up on the breadth of the earth and surrounded the camp of the saints and the beloved city. And fire came down from God out of heaven and devoured them. 10The devil, who deceived them, was cast into the lake of fire and brimstone where[b] the beast and the false prophet are. And they will be tormented day and night forever and ever." = One last rebellion by Satan is allowed at the end of the 1000 years Millennial Reign of Christ but this time fire from heaven devours the enemies and Judgment Day follows next. Notice how the Bible clearly describes that Satan only joins the "Beast" (last Antichrist) and "false prophet" in the "Lake of Fire" during this end of 1000 years meaning both the "Antichrist and false prophet" have been burning for 1000 years already.

Why is accuracy in prophecy important?

"10 ... Worship God! For the testimony of Jesus is the spirit of prophecy."[291]

THE THOUSAND YEARS

The **Chiliasm Church Fathers** unanimously affirm a **literal 1000-year period** between the **first resurrection** and the **general resurrection** of all mankind.[292] **Justin of Rome** declares plainly:

> "There will be a resurrection of the dead, and a thousand years in Jerusalem," and again, "those who believed in our Christ would dwell a thousand years in Jerusalem; and that thereafter the general, and, in short, the eternal resurrection and judgment of all men would likewise take place."[293]

Tertullian likewise writes:

> "Of the heavenly kingdom this is the process. After its thousand years are over, within which period is completed the resurrection of the saints."[294]

Victorinus of Pettau confirms this understanding by distinguishing the two resurrections:

> "For these are two resurrections. Therefore, however many were not previously to rise in the first resurrection and to reign with Christ over the world [Revelation 20:4–6], over all nations, will rise at the last trumpet, after the thousand years, that is, in the last resurrection, among the impious and sinners and perpetrators of various kinds [Revelation 20:11–15]."[295]

Methodius of Olympus offers a striking description of the **resurrection process**, affirming a **transformation into angelic glory** after the 1000 years:

---

[291] Revelation 19:10 (NKJV). biblehub.com/revelation/19-10.htm

[292] Revelation 20:5 reads, "But the rest of the dead did not live again until the thousand years were finished. This is the first resurrection" (NKJV). biblehub.com/revelation/20-5.htm

[293] Justin of Rome, *Dialogue with Trypho*, Chapters 80–81.
www.newadvent.org/fathers/01286.htm

[294] Tertullian, *Against Marcion*, Book 3, Chapter 25.
www.newadvent.org/fathers/03123.htm

[295] Victorinus of Pettau, *Commentary on the Apocalypse*, Revelation Chapter 20 (p. 18). earlychurchrevival.files.wordpress.com/2013/11/st-victorinus-of-poetovio-translated-by-kevin-edgecomb.pdf

> "For I also, taking my journey, and going forth from the Egypt of this life, came first to the resurrection, ... which is the true Feast of the Tabernacles, ... not continuing to remain in tabernacles—that is, my body not remaining as it was before, but, after the space of a thousand years, changed from a human and corruptible form into angelic size and beauty, where at last we virgins, when the festival of the resurrection is consummated."[296]

A **popular objection** argues that **Irenaeus** never explicitly mentions a **1000-year period**. However, this is clarified by **Professor Philip Schaff**, who explains that Irenaeus refers to *"the times of the kingdom"* as the **hallowed seventh day**, and equates one **prophetic day with a thousand years**:

> "Irenaeus speaks about 'the times of the kingdom' as equivalent to 'the hallowed seventh day,' and elsewhere he has equated one prophetic day with a thousand years (Against Heresies: V.28.3; cf. V.33.2)."[297]

Irenaeus places the **millennium** as commencing **at the Second Coming of Christ**.[298] This 1000-year span follows the **6000-year reign of mankind**, totaling **7000 years**, which is a fundamental feature of Chiliasm and appears in the **Epistle of Barnabas**.[299]

This framework parallels **Daniel's 70 Weeks Prophecy**, which divides prophetic history into **69 weeks** fulfilled in Christ's first coming and a **final week** (i.e., **7 literal years**) reserved for the **Antichrist** at the end of the age.[300] This **last week**, associated with the **final beast**, is future and yet to be fulfilled.[301]

---

[296] Methodius of Olympus, *Banquet of the Ten Virgins*, Discourse 9, Chapter 5. www.newadvent.org/fathers/062309.htm

[297] A. Skevington Wood, "The Eschatology of Irenaeus," *The Evangelical Quarterly* 41.1 (UK, Jan.–Mar. 1969): 36. biblicalstudies.org.uk/pdf/eq/1969-1_030.pdf

[298] Irenaeus of Lyons writes: "But when this Antichrist shall have devastated all things in this world ... then the Lord will come from heaven ... and bring in for the righteous the times of the kingdom, that is, the rest, the hallowed seventh day ..." (Against Heresies, Book 5, Chapter 30). www.newadvent.org/fathers/0103530.htm

[299] Hans Bietenhard, "The Millennial Hope in the Early Church," *Scottish Journal of Theology* 6, no. 1 (1953): 12–30. doi.org/10.1017/S0036930600005317

[300] Nathan Jarrett, "The Prophecy of Prophecies: Correcting Harold Hoehner's Interpretation of Daniel's 70 Weeks," *Eleutheria: John W. Rawlings School of Divinity Academic Journal* 5, no. 2 (2021): 289, 290, 305. doi.org/10.70570/QNLJ6499

[301] Ibid., 289.

Skeptics often assert that the **literal 1000 years** necessitate a **young earth timeline** capped at 6000 years, which not all accept.[302] A reasonable interpolation is that **6000 years** of world history may have elapsed **consecutively**, while the **last 1000 years**—the **Chiliasm Millennium**—is cut out and reserved **non-consecutively** for **after Christ's return**. In Daniel's prophecy, **seven days** are interpreted as **seven literal years** (as confirmed in Revelation). Thus, by consistent interpretation, the **"1000 years"** in Revelation 20:5 should also be taken as **literal**, either directly or by consistent prophetic equivalence.

NON-ELECT SALVATION POSSIBILITY QUOTES

This is not an exhaustive list but an **instructional survey** highlighting early fathers who also affirmed **Chiliasm**, which strengthens the possibility that they recognized **two types of salvation**—**elect** and **non-elect**. This distinction becomes vital when considered within the **1000-year gap** between the **first resurrection** and the **second resurrection**, since only through this interval can we scripturally position the second resurrection to life as separate from the first. The correlation of these patristic statements with the latter references to the **water of life** may therefore support a **non-elect salvation** interpretation for the recipients involved.

Justin of Rome

Possible non-elect salvation is suggested in Justin's interpretation of Isaiah, in which the **wicked become obedient** and are **subjected** to Christ—as **"one child"**, implying **non-elect inclusion** under submission rather than reward:

> "We have preached before Him as if [He were] a child, as if a root in a dry ground." (And what follows in order of the prophecy already quoted.) But when the passage speaks as from the lips of many, "We have preached before Him," and adds, "as if a child," it signifies that the wicked shall become subject to Him, and shall obey His command, and that all shall become as one child ... and of those things which would also be done by Christ Himself."[303]

Elect salvation, on the other hand, is likened to the unified **church**—those foreknown to believe:

---

[302] Victor Christianto, Isak Suria, & S. Simbolon, "On the Age of Earth," *Scientific God Journal*, 11, no. 4 (July 2020): 286–295. scigod.com/index.php/sgj/article/view/734

[303] Justin of Rome (Justin Martyr), *Dialogue with Trypho*, Chapter 42. www.newadvent.org/fathers/01283.htm

> "Such a thing [analogy] as you may witness in the body [Christians]: although the members are enumerated as many, all are called one, and are a body. For, indeed, a commonwealth and a church, though many individuals in number, are in fact as one, called and addressed by one appellation ... of those who it was foreknown were to believe in Him."[304]

Irenaeus of Lyons

Interestingly, **Irenaeus** speaks of certain **sheep being set free on judgment day**, the time associated with the **second resurrection** (after the 1000-year reign), rather than in the earlier marriage of the Lamb. These appear to be **non-elect**, as they are saved only **after** the millennial kingdom has concluded:

> "When God takes vengeance, in the one case indeed typically, temporarily, and more moderately ... For those points to which they call attention with regard to the God who then awarded temporal punishments to the unbelieving ... these same [facts, I say,] shall nevertheless repeat themselves in the Lord, who judges for eternity those whom He does judge, and lets go free for eternity those whom He does let go free."[305]

In the **same chapter**, he contrasts this with those who receive **elect salvation**—a group described as being saved **now**, in their earthly lifetime, by faith:

> "And again, who are they that have been saved and received the inheritance? Those, doubtless, who do believe God, and who have continued in His love; as did Caleb [the son] of Jephunneh and Joshua [the son] of Nun, Numbers 14:30 and innocent children, who have had no sense of evil. But who are they that are saved now, and receive life eternal? Is it not those who love God, and who believe His promises, and who in malice have become as little children?"[306]

The phrase **"saved now, and receive life eternal"** clearly emphasizes **present-tense faith-based salvation**, aligning with **elect status**, which differs from the **"let go free"** language applied to others **after** the kingdom. The **elect are rewarded for faith**, but the **non-elect** are merely **released**

---

[304] Ibid.

[305] Irenaeus of Lyons, *Against Heresies*, Book 4, Chapter 28, Points 1 to 3. www.newadvent.org/fathers/0103428.htm

[306] Ibid., Point 3.

from judgment, indicating **a lesser form of mercy**, not the glory of inheritance.

Furthermore, these individuals appear to be those who are **"let go" at the great white throne judgment** without receiving any **inheritance**, meaning that different judgment outcomes are being described across various passages. For instance, **1 Corinthians 3:15's** phrase, **"saved by fire"**, may correlate to **this kind of release**, potentially representing a **non-elect salvation** category. In contrast, those who **receive an inheritance** in **1 Corinthians 3:14** clearly represent a different group, one rewarded for works of enduring value—an idea further reinforced in **Colossians 3:23–24**, which identifies this **reward** as an **"inheritance"** from the Lord.[307]

Moreover, the reality that **faith without works is dead** (James 2:26) confirms that **living faith** must be **accompanied by works of holiness and charity**. Therefore, those in **1 Corinthians 3:14**, whose works endure, reflect such **living faith**, whereas those in **1 Corinthians 3:15** may instead represent **those without faith**, being **saved only by fire** and suffering **loss**, without receiving reward.

This interpretation harmonizes with the **threefold harvest** from **"good ground"** found in the **Parable of the Sower**, namely the **thirtyfold, sixtyfold**, and **hundredfold** categories (Matthew 13:8). These three levels are not about mere entrance into life but **degrees of reward**—a point underscored by **Matthew 19:29**, where Christ specifically distinguishes **"hundredfold"** reward from the phrase **"inherit eternal life"**, indicating that **eternal life** is common to all believers, but **reward** is measured in degrees.[308]

Thus, it is logical to assign **1 Corinthians 3:14** to such rewarded believers (elect), and **1 Corinthians 3:15** to a **separate class** that **lacks reward** entirely. The expression **"suffer loss"** in 1 Corinthians 3:15 inherently implies **zero reward**, confirming that these are **not included among the thirtyfold, sixtyfold, or hundredfold**, since **even the lowest**

---

[307] 1 Corinthians 3:15, "If anyone's work is burned, he will suffer loss; but he himself will be saved, yet so as through fire." (NKJV). biblehub.com/1_corinthians/3-15.htm 1 Corinthians 3:14, "If anyone's work which he has built on it endures, he will receive a reward." (NKJV). biblehub.com/1_corinthians/3-14.htm Colossians 3:23–24, "...you will receive the reward of the inheritance." (NKJV). biblehub.com/nkjv/colossians/3.htm James 2:26, "Faith without works is dead." (NKJV). biblehub.com/james/2-26.htm

[308] Matthew 13:8, "Some a hundredfold, some sixty, some thirty." (NKJV). biblehub.com/matthew/13-8.htm
Matthew 19:29, "...shall receive a hundredfold, and inherit eternal life." (NKJV). biblehub.com/matthew/19-29.htm

reward would contradict the language of complete **loss**. Therefore, the one **saved by fire** in **1 Corinthians 3:15** may be more rightly viewed as partaking in a **non-elect salvation** scenario, especially as he receives **no inheritance**, unlike those mentioned in Colossians.

Furthermore, the Lord Himself testifies that **those who believe** in Him on earth **"shall not come into judgment"** (John 5:24). This disqualifies the "saved by fire" individual of **1 Corinthians 3:15** from being classified among the **faithful**, since that verse explicitly describes one who is **judged, burned**, and only then **saved**, in stark contrast to the **good ground** believers, who **should not be judged** at all, let alone **burned** or forced to **suffer loss**.[309]

Is there any notable **early church father** who applies the **"water of life"** context to the **wicked or sinners** rather than the righteous? Yes—**Cyril of Alexandria** provides such an example when he applies the language of **Isaiah 49:9–10** to those formerly in **disobedience and darkness**, rather than the elect:

> "What occasion will we still have for weeping? On the contrary, will not what has happened to us, thanks to the Savior, cause us boundless rejoicing? He it was Who showed the way of salvation not only to us, but also went as herald to the once disobedient spirits of the underworld, as Peter says (1 Pet. 3:19–20). For it would not have done for His loving-kindness to be shown only to some; the manifestation of the gift had to be extended to all of nature… Having proclaimed His message, then, to the spirits in the underworld and having said to those in fetters, 'Come forth!' and to those in darkness, 'Show yourselves!' (cf. Isa. 49:9) … Even by the springs of water He will guide them"[310]

Cyril here connects this moment with **Christ's descent into Hades**, but what is noteworthy is his application of **Isaiah 49:9–10** to the **spirits in prison**—the disobedient, not the righteous. Though his historical setting may place it during or just after the resurrection, this same passage might be reinterpreted **within the Chiliasm timeline**. If so, these individuals—formerly imprisoned in darkness—could be recipients of **"water of life"** during the **post-millennial era**, after the **final judgment**.

---

[309] John 5:24, "He who hears My word and believes in Him who sent Me … shall not come into judgment." (NKJV). biblehub.com/john/5-24.htm

[310] Cyril of Alexandria, *Festal Letter* 2.8. Catholic University of America Press. archive.org/details/festalletters1120000cyri/page/n271/mode/2up; classicalchristianity.com/category/bysaint/st-cyril-of-alexandria-ca-376-444/

In Isaiah 49:9–10, the Scripture reads:

"'Go forth,' to those who are in darkness, 'Show yourselves.' They shall feed along the roads, and their pastures shall be on all desolate heights. They shall neither hunger nor thirst ... Even by the springs of water He will guide them."[311]

This **literal reading** suggests that some **who were imprisoned or punished** may later be **shown mercy, led by springs of water**, and granted **limited access** to dwell **outside the city**, "along the roads" and "on desolate heights"—imagery fitting for **non-elect salvation**.

However, others object to this view, citing **Revelation 20:15**, which states: "Anyone not found written in the Book of Life was cast into the lake of fire."[312] Yet perhaps this casting into the **lake of fire** does not preclude the possibility of being **"saved by fire"**, as described in **1 Corinthians 3:15**, suggesting a **fiery purification** rather than eternal destruction. This would align with a threefold division: the **righteous saved without judgment**, the **sinners saved by fire**, and the **wicked (ungodly) who perish**.[313]

This view is supported by **Psalm 1:5–6**, which distinguishes between **the righteous, sinners,** and **ungodly**—indicating three categories of outcome.[314] Moreover, **Revelation 22:1–2** links the **water of life** and **tree of life**, both of which appear after judgment, providing healing to the nations.[315] Those **requiring healing** at that point would not be the glorified elect, but perhaps **those saved through fire**, harmed by the **second death** but not destroyed by it.[316]

Therefore, **1 Corinthians 3:15** could reflect **non-elect salvation**: those **cast into fire** (Revelation 20:15) may **not be eternally condemned**, but merely **hurt by the second death**,[317] and yet **saved by fire** if God permits.[318] The typical rebuttal that **1 Corinthians 3** applies only to Christians because of verse 11—"no other foundation can anyone lay than Jesus Christ"[319]—

---

[311] Isaiah 49:9–10 (NKJV). biblehub.com/nkjv/isaiah/49.htm
[312] Revelation 20:15 (NKJV). biblehub.com/nkjv/revelation/20.htm
[313] John 5:24 (NKJV). biblehub.com/john/5-24.htm
[314] Psalm 1:5–6 (NKJV). biblehub.com/nkjv/psalms/1.htm
[315] Revelation 22:1–3 (NKJV). biblehub.com/revelation/22.htm
[316] Revelation 2:11 (NKJV). biblehub.com/revelation/2-11.htm
[317] Revelation 20:15 (NKJV).
[318] 1 Corinthians 3:15 (NKJV). biblehub.com/1_corinthians/3-15.htm
[319] 1 Corinthians 3:11 (NKJV). biblehub.com/1_corinthians/3-11.htm

can be addressed by considering **Romans 2:6–11**, which teaches that God renders to each man according to his deeds.[320]

This includes **those who never heard the Gospel**, but **did some of God's will** through the **conscience**, as described in **Romans 2:14–16**, showing that the **law is written on their hearts**.[321] Such individuals are judged **according to Christ's Gospel**, even if they never knew His name during their earthly life. Therefore, they may be the ones **excused on that Day**—not because of works, but because **Christ's atonement is applied to them posthumously**, by His sovereign mercy. This is perhaps why **some Church Fathers** interpret these passages differently, given the **difficulty** and **depth** of such a mysterious salvation category.

POSTMORTEM SALVATION

Tertullian appears to affirm a form of **postmortem purgation** in Hades. In several of his works, he interprets Christ's judgment sayings—such as the "till the last penny" passages—as referencing a process of correction or payment even after death.[322] Tertullian explicitly describes **a prison-like realm** in the afterlife where souls are detained until they fulfill the required judgment.[323] He associates this with Hades, arguing that the soul remains there until it is reunited with the resurrected body.[324] In this framework, the "prison" and "payment" described by Christ would apply to more than earthly consequences, extending into the **spirit world's penal dimension**.

Christ's words are striking:

> "Agree with your adversary quickly, while you are on the way with him, lest your adversary deliver you to the judge, the judge hand you over to the officer, and you be thrown into prison. Assuredly, I say to you, you will by no means get out of there till you have paid the last penny."[325]

While **Irenaeus** also references this passage, he does not comment directly on whether this judgment could end in **posthumous salvation**.[326] In

---

[320] Romans 2:6–11 (NKJV). biblehub.com/nkjv/romans/2.htm
[321] Romans 2:14–16 (NKJV). biblehub.com/nkjv/romans/2.htm
[322] Tertullian, *A Treatise on the Soul*, Chapter 35. www.newadvent.org/fathers/0310.htm
[323] Tertullian, *A Treatise on the Soul*, Chapter 58. www.newadvent.org/fathers/0310.htm
[324] Tertullian, *On the Resurrection of the Flesh*, Chapter 42. www.newadvent.org/fathers/0316.htm
[325] Matthew 5:25–26 (NKJV). biblehub.com/nkjv/matthew/5.htm
[326] Irenaeus of Lyons, *Against Heresies*, Book 1, Chapter 25.

contrast, **Justin of Rome** provides a more nuanced idea. In *Hortatory Address to the Greeks*, he mentions that **some of the severely wicked cannot escape the lower parts of Hades "unless they had paid the full penalty"**—a phrase which, though not affirming postmortem salvation directly, **logically implies that others may have escaped** after satisfying divine justice.[327] This opens the possibility of a **non-elect salvation** granted after afterlife punishments.

Christ Himself uses the term **"torturers"** in this context, suggesting a strong image of afterlife correction, especially in the case of those He labels **"wicked"**. The parable of the unforgiving servant reinforces this:

> "'You wicked servant! I forgave you all that debt because you begged me. Should you not also have had compassion on your fellow servant…?' And his master was angry, and delivered him to the torturers until he should pay all that was due to him. So My heavenly Father also will do to you if each of you… does not forgive his brother."[328]

If **Tertullian** is correct—that some souls undergoing this judgment are ultimately saved—then this "wicked servant," though judged, might still be **redeemed after full payment**. However, it is crucial to distinguish this type of salvation from the **elect**, the **bride of Christ**, whose **righteous acts and repentance on earth** qualify them for a **place in the wedding supper** of the Lamb:

> "His wife has made herself ready… the fine linen is the righteous acts of the saints."[329]

This distinction implies that the **wicked servant**, though saved eventually, is **excluded from the bride category**—a concept in line with **non-elect salvation**. Christ's use of the term "wicked" also undercuts Roman Catholic attempts to limit purgatory to the **righteous with minor sins**. After all, the "wicked servant" here is likened to an **unbeliever** in **Luke 12:46**:

---

www.newadvent.org/fathers/0103125.htm

[327] Justin of Rome, *Hortatory Address to the Greeks*, Chapter 27. www.newadvent.org/fathers/0129.htm

[328] Matthew 18:32–35 (NKJV). biblehub.com/nkjv/matthew/18.htm

[329] Revelation 19:7–8 (NKJV). biblehub.com/nkjv/revelation/19.htm

"The master... will cut him in two and appoint him his portion with the unbelievers."[330]

This interpolation leads to a thought-provoking implication: if a **"servant" who is wicked** receives the same portion as **"unbelievers,"** and yet Tertullian thinks such a one might be saved after judgment, then **unbelievers** themselves may likewise be granted **postmortem salvation**, if God wills it.

Irenaeus of Lyons affirms the possibility of spirit-world salvation through the language of Christ's descent and the recovery of perished souls. He writes that Christ **"descend[ed] to those things which are of the earth beneath, seeking the sheep which had perished"**, connecting this descent with a salvation timeline that includes those who had already died:

> "As the Head rose from the dead, so also the remaining part of the body — [namely, the body] of every man who is found in life — when the time is fulfilled of that condemnation which existed by reason of disobedience, may arise... each of the members having its own proper and fit position in the body. For there are many mansions in the Father's house, inasmuch as there are also many members in the body."[331]

This passage emphasizes that Christ's redemptive mission extends even to those previously under **condemnation**, implying a **delayed resurrection** for some who perished under judgment. His phrase **"seeking the sheep which had perished"** is particularly important because it is applied to Christ's descent into **the lower parts of the earth**, an expression commonly understood as Hades or the spirit world.[332]

Irenaeus refutes the Gnostic claim that these "lower parts" simply refer to our earthly life. He insists that they are **literal realms of the dead**, clarifying:

> "[If all these things occurred, I say], how must these men not be put to confusion, who allege that the lower parts refer to this

---

[330] Luke 12:46–48 (NKJV). biblehub.com/nkjv/luke/12.htm

[331] Irenaeus of Lyons, *Against Heresies*, Book 3, Chapter 19, Point 3. www.newadvent.org/fathers/0103319.htm

[332] Ephesians 4:9–10 (NKJV). biblehub.com/nkjv/ephesians/4.htm

world of ours…? For as the Lord went away in the midst of the shadow of death, where the souls of the dead were."[333]

From this, it becomes clear that Irenaeus considered the **descent of Christ into Hades** not symbolic, but a real event to **seek and redeem** those sheep who had perished in disobedience and condemnation.

Now, if we compare this to the phrase "other sheep which are not of this fold"[334] in John 10:16, the common interpretation is that this refers to **Gentile believers**, while the sheep of the present fold refer to **believing Israelites**. However, this interpretation is **not supported** by either **Justin of Rome** or **Irenaeus**, both of whom are strong proponents of **Chiliasm**. Instead, they present a two-stage resurrection framework consistent with **Revelation 20:5**[335] — separating two distinct groups by a **1,000-year gap**.

Irenaeus describes the first group, the **elect sheep**, as those saved during **the times of the kingdom**, i.e., during the **millennial reign**.[336] This is in contrast to another group raised only **after** the thousand years, which could refer to the **non-elect sheep** saved at the **general resurrection**.[337] This second group may be the ones referred to as the "other fold," distinct in **timing** and possibly in **inheritance status**. Irenaeus associates the **general resurrection** with the **last trumpet**[338] — indicating the final call of salvation after judgment.

Interestingly, **Justin Martyr** and **Irenaeus** do not label Gentile believers as the "other sheep." Instead, they refer to Gentiles as **"spotted"** or **"colored"** sheep. Justin writes:

> "As, therefore, from the varied colors of the sheep of Laban, there were produced speckled and many-spotted sheep… so also from the varied and many-formed errors of the Gentile race."[339]

---

[333] Irenaeus of Lyons, *Against Heresies*, Book 5, Chapter 31, Point 2. www.newadvent.org/fathers/0103531.htm

[334] John 10:16 (NKJV). biblehub.com/john/10-16.htm

[335] Revelation 20:5 (NKJV). biblehub.com/revelation/20-5.htm

[336] Irenaeus of Lyons, *Against Heresies*, Book 5, Chapters 30, 33, 36. www.newadvent.org/fathers/0103530.htm

[337] Irenaeus of Lyons, *Against Heresies*, Book 5, Chapter 35 and Book 4, Chapter 40. www.newadvent.org/fathers/0103535.htm

[338] Irenaeus of Lyons, *Against Heresies*, Book 5, Chapter 13. www.newadvent.org/fathers/0103513.htm

[339] Justin of Rome, *Dialogue with Trypho*, Chapter 134. www.newadvent.org/fathers/01289.htm

Irenaeus similarly uses the imagery of **"diverse and many-colored sheep"** in reference to Gentiles.[340] This is important because a **spot or color** speaks of a **physical trait** or **racial identity**, while the term for **"fold"** used in John 10:16 is αὐλῆς (*aulēs*) — which means **enclosure, sheepfold**, or **court**, indicating an **external dwelling or domain**.[341] This linguistic precision may support the idea that the **two folds** refer to **two eschatological households** — one in the **new heavens** (elect sheepfold) and one on the **new earth** (non-elect sheepfold), with both under one Shepherd but distinguished by their inheritance levels.

Thus, the structure of **elect vs non-elect salvation**, with sheep saved at **two distinct times**, is consistent with the literal timeline of **Chiliasm** held by these early church fathers and further supported by Irenaeus' teaching on Christ's descent to recover perished souls from Hades.

Around this same period, **Clement of Alexandria** interprets the "sheep of another fold"[342] as referring to those undergoing **afterlife judgment** and consigned to an **inferior final place**, which Roman Catholic doctrine later incorporated into its notion of **purgatory**. However, Clement's original context suggests more of an early Christian curiosity about varying afterlife destinies rather than any formalized dogma. The theological implications of this concept become more complex in the writings of **Irenaeus of Lyons**.

A particularly intriguing passage by Irenaeus appears in his refutation of Gnostic interpretations, yet it contains a peculiar admission:

> "They also affirm that the Saviour came to the lost sheep, in order to transfer it to the right hand, that is, to the ninety and nine sheep which were in safety, and perished not, but continued within the fold, yet were of the left hand."[343]

Here, Irenaeus acknowledges the **Gnostic claim** that the lost sheep were to be transferred from the **left hand to the right**, which correlates clearly with **Matthew 25:31–46**, where Christ separates the nations at the judgment, placing the **sheep at His right** and the **goats at His left**. The

---

[340] Irenaeus of Lyons, *Against Heresies*, Book 4, Chapter 21. www.newadvent.org/fathers/0103421.htm

[341] Strong's Concordance, 833: *aule* (αὐλή). "A yard... by implication, a mansion:—court, (sheep-)fold, hall, palace." (James Strong, *Strong's Exhaustive Concordance*, 1890, public domain).

[342] Clement of Alexandria, *The Stromata*, Book 6, Chapter 14. www.newadvent.org/fathers/02106.htm

[343] Irenaeus of Lyons, *Against Heresies*, Book 2, Chapter 24, Point 6. www.newadvent.org/fathers/0103224.htm

Gnostics err, however, in introducing an esoteric numerology—asserting that only sheep whose symbolic names add up to a numeric value of one hundred are saved—while those "on the left" who fail to meet this numeric threshold are considered corruptible. Irenaeus rebukes this nonsense, yet his critique reveals something profound:

> "They must acknowledge that the enjoyment of rest did not imply salvation."[344]

Although Irenaeus rejects their numerology, his use of their framework hints that there may be those who experience **a form of rest in the afterlife**, yet **do not attain salvation**. By extension, if there is such a distinction, then conversely, there could be some who are judged **but later saved**, aligning with the idea of **non-elect salvation** occurring **after** resurrection judgment.

This transfer from **left to right** in Irenaeus' discussion strongly mirrors **Matthew 25**'s end-times judgment imagery. Importantly, in that passage, Christ separates the sheep from the goats **at the resurrection**, which appears to be the **second resurrection** since both groups—righteous and wicked—are raised together.[345] This suggests that the sheep of Matthew 25 are **not the same** as the sheep raised in the **first resurrection**, who reign with Christ for a thousand years, but rather another group appearing **after** the millennial reign. Therefore, these may be the **sheep of the other fold**, representing **non-elect salvation**.

Supporting this reading are the soteriological distinctions found in **Athenagoras of Athens** (c. 133–190 C.E.), a contemporary of the above Church Fathers and a formidable apologist. In his work *On the Resurrection of the Dead*, Athenagoras offers what could be read as two contrasting destinies: one for the **elect**, and another for those who fall short of that mark.

Regarding the **elect**, he writes:

> "And we shall make no mistake in saying, that the final cause of an intelligent life and rational judgment, is to be occupied uninterruptedly with those objects to which the natural reason is chiefly and primarily adapted, and to delight unceasingly in the contemplation of Him who is, and of His decrees."[346]

---

[344] Ibid.

[345] Matthew 25:31–46 (NKJV). biblehub.com/nkjv/matthew/25.htm

[346] Athenagoras of Athens, *On the Resurrection of the Dead*, Chapter 25. www.newadvent.org/fathers/0206.htm

Here Athenagoras describes a state of **constant divine contemplation**, a reward reserved for those who attain the **full end of their created purpose**—likely a reference to the **elect** and their heavenly inheritance. However, he also includes a contrasting picture:

> "Majority of men, because they are affected too passionately and too violently by things below, pass through life without attaining this object. For the large number of those who fail of the end that belongs to them does not make void the common lot, since the examination relates to individuals, and the reward or punishment of lives ill or well spent is proportioned to the merit of each."[347]

This second statement is significant. Athenagoras admits that **"the majority of men"** will **fail to attain the contemplative destiny** reserved for the elect, but he does not consign them to utter destruction. Instead, he allows that they may still participate in a **"common lot"**, wherein **judgment is individual** and **proportionate** to one's earthly conduct. This statement allows for the possibility of **postmortem discipline**, with **rewards or punishments** assessed **after the full span of a person's life**, and seems to leave open the door for **a non-elect salvation** consistent with justice, mercy, and proportionate response.

Thus, when placed alongside **Clement's lesser view of the sheep of another fold, Irenaeus' post-resurrection sorting**, and **Athenagoras' two-tiered assessment**, a unified trajectory emerges. The early Church's theological landscape, while varied, allows for the possibility that **some may be saved after judgment**, even if they **failed to live as elect** in this life. In that light, the sheep of the other fold may represent the **redeemed from judgment**, who were not originally part of the elect bride but who are **granted life** in accordance with **God's mercy** and **righteous judgment**.

This is why we encourage **non-Christians** to engage in **acts of charity** toward Christians: with the hope that they may receive **mercy from Jehovah**. While we never obscure the reality of **eternal condemnation**, we also do not preclude the **possibility** of **postmortem salvation**. Both views exist in early Christian thought, and we present each honestly. Our aim is not to discourage belief, but rather to proclaim the full scope of the **Scriptural consequences**—whether salvation through faith in Christ or judgment for rejection of truth.

---

[347] Ibid.

The teaching of **two kinds of final resurrection bodies with "glory"** aligns with this duality. One is **heavenly**, referring to the **elect**, and the other is **earthly**, possibly referring to the **non-elect saved**. In both cases, **resurrection in glory** cannot describe the **unsaved**, for the wicked are raised to **judgment and shame**, not incorruption. As Paul explains:

> "There are also celestial bodies and terrestrial bodies; but the glory of the celestial is one, and the glory of the terrestrial is another. There is one glory of the sun, another glory of the moon, and another glory of the stars; for one star differs from another star in glory. So also is the resurrection of the dead. The body is sown in corruption, it is raised in incorruption."[348]

Let us map this **dual-glory resurrection** framework to the final eschatological scene depicted in Revelation 21 and make a theological interpolation:

i) The Overcomers = Christians (Elect Salvation)

> "He who overcomes shall inherit all things, and I will be his God and he shall be My son".[349]

ii) The Thirsty = Non-Elect Salvation Possibility for Some Non-Christians

> "I will give of the fountain of the water of life freely to him who thirsts."[350]

iii) The Damned = The Unsaved Remaining in the Lake of Fire

> "But the cowardly, unbelieving, abominable, murderers, sexually immoral, sorcerers, idolaters, and all liars shall have their part in the lake which burns with fire and brimstone, which is the second death."[351]

In these verses, the **"overcomers"** clearly enjoy a superior inheritance. Their promises are exclusive and intimate—**"My son"**, **"inherit all things"**—which distinguishes them from the **"thirsty"**, who are offered **only the water of life freely**. This indicates that the **overcomers** are not the

---

[348] 1 Corinthians 15:40–42 (NKJV). biblehub.com/nkjv/1_corinthians/15.htm
[349] Revelation 21:7 (NKJV). biblehub.com/revelation/21-7.htm
[350] Revelation 21:6 (NKJV). biblehub.com/revelation/21-6.htm
[351] Revelation 21:8 (NKJV). biblehub.com/revelation/21-8.htm

same as the **thirsty**, and so the **"thirsty"** likely refer to a **lesser class of saved**, possibly those of **non-elect salvation**.

Support for this conclusion comes from the Scriptural contrast between the "overcomers" and others. For instance, **1 John 5:4** defines the overcomer as **the one who has faith in Christ**.[352] Meanwhile, Christ Himself declares that **those who believe in Him will never thirst**:

> "He who comes to Me shall never hunger, and he who believes in Me shall never thirst."[353]

Therefore, if the **"thirsty"** are still thirsty in Revelation 21, then they cannot be the **faithful elect**, who are promised to thirst no more. If they had already believed in Christ before death, they would no longer be characterized as "thirsty." Their continued thirst suggests that they **did not believe during their lifetime**, and hence, this group could correspond to the **non-elect saved after judgment**—those who come to faith only after death, **possibly in the spirit world**.

This harmonizes with the principle in **John 6:40**:

> "This is the will of Him who sent Me, that everyone who sees the Son and believes in Him may have everlasting life; and I will raise him up at the last day."[354]

The Lord rebukes the Jews not simply for disbelieving, but for doing so **after seeing Him**[7]. This distinction implies that **some** may **believe after seeing**—as in the case of **Thomas**, who only believed upon seeing the resurrected Christ:

> "Jesus said to him, 'Thomas, because you have seen Me, you have believed. Blessed are those who have not seen and yet have believed.'"[355]

Those who come to believe **after seeing**, though not "blessed" in the same way as those who believed by faith, may still be **granted mercy**, and perhaps this is what qualifies them for **non-elect salvation**. This aligns with **1 Corinthians 3:15**, where some are **"saved by fire"**—implying salvation through judgment, not apart from it.

---

[352] 1 John 5:4 (NKJV). biblehub.com/1_john/5-4.htm
[353] John 6:35 (NKJV). biblehub.com/john/6-35.htm
[354] John 6:29, 35–36, 40 (NKJV). biblehub.com/nkjv/john/6.htm
[355] John 20:29 (NKJV). biblehub.com/john/20-29.htm

Thus, we must consider that **the thirsty in Revelation 21** might represent those **saved after judgment**, not condemned with the damned, but **distinct** from the overcomers. The overcomers inherit the **heavenly glory**, while the thirsty may be raised to the **terrestrial glory**, as Paul says—both glorious, but not equal.

This interpretation reinforces the **non-elect salvation possibility**, particularly as drawn from the final two chapters of Revelation. In **Revelation 21**, there is a deliberate distinction made between the **Bride (the Church)** and **"the nations who are saved"**. The **Bride** is shown descending from heaven and is described as the **"holy city, new Jerusalem"**, which is entirely **heavenly** in origin and constitution.[356] The **Bride** represents the **elect**, those who are **glorified** with **celestial (heavenly) bodies**, as Paul wrote:

> "There are also celestial bodies and terrestrial bodies; but the glory of the celestial is one, and the glory of the terrestrial is another."[357]

In contrast, the **"nations who are saved"**—mentioned in **Revelation 21:24**—are said to **walk in the light of the city**, but they are **not identified as the Bride**, nor as those who have **entered** that city in the same manner. Rather, they appear to dwell **outside** the heavenly city, in the **new earth**, under the reign of its **kings**, who themselves are permitted access into that holy city.[358] This **distinction** between the **nations** and the **Bride** suggests the possibility that these saved nations possess **terrestrial resurrection bodies**, glorified in a different and **inferior measure**, consistent with the principle of differing glories articulated in **1 Corinthians 15:40–42**.[359]

The **gates** of the city, while "never shut",[360] still imply **boundary and distinction**. That there are **gates** at all suggests **not all** have access to **enter**. This is explicitly confirmed in **Revelation 21:27**, where it is written that **nothing defiling**, and only those **written in the Lamb's Book of Life**, may enter.[361] Thus, while the nations are "saved," their **access to the heavenly Jerusalem** seems to be **conditional**, and their salvation of a **lesser inheritance**—possibly non-elect.

---

[356] Revelation 21:9–10 (NKJV). biblehub.com/nkjv/revelation/21.htm
[357] 1 Corinthians 15:40–42 (NKJV). biblehub.com/nkjv/1_corinthians/15.htm
[358] Revelation 21:24–27 (NKJV). biblehub.com/nkjv/revelation/21.htm
[359] 1 Corinthians 15:40–42 (NKJV). biblehub.com/nkjv/1_corinthians/15.htm
[360] Revelation 21:24–27 (NKJV). biblehub.com/nkjv/revelation/21.htm
[361] Revelation 21:24–27 (NKJV). biblehub.com/nkjv/revelation/21.htm

Further confirmation of this interpretation comes from **Revelation 22:17**, where **"the Spirit and the Bride"** jointly call to **others** to **"Come"**, inviting **"him who thirsts"** to take of the **water of life freely**:

> "And the Spirit and the bride say, 'Come!' And let him who hears say, 'Come!' And let him who thirsts come. Whoever desires, let him take the water of life freely."[362]

This final invitation occurs **after** the great judgment scene. The **Bride**, already perfected, now extends the call. But **to whom?** The **overcomers** have already inherited all things (Revelation 21:7), and the **wicked** have already been cast into the lake of fire (Revelation 21:8). Therefore, this **thirsty group** must be a **third class—not condemned**, yet also **not of the Bride**. Their desire and thirst, even at this late stage, is still being met with **mercy**, suggesting that the **"water of life"** is **extended to them**.

This agrees with the broader possibility that these are those who, though not part of the elect (the Bride), are nonetheless saved by **divine mercy**—perhaps through **postmortem repentance**, **charity shown to believers**, or some other righteous deed as **measured by conscience** (cf. Romans 2:14–16). Their resurrection bodies are **not celestial**, but **terrestrial**, glorified to a **lesser degree**—still incorruptible, but not partaking of the **full inheritance** of the saints.

Thus, **Revelation 21–22** presents a framework in which the **Bride** (elect) is **distinct from** the **saved nations** (non-elect), and where the **invitation to salvation** continues even after the judgment, directed toward those who **desire** and **thirst**, in accordance with God's will and mercy.

CONCLUSION

What if **non-elect salvation** turns out to be false?

Jehovah warned through the prophet Jeremiah that if a man gives a prophetic claim as his own reasoning—even if it proves wrong—it is not a sin, for he did not misuse the name of Jehovah.[363] However, if someone asserts, *"Jehovah has said,"* and the message is not from Him or does not come to pass, such a person incurs **divine judgment**. The punishment for this presumption is described with solemn severity: "an everlasting reproach and a perpetual shame."[364] The **Hebrew word "olam"**—translated here as

---

[362] Revelation 22:17 (NKJV). biblehub.com/revelation/22-17.htm
[363] Jeremiah 23:36.
[364] Jeremiah 23:38–40.

"everlasting" and "perpetual"—is used twice in that warning, indicating the seriousness of falsely invoking divine authority.

What if **non-elect salvation** turns out to be true?

If non-elect salvation is indeed true, then the "few" who are saved refer specifically to **elect salvation**.[365] These are those who become **the Bride** of Christ,[366] enter **heaven**,[367] and inherit **all things**. Meanwhile, Christ's ransom for "many"[368] could include **non-elect saved individuals**, who are not part of the Bride but receive their portion on the **final new earth**.[369] These may be the ones to whom the **Bride calls**, saying, *"Come ... let him who thirsts come. Whoever desires, let him take the water of life freely"*.[370] This water flows into the new earth in that **final scene**, along with **the leaves of the tree of life**, which are explicitly said to be "for the healing of the nations."[371]

This healing cannot logically apply to the **Bride**, who has already been glorified and reigning for 1,000 years. In **Chiliasm's framework**, this would apply instead to those who are **saved after the Great White Throne Judgment**, raised only in the **second resurrection**, and are **not condemned**, but have been **"saved by fire."**[372] It is unlikely that Christians—resurrected and glorified in the **first resurrection**—would require healing from the tree's leaves in this post-judgment context. Thus, **non-elect salvation** is the more coherent explanation.

Perhaps this is what the prophet Daniel meant when he said, *"many shall be purified"*—a phrase that could allude to the **refining fire** of final judgment.[373] This theory helps reconcile how certain verses imply a **larger group being saved**,[374] while the **believers** are clearly a **subset** of that larger group.[375]

---

[365] Matthew 7:14.
[366] Revelation 21:9.
[367] Matthew 7:21.
[368] Matthew 26:28.
[369] Revelation 21:24, 27.
[370] Revelation 22:17.
[371] Revelation 22:1–2.
[372] 1 Corinthians 3:15.
[373] Daniel 12:10.
[374] 1 Timothy 2:4.
[375] 1 Timothy 4:10.

The **academic concept of Non-Elect Salvation**[376] is admittedly **new**, developed from recent theological research and interpretation. It is **not doctrine**, since it cannot be confirmed with certainty. Rather, it is a **scholarly interpolation**, offered here cautiously as a **possibility**—not a dogma. Its inclusion in this work is to **highlight a literal reading** of relevant Bible passages and to suggest that **this framework aligns naturally** with what is written.

A study of prophecy must not rest on **private interpretation**, which is why I have drawn from the writings of **distinguished Chiliasm Church Fathers**. Even if this interpretation proves to be incorrect, it has been constructed with **honesty and documented historical testimony**. If non-elect salvation is false, then at worst this attempt is a **speculative effort** rooted in **honest scholarship**, and Jehovah, who judges justly, would see that the claim was **never made presumptuously**.

BIBLIOGRAPHY

A. Skevington Wood. "The Eschatology of Irenaeus" *The Evangelical Quarterly*, 41.1 (UK, Jan.-Mar. 1969): 36. biblicalstudies.org.uk/pdf/eq/1969-1_030.pdf

Athenagoras of Athens. *On the Resurrection of the Dead*. Chapter 25.

Augustine of Hippo. (*Catena Aurea*, Commentary on Matthew 25:1 – 13's Parable of the Five Wise/Foolish Virgins).

Augustine of Hippo. *The City of God*. Book 13. Chapters 20 – 23.

Bible. biblehub.com

Christianto, Victor & Suria, Isak & Simbolon, S., "On the Age of Earth," *Scientific God Journal*, Volume 11, Issue 4 (July 2020): 286-295. scigod.com/index.php/sgj/article/view/734

Clement of Alexandria. *The Stromata*. Book 6. Chapter 14.

Congregation for the Doctrine of the Faith (CDF), a Vatican's department, "Catechism 1137 of the Catholic Church", *Instruction, Pastoralis action* (Acta Apostolicae Sedis (AAS), 72, 1980).

Cyril of Alexandria. *Festal Letter 2.8*. (Catholic University of America Press. Washington, D.C., 2009).

---

[376] Jonathan Ramachandran, "Non Elect Salvation Possibility" (NESP), *The American Journal of Biblical Theology*, Vol 26, No. 6 (February 9, 2025).
www.biblicaltheology.com/Research/RamachandranJ01.pdf

Hans Bietenhard. "The Millennial Hope in the Early Church." *Scottish Journal of Theology* 6, no. 1 (1953): 12–30.

doi.org/10.1017/S0036930600005317

Ignatius of Antioch. *Epistle to the Romans*. Chapter 7.

Irenaeus of Lyons. *Against Heresies*. Book 1. Chapter 25.

Irenaeus of Lyons. *Against Heresies*. Book 2. Chapter 24.

Irenaeus of Lyons. *Against Heresies*. Book 3. Chapter 4.

Irenaeus of Lyons. *Against Heresies*. Book 3. Chapter 19.

Irenaeus of Lyons. *Against Heresies*. Book 4. Chapter 21.

Irenaeus of Lyons. *Against Heresies*. Book 4. Chapter 28.

Irenaeus of Lyons. *Against Heresies*. Book 4. Chapter 38.

Irenaeus of Lyons. *Against Heresies*. Book 4. Chapter 40.

Irenaeus of Lyons. *Against Heresies*. Book 5. Chapter 13.

Irenaeus of Lyons. *Against Heresies*. Book 5. Chapter 18.

Irenaeus of Lyons. *Against Heresies*. Book 5. Chapter 30.

Irenaeus of Lyons. *Against Heresies*. Book 5. Chapter 31

Irenaeus of Lyons. *Against Heresies*. Book 5. Chapter 32.

Irenaeus of Lyons. *Against Heresies*. Book 5. Chapter 33.

Irenaeus of Lyons. *Against Heresies*. Book 5. Chapter 34.

Irenaeus of Lyons. *Against Heresies*. Book 5. Chapter 35.

Irenaeus of Lyons. *Against Heresies*. Book 5. Chapter 36.

James Strong. *Strong's Exhaustive Concordance*, 1890, public domain.

John Calvin, "Genesis 2:9", in *Commentary on Genesis*, translated by John King (Baker, 2009).

Johnson E. Maxwell, *The rites of Christian initiation: their evolution and interpretation*, (Johnson - Liturgical Press, 2007).

Jonathan Ramachandran, "Non Elect Salvation Possibility" (NESP), *The American Journal of Biblical Theology* (AJBT, Theological Research), Vol 26, No. 6 (February 9, 2025).

www.biblicaltheology.com/Research/RamachandranJ01.pdf

Justin of Rome (Justin Martyr). *Dialogue with Trypho*. Chapter 42.

Justin of Rome (Justin Martyr). *Dialogue with Trypho*. Chapter 80.

Justin of Rome (Justin Martyr). *Dialogue with Trypho*. Chapter 81.

Justin of Rome (Justin Martyr). *Dialogue with Trypho*. Chapter 124.

Justin of Rome (Justin Martyr). *Dialogue with Trypho*. Chapter 134.

Justin of Rome (Justin Martyr). *Hortatory Address to the Greeks*. Chapter 27.

Luke A. Powery, "Revelation 7:9-17," *Interpretation*, 79, No. 1 (2025): 75-77. doi.org/10.1177/00209643241285801

Methodius of Olympus. *Banquet of the Ten Virgins*. Discourse 9. Chapter 5.

Nathan Jarrett. "The Prophecy of Prophecies: Correcting Harold Hoehner's Interpretation of Daniel's 70 Weeks." *Eleutheria: John W. Rawlings School of Divinity Academic Journal*, 5, (2), (USA, 2021): 289, 290, 305. doi.org/10.70623/QNLJ6499

Saint Augustine and Edmund Hill, *Homilies on the Gospel of John 1–40 (Works of Saint Augustine: A Translation for the 21st Century*, (Augustinus et al. - New City Press, 2009).

Theo M. M. A. C. Bel, "Man is a Microcosmos: Adam and Eve in Luther's Lectures on Genesis (1535-1545)," *Concordia Theological Quarterly*, Volume 69, No. 2 (April 2005): 170 – 171, 175 – 176. ctsfw.net/media/pdfs/BellManMicrocosmos.pdf

Tertullian. *A Treatise on the Soul*. Chapter 35.

Tertullian. *A Treatise on the Soul*. Chapter 58.

Tertullian. *An Answer to the Jews*. Chapter 13.

Tertullian. *Against Marcion*. Book 3. Chapter 25.

Tertullian. *Against Marcion*. Book 5. Chapter 10.

Tertullian. *On the Resurrection of the Flesh*. Chapter 42.

Thomas Aquinas, Daniel Keating, Matthew Levering, *Commentary on the Gospel of John, Chapters 1–5, Books 1–5* (Larcher et al. - Catholic University of America Press; Eurospan distributor, 2010).

Victorinus of Pettau. *Commentary on the Apocalypse*.

Jonathan Ramachandran

Essay 4: Shadow of Death Possibly Describing Non-Elect Salvation

KEYWORDS

Shadow of Death, Non-Elect Salvation, Chiliasm, Prophecy, Spirit World, Non-Christians, Salvation from Hell, Hades, Church Fathers, Early Christian Writings

ABSTRACT

This paper examines the occurrences of the phrase **"shadow of death"** in the Bible, analyzing its potential meaning in relation to **non-elect salvation**. Traditional interpretations are weighed against lesser-known possibilities using quotes from early church fathers to argue that this phrase may describe postmortem salvation for non-Christians. If correct, this would constitute a significant exegetical discovery with implications for the doctrine of **soteriology**. Since this phrase is directly tied to prophecies about the **Lord Jesus Christ**, it warrants close analysis from multiple interpretive angles. This research utilizes word-for-word translations of the Bible and primary church father sources, assuming that occurrences of this phrase in English reflect the original meanings conveyed in the biblical Hebrew and Greek texts.

INTRODUCTION

The Hebrew word וְצַלְמָוֶת (*transliterated: wə·ṣal·mā·weṯ*),[377] translated as **"shadow of death,"** appears frequently in Scripture. This study refers to it as **"the phrase"** throughout. Linguistically and contextually, this expression may describe **spirit world judgment regions of Hades**.[378] If so, then a literal reading of **Psalm 107:10–15** could imply the possibility of **non-elect salvation** for some who are delivered after undergoing judgment in **Hell**.

In modern English, this phrase often refers to those near physical death due to terminal illness.[379] Within biblical usage, it has also been interpreted as

---

[377] https://biblehub.com/hebrew/vetzalmavet_6757.htm

[378] Hermann Gunkel writes, "place through which the ancient Hebrew supposed the soul had to pass on the way to the underworld [i.e., the abode of the dead]," in *Dictionary of the Bible*, ed. James Hastings (New York: Charles Scribner's Sons, 1963).

[379] Asgeirsdottir, G. H., Sigurbjörnsson, E., Traustadottir, R., Sigurdardottir, V., Gunnarsdottir, S., & Kelly, E. "In the Shadow of Death: Existential and Spiritual Concerns

describing a spiritual state of sin[380] or the emotional grief associated with bereavement.[381]

SHADOW OF DEATH IN THE BIBLE

God personally used this mysterious Hebrew term, translated as **"shadow of death,"** only once in direct speech—to **Job**. This singular usage strongly suggests a **spirit world context**, as the word **death** is explicitly mentioned twice in this verse. One mention is tied to the **"gate"**, implying entry or exit into **regions of punishment or death**, and the other to **"shadow"**, which may signify the **intermediate state** between death and resurrection:

"Have the gates of death been revealed to you? Or have you seen the doors of the shadow of death?"[382]

Next, consider the principal passage that may describe a **non-elect salvation possibility**. This psalm references the **shadow of death** directly and applies it to those who had **rebelled against God** and **rejected His plan** for their lives. Yet, even in that condemned state, some are described as being **delivered by Jehovah** after calling upon Him:

"10There were those who lived in darkness and in the shadow of death,
Prisoners in misery and chains,
11Because they had rebelled against the words of God
And rejected the plan of the Most High.
12Therefore He humbled their heart with labor;
They stumbled and there was no one to help.
13Then they cried out to the LORD in their trouble;
He saved them from their distresses.
14He brought them out of darkness and the shadow of death
And broke their bands apart.
15They shall give thanks to the LORD for His mercy,
And for His wonders to the sons of mankind!

---

among Persons Receiving Palliative Care," *Journal of Pastoral Care & Counseling*, 68(1) (2014): 1–11. https://doi.org/10.1177/154230501406800104

[380] Harold Ray Stevens, "Byron, Original Sin, Shadows of Death and the Dramas of 1821," *The Byron Journal*, 43(1) (2015): 29–42. https://doi.org/10.3828/bj.2015.5

[381] Cambria Kaltwasser, "Meeting Christ in the Shadow of Death," *Reformed Journal*, March 16, 2025. https://reformedjournal.com/2025/03/16/meeting-christ-in-the-shadow-of-death

[382] Job 38:17 (NKJV).

16For He has shattered gates of bronze
And cut off bars of iron."[383]

We know this Old Testament passage is textually reliable, as the **Septuagint**—despite being a rival manuscript tradition—retains the **same essential meaning**. Compare the translation of the same verses from the LXX below:

"10(106:10) even them that sit in darkness and the shadow of death, fettered in poverty and iron;
11(106:11) because they rebelled against the words of God, and provoked the counsel of the Most High.
12(106:12) So their heart was brought low with troubles; they were weak, and there was no helper.
13(106:13) Then they cried to the Lord in their affliction, and he saved them out of their distresses.
14(106:14) And he brought them out of darkness and the shadow of death, and broke their bonds asunder.
15(106:15) Let them acknowledge to the Lord his mercies, and his wonders to the children of men.
16(106:16) For he broke to pieces the brazen gates, and crushed the iron bars."[384]

This passage, taken literally, may offer a rare glimpse into **postmortem mercy** shown to those who had rejected God during their earthly lives. The reference to **gates, bonds, darkness,** and the **shadow of death**—followed by their **deliverance**—supports the view that **Jehovah's mercy** may extend even into **judgment regions** of the **spirit world**, consistent with a **non-elect salvation** possibility.

The exact Hebrew phrase וְצַלְמָוֶת (wə·ṣal·mā·weṯ), translated "**shadow of death,**" appears in several other passages of the Old Testament. This can be easily verified using interlinear and concordance tools available today.[385] The consistent context of this phrase strengthens the case for interpreting it as describing the **gloomy regions of the spirit world**, especially in relation to **postmortem judgment or non-elect salvation possibilities.**

---

[383] Psalm 107:10–16 (NKJV).

[384] Psalm 106[107]:10–16, in *The English Translation of the Septuagint*, by Lancelot Charles Lee Brenton (1851). https://biblehub.com/sep/psalms/107.htm

[385] "Shadow of Death" (wə·ṣal·mā·weṯ — 7 Occurrences), in *Englishman's Hebrew Concordance of the Old Testament*, by George Wigram (1840), s.v. "vale, valley." https://biblehub.com/hebrew/vetzalmavet_6757.htm

I. Job 3: A Gloomy View of the Spirit World

Job laments the day of his birth, wishing it had been overtaken by darkness and the **shadow of death**, placing this phrase in contrast with life and celebration. His wording implies a desire for nonexistence or for the peace of the grave—what he considers the **opposite of life**:

"3May the day perish on which I was born,
And the night in which it was said,
'A male child is conceived.' ...
5May darkness and the shadow of death claim it;
May a cloud settle on it;
May the blackness of the day terrify it."[386]

Scholars have long recognized this passage as deeply saturated with **psychological despair**. Job's emotional intensity here has been studied in light of **modern trauma theory**, highlighting how this speech echoes the suffering of many who face overwhelming darkness.[387] Others note that Job's language includes what appears to be an **ironic praise of death and the underworld**, drawing deliberate parallels to the **Genesis creation account**, as if reversing creation's order and light.[388]

II. Job 10: A Literal Journey Toward Death and the Spirit World

Later in the same book, Job returns to this theme. Here, he contemplates his mortality and speaks of death as a **destination**, a literal **"land of darkness"** and **"shadow of death"** from which none return:

"19 I would have been as though I had not been.
I would have been carried from the womb to the grave.
20Are not my days few? Cease! Leave me alone, that I may take a little comfort,
21Before I go to the place from which I shall not return,
To the land of darkness and the shadow of death,
22A land as dark as darkness itself,

---

[386] Job 3:3, 5 (NKJV).

[387] Abbie F. Mantor, "Caring for the Sufferers Among Us: Job 3 Through the Lens of Classical Rhetorical Theory and Modern Psychological Trauma Studies," *The Asbury Theological Journal*, 75(2), (2020): 232.

https://place.asburyseminary.edu/asburyjournal/vol75/iss2/5

[388] Tobias Häner, "Job's Dark View of Creation: On the Ironic Allusions to Genesis 1:1–2:4a in Job 3 and Their Echo in Job 38–39," *Old Testament Essays*, 33(2), (2020): 275. https://doi.org/10.17159/2312-3621/2020/v33n2a7

As the shadow of death, without any order,
Where even the light is like darkness."[389]

Here, Job's use of "shadow of death" moves beyond metaphor—it **defines the afterlife as a region of disarray and obscurity**, a realm utterly unlike the order and light of life on earth. God's **sovereign rule** over this domain is implied by the finality of verse 21, where Job affirms that **God alone governs access** to that place.[390] This reinforces the point that **salvation from such a domain would require divine intervention**, which opens up the possibility that those held there—perhaps even some of the non-elect—could experience **God's mercy** after judgment.

III. Job 28: The Shadow of Death in the Depths of the Earth

In Job 28:3, the phrase **"shadow of death"** is used metaphorically to describe the deep, dark regions of the earth where miners search for precious minerals. While this imagery refers to **literal mining**, it may **symbolically mirror the spiritual world**, which is also described in Scripture as residing in the "lower parts of the earth."[391]

"3Man puts an end to darkness,
And searches every recess
For ore in the darkness and the shadow of death."[392]

This poetic verse implies **descending into hidden, shadowy places beneath the surface**, which may figuratively suggest a **connection to the spirit world**, traditionally located in subterranean realms according to both **Hebrew thought** and early **Christian cosmology**.[393]

Modern physics has also shown curiosity about dimensions beyond our perception. Some researchers theorize about **parallel universes or invisible dimensions**, but these remain **theoretical constructs**, not empirically proven realities. Any **scientific validation of a spirit world** would require a way to detect immaterial imprints that interact with our known laws of

---

[389] Job 10:19–22 (NKJV).

[390] N.F. Schmidt & P.J. Nel, "Divine Darkness in the Human Discourses of Job," *Acta Theologica*, 36(2), (2016): 135.
https://doi.org/10.4314/actat.v36i2.7

[391] Ephesians 4:9–10 (NKJV), "Now this, 'He ascended'—what does it mean but that He also first descended into the lower parts of the earth?"

[392] Job 28:3 (NKJV).

[393] Ming Tian, "On the Existence of Parallel Universe: Scientific Research on Life's Karma," *American Journal of Biomedical Science & Research*, 25(3), (2025): 393. DOI: 10.34297/AJBSR.2025.25.003329

physics. Until then, the idea of a spiritual realm remains a **truth accepted by faith,** for **"faith is the substance of things hoped for, the evidence of things not seen"** (Hebrews 11:1).³⁹⁴

IV. Psalm 44:19—Dragons and the Shadow of Death

Psalm 44:19 provides another compelling use of the **shadow of death**, this time coupled with the word translated "dragons" in the **King James Version (KJV):**

"Though thou hast sore broken us in the place of dragons, and covered us with the shadow of death."³⁹⁵

The KJV's use of **"dragons"** (from the Hebrew word תַּנִּין – *tannin*), is notable. Many modern translations opt for **"jackals"**, which may reflect a metaphorical or zoological interpretation, but the **original root** supports the possibility of **mythical or monstrous imagery** such as sea serpents or chaos creatures.³⁹⁶ This could imply a **literal or figurative realm of destruction**, possibly the **abyss or judgment regions** within the unseen world.

The **Septuagint** translation omits any mention of dragons or jackals, offering a more generalized rendering:

"19(43:19) For thou hast laid us low in a place of affliction, and the shadow of death has covered us."³⁹⁷

Despite the variation, the idea of being **"covered by the shadow of death"** is retained. It is understood in most commentaries to **symbolize divine judgment** or **national chastisement**, but it may also be applied in a **spirit world context**. Various commentators offer a range of symbolic interpretations:

Ellicott views the reference to **"dragons"** as **a metaphor for dangerous wilderness regions.**³⁹⁸

---

³⁹⁴ Hebrews 11:1 (NKJV).

³⁹⁵ Psalm 44:19 (KJV).

³⁹⁶ "Psalm 44:19," BibleHub.

ames Strong, *Strong's Expanded Exhaustive Concordance of the Bible* (Nashville: Thomas Nelson, 2009), s.v. "tannin" – serpent, dragon, sea monster. https://biblehub.com/hebrew/8577.htm

³⁹⁷ Psalm 44:19, *Brenton Septuagint Translation*.

https://biblehub.com/sep/psalms/44.htm

³⁹⁸ C. J. Ellicott, "Commentary on Psalm 44:19," *A New Testament Commentary for English Readers* (London: Cassell, 1896).

Spence-Jones interprets it as being **near the brink of destruction or divine wrath**.[399]

Matthew Henry sees it as **a spiritual state of sin and darkness**.[400] John Gill links it to **Israel's captivity and even allegorically to Papal Rome**, indicating long-standing affliction under hostile powers.[401]

Although the phrase "shadow of death" in this context is often read symbolically, it may carry a **dual literal-figurative application**, particularly if it evokes **a postmortem punishment context** within the spiritual geography implied in other biblical texts.

V. Psalm 107: Shadow of Death as a Punishment and Deliverance Zone

Our **principal text** in Psalm 107:10–12 offers one of the clearest **judgment-related uses** of the phrase **"shadow of death,"** and strongly aligns with the idea of the **spirit world**. The use of terms like **"darkness," "affliction," "irons,"** and **"shadow of death"** implies incarceration in a realm of postmortem punishment. This is not describing the faithful, but rather those explicitly said to have **"rebelled against the words of God"** and **"despised the counsel of the Most High."**

"10Those who sat in darkness and in the shadow of death,
Bound in affliction and irons—
11Because they rebelled against the words of God,
And despised the counsel of the Most High,
12Therefore He brought down their heart with labor;
They fell down, and there was none to help."[402]

This passage paints a picture of **divine judgment**—a deliberate affliction on those who defied God's Word. If this were merely a reference to an earthly captivity, it would not as readily explain the direct association with the **"shadow of death,"** a term already used in Job and Psalms for **postmortem or subterranean regions**.

---

[399] H. D. M. Spence-Jones, ed., "Commentary on Psalm 44:19," *The Pulpit Commentary* (New York & London: Anson D. F. Randolph; Kegan Paul, Trench, 1883).

[400] Matthew Henry, "Commentary on Psalm 44:19," *The Concise Commentary on the Whole Bible* (1706). https://ccel.org/ccel/henry/mhcc/mhcc.xx.xliv.html

[401] John Gill, "Commentary on Psalm 44:19," *Gill's Exposition of the Entire Bible* (1748–63). https://www.biblestudytools.com/commentaries/gills-exposition-of-the-bible/psalms-44-19.html

[402] Psalm 107:10–12 (NKJV).

In the **next portion** of this same Psalm (verses 13–15), we see an act of divine mercy where the **same group of rebels** are **delivered** from this affliction. The dramatic reversal seems to imply a **salvation event**, possibly even **after death**, reinforcing the idea of a **non-elect salvation possibility**:

"13Then they cried out to the LORD in their trouble,
And He saved them out of their distresses.
14He brought them out of darkness and the shadow of death,
And broke their chains in pieces.
15Oh, that men would give thanks to the LORD for His goodness,
And for His wonderful works to the children of men!"[403]

Here, those who **despised God's Word** and were cast into affliction are later **rescued**, not based on prior obedience, but upon their **cry to Jehovah in their trouble**. This moment of **grace extended to those formerly under wrath** may be pointing to a **literal spiritual salvation from Hades**—the "shadow of death"—and thus may fit into a **Chiliasm model** of **non-elect salvation after judgment**.

Some scholars interpret Psalm 107 through the lens of **Israel's historical captivity**, especially that in Egypt or Babylon.[404] However, even if such an **allegorical interpretation** is valid, it does not **eliminate** the **possibility of a literal application** to **postmortem realities**, especially since the **imagery is consistent** with the spirit world context laid out in earlier texts from Job and Psalms.

VI. Jeremiah 2:6 and the Shadow of Death in National Deliverance

The final direct occurrence of the **"shadow of death"** phrase appears in **Jeremiah 2:6**, where it is mentioned in the context of **God's historical deliverance of Israel** from Egypt, and possibly alluding to the **Babylonian Exile**.[405] Some scholars argue from this verse that the phrase must always refer to **earthly suffering**, such as physical exile or hardship.

Yet, such an assumption **overlooks** the wide **semantic range** the phrase holds in the rest of Scripture. In Jeremiah's usage, the **description of uninhabited lands**—"**a land that no one crossed and where no one**

---

[403] Psalm 107:13–15 (NKJV).

[404] G.T.M. Prinsloo, "From Desperation to Adoration: Reading Psalm 107 As a Transforming Spatial Journey," *Acta Theologica* (December 2021): 392–425. doi.org/10.38140/at.vi.5855

[405] Joseph M. Henderson, "Jeremiah 2–10 as a Unified Literary Composition," in *Uprooting and Planting: Essays on Jeremiah for Leslie Allen*, LHBOTS 459 (London and New York: T&T Clark, 2007): 116–152.

dwelt"—can still allow for a **spirit world application**, either **allegorical or literal**, especially if it conveys a **place of death or desolation**.

"Neither did they say, 'Where is the LORD,
Who brought us up out of the land of Egypt,
Who led us through the wilderness,
Through a land of deserts and pits,
Through a land of drought and the shadow of death,
Through a land that no one crossed
And where no one dwelt?'"[406]

The **"shadow of death"** is not described merely as a metaphor for national exile but as **an otherworldly desert**, a barren wilderness of **despair and divine absence**, possibly **symbolic of the abyss** or **Hades-like places** in Old Testament cosmology. Even if not every use of the term is literal, **some clearly are**, and thus, a **uniform metaphorical reading** cannot be maintained without dismissing strong lexical and contextual evidence from earlier passages.

SHADOW OF DEATH IN THE GOSPEL OF NICODEMUS

The phrase **"shadow of death"** can plausibly refer to the **spirit world** or **judgment regions** of the afterlife. If this contextual interpretation is valid, it strengthens the possibility that **Psalm 107:10–15** depicts a form of **non-elect salvation** for some—not all—depending upon God's will. For this academic hypothesis to hold any merit, we must demonstrate that **"shadow of death"** was used by early Christian sources in this same way. If that connection can be made, then the reading of **non-elect salvation** becomes at least a **possibility of truth**, even if it is not doctrinal certainty.

Although **Justin Martyr** and **Tertullian** do not preserve a direct quote that ties the phrase "shadow of death" to Hades or Hell regions, early church historian **Eusebius** affirms that both men referenced a document called the **"Acts of Pilate" (Acta Pilati)**—a text also known by its later name, **"The Gospel of Nicodemus."** While this document is not considered canonical, **Roman Catholic scholars** have admitted that it is **orthodox and free from Gnostic taint.**[407]

In this **Acts of Pilate / Gospel of Nicodemus**, the phrase **"shadow of death"** is applied directly to the **spirit world regions**, and the author

---

[406] Jeremiah 2:6 (NKJV).

[407] George Reid, "Acta Pilati (Gospel of Nicodemus)," *The Catholic Encyclopedia*, Vol. 1 (New York: Robert Appleton Company, 1907), www.newadvent.org/cathen/01111b.htm

quotes both **Psalm 107:10–16** and **Matthew 4:15–16** to establish the biblical basis:

> "The land of Zabulon and the land of Nephthalim across Jordan, Galilee of the nations, the people who sat in darkness, have seen a great light; and light was shining among those who are in the region of the shadow of death. And now it has come and shone upon us sitting in death."[408]
>
> ... And when all the saints heard this from Esaias, they said to Hades: Open your gates. Since you are now conquered, you will be weak and powerless. And there was a great voice, as of thunders, saying: Lift up your gates, you princes; and be lifted up, you infernal gates; and the King of glory shall come in. Hades, seeing that they had twice shouted out this, says, as if not knowing: Who is the king of glory?
>
> David says, in answer to Hades: I recognize those words of the shout, since I prophesied the same by His Spirit. And now, what I have said above I say to you, The Lord strong and mighty, the Lord mighty in battle; He is the King of glory.
>
> And the Lord Himself has looked down from heaven upon earth, to hear the groans of the prisoners, and to release the sons of the slain. And now, most filthy and most foul Hades, open your gates, that the King of glory may come in.
>
> While David was thus speaking, there came to Hades, in the form of a man, the Lord of majesty, and lighted up the eternal darkness, and burst asunder the indissoluble chains; and the aid of unconquered power visited us, sitting in the profound darkness of transgressions, and in the shadow of death of sins."[409]

This ancient text not only supports the **interpretation of "shadow of death" as referring to Hades**, but it also distinguishes between the **elect saints** who awaited Christ in the **comfort section** and others in **groaning,**

---

[408] Matthew 4:15–16, "15'The land of Zebulun and the land of Naphtali, By the way of the sea, beyond the Jordan, Galilee of the Gentiles: 16The people who sat in darkness have seen a great light, And upon those who sat in the region and shadow of death Light has dawned'" (NKJV).

[409] *Gospel of Nicodemus*, Part II, Chapters 2(18) and 5(21). Translated by Alexander Walker. In *Ante-Nicene Fathers*, Vol. 8. Edited by Alexander Roberts, James Donaldson, and A. Cleveland Coxe (Buffalo, NY: Christian Literature Publishing Co., 1886), www.newadvent.org/fathers/08072b.htm

chains, sins, and transgressions—clearly in **punishment regions** of Hades. The text speaks of these others being **freed**, but not as the **bride of Christ**.[410] Therefore, these released souls may fall under the category of **non-elect salvation**, distinguished from the **Old Testament saints** who were ransomed into glory.

This aligns closely with **Christ's own description of Hades** in **Luke 16:19–31**, where He speaks of **two compartments**: one of **comfort**, the other of **torment**. This idea reflects early Jewish concepts of the afterlife, where the righteous and unrighteous dead await judgment in separate chambers.[411]

Using slightly different wording, **all known variants of Part II** of the *Gospel of Nicodemus* maintain this same theme of a **possible non-elect salvation**. Let us now examine the two remaining variants: **Part II (Greek form)** and **Part II (Second Latin form)**.

In the **Part II (Greek form)**, non-elect salvation is implied where **"all the dead who had been bound came out of the prisons,"** including those from the **"dark places of Hades."** Meanwhile, the **saints** are identified and come out **separately**, suggesting a **distinction** between groups:

> "Hades answered: ... For, lo, all those that I have swallowed from eternity I perceive to be in commotion, and I am pained in my belly. And the snatching away of Lazarus beforehand seems to me to be no good sign: for not like a dead body, but like an eagle, he flew out of me; for so suddenly did the earth throw him out. Wherefore also I adjure even you, for your benefit and for mine, not to bring him here; for I think that he is coming here to raise all the dead. And this I tell you: by the darkness in which we live, if you bring him here, not one of the dead will be left behind in it to me. ...
>
> There came, then, again a voice saying: Lift up the gates. Hades, hearing the voice the second time, answered as if forsooth he did not know, and says: Who is this King of glory? The angels of the Lord say: The Lord strong and mighty, the Lord mighty in

---

[410] Revelation 19:7–8, "7Let us be glad and rejoice and give Him glory, for the marriage of the Lamb has come, and His wife has made herself ready." 8"And to her it was granted to be arrayed in fine linen, clean and bright, for the fine linen is the righteous acts of the saints." (NKJV)

[411] Sławomir Szkredka, "Postmortem Punishment in the Parable of Lazarus and the Rich Man (Luke 16:19–31): Between Coherence and Indeterminacy of Luke's Eschatology," *Verbum Vitae*, 36 (December 2019): 122–123. doi.org/10.31743/vv.4832

battle. And immediately with these words the brazen gates were shattered, and the iron bars broken, and **all the dead who had been bound came out of the prisons, and we with them**. And the King of glory came in in the form of a man, and **all the dark places of Hades were lighted up.**"[412]

The text portrays a universal disturbance within Hades and a mass liberation that seems to **include more than just the saints**, supporting a framework where **non-elect individuals**—though not among the righteous—are still granted **release**.

In the **Part II (Second Latin form)**, the **phrase "shadow of death"** appears explicitly and again seems to describe the **punishment regions of Hades**. Here, **all the saints** rejoice, but the context also implies the **salvation of others** beyond them:

> "I Karinus. O Lord Jesus Christ, Son of the living God, permit me to speak of Your wonders which You have done in the lower world. When, therefore, we were kept in **darkness and the shadow of death in the lower world**, suddenly there shone upon us a great light, and Hades and the gates of death trembled. And then was heard the voice of the Son of the Father most high, as if the voice of a great thunder; and loudly proclaiming, He thus charged them: Lift up your gates, you princes; lift up the everlasting gates; the King of glory, Christ the Lord, will come up to enter in.
>
> Then Satan, the leader of death, came up, fleeing in terror, saying to his officers and the powers below: My officers, and all the powers below, run together, shut your gates, put up the iron bars, and fight bravely, and resist, lest they lay hold of us, and keep us captive in chains. …
>
> Then all the saints, hearing this again, exulted in joy. And one of those standing round, Isaias by name, cried out aloud, and thundered: Father Adam, and all standing round, hear my declaration. When I was on earth, and by the teaching of the Holy Spirit, in prophecy I sang of this light: *The people who sat in darkness have seen a great light; to them dwelling in the region of the shadow of death light has arisen.* …

---

[412] *Gospel of Nicodemus*, Part II, Chapters 4(20)–5(21). Translated by Alexander Walker. In *Ante-Nicene Fathers*, Vol. 8. Edited by Alexander Roberts, James Donaldson, and A. Cleveland Coxe (Buffalo, NY: Christian Literature Publishing Co., 1886). www.newadvent.org/fathers/08072a.htm

> Then all the saints, adoring Him, cried out, saying: Blessed is He who comes in the name of the Lord! ... Praise, honour, power, glory! Because You have come from on high to visit us. Singing Alleluia continually, and rejoicing together concerning His glory, they ran together under the hands of the Lord. **Then the Saviour, inquiring thoroughly about all, seized Hades, immediately threw some down into Tartarus, and led some with Him to the upper world.**"[413]

The **final portion** of this account shows that **not all souls** in Hades were saved—**some were cast into Tartarus**, while **some were led to the upper world**. The use of **"us"** in reference to those who had been **kept in chains** but were **freed**, suggests that **not all saved individuals were saints**, hinting at a **non-elect group** delivered by mercy.

Even if this passage refers only to **those who lived prior to Christ**, it still aligns with the possibility revealed in **Psalm 107:10–16**, where individuals who **rebelled** and were **afflicted in judgment** still cried out and were **delivered**. These individuals are unlikely to be part of the **bride of Christ**, for Scripture affirms that His bride is clothed with **righteous acts**.[414]

This further suggests the existence of **lower-tier salvation**, involving those who are **neither priests nor kings**, and possibly destined to inhabit the **new earth** rather than enter **heaven**. These could be the **"nations of those who are saved"**, who walk in the light of the New Jerusalem but are **distinct** from it.[415]

---

[413] *Gospel of Nicodemus*, Part II, Chapters 2(18), 5(21), 9(25). Translated by Alexander Walker. In *Ante-Nicene Fathers*, Vol. 8. Edited by Alexander Roberts, James Donaldson, and A. Cleveland Coxe (Buffalo, NY: Christian Literature Publishing Co., 1886). www.newadvent.org/fathers/08072c.htm

[414] Revelation 19:7–8, "Let us be glad and rejoice and give Him glory, for the marriage of the Lamb has come, and His wife has made herself ready. And to her it was granted to be arrayed in fine linen, clean and bright, for the fine linen is the righteous acts of the saints" (NKJV).

[415] Revelation 21:24–27, "And the nations of those who are saved shall walk in its light... But there shall by no means enter it anything that defiles... but only those who are written in the Lamb's Book of Life" (NKJV); Revelation 21:9–10, "Come, I will show you the bride, the Lamb's wife... the great city, the holy Jerusalem, descending out of heaven from God" (NKJV).

Scripture teaches that **all Christians are priests**,[416] and the early church fathers echoed this understanding.[417] Therefore, anyone not included in that royal priesthood likely belongs to a different classification altogether.

SHADOW OF DEATH IN CHURCH FATHERS

Let us consider how the phrase **"shadow of death"** was used among the church fathers, particularly in reference to the **spirit world** or **intermediate place of the dead**. This usage reinforces the possibility that **Psalm 107:10–16** refers not only to Israel's earthly suffering but also potentially to **non-elect salvation** in the afterlife under God's mercy.

Irenaeus of Lyons (c. 130–202) uses this phrase in close proximity with **Ephesians 4:9–10** ("lower parts of the earth") to describe the intermediate state where the **souls of the dead**—including His disciples— wait for the resurrection. While Irenaeus focuses here on the **comfort regions of Hades** rather than its punitive compartments, the phrase **"shadow of death"** appears to describe this invisible realm for disembodied souls:

> "...how must these men not be put to confusion, who allege that the lower parts refer to this world of ours, but that their inner man, leaving the body here, ascends into the super-celestial place? For as the Lord went away in the midst of the **shadow of death**, where the souls of the dead were, yet afterwards arose in the body, and after the resurrection was taken up into heaven, it is manifest that the souls of His disciples also, upon whose account the Lord underwent these things, shall go away into the **invisible place** allotted to them by God, and there remain until the resurrection, awaiting that event; then receiving their bodies, and rising in their entirety, that is bodily, just as the Lord arose, they shall come thus into the presence of God."[418]

An ancient **Homily for Holy Saturday**, often attributed to **Melito of Sardis**, also speaks of Christ descending into **Hades** to deliver those in **darkness and the shadow of death**, confirming that the phrase refers to the **spirit world**:

---

[416] Revelation 1:6; 5:10; 20:6; and 1 Peter 2:5 (NKJV).
[417] Irenaeus of Lyons, *Against Heresies*, Book 5, Chapter 34, Point 3. www.newadvent.org/fathers/0103534.htm
[418] Irenaeus of Lyons, *Against Heresies*, Book 5, Chapter 31, Point 2. www.newadvent.org/fathers/0103531.htm

"Something strange is happening — there is a great silence on earth today, a great silence and stillness. The whole earth keeps silence because the King is asleep. ... He has gone to search for our first parent, as for a lost sheep. Greatly desiring to visit those who live in **darkness and in the shadow of death**, He has gone to free from sorrow the captives Adam and Eve, He who is both God and the son of Eve."[419]

Gregory Thaumaturgus (c. 213–270)[420] likewise uses the term **"shadow of death"** in reference to those in the underworld, whom Christ—the **"illumining Pearl"**—comes to raise up into eternal light:

"...the illumining Pearl cometh forth, to the end that it may raise up again into the ever-streaming light them that were gone down into **darkness and the shadow of death**."[421]

Melito of Sardis (c. 100–180)[422] clearly affirms that the "shadow of death" describes **spiritual captivity** in the realm of the dead, pointing again to an intermediate condition where God's deliverance is revealed:

"Humanity was doled out by death, for a strange disaster and captivity surrounded him; he was dragged off a captive under the **shadow of death**, and the father's image was left desolate. For this reason in the body of the Lord is the paschal mystery completed."[423]

John of Damascus (c. 675–749) provides the most developed theological use of the phrase **"shadow of death"** in this context. He directly connects it with **punishment regions** of Hades, stating that **some who were bound for ages** were set free when they **believed in Christ** during His descent. This indicates that **salvation was available even there**, though

---

[419] "From an Ancient Homily for Holy Saturday: The Lord's Descent Into Hell." www.vatican.va/spirit/documents/spirit_20010414_omelia-sabato-santo_en.html

[420] "St. Gregory Thaumaturgus," in *Encyclopedia Britannica*, July 20, 1998. www.britannica.com/biography/Saint-Gregory-Thaumaturgus

[421] Gregory Thaumaturgus, *Homily concerning the Holy Mother of God*, Point 11. Translated by F.C. Conybeare. *The Expositor*, 5th series, vol. 3 (1896): 161–173.

[422] "This Catholic source calls this work as belonging to Melito of Sardis." www.catholic.org/lent/story.php?id=33117

[423] Melito of Sardis, *On Pascha and Fragments*. Ed. Alistair Stewart-Sykes. (Crestwood, NY: St Vladimir's Seminary Press, 2001), Point 56, p. 52. sachurch.org/wp-content/uploads/2017/04/On-Pascha-Melito-of-Sardis.pdf

others rejected Him and thus suffered reproach. This clearly opens the possibility of **non-elect salvation** in the intermediate state:

> "The soul when it was deified descended into Hades, in order that, just as the Sun of Righteousness rose for those upon the earth, so likewise He might bring light to those who sit under the earth in **darkness and shadow of death**: in order that just as He brought the message of peace to those upon the earth, and of release to the prisoners, and of sight to the blind, and became to those who believed the Author of everlasting salvation and to those who did not believe a reproach of their unbelief, so He might become the same to those in Hades: that every knee should bow to Him, of things in heaven, and things in earth and things under the earth. And thus after He had freed those who had been **bound for ages**, straightway He rose again from the dead, shewing us the way of resurrection."[424]

This quote harmonizes with the **Old Testament usage** of "shadow of death" in passages like Psalm 107:10–16, where those who were judged were later delivered when they **cried out** to Jehovah. It also validates the pattern seen in early Christian writings such as the *Gospel of Nicodemus*, where some prisoners in Hades—though not saints—were set free by Christ. Such a doctrine implies that while **not all** are saved, **some of the non-elect** may yet find mercy **after death**, according to God's sovereign will.

SHADOW OF DEATH IN MODERN USAGE

In more recent times, the phrase **"shadow of death"** has continued to be employed in literature to describe the **spirit world**, including **intermediate states** between life and the final resurrection. One such usage appears in the writings of **C. S. Lewis**, a respected Christian apologist and the author of *The Chronicles of Narnia*. Although not a church father, Lewis's literary influence in Christian thought is significant, and his usage of this biblical phrase further demonstrates its adaptability in eschatological contexts.

In his allegorical work *The Great Divorce*, Lewis presents a conversation between the narrator and George MacDonald, wherein the term **"Valley of the Shadow of Death"** is applied to a spiritual state representing the experience of those who remain in separation from God:

---

[424] John of Damascus, *An Exposition of the Orthodox Faith*, Book III, Chapter 29. Translated by E.W. Watson and L. Pullan. In *Nicene and Post-Nicene Fathers*, Second Series, Vol. 9. Edited by Philip Schaff and Henry Wace. www.newadvent.org/fathers/33043.htm

"I don't understand. Is judgment not final? Is there really a way out of Hell into Heaven?" MacDonald answers:

> "It depends on the way ye're using the words. If they leave that grey town behind it will not have been Hell. To any that leaves it, it is Purgatory. And perhaps ye had better not call this country Heaven. Not Deep Heaven, ye understand." (Here he smiled at me.) "Ye can call it the Valley of the Shadow of Life. And yet to those who stay here it will have been Heaven from the first. And ye can call those sad streets in the town yonder the Valley of the Shadow of Death: but to those who remain there they will have been Hell even from the beginning."[425]

Lewis's allusion to the "Valley of the Shadow of Death" as a realm that may, for some, become **Purgatory** rather than **Hell**, reflects his personal belief in **an intermediate purification**—a belief which goes beyond mere fiction. While **George MacDonald**[426] is presented as a character in this dialogue, Lewis's[427] own published writings confirm that he himself believed in **a kind of Purgatory**, despite his Protestant background. He explains:

> "Of course I pray for the dead. ... At our age the majority of those we love best are dead. ... I believe in Purgatory. Mind you, the Reformers had good reasons for throwing doubt on *'the Romish doctrine concerning Purgatory'* as that Romish doctrine had then become."[428]

Lewis's view does not necessarily align with traditional Roman Catholic teachings on Purgatory, but rather opens the door to a more **biblically-grounded** and **philosophically modest** view of **postmortem cleansing or refinement**. This belief, while not a doctrine, echoes the **non-elect salvation possibility** described throughout this essay—namely, that some

---

[425] C. S. Lewis, "Purgatory" (Chapter 9), in *The Great Divorce* (New York: Collier Books, 1984). www.discovery.org/a/507/

[426] *George MacDonald* biography in *Encyclopedia Britannica* (July 20, 1998). www.britannica.com/biography/George-Macdonald

[427] *C.S. Lewis* biography in *Encyclopedia Britannica* (March 14, 2025). www.britannica.com/biography/C-S-Lewis

[428] C. S. Lewis, "Letter 20," in *Letters to Malcolm: Chiefly on Prayer* (London: Geoffrey Bles, 1964).

www.gutenberg.ca/ebooks/lewiscs-letterstomalcolm/lewiscs-letterstomalcolm-00-h.html

who are not part of the bride of Christ might still be shown **mercy after death**, if Jehovah wills it.

In using the phrase **"Valley of the Shadow of Death"** as a spiritual designation, Lewis's narrative language aligns with the ancient scriptural and patristic tradition which sees this phrase as referencing more than just earthly peril—it refers to the **unseen realms** where **judgment, hope,** and **mercy** intersect in the unfolding of God's purposes.

CONCLUSION

Even if the literal phrase **"shadow of death"** refers to this present world, as some argue,[429] Scripture frequently contains a **twofold meaning**—both literal and prophetic or allegorical—without contradiction. In this case, whether the "literal" or "allegorical" label is applied to the **spirit world interpretation** or the **earthly meaning**, the conclusion remains the same: **Scripture allows the phrase "shadow of death" to refer to the unseen realm of the dead** as supported by various verses.[430]

A biblical precedent for this twofold approach is found in the prophecy of **Hosea**, which speaks historically of **Israel's deliverance from Egypt**:

> "When Israel was a child, I loved him, And out of Egypt I called My son."[431]

Yet the **Gospel of Matthew** reveals its deeper **Christological fulfillment**, showing how the same verse foretold the **Messiah's return from Egypt**:

> "He took the young Child and His mother by night and departed for Egypt … that it might be fulfilled which was spoken by the Lord through the prophet, saying, 'Out of Egypt I called My Son.'"[432]

A word of caution is appropriate here. Allegorical readings should **not be inserted carelessly** or elevated to doctrine unless they are **clearly supported** by the overall witness of Scripture. Nevertheless, to present such interpretations as **possibilities**, when consistent with Scripture, is valid and should be handled reverently.

---

[429] Matthew 4:15–16.
[430] Job 10:19–22.
[431] Hosea 11:1.
[432] Matthew 2:14–15.

If the **non-elect salvation** interpretation of the **shadow of death** proves accurate, it opens the door to reconsider certain passages. For example, **1 Corinthians 3:15** describes one who is **"saved, yet so as through fire"**,[433] suggesting a form of **postmortem refinement** rather than full reward. This may correspond with **"believing after seeing"** as implied in **John 6:29, 35–36, 40**,[434] in contrast to Christians, who believe **without seeing** and receive a **greater reward**[435]—namely, the "reward of the inheritance"[436] as those who are the **"good ground"** in the parable of the sower.[437]

In the final state, **elect salvation**—those who are in Christ—may be identified as **the bride of the Lamb**,[438] dwelling in the **heavenly city**. In contrast, the "nations of those who are saved"[439] appear to be **separate from the bride**, dwelling **outside** the heavenly city. These may represent **non-elect believers**—saved, but not glorified in the same way. Supporting this, **1 Corinthians 15:40–42** distinguishes between **celestial bodies** and **terrestrial bodies**, both described as resurrected bodies with **glory**, but of differing kinds.[440] This distinction could correspond to **elect versus non-elect salvation**, suggesting that **only Christians**—those with true faith and righteousness—**enter heaven**, while **many of the non-elect**, though shown mercy, **do not**.

BIBLIOGRAPHY

Asgeirsdottir, G. H., Sigurbjörnsson, E., Traustadottir, R., Sigurdardottir, V., Gunnarsdottir, S., & Kelly, E. "In the Shadow of Death: Existential and Spiritual Concerns among Persons Receiving Palliative Care". *Journal of Pastoral Care & Counseling.* 68(1). (2014): 1-11. doi.org/10.1177/154230501406800104

Bible. biblehub.com

Brenton, Lancelot Charles Lee (Sir). *The English translation of The Septuagint* (1851).

---

[433] 1 Corinthians 3:15.
[434] John 6:29, 35–36, 40.
[435] 1 Corinthians 3:14.
[436] Colossians 3:23–24.
[437] Matthew 13:8.
[438] Revelation 21:9–10.
[439] Revelation 21:24–27.
[440] 1 Corinthians 15:40–42.

Ellicott, C. J.. *A New Testament Commentary for English Readers*. (London: Cassell, 1896).

"From an Ancient Homily for Holy Saturday: The Lord's Descent Into Hell," n.d. www.vatican.va/spirit/documents/spirit_20010414_omelia-sabato-santo_en.html

Gill, John. *Gill's Exposition of the Entire Bible*. (1748-63).

Gospel of Nicodemus (Part II, First Latin Form). Translated by Alexander Walker. From Ante-Nicene Fathers, Vol. 8. Edited by Alexander Roberts, James Donaldson, and A. Cleveland Coxe. (Buffalo, NY: Christian Literature Publishing Co., 1886).

Gospel of Nicodemus (Part II, Greek Form). Translated by Alexander Walker. From Ante-Nicene Fathers, Vol. 8. Edited by Alexander Roberts, James Donaldson, and A. Cleveland Coxe. (Buffalo, NY: Christian Literature Publishing Co., 1886).

Gospel of Nicodemus (Part II, Second Latin Form). Translated by Alexander Walker. From Ante-Nicene Fathers, Vol. 8. Edited by Alexander Roberts, James Donaldson, and A. Cleveland Coxe. (Buffalo, NY: Christian Literature Publishing Co., 1886).

Gregory Thaumaturgus. *Homily concerning the Holy Mother of God*. Translated by F. C. Conybeare. The Expositor, 5th series, vol.3, (1896).

Gunkel, Hermann. *Dictionary of the Bible*, ed. James Hastings (New York: Charles Scribner's Sons, 1963).

Häner, Tobias. "Job's Dark View of Creation: On the Ironic Allusions to Genesis 1:1-2:4a in Job 3 and their Echo in Job 38-39", *Old Testament Essays*, 33(2), (2020): 266-284. doi.org/10.17159/2312-3621/2020/v33n2a7

Henderson, Joseph M. "Jeremiah 2–10 as a Unified Literary Composition". In *Uprooting and Planting: Essays on Jeremiah for Leslie Allen*. (London and New York: T&T Clark, 2007).

Henry, Matthew. *The Concise Commentary on the Whole Bible*. (1706).

Irenaeus of Lyons. *Against Heresies*. Translated by Alexander Roberts and William Rambaut. From Ante-Nicene Fathers, Vol. 1. Edited by Alexander Roberts, James Donaldson, and A. Cleveland Coxe. (Buffalo, NY: Christian Literature Publishing Co., 1885).

John of Damascus. *An Exposition of the Orthodox Faith (Book III)*. Translated by E.W. Watson and L. Pullan. From Nicene and Post-Nicene

Fathers, Second Series, Vol. 9. Edited by Philip Schaff and Henry Wace. (Buffalo, NY: Christian Literature Publishing Co., 1899).

Kaltwasser, Cambria. "Meeting Christ in the Shadow of Death". *Reformed Journal*. (March 16, 2025).

reformedjournal.com/2025/03/16/meeting-christ-in-the-shadow-of-death/

Lewis, C.S.. *Letters To Malcolm: Chiefly on Prayer*. (London: Geoffrey Bles, 1964 [first edition]).

Lewis, C. S.. *The Great Divorce*. (New York: Collier Books, 1984).

Mantor, Abbie F. "Caring for the Sufferers Among Us: Job 3 Through the Lens of Classical Rhetorical Theory and Modern Psychological Trauma Studies," *The Asbury Theological Journal*, 75(2), (2020): 226-240.

Melito of Sardis, *On Pascha and Fragments*. Ed. Alistair Stewart-Sykes. Crestwood, (NY: St Vladimir's Seminary Press, 2001).

Prinsloo, G.T.M., "From Desperation to Adoration: Reading Psalm 107 As a Transforming Spatial Journey", *Acta Theologica*, (December, 2021): 392-425. doi.org/10.38140/at.vi.5855

Reid, George. "Acta Pilati" (Gospel of Nicodemus). *The Catholic Encyclopedia*. Vol. 1. (New York: Robert Appleton Company, 1907).

Schmidt, N.F., & Nel, P.J.. "Divine darkness in the human discourses of Job", *Acta Theologica*, 36(2), (2016): 125-147. doi.org/10.4314/actat.v36i2.7

Szkredka, Sławomir, "Postmortem Punishment in the Parable of Lazarus and the Rich Man (Luke 16:19-31): Between Coherence and Indeterminacy of Luke's Eschatology", *Verbum Vitae, 36,* (December, 2019):109-32. doi.org/10.31743/vv.4832

Spence-Jones, H. D. M. (Henry Donald Maurice), 1836-1917, editor. *The Pulpit Commentary*. (New York: London: Anson D.F. Randolph; Kegan Paul, Trench, 1883).

Stevens, Harold Ray. "Byron, Original Sin, Shadows of Death and the Dramas of 1821". *The Byron Journal*. 43 (1). (2015): 29-42. doi.org/10.3828/bj.2015.5

Strong, James. *Strong's Expanded Exhaustive Concordance of the Bible*. (Nashville: Thomas Nelson, 2009).

The Editors of Encyclopedia Britannica. *Encyclopedia Britannica*. (July 20, 1998).

Tian, Ming. "On the Existence of Parallel Universe: Scientific Research on Life's Karma", *Am J Biomed Sci & Res,* 25(3), (2025): 391-394. DOI: 10.34297/AJBSR.2025.25.003329

Jonathan Ramachandran

Essay 5: Does Thief in the Night Phrase refer to Secret Coming of Christ?

ABSTRACT

This essay aims to **refute the popular teaching** that the phrase **"thief in the night"** refers to a **secret coming of Christ**. This idea has gained traction largely through the influence of modern prophecy movements, particularly within Pentecostal circles. By examining the **biblical usage of the phrase**, its **historical interpretations**, and citations from **early Christian writings**—especially those of **Chiliasm Church Fathers**—this study demonstrates that the phrase more accurately refers to **Christ's public and singular Second Coming**, not a hidden or secret event.

The distinctive contribution of this paper lies in the **logical analysis** of key texts, supported by direct quotations and relevant Scriptures. Some of the arguments presented here may offer **new perspectives** not often explored in mainstream eschatological debate. The study proceeds from a **literal biblical hermeneutic** and a **historical-grammatical approach**, rejecting allegorism or speculative interpretations that lack primary source support.

INTRODUCTION

The teaching of a **secret coming of Christ**, typically tied to a **pre-tribulation rapture**, was **popularized by the Pentecostal movement** but was **first formally articulated by John Nelson Darby (1800–1882)**, a preacher affiliated with the **Plymouth Brethren**.[441] While proponents often attempt to argue for its antiquity, **no verifiable quotations from the early Church Fathers** nor any historical creeds or confessions demonstrate this view as a doctrinal tenet of the early Church. It only appears as a developed position **in the 19th century**, and even then, **without endorsement from any major church tradition** prior to that era.

This essay will focus particularly on the **phrase "thief in the night"**, evaluating each biblical occurrence and its **contextual significance**. It will also bring in the **voices of ancient Christian writers**, especially those aligned with **Chiliasm**, to demonstrate that the early Church understood the

---

[441] *Dictionary of Premillennial Theology*, (Grand Rapids, MI: Kregel Publications, 1996): 82.

return of Christ to be **a single, visible, and public event**, rather than a two-phase secret and visible return.

If the quotations and biblical analysis presented here are accurate, then Christians who hold to a secret rapture doctrine may be **spiritually unprepared** for the **great tribulation** and the **deception of the final Antichrist**, being falsely assured that they will be removed before it begins. This **false sense of security** could lead to **spiritual complacency**, increasing the risk of being caught off guard when tribulation does come.

Furthermore, having a **sound understanding** of the doctrine of Christ's coming is important to avoid **misusing Jehovah's name** by making **untrue prophetic claims**, which may constitute a **violation of the Third Commandment**. A proper grasp of this doctrine enables believers to discern the **true nature of Christ's return**, guiding them to more faithful choices regarding the **teachers they follow** and the **prophetic materials they consume**.

PRE-TRIBULATION RAPTURE CLAIMS IN ANTIQUITY

Some have argued that the doctrine of a *pre-tribulation rapture* was taught in the early Church, later lost, and only recently recovered. The primary argument in support of this claim centers on phrases implying *imminency*.[442] However, this reasoning is weak. In Scripture, the same language of imminency is used by Christ Himself in addressing the first-century Church at Sardis,[443] where the emphasis is not on a hidden rapture but rather a call to *repentance*. Pre-tribulational scholars acknowledge this point,[444] but insist that the future tense used implies that such language could be applied typologically to a pre-tribulational rapture as well.[445] This is an unwarranted expansion of the text's meaning. Such an interpretation would absurdly suggest that Christ's warning to Sardis implied a secret rapture exclusive to that church—something that clearly never occurred.

Some also appeal to the *Shepherd of Hermas* as supporting the idea of a secret coming of Christ, particularly its use of the phrase "escaped from great

---

[442] Thomas D. Ice, "A Brief History of the Rapture", *Article Archives*, 4 (2019): 1. digitalcommons.liberty.edu/pretrib_arch/4

[443] Revelation 3:1, 3, "And to the angel of the church in Sardis write, ... hold fast and repent. Therefore if you will not watch, I will come upon you as a thief, and you will not know what hour I will come upon you" (NKJV).

[444] Robert L. Thomas, "The 'Comings' of Christ in Revelation 2–3," *The Master's Seminary Journal* 7/2 (Fall 1996): 163. tms.edu/wp-content/uploads/2021/09/tmsj7f.pdf

[445] Ibid., 164.

tribulation."[446] However, this interpretation fails to account for the broader context of the writing, which teaches that the elect endure the great tribulation in order to escape it, not that they are removed beforehand.

The *Shepherd of Hermas* declares:

> "Happy you who endure the great tribulation that is coming on, and happy they who shall not deny their own life. For the Lord has sworn by His Son, that those who denied their Lord have abandoned their life in despair, for even now these are to deny Him in the days that are coming. To those who denied in earlier times, God became gracious, on account of His exceeding tender mercy."[447]

Thus, the true meaning of "escape" in this context is the preservation of faith in Christ under pressure, not removal from tribulation. The explanation continues:

> "The black is the world in which we dwell: but the fiery and bloody points out that the world must perish through blood and fire: but the golden part are you who have escaped from this world. For as gold is tested by fire, and thus becomes useful, so are you tested who dwell in it. Those, therefore, who continue steadfast, and are put through the fire, will be purified by means of it. For as gold casts away its dross, so also will you cast away all sadness and straitness, and will be made pure so as to fit into the building of the tower. But the white part is the age that is to come, in which the elect of God will dwell, since those elected by God to eternal life will be spotless and pure. Wherefore cease not speaking these things into the ears of the saints. This then is the type of the great tribulation that is to come. If you wish it, it will be nothing."[448]

This passage clearly portrays the "escape" as something achieved *through* tribulation—not as deliverance *from* it. Those tested by fire and found steadfast are the ones who "escape," while the rest of the world perishes "through blood and fire." The elect are not divided into two groups—some who endure and others who bypass the tribulation—but are instead portrayed as a unified body who pass through it.

---

[446] Ice, "Brief History of the Rapture", 1.

[447] *Shepherd of Hermas*, Vision 2 (chapter 2), trans. F. Crombie, in *Ante-Nicene Fathers*, Vol. 2, eds. Alexander Roberts, James Donaldson, and A. Cleveland Coxe (Buffalo, NY: Christian Literature Publishing Co., 1885). www.newadvent.org/fathers/02011.htm

[448] *Shepherd of Hermas*, Vision 4 (chapter 3), ibid.

Another writing often cited to support the antiquity of the pre-tribulation view is the **Sermon on the Last Times, the Antichrist, and the End of the World**, attributed by some to *Pseudo-Ephraem* (so-called because the authenticity of its attribution to Ephraem the Syrian, d. c. 373, is questioned). A key passage cited by pre-tribulation advocates reads:

> "For all the saints and elect of God are gathered, prior to the tribulation that is to come, and are taken to the Lord lest they see the confusion that is to overwhelm the world because of our sins."[449]

The first and most critical issue with this claim lies in the qualifier "*all* the saints and elect." Pre-tribulational proponents typically argue that only *some* believers are removed in a secret coming, while others—deemed unprepared—remain and endure the tribulation. But this passage contradicts that notion by including the *entire* body of saints in the gathering. If only a portion were raptured, then "all" could not be said to escape.

Compounding the problem, other sections of the same sermon describe Christians suffering amid the great tribulation:

> "In those days people shall not be buried, neither Christian, nor heretic, neither Jew, nor pagan, because of fear and dread there is not one who buries them; because all people, while they are fleeing, ignore them."[450]

This statement plainly indicates that Christians are among the dead during this time, which directly contradicts the idea that *all* saints were previously gathered to the Lord.[451] It becomes even clearer in the passage that follows:

> "In these three years and a half the heaven shall suspend its dew; because there will be no rain upon the earth, ... and there will be a great tribulation, as there has not been, since people began to be upon the earth, and there will be famine and an insufferable thirst. ... But those who wander through the deserts, fleeing from the face of the serpent, bend their knees to God, just as lambs to

---

[449] *Pseudo-Ephraem, On the Last Times, the Antichrist, and the End of the World*, Latin text in C.P. Caspari, *Briefe, Abhandlungen und Predigten* (Christiania, 1890): 208–220; English trans. by Cameron Rhoades, Tyndale Theological Seminary, Ft. Worth, TX. www.pre-trib.org/pretribfiles/pdfs/Ephraem-OntheLastTimestheAnt.pdf

[450] Ibid., section 4.

[451] Ibid., sections 1–5.

the adders of their mothers, being sustained by the salvation of the Lord, and while wandering in states of desertion, they eat herbs."[452]

These are clearly believers "bending their knees to God" and sustained by divine help during the tribulation—not removed beforehand. If this group includes Christians undergoing such afflictions, the earlier phrase about all the elect being "gathered" must refer instead to the *post-tribulational* return of Christ, when no further elect are added and the gathering is complete.

Another telling passage adds:

> "Then, when this inevitability has overwhelmed all people, just and unjust, the just, so that they may be found good by their Lord; and indeed the unjust, so that they may be damned forever with their author the Devil, ... he sends to them consolatory proclamation by his attendants, the prophets Enoch and Elijah ... and when those just ones have appeared, they confuse indeed the antagonistic serpent ... in order to (free them) from his seduction."[453]

Here again, the text speaks of the "just"—that is, believers[454]—being among those caught up in the widespread affliction brought by the Antichrist. Thus, the idea that "all the elect" are removed before the tribulation becomes untenable.[455] The only consistent interpretation is that the elect are gathered at the Second Coming, and their "escape" refers to deliverance through endurance, not avoidance.

One final question must be considered: what does it mean for the elect to "escape" if they are present during the tribulation? The key to understanding lies in comparing sections 2 and 10 of the Pseudo-Ephraem sermon. Pre-tribulation proponents often associate phrases like "no one knows the day or hour"[456] with a secret rapture, likening it to the phrase "thief in the night" in Matthew 24.[457] However, Pseudo-Ephraem uses the very

---

[452] Ibid., sections 4–5.

[453] Ibid., section 5.

[454] Hebrews 10:38, "The just shall live by faith" (NKJV).

[455] Thomas D. Ice, "The Rapture in Pseudo-Ephraem", *Article Archives*, 32 (2009): 1, 5. digitalcommons.liberty.edu/pretrib_arch/32

[456] Matthew 24:36 (NKJV).

[457] Matthew 24:40–44, "Then two men will be in the field: one will be taken and the other left... Therefore you also be ready, for the Son of Man is coming at an hour you do not expect" (NKJV).

same kind of language in reference to the *public* coming of Christ at the *end* of the Antichrist's reign:

> "In the hour which the world does not know, and on the day which the enemy of son of perdition does not know" [19].

This occurs *after* the three and a half years of tribulation, making it incompatible with both pre-tribulation[458] and mid-tribulation[459] theories. Instead, it aligns with post-tribulational expectations.

This later passage also clarifies what the "confusion" is that the elect escape—not the tribulation itself, but the divine judgment that befalls the wicked:

> "For all the saints and elect of God are gathered, prior to the tribulation that is to come, and are taken to the Lord lest they see the confusion that is to overwhelm the world because of our sins. ... [Later] the Lord shall appear with great power and much majesty ... and the enemy shall be thrown into confusion, and the Lord shall destroy him by the spirit of His mouth."[460]

Thus, the "escape" is from divine vengeance upon the wicked at Christ's return, not a secret removal from tribulation. The passage is fully consistent with a post-tribulational, public Second Coming of Christ and contradicts the notion of a secret rapture.

POST-TRIBULATION RAPTURE BELIEF IN KEY SCHOLARS OF THE CHURCH

All major theologians and Church Fathers of early Christianity affirmed a **post-tribulation rapture**, meaning they rejected any notion of a *secret coming* of Christ prior to the tribulation. Their writings consistently reflect the view that the Church will suffer persecution under the Antichrist before the return of Christ, and no portion of the faithful is described as being removed beforehand. The following quotations provide direct testimony to this belief:

---

[458] Samuele Bacchiocchi, *The Advent Hope for Human Hopelessness: A Theological Study of the Meaning of the Second Advent for Today* (Berrien Springs, MI: Biblical Perspectives, 1986): 2012.

[459] Colin D. Standish and Russell R. Standish, *The Evangelical Dilemma* (Rapidan, VA: Hartland Publications, 1994): 170–171.

[460] *Pseudo-Ephraem, On the Last Times*, sections 1–2, 5, 10.

"The kingdom of Antichrist shall fiercely, though for a short time, assail the Church before the last judgment of God" (Augustine of Hippo, c. 354–430).[461]

"He [Christ] shall come from heaven with glory, when the man of apostasy, who speaks strange things against the Most High, shall venture to do unlawful deeds on the earth against us the Christians" (Justin of Rome, c. 100–165).[462]

"And that he shall be himself the eighth among them. And they shall lay Babylon waste, and burn her with fire, and shall give their kingdom to the beast, and put the Church to flight. After that they shall be destroyed by the coming of our Lord" (Irenaeus of Lyons, c. 130–202).[463]

"The beast Antichrist with his false prophet may wage war on the Church of God" (Tertullian, c. 155–220).[464]

"That refers to the one thousand two hundred and threescore days (the half of the week) during which the tyrant is to reign and persecute the Church" (Hippolytus of Rome, c. 170–235).[465]

"That the day of affliction has begun to hang over our heads, and the end of the world and the time of Antichrist to draw near,

---

[461] Augustine of Hippo, "Chapter 23," in *The City of God* (Book XX), trans. Marcus Dods, from *Nicene and Post-Nicene Fathers*, First Series, Vol. 2, ed. Philip Schaff (Buffalo, NY: Christian Literature Publishing Co., 1887). www.newadvent.org/fathers/120120.htm

[462] Justin of Rome, "Chapter 110," in *Dialogue with Trypho*, trans. Marcus Dods and George Reith, from *Ante-Nicene Fathers*, Vol. 1, eds. Alexander Roberts, James Donaldson, and A. Cleveland Coxe (Buffalo, NY: Christian Literature Publishing Co., 1885). www.newadvent.org/fathers/01288.htm

[463] Irenaeus of Lyons, "Book 2, Chapter 34, Point 1," in *Against Heresies*, trans. Alexander Roberts and William Rambaut, from *Ante-Nicene Fathers*, Vol. 1, eds. Alexander Roberts, James Donaldson, and A. Cleveland Coxe (Buffalo, NY: Christian Literature Publishing Co., 1885). www.newadvent.org/fathers/0103526.htm

[464] Tertullian, "Chapter 25," in *On the Resurrection of the Flesh*, trans. Peter Holmes, from *Ante-Nicene Fathers*, Vol. 3, eds. Alexander Roberts, James Donaldson, and A. Cleveland Coxe (Buffalo, NY: Christian Literature Publishing Co., 1885). www.newadvent.org/fathers/0316.htm

[465] Hippolytus of Rome, "Point 61," in *On Christ and Antichrist*, trans. J.H. MacMahon, from *Ante-Nicene Fathers*, Vol. 5, eds. Alexander Roberts, James Donaldson, and A. Cleveland Coxe (Buffalo, NY: Christian Literature Publishing Co., 1886). www.newadvent.org/fathers/0516.htm

so that we must all stand prepared for the battle" (Cyprian of Carthage, c. 210–258).[466]

"The times of Antichrist, when there shall be a great famine, and when all shall be injured ... He speaks of Elias the prophet, who is the precursor of the times of Antichrist, for the restoration and establishment of the churches from the great and intolerable persecution" (Victorinus of Pettau, d. c. 303).[467]

"Then he [Antichrist] will attempt to destroy the temple of God, and persecute the righteous people; and there will be distress and tribulation, such as there never has been from the beginning of the world. ... When these things shall so happen, then the righteous and the followers of truth shall separate themselves from the wicked, and flee into solitudes" (Lactantius, c. 250–325).[468]

"We preach not one advent only of Christ, but a second also, far more glorious than the former. ... In His first coming, He endured the Cross, despising shame (Hebrews 12:2); in His second, He comes attended by a host of angels, receiving glory. ... The Church now charges you before the Living God; she declares to you the things concerning Antichrist before they arrive. Whether they will happen in your time we know not, or whether they will happen after you we know not; but it is well that, knowing these things, you should make yourself secure beforehand. ... As though he [Antichrist] were the expected Christ, he shall afterwards be characterized by all kinds of crimes of inhumanity and lawlessness, so as to outdo all unrighteous and ungodly men who have gone before him; displaying against all men, but especially against us Christians, a spirit murderous and most cruel, merciless and crafty. And after perpetrating such things for three years and six months

---

[466] Cyprian of Carthage, "Point 1," in *Epistle 55*, trans. Robert Ernest Wallis, from *Ante-Nicene Fathers*, Vol. 5, eds. Alexander Roberts, James Donaldson, and A. Cleveland Coxe (Buffalo, NY: Christian Literature Publishing Co., 1886).
www.newadvent.org/fathers/050655.htm

[467] Victorinus of Pettau, "Point 5, From the Sixth Chapter" and "Point 2, From the Seventh Chapter," in *Commentary on the Apocalypse*, trans. Robert Ernest Wallis, from *Ante-Nicene Fathers*, Vol. 7, eds. Alexander Roberts, James Donaldson, and A. Cleveland Coxe (Buffalo, NY: Christian Literature Publishing Co., 1886). www.newadvent.org/fathers/0712.htm

[468] Lactantius, "Chapter 17," in *Divine Institutes*, Book VII (*Of a Happy Life*), trans. William Fletcher, from *Ante-Nicene Fathers*, Vol. 7, eds. Alexander Roberts, James Donaldson, and A. Cleveland Coxe (Buffalo, NY: Christian Literature Publishing Co., 1886).
www.newadvent.org/fathers/07017.htm

only, he shall be destroyed by the glorious second advent from heaven of the only-begotten Son of God, our Lord and Saviour Jesus, the true Christ, who shall slay Antichrist with the breath of His mouth, and shall deliver him over to the fire of hell" (Cyril of Jerusalem, c. 313–386).[469]

Notably, the principal leaders of the Protestant Reformation also affirmed a **post-tribulation eschatology**, holding that the Church must endure the final tribulation. Nowhere in their writings is a secret coming of Christ or partial rapture ever proposed.

"[The Revelation of John] is intended as a revelation of things that are to happen in the future, and especially of tribulations and disasters for the Church" (Martin Luther, 1483–1546).[470]

"Though all the heresies and schisms which have existed from the beginning belong to the kingdom of Antichrist, yet when Paul predicts an approaching apostasy, he signifies by this description that that seat of abomination shall then be erected, when a universal defection shall have seized the Church ... this is the principal indication which we ought to follow in our inquiries after Antichrist, especially where such pride proceeds to a public desolation of the Church" (John Calvin, 1509–1564).[471]

"Then shall be great tribulation—Have not many things spoken in the chapter, as well as in Mark xiii, Luke xxi, a farther and much more extensive meaning than has been yet fulfilled? And unless those days were shortened—by the taking of Jerusalem sooner than could be expected: no flesh would be saved—the whole nation would be destroyed. But for the elect's sake—that is, for the sake of the Christians ... Immediately after the tribulation

---

[469] Cyril of Jerusalem, "Point 1," "Point 9," and "Point 12," in *Catechetical Lecture 15*, trans. Edwin Hamilton Gifford, from *Nicene and Post-Nicene Fathers*, Second Series, Vol. 7, eds. Philip Schaff and Henry Wace (Buffalo, NY: Christian Literature Publishing Co., 1894). www.newadvent.org/fathers/310115.htm

[470] Martin Luther, "Preface to the Revelation of St. John," in *Luther's Works*, Volume 35: *Word and Sacrament I*, ed. E. Theodore Bachmann (Philadelphia: Fortress, 1960), 398–399. media.sabda.org/alkitab-8/LIBRARY/LUT_WRK6.PDF (see pages 376–377)

[471] John Calvin, "Point XXV, Chapter VII, Book III," in *Institutes of the Christian Religion*, trans. John Allen, 6th American ed., Vol. II (Philadelphia: Presbyterian Board of Publication, 1841). www.gutenberg.org/ebooks/64392

of those days—Here our Lord begins to speak of His last coming" (John Wesley, 1703–1791).[472]

These authoritative witnesses—spanning both ancient and Reformation eras—clearly reject the doctrine of a pre-tribulational rapture. Instead, they uniformly anticipate the Church's visible endurance through tribulation under the final Antichrist, followed by the *public*, glorious return of Christ.

TESTIMONY OF CHILIASM CHURCH FATHERS

Since "no prophecy of Scripture is of any private interpretation",[473] it is appropriate to examine the writings of the earliest Christian authors—specifically, the **Chiliasm Church Fathers**—to understand how they interpreted eschatological matters. These fathers are among the most trustworthy sources for interpreting prophecy, as they represent the earliest theological witnesses following the apostolic age.[474] By *Chiliasm Fathers*, we refer especially to three prominent theologians: **Justin of Rome** (commonly known as Justin Martyr), **Irenaeus of Lyons**, and **Tertullian**.

When these Church Fathers speak of only **two advents** of Christ—one already fulfilled in His first coming, and the other yet to occur—they effectively rule out the possibility of a third, secret coming. Therefore, any biblical phrase such as "thief in the night" must refer to the single, public second coming of Christ, since no other future coming is acknowledged in their theology.

Justin of Rome states:

> "For the prophets have proclaimed **two advents** of His: the one, that which is already past, when He came as a dishonoured and suffering Man; but the second, when, according to prophecy, He shall come from heaven with glory, accompanied by His angelic host, when also He shall raise the bodies of all men who have lived, and shall clothe those of the worthy with immortality, and shall send those of the wicked, endued with eternal sensibility, into everlasting fire with the wicked devils. And that these things also have been foretold as yet to be, we will prove."[475]

---

[472] John Wesley, "Matthew 24," in *Explanatory Notes upon the New Testament* (London: William Boyer, 1755). www.ccel.org/ccel/wesley/notes.all.html

[473] 2 Peter 1:20 (NKJV).

[474] John F. Walvoord, *The Millennial Kingdom* (Grand Rapids: Zondervan, 1959), 121–122.

[475] Justin of Rome (Justin Martyr), "Chapter 52," in *The First Apology*, trans. Marcus Dods and George Reith, from *Ante-Nicene Fathers*, Vol. 1, eds. Alexander Roberts, James Donaldson,

Irenaeus of Lyons likewise affirms:

> "...and do not recognise the advent of Christ, which He accomplished for the salvation of men, nor are willing to understand that all the prophets announced **His two advents**: the one, indeed, in which He became a man subject to stripes, and knowing what it is to bear infirmity (Isaiah 53:3) ... but the second in which He will come on the clouds (Daniel 7:13), bringing on the day which burns as a furnace (Malachi 4:1), and smiting the earth with the word of His mouth (Isaiah 11:4), and slaying the impious with the breath of His lips, and having a fan in His hands, and cleansing His floor, and gathering the wheat indeed into His barn, but burning the chaff with unquenchable fire (Matthew 3:12; Luke 3:17)."[476]

Tertullian's statement, which explicitly associates the phrase "thief in the night" with the second coming of Christ, will be discussed in the following section.

THIEF IN THE NIGHT PHRASE

When the relevant passages are read plainly and literally, it becomes evident that the phrase "thief in the night" is uttered by Christ **after** the sixth bowl of God's wrath is poured out. This chronology is significant: it places the warning **after** a large portion of the antichrist's reign has already unfolded. Accordingly, this reading is often cited by **post-tribulation scholars** as supporting evidence that Christ's return occurs **after** the reign of the antichrist has concluded.[477] By contrast, **pre-tribulation scholars** tend to interpret this phrase symbolically—either as referring to the spiritual unawareness of unbelievers, or they claim that it pertains not to the rapture but to the Battle of Armageddon.

> "So the first went and poured out his bowl upon the earth, and a foul and loathsome sore came upon the men who had the mark of the beast and those who worshiped his image. ...

---

and A. Cleveland Coxe (Buffalo, NY: Christian Literature Publishing Co., 1885). www.newadvent.org/fathers/0126.htm

[476] Irenaeus, "Book 4, Chapter 33, Point 1," in *Against Heresies*. www.newadvent.org/fathers/0103433.htm

[477] G.H. Lang, *The Revelation of Jesus Christ* (Self-published, Oliphants Ltd., London & Edinburgh, 1945): 253–254. www.brethrenarchive.org/people/gh-lang/pamphlets/the-revelation-of-jesus-christ-select-studies

> Then the sixth angel poured out his bowl on the great river Euphrates, and its water was dried up, so that the way of the kings from the east might be prepared.
>
> And I saw three unclean spirits like frogs coming out of the mouth of the dragon, out of the mouth of the beast, and out of the mouth of the false prophet.
>
> For they are spirits of demons, performing signs, which go out to the kings of the earth and of the whole world, to gather them to the battle of that great day of God Almighty.
>
> "Behold, I am coming as a thief. Blessed is he who watches, and keeps his garments, lest he walk naked and they see his shame." And they gathered them together to the place called in Hebrew, Armageddon".[478]

Here we see a critical flaw in the **allegorical method** used by many pre-tribulation scholars. Some suggest that the "thief in the night" warning refers to the spiritual **blindness of unbelievers** who fail to realize that a secret rapture has already occurred.[479] Others maintain that this phrase refers to the final judgment at **Armageddon**, occurring at the end of the seven-year period.[480] Yet both camps concede—at least implicitly—that the phrase occurs **after** the sixth bowl is poured out, and therefore must be placed in a **specific chronological context**.

A major problem with the pre-tribulation view is that Christ pronounces a **blessing** upon those "who watch" in this passage. That group cannot be unbelievers, since they are precisely the ones who **do not** watch. But if the truly watchful believers were already taken in a secret rapture before the tribulation, then who are these blessed ones who remain? Are they the so-called **tribulation saints**[481] who survive until the visible return of Christ? If so, they are still classified as "blessed," even though they apparently failed to "watch" during the earlier rapture event. This undercuts the theological weight often placed on the distinction between a **secret** coming and a **public** second advent.

---

[478] Revelation 16:2, 12–16 (NKJV).

[479] Andrew M. Woods, "Jesus and the Rapture Part 1: Matthew 24:40–41 Reconsidered," *Pneumatikos* 15.1 (Spring 2024): 18–19. doi.org/10.62075/chafer.15.1.p3q9zf

[480] Charles Cooper, "The Meaning and Significance of Revelation 16:15 | Sola Scriptura," n.d. www.solagroup.org/the-meaning-and-significance-of-revelation-1615

[481] Richard Shalom Yates, "The Identity of the Tribulation Saints," *Bibliotheca Sacra* 163:649 (January 2006).

Furthermore, if the phrase "thief in the night" is applied to **both** the supposed secret coming and the visible return, then the linguistic basis for separating the two is lost. The idea that "thief" denotes imminency or secrecy, while signs accompany the public event, collapses under its own inconsistency.[482]

In Revelation 16, the phrase "I am coming as a thief" is spoken only **after** the sixth bowl has been poured out. If the secret rapture had truly occurred earlier, as pre-tribulationism teaches, then one would expect Christ's warning to come **before** the first bowl, not afterward. Nor does this support the **mid-tribulation** view, since the "mark of the beast" is introduced during the final 3.5 years of the antichrist's reign—the period commonly known as the **Great Tribulation**. According to Revelation 13, these events unfold **before** the bowls of wrath, not after, thus eliminating the mid-tribulation rapture theory as well.

> "And I saw one of his heads as if it had been mortally wounded, and his deadly wound was healed. And all the world marveled and followed the beast. So they worshiped the dragon who gave authority to the beast; and they worshiped the beast, saying, 'Who is like the beast? Who is able to make war with him?'
>
> And he was given a mouth speaking great things and blasphemies, and he was given authority to continue for **forty-two months**.
> ...
>
> He was granted power to give breath to the image of the beast, that the image of the beast should both speak and cause as many as would not worship the image of the beast to be killed.
>
> He causes all, both small and great, rich and poor, free and slave, to receive a mark on their right hand or on their foreheads, and that no one may buy or sell except one who has the mark or the name of the beast, or the number of his name.
>
> Here is wisdom. Let him who has understanding calculate the number of the beast, for it is the number of a man: His number is 666".[483]

---

[482] Robert L. Thomas, "Imminence in the NT, Especially Paul's Thessalonian Epistles," *The Master's Seminary Journal* 13.2 (2002): 191–214.

[483] Revelation 13:3–5, 15–18 (NKJV).

Let us next examine other passages in Scripture that use the **"thief in the night"** motif for comparison. The assumption that every such phrase refers to the same event—the **public Second Coming of Christ**—is a consistent interpretive approach, frequently upheld by **post-tribulation rapture proponents** as well.[484] If the words regarding the "day and hour" are understood literally in the context of imminency, such verses can indicate that believers, though unable to determine the exact timing, will nonetheless anticipate Christ's return during the persecution of the final antichrist. This would follow their refusal to receive the mark of the beast or worship his image, and they would remain in watchful expectation even amid tribulation. It should also be noted that Christ always uses the **singular** form in reference to His coming, never the plural, which further supports the position that there is **only one public return of Christ** in view throughout these passages.[485]

> "But of that day and hour no one knows, not even the angels of heaven, but My Father only. But as the days of Noah were, so also will the coming of the Son of Man be. For as in the days before the flood, they were eating and drinking, marrying and giving in marriage, until the day that Noah entered the ark, and did not know until the flood came and took them all away, so also will the coming of the Son of Man be. Then two men will be in the field: one will be taken and the other left. Two women will be grinding at the mill: one will be taken and the other left. Watch therefore, for you do not know what hour your Lord is coming. But know this, that if the master of the house had known what hour the thief would come, he would have watched and not allowed his house to be broken into. Therefore you also be ready, for the Son of Man is coming at an hour you do not expect."[486]

The Apostle Peter likewise uses the phrase **"thief in the night"**, and in this instance it unmistakably refers to a **public return of Christ**, not a secret one. This is evident from the **cataclysmic events** it describes—melting elements, global fire, and a great noise—all of which point toward a

---

[484] Douglas Hamp and Chris Steinle, *"Chapter 2: Coming Like a Thief in the Night"*, in *Reclaiming the Rapture: Restoring the Doctrine of the Gathering of the Commonwealth of Israel* (Memorial Crown Press, Phoenix, AZ, USA, 2017), 23–30.
cdn.subsplash.com/documents/868V8V/_source/16a21aeb-614b-4506-b8ed-d02c91cba1d9/document.pdf

[485] James Strong, *Strong's Expanded Exhaustive Concordance of the Bible* (Nashville: Thomas Nelson, 2009), s.v. "Coming." https://biblehub.com/greek/3952.htm

[486] Matthew 24:36–44 (NKJV).

worldwide renewal of the earth, consistent with the **Chiliasm** understanding of the beginning of the **Millennial Reign** of Christ.[487]

> "But the day of the Lord will come as a thief in the night, in which the heavens will pass away with a great noise, and the elements will melt with fervent heat; both the earth and the works that are in it will be burned up."[488]

What is particularly striking is that **mortals and sinners still exist** during this millennial period, confirming that this is **not the Great White Throne Judgment** scene. Rather, sinful mankind continues to exist alongside the **immortal saints** of the **First Resurrection**. Divine judgment remains active, but so too does human **free will**, with nations still being held accountable even while permitted to survive. The **prophet Zechariah** describes how some survivors from the nations that fought against Jerusalem are still present, indicating clearly that **mortal sinners** remain during this period. This implies that the events described in **2 Peter 3:10** refer to a **selective judgment** and **earthly purification**, not complete annihilation. The **resulting renewed order** is reflected in the following prophecy from Zechariah:

> "And it shall come to pass that everyone who is left of all the nations which came against Jerusalem shall go up from year to year to worship the King, Jehovah of hosts, and to keep the Feast of Tabernacles. And it shall be that whichever of the families of the earth do not come up to Jerusalem to worship the King, Jehovah of hosts, on them there will be no rain. If the family of Egypt will not come up and enter in, they shall have no rain; they shall receive the plague with which Jehovah strikes the nations who do not come up to keep the Feast of Tabernacles. This shall be the punishment of Egypt and the punishment of all the nations that do not come up to keep the Feast of Tabernacles."[489]

A similar usage of the phrase "thief" is found in Christ's **rebuke to the church at Sardis**. There, Christ declares, **"I will come upon you as a thief"**, and **"you will not know what hour I will come upon you"**—not in the context of a global end-time event, but in a **local warning** to first-century Christians. This raises the question of whether the phrase can

---

[487] J. P. Kirsch, *"Millennium and Millenarianism,"* in *The Catholic Encyclopedia* (New York: Robert Appleton Company, 1911). https://www.newadvent.org/cathen/10307a.htm

[488] 2 Peter 3:10 (NKJV).

[489] Zechariah 14:16–19 (NKJV).

function **allegorically** to apply to **any believer,** calling for **ongoing spiritual vigilance** and **completion of good works** before the Lord.[490] Since no secret or public coming of Christ occurred for that church in that generation, it implies a **general principle of preparedness**, not an eschatological event. Even so, this passage can still support the **single-coming** view in allegorical form—since there is **no second chance** for repentance or later identification as a "tribulation saint" for those unprepared at His coming:

> "And to the angel of the church in Sardis write, 'These things says He who has the seven Spirits of God and the seven stars: "I know your works, that you have a name that you are alive, but you are dead. Be watchful, and strengthen the things which remain, that are ready to die, for I have not found your works perfect before God. Remember therefore how you have received and heard; hold fast and repent. Therefore if you will not watch, I will come upon you as a thief, and you will not know what hour I will come upon you. You have a few names even in Sardis who have not defiled their garments; and they shall walk with Me in white, for they are worthy."[491]

The overall biblical usage of the phrase **"thief in the night"** strongly supports **only one future Second Coming**, occurring after the chaos of the **final antichrist**. At the same time, the phrase can be used **allegorically** to emphasize spiritual vigilance, readiness, and holy conduct at all times. Tertullian's testimony is highly instructive. When he cites both letters to the Thessalonians, he does not divide them into two separate events—as if one were secret and one public—but views both as describing **a single eschatological return of Christ**, which follows the rise of **the man of sin**. He interprets the **Roman state's dissolution** and the **emergence of the antichrist** as **prerequisites** to this event, which is described using the same **"thief in the night"** language:

> "But of the times and the seasons, brethren, there is no necessity for my writing unto you. For you yourselves know perfectly, that the day of the Lord comes as a thief in the night. For when they shall say, 'Peace,' and 'All things are safe,' then sudden destruction shall come upon them (1 Thessalonians 5:1–3). Again,

---

[490] W. O. Vaught, *"The Churches of Thyatira and Sardis"*, in *Vaught Sermon Notes: A Study of the Book of Revelation*, vol. 17 (1981), 2, 4.
https://scholarlycommons.obu.edu/vn_revelation/17
[491] Revelation 3:1–4 (NKJV).

in the second epistle he addresses them with even greater earnestness: 'Now I beseech you, brethren, by the coming of our Lord Jesus Christ, and by our gathering together unto Him, that you be not soon shaken in mind, nor be troubled, either by spirit, or by word, that is, the word of false prophets, or by letter, that is, the letter of false apostles, as if from us, as that the day of the Lord is at hand. Let no man deceive you by any means. For that day shall not come, unless indeed there first come a falling away'—he means indeed of this present empire—'and that man of sin be revealed, that is to say, Antichrist, the son of perdition, who opposes and exalts himself above all that is called God or religion; so that he sits in the temple of God, affirming that he is God. Do you not remember, that when I was with you, I used to tell you these things? And now you know what detains, that he might be revealed in his time. For the mystery of iniquity does already work; only he who now hinders must hinder, until he be taken out of the way.' (2 Thessalonians 2:1–7) What obstacle is there but the Roman state, the falling away of which, by being scattered into ten kingdoms, shall introduce Antichrist upon its own ruins? And then shall be revealed the wicked one, whom the Lord shall consume with the spirit of His mouth, and shall destroy with the brightness of His coming—even him whose coming is after the working of Satan, with all power, and signs, and lying wonders, and with all deceivableness of unrighteousness in them that perish."[492]

CONCLUSION

What remains unproven is the opposite claim—namely, the existence of a single quote from any **Chiliasm Church Father** that interprets any "thief in the night" Bible verse as referring to a **secret** coming of Christ, as taught by **pre-tribulation rapture** proponents. In fact, with regard to the primary verse often cited in support of the pre-tribulation rapture, **1 Thessalonians 4:17**, we have already demonstrated that every **Chiliasm Church Father** who commented on this passage—or on the broader context of the **second coming of Christ**—affirmed **only one** future coming. That coming is **public** and **postdates the reign of the final antichrist or beast**.

Furthermore, none of their writings about the last antichrist contain even a hint of a secret coming of Christ. Accordingly, based on both **Scripture** and **Chiliasm Church Father testimony**, the **post-tribulation**

---

[492] Tertullian, *On the Resurrection of the Flesh*, chapter 24.
https://www.newadvent.org/fathers/0316.htm

rapture interpretation remains the most consistent explanation of the "thief in the night" phrase within the early Christian prophetic framework.

BIBLIOGRAPHY

Augustine of Hippo. *The City of God (Book XX)*. Translated by Marcus Dods. From Nicene and Post-Nicene Fathers, First Series, Vol. 2. Edited by Philip Schaff. (Buffalo, NY: Christian Literature Publishing Co., 1887).

Bacchiocchi, Samuele. *The Advent Hope for Human Hopelessness: A Theological Study of the Meaning of the Second Advent for Today*. (Berrien Springs, Michigan: Biblical Perspectives, 1986).

Bible. biblehub.com

Cooper, Charles. "The Meaning and Significance of Revelation 16:15 | Sola Scriptura," n.d., www.solagroup.org/the-meaning-and-significance-of-revelation-1615/

Cyril of Jerusalem. *Catechetical Lecture 15*. Translated by Edwin Hamilton Gifford. From Nicene and Post-Nicene Fathers, Second Series, Vol. 7. Edited by Philip Schaff and Henry Wace. (Buffalo, NY: Christian Literature Publishing Co., 1894).

Cyprian of Carthage. *Epistle 55*. Translated by Robert Ernest Wallis. From Ante-Nicene Fathers, Vol. 5. Edited by Alexander Roberts, James Donaldson, and A. Cleveland Coxe. (Buffalo, NY: Christian Literature Publishing Co., 1886).

Dictionary of Premillennial Theology. (Grand Rapids, MI: Kregel Publications, 1996): 82.

Hamp, Douglas and Steinle, Chris. *Reclaiming the Rapture: Restoring the Doctrine of the Gathering of the Commonwealth of Israel*. (Memorial Crown Press Phoenix, AZ, USA, 2017).

Hippolytus of Rome. *On Christ and Antichrist*. Translated by J.H. MacMahon. From Ante-Nicene Fathers, Vol. 5. Edited by Alexander Roberts, James Donaldson, and A. Cleveland Coxe. (Buffalo, NY: Christian Literature Publishing Co., 1886).

Ice, Thomas D., "A Brief History of the Rapture", *Article Archives*, 4, (2019). digitalcommons.liberty.edu/pretrib_arch/4

Ice, Thomas D., "The Rapture in Pseudo-Ephraem", *Article Archives*, 32, (2009). digitalcommons.liberty.edu/pretrib_arch/32

Irenaeus of Lyons. *Against Heresies*. Translated by Alexander Roberts and William Rambaut. From Ante-Nicene Fathers, Vol. 1. Edited by Alexander Roberts, James Donaldson, and A. Cleveland Coxe. (Buffalo, NY: Christian Literature Publishing Co., 1885).

John Calvin. *Institutes of the Christian Religion*. Translated from the original Latin by John Allen. 6th American edition. Volume II. (Philadelphia: Presbyterian Board of Publication, 1841).

John Wesley. *Explanatory Notes upon the New Testament*. (London: William Boyer, 1755).

John F. Walvoord. *The Millennial Kingdom*. (Grand Rapids: Zondervan, 1959).

Justin of Rome (Justin Martyr). *Dialogue with Trypho*. Translated by Marcus Dods and George Reith. From Ante-Nicene Fathers, Vol. 1. Edited by Alexander Roberts, James Donaldson, and A. Cleveland Coxe. (Buffalo, NY: Christian Literature Publishing Co., 1885).

Justin of Rome (Justin Martyr). *The First Apology*. Translated by Marcus Dods and George Reith. From Ante-Nicene Fathers, Vol. 1. Edited by Alexander Roberts, James Donaldson, and A. Cleveland Coxe. (Buffalo, NY: Christian Literature Publishing Co., 1885).

Kirsch, J.P.. *Catholic Encyclopedia*. (New York: Robert Appleton Company, 1911).

L. Thomas, Robert, "The 'Comings' of Christ in Revelation 2-3", *TMSJ*, 7/2, (Fall 1996): 153-181. tms.edu/wp-content/uploads/2021/09/tmsj7f.pdf

Lactantius. *Divine Institutes, Book VII (Of a Happy Life)*. Translated by William Fletcher. From Ante-Nicene Fathers, Vol. 7. Edited by Alexander Roberts, James Donaldson, and A. Cleveland Coxe. (Buffalo, NY: Christian Literature Publishing Co., 1886).

Lang, G.H.. *The Revelation of Jesus Christ*. (Self-published, Oliphants LTD, London & Edinburgh, 1945).

Martin Luther. "Preface to the Revelation of St. John", in *Luther's Works Volume 35: Word and Sacrament I* (ed. E. Theodore Bachmann; Philadelphia: Fortress, 1960): 398-399.

Shepherd of Hermas (Book I). Translated by F. Crombie. From Ante-Nicene Fathers, Vol. 2. Edited by Alexander Roberts, James Donaldson, and A. Cleveland Coxe. (Buffalo, NY: Christian Literature Publishing Co., 1885).

Standish, Colin D. and Standish, Russell R. *The Evangelical Dilemma*. (Rapidan, VA: Hartland Publications, 1994).

Strong, James. *Strong's Expanded Exhaustive Concordance of the Bible*. (Nashville: Thomas Nelson, 2009).

Tertullian. *On the Resurrection of the Flesh*. Translated by Peter Holmes. From Ante-Nicene Fathers, Vol. 3. Edited by Alexander Roberts, James Donaldson, and A. Cleveland Coxe. (Buffalo, NY: Christian Literature Publishing Co., 1885).

Thomas, Robert L., "Imminence in the NT, Especially Paul's Thessalonian Epistles", *TMSJ*, 13(2), (2002): 191-214.

Vaught, W. O., "The Churches of Thyatira and Sardis", in *Vaught Sermon Notes: A Study of the Book of Revelation*. 17 (1981). scholarlycommons.obu.edu/vn_revelation/17

Victorinus of Pettau. *Commentary on the Apocalypse*. Translated by Robert Ernest Wallis. From Ante-Nicene Fathers, Vol. 7. Edited by Alexander Roberts, James Donaldson, and A. Cleveland Coxe. (Buffalo, NY: Christian Literature Publishing Co., 1886).

Woods, Andrew, "Jesus and the Rapture Part 1: Matthew 24:40–41 Reconsidered", *Pneumatikos*, 15(1), (Spring 2024): 1–23. www.doi.org/10.62075/chafer.15.1.p3q9zf

Yates, Richard Shalom, "The Identity of the Tribulation Saints", *Bibliotheca Sacra* (BSAC), 163:649, (Jan 2006).

Jonathan Ramachandran

Essay 6: Non-Elect Salvation Possibility via Saved by Fire

ABSTRACT

This essay introduces the possibility of **non-elect salvation** through the concept of being **"saved by fire."** The primary focus is the interpretation of **1 Corinthians 3:15**, with the aim of evaluating whether this verse opens the door for God's grace to extend beyond the elect—even to certain **unbelievers**, though not all. This view is distinct from both **universalism**[493] and the Roman Catholic doctrine of **purgatory**,[494] as commonly understood. The key theological distinctions between these concepts will be outlined in this article.

There remains a grey area in theology concerning the post-mortem destiny of non-Christians. The majority of Christians deny the possibility of salvation after death for unbelievers. However, some believe that backslidden or imperfect believers might attain salvation through an intermediate process, such as purgatory, provided their sins are not grievous.

SAVED BY FIRE

We begin with **1 Corinthians 3:15**: **"If anyone's work is burned, he will suffer loss; but he himself will be saved, yet so as through fire"**.[495] Protestant interpreters generally reject a post-mortem reading of this verse, viewing it instead as metaphorical—a description of **trials and spiritual testing** in this life. The individual in view is saved before death, and the "fire" represents hardship or divine refinement. Roman Catholic theology, however, interprets this verse as referring to an imperfect catechumen who is ultimately saved after passing through purgatory.[496]

---

[493] Richard Bauckham, *"Universalism: A Historical Survey"*, in *Themelios*, 4.2 (September 1978): 47–54.

[494] Edward Hanna, *"Purgatory"*, in *The Catholic Encyclopedia*, Vol. 12 (New York: Robert Appleton Company, 1911). www.newadvent.org/cathen/12575a.htm

[495] 1 Corinthians 3:15, *"If anyone's work is burned, he will suffer loss; but he himself will be saved, yet so as through fire"* (NKJV).

[496] Augustine of Hippo, *"Chapter 69"*, in *Enchiridion (Handbook on Faith, Hope and Love)*, trans. J.F. Shaw, from *Nicene and Post-Nicene Fathers*, First Series, Vol. 3, ed. Philip Schaff (Buffalo, NY: Christian Literature Publishing Co., 1887).
www.newadvent.org/fathers/1302.htm

In the context of **non-elect salvation**, the verse could plausibly apply to someone who is not a Christian. How so? Scripture affirms that **living faith** is proven by **works**.[497] A Christian with living works will receive the **reward of the inheritance**,[498] consistent with **1 Corinthians 3:14**.[499] But if both verses—1 Corinthians 3:14 and 3:15—result in reward, then the distinction collapses. Yet 3:15 clearly describes a person who suffers **loss**, indicating the absence of reward, in contrast to the rewarded individual in 3:14.

This difference can be mapped onto the **Parable of the Sower**, in which the **"good ground"** represents Christians who yield a harvest starting at **thirtyfold**,[500] with some reaching **hundredfold**.[501] This suggests that **reward is inherent to true faith**, making it difficult to classify someone who is **"saved by fire" and suffers loss** as a genuine Christian. Moreover, such a person may not undergo further **afterlife judgment**,[502] indicating a category outside the elect—perhaps a **non-elect individual** shown mercy by God.

If this understanding is accurate, what then differentiates **elect salvation** from **non-elect salvation**? The distinction lies in the nature of the resurrection body. Elect believers are granted a **celestial (heavenly)** body necessary to enter heaven, while non-elect individuals are raised with a **terrestrial (earthly)** body.[503] Both possess glory, but of distinct kinds. The terrestrial body may belong to the saved-by-fire category.

In the second-to-last chapter of Revelation, the **bride of Christ**—that is, the elect—is described as residing in **heaven**,[504] whereas a separate group,

---

[497] James 2:26, *"For as the body without the spirit is dead, so faith without works is dead also"* (NKJV).

[498] Colossians 3:23–24, *"And whatever you do, do it heartily, as to the Lord and not to men, knowing that from the Lord you will receive the reward of the inheritance"* (NKJV).

[499] 1 Corinthians 3:14, *"If anyone's work which he has built on it endures, he will receive a reward"* (NKJV).

[500] Matthew 13:8, *"But others fell on good ground and yielded a crop: some a hundredfold, some sixty, some thirty"* (NKJV).

[501] Matthew 19:29, *"And everyone who has left houses or brothers or sisters or father or mother or wife or children or lands, for My name's sake, shall receive a hundredfold, and inherit eternal life"* (NKJV).

[502] John 5:24, *"Most assuredly, I say to you, he who hears My word and believes in Him who sent Me has everlasting life, and shall not come into judgment, but has passed from death into life"* (NKJV).

[503] 1 Corinthians 15:40–42, *"There are also celestial bodies and terrestrial bodies; but the glory of the celestial is one, and the glory of the terrestrial is another... So also is the resurrection of the dead"* (NKJV).

[504] Revelation 21:9–10, *"Come, I will show you the bride, the Lamb's wife... and showed me the great city, the holy Jerusalem, descending out of heaven from God"* (NKJV).

called the **"nations who are saved,"** dwell upon the **new earth**.[505] These two groups are not conflated. The **Book of Life** is now opened (Rev. 21:27), indicating that this occurs **after** the **Great White Throne Judgment** (Rev. 20:11–15). The nations appear distinct from the bride, possibly signifying the **non-elect saved**.

Scripture also states that all Christians are **kings and priests**,[506] a view affirmed by various **early church fathers**.[507] Thus, the **bride of Christ** represents the **royal priesthood**, consistent with the **"kings of the earth"** in Revelation 21:24. If the saved nations are not kings or priests, then they could be **non-elect** individuals who receive grace and life, but not full heavenly inheritance. Revelation 21:27 confirms that only those whose names are written in the **Book of Life** enter the lowest heaven that descends to the earth.

Those **not written** in the **Book of Life** are cast into the **lake of fire** (Rev. 20:15). Yet, if **1 Corinthians 3:15** applies here, some may be **saved by fire**, if God wills. This implies **two classes** of condemned individuals: one that is ultimately **redeemed** after the second death,[508] and another that remains **forever unsaved**.[509] This may explain why some of the **saved nations** require healing from the **leaves of the tree of life**,[510] having been wounded by the fire of Gehenna.

It is possible that the **terrestrial resurrection body** of the non-elect can only **partake of life through Christ** by such indirect means—just as Christians also **partake for 1000 years** in the first resurrection.[511] God previously prevented fallen mankind from accessing the **tree of life** lest they live eternally in sin.[512] The **elect**, however, experience a **transformation** from **human (terrestrial)** to **angelic (celestial)** form at the end of the

---

[505] Revelation 21:24–27, *"And the nations of those who are saved shall walk in its light… but only those who are written in the Lamb's Book of Life"* (NKJV).

[506] Revelation 1:6, 5:10, 20:6; 1 Peter 2:5 (NKJV).

[507] Irenaeus of Lyons, *"Book 5, Chapter 34, Point 3"*, in *Against Heresies*. www.newadvent.org/fathers/0103534.htm

[508] Revelation 2:11, *"He who overcomes shall not be hurt by the second death"* (NKJV).

[509] Revelation 21:8, *"But the cowardly, unbelieving, abominable… shall have their part in the lake which burns with fire and brimstone, which is the second death"* (NKJV).

[510] Revelation 22:1–2, *"The leaves of the tree were for the healing of the nations"* (NKJV).

[511] Revelation 7:9–17 (NKJV).

[512] Genesis 3:22, *"Behold, the man has become like one of Us… lest he put out his hand and take also of the tree of life, and eat, and live forever"* (NKJV).

millennium, as testified by **Chiliasm church fathers**—a truth often neglected.[513]

This new **angelic body**, no longer made of **flesh and blood** (1 Cor. 15:50–52), may draw life directly from Christ.[514] This is the very goal of the **Marriage Supper of the Lamb**, in which believers become **one flesh** with Christ.[515] Notably, Christians remain in a **sinless human form** for 1000 years in order to receive **earthly recompense**—delights which are holy—before their final change at the **end of the millennium**, a view affirmed by both **Irenaeus of Lyons**[516] and **Tertullian**.[517]

SHEPHERD OF HERMAS

Did early Christians distinguish between **elect salvation** and **non-elect salvation** in a similar way? One important source that supports this possibility is the *Shepherd of Hermas*, a work which many in early Christianity regarded as either Scripture or very near to it.[518] The Shepherd describes **elect salvation** allegorically through the imagery of a **tower** built with stones, symbolizing the Church and its repentant members:

> "Many indeed shall hear, and hearing, some shall be glad, and some shall weep. But even these, if they hear and repent, shall also

---

[513] Justin Martyr, *Dialogue with Trypho*, Chapter 124,
  www.newadvent.org/fathers/01288.htm.
Irenaeus of Lyons, *Against Heresies*, Book 4, Chapter 38,
  www.newadvent.org/fathers/0103438.htm.
Tertullian, *Against Marcion*, Book 3, Chapter 25,
  www.newadvent.org/fathers/03123.htm; and Book 5, Chapter 10,
  ccel.org/ccel/schaff/anf03.v.iv.vi.x.html.
Victorinus of Pettau, *Commentary on the Apocalypse*, Chapter 18,
  earlychurchrevival.wordpress.com/...
Methodius of Olympus, *Banquet of the Ten Virgins*, Discourse 9, Chapter 5,
  www.newadvent.org/fathers/062309.htm.

[514] Irenaeus of Lyons, *Against Heresies*, Book 5, Chapter 32.
  www.newadvent.org/fathers/0103532.htm

[515] Ephesians 5:31–32, *"And the two shall become one flesh. This is a great mystery, but I speak concerning Christ and the church"* (NKJV).

[516] Irenaeus of Lyons, *Against Heresies*, Book 5, Chapter 32.
  www.newadvent.org/fathers/0103532.htm

[517] Tertullian, *Against Marcion*, Book 3, Chapter 25.
  www.newadvent.org/fathers/03123.htm

[518] G. M. Hahneman, "The Muratorian Fragment and the Origins of the New Testament Canon," in *The Canon Debate*, ed. L. M. McDonald and J. A. Sanders (Massachusetts: Hendrickson, 2002), 405–415.

rejoice. Hear, then, the parables of the tower... The tower which you see building is myself, the Church, who have appeared to you now and on the former occasion. Ask, then, whatever you like in regard to the tower, and I will reveal it to you, that you may rejoice with the saints."[519]

This idea of the **elect tower** is also cited by **Irenaeus of Lyons** in support of his own doctrine of the Church.[520] In contrast, the *Shepherd of Hermas* also presents another group—**rejected stones**—who, although unable to be incorporated into the elect tower, are still granted a chance at salvation. However, this possibility only becomes available to them **after some form of judgment**:

"Do you wish to know who are the others which fell near the waters, but could not be rolled into them? These are they who have heard the word and wish to be baptized in the name of the Lord; but when the chastity demanded by the truth comes into their recollection, they draw back, and again walk after their own wicked desires... But I, shameless as I yet was, asked her, Is repentance possible for all those stones which have been cast away and did not fit into the building of the tower, and will they yet have a place in this tower? Repentance, said she, is yet possible, but in this tower, they cannot find a suitable place. But in another and much inferior place they will be laid, and that, too, only when they have been tortured and completed the days of their sins. And on this account will they be transferred, because they have partaken of the righteous Word. And then only will they be removed from their punishments when the thought of repenting of the evil deeds which they have done has come into their hearts. But if it does not come into their hearts, they will not be saved on account of the hardness of their heart."[521]

---

[519] *Shepherd of Hermas*, "Book 1, Vision 3, Chapter 3," www.newadvent.org/fathers/02011.htm.
[520] Irenaeus of Lyons, *Against Heresies*, "Book 4, Chapter 36," www.newadvent.org/fathers/0103436.htm.
[521] *Shepherd of Hermas*, "Book 1, Vision 3, Chapter 7," www.newadvent.org/fathers/02011.htm.

Some Catholics cite this passage in support of **purgatory**.[522] However, the **linguistic emphasis** in the *Shepherd* seems to suggest that the final destination of these souls lies **outside** the elect tower, not within it. Catholic interpreters often view purgatory as **a chamber within the tower**, but the *Shepherd* speaks of these souls being placed in **another and much inferior place**. This distinction might point to a **non-elect salvation** scenario—where "outside the tower" represents the **final new earth**, while "inside the tower" represents the **final new heaven**, the realm of the elect, who are said to "go out no more" (Revelation 3:12–13).[523]

This also aligns with one of the **earliest extra-biblical chiliastic statements** by **Papias of Hierapolis**, who described differing eternal abodes for Christians based on their fruitfulness:

> "As the presbyters say, then those who are deemed worthy of an abode in heaven shall go there, others shall enjoy the delights of Paradise, and others shall possess the splendour of the city; for everywhere the Saviour will be seen, according as they shall be worthy who see Him. But that there is this distinction between the habitation of those who produce an hundredfold, and that of those who produce sixty-fold, and that of those who produce thirty-fold; for the first will be taken up into the heavens, the second class will dwell in Paradise, and the last will inhabit the city."[524]

Irenaeus of Lyons confirms this view, indicating that only those **deemed worthy** will enter heaven. He distinguishes between the **heavenly regions**—consisting of the **city, Paradise**, and the **heavens**—and the **new earth**, which might house those not considered worthy, possibly a category of **non-elect saved**:

> "But when this [present] fashion [of things] passes away, and man has been renewed, and flourishes in an incorruptible state... there shall be the new heaven and the new earth, in which the new man shall remain continually... And as the presbyters say, Then those who are deemed worthy of an abode in heaven shall go there,

---

[522] Phillip Campbell, "Catholic Elements in the Shepherd of Hermas," *Unam Sanctam Catholicam*, July 17, 2013. www.unamsanctamcatholicam.com/catholic-elements-in-the-shepherd-of-hermas.

[523] Revelation 3:11–13, "Behold, I am coming quickly! Hold fast what you have, that no one may take your crown... He who overcomes... shall go out no more" (NKJV).

[524] Papias of Hierapolis, "Fragment V," in *Fragments of Papias*, translated by Alexander Roberts and James Donaldson, from *Ante-Nicene Fathers*, Vol. 1 (Buffalo, NY: Christian Literature Publishing Co., 1885), www.newadvent.org/fathers/0125.htm.

others shall enjoy the delights of paradise, and others shall possess the splendour of the city; for everywhere the Saviour shall be seen according as they who see Him shall be worthy."[525]

CONCLUSION

Non-elect salvation may refer to those distinct from the "few" who attain **elect salvation**, who are identified as the **bride**[526] and who enter **heaven**.[527] In contrast, the **non-elect saved** may receive their final inheritance upon the **new earth**.[528] This distinction rests in the difference between those saved as the bride, and those for whom Christ died as a ransom for "many",[529] which could include those who believed after encountering Him in the **spirit world**.[530]

This layered distinction appears to be reflected in the penultimate chapter of the Apocalypse, which may be interpreted as presenting **three classes of humanity**:

i) The Overcomers / Christians / Elect Salvation (those of faith):

"He who overcomes shall inherit all things, and I will be his God and he shall be My son."[531]

ii) The Thirsty / Non-Christians / Non-Elect Salvation (those without faith, with no reward, saved by fire through God's mercy):

"I will give of the fountain of the water of life freely to him who thirsts."[532]

iii) The Damned (unsaved non-Christians / the wicked):

---

[525] Irenaeus of Lyons, *Against Heresies*, "Book 5, Chapter 36, Point 1," www.newadvent.org/fathers/0103536.htm.

[526] Revelation 21:9.

[527] Matthew 7:21, "Not everyone who says to Me, 'Lord, Lord,' shall enter the kingdom of heaven, but he who does the will of My Father in heaven" (NKJV).

[528] Revelation 21:24, 27.

[529] Matthew 26:28, "For this is My blood of the new covenant, which is shed for many for the remission of sins" (NKJV).

[530] John 6:29, 35–36, 40: "Jesus answered and said to them, 'This is the work of God, that you believe in Him whom He sent.'... 'And this is the will of Him who sent Me, that everyone who sees the Son and believes in Him may have everlasting life; and I will raise him up at the last day'" (NKJV).

[531] Revelation 21:7 (NKJV); cf. 1 John 5:4.

[532] Revelation 21:6 (NKJV).

"But the cowardly, unbelieving, abominable, murderers, sexually immoral, sorcerers, idolaters, and all liars shall have their part in the lake which burns with fire and brimstone, which is the second death."[533]

A similar threefold classification appears again in the final chapter of Revelation:

i) Elect Salvation (the Bride, who participates in the marriage of the Lamb and the first resurrection; cf. Matthew 25:1–13):

"And the Spirit and the bride say, 'Come!'"[534]

ii) Non-Elect Salvation for Israel (the "servants" in this final vision; cf. Matthew 25:14–30):

"And there shall be no more curse, but the throne of God and of the Lamb shall be in it, and His servants shall serve Him. They shall see His face, and His name shall be on their foreheads."[535]

iii) Non-Elect Salvation for Gentiles (the "thirsty"; cf. Matthew 25:31–46):

"And the Spirit and the bride say, 'Come!' And let him who hears say, 'Come!' And let him who thirsts come. Whoever desires, let him take the water of life freely."[536]

The academic model of **Non-Elect Salvation**[537] is relatively recent and speculative. It should not be taught as doctrine, since Scripture does not confirm it explicitly. Rather, it may be treated as a **possible scholastic interpretation** that harmonizes with a literal reading of Scripture. As such, it is offered here not as dogma but as an honest exegetical proposal, consistent with a conservative hermeneutic.

BIBLIOGRAPHY

Augustine of Hippo. *Enchiridion*. Translated by J.F. Shaw. From Nicene and Post-Nicene Fathers, First Series, Vol. 3. Edited by Philip Schaff. (Buffalo, NY: Christian Literature Publishing Co., 1887).

---

[533] Revelation 21:8 (NKJV).

[534] Revelation 22:17 (NKJV).

[535] Revelation 22:3–4 (NKJV).

[536] Revelation 22:17 (NKJV).

[537] Jonathan Ramachandran, "Non Elect Salvation Possibility" (NESP), in *The American Journal of Biblical Theology (AJBT)*, Vol. 26, No. 6 (February 9, 2025). www.biblicaltheology.com/Research/RamachandranJ01.pdf

Bauckham, Richard. "Universalism: a historical survey", in *Themelios*, 4.2 (September 1978): 47-54.

Bible. biblehub.com

Campbell, Phillip. "Catholic Elements in the Shepherd of Hermas", *Unam Sanctam Catholicam*, (July 17, 2013).

www.unamsanctamcatholicam.com/catholic-elements-in-the-shepherd-of-hermas

Hahneman, G. M.. *The Canon Debate*. Ed. L. M. McDonald and J. A. Sanders. (Massachusetts: Hendrickson, 2002).

Hanna, Edward. "Purgatory". In *The Catholic Encyclopedia*. Vol. 12. (New York: Robert Appleton Company, 1911).

Irenaeus of Lyons. *Against Heresies*. Translated by Alexander Roberts and William Rambaut. From Ante-Nicene Fathers, Vol. 1. Edited by Alexander Roberts, James Donaldson, and A. Cleveland Coxe. (Buffalo, NY: Christian Literature Publishing Co., 1885).

Justin of Rome (Justin Martyr). *Dialogue with Trypho*. Translated by Marcus Dods and George Reith. From Ante-Nicene Fathers, Vol. 1. Edited by Alexander Roberts, James Donaldson, and A. Cleveland Coxe. (Buffalo, NY: Christian Literature Publishing Co., 1885).

Methodius of Olympus. *Banquet of the Ten Virgins*. Translated by William R. Clark. From Ante-Nicene Fathers, Vol. 6. Edited by Alexander Roberts, James Donaldson, and A. Cleveland Coxe. (Buffalo, NY: Christian Literature Publishing Co., 1886).

Papias of Hierapolis. *Fragments of Papias*. Translated by Alexander Roberts and James Donaldson. From Ante-Nicene Fathers, Vol. 1. Edited by Alexander Roberts, James Donaldson, and A. Cleveland Coxe. (Buffalo, NY: Christian Literature Publishing Co., 1885).

Ramachandran, Jonathan. "Non Elect Salvation Possibility" (NESP), in *The American Journal of Biblical Theology* (AJBT, Theological Research), Vol 26, No. 6 (February 9, 2025).

www.biblicaltheology.com/Research/RamachandranJ01.pdf

Shepherd of Hermas. Translated by F. Crombie. From Ante-Nicene Fathers, Vol. 2. Edited by Alexander Roberts, James Donaldson, and A. Cleveland Coxe. (Buffalo, NY: Christian Literature Publishing Co., 1885).

Tertullian. *Against Marcion*. Translated by Peter Holmes. From Ante-Nicene Fathers, Vol. 3. Edited by Alexander Roberts, James Donaldson, and A. Cleveland Coxe. (Buffalo, NY: Christian Literature Publishing Co., 1885).

Victorinus of Pettau. *Ancient Bible Commentaries in English - Victorinus on Revelation Commentary on Revelation by St. Victorinus*. By John Litteral, Kevin P. Edgecomb. (Createspace Independent Publishing Platform, 2014).

Jonathan Ramachandran

Essay 7: Prophecy of 5 Wise and 5 Foolish Virgins in Chiliasm

KEYWORDS

Wise Virgins, Foolish Virgins, Parables, Second Coming of Christ, Bride, Wife of the Lamb, Elect Salvation, Wedding of the Lamb, Prophecy, Eschatology, Chiliasm

ABSTRACT

This essay defends the most ancient interpretation of the parable of the five wise and five foolish virgins, using quotations from **Chiliasm church fathers** to demonstrate that it refers to **right faith** accompanied by **good works**. Right faith is defined as obedience to the commandments found in the New Testament, particularly **nine of the Ten Commandments**—excluding the sabbath, which was not required for Gentile believers. Good works are understood primarily in terms of **charity** rather than tithing, with financial holiness being based on **voluntary giving**.

The **Holy Spirit dwells** in believers who maintain a living faith through such works. A correct understanding of this parable increases one's focus on obedience to Christ, both in **physical holiness** through the abstinence of sin and in **financial holiness** through giving, as modeled in the **charity doctrine**. These principles are not only taught in Scripture by Christ Himself but are also confirmed in the writings of the **Chiliasm church fathers**.

INTRODUCTION

The parable of the **five wise and five foolish virgins** (Matthew 25:1 – 13) is decisive because it identifies those who attain **elect salvation** and participate in the **wedding of the Lamb**. From the earliest centuries, Christian interpreters—East and West—have understood the virgins to symbolize believers who possess **faith combined with good works**. This reading is embedded in both **Catholic**[538] and **Orthodox**[539] tradition.

---

[538] Friedrich Justus Knecht, "The Parable of the Ten Virgins," in *A Practical Commentary on Holy Scripture* (B. Herder, 1910), 620 – 622.

[539] Fr. Evan Armatas, "Parables Bible Study 8: The Ten Virgins," *Orthodox Catechism Project*, n.d. www.orthodoxcatechismproject.org.

Scholars across confessions agree that the entire Olivet Discourse "is concerned with practicing and keeping that which has been commanded by Jesus."[540] The divergence lies in which commandments each individual, congregation, or communion emphasizes as indispensable for salvation.[541]

During the **Reformation**, Reformers retained the traditional link between faith and obedience but sharpened their insistence on **Scripture as the final authority**.[542] Their convictions were summarized in the **Five Solas**—*sola Scriptura, solus Christus, sola fide, sola gratia*, and *soli Deo gloria*—[543] which became foundational to Reformation theology and sought to align the **Fathers** with the **biblical text**.[544] Reformed polemicists frequently declared that certain Catholic and Orthodox practices—such as Marian veneration or justification by works—placed those communions outside salvation,[545] while Rome and Constantinople responded with reciprocal anathemas.[546]

At the dawn of the twentieth century, the **Pentecostal revival** emerged, claiming to be the restored end-time church.[547] Leaders such as **William J. Seymour** (1870 – 1922) advanced a fresh application of the parable, arguing that only believers who receive a **"double portion"** of the Holy Spirit—evidenced by glossolalia—correspond to the **wise virgins**.[548] The Azusa Street meetings (1906-1909) propelled this teaching worldwide, asserting that those who do **not** speak in tongues "have not the Spirit."[549] Pentecostal eschatology went on to teach that Christ will secretly rapture tongue-speaking believers before the great tribulation.[550] Critics note, however, that nineteen

---

[540] K. Paul Donfried, "The Allegory of the Ten Virgins (Matt 25:1-13) as a Summary of Matthean Theology," *Journal of Biblical Literature* 93/3 (1974): 420.

[541] Adam Mukabva, "The Parable of the Ten Virgins: Matthew 25:1-13," *DARE: Holy Trinity College Journal* 12 (2023): 57-58.

[542] Yerlin & Bobby Putrawan, "The History of the Reformation of the Church in the 16th Century," *Journal of Religious and Socio-Cultural* 2 (2021): 116.

[543] Ibid., 116-117; Mihai Androne, "The Five Solas," in *Martin Luther* (Springer, 2020).

[544] R. Ward Holder, "The Reformers and Tradition," *Religions* 8/6 (2017): 105.

[545] John Wolffe, "A Comparative Historical Categorisation of Anti-Catholicism," *Journal of Religious History* 39/2 (2015): 182-202.

[546] John F. Pollard, *The Vatican and Italian Fascism, 1929 – 32* (Cambridge UP, 2014), 109-111.

[547] Wolfgang Vondey, "Soteriology at the Altar," *Transformation* 34/3 (2016): 223-238.

[548] Stephen Williams, "Jesus Is Coming Soon: Revisioning Pentecostal Eschatology," *Vanguard Journal of Theology and Ministry* 1/2 (2022): 31.

[549] Christopher A. Stephenson, "Un-Speaking in Tongues," *Journal of Spiritual Formation and Soul Care* 13/1 (2019): 95, 99.

[550] Frank Small, ed., *Living Waters* 1/1 (Winnipeg: Old Knox Church, 1918), 3.

centuries of Christian exegesis furnish **no precedent** for this view, a point often raised by **post-tribulationists**.[551]

REFORMERS

Martin Luther (1483–1546), founder of the Lutheran churches, taught that the parable of the **five wise and five foolish virgins** applies directly to **all Christians**. He explained that Christ's use of the term "virgins" refers broadly to those professing Christianity. However, only the wise virgins possess both **true faith** and **active good works**, whereas the foolish maintain merely an external appearance of faith while continuing in selfishness and indifference toward the poor. For Luther, authentic faith consists not only of inward belief but also outward obedience that manifests in practical acts of love toward one's neighbor.

> "Now pay attention: this parable speaks of the time right before the Last Judgment of God, and thus it applies to all Christians. For many of them—the majority—will turn, some to the imaginary faith, and the others to the true faith. ... To expand further on the Gospel, notice that the lamps are intended to depict for us an outward thing and a bodily practice. But the lamps together with the oil are the inner treasures with the true faith. ... Five are wise, five foolish. Here He calls all Christians 'virgins.' ... Matthew writes (7:22), saying: 'Lord, Lord!'[552] The mouth is there, but the heart is far away (Matt. 15:8). The oil is not in the lamp, that is, faith is not in the heart. They give it no thought. Indeed, they know it not and imagine that their lamps are ready. Their nature is that they gladly hear the preaching about faith, and if they have heard the Word, they invent and fabricate for themselves a thought, a delusion in the heart which they consider to be oil, and yet they remain the same as before in their behavior. Following their old ways, they are just as wrathful as before, just as covetous, just as unmerciful toward the poor, just as discourteous, etc. ... Therefore, let each one see to it that he has these two together: the oil, which is true faith and trust in Christ; and the lamps, the vessel, which is the outward service toward your neighbor. The whole

---

[551] Craig L. Blomberg & Sung Wook Chung, eds., *A Case for Historic Premillennialism* (Baker, 2008).

[552] Notice how Luther quotes the context of the "Great Denial" as referring to Christians who did not have charity doctrine works in particular here. Bible reads, "22Many will say to Me in that day, 'Lord, Lord, have we not prophesied in Your name, cast out demons in Your name, and done many wonders in Your name?' 23And then I will declare to them, 'I never knew you; depart from Me, you who practice lawlessness!'" (Matthew 7:22–23, NKJV).

Christian life consists in these two things: **Believe God. Help your neighbor.** The whole Gospel teaches this. Parents should tell it to their children at home and everywhere. Children, too, should constantly foster this Word among themselves."[553]

Luther's interpretation clearly connects the warning in the parable with **Matthew 7:22–23**, where Christ rebukes professing believers who perform external religious acts but lack obedience to God's will. According to Luther, **the absence of charity doctrine works—such as mercy toward the poor—is the very lawlessness Christ condemns** in this "Great Denial" passage:

> "22Many will say to Me in that day, 'Lord, Lord, have we not prophesied in Your name, cast out demons in Your name, and done many wonders in Your name?' 23And then I will declare to them, 'I never knew you; depart from Me, you who practice lawlessness!'" (Matthew 7:22–23).

This shows that for Luther, **saving faith is never alone**; it is accompanied by **tangible acts of righteousness**, especially in service to others. Thus, **the foolish virgins lack charity**, while the wise are those who both **believe rightly** and **live righteously** through love.

John Calvin (1509–1564), founder of the Reformed churches and Calvinism, interpreted the parable of the **five wise and five foolish virgins** as emphasizing both **belief in Christ** and the **fruits of that belief**, particularly demonstrated through **mutual aid within the Church**. For Calvin, true faith is not a static profession but must manifest in **works of charity**, which he understood to be the proper use of God-given gifts for the benefit of others. This directly aligns with the principle of **"freely you have received, freely give"**[554] (Matthew 10:8) and what this work identifies as **charity doctrine**.

Calvin writes:

> "But I take it more simply as denoting earthly occupations, in which believers must be engaged, so long as they dwell in the body; and, though forgetfulness of the kingdom of God ought never to steal upon them, yet the distracting influence of the occupations of

---

[553] Martin Luther, *Sermon On Faith and Good Works*, preached in Erfurt at St. Michaeliskirche on the day of the 11,000 virgins (October 21, 1522), translated by Rev. Paul A. Rydecki (2013). www.godwithuslc.org/luther-sermon-for-trinity-27

[554] Matthew 10:8 reads, "Heal the sick, cleanse the lepers, raise the dead, cast out demons. Freely you have received, freely give" (NKJV).

this world is not inappropriately compared to sleep. For they cannot be so constantly occupied with the thought of meeting Christ, as not to be distracted, or retarded, or entangled by a variety of cares, in consequence of which, while they watch, they are partly asleep. ...

9. Lest there be not enough for you and us. We know that the Lord distributes his gifts so variously to each, according to his measure, in order that **they may give mutual aid to each other**, and may employ for the general advantage what has been entrusted to each individual; and that in this way is preserved **the sacred connection which exists among the members of the Church.** ... There is no other way of obtaining it, therefore, but to receive by faith what is offered to us."[555]

Calvin highlights that believers are entrusted with spiritual and material gifts **not for self-indulgence**, but for the **benefit of others**—maintaining the unity and function of the body of Christ. This statement directly connects faith to works in the context of **communal responsibility**, which is a central theme in the doctrine of **elect salvation**. For Calvin, **the wise virgins** are not just those who have faith, but those who **actively invest their resources in service to others**, confirming that **true faith results in love**.

John Wesley (1703–1791), key founder of the Methodist churches, interpreted the parable of the **five wise and five foolish virgins** as a call to active **faith working through love**. He taught that the **oil in the lamps** represents not merely a profession of faith, but faith that is sustained and made perfect through **spiritual love in action**—that is, good works.

Wesley explains:

"1: Then shall the kingdom of heaven—that is, the candidates for it—be like ten virgins. The bridesmaids on the wedding night were wont to go to the house where the bride was, with burning lamps or torches in their hands, to wait for the bridegroom's coming. When he drew near, they went to meet him with their lamps, and to conduct him to the bride.

3: The foolish took no oil with them—no more than kept them burning just for the present. None to supply their future want, to recruit their lamp's decay.

---

[555] John Calvin, *Calvin's Commentaries*, commentary on Matthew 25's parable of the five wise and five foolish virgins. biblehub.com/commentaries/calvin/matthew/25.htm

The lamp is faith. A lamp and oil with it, is faith working by love.

4: The wise took oil in their vessels—love in their hearts. And they daily sought a fresh supply of spiritual strength, till their faith was made perfect."[556]

Wesley's understanding of **"faith working by love"** was not limited to personal piety but extended deeply into what this paper terms **financial holiness**—the obedience to Christ's commands regarding money and possessions. For Wesley, a Christian's spiritual condition was tested by their generosity and compassion for the poor. He warned that increasing wealth without a proportional increase in giving could lead to spiritual ruin, even hell itself.

He warns:

"For the Methodists in every place grow diligent and frugal; consequently they increase in goods. Hence, they proportionably increase in pride, in the desire of the flesh, the desire of the eyes, and the pride of life. So, although the form of religion remains, the spirit is swiftly vanishing away.

Is there no way to prevent this?—this continual declension of pure religion?

We ought not to forbid people to be diligent and frugal; we must exhort all Christians, to gain all they can, and to save all they can: this is, in effect, to grow rich!

What way then, I ask again, can we take that our money may not sink us to the nethermost hell?

There is one way, and there is no other under heaven. **If those who gain all they can, and save all they can, will likewise give all they can**, then the more they gain, the more they will grow in grace, and the more treasure they will lay up in heaven."[557]

Wesley's concern echoes the core emphasis of this essay: that **faith without charity is incomplete,** and holiness includes how one stewards

---

[556] John Wesley, *John Wesley's Notes on the Bible*, commentary on Matthew 25's parable of the five wise and five foolish virgins. bible.christiansunite.com/wes.cgi?b=Mt&c=25

[557] Luke Tyerman, *Life and Times of Wesley*, Volume III, (Harper & Bros; 1872): 520. Quoted by Mark Dever: *The Pastor and the Community*, via Kevin DeYoung (11 June 2010). www.thegospelcoalition.org/blogs/kevin-deyoung/the-pastor-and-the-community-mark-dever/

resources in obedience to Christ. Thus, Wesley's interpretation complements both earlier Reformers and the Chiliasm church fathers who insisted on **almsgiving** as an indispensable part of the Christian life.

This view agrees with the writings of the **Chiliasm church fathers**, who emphasized that **pure religion** must consist of two inseparable elements: **personal holiness**—which involves abstinence from sin—and **charity doctrine**, defined here as love in action through material giving and care for the most vulnerable. This twofold righteousness begins with practical concern for **widows and orphans**,[558] as the apostle James writes:

> "Pure religion and undefiled before God and the Father is this, To visit the fatherless and widows in their affliction, and to keep himself unspotted from the world".[559]

This emphasis on good works must be practiced according to one's **relative measure**—a concept that accounts for varying circumstances among believers. For example, Lazarus in the parable was too impoverished to give, and therefore would be exempted from such requirements.[560] The **Chiliasm fathers** Irenaeus[561] and Tertullian[562] affirmed that this parable was based on real historical figures, making its moral teaching applicable to the faithful poor. Likewise, the apostle Paul, when writing instructions about the **church's financial support for widows**, laid down specific criteria: a Christian widow must have previously demonstrated **charity doctrine**, such as bringing up children, lodging strangers, or relieving the afflicted.[563]

Scripture also records that **Tabitha**, called a **disciple**, "was full of good works and charitable deeds",[564] showing that such works are not optional but essential in the Christian life. Since men are called to spiritual leadership,[565]

---

[558] Vukelić Jelisaveta & Stanojević Dragan, "Who should take care of the poor? Religion and social welfare in America", *Filozofija i društvo*, Volume 25, Issue 2, (Serbia, 2014): 137–156. doi.org/10.2298/FID1402137V

[559] James 1:27 (KJV).

[560] Luke 16:19–31.

[561] Irenaeus of Lyons, *Against Heresies*, Book 2, Chapter 34. www.newadvent.org/fathers/0103234.htm

[562] Tertullian, *Against Marcion*, Book 4, Chapter 34. www.newadvent.org/fathers/03124.htm

[563] 1 Timothy 5:10 (NKJV).

[564] Acts 9:36 (NKJV).

[565] 1 Corinthians 11:3.

they are held to an even higher standard in these matters. Paul's command to the **rich** especially reinforces the idea of **relative responsibility** in giving:

> "Command those who are rich in this present age not to be haughty, nor to trust in uncertain riches but in the living God ... Let them do good, that they be rich in good works, ready to give, willing to share".[566]

These good works are not merely outward acts of kindness but are part of **financial holiness**, a form of sanctification that has direct implications for **eternal life**. In this context, the **prophet of God** may serve not only as a **divinely inspired foreteller**[567] but also as one who speaks on behalf of God concerning social righteousness—what some call **social justice**, though it is properly grounded in the commands of Scripture.[568]

HOLINESS AND CHARITY DOCTRINE

Irenaeus of Lyons (c. 130–c. 202) offered a stern warning that those who obscure the interpretation of parables—especially those given by Christ—risk **exclusion from elect salvation**. He connects this failure to a lack of preparation for the **marriage-chamber**, symbolizing eternal union with Christ. This serious consequence underscores the importance of interpreting such parables in light of teachings preserved by the **Chiliasm church fathers**, particularly **Irenaeus, Justin, and Tertullian**. Any theological interpolation must be grounded in their writings, while always acknowledging that human conclusions may still fall short:

> "And when the Bridegroom (Matthew 25:5, etc.) comes, he who has his lamp untrimmed, and not burning with the brightness of a steady light, is classed among those who obscure the interpretations of the parables, forsaking Him who by His plain announcements freely imparts gifts to all who come to Him, and is excluded from His marriage-chamber".[569]

Tertullian, in mocking the heretics who presume forgiveness without holiness, implicitly reveals that the **oil** in the parable of the virgins signifies

---

[566] 1 Timothy 6:17–19 (NKJV).

[567] Ellen F. Davis and Sarah Musser, "Prophecy, Interpretation, and Social Criticism", in *St Andrews Encyclopaedia of Theology*, ed. Brendan N. Wolfe et al., University of St Andrews, Article published July 27, 2023: 6.
www.saet.ac.uk/Christianity/ProphecyInterpretationandSocialCriticism

[568] Ibid., 6, 9–12, 15–16, 20.

[569] Irenaeus of Lyons, *Against Heresies*, Book 2, Chapter 27.
www.newadvent.org/fathers/0103227.htm

personal purity and holy conduct. This includes what can be termed **financial holiness**, as evidenced in his broader writings where **charity doctrine** is plainly taught:

> "Himself pure from sin, and in all respects holy, He might undergo death on behalf of sinners. Similarly, you who emulate Him in condoning sins, if you yourself have done no sin, plainly suffer in my stead. If, however, you are a sinner, how will the oil of your puny torch be able to suffice for you and for me?"[570]

This rhetorical statement implies that **no sinner has surplus oil** (i.e., surplus holiness) to offer another. Therefore, the oil represents not mere profession, but **righteous living**, including almsgiving and obedience to Christ's financial commands.[571]

Methodius of Olympus confirms this same understanding of the **oil**—that it refers to **holiness and good works**. In his exposition, he teaches that the light of the virgins endured so long as they maintained purity and practical righteousness. When they abandoned such disciplines, the flame of continence was extinguished:

> "So long, then, as this people treasured up nourishment for the light, supplying oil by their works, the light of continence was not extinguished among them, but was ever shining and giving light in the lot of their inheritance. But when the oil failed, by their turning away from the faith to incontinence, the light was entirely extinguished, so that the virgins have again to kindle their lamps by light transmitted from one to another, bringing the light of incorruption to the world from above. Let us then supply now the oil of good works abundantly, and of prudence, being purged from all corruption which would weigh us down; lest, while the Bridegroom tarries, our lamps may also in like manner be extinguished".[572]

This call to **supply the oil of good works abundantly** aligns perfectly with the teachings of both Irenaeus and Tertullian, forming a unified voice

---

[570] Tertullian, *On Modesty (De pudicitia)*, Chapter 22. www.newadvent.org/fathers/0407.htm

[571] Tertullian, *Against Marcion*, Book 4, Chapter 27. www.newadvent.org/fathers/03124.htm

[572] Methodius of Olympus, *Banquet of the Ten Virgins*, Discourse 6, Chapter 4. www.newadvent.org/fathers/062306.htm

within **early Chiliasm**: the wise virgins are those whose **faith is proven by holiness and charity**.

While this work primarily focuses on the **Chiliasm Church Fathers**, it is valuable to note that several other early Church Fathers also interpret the **Parable of the Ten Virgins** in a way that confirms the same doctrinal conclusions—namely, that **the oil represents charity, almsgiving, and good works**. These quotations, compiled in the **Catena Aurea**[573] of Thomas Aquinas, strongly reinforce the teaching that **faith must be expressed in acts of mercy** if it is to result in salvation.

Hilary of Poitiers (c. 310 – c. 367) interprets the oil as referring to charitable giving to the poor. He teaches that those in need "sell" the opportunity for reward to the one giving, by receiving the relief of their affliction in exchange for eternal recompense:

> "They that sell are the poor, who, needing the alms of the faithful, made them that recompense which they desire, selling in return for the relief afforded to their wants, a consciousness of good works. This is the abundant fuel of an undying light which may be bought and stored up for the fruits of mercy".[574]

John Chrysostom (c. 347 – c. 407) likewise declares that the oil is **charity and almsgiving**, without which even the virtue of virginity (a higher calling in ascetic discipline) is not enough. He laments that some endure the greater toil of bodily chastity yet forfeit everything due to a lesser neglect—**the failure to help the poor**:

> "The 'oil' denotes charity, alms, and every aid rendered to the needy; the lamps denote the gifts of virginity; and He calls them 'foolish,' because after having gone through the greater toil, they lost all for the sake of a less; for it is greater labour to overcome the desires of the flesh than of money".[575]

Jerome of Stridon (c. 342 – c. 420), translator of the Latin Vulgate, emphasizes that this oil cannot be gained cheaply. It is acquired at a **high cost**, through effort, toil, and practice of **all virtues**, especially those taught by **biblical doctrine** and faithful teachers:

---

[573] Thomas Aquinas, *Catena Aurea – Gospel of Matthew*, translated by John Henry Parker, Vol. I (London: J.G.F. and J. Rivington, 1842).
www.ccel.org/ccel/aquinas/catena1.ii.xxv.html
[574] Hilary of Poitiers, as cited in *Catena Aurea*, Matthew 25.
[575] John Chrysostom, as cited in *Catena Aurea*, Matthew 25.

> "And this oil is sold, and at a high cost, nor is it to be got without much toil; so that we understand it not of alms only, but of all virtues and counsels of the teachers".[576]

The **scholia** attributed to **Thomas Aquinas** or possibly others summarize that the oil may mean either **good works**, **inner joy**, or **almsgiving** in a broader sense, but always includes **moral preparation**:

> "In the foregoing parable is set forth the condemnation of such as have not prepared sufficient oil for themselves, whether by oil is meant the brightness of good works, or inward joy of conscience, or alms paid in money".[577]

Augustine of Hippo (c. 354 – c. 430) likewise interprets the wise virgins as those who possessed not just lamps, but the "gladness of good works":

> "But the wise took oil with their lamps, that is, the gladness of good works".[578]

Finally, **Origen of Alexandria** (c. 185 – c. 253) offers a nuanced perspective, linking the oil to **comforting doctrine** and **good deeds**, showing how ignorance or neglect of **biblical teaching** can extinguish even the best intentions:

> "The 'foolish' took lamps, alight indeed at the first, but not supplied with so much oil as should suffice even to the end, being careless respecting the provision of doctrine which comforts faith, and enlightens the lamp of good deeds".[579]

These testimonies across a broad range of early Church fathers—spanning East and West—further validate the **Chiliasm interpretation** that the **oil symbolizes the fruit of righteous action**. It is not merely inward belief, but rather a **living, active faith** characterized by **sacrificial love, financial holiness, and consistent obedience** to Christ's commands. This unanimous voice across centuries of patristic witness confirms that **salvation cannot be secured apart from charity doctrine**.

---

[576] Jerome of Stridon, as cited in *Catena Aurea*, Matthew 25.

[577] Anonymous scholia, possibly by Thomas Aquinas, as cited in *Catena Aurea*, Matthew 25.

[578] Augustine of Hippo, as cited in *Catena Aurea*, Matthew 25.

[579] Origen of Alexandria, as cited in *Catena Aurea*, Matthew 25.

Among the most vivid and sobering teachings in Scripture is the requirement of the **wedding garment** at the **marriage supper of the Lamb** (Matthew 22:11–13; Revelation 19:7–9). This is not an arbitrary garment but has consistent interpretation across early Church writings as signifying either **good works, personal holiness,** or **both**, with failure to wear such a garment resulting in **exclusion** from the first resurrection and **being cast into outer darkness**. The **Chiliasm Fathers**—particularly **Tertullian** and **Irenaeus**—provide detailed exposition on this teaching.

Tertullian affirms that **those invited to the marriage** must be clothed in **raiment of good works** to be counted worthy to recline at the table of the Kingdom. Failure to wear such raiment results in damnation, specifically to be "bound hand and foot," implying **bodily resurrection for judgment**:

> "He also who shall not be clothed at the marriage feast in the raiment of good works, will have to be bound hand and foot,— as being, of course, raised in his body. So, again, the very reclining at the feast in the kingdom of God, and sitting on Christ's thrones, and standing at last on His right hand and His left, and eating of the tree of life: what are all these but most certain proofs of a bodily appointment and destination?"[580]

Irenaeus of Lyons confirms the same interpretation by linking the **indwelling of the Holy Spirit** with one's **works of righteousness**. He states unambiguously that **the wedding garment is righteousness**—and without it, there is no entrance into the marriage chamber. Those called to the banquet but **found without righteousness are cast out**, and the phrase "many are called, but few are chosen" is fulfilled:

> "Still further did He also make it manifest, that we ought, after our calling, to be also adorned with works of righteousness, so that the Spirit of God may rest upon us; for this is the wedding garment. ... But those who have indeed been called to God's supper, yet have not received the Holy Spirit, because of their wicked conduct shall be, He declares, cast into outer darkness. ... the same King who gathered from all quarters the faithful to the marriage of His Son, and who grants them the incorruptible banquet, [also] orders that man to be cast into outer darkness who has not on a wedding garment, that is, one who despises it."[581]

---

[580] Tertullian, *On the Resurrection of the Flesh*, chapter 35. www.newadvent.org/fathers/0316.htm
[581] Irenaeus of Lyons, *Against Heresies*, book 4, chapter 36.

Tertullian extends the symbolism of the wedding garment further. He presents a **dual meaning**: (1) **the sanctity of the flesh**, particularly those who practice virginity or remain unmarried for the Kingdom of Heaven's sake, and (2) **the hope of resurrection** for those whose works display holiness. Drawing on Revelation and Isaiah, he spiritualizes the garments as reflecting both **bodily sanctity** and **the reward of the resurrection**:

> "We have also in the Scriptures robes mentioned as allegorizing the hope of the flesh. Thus in the Revelation of John it is said: These are they which have not defiled their clothes with women,—indicating, of course, virgins, and such as have become eunuchs for the kingdom of heaven's sake. ... In the gospel even, the wedding garment may be regarded as the sanctity of the flesh. ... Then shall your light break forth as the morning, and your garments shall speedily arise ... where he has no thought of cloaks or stuff gowns, but means the rising of the flesh ... Thus we are furnished even with an allegorical defense of the resurrection of the body."[582]

Tertullian even interprets Isaiah 26:20—"enter into your closets for a little season"—as a veiled reference to **graves** in which the righteous rest until they rise again after **the final persecution of Antichrist**, affirming the **bodily resurrection** consistent with **Chiliasm eschatology**.

These consistent testimonies from two of the most authoritative Chiliasm teachers—**Irenaeus** and **Tertullian**—underscore that **holiness**, manifested outwardly through **righteous works**, is the **essential clothing** for participating in the **first resurrection** and **marriage of the Lamb**. This aligns precisely with the earlier section on the **oil of the virgins**, the **fruit of financial holiness**, and the **charity doctrine** requirements that accompany saving faith.

A careful reading of Scripture reveals that the command to keep our **"lamps burning"** (Luke 12:35) is closely tied to how we use **earthly possessions**, especially in relation to **charity** or **almsgiving**. Christ does not isolate this exhortation as a vague moral principle, but explicitly ties it to **selling what we have** and **giving alms**, showing that the **burning lamp** metaphor is a command to walk in **charity doctrine** as a form of spiritual readiness. This connection is often **ignored or diminished** by prosperity

---

www.newadvent.org/fathers/0103436.htm
[582] Tertullian, *On the Resurrection of the Flesh*, chapter 27.
www.newadvent.org/fathers/0316.htm

gospel preachers, who emphasize the "receiving" of material blessings without the equally emphasized responsibility of **distributing wealth for God's purposes** through sacrificial giving. As Christ states:

> "But seek the kingdom of God, and all these things shall be added to you. Do not fear, little flock, for it is your Father's good pleasure to give you the kingdom. Sell what you have and give alms; provide yourselves money bags which do not grow old, a treasure in the heavens that does not fail, where no thief approaches nor moth destroys. For where your treasure is, there your heart will be also. Let your waist be girded and your lamps burning"[583]

The implication is direct: if earthly money is not converted into **treasure in heaven** through **charity**, then the heart remains fixed on earth. Christ is not offering both **earthly treasure** and **heavenly treasure**, but only the latter. This directly **contradicts the so-called Law of Compensation** taught by some modern prosperity teachers, which asserts that God promises to return financial wealth to givers in this life.[584] Scripture teaches otherwise:

> "Do not lay up for yourselves treasures on earth, where moth and rust destroy and where thieves break in and steal; but lay up for yourselves treasures in heaven, where neither moth nor rust destroys and where thieves do not break in and steal. For where your treasure is, there your heart will be also"[585]

This theme is reinforced when Jesus counsels the rich young ruler:

> "If you want to be perfect, go, sell what you have and give to the poor, and you will have treasure in heaven; and come, follow Me." But when the young man heard that saying, he went away sorrowful, for he had great possessions"[586]

These passages together reinforce the truth that **charity doctrine** is not optional—it is a command for those seeking to be **"perfect"** and to **store treasure in heaven**. It also becomes a way of keeping one's **"lamp burning"**, as Christ instructed.

---

[583] Luke 12:31–35 (NKJV)

[584] Ogunlusi Clement Temitope, "Prosperity Gospel Preaching and its Implications on National Developments," *International Journal of Humanities and Cultural Studies*, 5(1), (June 2018): 320–321. ijhcs.com/index.php/IJHCS/article/viewFile/223/207

[585] Matthew 6:19–21 (NKJV)

[586] Matthew 19:21–22 (NKJV)

Further confirmation comes from **Methodius of Olympus**, who interprets the five wise virgins with lit lamps as those who adorn their lives with **good works**:

> "Whence sin being dead and destroyed, again I shall rise immortal; and I praise God who by means of death frees His sons from death, and I celebrate lawfully to His honour a festal-day, adorning my tabernacle, that is my flesh, with good works, as there did the five virgins with the five-lighted lamps."[587]

Thus, **"lamps burning"** is not a vague image of readiness but represents the continual **exercise of almsgiving and good works**, rooted in obedience to Christ. The **modern neglect of almsgiving** in favor of promises of personal financial gain stands in stark contrast to the clear teaching of the Lord Jesus and the early Church Fathers. Such imbalance distorts the biblical message and minimizes the **sanctifying role of sacrificial giving** in the Christian life.[588]

REGARDING SABBATH AND LAW OF MOSES

i) False Teachers Demanded Full Observance of the Law of Moses for Gentile Converts

In the early church, a significant doctrinal controversy arose when some **false teachers from Judea** insisted that Gentile believers were obligated to observe the entirety of the **Law of Moses**. This teaching included the requirement of **circumcision**, which they wrongly presented as a condition for salvation:

> "And certain men came down from Judea and taught the brethren, 'Unless you are circumcised according to the custom of Moses, you cannot be saved.' ... But some of the sect of the Pharisees who believed rose up, saying, 'It is necessary to circumcise them, and to command them to keep the law of Moses.'"[589]

This error prompted the Jerusalem Council to meet and clarify the apostolic position on the matter, ultimately rejecting this imposition on Gentile Christians.

---

[587] Methodius of Olympus, *Banquet of the Ten Virgins*, Discourse 9, Chapter 2. www.newadvent.org/fathers/062309.htm

[588] J. C. Harrod, "The Neglected Discipline of Almsgiving," *Journal of Spiritual Formation and Soul Care*, 12(1), (2018): 89–111. doi.org/10.1177/1939790918812460

[589] Acts 15:1, 5 (NKJV)

ii) True Apostolic Doctrine Taught that Jewish and Gentile Believers Do Not Have the Same Observances

In contrast, the **true apostles**, guided by the **Holy Spirit**, affirmed that Gentile believers were **not bound to keep the Law of Moses**. Their inspired conclusion was that the Gentiles were to observe only a few necessary commands that preserved **moral purity** and **fellowship unity** between Jewish and Gentile believers. The official letter from the Jerusalem Council reads:

> "To the brethren who are of the Gentiles in Antioch, Syria, and Cilicia: ... Since we have heard that some who went out from us have troubled you with words, unsettling your souls, saying, 'You must be circumcised and keep the law'—to whom we gave no such commandment—... For it seemed good to the Holy Spirit, and to us, to lay upon you no greater burden than these necessary things: that you abstain from things offered to idols, from blood, from things strangled, and from sexual immorality. If you keep yourselves from these, you will do well. Farewell."[590]

This passage proves that **Gentile believers** are **not under the Mosaic Law**, including the **Sabbath command**, which is never reiterated for them in any New Testament instruction. Yet it also shows that **some moral laws from the Mosaic code not included in the Ten Commandments**—such as **prohibitions against sexual immorality (e.g., LGBTQ practices in Leviticus 18:22, prostitution in Leviticus 19:29) and blood consumption**—still apply. These were singled out for inclusion in the Gentile instruction precisely because they **do not fall under the Ten Commandments** and might otherwise be overlooked.

Thus, the apostolic Church taught a **clear distinction** in **covenant observance** between Jewish and Gentile believers: **the Gentiles are not to be yoked to the ceremonial laws of Moses**, but are to keep themselves from what defiles and contradicts God's moral standards, as reemphasized through apostolic revelation.

A closer examination of Acts 21 reveals that the **early Jewish Christians** continued to observe portions of the **Mosaic Law**, while **Gentile believers** were **not held to the same requirements**. This clear distinction

---

[590] Acts 15:23–24, 28 (NKJV)

between Jewish and Gentile Christian observance of the Torah becomes evident in the following sequence:

The **accusation** against Paul was that he **"teaches all the Jews who are among the Gentiles to forsake Moses"** (Acts 21:21)—a serious charge in the eyes of the Judaizers and the Jewish believers in Jerusalem. To refute this claim, the elders proposed a solution demonstrating that Paul himself continued to walk in obedience to the Law:

> "Take them and be purified with them, and pay their expenses so that they may shave their heads, and that all may know that those things of which they were informed concerning you are nothing, but that **you yourself also walk orderly and keep the law**" (Acts 21:24).[591]

This example affirms that **Jewish Christians were permitted** to continue **practicing non-contradictory aspects of the Torah**, so long as they did not undermine the sufficiency of **Christ's atonement**. Practices such as **animal sacrifice for sin** were no longer acceptable since Jesus fulfilled the **sin offering** once for all (Hebrews 10:1–14). However, **ritual purifications, dietary practices**, or **Sabbath observance** could be followed by Jewish believers without conflict, provided they were not viewed as meritorious or salvific.

This apostolic decision also draws a **clear line** between **Jewish** and **Gentile believers**. The elders expressly wrote:

> "But concerning the Gentiles who believe, **we have written and decided that they should observe no such thing**" (Acts 21:25).[592]

This canonically distinguishes between the **Jewish practice of the Law** and the **Gentile call to liberty in Christ**, which does not include Torah observance.

Applying this principle, we observe that when Paul participates in **Sabbath observance**, it is **not a universal command** for all Christians, but a **cultural practice** in line with his **Jewish identity**. He affirms the liberty of Gentile believers regarding the Sabbath explicitly in **Colossians 2:16**, where he writes:

---

[591] Acts 21:21, 24–25 (NKJV).
[592] Acts 21:21, 24–25 (NKJV).

> "Let no one judge you in food or in drink, or regarding a festival or a new moon or sabbaths" (Colossians 2:16).[593]

Here, **Sabbath observance** is categorized along with **Old Covenant shadows**, and Gentile believers are instructed that **they are not to be judged for not observing** such things. Paul does **not command them** to **"keep the Sabbath"**—a command that, had it been obligatory, would have been plainly stated.

Moreover, the phrase **"let no one judge you"** appears to **defend those not observing the Sabbath**, not those who do. In fact, **only Sabbath-keepers** would have cause to **judge others** for failing to keep it. Therefore, this phrase seems to favor **liberty from the Sabbath command** more than permission for it. This again reinforces the interpretation that the **Fourth Commandment**, which is **not reaffirmed** in the New Testament for Gentiles,[594] **does not apply to them.**

Of the **Ten Commandments, nine** are **reaffirmed** clearly for Gentile Christians in the New Testament epistles. The **Sabbath** alone stands **absent**, which is telling. Gentile Christians instead observe the **Lord's Day**, which is mentioned once in **Revelation 1:10**,[595] not as a mandated Sabbath but as a day chosen to remember Christ's resurrection. There is **no command** to keep Sunday in the manner of a sabbath, and early Christians met **willingly** on this day as a matter of worship tradition, not legal obligation.

Therefore, the New Testament teaches that **Gentile Christians are not bound** to keep the Sabbath. The **apostolic council, Paul's letters**, and the **absence of a command** to "keep the Sabbath" for Gentiles all affirm this position. The **Sabbath was part of the Mosaic Covenant**, which Gentiles were **never under**, and **Christ's fulfillment** of the Law has freed all believers from its **ceremonial shadows**.

Hebrews 4 is not speaking about Sabbath-keeping in the present time but rather about the **"seventh day" as an allegorical reference to the 1,000-year millennial reign of Christ**. Irenaeus directly connects this passage to **elect salvation at the beginning of the 1,000 years**, which he calls the **"times of the kingdom."** He refers to the same **"seventh day"**

---

[593] GotQuestions.org, "Are the Ten Commandments repeated in the New Testament?", accessed March 14, 2025. www.gotquestions.org/Ten-Commandments-New-Testament.html

[594] R. J. Bauckham, "The Lord's Day" and "Sabbath and Sunday in the Postapostolic Church," in *From Sabbath to Lord's Day*, ed. D. A. Carson (Grand Rapids: Zondervan, 1982), 221–298.

[595] Revelation 1:10 (NKJV).

from Hebrews 4 in the context of the **second coming** and the **first resurrection**, indicating that it is not a present obligation but pertains to the future reign of Christ:

> "For in as many days as this world was made, in so many thousand years shall it be concluded. And for this reason the Scripture says: 'Thus the heaven and the earth were finished, and all their adornment. And God brought to a conclusion upon the sixth day the works that He had made; and God rested upon the seventh day from all His works.' This is an account of the things formerly created, as also it is a prophecy of what is to come. For the day of Jehovah is as a thousand years; and in six days created things were completed: it is evident, therefore, that they will come to an end at the sixth thousand year. ... For the Sabbath is the type and image of the future kingdom of the saints, when they shall reign with Christ, when He comes from heaven, as John says in the Apocalypse: 'For a day with the Lord is as a thousand years.' And he signifies to us that this is the day of which he said: 'And God rested on the seventh day from all His works'."[596]

In another place, Irenaeus explains that the apostles taught not to judge anyone regarding meat, drink, feast days, new moons, or sabbaths, quoting Colossians 2:16. He warns that **such judgment creates schisms in the Church of God** and **preserves only external observance** while **casting away the greater commands of faith and love**:

> "The apostles ordained, that 'we should not judge any one in respect to meat or drink, or in regard to a feast day, or the new moons, or the sabbaths.' Whence then these contentions? whence these schisms? We keep the feast, but in the leaven of malice and wickedness, cutting in pieces the Church of God; and we preserve what belongs to its exterior, that we may cast away these better things, faith and love. We have heard from the prophetic words that these feasts and fasts are displeasing to the Lord."[597]

Clearly, Irenaeus did not use this passage to compel Gentile believers to keep the Sabbath but rather to warn against using it as a standard for condemnation.

---

[596] Irenaeus of Lyons, *Against Heresies*, Book 5, Chapter 33, www.newadvent.org/fathers/0103533.htm

[597] Irenaeus of Lyons, *Fragments from the Lost Writings of Irenæus*, XXXVIII, www.ccel.org/ccel/schaff/anf01.ix.viii.xxxviii.html

Tertullian affirms the same understanding when he rebukes the arch-heretic Marcion, citing Colossians 2:16 to teach that the Sabbath has been **abolished** for Gentile believers. He explains that the passage speaks of the **transition from shadow to substance**—from **figurative types to their reality in Christ:**

> "Now tell me, Marcion, what is your opinion of the apostle's language, when he says, 'Let no man judge you in meat, or in drink, or in respect of a holy day, or of the new moon, or of the sabbath, which is a shadow of things to come, but the body is of Christ?' We do not now treat of the law, further than (to remark) that the apostle here teaches clearly how it has been abolished, even by passing from shadow to substance—that is, from figurative types to the reality, which is Christ."[598]

Furthermore, Christ did not deny that His disciples broke Sabbath laws but rather declared that they were **"guiltless"** even if they did:

> "But when the Pharisees saw it, they said to Him, 'Look, Your disciples are doing what is not lawful to do on the Sabbath!' But He said to them, 'Have you not read what David did when he was hungry, he and those who were with him … Or have you not read in the law that on the Sabbath the priests in the temple profane the Sabbath, and are blameless?'"[599]

Irenaeus echoes this very interpretation, stating that all true Christians are priests of God, and as priests who profane the Sabbath are considered **blameless** in the temple service, likewise, Christ's disciples are not judged for non-observance:

> "Now, in the preceding book I have shown that all the disciples of the Lord are Levites and priests, they who used in the temple to profane the Sabbath, but are blameless."[600]

Even the Reformers rejected a literal transfer of the Mosaic Sabbath to the Lord's-Day and treated Sunday chiefly as a **convenient weekly rhythm for worship and works of mercy,** not as a legal "seventh-day." John Calvin cautioned that, if Christians merely swapped Saturday for Sunday while

---

[598] Tertullian, *Against Marcion*, Book 5, Chapter 19, www.ccel.org/ccel/schaff/anf03.v.iv.vi.xix.html

[599] Matthew 12:2–5 (NKJV)

[600] Irenaeus of Lyons, *Against Heresies*, Book 5, Chapter 34, www.newadvent.org/fathers/0103534.htm

loading it with Judaic rigor, they would relapse "into the gross and carnal superstition of sabbatism." Instead, **"one day in seven"** is to be devoted to corporate or **private** devotion and "pious meditation on the works of God."[601] The Westminster divines echo this balance, requiring believers on the Lord's-Day to engage "in the public and private exercises of His worship, and in the duties of necessity and mercy."[602] Augustine agreed that the **only Mosaic precept not binding on Christians is the literal Sabbath-rest**: "I should like to be told what there is in these Ten Commandments, except the observance of the Sabbath, which ought not to be kept by a Christian."[603]

Acts portrays the first Lord's-Day gatherings as **charity-oriented**: believers "had all things in common … and divided them … as anyone had need."[604] The writer to the Hebrews exhorts the church not to forsake assembling, precisely so they might "stir up love and good works."[605] Many modern Christians follow this pattern by willing a portion of their estate to church and benevolence when present needs prevent large gifts in life—an application of the **relative-measure** principle you outlined earlier.

Irenaeus underscores that the **physical** sabbath and circumcision applied uniquely to Israel, whereas Christians fulfil the **spiritual Sabbath** that foreshadows the millennial kingdom by practising three habits:

1. **"Circumcise the hardness of your heart,"** renouncing inward sin.
2. **"Continue day by day in God's service,"** living each day as holy time.
3. **Minister continually to faith, persevering in it, and abstaining from all avarice,** refusing to "acquire or possess treasures upon earth."

These three points, he says, constitute the believer's true preparation for the **seventh-day rest—the 1,000-year reign of Christ.**

Hebrews 4 is not a command for weekly Sabbath observance but refers to the **allegorical meaning** of the **"seventh day"**—a prophecy of the **1,000-**

---

[601] John Calvin, *Institutes*, IV.x.34: "The moral part remains—viz., the observance of one day in seven … but not changing the day, and yet mentally attributing to it the same sanctity, lest we fall 'into the gross and carnal superstition of sabbatism.'"

[602] *Westminster Confession of Faith* 21.8: the Lord's-Day is to be spent "in the public and private exercises of His worship, and in the duties of necessity and mercy."

[603] Augustine, *On the Spirit and the Letter* 23.

[604] Acts 2 : 44-45.

[605] Hebrews 10 : 24-25.

year reign of Christ, or the **Millennial Kingdom**. Irenaeus points to this understanding when he connects **elect salvation** to the beginning of that **seventh day rest**, interpreting it in the context of the **Second Coming of Christ** and the **first resurrection** as the time when the righteous enter into the "times of the Kingdom".[606]

He also affirms that the Sabbath was never meant to be observed by Gentiles in the same way as Israel. Instead, it was a **sign** given specifically to Israel and fulfilled spiritually in Christian practice:

> "For it declares: God said to Abraham, Every male among you shall be circumcised; and you shall circumcise the flesh of your foreskins, as a token of the covenant between Me and you. This same does Ezekiel the prophet say with regard to the Sabbaths: Also I gave them My Sabbaths, to be a sign between Me and them, that they might know that I am the Lord, that sanctify them. And in Exodus, God says to Moses: And you shall observe My Sabbaths; for it shall be a sign between Me and you for your generations. These things, then, were given for a sign; but the signs were not unsymbolical, that is, neither unmeaning nor to no purpose, inasmuch as they were given by a wise Artist; but the circumcision after the flesh typified that after the Spirit. For we, says the apostle, have been circumcised with the circumcision made without hands. And the prophet declares, Circumcise the hardness of your heart. But the Sabbaths taught that we should continue day by day in God's service. For we have been counted, says the Apostle Paul, all the day long as sheep for the slaughter; that is, consecrated [to God], and ministering continually to our faith, and persevering in it, and abstaining from all avarice, and not acquiring or possessing treasures upon earth. Moreover, the Sabbath of God (requietio Dei), that is, the kingdom, was, as it were, indicated by created things; in which [kingdom], the man who shall have persevered in serving God (Deo assistere) shall, in a state of rest, partake of God's table."[607]

This interpretation shifts the focus away from physical observance of the Sabbath toward **spiritual perseverance and daily faithfulness**, especially **abstinence from greed and accumulation**, which is part of

---

[606] Irenaeus of Lyons, *Against Heresies*, Book 5, Chapter 33.
www.newadvent.org/fathers/0103533.htm
[607] Irenaeus of Lyons, *Against Heresies*, Book 4, Chapter 16, Point 1.
www.newadvent.org/fathers/0103416.htm

charity doctrine. The Sabbath is not ignored, but its true fulfillment is found **in living rightly and serving God daily**, with the final reward being **rest in the millennial kingdom**.

Irenaeus continues by showing how **Sabbath and circumcision were not part of moral law for all mankind**, but were **ceremonial signs** introduced at Sinai for Israel:

> "And that man was not justified by these things, but that they were given as a sign to the people, this fact shows — that Abraham himself, without circumcision and without observance of Sabbaths, believed God, and it was imputed unto him for righteousness; and he was called the friend of God. Then, again, Lot, without circumcision, was brought out from Sodom, receiving salvation from God. So also did Noah, pleasing God, although he was uncircumcised, receive the dimensions [of the ark], of the world of the second race [of men]. Enoch, too, pleasing God, without circumcision, discharged the office of God's legate to the angels although he was a man, and was translated, and is preserved until now as a witness of the just judgment of God... Moreover, all the rest of the multitude of those righteous men who lived before Abraham, and of those patriarchs who preceded Moses, were justified independently of the things above mentioned, and without the law of Moses. As also Moses himself says to the people in Deuteronomy: The Lord your God formed a covenant in Horeb. The Lord formed not this covenant with your fathers, but for you."[608]

This plainly shows that the **Sabbath is not a moral law** universally binding on all people. **Before Moses**, no one—including Abraham, Noah, or Enoch—was required to observe it. The **Sabbath was given to Israel**, as Deuteronomy 5:2 confirms, and not to the patriarchs. Thus, Gentile believers today, like the ancient saints, are **justified by faith and obedience to God**, not by observance of Israel's ceremonial signs.

This is reinforced further by Irenaeus' earlier quote in which he connects **Sabbath-breaking without condemnation** to the identity of believers as **spiritual priests**:

---

[608] Irenaeus of Lyons, *Against Heresies*, Book 4, Chapter 16, Point 2. www.newadvent.org/fathers/0103416.htm

"Now, in the preceding book I have shown that all the disciples of the Lord are Levites and priests, they who used in the temple to profane the Sabbath, but are blameless."[609]

Therefore, Gentile believers are not condemned for not keeping the Sabbath. The **moral fulfillment** of the Sabbath command is daily dedication, abstinence from greed, and faithful perseverance toward the Kingdom, where the true **Sabbath rest** awaits.

Tertullian affirms the same teaching that Gentile believers are **not bound to observe the Sabbath**, showing that from Adam onward, the righteous who pleased God did so **without sabbath observance or circumcision**. He uses powerful examples to underscore that these ceremonial signs were never prerequisites for salvation or righteousness in earlier eras:

"Let him who contends that the Sabbath is still to be observed as a balm of salvation ... consider that God originated Adam uncircumcised, and inobservant of the Sabbath. Consequently, his offspring also, Abel, offering Him sacrifices, uncircumcised and inobservant of the Sabbath, was by Him commended ... Noah also, uncircumcised—yes, and inobservant of the Sabbath—God freed from the deluge. For Enoch too, most righteous man, uncircumcised and inobservant of the Sabbath, He translated from this world; who did not first taste death, in order that, being a candidate for eternal life, he might by this time show us that we also may, without the burden of the law of Moses, please God. Melchizedek also, the priest of the most high God, uncircumcised and inobservant of the Sabbath, was chosen to the priesthood of God."[610]

Justin Martyr of Rome echoes the same doctrine in his famous conversation with Trypho the Jew, stating that Christians **understand the purpose** behind the ceremonial observances and **do not practice them** because they were given for a specific historical reason:

"For we too would observe the fleshly circumcision, and the Sabbaths, and in short all the feasts, if we did not know for what reason they were enjoined you—namely, on account of your

---

[609] Irenaeus of Lyons, *Against Heresies*, Book 5, Chapter 34. www.newadvent.org/fathers/0103534.htm

[610] Tertullian, *An Answer to the Jews*, chapter 2, "The Law Anterior to Moses." www.newadvent.org/fathers/0308.htm

transgressions and the hardness of your hearts. ... How is it, Trypho, that we would not observe those rites which do not harm us—I speak of fleshly circumcision, and Sabbaths, and feasts?"[611]

These statements from two major **Chiliasm-respecting** church fathers—**Tertullian** and **Justin**—affirm that sabbath observance was **never imposed on Gentile believers**. Even more so, they expose the theological error of judging non-Jewish Christians for not observing it. If Sabbath-keeping had been reimposed on Gentiles, even with a change of day to Sunday, the apostles would have stated it plainly, and surely would have issued **a warning of condemnation**. But no such command exists.

The apostle Paul's statement makes this very clear. Rather than reinforcing sabbath-keeping, he warns against allowing others to **judge or burden believers with it**:

> "So let no one judge you in food or in drink, or regarding a festival or a new moon or sabbaths"[612]

This is decisive: **Sabbath-keeping is not a command for Gentile Christians**, and the historic church fathers acknowledged it plainly.[613] The gospel invites believers to **walk daily in holiness and charity**, not in external ceremonial observances which were symbolic shadows of the substance found in Christ.

Let us examine a commonly misunderstood verse:

> "26 For you are all sons of God through faith in Christ Jesus. 27 For as many of you as were baptized into Christ have put on Christ. 28 There is neither Jew nor Greek, there is neither slave nor free, there is neither male nor female; for you are all one in Christ Jesus. 29 And if you are Christ's, then you are Abraham's seed, and heirs according to the promise."[614]

Comments:

---

[611] Justin of Rome, *Dialogue with Trypho*, chapter 18, "Christians would observe the law, if they did not know why it was instituted." www.newadvent.org/fathers/01282.htm

[612] Colossians 2:16 (NKJV)

[613] For broader references against sabbath observance by early church fathers, see: James Richardson, "Quotes From Early Church Fathers: The Sabbath, Lord's Day, and Worship," *Apostles Creed*, August 10, 2016. apostles-creed.org/confessional-reformed-christian-theology/ecclesiology/quotes-from-early-church-fathers-on-the-sabbath-and-the-lords-day/

[614] Galatians 3:26–28 (NKJV).

i) Some Christians appeal to the passage above to argue that there is no longer any distinction between male and female, thereby justifying the ordination of women as priests or pastors.[615] However, Acts 21:21–25 clearly demonstrates that gentile Christians were not regarded as identical to Jewish Christians. This suggests that the statement "There is neither Jew nor Greek" (Galatians 3:28) refers to the future fulfillment of the Abrahamic promise in the resurrection, as shown in Galatians 3:26 and 29, rather than to current earthly distinctions. This interpretation is confirmed by the writings of the **Chiliasm** Church Fathers, who place the fulfillment of the Abrahamic inheritance within the context of Christ's millennial reign. This corrects the error of prosperity gospel theology and other modern interpretations which impose a present-tense equality that contradicts the rest of Scripture.[616]

Irenaeus of Lyons clearly taught—based on the words of Christ, not his own opinion—that material wealth is not an evidence of faith. He affirms that the Abrahamic promise will be fulfilled at the bodily resurrection of believers, when they will be repaid in the millennial reign of Christ with good meals and non-sinful delights on a restored earth. For Irenaeus, the true Sabbath is thus the thousand-year reign of the righteous.[617]

ii) The same apostle Paul who wrote Galatians 3:26–28 also wrote extensively on gender distinctions within the church and in the context of

---

[615] Rebecca M. Groothuis, *Good News for Women: A Biblical Picture of Gender Equality*, (Grand Rapids, Mich.: Baker Books, 1996), 25.

Francois D. Tolmie, "Tendencies in the interpretation of Galatians 3:28 since 1990," *Acta Theologica*, 34 (Suppl. 19), (2014): 119. doi.org/10.4314/actat.v33i2S.6

[616] Eric Gbote and Selaelo Kgatla, "Prosperity gospel: A missiological assessment", *HTS Teologiese Studies / Theological Studies*, 70(1), (2014): 2–3. doi.org/10.4102/hts.v70i1.2105

Kate Bowler, "A Successful Calling: Women, Power, and the Rise of the American Prosperity Gospel", in *Women in Pentecostal and Charismatic Ministry*, (Leiden, The Netherlands: Brill, 2017): 184–185. doi.org/10.1163/9789004332546_016

[617] Irenaeus of Lyons writes, "For what are the hundred-fold [rewards] in this word, the entertainments given to the poor, and the suppers for which a return is made? These are [to take place] in the times of the kingdom, that is, upon the seventh day, which has been sanctified, in which God rested from all the works which He created, which is the true Sabbath of the righteous, which they shall not be engaged in any earthly occupation; but shall have a table at hand prepared for them by God, supplying them with all sorts of dishes. ... The predicted blessing, therefore, belongs unquestionably to the times of the kingdom, when the righteous shall bear rule upon their rising from the dead; when also the creation, having been renovated and set free, shall fructify with an abundance of all kinds of food, from the dew of heaven, and from the fertility of the earth: as the elders who saw John, the disciple of the Lord, related that they had heard from him how the Lord used to teach in regard to these times, and say ..." (*Against Heresies*, book 5, chapter 33, points 2 and 3).

www.newadvent.org/fathers/0103533.htm

marriage. If "male and female" were identical in function and authority now,[618] then how could the husband still be the head, as the New Testament declares?[619] Paul's teaching on male leadership and female submission remains in force and is part of God's intended church order.[620]

For example, women are explicitly forbidden to have spiritual authority over men,[621] which would exclude them from serving as pastors, elders, or bishops. These leadership roles were written with gender-specific qualifications, such as being "the husband of one wife":

> "12 And I do not permit a woman to teach or to have authority over a man, but to be in silence."[622]

Some claim that the verse previously cited applies **only** to marriage.[623] However, consider the logic of this: would God permit a woman pastor to exercise spiritual authority over men outside her household, while denying her such authority over her own husband? If God had intended to establish equal spiritual leadership between genders, surely He would have begun by instituting that equality within the marital relationship. But He did not. Instead, it is written:

> "For the husband is head of the wife, as also Christ is head of the church; and He is the Savior of the body."[624]

Women are further instructed to remain silent in churches specifically in the context of **preaching, theological instruction, or public questioning**—not in worship or singing, which are described using different Greek terms:

---

[618] Amanda A. Slowinski, "Christian Feminism: Female Pastors and Feminism," *Journal of Undergraduate Research at Minnesota State University, Mankato*: Vol. 7, Article 14 (2007). doi.org/10.56816/2378-6949.1101

[619] Jaclyn S. Wong & Allison Daminger, "The Myth of Mutuality: Decision-Making, Marital Power, and the Persistence of Gender Inequality", *Gender & Society*, 38(2), (2024): 157–186. doi.org/10.1177/08912432241230555

[620] 1 Timothy 3:2, 12, "A bishop then must be blameless, the husband of one wife … Let deacons be the husbands of one wife" (NKJV).

[621] Matthew C. Harrison and John T. Pless (Editors), *Women Pastors? The Ordination of Women in Biblical Lutheran Perspective*, (St. Louis: Concordia Publishing House, 2012): 75, 204, 450.

[622] 1 Timothy 2:12 (NKJV).

[623] Daniel Fajar Panuntun and Zulkifli Oddeng, "Vulnerability and Vulnerance: Marginalization of Women in 1 Timothy 2:12–15," *Evangelikal: Jurnal Teologi Injili Dan Pembinaan Warga Jemaat*, 8(2), (2024): 208–209. doi.org/10.46445/ejti.v8i2.841

[624] Ephesians 5:23 (NKJV).

> "33 For God is not the author of confusion but of peace, as in all the churches of the saints. 34 Let your women keep silent in the churches, for they are not permitted to speak; but they are to be submissive, as the law also says. 35 And if they want to learn something, let them ask their own husbands at home; for it is shameful for women to speak in church."[625]

This is not a cultural adaptation.[626] If God's instructions were meant to vary by culture, no command would be needed at all—since each society already has its own view of gender roles. However, God is not bound by human customs. It is we who must conform to **His Word**, not the reverse:

> "... making the word of God of no effect through your tradition which you have handed down. And many such things you do."[627]

Even Galatians 3:28's statement regarding "no more slaves" is clearly referring to the **equality of heavenly reward**, not to a redefinition of social or ecclesiastical structures. The "inheritance" promised in that passage is given in proportion to obedience and suffering borne in this life, as explained here:

> "22 Bondservants, obey in all things your masters according to the flesh, not with eyeservice, as men-pleasers, but in sincerity of heart, fearing God. 23 And whatever you do, do it heartily, as to the Lord and not to men, 24 knowing that from the Lord you will receive the reward of the inheritance; for you serve the Lord Christ. 25 But he who does wrong will be repaid for what he has done, and there is no partiality."[628]

God is not condoning slavery, as some mistakenly argue.[629] Rather, He promises that if a believer suffers unjustly—even under enslavement—He will reward their obedience with the **heavenly inheritance** referenced in Colossians 3:24.

God desires that masters voluntarily release their slaves or treat them justly, which is why He forbids violence and commands ethical treatment. In

---

[625] 1 Corinthians 14:33–35 (NKJV).

[626] Matthew C. Harrison and John T. Pless, *Women Pastors?*, 86, 343.

[627] Mark 7:13 (NKJV).

[628] Colossians 3:22–25 (NKJV).

[629] Jakobus M. Vorster, "The theological-ethical implications of Galatians 3:28 for a Christian perspective on equality as a foundational value in the human rights discourse," *In die Skriflig / In Luce Verbi*, 53(1), (2019): 2, 5, 7. doi.org/10.4102/ids.v53i1.2494

cases where a slave remains bound—especially under a non-Christian master—God promises **heavenly compensation** for the time endured in faithful service. The apostle Paul writes:

> "7 with goodwill doing service, as to the Lord, and not to men, 8 knowing that whatever good anyone does, he will receive the same from the Lord, whether he is a slave or free. 9 And you, masters, do the same things to them, giving up threatening, knowing that your own Master also is in heaven, and there is no partiality with Him."[630]

Therefore, Galatians 3:26–28 does **not** erase the distinct instructions applicable to each social or spiritual category. These distinctions are upheld in other Scriptures. Instead, the reward in heaven will be proportionate to the **obedience demonstrated**—and of even greater worth when one has endured **discrimination or unjust treatment** on earth. As it is written:

> "Behold, to obey is better than sacrifice."[631]

Consider also the following analogy-based reasoning:

If one argues that Christians today must "keep the same standards as Jesus kept," and includes **sabbath observance** within that standard, then logically, all 613 commandments of the Mosaic Law must also apply—since Christ fulfilled them all. However, this reasoning is refuted by several clear scriptural decisions from the apostolic era.

If that standard were true, then the decision recorded in Acts—that **Jewish believers may continue in the Law** (Acts 21:21, 24), but **gentile believers are not bound** to observe its ceremonial parts (Acts 21:25)—would be meaningless, since it would impose one law for all. Likewise, the **Jerusalem Council in Acts 15** would be irrelevant if there were no distinction in application between Jews and gentiles. These observations show that applying Jesus' Torah observance as a universal standard contradicts Scripture.

Further, if one insists on keeping Jesus' standard **including sabbath-keeping**, then **circumcision** must logically follow. Yet, the New Testament directly contradicts this requirement:

Only false teachers demanded that **gentile believers be circumcised** in order to be saved:

---

[630] Ephesians 6:7–9 (NKJV).
[631] 1 Samuel 15:22 (NKJV).

"1 And certain men came down from Judea and taught the brethren, 'Unless you are circumcised according to the custom of Moses, you cannot be saved.'"[632]

But the true apostolic teaching is clear: **circumcision is not required** for gentile believers—neither for **salvation** nor for **reward**:

"2 Indeed I, Paul, say to you that if you become circumcised, Christ will profit you nothing. 3 And I testify again to every man who becomes circumcised that he is a debtor to keep the whole law. 4 You have become estranged from Christ, you who attempt to be justified by law; you have fallen from grace."[633]

Thus, in the understanding of the **Chiliasm church fathers**, the **"good works"** that matter for gentile believers **did not include sabbath observance**, but rather emphasized acts of obedience, faithfulness, and charity in alignment with the teachings of Christ and His apostles.

CHILIASM CHURCH FATHERS DID NOT TEACH TITHING

Irenaeus of Lyons writes that the Lord did not bring up the tithe command toward gentile believers for the new testament. In his quote next, Irenaeus clearly even shows how some laws are extended such as giving to enemies without worrying about their evil intentions to emulate God the father. Also, no compulsion giving is commanded either and so no other replacement type of tithe teaching was observed either since tithing if commanded, becomes mandatory. The interesting thing is Irenaeus testifies that tithing was not commanded but charity doctrine of sharing all our possessions with the poor was commanded not just toward neighbours but to enemies as well and so, the level we do this will determine our gradation in his kingdom too and if it is not done at all or done hypocritically, then the love of God is absent.

"and instead of the law enjoining the giving of tithes, [He told us] to share Matthew 19:21 all our possessions with the poor; and not to love our neighbours only, but even our enemies; and not merely to be liberal givers and bestowers, but even that we should present a gratuitous gift to those who take away our goods. ... so that you may not follow him as a slave, but may as a free man go before him, showing yourself in all things kindly disposed and

---

[632] Acts 15:1 (NKJV).
[633] Galatians 5:2–4 (NKJV).

useful to your neighbour, not regarding their evil intentions, but performing your kind offices, assimilating yourself to the Father, who makes His sun to rise upon the evil and the good, and sends rain upon the just and unjust. Matthew 5:45"[634]

Irenaeus strikes an important point about giving here which is not "not regarding their evil intentions" as the core of Christ's commands here. Thus, if a person uses our giving to do evil, we are not held accountable for it. This issue about giving time and money to causes which are not local church related only but toward community as a whole[635] as Christ's commands here advocates is also important to be a wholesome Christian in this grace as well.[636]

Justin of Rome does not have a surviving quote on tithing directly but also taught that no compulsion giving exists implying naturally that no tithing doctrine seems more likely especially in light of both Irenaeus' quote earlier and Tertullian's quote next too which agrees.

> "And the wealthy among us help the needy … and there is a distribution to each, and a participation of that over which thanks have been given, and to those who are absent a portion is sent by the deacons. And they who are well to do, and willing, give what each thinks fit; and what is collected is deposited with the president, who succours the orphans and widows and those who, through sickness or any other cause, are in want, and those who are in bonds and the strangers sojourning among us, and in a word takes care of all who are in need."[637]

Tertullian clearly describes how the true Christian church was built upon charity doctrine. Church money was collected willingly where no tithes nor any obligatory giving is mentioned. Further, no prosperity gospel type of

---

[634] Irenaeus of Lyons, Against Heresies, book 4, chapter 13, point 3, www.newadvent.org/fathers/0103413.htm

[635] Steve Cheung & Kuah Khun Eng. "Being Christian through External Giving", Religions, (2019): 4-9. doi.org/10.3390/rel10090529

[636] 2 Corinthians 8:2-3,7, "2that in a great trial of affliction the abundance of their joy and their deep poverty abounded in the riches of their liberality. 3For I bear witness that according to their ability, yes, and beyond their ability, they were freely willing, … 7But as you abound in everything—in faith, in speech, in knowledge, in all diligence, and in your love for us—see that you abound in this grace also" (NKJV).

[637] Justin of Rome (Justin Martyr), The First Apology, chapter 67, www.newadvent.org/fathers/0126.htm

buying and selling of gospel things and neither any luxury lifestyle with church money either was lawful for any church leaders in his quote next.

> "The tried men of our elders preside over us, obtaining that honour not by purchase, but by established character. There is no buying and selling of any sort in the things of God. Though we have our treasure chest, it is not made up of purchase-money, as of a religion that has its price. On the monthly day, if he likes, each puts in a small donation; but only if it be his pleasure, and only if he be able: for there is no compulsion; all is voluntary. These gifts are, as it were, piety's deposit fund. For they are not taken thence and spent on feasts, and drinking-bouts, and eating-houses, but to support and bury poor people, to supply the wants of boys and girls destitute of means and parents, and of old persons confined now to the house; such, too, as have suffered shipwreck; and if there happen to be any in the mines, or banished to the islands, or shut up in the prisons, for nothing but their fidelity to the cause of God's Church, they become the nurslings of their confession. But it is mainly the deeds of a love so noble that lead many to put a brand upon us."[638]

Tertullian also clearly writes that it is charity (alms) which God has commanded as more important than tithes since only the former proves the love of God and cleansing context:

> "same God belongs the cleansing of a man's external and internal nature, both alike being in the power of Him who prefers mercy not only to man's washing, but even to sacrifice. For He subjoins the command: Give what you possess as alms, and all things shall be clean unto you. Luke 11:41 … In like manner, He upbraids them for tithing paltry herbs, but at the same time passing over hospitality and the love of God. Luke 11:42 The vocation and the love of what God, but Him by whose law of tithes they used to offer their rue and mint? For the whole point of the rebuke lay in this, that they cared about small matters in His service of course, to whom they failed to exhibit their weightier duties when He commanded them:"[639]

---

[638] Tertullian, Apology, chapter 39, www.newadvent.org/fathers/0301.htm
[639] Tertullian, Against Marcion, book 4, chapter 27, www.newadvent.org/fathers/03124.htm

The "good works" context understood by these chiliasm church fathers did not involve tithes doctrine either for Christians but involved charity doctrine with holiness to become one of the 5 wise virgins which makes it perfect.

CONCLUSION

It is worth noting that the father of the reformation, Martin Luther also did not believe in sabbath-keeping nor tithing as good works either as he wrote,

> "Tithing: But the other commandments of Moses, which are not [implanted in all men] by nature, the Gentiles do not hold. Nor do these pertain to the Gentiles, such as the tithe and others equally fine which I wish we had too. ... Sabbath: Again one can prove it from the third commandment that Moses does not pertain to Gentiles and Christians".[640]

The Augsburg Confession reads likewise:

> "Col. 2:16: Let no man, therefore, judge you in meat, or in drink, or in respect of an holy-day, or of the Sabbath-day; ... as of matrimony or of tithes, etc., they have it by human right ... For those who judge that by the authority of the Church the observance of the Lord's Day instead of the Sabbath-day was ordained as a thing necessary, 59 do greatly err ... example of Christian liberty, and might know that the keeping neither of the Sabbath nor of any other day is necessary."[641]

Notice when the Augsburg Confession was written, tithes were not collected by individual pastors but rather by the government which shared only a little with the church[642] meaning it involved secular spending and not a solely religious one in contrast to today's practice.

---

[640] Martin Luther, "How Christians Should Regard Moses," trans. and ed. by E. Theodore Bachmann, Luther's Works: Word and Sacrament I, vol. 35 (Philadelphia: Muhlenberg Press, 1960), 161-174. This sermon was preached on August 27, 1525. www.wordofhisgrace.org/LutherMoses.htm

[641] Robert Kolb and Timothy J. Wengert, eds. Article XXVI of the Distinction of Meats & Article XXVIII Of Ecclesiastical Power. In The Book of Concord: The Confessions of the Evangelical Lutheran Church. Minneapolis: Fortress Press, 2000.

bookofconcord.org/augsburg-confession/

[642] Matthew Vester. "Who Benefited from Tithe Revenues in Late-Renaissance Bresse?", The Catholic Historical Review, 96, no. 1 (2010): 1-26. doi.org/10.1353/cat.0.0596

ESSAYS IN EARLY CHRISTIANITY

By God's Grace, we can strive to be one of the 5 wise virgins instead of the 5 foolish virgins by understanding and following what the giants of faith have written by quoting the Bible verses here which includes chiefly the chiliasm church fathers and protestant reformers who all agree on holiness via abstinence of sin together with charity doctrine as the primary good works for love in action so that the Holy Spirit of God lives in us.

BIBLIOGRAPHY

Adam Mukabva. "The Parable of the Ten Virgins: Matthew 25:1-13", *DARE : Holy Trinity College Journal*, 12 (2023): 50-59.

journals.cuz.ac.zw/index.php/dare/article/view/286

Amanda A. Slowinski. "Christian Feminism: Female Pastors and Feminism," *Journal of Undergraduate Research at Minnesota State University, Mankato*: Vol. 7, Article 14, (2007). doi.org/10.56816/2378-6949.1101

Augustine of Hippo. *On the Spirit and the Letter*. Translated by Peter Holmes and Robert Ernest Wallis, and revised by Benjamin B. Warfield. From Nicene and Post-Nicene Fathers, First Series, Vol. 5. Edited by Philip Schaff. (Buffalo, NY: Christian Literature Publishing Co., 1887).

Allan Anderson. *An Introduction to Pentecostalism: Global Charismatic Christianity*. (Cambridge: Cambridge University Press, 2004).

Bible. biblehub.com

Christopher A. Stephenson. "Un-Speaking in Tongues: Glossolalia as Ascetical Prayer". *Journal of Spiritual Formation and Soul Care*, 13(1), (2019): 88-101. doi.org/10.1177/1939790919893278

Craig L. Blomberg & Sung Wook Chung. Eds., *A Case for Historic Premillennialism. An Alternative to "Left Behind" Eschatology*. (Grand Rapids: Baker, 2008).

Ellen F. Davis and Sarah Musser. "Prophecy, Interpretation, and Social Criticism". In *St Andrews Encyclopaedia of Theology*, edited by Brendan N. Wolfe et al. University of St Andrews, (2022–. Article published July 27, 2023). www.saet.ac.uk/Christianity/ProphecyInterpretationandSocialCriticism

Eric Gbote and Selaelo Kgatla. "Prosperity gospel: A missiological assessment", *HTS Teologiese Studies / Theological Studies*, 70(1), (2014): 01-10. doi.org/10.4102/hts.v70i1.2105

Francois D. Tolmie, "Tendencies in the interpretation of Galatians 3:28 since 1990", *Acta Theologica*, 34 (Suppl. 19), (2014): 105-129.

doi.org/10.4314/actat.v33i2S.6

Frank Small. *Living Waters*. Ed. Vol. 1, No.1. (Winnipeg: Old Knox Church, 1918).

Friedrich Justus Knecht. "LXI. The Parable of the Ten Virgins". In *A Practical Commentary on Holy Scripture*. (B. Herder – Publisher to the Holy Apostolic See, 1910).

GotQuestions.org. "GotQuestions.org", March 14, 2025.

www.gotquestions.org/Ten-Commandments-New-Testament.html

Irenaeus of Lyons. *Against Heresies*. Translated by Alexander Roberts and William Rambaut. From Ante-Nicene Fathers, Vol. 1. Edited by Alexander Roberts, James Donaldson, and A. Cleveland Coxe. (Buffalo, NY: Christian Literature Publishing Co., 1885).

Irenaeus of Lyons. *Fragments from the Lost Writings of Irenæus*, XXXVIII. Translated by Alexander Roberts. From Ante-Nicene Fathers, Vol. 1. Edited by Alexander Roberts, James Donaldson, and A. Cleveland Coxe. (Buffalo, NY: Christian Literature Publishing Co., 1885).

J. C. Harrod, "The Neglected Discipline of Almsgiving", *Journal of Spiritual Formation and Soul Care*, 12(1), (2018): 89-111.

doi.org/10.1177/1939790918812460

Jaclyn S. Wong & Allison Daminger, "The Myth of Mutuality: Decision-Making, Marital Power, and the Persistence of Gender Inequality", *Gender & Society*, 38(2), (2024): 157-186. doi.org/10.1177/08912432241230555

Jakobus M. Vorster, "The theological-ethical implications of Galatians 3:28 for a Christian perspective on equality as a foundational value in the human rights discourse", *In die Skriflig /In Luce Verbi*, 53(1), (2019): 1-9. doi.org/10.4102/ids.v53i1.2494

James Richardson. "Quotes From Early Church Fathers: The Sabbath, Lord's Day, and Worship - Apostles Creed." Apostles Creed, August 10,

2016. apostles-creed.org/confessional-reformed-christian-theology/ecclesiology/quotes-from-early-church-fathers-on-the-sabbath-and-the-lords-day/

John Calvin. *Calvin's Commentaries*. (Faithlife; Westminster, 1851–2010).

John Calvin. *Institutes*. Edited by John T. McNeill. (Westminster John Knox Press, 1 Jan 1960).

ESSAYS IN EARLY CHRISTIANITY

John F. Pollard. *The Vatican and Italian Fascism, 1929–32: A Study in Conflict.* (Cambridge: Cambridge University Press, 2014): 109–111.

John Wesley. *John Wesley's Notes on the Bible.* (Christian Classics Ethereal Library, 2011).

John Wolffe. "A Comparative Historical Categorisation of Anti-Catholicism". In Special Issue: Transnational Approaches to the History of anti-Catholicism in the Modern Era. Edited by Timothy Verhoeven. *Journal of Religious History,* 39.2 (2015): 182–202. doi.org/10.1111/1467-9809.12182

Justin of Rome (Justin Martyr). *Dialogue with Trypho.* Translated by Marcus Dods and George Reith. From Ante-Nicene Fathers, Vol. 1. Edited by Alexander Roberts, James Donaldson, and A. Cleveland Coxe. (Buffalo, NY: Christian Literature Publishing Co., 1885).

Justin of Rome (Justin Martyr). *The First Apology.* Translated by Marcus Dods and George Reith. From Ante-Nicene Fathers, Vol. 1. Edited by Alexander Roberts, James Donaldson, and A. Cleveland Coxe. (Buffalo, NY: Christian Literature Publishing Co., 1885).

K. Paul Donfried. "The Allegory of the Ten Virgins (Matt 25:1-13) as a Summary of Matthean Theology", *Journal of Biblical Literature (JBL),* 93 (3), (1974): 415-428. doi.org/10.2307/3263387

Kate Bowler. "A Successful Calling: Women, Power, and the Rise of the American Prosperity Gospel". In *Women in Pentecostal and Charismatic Ministry*, (Leiden, The Netherlands: Brill, 2017).

Landocalvinian. "WCF CHAPTER 21: of Religious Worship, and the Sabbath Day 21.5 – 21.8 : The Westminster Standards With Video and Audio Teaching Resources," n.d. thewestminsterstandards.com/wcf-chapter-21-of-religious-worship-and-the-sabbath-day-21-5-21-8/

Luke Tyerman. *Life and Times of Wesley.* Volume III. (Harper & Bros; 1872).

Matthew C. Harrison and John T. Pless (Editors). *Women Pastors? The Ordination of Women in Biblical Lutheran Perspective.* (St. Louis: Concordia Publishing House, 2012).

Martin Luther, "How Christians Should Regard Moses," trans. and ed. by E. Theodore Bachmann, *Luther's Works: Word and Sacrament I*, vol. 35 (Philadelphia: Muhlenberg Press, 1960).

Martin Luther. *Sermon On Faith and Good Works.* Preached in Erfurt at St. Michaeliskirche on the day of the 11,000 virgins (October 21st, 1522).

Translated by Rev. Paul A. Rydecki (2013). www.godwithuslc.org/luther-sermon-for-trinity-27/

Matthew Vester. "Who Benefited from Tithe Revenues in Late-Renaissance Bresse?", *The Catholic Historical Review*, 96, no. 1 (2010): 1-26. doi.org/10.1353/cat.0.0596

Methodius of Olympus. *Banquet of the Ten Virgins*. Translated by William R. Clark. From Ante-Nicene Fathers, Vol. 6. Edited by Alexander Roberts, James Donaldson, and A. Cleveland Coxe. (Buffalo, NY: Christian Literature Publishing Co., 1886).

Mihai Androne. "The Five Solas". In *Martin Luther*. (SpringerBriefs in Education, Springer, Cham, 2020). doi.org/10.1007/978-3-030-52418-0_2

Ogunlusi Clement Temitope, "Prosperity Gospel Preaching and its Implications on National Developments", *International Journal of Humanities and Cultural Studies*, 5(1), (June 2018): 320-321.

ijhcs.com/index.php/IJHCS/article/viewFile/223/207

Orthodox Catechism Project. "Parables Bible Study 8: the Ten Virgins - Orthodox Catechism Project", n.d. www.orthodoxcatechismproject.org/complete-title-list-n-z/-/asset_publisher/lSHf6HfdOOeQ/content/parables-bible-study-8-the-ten-virgins.

Panuntun, Daniel Fajar, and Zulkifli Oddeng, "Vulnerability and Vulnerance: Marginalization of Women in 1 Timothy 2:12-15", *Evangelikal: Jurnal Teologi Injili Dan Pembinaan Warga Jemaat*, 8 (2), (2024): 203-219. doi.org/10.46445/ejti.v8i2.841

R. J. Bauckham. "The Lord's Day" and "Sabbath and Sunday in the Postapostolic Church". In *From Sabbath to Lord's Day*, ed. D. A. Carson. (Grand Rapids: Zondervan, 1982).

R. Ward Holder. "The Reformers and Tradition: Seeing the Roots of the Problem", *Religions,* 8, no. 6 (2017):105. doi.org/10.3390/rel8060105

Rebecca M. Groothuis, *Good News for Women: a Biblical Picture of Gender Equality*, (Grand Rapids, Mich.: Baker Books, 1996).

Robert Kolb and Timothy J. Wengert, eds. *The Book of Concord: The Confessions of the Evangelical Lutheran Church*. Minneapolis: Fortress Press, 2000.

Stephen Williams, "Jesus is Coming Soon: Toward Revisioning Pentecostal Eschatology for Postmodern Ministry and Mission", *Vanguard*

Journal of Theology and Ministry, Volume 01, No. 2 (2022): 28- 39. vjtm.vanguardcollege.com/index.php/vjtm/article/view/49

Steve Cheung & Kuah Khun Eng. "Being Christian through External Giving", *Religions,* (2019): 4-9. doi.org/10.3390/rel10090529

Sutri, Yerlin & Bobby Putrawan. "The History of the Reformation of the Church in the 16th Century and Its Influence on the Church Today", *Journal of Religious and Socio-Cultural*, 2, (2021): 109-122.

doi.org/10.46362/jrsc.v2i2.84

Thomas Aquinas. *St. Thomas Aquinas: Catena Aurea - Gospel Of Matthew*. Translated by John Henry Parker, v. I, J.G.F. and J. Rivington. (London, 1842).

Tertullian. *An Answer to the Jews*. Translated by S. Thelwall. From Ante-Nicene Fathers, Vol. 3. Edited by Alexander Roberts, James Donaldson, and A. Cleveland Coxe. (Buffalo, NY: Christian Literature Publishing Co., 1885).

Tertullian. *Against Marcion*. Translated by Peter Holmes. From Ante-Nicene Fathers, Vol. 3. Edited by Alexander Roberts, James Donaldson, and A. Cleveland Coxe. (Buffalo, NY: Christian Literature Publishing Co., 1885).

Tertullian. *Apology*. Translated by S. Thelwall. From Ante-Nicene Fathers, Vol. 3. Edited by Alexander Roberts, James Donaldson, and A. Cleveland Coxe. (Buffalo, NY: Christian Literature Publishing Co., 1885).

Tertullian. *On Modesty ("De pudicitia")*. Translated by S. Thelwall. From Ante-Nicene Fathers, Vol. 4. Edited by Alexander Roberts, James Donaldson, and A. Cleveland Coxe. (Buffalo, NY: Christian Literature Publishing Co., 1885).

Tertullian. *On the Resurrection of the Flesh*. Translated by Peter Holmes. From Ante-Nicene Fathers, Vol. 3. Edited by Alexander Roberts, James Donaldson, and A. Cleveland Coxe. (Buffalo, NY: Christian Literature Publishing Co., 1885).

Vukelić Jelisaveta & Stanojević Dragan, "Who should take care of the poor? Religion and social welfare in America", *Filozofija i drustvo,* Volume 25, Issue 2, (Serbia, 2014): 137-156. doi.org/10.2298/FID1402137V

Wolfgang Vondey, "Soteriology at the Altar: Pentecostal Contributions to Salvation as Praxis". *Transformation: An International Journal of Holistic Mission Studies*, 34(3), (2016): 223-238. doi.org/10.1177/0265378816675831

Jonathan Ramachandran

Essay 8: Did Christ Imply Non-Elect Salvation in Matthew 19:16-22?

ABSTRACT

Matthew 19 contains the principal response by Christ for eternal life context. This passage illustrates what to believe and do to be saved. Christian doctrine of soteriology is derived from its content in regard to Christ's commandments as fruits for immortality. However, this paper seeks to see if we may understand Christ's words here to mean two types of salvation, namely elect vs non-elect salvation which may open up a possibility for some non-Christians to be saved with a much lower grade salvation.

CHRISTIAN SALVATION IN MATTHEW 19:16-22

Here's a sample scholarly translation for this text:

> "16Now behold, one came and said to Him, "Good[d] Teacher, what good thing shall I do that I may have eternal life?" 17So He said to him, [e]"Why do you call Me good? [f]No one is good but One, that is, God. But if you want to enter into life, keep the commandments." 18He said to Him, "Which ones?" Jesus said, "'You shall not murder,' 'You shall not commit adultery,' 'You shall not steal,' 'You shall not bear false witness,' 19'Honor your father and your mother,' and, 'You shall love your neighbor as yourself.'" 20The young man said to Him, "All these things I have kept [g]from my youth. What do I still lack?" 21Jesus said to him, "If you want to be perfect, go, sell what you have and give to the poor, and you will have treasure in heaven; and come, follow Me." 22But when the young man heard that saying, he went away sorrowful, for he had great possessions."[643]

A way to understand these verses is to look at the summary given at the end of that discussion in Matthew 19 itself[644] and map everything else to its

---

[643] Matthew 19:16-22 (NKJV).

[644] Matthew 19:28-30, "28So Jesus said to them, "Assuredly I say to you, that in the regeneration, when the Son of Man sits on the throne of His glory, you who have followed Me will also sit on twelve thrones, judging the twelve tribes of Israel. 29And everyone who has left houses or brothers or sisters or father or mother [h]or wife or children or [i]lands, for My name's sake, shall receive a hundredfold, and inherit eternal life. 30But many who are first will be last, and the last first." (NKJV).

context. The common ground which is affirmed by all Christians is that "there are requirements for entry into the kingdom" and "one must repent for the sins that were committed over one's lifetime".[645] So, more obedience is expected to get a greater reward in heaven.[646] Also, having "eternal life" and having "treasure in heaven" is seen as two distinct objects[647] where the former is free while the latter is by reward.

Christ speaks of holiness as the command for life here and it's interesting to note that "Jesus quoted those commandments that relate to our relationship with other people"[648] and that this rich man's "lack of generosity and love for others"[649] is already sin (implied) and that's why Christ commands him the "perfection" of sell all and give to the poor to demonstrate the sinless state in financial holiness context. In light of the future resurrection context mentioned in Matthew 19:28,[650] Christians are to those who obeyed these passages and are thus raised to life to reign with him during his second coming.[651] New believers enter a process to obtain "eternal life" which begins by believing in Jesus and "go on to follow Christ as dedicated disciples".[652]

Absolute assurance believers assert that Christians will attain eternal life regardless of fall in sin as long as they believe in Christ and the difference will be that some Christians will get rewards for faithfulness while others will not.[653] MacArthur confronts such a view and warns that not all who profess Christ for a limited time are really Christians stating, "lest the day come when, like the people of John 6:66, they walk no more with him, and like Judas, they

---

[645] Michael Koplitz, "Hebraic Analysis for Matthew 19:27-30", (2020): 20. DOI.org/10.13140/RG.2.2.27636.58243.

[646] Ibid., 22.

[647] Matthew Paul Earnhardt, "Exegetical Study of Matthew 19:16-26", in The American Journal of Biblical Theology (AJBT), (March 10, 2023): 3.

www.biblicaltheology.com/Research/EarnhardtMP01.pdf

[648] John W. (Jack) Carter, "The Cost of Discipleship", in The American Journal of Biblical Theology (AJBT), Volume 26(12), (March 3, 2025): 5.

www.biblicaltheology.com/printerfriendly.pdf

[649] Ibid., 6.

[650] Matthew 19:28, "So Jesus said to them, "Assuredly I say to you, that in the regeneration, when the Son of Man sits on the throne of His glory, you who have followed Me will also sit on twelve thrones, judging the twelve tribes of Israel." (NKJV).

[651] Robert Vacendak, "Is assurance of salvation of the essence of saving faith in the Gospel of John?", PhD diss., (Rawlings School of Divinity, Liberty University, USA, April 2023): 121. digitalcommons.liberty.edu/cgi/viewcontent.cgi?article=5359&context=doctoral

[652] Ibid., 135.

[653] Ibid., 210.

go to the place of everlasting judgment reserved for such traitors".[654] Calvinists warn of cultural Christians who profess Christ with their lips but deny him by their unholy lifestyle.[655] Even regular church attenders may find themselves to be unsaved unless they persevere in a living faith with works as Inserra serves this sharp rebuke containing the elements of Matthew 19:16-22 here as, "self-proclaimed Christians who worship a god that requires no self-sacrifice, no obedience, no submission, and no surrender are not worshiping the God of the Bible, no matter how much they claim they love Jesus".[656]

FINANCIAL HOLINESS AS CHRISTIAN PERFECTION IN MATTHEW 19:16-22

We find Christ making a startling invitation toward perfection[657] where a financial command toward giving to the poor was given to a rich man who generally kept the major parts of the Torah well but yet he was "lacking in this" (Matt. 19:20). The perfection commands of Christ extend to other areas of life[658] and not in finance only which is chiefly seen with the "beatitudes"[659] listed in the famous "sermon on the mount".[660]

Christians have struggled with its meaning since it's a whole big list of do and don'ts listed in chapters from Matthew 5 to 7 and some have been content to find its meaning as "achieving the purpose for which they are

---

[654] John MacArthur, Hard to Believe: The High Cost and Infinite Value of Following Jesus, (Nashville, TN: Nelson, 2003): 182.

[655] Justin of Rome, "And let those who are not found living as He taught, be understood to be no Christians, even though they profess with the lip the precepts of Christ; for not those who make profession, but those who do the works, shall be saved" ("Chapter 16", in The First Apology, translated by Marcus Dods and George Reith, from Ante-Nicene Fathers, Vol. 1, edited by Alexander Roberts, James Donaldson, and A. Cleveland Coxe. (Buffalo, NY: Christian Literature Publishing Co., 1885)). www.newadvent.org/fathers/0126.htm

[656] Dean Inserra, The Unsaved Christian: Reaching Cultural Christianity with the Gospel, (Moody Publishers, 2019): 38.

[657] Gerald O'Collins SJ, "Difficult texts: being made perfect according to Matthew 5 and 19", Theology, 124(6), (2021): 404-409. doi.org/10.1177/0040571X211056790

[658] Reinhard Feldmeier, "As Your Heavenly Father is Perfect: The God of the Bible and Commandments in the Gospel", in Interpretation, 70(4), (2016): 431-444. doi.org/10.1177/0020964316655109

[659] Dinh Van Chien, "Humanistic Thought in Jesus' Sermon on The Eight Beatens", in Pakistan Journal of Life and Social Sciences (Pak. j. life soc. Sci.), 2024, 22(2): 15166. doi.org/10.57239/PJLSS-2024-22.2.001095

[660] Carl G. Vaught, The Sermon on the Mount: A Theological Interpretation, (SUNY Press., 1986): 7-10.

intended to live" which varies from person to person.⁶⁶¹ Humans have struggled with the very concept of perfection studying it through the lens of secular thoughts to even Jewish cultural thoughts⁶⁶² in order to understand Christ's meaning of it. Any research using non-Christian views (even Jewish traditions) must be cautiously approached lest we regress into their errors because often times Christ has been correcting ancient misconceptions⁶⁶³ especially in his famous "you have heard it was said, … but I say to you" statements.⁶⁶⁴

In the money aspect, Korver makes it clear that "what Jesus said in Matthew 19:21 was concerning treasure in heaven not entrance into heaven".⁶⁶⁵ However, this superficial reading is dangerous unless one recognizes that if we likewise ignore helping the poor, we could end up in hell likewise. So, the difference in reward level argument does not negate the financial holiness requirement without which one cannot be saved either being a Christian who has not love. This idea is well expounded in the church fathers first and in reformers next too. The concept of Hell derived from Luke 16:19-31 which includes the financial context as well has been debated

---

⁶⁶¹ Gerald L. Borchert, "Matthew 5:48 - Perfection and the Sermon", Review & Expositor, 89(2), (1992): 265. doi.org/10.1177/003463739208900208

⁶⁶² Leslie Stevenson, "On the very idea of perfection", International Journal of Philosophy and Theology, 85(3–4), (2024): 111-123.
doi.org/10.1080/21692327.2024.2417091

⁶⁶³ Will Herberg, "Judaism and Christianity: Their Unity and Difference. The Double Covenant in the Divine Economy of Salvation", Journal of Bible and Religion, 21(2), (1953): 67–78. www.jstor.org/stable/1458587

⁶⁶⁴ Matthew 5:21-22, 27-28, 33-34, 38-39, 43-44, "21"You have heard that it was said to those [d]of old, 'You shall not murder, and whoever murders will be in danger of the judgment.' 22But I say to you that whoever is angry with his brother [e]without a cause shall be in danger of the judgment. 27"You have heard that it was said [i]to those of old, 'You shall not commit adultery.' 28But I say to you that whoever looks at a woman to lust for her has already committed adultery with her in his heart. 33"Again you have heard that it was said to those of [m]old, 'You shall not swear falsely, but shall perform your oaths to the Lord.' 34But I say to you, do not swear at all: neither by heaven, for it is God's throne; 38"You have heard that it was said, 'An eye for an eye and a tooth for a tooth.' 39But I tell you not to resist an evil person. But whoever slaps you on your right cheek, turn the other to him also. 43"You have heard that it was said, 'You shall love your neighbor and hate your enemy.' 44[o]But I say to you, love your enemies, bless those who curse you, do good to those who hate you, and pray for those who spitefully use you and persecute you," (NKJV).

⁶⁶⁵ Bill Fredric Korver, "Biblical use of rewards as a motivation for Christian service", PhD diss., (Liberty University, USA, August 2011): 46.
digitalcommons.liberty.edu/cgi/viewcontent.cgi?article=1495&context=doctoral

especially from the Jewish perspective to either contradict it[666] or to support it.[667]

Church fathers saw this parable as a real life event. Irenaeus (c.130-202) includes the reason for the rich man's condemnation to hades as being unmerciful to poor Lazarus.[668] Apostle James has warned that luxurious living without helping the poor in the context of hoarding earthly treasures leads to hell[669] and this is echoed likewise in Irenaeus.[670] Tertullian (c.155-220) gives a clever response to philosophers who think that this story is imaginary or a parable only by stating that even a made up story to illustrate a lesson must use real life elements and not things which do not exist which in turn, implies that such a place for torment in the afterlife is real.[671] Christ's

---

[666] Yusak Tanasyah, "The Development of Hell from Jewish to Christian Theology: A Biblical Guide to Hell and Its Existence", QUAERENS: Journal of Theology and Christianity Studies, 4 (1), (2022): 27-41. DOI.org/10.46362/quaerens.v4i1.80

[667] Jordan P. Ballard, "Defending the Doctrine of Hell", Eleutheria: John W. Rawlings School of Divinity Academic Journal, 8(2), (2025).

digitalcommons.liberty.edu/eleu/vol8/iss2/5

[668] Irenaeus of Lyons writes, "that Dives knew Lazarus after death, and Abraham in like manner, and that each one of these persons continued in his own proper position, and that [Dives] requested Lazarus to be sent to relieve him — [Lazarus], on whom he did not [formerly] bestow even the crumbs [which fell] from his table ... moreover, that the gift of prophecy was possessed by Abraham, and that each class [of souls] receives a habitation such as it has deserved, even before the judgment" ("Book 2. Chapter 34. Point 1.", in Against Heresies). www.newadvent.org/fathers/0103234.htm

[669] James 5:1-3, 5, "1Come now, you rich, weep and howl for your miseries that are coming upon you! 2Your riches [a]are corrupted, and your garments are moth-eaten. 3Your gold and silver are corroded, and their corrosion will be a witness against you and will eat your flesh like fire. You have heaped up treasure in the last days. 5You have lived on the earth in pleasure and [c]luxury;" (NKJV).

[670] Irenaeus of Lyons writes, "Now, He has not merely related to us a story respecting a poor man and a rich one; but He has taught us, in the first place, that no one should lead a luxurious life, nor, living in worldly pleasures and perpetual feastings, should be the slave of his lusts, and forget God. For there was, He says, a rich man, who was clothed in purple and fine linen, and delighted himself with splendid feasts." ("Book 4. Chapter 2. Point 4.", in Against Heresies). www.newadvent.org/fathers/0103402.htm

[671] Tertullian writes, "In hell the soul of a certain man is in torment, punished in flames, suffering excruciating thirst, and imploring from the finger of a happier soul, for his tongue, the solace of a drop of water. Luke 16:23-24 Do you suppose that this end of the blessed poor man and the miserable rich man is only imaginary? Then why the name of Lazarus in this narrative, if the circumstance is not in (the category of) a real occurrence? But even if it is to be regarded as imaginary, it will still be a testimony to truth and reality." ("Chapter 7", in A Treatise on the Soul, translated by Peter Holmes, from Ante-Nicene Fathers, Vol. 3, edited by Alexander Roberts, James Donaldson, and A. Cleveland Coxe. (Buffalo, NY: Christian Literature Publishing Co., 1885)). www.newadvent.org/fathers/0310.htm

particular mention of the real person Abraham is used by Tertullian to defend that these are actual and not dreamy ideas.[672] Indeed, Christ would not need to warn of a place like that and the reason for ignoring the poor if it was not so. Tertullian also affirms that lack of hospitality toward the poor can also cause bishops to be condemned in hell-fire as part of the message of "Moses and the prophets" meant in this principal passage.[673]

In light of the rich man who went to hell in Luke 16:19-31, father of the reformation Martin Luther (1483–1546) wrote that "it is not enough to 'depart from evil;' one must also 'do good'"[674] while John Calvin (1509–1564), the premier theologian for the reformed western world plainly stated that the rich man went to hell primarily for "refusing to raise a finger to help the poor man".[675]

Let's revisit the question as to why Christ pointed to financial perfection as living penniless? They who live in financial renunciation are free from the sin of not giving money to the poor because they only live by taking needs and do not keep any surplus hoarded for self[676] and so, cannot be blamed in any scenario for not giving out more since they don't have any extra.[677] God's perfection calls it sin even when we don't do any good that we are able in all areas of life[678] which includes even the financial context where we are already sinning whenever we do not give what we can to the poor.

---

[672] Ibid., "Chapter 57".

[673] Tertullian writes, "These will be warnings both to people and to bishops, even spiritual ones, in case they may ever have been guilty of incontinence of appetite. Nay, even in Hades the admonition has not ceased to speak; where we find in the person of the rich feaster, convivialities tortured; in that of the pauper, fasts refreshed; having — (as convivialities and fasts alike had)— as preceptors Moses and the prophets." ("Chapter 16", in On Fasting, translated by S. Thelwall, from Ante-Nicene Fathers, Vol. 4, edited by Alexander Roberts, James Donaldson, and A. Cleveland Coxe. (Buffalo, NY: Christian Literature Publishing Co., 1885). www.newadvent.org/fathers/0408.htm

[674] Thomas R. Shepherd, "The Parable of the Rich Man and Lazarus: A Narrative-Exegetical Study of Its Relationship to the Afterlife, Wealth, and Poverty–Part 1: The Afterlife", in Journal of the Adventist Theological Society, 32/1-2 (2021): 175. digitalcommons.andrews.edu/cgi/viewcontent.cgi?article=1621&context=jats

[675] Ibid.

[676] Luke 12:21, "So is he who lays up treasure for himself, and is not rich toward God." (NKJV).

[677] Acts 3:6, "Peter said, "Silver and gold I do not have,"" (NKJV).

[678] James 4:17, "Therefore, to him who knows to do good and does not do it, to him it is sin." (NKJV).

This is a reason why the first new testament church had all its earthly possessions in common[679] and since we cannot live like that due to other practical reasons like that today, we just give what we can by relative measure.[680] True unity of the church involves financial giving aspect since only then we are loving others as ourself which is part of fulfilling the greatest commands of God[681] by spending equally on both self and others as much as possible[682] instead of other prevalent human ways which teach to spend more for self-indulgences[683] while giving least to others[684] despite being outwardly holy.[685] It is also worth noting since love of God in action requires the sharing of this world's goods (be it spiritual goods[686] or physical goods[687]) as a

---

[679] Acts 2:44, "Now all who believed were together, and had all things in common," (NKJV).

[680] Luke 21:3-4, "Truly I [Jesus] say to you that this poor widow has put in more than all; 4for all these out of their abundance have put in offerings [b]for God, but she out of her poverty put in all the livelihood that she had." (NKJV).

[681] Mark 12:29-31, "29Jesus answered him, "The [k]first of all the commandments is: 'Hear, O Israel, the Lord our God, the Lord is one. 30And you shall love the Lord your God with all your heart, with all your soul, with all your mind, and with all your strength.' [l]This is the first commandment. 31And the second, like it, is this: 'You shall love your neighbor as yourself.' There is no other commandment greater than these." (NKJV).

[682] Luke 10:25, 33-37, "25And behold, a certain [h]lawyer stood up and tested Him, saying, "Teacher, what shall I do to inherit eternal life?" ... 33But a certain Samaritan, as he journeyed, came where he was. And when he saw him, he had compassion. 34So he went to him and bandaged his wounds, pouring on oil and wine; and he set him on his own animal, brought him to an inn, and took care of him. 35On the next day, [j]when he departed, he took out two denarii, gave them to the innkeeper, and said to him, 'Take care of him; and whatever more you spend, when I come again, I will repay you.' 36So which of these three do you think was neighbor to him who fell among the thieves?" 37And he said, "He who showed mercy on him." Then Jesus said to him, "Go and do likewise."'" (NKJV).

[683] Luke 11:39-41, "39Then the Lord said to him, "Now you Pharisees make the outside of the cup and dish clean, but your inward part is full of [k]greed and wickedness. 40Foolish ones! Did not He who made the outside make the inside also? 41But rather give alms of [l]such things as you have; then indeed all things are clean to you." (NKJV).

[684] Revelation 3:17, "Because you say, 'I am rich, have become wealthy, and have need of nothing'—and do not know that you are wretched, miserable, poor, blind, and naked" (NKJV).

[685] Matthew 23:25, "Woe to you, scribes and Pharisees, hypocrites! For you cleanse the outside of the cup and dish, but inside they are full of extortion and self-indulgence." (NKJV).

[686] 1 Corinthians 9:14-15, 18, "14Even so the Lord has commanded that those who preach the gospel should live from the gospel. 15But I have used none of these things, 18What is my reward then? That when I preach the gospel, I may present the gospel [d]of Christ without charge" (NKJV).

[687] Luke 12:33, "Sell what you have and give alms; ... a treasure in the heavens that does not fail" (NKJV).

tangible expression of it,[688] a person who lacks in almsgiving may thus be living in sin in this context and hence, is unsaved as the story of the rich man and Lazarus[689] demonstrates earlier.

Human greed can be observed in worldly men who have not Christ and find it strange that Christians are generous to both believers and unbelievers[690] (even enemies)[691] which sounds foolish to them.[692] John Chrysostom (c.347-407) wrote that charity doctrine[693] hits a higher mark than virginity[694] while correcting the error of some who thought that fasting and prayer is more important than almsgiving. The opposite is true since Chrysostom ranks the choirs of virtue as does Christ here in Matthew 19:21 calling only the virtue of almsgiving as a requirement for "perfection" as prophets like Isaiah have echoed likewise in the past.[695]

In fact, charitable giving is called one of the gift of grace in Scripture and is the only virtue which is profoundly praised when done "beyond one's ability" especially when one is poor too.[696] This is due to the fact that to earn

---

[688] 1 John 3:17.

[689] Luke 16:19-31.

[690] Galatians 6:10, "let us do good to all, especially to those who are of the household of faith." (NKJV).

[691] Luke 6:32-35, "if you love those who love you, what credit is that to you? ... if you do good to those who do good to you, what credit is that to you? ... if you lend to those from whom you hope to receive back, what credit is that to you? ... But love your enemies, do good, and lend, [h]hoping for nothing in return;" (NKJV).

[692] Carter, "Cost of Discipleship", 7.

[693] Charity doctrine refers to any new testament commands relating to almsgiving or those done for free. Matthew 10:8, "Freely you have received, freely give" (NKJV).

[694] John Chrysostom writes, "And all this I say, not to depreciate fasting, God forbid, but rather highly to commend it. But I grieve when other duties being neglected, you think it enough for salvation, having but the last place in the choir of virtue. For the greatest thing is charity, and moderation, and almsgiving; which hits a higher mark even than virginity. Wherefore, if you desire to become equal to the apostles, there is nothing to hinder you. For to have arrived at this virtue only suffices for your not at all falling short of them. Let no one therefore wait for miracles." ("Point 4" in Homily 46 on Matthew, translated by George Prevost and revised by M.B. Riddle, from Nicene and Post-Nicene Fathers, First Series, Vol. 10, edited by Philip Schaff, (Buffalo, NY: Christian Literature Publishing Co., 1888)). www.newadvent.org/fathers/200146.htm

[695] Isaiah 58:3, 6, 7, "3'Why have we fasted,' they say, 'and You have not seen? ... 6"Is this not the fast that I have chosen: ... 7Is it not to share your bread with the hungry, And that you bring to your house the poor who are [d]cast out; When you see the naked, that you cover him," (NKJV).

[696] 2 Corinthians 8:2-4, 7, "their deep poverty abounded in the riches of their liberality. 3For I bear witness that according to their ability, yes, and beyond their ability, they were freely

clean money in the first place, one works hard for it and so, giving it away to charitable causes is equivalent to giving one's life away (i.e. "lay down one's life") which is drawn as an analogy to Christ's perfect sacrifice for our sins too in Scripture for us to follow likewise in finance areas as well.[697]

NON-ELECT SALVATION POSSIBILITY WITH MATTHEW 19:16-22

Koplitz writes that in the Greek method of teaching, the instructor is always right and this is the standard adopted way in many Biblical institutions and churches as well.[698] The Hebraic way of teaching however, is different. The teacher wants the student to challenge "what they hear" to the point that the student eventually becomes a teacher as well.[699] We see this feature in Christ's reply in Matthew 19:16-22 since he doesn't just give a list of instructions directly when asked "what good thing shall I do that I may have eternal life?" but rather asks the opinion of the rich young ruler first regarding it. Thereafter, Christ affirms the parts which the ruler got right and after that, he corrects or expands on the themes where the ruler missed out.[700] Here are further thoughts in regard to Matthew 19:16-22:

Christ did not ask to keep "all" the 613 Torah commands for "eternal life" context.

When asked "which commandments?" Christ did not quote all the ten commandments even but only the last six commandments which related to men. Is this the gateway for non elect salvation[701] since the first four commandments relating to God context are not mentioned by Christ? Now, if the first four commands are kept by a person, they're considered elect salvation since these commands relate to God directly but Sabbath does not

---

willing, 4imploring us with much urgency [a]that we would receive the gift and the fellowship of the ministering to the saints…. see that you abound in this grace also." (NKJV).

[697] John 15:13, "Greater love has no one than this, than to lay down one's life for his friends." (NKJV). 1 John 3:16-17, "16By this we know love, because He laid down His life for us. And we also ought to lay down our lives for the brethren. 17But whoever has this world's goods, and sees his brother in need, and shuts up his heart from him, how does the love of God abide in him?" (NKJV).

[698] Koplitz, "Hebraic Analysis", 8.

[699] Ibid., 9.

[700] Ibid., 9.

[701] Jonathan Ramachandran, "Non Elect Salvation Possibility" (NESP), in The American Journal of Biblical Theology (AJBT), Vol 26, No. 6 (February 9, 2025). www.biblicaltheology.com/Research/RamachandranJ01.pdf

apply to gentile believers[702] as earliest church fathers[703] and protestant founders[704] taught likewise. Furthermore, Irenaeus taught that keeping this fourth commandment spiritually included the financial holiness aspect as he says, "Sabbaths taught that we should continue day by day in God's service

---

[702] Colossians 2:16, "So let no one judge you in food or in drink, or regarding a festival or a new moon or sabbaths" (NKJV).

[703] Irenaeus of Lyons writes, "that Abraham himself, without circumcision and without observance of Sabbaths, believed God, and it was imputed unto him for righteousness" ("Book 4. Chapter 16. Point 2.", in Against Heresies), www.newadvent.org/fathers/0103416.htm, Justin of Rome writes, "For we too would observe the fleshly circumcision, and the Sabbaths, and in short all the feasts, if we did not know for what reason they were enjoined you ... we would not observe those rites which do not harm us— I speak of fleshly circumcision, and Sabbaths, and feasts?" ("Chapter 18", in Dialogue with Trypho, translated by Marcus Dods and George Reith, from Ante-Nicene Fathers, Vol. 1, edited by Alexander Roberts, James Donaldson, and A. Cleveland Coxe. (Buffalo, NY: Christian Literature Publishing Co., 1885), www.newadvent.org/fathers/01282.htm, and Tertullian answers anyone, "who contends that the Sabbath is still to be observed as a balm of salvation" to say that specifically that Adam, Abel, Noah, Enoch & Melchizedek, were all commended by God though they were "uncircumcised, and inobservant of the Sabbath" ("Chapter 2", in An Answer to the Jews, translated by S. Thelwall, from Ante-Nicene Fathers, Vol. 3, edited by Alexander Roberts, James Donaldson, and A. Cleveland Coxe. (Buffalo, NY: Christian Literature Publishing Co., 1885)), www.newadvent.org/fathers/0308.htm

James Richardson, "Quotes From Early Church Fathers: The Sabbath, Lord's Day, and Worship - Apostles Creed", Apostles Creed, August 10, 2016. apostles-creed.org/confessional-reformed-christian-theology/ecclesiology/quotes-from-early-church-fathers-on-the-sabbath-and-the-lords-day/

[704] Martin Luther writes, "Sabbath: Again one can prove it from the third commandment that Moses does not pertain to Gentiles and Christians" ("How Christians Should Regard Moses," trans. and ed. by E. Theodore Bachmann, in Luther's Works: Word and Sacrament I, vol. 35 (Philadelphia: Muhlenberg Press, 1960): 161-174. This sermon was preached on August 27, 1525. www.wordofhisgrace.org/LutherMoses.htm), John Calvin writes not "changing the day, and yet mentally attributing to it the same sanctity" lest we fall "Of the observance of the Lord's day, in answer to those who complain that the Christian people are thus trained to Judaism. Objection. Ground of this institution. There is no kind of superstitious necessity. The sum of the Commandment." ("Points 33-34. Chapter 8. Fourth commandment.", in Institutes, edited by John T. McNeill. (Westminster John Knox Press, 1 Jan 1960), www.ccel.org/ccel/calvin/institutes.iv.ix.html) and the Augsburg Confession reads, "For those who judge that by the authority of the Church the observance of the Lord's Day instead of the Sabbath-day was ordained as a thing necessary, 59 do greatly err ... example of Christian liberty, and might know that the keeping neither of the Sabbath nor of any other day is necessary" (Robert Kolb and Timothy J. Wengert, eds. "Article XXVI of the Distinction of Meats & Article XXVIII Of Ecclesiastical Power", in The Book of Concord: The Confessions of the Evangelical Lutheran Church. Minneapolis: Fortress Press, 2000. bookofconcord.org/augsburg-confession/)

... abstaining from all avarice, and not acquiring or possessing treasures upon earth".[705]

Notice that Christ also included the "love your neighbour as yourself" command[706] which is not a 10 commandment in his reply here for "eternal life". Also, the context of this commandment was expanded by Christ to include "enemies level" too in his own definition during the discourse of the parable of good Samaritan (Luke 10:25-37).

The rich young ruler said he kept all these Torah commands and asked Christ what he lacked to which Christ replied "charity doctrine" to "following him generally too" meaning these are all in addition to those six commandments and together, make up the definition of elect salvation for both holiness and reward contexts as well.

Perhaps the parable of the good Samaritan[707] by Christ can refer to such non-elect salvation hope since Christ himself said that Samaritans "do not know God"[708] opening hope for such Samaritans who did charity doctrine toward their "enemies-Jews level" which can be analogous to a non-Christian doing charity doctrine likewise toward a Christian. The surprised sheep of the nations seem to not know Christ as they ask back, "when did we see you, Lord? being hungry, thirsty, stranger, naked, sick and in prison?" but Christ knows them based on their charity doctrine deeds done toward "his brethren" or Christians[709] and being righteous[710] which could based on the last 6 commandments for human interactions out of the 10 Commandments which we saw in discussions earlier.

If this interpretation is true, then it's not salvation by works for the "non elect salvation" part either but rather that these may get a chance to believe after seeing Christ in the spirit world. The "saved by fire" case ones of 1 Corinthians 3:15 also may refer to this class of "believing after seeing" case

---

[705] "Book 4. Chapter 16. Point 1." (Irenaeus of Lyons, in Against Heresies). www.newadvent.org/fathers/0103416.htm

[706] Leviticus 19:18, 34, "18You shall not take vengeance, nor bear any grudge against the children of your people, but you shall love your neighbor as yourself: I am the Lord. ... 34The stranger who dwells among you shall be to you as one born among you, and you shall love him as yourself; for you were strangers in the land of Egypt: I am the Lord your God" (NKJV).

[707] Luke 10:25-37.

[708] John 4:22, "22You worship what you do not know; we know what we worship, for salvation is of the Jews" (NKJV).

[709] Matthew 12:50.

[710] Matthew 25:31-46.

of John 6:29, 36, 40[711] where Christ was only angry with the Jews for not believing him even after seeing him and his miracles and other works. The context of seeing the risen Christ and then given a chance to believe is also evidenced in apostle Thomas' conversion too.[712] In comparison, Christians could be those saved with reward which is the 1 Corinthians 3:14 case.[713] In short, a living faith is not dead[714] and thus produces works at a minimum thirtyfold level[715] of the gospel's commands and are thus different from the no reward case of 1 Corinthians 3:15.[716]

Next, Christ did not say that old testament prophets were until Malachi but rather until John the Baptist[717] meaning it could include even Deuterocanonical books such as "Wisdom of Solomon" and even "2 Esdras" which some of the Roman Catholics and Orthodox consider as Scripture in their Bible since all these happened between the time Malachi to John the Baptist.

This can support non-elect salvation in some way but it's not necessary since other arguments presented here are independent of this. Here is a purgatory quote from Maccabees:

"42Betook themselves unto prayer, and besought him that the sin committed might wholly be put out of remembrance. Besides, that noble Judas exhorted the people to keep themselves from sin, forsomuch as they saw before their eyes the things that came to pass for the sins of those that were slain. 43And when he had made a gathering throughout the company to the sum of two thousand drachms of silver, he sent it to Jerusalem to offer a sin offering, doing therein very well and honestly, in that he was mindful of the resurrection: 44For if he had not hoped that they that were slain should

---

[711] John 6:29, 36, 40, "29Jesus answered and said to them, 'This is the work of God, that you believe in Him whom He sent.' 36But I said to you that you have seen Me and yet do not believe. 40And this is the will of Him who sent Me, that everyone who sees the Son and believes in Him may have everlasting life; and I will raise him up at the last day." (NKJV).

[712] John 20:29, "Jesus said to him, 'Thomas, because you have seen Me, you have believed. Blessed are those who have not seen and yet have believed.'" (NKJV).

[713] 1 Corinthians 3:14, "If anyone's work which he has built on it endures, he will receive a reward" (NKJV).

[714] James 2:17, "Thus also faith by itself, if it does not have works, is dead." (NKJV).

[715] Matthew 13:8, "But others fell on good ground and yielded a crop: some a hundredfold, some sixty, some thirty." (NKJV).

[716] 1 Corinthians 3:15, "If anyone's work is burned, he will suffer loss; but he himself will be saved, yet so as through fire." (NKJV).

[717] Luke 16:16, "The law and the prophets were until John. Since that time the kingdom of God has been preached, and everyone is pressing into it" (NKJV).

have risen again, it had been superfluous and vain to pray for the dead. 45And also in that he perceived that there was great favour laid up for those that died godly, it was an holy and good thought. Whereupon he made a reconciliation for the dead, that they might be delivered from sin."[718]

Notice that this is a "prayer for the dead" with charity doctrine and not a "prayer to the dead" which is found nowhere in Scripture. Now, Christ may have celebrated Hanukkah (feast of dedication or the festival of lights which is sometimes called the "second Sukkot or the second feast of tabernacles") which is not a canonical old testament feast but was one derived from the life of Judas Maccabees during this same window time period.

"22Now it was the Feast of Dedication in Jerusalem, and it was winter. 23And Jesus walked in the temple, in Solomon's porch."[719]

The point is this: if Maccabees was a false prophet or his purgatory belief false, then why did Christ celebrate Hanukkah which originated from this same Maccabees as apostle John records here? Thus, a refinement of the concept of purgatory can be a possibility for non elect salvation concept.

Here's a question to ponder: Why did Christ not correct this writing or comment on it since some of the Jews of his time were practicing this due to this Maccabees' writing? Now, since Christ did not comment directly regarding it, we have to leave the question answered from a Sola Scriptura point of view but may speculate it to refer to non elect salvation since elect salvation does not undergo any type of spirit world judgment.[720]

Other early church writings from the orthodox and Catholic community (and not from heretical sources) may also have quotes in support of non elect salvation.[721] Here, we will just see a brief sample next especially in light of chiliasm timeline for prophecy.

i) First resurrection quote comparison.

---

[718] 2 Maccabees 12:42-45 (KJV). www.kingjamesbibleonline.org/2-Maccabees-Chapter-12/

[719] John 10:22-23 (NKJV).

[720] John 5:24, "Most assuredly, I say to you, he who hears My word and believes in Him who sent Me has everlasting life, and shall not come into judgment, but has passed from death into life" (NKJV).

[721] Ramachandran, "Non Elect Salvation Possibility", 4-40.

Both Lactantius (c. 250-325)[722] and Irenaeus[723] agree that all Christians and righteous of the past participate in the first bodily resurrection during Christ's public second coming which destroys the antichrist marking the beginning of the thousand years reign of Christ.

ii) Second resurrection quote to compare next.

However, after these 1000 years are over, Lactantius writes that all those of the second resurrection are raised to judgment and are unsaved with no more hope for them.

"But when the thousand years shall be completed, the world shall be renewed by God, and the heavens shall be folded together, and the earth shall be changed, and God shall transform men into the similitude of angels, and they shall be white as snow; and they shall always be employed in the sight of the Almighty, and shall make offerings to their Lord, and serve Him forever. At the same time shall take place that second and public resurrection of all, in which the unrighteous shall be raised to everlasting punishments. ... But their lord with his servants shall be seized and condemned to punishment, together with whom all the band of the wicked, in accordance with their deeds, shall be burnt for ever with perpetual fire in the sight of angels and

---

[722] Lactantius writes, "But He, when He shall have destroyed unrighteousness, and executed His great judgment, and shall have recalled to life the righteous, who have lived from the beginning, will be engaged among men a thousand years, and will rule them with most just command. ... Then they who shall be alive in their bodies shall not die, but during those thousand years shall produce an infinite multitude, and their offspring shall be holy, and beloved by God; but they who shall be raised from the dead shall preside over the living as judges. But the nations shall not be entirely extinguished, but some shall be left as a victory for God, that they may be the occasion of triumph to the righteous, and may be subjected to perpetual slavery. About the same time also the prince of the devils, who is the contriver of all evils, shall be bound with chains, and shall be imprisoned during the thousand years of the heavenly rule in which righteousness shall reign in the world, so that he may contrive no evil against the people of God", ("Book 7, Chapter 24.", in Divine Institutes). www.newadvent.org/fathers/07017.htm

[723] Irenaeus of Lyons writes, "But when this Antichrist shall have devastated all things in this world, he will reign for three years and six months, and sit in the temple at Jerusalem; and then the Lord will come from heaven in the clouds, in the glory of the Father, sending this man and those who follow him into the lake of fire; but bringing in for the righteous the times of the kingdom, that is, the rest, the hallowed seventh day; and restoring to Abraham the promised inheritance, in which kingdom the Lord declared, that many coming from the east and from the west should sit down with Abraham, Isaac, and Jacob. Matthew 8:11" ("Book 5. Chapter 30. Point 4", in Against Heresies). www.newadvent.org/fathers/0103530.htm

the righteous. This is the doctrine of the holy prophets which we Christians follow;"[724]

On the other hand, Irenaeus seems to quote the "surprised sheep of the nations" passage to refer to the "whole human race" where some seem to be only saved during this second resurrection. Since the first and second resurrection are separated by 1000 years in his eschatology,[725] hence this must be a different badge of righteous which did not participate in the first resurrection and hence could be recipients of the non elect salvation possibility. Compare:

"But inasmuch as one and the same Lord has pointed out that the whole human race shall be divided at the judgment, as a shepherd divides the sheep from the goats, Matthew 25:32 and that to some He will say, Come, you blessed of My Father, receive the kingdom which has been prepared for you, Matthew 25:34 but to others, Depart from me, you cursed, into everlasting fire, which My Father has prepared for the devil and his angels, Matthew 25:41."[726]

The idea of a righteous gentile abiding by the 7 Noahide laws in rabbinical Judaism (instead of the refinement of 6 of the last ten commandments presented in this study based on Matthew 19), may also be seen as a precursor to non elect salvation possibility thought.[727] Note that the missing law matching these two ideas is the one relating to not having idols (linking it to the first two of the ten commandments) which may then make a person to be an elect salvation instead, if observed.

CONCLUSION

Non elect salvation possibility may only be aimed at righteous gentiles who may have fulfilled the last six of the 10 commandments relating to man in some way in their lifetime. If this interpretation is true, then in Matthew 19:16-22, Christ in his foreknowledge may be demonstrating why that rich man who could not fulfil the six of 10 commandments in the context of finance toward his fellow man satisfactorily may still be saved into a non elect

---

[724] Lactantius, "Divine Institutes", Book 7, Chapter 26.

[725] A. Skevington Wood, "The Eschatology of Irenaeus", in The Evangelical Quarterly, 41.1 (UK, Jan.-Mar. 1969): 36. biblicalstudies.org.uk/pdf/eq/1969-1_030.pdf

[726] Irenaeus of Lyons, "Book 4. Chapter 40. Point 2.", in Against Heresies. www.newadvent.org/fathers/0103440.htm

[727] Philip La Grange Du Toit, "The Radical New Perspective on Paul, Messianic Judaism and their connection to Christian Zionism", in HTS Theological Studies, 73(3), (2017): 2-3,5-6. doi.org/10.4102/hts.v73i3.4603

salvation. It can explain why Christ did not quote the first four commandments to him especially since to fulfil the greatest commandment (Mark 12:29-31) requires the fulfilment of "love your neighbour as yourself" together with it, meaning the commands toward men are a prerequisite and those who do not fulfil it cannot fulfil the "love God" command independently.

This fulfilment of those six commands is possible since it only relates to humans and imperfect Christians too strive for it likewise. The ability to produce such fruits of good works is solely due to the grace of God which may be a proof that these are marked for this lower grade salvation. In the Bible, apart from the "surprised sheep of the nations" earlier (Matthew 25:31-46), Cyrus the great[728] has been used by God to do such charity doctrine act to liberate the Jews[729] where he never knew the true God either before nor after doing it[730] together with the example of Cornelius whose charity doctrine works were accepted whilst he was an unbeliever could be matched to non elect salvation.[731] The fact that Cornelius repents later and believes via a divine encounter proves God's higher call in his life into being selected for elect salvation.[732]

We must be careful in prophecy considerations lest the warning mentioned for adding or manipulating any prophecy in Holy Scripture condemn us, verses:

"17And the Spirit and the bride say, "Come!" And let him who hears say, "Come!" And let him who thirsts come. Whoever desires, let him take the water of life freely. 18[i]For I testify to everyone who hears the words of the prophecy of this book: If anyone adds to these things, [j]God will add to him the plagues that are written in this book; 19and if anyone takes away from the words of the book of this prophecy, God[k] shall take away his part

---

[728] Isaiah 45:1, "Thus says the Lord to His anointed, To Cyrus, whose right hand I have [a]held" (NKJV).

[729] Simon John De. Vries, From old Revelation to new: a tradition-historical and redaction-critical study of temporal transitions in prophetic prediction, (Wm. B. Eerdmans Publishing, 1995): 126.

[730] Isaiah 45:4, "For Jacob My servant's sake, And Israel My elect, I have even called you by your name; I have named you, though you have not known Me." (NKJV).

[731] Acts 10:31, "Cornelius, your prayer has been heard, and your alms are remembered in the sight of God." (NKJV).

[732] Acts 10:34-35, "34Then Peter opened his mouth and said: "In truth I perceive that God shows no partiality. 35But in every nation whoever fears Him and works righteousness is accepted by Him." (NKJV).

from the [l]Book of Life, from the holy city, and from the things which are written in this book."[733]

Regarding non elect salvation possibility, doesn't Revelation 22:17 here literally seems to refer to it since the bride (church, Christians) seem to call to the thirsty (non-Bride, others) here to partake of the water of life freely at the end of time? Remember that you cannot partake of the water of life until a person is in their final sinless resurrection body and such ones seem to need healing from the leaves of the tree of life too (Revelation 22:2)[734] which comes straight from Christ and God's throne at that time.

Remember that in chiliasm timeline (as per Lactantius' and more importantly, Irenaeus' resurrection quotes earlier), Christians already partook of the water of life 1000 years earlier[735] during the millennial reign first resurrection timeline (which is prior to great white throne judgment day, Revelation 20:11-15) and so, it's difficult to imagine any Christian still needing healing after 1000 years of bodily resurrection where this occurrence is happening after judgment day (since book of life results are revealed already, Revelation 21:27) in the final new earth and heavens. Those saved non-Christians could be part of the nations of those who are saved (Revelation 21:24-26) with kings of the earth ruling over them (Revelation 21:24) while Christians could be mentioned differently here as being in heaven at this time (Revelation 21:9) as kings and priests too (Revelation 1:6).

Now, here's the main point which may help us not to be judged at all even if my writing here turns out false regarding the non elect salvation possibility part: we presented it as an academic possibility and not as a doctrine and did not claim the Holy Spirit told me which would directly mean adding/removing from Scripture if wrong.

BIBLIOGRAPHY

Ballard, Jordan P., "Defending the Doctrine of Hell", *Eleutheria: John W. Rawlings School of Divinity Academic Journal*, 8(2), (2025).

---

[733] Revelation 22:17-19 (NKJV).

[734] Revelation 22:1-2, "1And he showed me a pure river of water of life, clear as crystal, proceeding from the throne of God and of the Lamb. 2In the middle of its street, and on either side of the river, was the tree of life, which bore twelve fruits, each tree yielding its fruit every month. The leaves of the tree were for the healing of the nations" (NKJV).

[735] Revelation 7:9-17, "I looked, and behold, a great multitude which no one could number, … These are the ones who come out of the great tribulation … 17for the Lamb who is in the midst of the throne will shepherd them and lead them to living fountains of waters" (NKJV).

digitalcommons.liberty.edu/eleu/vol8/iss2/5

Bible. Unless noted, all Scripture is taken from the New King James Version (NKJV). Nashville: Published by Thomas Nelson, 1996, c1982. NKJV and other translations used are from biblehub.com

Borchert, G. L., "Matthew 5:48 - Perfection and the Sermon", *Review & Expositor*, 89(2), (1992): 265-269. doi.org/10.1177/003463739208900208

Calvin, John. *Institutes*. Edited by John T. McNeill. (Westminster John Knox Press, 1 Jan 1960).

Carter, John W. (Jack)., "The Cost of Discipleship", in *The American Journal of Biblical Theology* (AJBT), Volume 26(12), (March 3, 2025). www.biblicaltheology.com/printerfriendly.pdf

Chien, Dinh Van., "Humanistic Thought in Jesus' Sermon on The Eight Beatens", in *Pakistan Journal of Life and Social Sciences* (Pak. j. life soc. Sci.), 2024, 22(2): 15165-15170. doi.org/10.57239/PJLSS-2024-22.2.001095

Chrysostom, John. *Homily 46 on Matthew*. Translated by George Prevost and revised by M.B. Riddle. From Nicene and Post-Nicene Fathers, First Series, Vol. 10. Edited by Philip Schaff. (Buffalo, NY: Christian Literature Publishing Co., 1888).

Du Toit, Philip La Grange., "The Radical New Perspective on Paul, Messianic Judaism and their connection to Christian Zionism", in *HTS Theological Studies*, 73(3), (2017): 1-8. doi.org/10.4102/hts.v73i3.4603

Earnhardt, Matthew P., "Exegetical Study of Matthew 19:16-26", in *The American Journal of Biblical Theology* (AJBT), (March 10, 2023). www.biblicaltheology.com/Research/EarnhardtMP01.pdf

Feldmeier, R., "As Your Heavenly Father is Perfect: The God of the Bible and Commandments in the Gospel", in *Interpretation*, 70(4), (2016): 431-444. doi.org/10.1177/0020964316655109

Herberg, Will., "Judaism and Christianity: Their Unity and Difference. The Double Covenant in the Divine Economy of Salvation", *Journal of Bible and Religion*, 21(2), (1953): 67–78. www.jstor.org/stable/1458587

Inserra, Dean. *The Unsaved Christian: Reaching Cultural Christianity with the Gospel*. (Moody Publishers, 2019).

Irenaeus of Lyons. *Against Heresies*. Translated by Alexander Roberts and William Rambaut. From Ante-Nicene Fathers, Vol. 1. Edited by Alexander

Roberts, James Donaldson, and A. Cleveland Coxe. (Buffalo, NY: Christian Literature Publishing Co., 1885).

Justin of Rome (Justin Martyr). *Dialogue with Trypho.* Translated by Marcus Dods and George Reith. From Ante-Nicene Fathers, Vol. 1. Edited by Alexander Roberts, James Donaldson, and A. Cleveland Coxe. (Buffalo, NY: Christian Literature Publishing Co., 1885).

Justin of Rome (Justin Martyr). *The First Apology.* Translated by Marcus Dods and George Reith. From Ante-Nicene Fathers, Vol. 1. Edited by Alexander Roberts, James Donaldson, and A. Cleveland Coxe. (Buffalo, NY: Christian Literature Publishing Co., 1885).

Kolb, Robert. and Wengert, Timothy J., eds. *The Book of Concord: The Confessions of the Evangelical Lutheran Church.* (Minneapolis: Fortress Press, 2000).

Koplitz, Michael., "Hebraic Analysis for Matthew 19:27-30", (2020). DOI.org/10.13140/RG.2.2.27636.58243

Korver, Bill Fredric. "Biblical use of rewards as a motivation for Christian service". PhD diss.. Liberty University, USA, August 2011. digitalcommons.liberty.edu/cgi/viewcontent.cgi?article=1495&context=doctoral

Lactantius. *Divine Institutes.* Translated by William Fletcher. From Ante-Nicene Fathers, Vol. 7. Edited by Alexander Roberts, James Donaldson, and A. Cleveland Coxe. (Buffalo, NY: Christian Literature Publishing Co., 1886).

MacArthur, John. *Hard to Believe: The High Cost and Infinite Value of Following Jesus.* (Nashville, TN: Nelson, 2003).

O'Collins SJ, G., "Difficult texts: being made perfect according to Matthew 5 and 19", *Theology*, 124(6), (2021): 404-409.

doi.org/10.1177/0040571X211056790

Ramachandran, Jonathan., "Non Elect Salvation Possibility" (NESP), in *The American Journal of Biblical Theology* (AJBT), Vol 26, No. 6 (February 9, 2025). www.biblicaltheology.com/Research/RamachandranJ01.pdf

Richardson, James., "Quotes From Early Church Fathers: The Sabbath, Lord's Day, and Worship - Apostles Creed", Apostles Creed, August 10, 2016.

apostles-creed.org/confessional-reformed-christian-theology/ecclesiology/quotes-from-early-church-fathers-on-the-sabbath-and-the-lords-day/

Shepherd, Thomas R., "The Parable of the Rich Man and Lazarus: A Narrative-Exegetical Study of Its Relationship to the Afterlife, Wealth, and Poverty–Part 1: The Afterlife", in *Journal of the Adventist Theological Society*, 32/1-2 (2021): 171-189.

digitalcommons.andrews.edu/cgi/viewcontent.cgi?article=1621&context=jats

Stevenson, L., "On the very idea of perfection", *International Journal of Philosophy and Theology*, 85(3–4), (2024): 111-123.

doi.org/10.1080/21692327.2024.2417091

Tanasyah, Yusak., "The Development of Hell from Jewish to Christian Theology: A Biblical Guide to Hell and Its Existence", *QUAERENS: Journal of Theology and Christianity Studies,* 4 (1), (2022): 27-41. DOI.org/10.46362/quaerens.v4i1.80

Tertullian. *A Treatise on the Soul.* Translated by Peter Holmes. From Ante-Nicene Fathers, Vol. 3. Edited by Alexander Roberts, James Donaldson, and A. Cleveland Coxe. (Buffalo, NY: Christian Literature Publishing Co., 1885).

Tertullian. *An Answer to the Jews.* Translated by S. Thelwall. From Ante-Nicene Fathers, Vol. 3. Edited by Alexander Roberts, James Donaldson, and A. Cleveland Coxe. (Buffalo, NY: Christian Literature Publishing Co., 1885).

Tertullian. *On Fasting.* Translated by S. Thelwall. From Ante-Nicene Fathers, Vol. 4. Edited by Alexander Roberts, James Donaldson, and A. Cleveland Coxe. (Buffalo, NY: Christian Literature Publishing Co., 1885).

Vacendak, Robert. "Is assurance of salvation of the essence of saving faith in the Gospel of John?". PhD diss.. Rawlings School of Divinity, Liberty University, USA, April 2023.

digitalcommons.liberty.edu/cgi/viewcontent.cgi?article=5359&context=doctoral

Vaught, Carl G.. *The Sermon on the Mount: A Theological Interpretation.* (SUNY Press., 1986).

Vries, Simon John De. *From old Revelation to new: a tradition-historical and redaction-critical study of temporal transitions in prophetic prediction*. (Wm. B. Eerdmans Publishing, 1995).

Wood, A. Skevington., "The Eschatology of Irenaeus", in *The Evangelical Quarterly*, 41.1 (UK, Jan.-Mar. 1969). biblicalstudies.org.uk/pdf/eq/1969-1_030.pdf

ESSAYS IN EARLY CHRISTIANITY

Essay 9: Other Church Fathers or Quotes for Non-Elect Salvation

Any Church Father quotes regarding someone saved in the Spirit World be it in Hades or Lake of Fire could be candidates for **Non Elect Salvation** *possibility* since we maintain the classical Protestant position that **Elect Salvation** does not undergo any *Spirit World* Judgment at all based on Bible verses like John 5:24 and Revelation 2:11.

Some (if not all) of the fallen Christians and fake Christians whom the Lord denies together with non-Christians who end up saved in the *Spirit World after Judgment first* could be the recipients of this **Non Elect Salvation** if my *interpolations* in light of these *Church Fathers* quotes presented next is true.

i) **Elect Salvation** does not undergo any *Hades Judgment*:

"Most assuredly, I say to you, he who **hears** My word and **believes** in Him who sent Me has **everlasting life**, and shall **not come into judgment**, but has **passed from death into life.**"[736]

ii) **Elect Salvation** does not undergo any *Lake of Fire Judgment*:

"He who has an ear, let him hear what the Spirit says to the **churches**. He who **overcomes** shall **not be hurt** by the **second death**." [737]

"Blessed and holy is he who has part in the **first resurrection**. Over such the **second death has no power**, but they shall be **priests** of God and of Christ, and shall **reign** with Him a **thousand years**." [738] [739]

1. Book of 1 Enoch

---

[736] John 5:24 (NKJV). biblehub.com/john/5-24.htm

[737] Revelation 2:11 (NKJV). biblehub.com/revelation/2-11.htm

[738] Revelation 20:6 (NKJV). biblehub.com/revelation/20-6.htm

[739] Revelation 20:14 – 15, "14Then Death and Hades were cast into the **lake of fire**. This is the **second [d]death.** 15And anyone **not** found **written** in the **Book of Life** was **cast into the lake of fire.**" (NKJV). biblehub.com/nkjv/revelation/20.htm versus Revelation 3:5, "He who **overcomes** shall be clothed in **white garments**, and I will **not** blot out his name from the **Book of Life**; but I will confess his name before My Father and before His angels." (NKJV). biblehub.com/revelation/3-5.htm

In the **Book of 1 Enoch**, (which is considered canonical by some Christians such as the isolated Ethiopian Orthodox Church[740]), chapter 50 could be describing this *Chiliasm* Prophecy "change" happening to the "elect" (Christians, Verse 1) from "human" to "no more flesh and blood" to some type of *heavenly shining body* with "light of days", "glory" and "honour" on "Judgment Day" when sinners are judged (Verse 2, so *Second* Resurrection timeline implied intrinsically) which seems to be shown alongside **Non Elect Salvation** *possibility* toward "some" sinners who repent via "believing after seeing" and it *cannot* be elect salvation since it is called as "no honour" (Verse 3) while those who do not repent "perish" thereafter eternally with no more hope in Hell as God stops His Mercy henceforth (Verses 4 & 5).

"1 And in those days a **change** shall take place for the **holy** and **elect**,

And the **light of days** shall abide upon them,

2 On the **day of affliction** on which **evil** shall have been treasured up against the **sinners**.

And the **righteous** shall be victorious in the **name** of the Lord of Spirits:

And He will cause the **others** to witness (this)

That **they may repent**

And forgo the works of their hands.

3 They shall have **no honour** through the **name** of the **Lord of Spirits**,

Yet **through His name** shall **they be saved**,

And the Lord of Spirits will have compassion on them, For His compassion is great.

4 And He is righteous also in His judgement,

And in the presence of His glory unrighteousness also shall not maintain itself: At **His judgment** the **unrepentant shall perish** before Him.

---

[740] Ethiopian Orthodox Tewahido Church Holy Synod. *A short history, faith and order of the Ethiopian Orthodox Tewahido Church*, Canonical Books, Addis Ababa 1983. www.ethiopianorthodox.org/english/canonical/books.html

5And from henceforth I will have **no mercy on them**, saith the Lord of Spirits."[741]

2. Shepherd of Hermas

Tertullian himself had trouble with the **Non Elect Salvation** quotes of the **Shepherd of Hermas** (which **proves** this part is **preserved authentically** according to even Tertullian himself who is *disagreeing or having trouble with its meaning*) but yet please observe carefully Tertullian's wise and scholarly reply (no wonder Tertullian is the *Father of Latin Christianity* and *Founder of Western Theological Scholarship*) since he writes as follows,[742]

> "But I would yield my ground to you, if the **scripture** of the **Shepherd**, which is the only one **which favours adulterers**, had deserved to find a place in the **Divine canon**; if it had not been habitually judged by every council of Churches (even of your own) among apocryphal and false (writings); ... I, however, **imbibe the Scriptures of that Shepherd who cannot be broken**."[743]

Basically, **Tertullian** in his discussion here (with Bishop of Rome, Pope St. Callixtus I at that time) is saying he has **problem** because the **Shepherd of Hermas since it gives some type of Non Elect Salvation to "adulterers"** (implied) and that's a reason for his hesitance that it has been included in the Divine Canon (e.g. *Muratorian/Roman Canon which are first oldest known Bible Canon, etc.*) but yet he says that he will "**imbibe**" (absorb) it since it is "**Scripture which cannot be broken**".

Similarly, I am doing academic reporting and commenting honestly in this book based on evidence like this regardless if I agree to the Shepherd of Hermas or not **like how Tertullian did and that's exactly the methodology I follow decided to follow here**. There is only one part of the Shepherd of Hermas which has this *Non Elect Salvation possibility* quotes which I will present soon.

---

[741] From-*The Apocrypha and Pseudepigrapha of the Old Testament* R.H. Charles Oxford: The Clarendon Press, UK, 1913. Book of 1 Enoch. Chapter 50. www.ccel.org/c/charles/otpseudepig/enoch/ENOCH_2.HTM

[742] A *Catholic encyclopedia* writes, "St. Irenaeus and Tertullian (in his Catholic days) cite the "Shepherd" as Scripture. Tertullian, when a Montanist, implies that Pope St. Callistus had quoted it as an authority (though evidently not as Scripture)," in his reply here. www.catholic.com/encyclopedia/hermas

[743] Tertullian. *On Modesty* ("De pudicitia"). Chapter 10. www.newadvent.org/fathers/0407.htm

Firstly, the Shepherd of Hermas (*The Pastor*) writing has been called as "Scripture" by some early church fathers including *Chiliasm* church fathers such as St. Irenaeus of Lyons and even Tertullian and was also in the "first known Bibles" of Christianity such as the Roman Canon/Muratorian Canon in the West and Codex Sinaiticus [744] (4th century) in the East.

A greater witness is St. Irenaeus of Lyons who called the Shepherd of Hermas as Scripture when he quoted it as follows:

> "2. Truly, then, the **Scripture** declared, which says, First of all believe that there is one God, who has established all things, and completed them, and having caused that from what had no being, all things should come into existence: He who contains all things, and is Himself contained by no one."[745]

Compare this against the preserved Shepherd of Hermas quote to see the match [746].

The Roman Canon ("Muratorian Canon" c. 170 AD) which is the oldest known canonical list of New Testament Scripture whose surviving fragment lists the Shepherd of Hermas as Scripture and says,

> "But **Hermas** wrote **The Shepherd** very recently, in our times, in the city of Rome, while bishop Pius, his brother, was occupying the chair of the church of the city of Rome. And therefore, **it ought indeed to be read**; but it **cannot be read publicly** to the people in **church** either among the **Prophets**, whose **number is complete**, or among the **Apostles**, for it is **after their time**."[747]

St. Athanasius the Great did not classify Shepherd of Hermas as Scripture in his famous letter which lists all 27 New Testament books but yet he approved it for usage. Few have noticed that in this same letter, St. Athanasius places the "Shepherd of Hermas" (called the *Shepherd* or *Pastor*) in

---

[744] Bible Canon. *Codex Sinaiticus*. codexsinaiticus.org/en/codex/content.aspx

[745] St. Irenaeus of Lyons. *Against Heresies*. Book 4. Chapter 20. Point 2. www.newadvent.org/fathers/0103420.htm

[746] *Shepherd of Hermas*, Book 2, Commandment 1, reads, "First of all, believe that there is one God who created and finished all things, and made all things out of nothing. He alone is able to contain the whole, but Himself cannot be contained", www.newadvent.org/fathers/02012.htm

[747] G. M. Hahneman. *The Muratorian Fragment and the Origins of the New Testament Canon in "The Canon Debate"* (ed. L. M. McDonald and J. A. Sanders, Massachusetts: Hendrickson, 2002), 405–415.

the same level as "Esther" where today, "Esther" is considered one of the 66 books in the protestant Bible. This means "Shepherd of Hermas" too has such a potential though we cannot say for sure hence it remains a possibility only[748]. Interestingly, the Shepherd of Hermas has never been condemned by any church council and earliest Bible canons listed it as Scripture. It just went out of use and so it remains a mystery as such.

The Shepherd of Hermas calls the elect salvation as the salvation in the "Tower [of Repentance]" parabolically as representing the "Church".

> "Many indeed shall hear, and hearing, some shall be glad, and some shall weep. But even these, if they hear and repent, shall also rejoice. Hear, then, the **parables of the tower**; ... The **tower** which you see building is myself, the **Church**, who have appeared to you now and on the former occasion. Ask, then, whatever you like in regard to the **tower**, and I will reveal it to you, that you may rejoice with the **saints**."[749]

This same "Elect Tower" concept is quoted by *Chiliasm* church father St. Irenaeus of Lyons too.

> "the beautiful **elect tower** being also raised everywhere. For the **illustrious Church** is [now] everywhere, and everywhere is the winepress dug: because those who do receive the Spirit are everywhere."[750]

However, during this same vision, the Shepherd of Hermas reveals further that there is a *non-elect salvation* possibility outside the "Elect Tower" for "all the rejected stones" where "stones" refer to "people" parabolically throughout these visions including those who have "heard the Gospel and

---

[748] After listing the 27 New Testament books, St. Athanasius the Great writes, "These are the springs of salvation, in order that he who is thirsty may fully refresh himself with the words contained in them. In them alone is the doctrine of piety proclaimed. Let no one add anything to them or take anything away from them ... But for the sake of greater accuracy I add, being constrained to write, that there are also other books besides these, which have not indeed been put in the canon, but have been appointed by the Fathers as reading-matter for those who have just come forward and which to be instructed in the doctrine of piety: the Wisdom of Solomon, the Wisdom of Sirach, Esther, Judith, Tobias, the so-called Teaching [Didache] of the Apostles, and the Shepherd. And although, beloved, the former are in the canon and the latter serve as reading matter," (*39th Festal Letter*, c. 367 AD), www.ntcanon.org/Athanasius.shtml

[749] Shepherd of Hermas. Book 1. Vision 3. Chapter 3. www.newadvent.org/fathers/02011.htm

[750] St. Irenaeus of Lyons. *Against Heresies*. Book 4. Chapter 36. Point 2. www.newadvent.org/fathers/0103436.htm

wished to be baptized" but remain "unbaptized" and regressed into their "wicked sins". This is the part I think Tertullian speaks of earlier:

> "Do you wish to know who are the others which fell near the waters, but could not be rolled into them? These are **they who have heard the word** and **wish to be baptized** in the name of the Lord; but when the **chastity** demanded by the truth comes into their recollection, **they draw back**, and **again walk after their own wicked desires**. She **finished** her **exposition of the tower**. But I, shameless as I yet was, asked her, Is **repentance possible** for **all those stones** which have been **cast away** and did **not fit** into the building of the **tower**, and **will they yet have a place in this tower? Repentance**, said she, is **yet possible**, but **in this tower**, they **cannot** find **a suitable place**. But **in another** and **much inferior place** they will be laid, and that, too, only when they have been **tortured** and **completed** the days of **their sins**. And on this account will they be transferred, because they have **partaken of the righteous Word**. And then only will they be **removed** from **their punishments** when the thought of **repenting** of the evil deeds which they have done has come into their hearts. But if it does not come into their hearts, they will **not be saved** on account of the **hardness** of their heart."[751]

It is to be noted that this **Non Elect Salvation** in another much more inferior place is only attainable if they repent in fire of punishment first and have partaken of the righteous word (possibly Christ's Commands during some period of their lives which I personally think is the holiness and charity doctrine commands).

We can match the "elect tower salvation" as referring to the "final new heavens" abode while the **Non Elect Salvation** outside the tower salvation to the "final new earth" abode in our previous discussions. Also, notice that if the Roman Catholic doctrine of purgatory is true, then these must be placed back "into the tower" after purgatory as that's how they teach it but it is not the case here as the salvation is not in the tower (church) after this anymore implying *non-elect salvation* possibility only. Notice that these are not said to repent on earth "despite having heard of the Gospel since they walk back according to their evil desires" meaning that this is not the unlearnt case or equivalent either.

---

[751] Shepherd of Hermas. Book 1. Vision 3. Chapter 7. www.newadvent.org/fathers/02011.htm

3. St. Ambrose (c. 340 AD – c. 397 AD), archbishop of Milan.

Elect Salvation here is those of "First Resurrection" who *come to grace without the judgment* while **Non Elect Salvation** here is those of "Second Resurrection" who are *disciplined* first before being saved later.

> "Our Savior has appointed **two kinds of resurrection** in the Apocalypse. 'Blessed is he that hath part in the **first resurrection**,' for such **come to grace without the judgment**. As for those who **do not come to the first**, but are reserved unto the **second resurrection**, these shall be **disciplined** until their appointed times, **between** the **first** and the **second resurrection**."[752]

Elect Salvation here is those who believe on earth itself without seeing (which is the definition of *faith* [753]) as he calls that *now* in quote next while **Non Elect Salvation** here is those who *believe after seeing* sometime later in the "Spirit World" Judgments (implied against "now"):

> "182. Let us then shortly sum up our **conclusion** on the whole matter. A unity of power puts aside all idea of a degrading subjection. His giving up of power, and His victory as conqueror won over death, have not lessened His power. Obedience works out subjection. Christ has taken obedience upon Himself, obedience even to taking on Him our flesh, the cross even to gaining our salvation. Thus where the work lies, there too is the Author of the work. When therefore, **all things** have become **subject** to **Christ**, through Christ's obedience, so that **all bend their knees** in His name, then He Himself will be **all in all**. For **now**, since **all** do **not believe**, **all** do **not seem** to be in **subjection**. But **when all have believed** and **done** the **will of God**, then **Christ will be all** and **in all**. And when Christ is all and in all, then will God be all and in all; for the Father abides ever in the Son. How, then, is He shown to be weak, Who redeemed the weak? 183. And lest you should by chance attribute to the weakness of the Son, that it is written, that God has put all things in subjection under Him; learn that He has Himself brought all things into subjection to Himself, for it is written: Our conversation is in heaven, from whence also we look for the Saviour, the Lord Jesus,

---

[752] Source (no one seems to quote the original source but rather only this): www.tentmaker.org/Quotes/churchfathersquotes.htm

[753] Hebrews 11:1, "Now **faith** is the substance of things **hoped for**, the evidence of things **not seen**" (NKJV). biblehub.com/hebrews/11-1.htm

Who shall change our vile body that it may be fashioned like His glorious body according to the working, whereby He is able to **subdue all things unto Himself.** Philippians 3:20-21 You have learned, therefore, that He can subdue all things unto Himself according to the working of His Godhead"[754]

4. St. Augustine (c. 354 AD – c. 430 AD), bishop of Hippo.

St. Augustine initially believed in *Chiliasm* and then became *non-Chiliast*. In his quote next, he implies that those of *Prosperity Gospel* type (i.e. those who love the *goods of this world*) have to go through *purgatory* before being saved unless they have done *sufficient Charity Doctrine*. My *interpolation* is that anyone *saved* through *purgatory* is part of **Non Elect Salvation** possibility.

> "And it is not impossible that something of the same kind may take place even **after this life.** It is a matter that may be inquired into, and either ascertained or left doubtful, whether some **believers** shall pass through a **kind of purgatorial fire,** and in **proportion** as they have **loved** with more or less **devotion the goods** that **perish,** be less or more quickly **delivered from it.** This cannot, however, be the case of any of those of whom it is said, that they shall not inherit the kingdom of God, unless after suitable repentance their sins be forgiven them. When I say suitable, I mean that they are **not to be unfruitful in almsgiving**; for **Holy Scripture** lays so much **stress** on this **virtue,** that our Lord tells us beforehand, that He will ascribe **no merit** to those on His right hand **but that they abound in it**, and no defect to those on His left hand but their want of it, when He shall say to the former, Come, you blessed of my Father, inherit the kingdom, and to the latter, Depart from me, you cursed, into everlasting fire. We must beware, however, lest any one should suppose that gross sins, such as are committed by those who shall not inherit the kingdom of God, may be daily perpetrated, and daily atoned for by almsgiving. The life must be changed for the better; and **almsgiving** must be used to **propitiate God for past sins, not to purchase impunity** for the commission of such **sins in the future.** For He has given no man license to sin, although in His mercy He may blot out sins

---

[754] St. Ambrose of Milan. *Exposition of the Christian Faith*. Book 5. Chapter 15. Points 182 – 183. www.newadvent.org/fathers/34045.htm

that are already committed, if we do not neglect to make proper satisfaction."[755]

Non Elect Salvation could be those who suffer *temporal* punishments in the *Spirit World* while **Elect Salvation** refers to those who do not come into such judgments.

> "But **temporary punishments** are suffered by some in this life only, **by others after death,** by **others both now and then**; but all of them **before** that **last** and **strictest judgment**. But of those who suffer **temporary punishments after death**, all are **not doomed** to those **everlasting pains** which are to follow that judgment; for to some, as we have already said, **what is not remitted in this world is remitted in the next,** that is, they are **not punished** with the **eternal punishment** of the world to come." [756]

St. Augustine does **not** call even *universalism* type of Christians as *heretics* and **nor** does he say that they *deny Holy Scripture*. I believe in either Eternal Hell or Annihilation for the Wicked, i.e. am open to both *possibilities* (different topic). The *new* difference is, **Non Elect Salvation** could be *sinners* who are **not Elect Salvation** and neither are they the **Wicked**.

> "It is in vain, then, that **some, indeed very many**, make moan over the **eternal punishment**, and perpetual, unintermitted torments of the lost, and say **they do not believe it shall be so; not, indeed, that they directly oppose** themselves to **Holy Scripture,** but, at the suggestion of their own feelings, they soften down everything that seems hard, and give a milder turn to statements which they think are rather designed to terrify than to be received as literally true. ... But let them suppose, if the thought gives them pleasure, that the pains of the damned are, at certain intervals, in some degree assuaged. For even in this case the wrath of God, that is, their condemnation (for it is this, and not any disturbed feeling in the mind of God that is called His wrath), abides upon them; that is, His wrath, though it still remains, does not shut up His tender mercies; though **His tender mercies** are exhibited, not in putting an end to their eternal punishment, but in

---

[755] St. Augustine of Hippo. The *Enchiridion* on Faith, Hope and Love. Chapters 69 and 70. www.newadvent.org/fathers/1302.htm

[756] St. Augustine of Hippo. *The City of God*. Book 21. Chapter 13. www.newadvent.org/fathers/120121.htm

mitigating, or in granting them a respite from, their torments; for the psalm does not say, to put an end to His anger, or, when His anger is passed by, but in His anger. Now, if this anger stood alone, or **if it existed** in the **smallest conceivable degree,** yet to be **lost out of the kingdom of God,** to be an exile from the city of God, to be alienated from the life of God, to have no share in that great goodness which God has laid up for them that fear Him, and has wrought out for them that trust in Him, would be a punishment so great, that, supposing it to be eternal, no torments that we know of, continued through as many ages as man's imagination can conceive, could be compared with it."[757]

The important thing is that even St. Augustine of Hippo who is considered as having a *high* level of *spiritual anointing* by many Christians (including Catholic, Orthodox and Protestants alike) does **not** see even *universalism* believing type of Christians as *possessed by the devil* or *unsaved* while our **Non Elect Salvation** position is much better than *universalism* (from St. Augustine's view, implied) and it's only a *possibility and not doctrine*, hence risking no one's faith in such discussions.

5.   St. Jerome of the Vulgate (c. 343 AD – 420 AD).

St. Jerome initially believed in Christ centred universalism but after the time when this letter was written (c. 394 AD), he began to believe in eternal hell only for the unsaved. However, it is interesting to note that he is quoting St. Hilary of Poitiers (c. 310 AD – c. 368 AD who is already dead for at about 30 years by now) as a *Christian universalist* which is important since it is well known that God used St. Hilary to being back the *Doctrine of Trinity* in "Western Christianity" and so St. Hilary is sometimes honoured with the title *the Athanasius of the West*. So if God can use a person who believed in Universalism for such important doctrinal correction in another topic, no Churches should discriminate us either for considering the weaker **Non Elect Salvation** as a *possibility only (not doctrine)*. Notice also how St. Jerome quotes St. Hilary's defence of *Trinity* doctrine for some parts below which was made on *Universalism* grounds as well.

> "5. Your third and last question relates to the passage in the same epistle where the apostle in discussing the **resurrection** … 28 I am surprised that you have resolved to question me about this passage when that **reverend man, Hilary, bishop of Poictiers,**

---

[757] St. Augustine of Hippo. The *Enchiridion* on Faith, Hope and Love. Chapter 112. www.newadvent.org/fathers/1302.htm

has occupied the **eleventh book of his treatise against the Arians** with a **full examination and explanation of it.** Yet I may at least say a few words. … and I, if I be lifted up from the earth, will draw all men unto me. John 12:32 Christ then is subject to the Father in the faithful; for all believers, nay the **whole human race,** are accounted members of His body. But in **unbelievers,** that is in Jews, heathens, and heretics, He is said to be **not subject;** for these members of His body are **not subject to the faith.** But in the **end of the world** when all His members shall **see Christ,** that is their own body, reigning, **they also shall be made subject to Christ,** that is to their own body, that the whole of Christ's body may be subject unto God and the Father, and that God may be all in all. He does not say that the Father may be all in all but that God may be, a title which properly belongs to the **Trinity** and may be referred not only to the Father but also to the Son and to the Holy Ghost. His **meaning** therefore is **that humanity may be subject to the Godhead.** By **humanity** we here intend **not** that gentleness and kindness which the Greeks call **philanthropy** but **the whole human race.** Moreover when **he says** that **God may be all in all,** it is to be **taken in this sense."**[758]

St. Jerome of the Vulgate was used by God to do the "Latin Vulgate" translation of the Bible which was the *only one* used to convert people into salvation in the Western World for at least 1000 years! (i.e. between c. 500 AD to c. 1500 AD). Rival Bible translations only appeared after the Protestant Reformation. Even such an important influencer in Christianity as a whole may have believed in **Non Elect Salvation** in his quote below which refers clearly to *non-Christians* context since he is quoting Christ's Parable regarding where the "Gospel Seed was sowed not" (perhaps this refers to the *unlearnt case and also where the ground did not receive it*):

> "Also, by this which this servant dared to say, Thou, **reapest** where **thou sowedst not,** we **understand** that the **Lord accepts** the **good life** of the **Gentiles** and of the **Philosophers.**"[759]

---

[758] St. Jerome of the Vulgate. Letter 55. *To Amandus.* Point 5. www.newadvent.org/fathers/3001055.htm

[759] Commentary On the Four Gospels Collected Out of the Works of the Fathers: Volumes 1 to 4. *Catena Aurea* by St. Thomas Aquinas. *Commentary on Matthew 25:14 – 30.* Oxford: John Henry Parker; J. G. F. and J. Rivington. London. 1841. www.ecatholic2000.com/catena/

St. Jerome of the Vulgate's **Non Elect Salvation** quote toward *non-Christians* is clearest in his *Commentary on Prophet Amos* below because he applies the context of 1 Corinthians 3:15's **Baptism by Fire** with judgment first which is followed by being **Saved by Fire** case to apply as an **extreme medicine,** [to the] **ten tribes, and heretics, and all sinners** as follows:

> "When he did these things for the healer, they did not even return to him, says the Lord. I overthrew you as God overthrew **Sodom and Gomorrah**, and you have become like a furnace taken from the fire, and you have not returned to me, says the Lord. 70; You have been overthrown as God overthrew Sodom and Gomorrah, and you have **become like a furnace taken out of the fire**, and you have not even come to me like this, says the Lord. it is an **extreme medicine, and ten tribes, and heretics, and all sinners**, as after he sent death in the ways of Egypt, and smote their young men with the sword, the horses which he had consumed, and caused the rottenness of the camp to come up into their nostrils, and they did not even so return to him , overthrow them as God overthrew Sodom and Gomorrah; and when they have been overthrown, because of the **likeness of the crimes of Sodom and Gomorrah,** the **worst** in which the **divine fire burned up** the edifices, **they themselves will be freed as if caught in a burning furnace.** and how the lot, having reached Sodom, he was buried, losing his substance and part of his body, which we understand to be his wife, so let **all these men of Sodom, losing their riches, escape naked**, according to what we read in the **apostle: if his work remains that which he has built up, he will receive a reward; but if his work burns, he will suffer loss,** but he **himself will be saved, even so as though by fire.** He therefore **who is saved by fire** is **snatched away as if by a burning torch**. and to such men as the Salvator [*Saviour*] spoke in the Gospel arguing: if you were Abraham's children, you would do Abraham's works. John the Baptist says: descendants of the Jews, who has shown you to flee from the wrath to come? therefore bear fruit worthy of repentance, and do not be unwilling to say that we have Abraham as our father within. for I say unto you, since God can raise up Abraham's children from these stones? therefore both Israel and all the heretics because they had the works of Sodom and Gomorrah, they are **overthrown like Sodom and Gomorrah,** that **they may be delivered from the fire** as though **they had been snatched away from the fire**. and this is what we read in the **prophet: Sodom** shall be **restored** to its

former state, so that he who is a **Sodomite by his own will, after the works of Sodom have burned in him, shall be restored to his former state**. therefore I will do these things to you, Israel; But after I have done these things for you, prepare to meet your God, O Israel; for behold, he forming the mountains, and creating the wind, and declaring his speech to man, making the morning mist, and walking on the heights of the earth, the Lord of Hosts is his name. 70: therefore I will do this to you, O Israel; indeed, because I will do this to you, to prepare that you may call upon your god, Israel"[760]

Notice carefully this part where St. Jerome of the Vulgate *differentiates* 1 Corinthians 3:14 to refer to a *reward* case (hence **Elect Salvation** with minimum *thirtyfold* reward level for "good ground", Matthew 13:8, implied] as opposed to 1 Corinthians 3:15's case of **Saved by Fire** with "no reward" and "suffered loss" in comparison [so **Non Elect Salvation** with "no inheritance"]as he further states that their *sin level* matches even the *worst* type of *Sodom and Gomorrah* type of "sinners" in the above [compare with my *interpolation* in pages 134 – 135 with St. Irenaeus' *let go* on Judgment Day case]:

"so let **all these men of Sodom, losing their riches, escape naked**, according to what we read in the **apostle: if his work remains that which he has built up, he will receive a reward**; but **if his work burns, he will suffer loss**, but he **himself will be saved, even so as though by fire**. He therefore **who is saved by fire is snatched away as if by a burning torch**."

Some Bible verses quoted by St. Jerome here:

"14If anyone's **work** which he has built on it **endures**, he will receive a **reward**. 15If anyone's **work** is **burned**, he will **suffer loss**; but **he himself** will be **saved**, yet so as **through fire**"[761]

---

[760] St. Jerome of the Vulgate. *Commentary on Prophet Amos*. Chapter 4. www.documentacatholicaomnia.eu/02m/0347-0420,_Hieronymus,_Commentariorum_In_Amos_Prophetam_Libri_Tres,_MLT.pdf [Note: I *cannot* read Latin either. I used *Google Translate* to do it from this source which is non-existent now: sites.google.com/site/aquinasstudybible/home/amos/st-jerome-on-amos—latin]. The English translation is copyrighted but the Latin one is available for *public* use as stated in these official Orthodox and Roman Catholic sources respectively: www.fourthcentury.com/jerome-commentary-on-amos/ pointing to www.documentacatholicaomnia.eu/04z/z_0347-0420__Hieronymus__Commentariorum_In_Amos_Prophetam_Libri_Tres__MLT.pdf.html which I believe is the same Latin version I used for my quote here.

[761] 1 Corinthians 3:14 – 15 (NKJV). biblehub.com/nkjv/1_corinthians/3.htm

> "53"When I bring back their captives, the captives of Sodom and her daughters, and the captives of Samaria and her daughters, then I will also bring back the captives of your captivity among them, 54that you may **bear your own shame** and be **disgraced by all** that you did when you comforted them. 55When your sisters, **Sodom and her daughters, return to their former state**, and **Samaria** and her daughters **return to their former state**, then you and **your daughters** will **return to your former state.**"[762]

"11"I overthrew some of you, As God overthrew **Sodom and Gomorrah**, And you were like a **firebrand plucked from the burning**; Yet you have **not returned to Me**," Says the Lord. 12"Therefore thus will I do to you, O Israel; Because I will do this to you, Prepare to meet your God, O Israel!"[763]

6. St. Gregory the Great (c. 540 AD – c. 604 AD), bishop of Rome (Pope).

Just like St. Augustine, St. Gregory the Great also only applies purgatory for *Christians* context and limits it some small sins.

> "But yet we must believe that **before** the day of **judgment** there is a **Purgatory fire** for certain small sins: because our Saviour saith, that he which speaketh blasphemy against the holy Ghost, that it shall not be forgiven him, neither in this world, nor in the world to come.66 Out of which sentence we learn, that some sins are forgiven in this world, and **some other may be pardoned in the next:** for that which is **denied** concerning one sin, is consequently understood to be **granted** touching some other." [764]

However, there is a *mysterious* event reported in his lifetime by some credible sources including St. John of Damascus ("last father of the church") who state this real-life event where **Non Elect Salvation** could have been granted to the *evil Emperor Trajan* who *killed many Christians* after the prayers of St. Gregory the Great for him based on some *Charity Doctrine* defence Trajan did during his life by avenging the unjust death of a son of a widow.

---

[762] Ezekiel 16:53 – 55 (NKJV). biblehub.com/nkjv/ezekiel/16.htm

[763] Amos 4:11 – 12 (NKJV). biblehub.com/nkjv/amos/4.htm

[764] St. Gregory the Great. *Dialogues* (1911). Book 4. Chapter 39. pp. 177-258. www.tertullian.org/fathers/gregory_04_dialogues_book4.htm

If this story is true and since God has no partiality, isn't most of our *non-Christian* friends much better than Trajan since they would never 'kill a Christian', right? So, the reason why God asked Trajan to stop praying for ones like Trajan (as the story goes) is probably because He might save them due to prayers by Christians which is probably only fair at the end of time when the Bride calls such *thirsty* ones to partake of the water at the Final Scene only (Revelation 22:17). Here's that story:

> "Remember that **Pope Saint Gregory the Great prayed for the Emperor Trajan and his prayer was heard**...Trajan was saved: the Roman emperor, he who was a pagan, he who killed Christians in the Colosseum! Why did this great Pope of Rome pray for Trajan? Because there was a time when the holy Church of Rome was joined with her sister Churches and there was a time **when the Romans believed that God would deliver souls from hell. But in later centuries this teaching has been lost.** We see the belief in the great prayer which still remains in the **Roman liturgy for the dead:** "Libera animas omnium fidelium defunctorum de poenis inferni et de profundo lacu." Roman scholars will say that this prayer means exactly what it says. Roman theologians will say that this was an error in the belief of the ancient Church and they have corrected it. **They have retained the prayer but they no longer understand it as their ancestors in the faith understood it.** There is no doubt that **our ancestors in the faith, from the Emerald Isle, during the first millennium believed that souls could be released from hell.**"[765]

Now, here's that story from a Roman Catholic source which objects that this incident can be applied generally to every other case for *Non Elect Salvation* possibility. Regardless of their objections, they do not deny that it happened and so let God decide which is it one day.

> "Objection 5. Further, the **Damascene** in the same **sermon** relates that **Gregory**, while **praying** for **Trajan**, heard **a voice from heaven** saying to him: "I have heard thy voice, and **I pardon Trajan**": and of this fact the Damascene adds in the same sermon, "the **whole East and West are witnesses**." Yet it is clear that **Trajan was in hell**, since "he put **many martyrs to a cruel**

---

[765] Orthodox Christianity. Online Forum. Via user: Hieromonk Ambrose. www.byzcath.org/forums/ubbthreads.php/topics/339693/Praying%20people%20out%20of%20hell

death" [De his qui fide dormierunt]. Therefore the **suffrages of the Church** avail even for **those** who are in **hell**."⁷⁶⁶ ⁷⁶⁷

7. St. Athanasius (c. 297 AD – c. 373 AD), bishop of Alexandria.

Here, St. Athanasius the Great writes the *love of God* which surpasses knowledge includes the context of Christ being known even in *Hades* context:

> "2. This, too, is what Paul means to point out when he says: That ye being rooted and grounded in love, may be strong to apprehend with all the saints what is the breadth and length, and height and depth, and to know the **love of Christ which passes knowledge**, ... 3. For by the **Word revealing Himself everywhere**, both above and **beneath**, and in the depth and in the breadth — above, in the creation; beneath, in becoming man; **in the depth, in Hades**; and in the breadth, in the world — all things have been filled with the knowledge of God."⁷⁶⁸

The context in which St. Athanasius the Great meant in regard to Christ being known even in *Hades* is explained later in this same famous book on which he defended the *Doctrine of Trinity* and earned the title *Father of Orthodoxy*, that is done also on the grounds of possibly referring to **Non Elect Salvation** regarding those *believing after seeing* Christ in *Hades* as it seems to be *literally* implied next, because St. Athanasius says that even *in Hades* that man can *worship God rightly* and be *undeceived* which is seen as follows:

> "Or if a man is gone astray among demons, and is in fear of them, he may see this man drive them out, and make up his mind that He is their Master. Or if a man has sunk to the waters , and thinks that they are God — as the Egyptians, for instance, reverence the water — he may see its nature changed by Him, and learn that the Lord is Creator of the waters. 4. **But if a man is gone down even to Hades**, and stands in awe of the heroes who have descended there, regarding them as gods, yet he may see the **fact of Christ's Resurrection and victory over death**, and infer

---

⁷⁶⁶ St. Thomas Aquinas (1225 AD – 1274 AD). *Summa Theologiae*. Supplement to the Third Part (Supplementum Tertiæ Partis). Article 5. Objection 5. www.newadvent.org/summa/5071.htm

⁷⁶⁷ St. John of Damascus. Sermon. *De his qui in fide dormierunt*. PG 95:264. www.biblindex.org/en/work-editions/oratio-de-his-qui-in-fide-dormierunt/patrologia-graeca-95

⁷⁶⁸ St. Athanasius the Great. *On the Incarnation of the Word*. Chapter 16. Points 2 and 3. www.newadvent.org/fathers/2802.htm

that among them also **Christ alone is true God** and Lord. 5. For the **Lord touched all** parts of **creation**, and **freed** and **undeceived** all of them from every illusion; as Paul says: Having Colossians 2:15 put off from Himself the principalities and the powers, He triumphed on the Cross: that **no one might by any possibility be any longer deceived**, but **everywhere** might find the **true Word of God**. 6. For thus man, shut in on every side, and beholding the **divinity of the Word unfolded everywhere**, that is, in heaven, **in Hades**, in man, upon earth, **is no longer exposed to deceit concerning God, but is to worship Christ alone,** and **through Him come rightly to know the Father.** 7. By these arguments, then, on grounds of reason, the Gentiles in their turn will fairly be put to shame by us. But if they deem the arguments insufficient to shame them, let them be assured of what we are saying at any rate by facts obvious to the sight of all."[769]

The **Non Elect Salvation** part of *Worshipping Christ* rightly and coming to *know the Father* via *believing after seeing* in *Hades* seems to be implied here by St. Athanasius is (I re-emphasize):

"**4. But if a man is gone down even to Hades,** ... For the **Lord touched all** parts of **creation,** ... that **no one might by any possibility be any longer deceived,** but **everywhere** might find the **true Word of God** ... beholding the **divinity of the Word unfolded everywhere,** that is, in heaven, **in Hades** ... **is no longer exposed to deceit concerning God, but is to worship Christ alone,** and **through Him come rightly to know the Father.**"

8. St. John Chrysostom (c. 347 AD – c. 407 AD), archbishop of Constantinople.

St. John Chrysostom was nicknamed "Golden-Mouthed" due to his eloquence in preaching. The Catholics use this vague quote by him next in support of purgatory too. I say vague because he implies that *some* of those prayed for via Christians who do *Charity Doctrine* get some type of *comfort* in the *Spirit World* as a result which I infer as **Non Elect Salvation** *possibility* because I don't think such delivered ones would be in the same regions as Christians who lived holy, believed and suffered for Christ which he himself calls this **Elect Salvation** *regions* differently as *perfect deliverance* below.

---

[769] St. Athanasius the Great. *On the Incarnation of the Word.* Chapter 45. Points 3 – 7. www.newadvent.org/fathers/2802.htm

"By **means of his substance**, by means of your own, by what means you will, aid him: ... Has he **no almsdeeds of his own** to exhibit? Let him have at least those of his kindred. ... The **more sins** he has to answer for, the **greater need has he of alms**, not only for this reason, but because the **alms** has not the same virtue now, but far less: for it is not all one to have done it himself, and to have another do it for him; therefore, the virtue being less, let us by quantity make it the greatest. Let us not busy ourselves about monuments, not about memorials. This is the greatest memorial: set widows to stand around him. Tell them his name: bid them all make for him their prayers, their supplications: this will overcome God: though it have not been done by the man himself, yet because of him another is the author of the **almsgiving**. Even this pertains to the **mercy of God**: widows standing around and weeping know how to **rescue, not** indeed from the **present death**, but from **that which is to come. Many** have **profited even by the alms done by others on their behalf**: for even **if they have not got perfect (deliverance),** at least **they have found some comfort thence.** If it be not so, how are children saved? And yet there, the children themselves contribute nothing, but their parents do all: and often have women had their children given them, though the children themselves contributed nothing. Many are the ways God gives us to be saved, only let us not be negligent."[770]

9. St. Basil the Great (c. 329 AD – c. 379 AD), bishop of Caesarea.

St. Basil the Great is probably revealing what his predecessors taught regarding the *prayer for the dead* where a class of those released from the prison of Hades could be **Non Elect Salvation** even if he applies it only to believers since beliefs could change over time. So, no harm in trying and let God decide.

"O Christ our God ... (who) on this all-perfect and saving Feast, art graciously pleased to accept **propitiatory prayers for those who are imprisoned in hades,** promising unto us who are held in bondage **great hope of release** from the vilenes that doth hinder us and did hinder them, ... send down Thy consolation ... and establish their souls in the mansions of the Just; and graciously vouchsafe unto them peace and **pardon**; for not the dead shall praise thee, O Lord, neither shall they who are in **Hell** make bold

---

[770] St. John Chrysostom. *Homily 21 on the Acts of the Apostles.* Acts 9:26, 27. www.newadvent.org/fathers/210121.htm

to offer unto thee confession. But we who are living will bless thee, and will pray, and offer unto thee propitiatory prayers and sacrifices for their souls."[771]

10. St. Hilary of Poitiers (c. 315 AD – c. 368 AD), the Athanasius of the West.

In his famous book, Professor Philip Schaff reveals that St. Hilary of Poitiers argues that the baptized will eventually be saved since even *Sodom and Gomorrah* can be *saved after some Spirit World Judgments* in analogy which can be **Non Elect Salvation** again since those of Sodom are not going to be part of the "Bride of Christ":

> "Hence a prevalent tone of hopefulness about the **future state of the baptized**; even **Sodom** and **Gomorrah**, their **punishment** in history having satisfied the righteousness of God, **shall ultimately be saved**359. Yet God has a perfect, immutable goodness of which human goodness, though real, falls infinitely short, because He is steadfast and we are driven by varying impulses360. This Divine goodness is the standard and the hope set before us. It can only be attained by grace361, and grace is freely offered. But just as **the soul, being free**, advances to meet sin, so it **must advance to meet grace**."[772]

Even a holy Christian man whom God used to bring back and establish the *Doctrine of Trinity* in the West, such as St. Hilary of Poitiers wrote in that very famous book of his which defended Trinity, that the subjection of his *enemies* causes death to cease and they too *seem to* experience immortality thereafter, in his quote next which sounds more like *universalism* than even the weaker **Non Elect Salvation** possibility here:

> "35. But we must not forget what follows the subjection, namely, **Last** of all is **death** conquered by Him. 1 Corinthians 15:26 This victory over death is nothing else than the **resurrection from the dead**: for when the corruption of death is stayed, the

---

[771] St. Basil the Great. *Third Kneeling Prayer at Pentecost*. Isabel F. Hapgood, Service Book of the Holy Orthodox-Catholic Apostolic Church (Antiochian Orthodox Christian Archdiocese, Englewood, New Jersey, 1975, 5th edition), p. 255. www.ccel.org/ccel/schaff/encyc09.html?term=Purgatory

[772] Schaff, Philip. *Hilary of Poitiers, John of Damascus*. The Theology of St. Hilary of Poitiers. Nicene and Post-Nicene Fathers: Series II, Volume 9. USA, Grand Rapids, MI: Christian Classics Ethereal Library. 1899. Page 123. ccel.org/ccel/s/schaff/npnf209/cache/npnf209.pdf

quickened and now heavenly nature is made eternal, as it is written, For this corruptible must put on incorruption, and this mortal must put on immortality. But when this mortal shall have put on immortality, then shall come to pass the saying that is written, Death is swallowed up in strife. O death, where is your sting? O death, where is your strife ? **In the subjection of His enemies death is conquered**; and, **death conquered, life immortal follows**. The Apostle tells us also of the special reward attained by this subjection which is made perfect by the subjection of belief: Who shall fashion anew the body of our humiliation, that it may be conformed to the body of His glory, according to the works of His power, whereby He is able to subject all things to Himself. Philippians 3:21 There is then another subjection, which consists in a transition from one nature to another, for our nature ceases, so far as its present character is concerned, and is subjected to Him, into Whose form it passes. But by 'ceasing' is implied not an end of being, but a promotion into something higher. Thus our nature by being merged into the image of the other nature which it receives, becomes subjected through the imposition of a new form."[773]

11. St. Cyril (c. 376 AD – c. 444 AD), archbishop of Alexandria.

St. Cyril of Alexandria writes that during Christ's descent into Hades, He did not just save the *righteous* Old Testament faithful and unlearnt Gentiles but also *freed* those who were *sinners* where if true, together with my *interpolation* that I don't think these *freed sinners* would be "His Bride" nor enter Heaven (since some of them are actually getting a *second* chance in Hades since they heard the "preaching of Noah" which is allegory for "preaching the Gospel" on earth, but yet "refused to repent on earth" and so *likewise* such hope *may* be available even today) so, this means these could be part of the "final saved nations who don't enter heaven on that final new earth" (Revelation 21:24 – 27) in our *Chiliasm* Model being **Non Elect Salvation** possibility only.

"What occasion will we still have for weeping? On the contrary, will not what has happened to us, thanks to the Savior, cause us boundless rejoicing? He it was Who showed **the way of salvation not only to us,** but also went as herald to the **once disobedient spirits of the underworld,** as Peter says (1 Pet. 3:19-

---

[773] St. Hilary of Poitiers. *On the Trinity*. Book 11. Point 35. www.newadvent.org/fathers/330211.htm

20). For it would not have done for His loving-kindness to be shown only to some; the manifestation of the gift had to extended to all of nature. For He spoke opportunely through the **Prophets**, "One part shall be rained upon, and the part on which I shall not rain shall be dried up." (Amos 4:7) But the word which befits the Savior is: "Come to me, all you who labor and are weary, and I will give you rest." (Mt. 11:28) Having proclaimed His message, then, to the **spirits in the underworld** and **having said to those in fetters, "Come forth!"** and to **those in darkness, "Show yourselves!"** (cf. Isa. 49:9) He raised up the temple of Himself in three days, (cf. Jn. 2:19) and renewed for nature even the ascent into heaven, presenting Himelf to the Father as a kind of first-fruits of humanity, having endowed those on earth with a share of the Spirit as a pledge of grace. (cf. 2 Cor. 5:5) (Festal Letter 2.8)"[774]

St. Cyril is quoting these Bible verses where notice that these "spirits in prison" refers to not Old Testament righteous but more likely to those who are "punished" in Hades which is signified by the word "prison", "no word calling them just/righteous is used" and that they "heard the [Gospel allegory] via the preaching of Noah on earth and rejected it" but now, when Christ preaches a *Second* time to them in the *Spirit World*, they "repent" which is stated here as "formerly were disobedient" which simply means they're not disobedient anymore and so are likely to be *saved* which could be **Non Elect Salvation:**

"18For Christ also suffered once for sins, the just for the unjust, that He might bring [f]us to God, being put to **death** in the **flesh** but made **alive** by the **Spirit**, 19by whom also He went and preached to the **spirits in prison**, 20who **formerly were disobedient**, [g]when once the **Divine longsuffering waited** in the **days of Noah**, while the ark was being prepared, in which a few, that is, eight souls, were saved through water."[775]

Its continuation today may be marked by this Bible verse from this same 1 Peter letter too since it's clearly mentioned that these ones are *judged first before being saved* which can indicate that this "Gospel Preaching" seems to be done to those "literally dead" and not those 'spiritually dead' since the earlier

---

[774] St. Cyril of Alexandria. *Festal Letter 2.8*. Catholic University of America Press. 2009. Washington, D.C. archive.org/details/festalletters1120000cyri/page/n271/mode/2up or Orthodox quotation here: classicalchristianity.com/category/bysaint/st-cyril-of-alexandria-ca-376-444/

[775] 1 Peter 3:18 – 20 (NKJV). biblehub.com/nkjv/1_peter/3.htm

consecutive verses with it do indicate that such ones are 'spiritually dead' and no indication is given as to any repentance of them on earth.

So, these verses may be speaking of a *Second* chance for "Gospel preaching in Hades likewise" after they're dead (since they did not repent on earth being spiritually dead there first in their sins) and thereafter are judged and saved in Spirit World context which can link to the *Baptism by Fire* especially since the "judged in the flesh" part before being *saved* in *Chiliasm* Model can refer to Matthew 3:11 – 12's context as discussed in Essay 10 later.

> "3For we have spent enough of our past [b]lifetime in doing the will of the Gentiles—when we walked in lewdness, lusts, drunkenness, revelries, drinking parties, and abominable idolatries. 4In regard to these, they think it strange that you do not run with them in the same flood of dissipation, **speaking evil of you**. **5They** will give an account to Him who is ready to **judge** the **living** and the **dead**. 6For this reason the **gospel was preached also to those who are dead**, that they might be **judged** according to men in the **flesh**, but **live** according to God in the **spirit**."[776]

Notice that Apostle St. Paul also mentioned something similar in regard to a *fallen Christian* living in *sexual immorality* to be "judged in the flesh and saved" thereafter not now on earth but in the *future* **Day of Lord Jesus** which can refer to this 1000 years Millennial Reign timeline meaning that *Cleansing Fire* can apply to such before they're saved. The "dead" in verse 5 and 6 are same and words like "who are dead" are added by some translators (but not others, both scholars) as you can read and compare with the original Interlinear too.

> "deliver such a one to Satan for the **destruction of the flesh,** that **his spirit** may be **saved** in the **day** of the **Lord Jesus**."[777]

Also, if the context of this person's salvation included being judged in the flesh *now*, then wouldn't his salvation in the *spirit world* be immediate, i.e. *absent in the body and present in the Lord* case [778] for **Elect Salvation** instead of the specific mention of 'future Day of Lord Jesus' here? Another important

---

[776] 1 Peter 4:3 – 6 (NKJV). biblehub.com/nkjv/1_peter/4.htm

[777] 1 Corinthians 5:5 (NKJV). biblehub.com/1_corinthians/5-5.htm

[778] 2 Corinthians 5:8, "We are confident, yes, well pleased rather to be **absent from the body** and to be **present with the Lord**" (NKJV). biblehub.com/2_corinthians/5-8.htm

point is that some scholars point that he repented on earth [779] but this 2 Corinthians letter was written *later* (about 2 – 3 years gap [780]) than this 1 Corinthians letter and *separately* meaning that at the *time of the writing*, only a "sexually immoral Christian sinner" seems to be implied and so, Apostle St. Paul's 1 Corinthians verses seem to point to post-mortem salvation after judgment, right?

If these *interpolations* are true, then the *Baptism by Fire* described in Essay 10 with *Chiliasm* quotes can refer to either done for *souls (spirit)* or *bodily* case unto *Judgment* and they're *saved* in *Second Resurrection* thereafter *bodily*. It is also possible in light of say 1 Peter 4:5 here, that two such judgments run in parallel in the Millennium (one earthly and one Spirit World context as some of these verses are interpreted by scholars and Church Father quotes both ways too where *maybe* both are true since Scripture can have both is *literal and allegorical* meaning at the same time).

Back to St. Cyril, here's another quote of his which proves **Non Elect Salvation** since if it's true and something which is preserved through *apostolic succession* of leadership before him, then due to the fact that it involves *all wicked*, it sounds more like *universalism* which could also mean St. Cyril generalized too much making no distinction between *sinners* vs *wicked* (but which is *accurate*, only God knows).

> "For having destroyed hell and opened the impassable gates for the departed spirits, He left the devil there abandoned and lonely" [781]

12. St. Cyril (c. 315 AD – c. 386 AD), archbishop of Jerusalem.

St. Cyril of Jerusalem seems to hint on **Non Elect Salvation** possibility for "some" via *believing after seeing* in the context of *Spirit World* for those *punished* in *Hades* in his famous quote next but notice carefully how he says that this is a **Mystery** meaning *not many Christians too may know it* but he is an archbishop of **Jerusalem** where the **Gospel was born** and so may be

---

[779] 2 Corinthians 2:5 – 8, "5But if anyone has caused grief, he has not grieved me, but all of you to some extent—not to be too severe. 6This punishment which was inflicted by the majority is sufficient for such a man, 7so that, on the contrary, you ought rather to forgive and comfort him, lest perhaps such a one be swallowed up with too much sorrow. 8Therefore I urge you to reaffirm your love to him" (NKJV). biblehub.com/nkjv/2_corinthians/2.htm

[780] Encyclopedia. Britannica. *Letters of Paul to the Corinthians*. www.britannica.com/topic/The-Letter-of-Paul-to-the-Corinthians

[781] St. Cyril of Alexandria. *7th Paschal Homily 2*. PG 77, 552 A. orthodoxeurope.org/page/11/1/5.aspx

acquainted with such hidden mysteries. (Notice that those of **Elect Salvation** in comparison are saved "before they die" and "do not endure any Spirit World Judgment" having attained to the minimum "thirtyfold reward level" for "good ground" where "good" ones don't get punished more, right?). Here is that possibility if he means this since he talks about a **twofold** descent of Christ with an implication in **Hades** where he doesn't conclude whether Christ Saved all there or only those who believed when they say Christ in Hadees during His Descent:

> "And if, like a Thomas, you were left out when the disciples were assembled to whom Christ shews Himself, when you do see Him be not faithless;4674 and if you do not believe, then believe those who tell you; and if you cannot believe them either, then have confidence in the print of the nails. **If He descend into Hell**,4675 descend with Him. Learn to know the **mysteries of Christ there also**, what is the providential purpose of the **twofold** descent, to **save all men** absolutely by His manifestation, **or there too only them that believe**."782

Some may argue that this is a special case for those who existed before Christ. This could be true but St. Cyril of Jerusalem's next quote seem to imply that he does believe in some type of *Spirit World Salvation after Judgment* which could be **Non Elect Salvation** where this must happen in the "same way" it happened to those mentioned for 'before Christ' timeline, right? Notice that the next quote is not time-limited for the past since it involves *prayers for the dead* even **now** and so seems to include non-Christians too as I will highlight next (as per the phrase **"or there [Hades] too only them that believe"** by him earlier), here:

> "9. Then we commemorate also **those who have fallen asleep** before us, first Patriarchs, Prophets, Apostles, Martyrs, that at their prayers and intercessions God would receive our petition. Then on behalf also of the Holy Fathers and Bishops who have fallen asleep before us, and **in a word of all who in past years have fallen asleep among us**, believing that it will be a very great benefit to the souls, for whom the supplication is put up, while that holy and most awful sacrifice is set forth. 10. And I wish to

---

782 Schaff, Philip. St. Cyril of Jerusalem. *The Second Oration on Easter.* Oration 45 (XLV). Point 24 (XXIV). Nicene and Post-Nicene Fathers (NPNF2 – 07): Series II, Volume 7. USA, Grand Rapids, MI: Christian Classics Ethereal Library. 1893. Page 641. www.documentacatholicaomnia.eu/03d/1819-1893,_Schaff._Philip,_3_Vol_07_Cyril_Of_Jerusalem._Gregory_Nazianzen,_EN.pdf.

persuade you by an illustration. For I know that many say, what is a soul profited, which departs from this world either with sins, or without sins, if it be commemorated in the prayer? For if a king were to banish certain who had given him offense, and then **those who belong to them should weave a crown** and **offer it to him on behalf of those under punishment**, would **he not grant a remission of their penalties?** In the same way we, when we offer to Him our supplications for **those who have fallen asleep, though they be sinners, weave no crown**, but offer up Christ sacrificed for our sins, propitiating our merciful God for them as well as for ourselves."[783]

i. **Elect Salvation** highlight here (Christians/the Bride with "crowns" with minimum thirtyfold level "good ground" harvest of the Gospel, Matthew 13:8 up to "hundredfold" level, Matthew 19:29 in heavens' final dwellings, I *interpolate* in support):

"9. Then we commemorate also **those who have fallen asleep** before us, first Patriarchs, Prophets, Apostles, Martyrs, that at their prayers and intercessions God would receive our petition. Then on behalf also of the Holy Fathers and Bishops who have fallen asleep before us, and **in a word of all who in past years have fallen asleep among us** … For if a king were to banish certain who had given him offense, and then **those who belong to them should weave a crown**"

ii. **Non Elect Salvation** highlight here for those in *Hades* now (i.e. among those who have "fallen asleep" or "dead") who have "no crowns" and are "sinners" but may be "saved by fire" only with "no reward" at the Mercy of God and prayer requests of Christians who may have known them earlier in life who are "judged (punished) first in Hades" who may get an abode in the final new earth as part of the nations saved but not enter heaven too with "kings" (maybe Christians meant) ruling over them as Revelation 21:24 – 27 prophesies:

"For if a king were to banish certain who had given him offense, and then those who belong to them should weave a crown and offer it to him on behalf of those under punishment, would he not grant a remission of their

---

[783] St. Cyril of Jerusalem. *Catechetical Lecture 23* (On the Mysteries. V.). On the Sacred Liturgy and Communion. Points 9, 10. www.newadvent.org/fathers/310123.htm

penalties? In the same way we, when we offer to Him our supplications for **those who have fallen asleep, though they be sinners, weave no crown**, but offer up Christ sacrificed for our sins, propitiating our merciful God for them as well as for ourselves."

Compare with these Bible verses:

"Come, I will show you **the bride, the Lamb's wife** ... and showed me the great city, the holy Jerusalem, descending out of **heaven** from God [784]... 6 ... I will **give** of the fountain of the **water of life freely to him who thirsts.** ... 24And the **nations [n]of those who are saved** shall walk in its light, and the kings of the earth bring their glory and honor [o]into it. ... ... 2In the middle of its street, and on either side of the river, was the **tree of life**, which bore twelve fruits, each tree yielding its fruit every month. The **leaves of the tree** were for the **healing of the nations**. ... 17And the Spirit and the bride say, "Come!" And let him who hears say, "Come!" And **let him who thirsts come. Whoever desires,** let him **take the water of life freely**" [785]

Notice that Bible verses such as the one below prohibits any "salvation" from "judgment" and no participation apart from Christians *only* in the First Resurrection (Ezekiel 14:14, 16, 18, 20) together with some "remnant mortals" (Ezekiel 14:22) and "Baptism by Fire" during the Millennium Judgment in the *Chiliasm* Prophecy Model meaning they do not contradict each other since these (next, Ezekiel prophecy or Matthew 3:11 – 12) parts happen on Old Earth and Old Heavens timeline where the Bible verses quoted earlier (Revelation 21, 22) occur *after* the times of the kingdom in the final New Earth and New Heavens during the "Final Scene" instead, compare:

"19"Or if I send a pestilence into that land and **pour out My fury** on it in blood, and cut off from it man and beast, 20even though **Noah, Daniel, and Job** were in it, as I live," says the Lord God, "they **would deliver neither son nor daughter; they would deliver only themselves** by **their righteousness.**"

21For thus says the Lord God: "How much more it shall be when **I send My four [c]severe judgments on Jerusalem**—the

---

[784] Revelation 21:9 – 10 (NKJV). biblehub.com/nkjv/revelation/21.htm

[785] Revelation 21:6, 24 (NKJV), biblehub.com/nkjv/revelation/21.htm and Revelation 22:2, 17 (NKJV), biblehub.com/nkjv/revelation/22.htm

sword and famine and wild beasts and pestilence—to cut off man and beast from it? 22Yet behold, **there shall be left in it a remnant** who will be brought out, **both sons and daughters**; surely they will come out to you, and you will see their ways and their doings. Then you will be comforted concerning the disaster that I have brought upon Jerusalem, all that I have brought upon it. 23And they will comfort you, when you see their ways and their doings; and you shall know that I have done nothing without cause that I have done in it," says the Lord God."[786]

13. St. John of Damascus (c. 675 AD – c. 749 AD), monk and priest.

St. John of Damascus (John of Damascene) who is sometimes called the "last Church Father" clearly allows praying for the salvation of *non-Christians* even supporting our **Non Elect Salvation** *possibility* in the *Chiliasm* Prophecy Model presented consistently.

> "Did not the Protomartyr save **Falconilla** after the **latter had reposed**? Perhaps you may say that her prayer was heard because she was a martyr. To this I reply that it was indeed fitting that her prayer was heard since she was a martyr. But **consider also on whose behalf the supplication was made. Was it not** for a **pagan**, an **idolater**, altogether **profane** and **estranged from the Lord?**" … One day, as Gregory the Dialogist, Bishop of Old Rome (a man known to all for his holiness and wisdom, of whom it is said that an angel from heaven served with him when he celebrated the Divine Liturgy), was traveling along a paved stone road, he halted and prayed to God, who loves the souls of men, to **forgive the Emperor Trajan his sins.** The Saint straightway heard the **voice of the most heavenly God,** which said to him, 'I have heard your supplication and **shall grant Trajan forgiveness, but I command you to cease your entreaties to Me on behalf of the impure.'** To the **veracity** of this account East and West alike bear witness … The same is true of Falconilla, of whom we spoke before. She was **guilty** only of **worshipping idols, but Trajan sent numerous martyrs to cruel death.** You are wonderful, O Master, and marvelous are Your works, and Your inexpressible compassions do we glorify!"[787]

---

[786] Ezekiel 14:19 – 23 (NKJV). biblehub.com/nkjv/ezekiel/14.htm

[787] St. John of Damascus. *Homily for Meat-Fare Saturday.* arizonaorthodox.com/pray-reposed-non-christians-non-orthodox/

Jonathan Ramachandran

14. St. Bede the Venerable (c. 673 AD – c. 735 AD), monk and scholar.

St. Bede the Venerable is known for his historical accounts and some level of scholastic accuracy which is the reason why he is given the title "Father of English History". In his famous book on *English History*, St. Bede writes about a man who died and came back to life who *may* have seen the *Spirit World* as follows where this man upon coming back to life, even split his possessions equally between his wife, his children and the poor which is clearly a notable *Charity Doctrine* act:

> "At this time a memorable **miracle**, and like to those of former days, was wrought in **Britain**; for, to the end that the living might be roused from the death of the soul, a **certain man, who had been some time dead, rose again to the life of the body**, and related many memorable things that he had seen; some of which I have thought fit here briefly to describe. There was a certain householder in that district of the Northumbrians which is called Incuneningum,841 who led a godly life, with all his house. … Then rising immediately, he went to the oratory of the little town, and continuing in prayer till day, forthwith **divided all** his **substance** into **three parts**; one whereof he gave to **his wife**, another to **his children**, and the **third**, which he kept himself, he straightway **distributed among the poor**. … [*Quoting halfway from this Spirit World Vision part*] … In our return, when we came to those joyous mansions of the white-robed spirits, he said to me, 'Do you know what all these things are which you have seen?' I answered, 'No,' and then he said, 'That **valley** which you beheld **terrible with flaming fire** and **freezing cold**, is the **place** in which **the souls of those are tried and punished**, who, delaying to confess and amend their crimes, at length have **recourse to repentance at the point of death**, and so **go forth from the body**; but nevertheless because they, even **at their death, confessed and repented**, they shall all be **received into the kingdom of Heaven at the day of judgement**; but many are succoured before the day of judgement, by the prayers of the living and their alms and fasting, and more especially by the celebration of Masses. Moreover that foul flaming pit which you saw, is the mouth of **Hell**, into which **whosoever falls** shall **never be delivered** to **all eternity**. This flowery place, in which you see this fair and youthful company, all bright and joyous, is that into which the **souls of those are received** who, indeed, when they **leave the**

body have done good works, but who are **not so perfect** as to deserve to be **immediately admitted** into the **kingdom of Heaven**; yet they shall all, **at the day of judgement, behold Christ**, and **enter** into the joys of **His kingdom**; for such as are **perfect in every word and deed and thought, as soon as they quit the body**, forthwith **enter into the kingdom of Heaven**; in the neighbourhood whereof that place is, where you heard the sound of sweet singing amidst the savour of a sweet fragrance and brightness of light. **As for you, who must now return to the body,** and again live among men, if you will seek diligently to examine your actions, and preserve your manner of living and your words in righteousness and simplicity, you shall, after death, have a place of abode among these joyful troops of blessed souls which you behold. For when I left you for a while, it was for this purpose, that I might learn what should become of you.' When he had said this to me, I much abhorred returning to the body, being delighted with the sweetness and beauty of the place which I beheld, and with the company of those I saw in it. Nevertheless, I durst not ask my guide anything; but thereupon, on a sudden, I found myself, I know not how, alive among men" [788]

Let me highlight again the 4 classes of "souls" revealed in this vision (if true).

i. The **Damned**.

"Moreover that foul flaming pit which you saw, is the mouth of **Hell**, into which **whosoever falls** shall **never** be **delivered** to **all eternity**."

ii. The **Elect**.

"for such as are **perfect in every word and deed and thought, as soon as they quit the body**, forthwith **enter into the kingdom of Heaven**; in the neighbourhood whereof that place is, where you heard the sound of sweet singing amidst the savour of a sweet fragrance and brightness of light."

iii. The **Non Elect Salvation** for "punished" case or "saved by fire" (1 Corinthians 3:15, Daniel 12:10's many "purified", Matthew 3:11

---

[788] St. Bede the Venerable. *Ecclesiastical History of England.* Chapter 12 (Chap. XII. How one in the province of the Northumbrians, rose from the dead, and related many things which he had seen, some to be greatly dreaded and some to be desired. [Circ. 696 a.d.]). Pages 326, 330. A Revised Translation with Introduction, Life, and Notes by A. M. Sellar, Late Vice-Principal of Lady Margaret Hall, Oxford. London. George Bell and Sons. 1907. www.gutenberg.org/files/38326/38326-h/38326-h.html

– 12's Baptism by Fire and John 10:16's sheep of the "other fold"?).

"then he said, 'That **valley** which you beheld **terrible with flaming fire** and **freezing cold**, is the **place** in which **the souls of those are tried and punished**, who, delaying to confess and amend their crimes, at length have **recourse to repentance at the point of death**, and so **go forth from the body**; but nevertheless because they, even **at their death, confessed and repented**, they shall all be **received into the kingdom of Heaven at the day of judgement**"

    iv.   The **Non Elect Salvation** for "not punished" case (Matthew 25:31 – 46's surprised sheep of the nations? John 10:16's sheep of the "other fold"?).

"This flowery place, in which you see this fair and youthful company, all bright and joyous, is that into which the **souls of those are received** who, indeed, when they **leave the body have done good works,** but who are **not so perfect** as to deserve to be **immediately admitted** into the **kingdom of Heaven**; yet they shall all, **at the day of judgement, behold Christ**, and **enter** into the joys of **His kingdom**"

Notice a key difference for the **Non Elect Salvation** part regarding those who repented last minute are punished in fire first but may be saved later (Case iii) where no indication of "Spirit World confession" is mentioned.

Also, notice that the **Non Elect Salvation** possibility for Case iv above only seems to mention **good works** part with *no mention of faith nor of confession* even though in Case iii it is mentioned, meaning Case iv ones could also "include" (but not limited to), those **not perfect** in this aspect or due to any other *sin* reasons likewise (since it's generally mentioned, so I *interpolate*). Thus, despite their "good works" lifestyle in general (perhaps keeping say the keeping of last 6 of the 10 Commandments, see Essay 8), they are still **not Elect Salvation** (who are written earlier to mean **perfect** in the context of **word, thought** and **deed** in comparison).

I mean **imperfect** in "word, thought or deed" **possibly** can include **Non-Christians**, right? In fact, they're specifically mentioned only to **behold Christ** on Judgment Day which seems strange if it is for "Elect Salvation" because all Christians get to meet Christ *right* after death, right? Entering "Kingdom of Heaven" can also mean separation between final "New Heavens" and "New Earth" as Book of Revelation distinguishes.

Could **behold Christ** in Case iv above speak of the Mysterious **believing after seeing** possibility of John 6:29, 35, 36, 40? Compare:

> "29Jesus answered and said to them, "This is the **work of God**, that you **believe in Him** whom He sent." 35And **Jesus** said to them, "I am the bread of life. He who comes to Me shall never hunger, and **he who believes in Me shall never thirst**. 36But I said to you that you have **seen Me** and yet **do not believe**. 40And this is the **will of Him** who sent Me, that **everyone who sees the Son** and **believes in Him** may have **everlasting life**; and I **will raise him up** at the **last day**"[789]

15. St. Maximus the Confessor (c. 580 AD - c. 662 AD), monk and scholar.

St. Maximus the Confessor writes that while some are saved without Judgment (**Elect Salvation**) others can only be saved after Judgment (**Non Elect Salvation**).

> "They who have acquired the **perfection of love for God** and have elevated the wing of the soul through the **virtues**, according to Apostle "are caught up in the clouds" and **do not come into judgment.** And they **who did not completely acquire perfection** but have **acquired both sin and good works**, come into the court of **judgment**; there, **they are scorched as by a fire** by the comparison of their **good** and **evil** deeds, and if, in fact, the scale of their **good deeds weighs downwards**, they are **cleansed** of **punishment**."[790]

Notice that St. Maximus points the context of this passage toward *fallen* Christians and not non-Christians. I wonder if originally such a concept included any man in general but as time went on, the later scholars narrowed it down to include the "saved after Spirit World judgment" case to be only for *fallen* Christians just like Lactantius' quote also rings similarly (shown next).

16. Lactantius (c. 250 AD – c. 325 AD), scholar and advisor to Roman Emperor Constantine I.

---

[789] John 6:29, 35, 36, 40 (NKJV). biblehub.com/nkjv/john/6.htm

[790] St. Maximus the Confessor. *Questions and Doubts*. pg. 143. Various Questions and Selections from Various Passages that are Perplexing, Question I, 10. classicalchristianity.com/2013/12/10/st-maximus-on-the-fire-of-god/

"**Not all men**, however, shall then be judged by God, but those **only** who have been **exercised in the religion of God**. For they who have not known God, since sentence cannot be passed upon them for their acquittal, are already judged and condemned, since the **Holy Scriptures testify that the wicked shall not arise to judgment**. Therefore they who have known God shall be judged, and their deeds, that is, their **evil works**, shall be **compared** and **weighed** against their **good ones**: so that if those which are **good** and **just** are **more** and **weighty**, they may be **given** to a **life** of **blessedness**; but if the **evil exceed**, they may be **condemned** to **punishment**."[791]

Notice that Lactantius is quoting Psalm 1:5's context as the *wicked will not rise in Judgment*. Compare with the *Masoretic* and *Septuagint* Bible translations below:

"4The **ungodly** are not so, But are like the **chaff** which the wind drives away. 5Therefore the **ungodly** shall **not stand** in the **judgment**, Nor **sinners** in the congregation of the **righteous**."[792]

"4Not so the **ungodly**; - not so: but rather as the **chaff** which the **wind scatters away** from the face of the earth. 5Therefore the **ungodly** shall **not rise in judgment, nor sinners** in the counsel of the **just**."[793]

With this too,

"12His winnowing fan is in His hand, and He will thoroughly **clean out His threshing floor**, and **gather** His **wheat** into the barn; but He will **burn** up the **chaff** with **unquenchable fire**."[794]

Firstly, we see that the "wicked (ungodly)" are the "chaff" which has no hope in God's Judgment. Next, in Psalm 5, *sinners* are mentioned with a "different" word which can imply the *possibility* that "sinners" could be "cleansed in that Judgment Fire" (as proposed with quotes in Essay 10's

---

[791] Lactantius. *Divine Institutes*. Book 7 (VII, Of a Happy Life). Chapter 20. www.newadvent.org/fathers/07017.htm

[792] Psalm 1:4 – 5 (NKJV). biblehub.com/nkjv/psalms/1.htm

[793] Psalm 1: 4 – 5 (Brenton's Septuagint Translation). biblehub.com/sep/psalms/1.htm

[794] Matthew 3:12 (NKJV). biblehub.com/matthew/3-12.htm

"Baptism by Fire") but the "righteous/just" meaning those of "faith" [795] are not mingled with sinners either (implying different final abodes e.g. in *Chiliasm* Prophecy Model, the "righteous/just" get the "final new heavens" while the "saved by judgment sinners" only get the "final new earth"). I mean the *Chiliasm* model matches this verse well but whether it is true or not, remains unsure.

Lactantius himself was a *Chiliast* and here are some of his fascinating quotes agreeing to many things I quoted in the previous chapters of *my* writing. These are stated next in *chronological order of time* as he wrote. Firstly, he says that Most Blessed Lord Jesus Christ will Return at the end of the Reign of the final Antichrist and destroy him in stages as follows (i.e. Lactantius may have gotten the picture of *Chiliasm* right but sometimes his details are mixed with interpolations of the *Sibyl* and others):

> "This is the night which is celebrated by us in watchfulness on account of the **coming of our King and God:** of which night there is a twofold meaning; because in it He then received life when He suffered, and hereafter He is about to receive the kingdom of the world. For He is the **Deliverer,** and **Judge, and Avenger,** and **King, and God,** whom we call **Christ,** who before He descends will give this sign: There shall suddenly fall from heaven a sword, that the righteous may know that the leader of the sacred warfare is about to descend; and He shall descend with a company of angels to the middle of the earth, and there shall go before Him an **unquenchable fire,** and the power of the angels shall deliver into the hands of the just that multitude which has surrounded the mountain, and they shall be slain from the third hour until the evening, and blood shall flow like a torrent; and all his forces being destroyed, the wicked one shall alone escape, and his power shall perish from him. **Now this is he who is called Antichrist; but he shall falsely call himself Christ**, and shall fight against the truth, and being overcome shall flee; and shall often renew the war, and often be conquered, until in the fourth battle, all the wicked being slain, subdued, and captured, he shall at length pay the penalty of his crimes. But other princes also and tyrants who have harassed the world, together with him, shall be led in chains to the king; and he shall rebuke them, and reprove them, and upbraid

---

[795] Hebrews 10:38, "Now the **just** shall **live by faith**; But if anyone draws back, My soul has no pleasure in him" (NKJV). biblehub.com/kjv/hebrews/10-38.htm

them with their crimes, and **condemn them, and consign them to deserved tortures.**"[796]

Lactantius is describing this *Chiliasm* Prophecy Model timeline and big picture very accurately when compared to what I have written (minus some of his interpolation details) where for example his view of "Baptism of Fire" (just that the word is not used) is to occur *immediately* after the Second Coming of Christ is very clear next:

"After these things the **lower regions shall be opened,** and **the dead shall rise again**, on whom the same King and God shall pass judgment, to whom the supreme Father shall give the great power both of judging and of reigning. And **respecting this judgment** and reign, it is thus found in the Erythræan Sibyl: —

When this shall receive its fated accomplishment, and the judgment of the immortal God shall now come to mortals, the great judgment shall come upon men, and the beginning.

Then in another:—

And then the gaping earth shall show a Tartarean chaos; and all kings shall come to the judgment-seat of God.

And in another place in the same:—

Rolling along the heavens, I will open the caverns of the earth; and then I will raise the dead, loosing fate and the sting of death; and afterwards I will call them into judgment, judging the life of pious and impious men.

Not all men, however, shall then be judged by God, but those **only** who have been **exercised in the religion of God**. For they who have not known God, since sentence cannot be passed upon them for their acquittal, are already judged and condemned, since the **Holy Scriptures testify that the wicked shall not arise to judgment**. Therefore they who have known God shall be judged, and their deeds, that is, their **evil works**, shall be **compared** and **weighed** against their **good ones**: so that if those which are **good** and **just** are **more** and **weighty**, they may be **given** to a **life** of **blessedness**; but if the **evil exceed**, they may be **condemned** to **punishment**."[797]

---

[796] Lactantius. *Divine Institutes.* Book 7 (VII, Of a Happy Life). Chapter 19. www.newadvent.org/fathers/07017.htm

[797] Lactantius. *Divine Institutes.* Book 7 (VII, Of a Happy Life). Chapter 20. www.newadvent.org/fathers/07017.htm

Notice how Lactantius' quote here *(which I also quoted at the start)* is so similar to both St. Justin of Rome and St. Irenaeus of Lyons' quote using Matthew 3:11 – 12's context of "Baptism by Fire" (in Essay 10) which is to occur in this 1000 years (Millennial Reign) timeline where the only *interpolation* I bring is that those "saved by fire" here could be more than just *fallen* Christians when compared to say St. Irenaeus (page 330) and St. Gregory Nazianzus' quotes for this part (page 320).

Next, he says that those of *First Resurrection* rise and live among *mortal men* (alongside with beasts on *renewed old earth*) with Satan locked up for 1000 years:

> "But He, when He shall have destroyed unrighteousness, and executed His great judgment, and shall have **recalled to life the righteous**, who have lived from the beginning, will be **engaged among men** a **thousand years**, and will rule them with most just command. ... Then they **who shall be alive in their bodies shall not die,** but during those **thousand years** shall produce an infinite multitude, and their offspring shall be holy, and beloved by God; but they who shall be **raised from the dead** shall preside over the living as judges. But the **nations shall not be entirely extinguished**, but **some shall be left** as a victory for God, that they may be the occasion of triumph to the righteous, and may be subjected to perpetual slavery. About the same time also the **prince of the devils**, who is the contriver of all evils, shall be **bound with chains**, and shall be **imprisoned** during the **thousand years** of the heavenly rule in which righteousness shall reign in the world, so that he may contrive no evil against the people of God. After His coming the righteous shall be collected from all the earth, and the judgment being completed, the sacred city shall be planted in the middle of the earth, in which God Himself the builder may dwell together with the righteous, bearing rule in it. ... and the moon will receive the brightness of the sun, nor will it be further diminished: but the sun will become seven times brighter than it now is; and the earth will open its fruitfulness, and bring forth most abundant fruits of its own accord; the rocky mountains shall drop with honey; streams of wine shall run down, and rivers flow with milk: in short, the world itself shall rejoice, and all nature exult, being rescued and set free from the dominion of evil and impiety, and guilt and error. Throughout this time beasts shall not be nourished by blood, nor birds by prey; but all things shall be peaceful and tranquil. Lions and calves shall stand together

at the manger, the wolf shall not carry off the sheep, the hound shall not hunt for prey; hawks and eagles shall not injure; the infant shall play with serpents. ... Therefore men will live a most tranquil life, abounding with resources, and will reign together with God; and the kings of the nations shall come from the ends of the earth with gifts and offerings, to adore and honour the great King, whose name shall be renowned and venerated by all the nations which shall be under heaven, and by the kings who shall rule on earth."[798]

At the end of this 1000 years, Satan will be released and will do one last deception which fails and thereafter the Great White Throne Judgment Day follows next.

"We have said, a little before, that it will come to pass at the commencement of the sacred reign, that the prince of the devils will be bound by God. But he also, when the **thousand years of the kingdom**, that is, seven thousand of the world, shall begin to be **ended**, will be loosed afresh, and being sent forth from prison, will go forth and assemble all the nations, which shall then be under the dominion of the righteous, that they may make war against the holy city; and there shall be collected together from all the world an innumerable company of the nations, and shall besiege and surround the city. Then the last anger of God shall come upon the nations, and shall utterly destroy them; and first He shall shake the earth most violently, and by its motion the mountains of Syria shall be rent, and the hills shall sink down precipitously, and the walls of all cities shall fall, and God shall cause the sun to stand, so that he set not for three days, and shall set it on fire;"[799]

Amazingly, Lactantius also mentions this *Chiliasm* Prophecy that those of First Resurrection (implied) **change** from **human** to **angelic** as the end of this 1000 years (or *millennium*) as the meaning of 1 Corinthians 15:52's "twinkling of an eye change" (which I detailed out with other *Chiliasm* Church Fathers in Chapter 15 that **1 Thessalonians 4:17 and 1 Corinthians 15:52 are separated by 1000 years**) and he ends by saying **holy prophets** and **Christians** follow these details accurately in his quote below.

---

[798] Lactantius. *Divine Institutes.* Book 7 (VII, Of a Happy Life). Chapter 24. www.newadvent.org/fathers/07017.htm

[799] Lactantius. *Divine Institutes.* Book 7 (VII, Of a Happy Life). Chapter 26. www.newadvent.org/fathers/07017.htm

"Then the righteous shall go forth from their hiding-places, and shall find all things covered with carcasses and bones. But the whole race of the wicked shall utterly perish; and there shall no longer be any nation in this world, but the nation of God alone. Then for seven continuous years the woods shall be untouched, nor shall timber be cut from the mountains, but the arms of the nations shall be burnt; and now there shall be no war, but peace and everlasting rest. But when the **thousand years shall be completed**, the world shall be renewed by God, and the heavens shall be folded together, and the earth shall be changed, and God shall **transform men into the similitude of angels**, and **they shall be white as snow;** and they shall always be employed in the sight of the Almighty, and shall make offerings to their Lord, and serve Him forever. At the same time shall take place that **second and public resurrection of all,** in which the **unrighteous shall be raised to everlasting punishments.** These are they who have worshipped the works of their own hands, who have either been ignorant of, or have denied the Lord and Parent of the world. But their lord with his servants shall be seized and condemned to punishment, together with whom all the band of the wicked, in accordance with their deeds, shall be burnt for ever with perpetual fire in the sight of angels and the righteous. This is the **doctrine** of the **holy prophets** which we **Christians** follow;"[800]

17. Ambrosiaster (c. 366 AD – c. 384 AD), roman clergy.

Ambrosiaster (translated *would be Ambrose*) is a name given to an unknown clergy at Rome who did the first complete Latin commentary on the Pauline epistles. How did Ambrosiaster understand this verse?

"For this is **My blood** of the **new covenant**, which is **shed** for **many** for the **remission of sins**." [801]

Ambrosiaster writes that the **majority of men** *literally* from *all nations* must believe in Christ eventually (and if true, doesn't it imply most must be **Non Elect Salvation** since *most* men even today or in any timeline of history are not Christians?):

---

[800] Lactantius. *Divine Institutes*. Book 7 (VII, Of a Happy Life). Chapter 26. www.newadvent.org/fathers/07017.htm

[801] Matthew 26:28 (NKJV). biblehub.com/matthew/26-28.htm

"— The words are different, it is true, but the meaning is the same; at other times, on the other hand, words that seem the same have quite a different meaning, such as these: "All that is not done in good faith (ex fide) is a sin." (Rom. 14:23) and these others: "The law does not come from faith," (Gal. 3:12) although the law is not a sin. This great number of which the Savior speaks is **all the men** of whom St. Paul speaks: They are in **great numbers**, because the **greater part of all peoples and all nations** ought to **believe in the Savior**. It is **this great number** of those who must believe that the **Apostle calls all men**. "He is dead for all," he says, "that is, **for those who believe and must believe.**""[802]

Ambrosiaster's next quote looks similar to Book of 1 Enoch's quote at the start of this chapter (page 245) where in God's *Judgment Court*, he seems to also see *three* categories of men: *righteous, sinners and ungodly* (wicked). The righteous are "honoured and rewarded" with Salvation (1 Corinthians 3:14) while *some* of the *sinners* he mentions includes *fallen* Christians and also those who regarded the *Christian faith as madness* (which means must refer to some *non-Christians* , right?) who **repent of their unbelief** only on that 'judgment time' implying *believing after seeing* possibility and thereby *could be saved* (hence **Non Elect Salvation** possibility, 1 Corinthians 3:15's case can match it) as he only seems to mention the *ungodly* (differently) to perish:

"In fact, the knowledge of God must inspire the fear of the **just judge**, in **whose court** he teaches us that the **faithful** will **receive** the **reward of their righteousness**, and the **ungodly**, that is to say the **unbelievers**, the **just punishment** of their infidelity. It is of all justice, indeed, that the good ones be filled with joy in the future life in which Jesus Christ must reign with his chosen ones. They have been exposed to scorn, outrages in this world where the devil reigns, they will appear surrounded by glory in the kingdom of Jesus Christ for which they have borne the contempt of the worldly. **Sinners**, on the contrary, who seemed to shine here below a false brilliance, **opposing falsehood to truth**, have to **wait** for **tribulation** and an imaginary glory to succeed for them a

---

[802] Ambrosiaster. *Questions And Answers On The Old And New Testaments*. QUESTION 54. THE APOSTLE TEACHES THAT JESUS CHRIST DIED FOR ALL MEN. "ALL ARE THEREFORE DEAD," SAID HE, "AND HE DIED FOR ALL." THE SAVIOR SAYS, ON THE CONTRARY: THE SON OF MAN HAS COME TO GIVE HIS LIFE FOR THE REDEMPTION OF MANY. (MATT 20:28) THERE IS HERE A CONTRADICTION. Page 282. By John Litteral. 2018-07-29. Litteral Truth. Opensource. archive.org/details/ambrosiaster-questions-and-answers-on-the-old-and-new-testaments

contempt, a **humiliation** too real. The **righteous** will rejoice in **having believed,** when they witness the **chastisements of the unbelieving**, and the **unfaithful will repent of their unbelief** only when they see both **their own chastisement** and the **glory** of those **whose faith they** had **regarded** as an **act of madness**, which was only worthy of **their contempt.**"[803]

I don't think that I'm *interpolating* too far out for the *sinners* category above when I say that they could be **Non Elect Salvation** since Ambrosiaster's own definition for "sinners" has already been explained in an earlier question as follows (where he clearly states that this **sinners** category [including perhaps of those he mentioned earlier to *repent of their unbelief only via believing after seeing on that future Judgment time which is most likely the Baptism by Fire type*] where it involves those who are **punished** but they **do not have complete ruin but may be amended** which is a hope *not* available to the *ungodly (wicked)* which seems to be implied below:

> "Blessed is the man who did not stop in the way of **sinners.**" If he stops there, he **stops being blessed** to become **guilty** and **worthy of punishment**. Yet **he** still retains some **hope of amendment**, because he is **not impious**, but **simply sinful**. If a man is found who has not entered the council of the **wicked** and has not stopped in the way of **sinners**, he is doubly blessed. For he cannot be blessed, if without entering into the counsel of the **wicked**, he stops in the path of **sinners**, because if he **does not then have a complete ruin,** he is nevertheless **worthy of punishment.** The Psalmist adds: "nor sits in the seat of scoffers." Happiness, according to him, consists of these three degrees together, and is based on a triple reason, not to enter the counsel of the **ungodly**, not stopping in the path of **sinners**, nor sits in the seat of scoffers"[804]

Compare with Bible verses below:

---

[803] Ambrosiaster. *Questions And Answers On The Old And New Testaments.* QUESTION 126. FROM THE ONE WHO RECEIVED THE FAITH OF JESUS CHRIST. Pages 394 – 395. By John Litteral. 2018-07-29. Litteral Truth. Opensource.
archive.org/details/ambrosiaster-questions-and-answers-on-the-old-and-new-testaments

[804] Ambrosiaster. *Questions And Answers On The Old And New Testaments.* QUESTION 110. ON THE FIRST PSALM. Page 117. By John Litteral. 2018-07-29. Litteral Truth. Opensource. archive.org/details/ambrosiaster-questions-and-answers-on-the-old-and-new-testaments

"18Now "If the **righteous** one is scarcely **saved**, Where will the **ungodly** and the **sinner** appear?"[805]

Indeed, the righteous are "scarcely saved" from "judgment" meaning they're spared of it while both the "ungodly" and "sinner" must go through it. The *interpolation* here even based on Ambrosiaster's quotes earlier is that *some* "sinners" may be "saved by fire" while the "ungodly" perish eternally in that same fire.

My claim that Ambrosiaster's "saved after punishment" quotes earlier includes those *saved from Hell* (or Hades now) during Christ's Second Coming can be seen clearly in his own words below:

> "The **prophet Joel** also predicted this phenomenon so that one cannot doubt the fulfillment of a fact attested by several witnesses. "And the sun," he says, "will be changed into darkness and the moon into blood before the great" and terrible day of the Lord's coming." (Joel 2:31) As far as the **literal meaning** of these words indicates, they seem to be more fitting for the **second advent, for then the Lord will manifest himself publicly to all men**, to the testimony of Scripture: "Then every eye will see him, and all the tribes of the earth and those who have crucified him will strike their breast." (Rev. 1:7) Now, if according to the **oracles** of the **prophets** the sun is to be covered with darkness in the **two events** of the Lord, what is the day when, according to the prophet Isaiah, the sun and the moon must shine with greater brilliance?" ... And while **their unbelief was the cause of their ruin,** others arose by the faith that negligence retained powerlessness and infirmity. That is why the Savior said: "I have come to this world for **judgment**, that those who do not see shall see, and those who see, blind; (Jn. 9:39) That is to say, those whom their knowledge and skill in the law made shine like lights became blind and the eyes of the blind, that is to say ignorant and publicans, open to the light by faith. So the **prophet** foretold that the Savior would take care of their infirmities, and this **prophecy** is fulfilled in his time, as we see in the **Gospel**: "He really has borne our torpor, of our sufferings." (Isa. 1:4) All these predictions have received their consummation and fulfillment in the **Savior's passion**, and thus the **salvation of the human race** has been done in a true way for those who were **on earth or in hell**, for the **prophecy** of

---

[805] 1 Peter 4:18 (NKJV). biblehub.com/1_peter/4-18.htm

Zachariah embraces both of them at once. On earth, men have been freed from the oppression of their enemies by the intervention of the mercy of God, and in hell they were delivered from the sorrows they endured. Indeed, all those who hoped in Christ who had been promised to them awaited the coming of him who was to triumph over death and deliver them from hell. This is why Zechariah says: "To fulfill his mercies toward our fathers." (Luke 1:72) But if it is understood that this salvation must also come in the second advent, but it 1s especially in the second that the sun will be covered with darkness and the moon will not give its light, how to admit that the light of the sun and the moon will shine more brightly in the day when God will visit his people, since, in one as in the other time when the deliverance of this people begins and ends, we read that not only the light of the sun and the moon will be weakened, but that these stars will be completely obscured. We must therefore understand that the **sun and the moon represent the saints here,** just as in another place they are compared to the **stars of heaven**, to the testimony of the Apostle St. Paul, who declares that the **saints shine** in this world like the **stars of the faith**. We also read in the Gospel that the righteous will shine like the sun (Matt. 13:43),"[806]

Non-Elect Salvation part here is:

"in the **Savior's passion,** and thus the **salvation of the human race** has been done in a true way for those who were … **in hell,** for the **prophecy** of **Zachariah embraces both** of them **at once.** … and **in hell** they were delivered from the **sorrows they endured**. Indeed, all those who hoped in Christ who had been promised to them **awaited the coming of him** who was to **triumph over death** and **deliver them from hell**. This is why Zechariah says: "To fulfill his mercies toward our fathers." (Luke 1:72) But if it is **understood** that **this salvation must also come in the second advent,**"

Notice how Ambrosiaster comments that this "salvation from hell" after *Spirit World* judgments (since it's in hell!) must occur during the "Second

---

[806] Ambrosiaster. *Questions And Answers On The Old And New Testaments.* QUESTION 105. HOW TO RECONCILE THE PROPHECIES WITH THE GOSPEL ON THE OBSCURATION OF THE SUN AND ON SOME OTHER POINTS?. Pages 211 – 213. By John Litteral. 2018-07-29. Litteral Truth. Opensource. archive.org/details/ambrosiaster-questions-and-answers-on-the-old-and-new-testaments

Coming" future timeline. Ambrosiaster is also telling that in Christ's "First Coming" (which is past), there was also such a *harrowing of hell*.

He is revealing that the "prophets" have foretold in the Bible two times of salvation from Hell after judgment for some likewise by the Messiah. The salvation of earth when Christ Returns during His Second Coming which is *paralleled* to happen at the *same time* as the 'Salvation from Hell' in that future time agrees with **Chiliasm Prophecy Model** that I have presented perfectly for this **Non Elect Salvation** part since "good ground" of Matthew 13:8 representing Christians are already "good" and so, I think those delivered from "punishment" (i.e. **sorrows** in **hell** as Ambrosiaster says) could be **Non Christians**.

18. Book of Esdras by Prophet Ezra

Firstly, the Book of Esdras part which I am quoting is found in all Roman Catholic and Orthodox Bibles while during the Protestant Reformation, these were pushed into the *Apocrypha* section (where *Apocrypha* means "hidden"). Whether Esdras is Scripture or not, its account is believed as true by Christians and Jews and so, I am not going to argue about that but just present the implication *assuming that its contents turned out true*.

Here is that a quote from Esdras which states the existence of certain 70 secret books though "canonical Scripture", but cannot be included in the "public" canon as God instructed to Prophet Ezra who recreated the entire Old Testament Scripture via *Divine Inspiration* during that time since it was lost/destroyed:

> "41And my mouth was opened, and shut no more. 42The Highest gave understanding unto the five men, and they wrote the wonderful visions of the night that were told, which they knew not: and they sat forty days, and they wrote in the day, and at night they ate bread. 43As for me. I spake in the day, and I held not my tongue by night. **44In forty days they wrote two hundred and four books.** 45And it came to pass, when the forty days were filled, that the **Highest spake**, saying, **The first that thou hast written publish openly,** that the **worthy and unworthy may read it:** 46But **keep the seventy last,** that thou mayest deliver them **only to such as be wise** among the people: 47For in them is the spring of understanding, the fountain of wisdom, and the stream of knowledge."[807]

---

[807] 2 Esdras 14:41 – 47 (KJV). www.kingjamesbibleonline.org/2-Esdras-Chapter-14/

So, to agree to the 24 (or 39) Books of the Old Testament is to take this record as true in 2 Esdras which in turn implies in its same sentence the truth of the '70 hidden/secret books to the wise[808]. Among these, the books to the "wise" could include "Book of 1 Enoch" (which I quoted at the start, page 245" and "Apocalypse of Elijah" (which I will quote later, see page 288) according to some orthodox Jewish traditions [809] where both have very clear **Non Elect Salvation** claims.

Here is a section where Prophet Ezra is asking for salvation for some *sinners* who are *unsaved* where God in His Reply, clearly denies the "Messianic Age" (*Olam Ha-ba* or World (age/olam/aeon) to come) to such *sinners* (implied, which is *First Resurrection* in *Chiliasm* Christian timeline):

"31For we and our fathers do languish of such diseases: but because of us **sinners** thou shalt be called merciful. 32For if thou hast a desire to have **mercy upon** us, thou shalt be called merciful, to us namely, that have **no works of righteousness**. 33For the **just**, which **have many good works** laid up with thee, shall out of their own deeds **receive reward**. 34For what is man, that thou shouldest take displeasure at him? or what is a corruptible generation, that thou shouldest be so bitter toward it? 35For in truth them is no man among them that be born, but he hath dealt **wickedly**; and among the faithful there is none which hath not done amiss."[810]

Next, notice this mysterious reply to the above which can mean **Non Elect Salvation** for *some* (if God Wills) as these verses continue next, for God did not entirely say that He rejects all these petitions for this *only topic here* but rather says that '*something can be done* according to the words of Prophet Ezra who is *repeatedly* asking for the *salvation of some sinners who have no good works* to be "saved" (*Spirit World* and future context, implied)', which is stated as follows:

"36For in this, O Lord, thy righteousness and thy goodness shall be declared, if thou be merciful unto them which have not

---

[808] Encyclopedia. Jewish. *Esdras*. Apocryphal writings ascribed to Ezra by Richard Gottheil, Enno Littmann and Kaufmann Kohler.

www.jewishencyclopedia.com/articles/5852-esdras-books-of

[809] Apocrypha. *The 70 Apocrypha Books of Ezra*. This list by Onieh lists both the **Book of 1 Enoch** and **Apocalypse of Ezra**.

orthodoxessenejudaism.wordpress.com/2016/04/25/the-70-apocrypha-books-of-ezra/comment-page-1/

[810] 2 Esdras 8:31 – 35 (KJV). www.kingjamesbibleonline.org/2-Esdras-Chapter-8/

the confidence of good works. 37Then answered he me, and said, Some things hast thou spoken aright, and according unto thy words it shall be." [811]

No details are given for this part and so we may only *speculate*. Notice also that instead of condemning Prophet Ezra to Hell for asking for **Non Elect Salvation** *possibility* even *repeatedly* and despite given the divine answer as "no", the opposite is recorded next where God "praises" Prophet Ezra for asking it (and so I decide to *follow likewise* and see "no" condemnation in *trying*):

> "46Then answered he me, and said, Things present are for the present, and things to cometh for such as be to come. 47For thou comest far short that thou shouldest be able to love my creature more than I: but I have ofttimes drawn nigh unto thee, and unto it, but never to the unrighteous. 48In this also **thou art marvellous** before the **most High**: 49In that thou hast **humbled** thyself, as it becometh thee, and hast **not judged thyself** worthy to be **much glorified** among the righteous."[812]

Here's another mysterious verse from this same 2 Esdras which seem to speak of *some* escaping the final judgments through "faith" *or* "good works". If the translations quoted below are accurate for the usage of word "or" instead of "and" and if I'm reading it right, this could mean **Elect Salvation** for those of "faith" (Matthew 25:1 – 13) while **Non Elect Salvation** for those of "works" (Matthew 25:14 – 46). Also, these verses in Matthew seem to match the *possibility* given here since for example, strangely, only Matthew 25:1 – 13 mentions words like "wedding", "virgins", "bridegroom" which all parabolically relate to *Elect Salvation* while Matthew 25:14 – 30 only uses the lower words "servant" while Matthew 25:31 – 46 only uses just the plain "righteous *surprised* sheep" who did "not even know the Lord as they ask back, *'When did we see you Lord hungry, thirsty, naked, homeless, etc.?'* which can be *Non Elect Salvation*.

"All this—who **will be saved**, who will be able to **escape** through **their works or through the faith** with which they **believe**" [813]

---

[811] 2 Esdras 8:36 – 37 (KJV). www.kingjamesbibleonline.org/2-Esdras-Chapter-8/

[812] 2 Esdras 8:46 – 49 (KJV). www.kingjamesbibleonline.org/2-Esdras-Chapter-8/

[813] 2 Esdras 9:7 (CEB). Compare with other translations here: NRSVA, 'It shall be that all who will be **saved** and will be able to escape on account of their **works, or** on account of the **faith** by which they have believed,'

Note: **"will be saved"** can mean different timelines.

So, an *interpolation* in light of these evidences could be those of *good works* but "no faith", are judged first and can be "saved by fire" thereafter via *believing* after seeing.

19. Apocalypse of Elijah (Coptic Christian preservation)[814]

As mentioned, this could be one of the 70 secret books to the "wise" which 2 Esdras 14:41 – 47 mentions. Isn't it strange that the two books which bear the names generally believed to be the two final *prophetic* witness before the times of the "final Antichrist (Beast)" and before the Second Coming of Lord Jesus Christ which are **Enoch** (of which we saw *Book of 1 Enoch* earlier, page 245) and now **Elijah** here both have clear **Non Elect Salvation** quotes for different classes of men where this next one seems to mean *some* (not all) are *saved from some type of future fire judgments* (be it the "Baptism by Fire" of Matthew 3:11 – 12 or the final "Lake of Fire" of Revelation 20:11 – 15) but only for those whom the **Elect Salvation** ask for *individually**:

> "22. It will come to pass on that **day that the Lord** will hear and command the heaven and the earth with great wrath. And they will send for **fire**. 23. And the **fire** will prevail over the earth seventy-two cubits. It will consume the **sinners** and the devils like stubble. 24. A true **judgment** will occur. 25. On that day, the mountains and the earth will utter speech. The byways will speak with one another, saying, "Have you heard today the voice of a man who walks who has not come to **the judgment of the Son of YHWH**." 26. The sins of each one will stand against him in the place where they were committed, whether those of the day or of the night. 27. Those who belong to the **righteous** and ... will see the **sinners** and **those who persecuted them** and **those who handed them over to death in their torments**. 28. Then the **sinners** [in torment] will see the place of the righteous. 29. And

---

NRSVUE, "It shall be that all who will be **saved** and will be able to escape on account of their **works or** on account of the **faith** by which they have believed"

RSV, 'And it shall be that every one who will be **saved** and will be able to escape on account of his **works, or** on account of the **faith** by which he has believed,' www.biblegateway.com/verse/en/2%20Esdras%209%3A7

[814] Lundhaug, Hugo. "The Apocalypse of Elijah in the Context of Coptic Apocrypha". *The Chester Beatty Biblical Papyri at Ninety: Literature, Papyrology, Ethics*, edited by Garrick Vernon Allen, Usama Ali Mohamed Gad, Kelsie Gayle Rodenbiker, Anthony Philip Royle and Jill Unkel, Berlin, Boston: De Gruyter, 2023, pp. 161-174. doi.org/10.1515/9783110781304-012

thus grace will occur. In those days, that which the **righteous will ask for many times will be given to them**." ⁸¹⁵

*Notice the specific type of *Non Elect Salvation* here where the *Elect Salvation* ones who ask for it via prayer requests at that time seem to ask "many times" before it is granted. Also, they can "only ask for the non-elect who has wronged them first in life including killing them too!" which is *fair* in *human logic* perspective also because you (the elect) can decide their fate of those who did worst to them (and if you [the elect] don't want them to be saved, it's okay as no forcing is involved; thus non-Christians really need to be careful when they *wrong Christians* as perhaps some may never be forgiven by whom they wronged and so remain *eternally in hell* thereafter). Compare with these Bible verses which seem to echo likewise for these *possibilities* even in the "Final Scene":

> "21So **Jesus** said to them again, "**Peace to you!** As the Father has sent Me, I also send you." 22And when He had said this, He breathed on them, and said to them, "**Receive** the **Holy Spirit.** 23If you **forgive the sins of any, they are forgiven them; if you retain the sins of any, they are retained.**" ⁸¹⁶

Could this be the final forgiveness implied for some where the "Bride" (Elect) calls for them in the future?

> "17And the Spirit and the **bride** say, "Come!" And let him who hears say, "Come!" And let him **who thirsts come**. Whoever desires, let him **take the water of life freely.**"⁸¹⁷

Regarding the Apocalypse of Elijah's Coptic vs Jewish version and its reliability, I will quote from a website (since whether it's true or not cannot be determined in 100% certainty, so I will just consider it a *possibility*):

> "Two versions are known today, a Coptic Christian fragmentary version and a Hebrew Jewish version. The title derives from mentions of Elijah within the text, although there is no other reason to assume that he is meant to be the author. This apocalypse

---

⁸¹⁵ Pseudepigrapha. *Apocalypse of Elijah* (Coptic).

www.3-in-1.net/Pseudepigrapha/Apocalypse%20of%20Elijah/The%20Apocalypse%20of%20Elijah.htm

⁸¹⁶ John 20:21 – 23 (NKJV). biblehub.com/nkjv/john/20.htm

⁸¹⁷ Revelation 22:17 (NKJV). biblehub.com/nkjv/revelation/22.htm

is mentioned in the Apostolic Constitutions, the List of Sixty Books, the Synopsis of Pseudo-Athanasius, the Stichometry of Nicephorus, and the Armenian list of Mechithar. **Origen, Ambrosiaster, and Euthalius** ascribe I Cor. 2:9 to it: "Eye hath not seen, nor ear heard, neither have entered into the heart of man, the things which God hath prepared for them that love him." If they are right, the apocalypse is pre-Pauline. The peculiar form in which this quotation appears appears in **Clement of Alexandria**, Protrepticus x. 94, and the Apostolic Constitutions vii. 32, shows that both have the same source, probably this apocalypse. **Epiphanius** ascribes to this work Eph. 5:14: "Awake thou that sleepest, and arise from the dead, and Christ shall give thee light."[818]

20. Apocalypse of Ezra (Armenian Christian preservation).

This may not be a solid preserved source since it has a few versions and scholars note the contradictions between them. However, one of the versions has the *Questions of Ezra* part[819] which describes a "possible" **Non Elect Salvation** quote (**Question 6** below) for *non-Christians* under the condition that *Christians* (who probably knew them earlier in life, implied by usage) pray for their salvation or do some act of righteous on their behalf (I *interpolate* perhaps via some good deeds be it either workwise or charity done by that *non-Christian* toward a *Christian* first prior in life. This is because I don't think that any Christian would randomly think of a non-Christian at that future time unless that *non-Christian* has been kind, helpful and loving toward him).

"James Charlesworth writes (The Pseudepigrapha and Modern Research, pp. 117-118): 'The one extant Armenian manuscript of the Questions of Ezra has not been edited, but parts of it were translated into English by J. Issaverdens (UWOT. Pp. 457-61). The work is Christian, rather late, and apparently influenced by traditions recorded in 1 Enoch, 2 Enoch, the Apocalypse of Abraham, and the Apocalypse of Zosimus. Issaverdens translates six of the questions Ezra asks 'the Angel of God'; these can be paraphrased as follows:

---

[818] Apocalypse of Elijah. *Comments*. rejectedscriptures.weebly.com/pseudepigraphic-apocalypses.html

[819] Charlesworth, James H. *The pseudepigrapha and modern research*, with a supplement. Chico, CA: Published by Scholars Press for the Society of Biblical Literature. 1981. Pages 117 – 118. archive.org/details/pseudepigraphamo0000char/page/n9/mode/2up

1. What has God prepared for the **righteous** and **sinners**? Ans. For the **righteous** are prepared **rejoicing** and **light**, for **sinners darkness** and **fire.**

2. If all men living are sinners and hence deserve condemnation, are not beasts more blessed? Ans. Do not repeat these words to "Him who is above you."

3. Where does the soul go after death? Ans. A good angel comes to a good soul, and a wicked one to a bad soul (cf. ApAb). The soul is taken eastward.

4. What is that way like? Ans. There are seven steps to the Divinity; the righteous soul passes through four steps of terror, one of enlightenment, and two of blessing.

5. Why do you not take the soul to the Divinity?

Ans. Ezra is called a vain man (cf. ApZos) who thinks according to human nature. No man or angel can see the face of God, but only the place of God's throne, which is fiery (cf. 1En 14:18-23, 2En 20).

6. What shall become of "us **sinners**"? Ans. When **you die** you **will obtain mercy and rest** if a **Christian prays or performs some act of devotion for you.**' "[820]

Whether it's true or not, some orthodox Christians did preserve it with this meaning and notice that both points 1 and 6 refer to these same "sinners" who by default end up in "fire".

21. Apocalypse of Abraham

Such an idea of **Non-Elect Salvation** for *some sinners after judgment* from the **left side** to undergo **judgement and restoration** is found in a non-canonical Jewish writing called the *Apocalypse of Abraham*. Though not canonical, such writings demonstrate that such ideas are within the realm of possibilities especially if they can match say in this case the "transfer from left hand to right hand after judgment to be restored and saved by judgment day" as literal reading of Matthew 25:31 – 46 can mean likewise.

> "A Vision of Sin and Paradise: the Mirror of the World (Chapter XXI.). XXI. ... And I saw there the Garden of Eden and its fruits, the source4 of the stream issuing from it, and its trees and their bloom, and those who behaved righteously. And I saw therein

---

[820] Early Jewish Writings. *Questions of Ezra*.
www.earlyjewishwritings.com/questionsezra.html

their foods and blessedness. 5 And I saw there a great multitude—men and women and children [half of them on the right side of the picture]6 and half of them on the left side of the picture.7 The Fall of Man and its Sequel (Chapters XXIL-XXV.). XXII. ... "10 And I said: "O Lord, mighty and eternal! Who are the people in this picture on this side and on that?" And He said to me: "These which are on the **left side** are the multitude of the peoples which have formerly been in existence and which are after thee destined,1 **some for judgement and restoration, and others for vengeance and destruction at the end of the world.** 2 But these which are on the **right side** of the picture—they are the **people set apart for me of the peoples with Azazel.**3 These are they whom I have ordained to be born of thee and to be called **My People**"[821]

Compare this "left hand" to "right hand" transfer for "sheep of other fold" possible context with St. Irenaeus quote in Essay 1, pages 47 – 48 earlier. Here's another translation for it for comparison where this source also contains the translation above and this "left side" to "right side" transfer applies to *both* those who existed *before Abraham* and *after Abraham*. The people on the "right side" are called "God's people" who are "born of Abraham" but this is *not physically* meant as Bible verses* also have similar words like "seed of Abraham" to attain to the *promise of right hand Elect Salvation* which we understand as referring to "Christians today [be it Jews or Gentiles] together with Old Testament Faithful with some unlearnt Gentiles too" since *New Testament* refers to those "born of faith":

"And I said, "O sovereign, mighty and eternal! Why are the people in this picture on this side and on that?" And he said to me, "These who are on the **left side** are a multitude of tribes who existed previously...and after you some (who have been) **prepared for judgment and order, others for revenge and perdition** ... 5. at the end of the age. Those on the **right side** of the picture are the **people set apart for me** of the people with Azazel; these are the ones I have prepared to be born of you and to be called **my people.**"[822]

---

[821] *Apocalypse of Abraham.* Chapters 21 – 22. Society for promoting Christian Knowledge, translated by G.H. Box, London, Macmillan Company. 1919. Pages 42 – 44; www.marquette.edu/maqom/box.pdf

[822] Jewish Pseudepigrapha. *Apocalypse of Abraham.* Chapter 22. www.pseudepigrapha.com/pseudepigrapha/Apocalypse_of_Abraham.html

Here are New Testament verses clearing out the ancient misconception that "children born of Abraham" are not meant as by "flesh or *race*" but rather those "spiritually born" to be on the "right side" or Elect Salvation:

> "6But it is not that the word of God has taken no effect. For they are **not all Israel who are of Israel, 7nor are they all children** because they are the **seed of Abraham**; but, "In Isaac your seed shall be called." 8That is, those who are the **children of the flesh**, these are **not the children of God; but the children** of the **promise** are counted as the **seed**."[823]

> "16Now to **Abraham** and his Seed were the promises made. He does not say, "And to seeds," as of many, but as of one, "And to your **Seed**," who is **Christ**. ... 26For you are **all sons of God through faith in Christ Jesus**. 27For as many of you as were baptized into Christ have put on Christ. 28There is **neither Jew nor Greek**, there is neither slave nor free, there is neither male nor female; for you are all one in Christ Jesus. 29And **if you are Christ's**, then you are **Abraham's seed**, and **heirs** according to the **promise**."[824]

22. Sibyline Oracles Book 2 (Christian revision).

Sibyls are quoted and rephrased in a Christian way by Church Fathers such as St. Theophilus of Antioch, St. Clement of Alexandria, Lactantius and St. Augustine of Hippo and even *chiliasm* church father St. Justin of Rome. Here's an example quote by St. Justin of Rome,

"We must also mention what the ancient and exceedingly **remote Sibyl**, whom Plato and Aristophanes, and others besides, mention as a **prophetess**, taught you in her **oracular** verses concerning one only God. And she speaks thus:—

There is one only unbegotten God,

Omnipotent, invisible, most high,

All-seeing, but Himself seen by no flesh.

Then elsewhere thus:—

---

[823] Romans 9:6 – 8 (NKJV). biblehub.com/nkjv/romans/9.htm

[824] Galatians 3:16, 26 – 29 (NKJV). biblehub.com/nkjv/galatians/3.htm

But we have strayed from the Immortal's ways, And worship with a dull and senseless mind Idols, the workmanship of our own hands, And images and figures of dead men. ...

And you may in part easily learn the **right religion** from the **ancient Sibyl,** who by some kind of potent inspiration teaches you, through her **oracular predictions,** truths which seem to be much akin to the **teaching of the prophets.**"[825]

St. Justin of Rome also wrote that quoting the *Sibyl* or persuading others to do so is blocked by the Devil and may even be *rewarded* greatly by God even if we just managed to persuade a few with its contents:

> "But by the **agency of the devils death** has been decreed **against** those who **read the books of Hystaspes, or of the Sibyl,** or of the **prophets,** that through fear they may prevent men who read them from receiving the knowledge of the good, and may retain them in slavery to themselves; which, however, they could not always effect. For not only do **we fearlessly read them**, but, as you see, **bring them for your inspection**, knowing that their contents will be pleasing to all. And if we **persuade even a few, our gain will be very great;** for, as good husbandmen, we shall receive the **reward from the Master.**"[826]

Why such a motivation to preach from the *Sibyls*? Around that same time period, St. Clement of Alexandria writes that such a *verbal tradition* to do so may have originated from *Apostle St. Paul's* preaching to "read the Sibyl" in "future" (prophecy context) as he writes,

> "He distinguished the most excellent of the Greeks from the common herd, in addition to Peter's Preaching, the **Apostle Paul** will show, saying: Take also the Hellenic books, **read the Sibyl**, how it is shown that God is one, and **how the future is indicated.** And taking Hystaspes, read, and you will find much more luminously and distinctly the Son of God described, and how many kings shall draw up their forces against Christ, hating Him and

---

[825] St. Justin of Rome (Justin Martyr). *Hortatory Address to the Greeks.* Chapters 16 and 37. www.newadvent.org/fathers/0129.htm

[826] St. Justin of Rome (Justin Martyr). *First Apology.* Chapter 44. www.newadvent.org/fathers/0126.htm

those that bear His name, and His faithful ones, and His patience, and His coming."[827]

The Sibyls themselves are a collection of such prophecies and it spans some time. The one I'm quoting next has clear **Non Elect Salvation** for *some* whom the **Elect Salvation** (called *immortals*) pray or ask for from the *Judgment of Fire* context and notice how these saved ones at that time are placed on a "different" salvation location (similar to *Shepherd of Hermas'* in page 249 earlier) just that the parabolic name given here is *Elysian Fields* which can mean the "final new earth" regions instead of "heaven" (in comparison) which is only for "Elect Salvation" as I have *interpolated* repeatedly before:

> "for a long day will God make. And to the **pious** will the almighty God 405 **Imperishable** grant another thing, When **they shall ask** the imperishable God: That **he will suffer men** from **raging fire** And **endless gnawing anguish** to be **saved**; And **this will he do**. For hereafter he 410 Will **pluck them** from the **restless flame**, elsewhere **Remove them**, and for **his own people's sake** Send them to **other** and **eternal life** With the **immortals, in Elysian field**,"[828]

Could this be the part in the Book of Revelation where the "thirsty" get the "water of life" freely after being "hurt by the Second Death" first in Judgment? (Revelation 21:6) where the "Bride" (Elect, Immortals) also calls at that future time (Revelation 22:17)?

23. Epistle of Apostles (*Epistula Apostolorum*).

This writing is preserved in the *isolated* Ethiopic Orthodox Church. The clearest quote of it is by St. Clement of Alexandria who makes an identical quote found in this with a writing which he did not name but just called it as "Scripture" [829]. Scholar, Professor Brandon Hawk writes,

"Other **apocrypha** survive in full only in Geʻez because of their significance in **Ethiopic Judaism and Christianity**, including:

Letter of the Apostles (survives in fragments in Coptic and Latin)

---

[827] St. Clement of Alexandria. *The Stromata*. Book 6. Chapter 5. www.newadvent.org/fathers/02106.htm

[828] Sibyl. *Sibyline Oracles*. Book 2. Sections 297 – 322. Page 51. sacred-texts.com/cla/sib/sib04.htm

[829] Montague Rhode James. *The Apocryphal New Testament*. Oxford: Clarendon Press 1924. pages 485-503. www.earlychristianwritings.com/text/apostolorum.html

Apocalypse of Peter (survives in fragments in Greek)"[830]

The word "Epistle" means "Letter" here so it's referring to the same writing. Whether it is canonical or not, we don't know for sure and so, I present it under the *assumption* if this part was preserved or is accurate in its prophecy which has possible **Non Elect Salvation (non-Christians)** for *some* **sinners** for whom the **Elect Salvation (Christians)** pray for which again can correlate with Revelation 21:6 and Revelation 22:17 [while the rest may *go astray forever* in punishment]:

> "For I will say unto him: As thou soughtest, so hast thou found, and as thou askedst, so hast thou received. Therefore condemnest thou me, O man? Wherefore hast thou departed from me and denied me? And wherefore hast thou confessed me and yet denied me? hath not every man power to live and to die? **Whoso then hath kept my commandments shall be a son of the light**, that is, of the Father that is in me. But because of them that corrupt my words am I come down from heaven. I am the word: I became flesh, and I wearied myself (or, suffered) and taught, saying: The heavy laden shall be saved, and **they that are gone astray shall go astray for ever.** They shall be **chastised and tormented in their flesh** and in **their soul**. ... 40 And we said unto him: O Lord, verily **we are sorrowful for their sake**. And he said unto us: Ye do rightly, for **the righteous are sorry for the sinners**, and **pray for them**, making prayer unto my Father. Again we said unto him: Lord, is there **none** that **maketh intercession unto thee** (so Eth.)? And he said unto us: **Yea, and I will hearken unto the prayer of the righteous which they make for them.**" [831]

I think the above is preserved in both *Ethiopic* and *Coptic* versions as the source also indicates that the "Coptic resumes" for this part. Notice that the Ethiopian Canon (or Apocrypha) includes the *Apocalypse of Peter as well* in Prof. Brandon's quote earlier which also contains a similar statement which we will discuss next.

---

[830] Hawk, Brandon. *Ethiopian Biblical Canons and Apocrypha.*
brandonwhawk.net/2021/03/22/ethiopian-biblical-canons-and-apocrypha/
[831] Epistle of the Apostles. *Epistula Apostolorum.* Verses 39 – 40.
www.earlychristianwritings.com/text/apostolorum.html

24. Apocalypse of Peter

The *Apocalypse of Peter* was a recent discovery. However, it is mentioned to be "Scripture" in the first oldest known Bible Canon in all of Christianity namely the *Roman Canon* or *Muratorian Fragment* (it's called a fragment and some New Testament books are not printed on it simply because only a portion of it exists and so we cannot limit its content based on this surviving piece of manuscript only). Here's an attestation of it from an abstract:

> "This **Apocalypse of Peter** has no connection with the Gnostic Apocalypse of Peter from Nag Hammadi (now included in Hennecke5, ii. 633–43; Eng. trans. ii. 700–12). The **existence of** this **apocalypse** was **known in antiquity**. The **Muratorian Fragment** and the **Stichometry of Nicephorus** include it among their 'disputed' texts. The catalogue of **Biblical** writings in **Codex Claromontanus** (Paris gr. 107) includes the **Shepherd of Hermas**, the Acts of Paul, and the **Apocalypse of Peter** among its **canonical** writings, but Eusebius, HE 6. 14. 1 and especially 3. 3. 2 and 3. 25. 4 (Schwartz, GCS 9.2, pp. 548–60, 188, 252), classes it as 'spurious' (cf. also Origen, on John 13. 7 (Preuschen, pp. 231–2)). **Sozomen** in the fifth century, HE 7. 19 (ed. J. Bidez and G. C. Hansen, GCS 50 (Berlin, 1960), p. 331), **refers to its being used in public worship on Good Friday**. (It is not listed in the Gelasian Decree.) Thus it is clear that the **book was popular and widespread in use** in the **early centuries of Christianity** and hovered on the edges of **canonical scripture**. The Akhmim manuscript (see below) testifies to the popularity of the text up to the eighth or ninth century, when that manuscript was copied."[832]

The *Apocalypse of Peter*'s manuscript is well studied and documented [833]. The Ethiopian version of it contained the **Non Elect Salvation** part which may be granted for *some* after the "prayers of the **Elect Salvation** for them" at that future time (*not now*) as follows:

---

[832] Elliott, J. K. (ed.), 'The *Apocalypse of Peter*', in J. K. Elliott (ed.), The Apocryphal New Testament: A Collection of Apocryphal Christian Literature in an English Translation (Oxford, 1993; online edn, Oxford Academic, 1 Nov. 2003), doi.org/10.1093/0198261829.003.0032

[833] NASSCAL. Apocalypse of Peter. *Apocalypsis Petri.* Manuscript details by North American Society for the Study of Christian Apocryphal Literature. www.nasscal.com/e-clavis-christian-apocrypha/apocalypse-of-peter/

"Next: ' The Father hath committed all judgement unto the Son.' The destiny of **sinners** -their **eternal doom**- is **more than Peter can endure: he appeals to Christ to have pity on them.** And my **Lord answered me** and said to me: 'Hast thou understood that which I said unto thee before? It is permitted unto thee to know that concerning which thou askest: but thou **must not tell that which thou hearest unto the sinners** lest they transgress the more, and sin.' Peter weeps many hours, and is at last consoled by an answer which, though exceedingly diffuse and vague does seem to **promise ultimate pardon for all**: 'My Father will give unto them all the life, the glory, and the kingdom that passeth not away,' . . . 'It is **because of them that have believed in me** that I am come. It is **also because of them** that have **believed in me,** that, **at their word, I shall have pity on men.**"[834]

Some scholars noted that this claim is not consistent with their current orthodoxy. So, they claimed that the Ethiopian version was corrupted or interpolated. Then, came along a scholar with the *Rainer Fragment* discovery which was found in a tomb of a Christian monk or priest who was buried with it (which seems to suggest that he probably held it dear to him). You can read an account of this in the *freely* available part of the distinguished journal which published it (and others reprinted it) together with the quote stated next. The difference here is that the *Rainer Fragment* discovery is showing the text in *Greek* implying it could be a copy of the original *Apocalypse of Peter* and the most interesting part is this *fragment* that survived is *earliest known* and it contained "exactly" this **Non Elect Salvation** part as follows:

"Then will I **give** unto **my called and my chosen whomsoever they shall ask me for, out of torment**, and will **give** them a **fair baptism** in (or unto) **salvation** from the **Acherusian lake** which **men** so call in the **Elysian field**, even a **portion** of **righteousness** with **my holy ones**. And I will depart, I and my chosen, rejoicing, with the patriarchs, unto mine eternal kingdom, and I will perform for them the promises which I promised them, I and my Father which is in heaven. Lo, I have manifested unto thee, **Peter,** and have expounded all this. And go thou into a city that ruleth over the west, and drink the cup which I promised thee, at the hands of the **son of him that is in Hades,**

---

[834] M. R. James. *Apocalypse of Peter*. The Apocryphal New Testament. Translation and Notes. Oxford: Clarendon Press. 1924.

www.earlychristianwritings.com/text/apocalypsepeter-mrjames.html

that his destruction may have a beginning; and (lit.) thou acceptable of the promise .... (perhaps (become)a receiver of the promise)."[835]

Notice how it details out "My chosen" which is the "Elect" and their salvation in heaven (the "Bride" of Revelation 21:9 – 10) while describing that the saved "Non Elect" do not enter heaven but may get only a "portion" of the kingdom (overall) which correlates well with my possibility *interpolation* that this refers to the "final new earth" regions who become part of the "saved nations" who do not enter heaven (Revelation 21:24 – 27).

It's also a mystery whether Matthew 3:11 – 12's Baptism by Fire (described in Essay 10) can correlate with it or whether Revelation 21:6 and Revelation 22:17 in the "Final Scene" correlates independently with it as the "Bride" calls to these newly saved "thirsty" ones from the "Lake of Fire". Also, notice an important point where this **may not be Universalism** because that *not all* are delivered from that Fire but rather only **whom** the **Elect** shall **pray or ask for** (maybe their unbelieving friends or non-Christian acquaintances on earth earlier?). Since we cannot say for sure whether this writing is *Canonical Scripture* or not, or even whether is it the "original" mentioned in early Christian literature or not, all we can do is let God decide but this is *honesty* presented with *evidence* again and so we can be exempted even if *wrong*.

25. Martin Luther (10 November 1483 – 18 February 1546), Protestant Reformer.

Martin Luther is the *Father of Protestantism* and founder of the Lutheran churches. He never believed in Universalism but neither did he consider those of the *Origen* type as he implies to be 'heretics' based on that belief alone. This is what he wrote about this topic:

> "There are those among us, since the times of **Origen** and his followers, who have considered it too hard, too severe, and contrary to God's goodness that he should cast people away and create them for **eternal torment**. ... It would be a **completely different question to ask** whether God could **grant faith to a few** at the moment of **their death** or **after death and thereby save them through faith**. Who would doubt that he could do this? But **no one can prove** that **he does do this** ... St. Paul

---

[835] M. R. James. *The Rainer Fragment of the Apocalypse of Peter*. The Journal of Theological Studies. Volume os-XXXII, Issue 127. April 1931. Pages 270–279. doi.org/10.1093/jts/os-XXXII.127.270. Available *freely* here: biblicalstudies.org.uk/pdf/jts/032_270.pdf

speaks the truth: it is God's will that everyone be made well - for without his will it does not happen. **But it does not follow from this that all people are saved.**"[836]

Notice carefully how Dr. Luther differentiates between "Universalism" (no possibility) from **Non Elect Salvation** ("possible", but no one can prove it). So, the first universally accepted Spirit-Filled Protestant Christian did not consider it a *heresy* to consider the *Non Elect Salvation as a possibility* (not doctrine since none can prove it). This supports my position for this writing itself since I attempt to "prove" it by presenting evidence from other First Christianity writings together with *my interpolations* but yet, since this is a **prophecy** context, it "cannot" be proven until we see it *come to pass or not*.

However, the particular phrase used by Dr. Luther here, "**grant faith to a few** at the moment ... **after death and thereby save them through faith**" easily means the *believing after seeing* possibility in the *Spirit World* for **Non Elect Salvation** where viewing the *context* of John 6:29, 35, 36, 40 [837] can mean so (if God Wills it). But whether, this means so or not, cannot be proven and so Martin Luther doesn't pursue this thought further. In his footsteps, I intend to present it as a *possibility* with *evidence* responsibly and state the fact that it can be *either way* (true or false) for we cannot see it from here.

26. John Wesley (28 June 1703 – 2 March 1791), Protestant Reformer.

John Wesley was the main founder of the Methodist churches who was renown for his almost penniless lifestyle by giving away so much of the money earned through ministry to both churches and for *Charity Doctrine*

---

[836] Luther, Martin. *Letter from Martin Luther to Hans von Rechenberg.* Issued from Wittenberg on the Monday after the assumption of Mary [August 18], 1522. Translated by Rev. William Wangelin of Hudsonville, MI.

storage.cloversites.com/holycrosslutheranchurch2/documents/Martin%20Luther%20to%20Hans%20von%20Rechenberg%201522_2.pdf . Note: This translation of Luther's letter is based on the St. Louis edition of Martin Luther's works (St. Louis: Concordia Publishing House (1903), 2002 ff.) with consultation of the Weimar Ausgabe (WA 10II, 322-326) and is intended to be copied and distributed freely. Another English translation, which is under copyright, may be found published in Luther's Works, (Philadelphia: Fortress Press (1968), 43:51-55).

[837] John 6:29, 35, 36, 40, "29Jesus answered and said to them, "This is the work of God, that you believe in Him whom He sent." 35And Jesus said to them, "I am the bread of life. He who comes to Me shall never hunger, and he who believes in Me shall never thirst. 36But I said to you that you have seen Me and yet do not believe. 40And this is the **will of Him who sent Me, that everyone who sees the Son and believes in Him may have everlasting life**; and I will raise him up at the last day." (NKJV).

which proved his sincerity while preaching the Gospel in words too bringing revival in England during those times. He is my favourite reformer for sure.

The influence of a Moravian Bishop namely Peter Bohler (31 December 1712 – 27 April 1775) toward the conversion of the great Methodist Churches co-founder John Wesley (28 June 1703 – 2 March 1791) is undeniable. We can read this not from an interpretation but directly from the words of Wesley himself since he kept a journal. Bohler encouraged Wesley early on to *"preach faith till you have it"*[838].

John Wesley certainly held Bohler in high regard and called him a man with "fruits of a living faith" [839]. Interestingly, Wesley was converted to Christianity during the "Aldersgate Conversion Experience" which happened in a Moravian setting and included even Bohler's presence and encouragements prior mainly and it impacted him to the point that he visited the Moravians for the next 3 months in Germany[840].

Peter Bohler was a Christian Universalist meaning he did not believe in eternal hell for anyone and probably so did some of the Moravians who were present during Wesley's "Aldersgate Conversion Experience". Far from the usual claim that if such Christians were present, they might invite the presence of the "devil" due to the error of "full universalism", it was there where one of the greatest Protestant founders, John Wesley himself was converted. Why would God choose such a person like Bohler to influence and convert Wesley?

In fact, Bohler's *universalism* was well known and the other Methodist Churches' founder, George Whitefield who is an ardent Calvinist clearly wrote a letter to John Wesley to keep away from Bohler due to the fact that Bohler is a Christian Universalist[841]. Wesley probably knew this all along and

---

[838] Wesley, John. The Tyndale Series of Great Biographies. *The Journal of John Wesley.* By Hugh Price Hughes, Augustine Birrell, K. C. and edited by Percy Livingstone Parker. Published by Moody Press (Chicago, 1951). Page 49. ccel.org/w/wesley/journal/cache/journal.pdf

[839] Wesley, John. … *The Journal of John Wesley* … 52.

[840] Wesley, John. … *The Journal of John Wesley* … 55.

[841] Journal of Moravian History. *Peter Boehler's Universalist Letter* by Jared S. Burkholder. Volume 23, Issue 2, October 2023. 129–142. The Abstract reads, "Although the belief in universalism has been attributed to Peter Boehler since the eighteenth century, the matter has not been clearly documented. However, a letter, written by Boehler and preserved in the Moravian Archives, provides greater clarity as it contains a defense of a future "restitution of all things." Possibly sent to George Whitefield, the letter detailed in this article not only provides evidence of Boehler's restorationist beliefs, but also points to the role that

it did not bother him much and we can probably see Wesley's own words in his journal possibly regarding this letter too as follows, to quote:

"1741. Sunday, February 1.—A private letter, written to me by Mr. Whitefield, was printed without either his leave or mine, and a great numbers of copies were given to our people, both at the door and in the Foundry itself.

Having procured one of them, I related (after preaching) the naked fact to the congregation and told them, "I will do just what I believe Mr. Whitefield would, were he here himself." Upon which I tore it in pieces before them all. Everyone who had received it, did the same. So that in two minutes there was not a whole copy left.

Saturday, March 28.—Having heard much of **Mr. Whitefield's unkind behavior,** since his return from Georgia, I went to him to hear him speak for himself that I might know how to judge. I much approved of his plainness of speech. **He told me that he and I preached two different gospels;** and therefore he not only would **not join** with or **give** me the **right hand of fellowship,** but was resolved **publicly** to **preach against** me and my brother, wheresoever he preached at all. ...

Monday, April 6.—I had a long conversation with **Peter Bohler.** I marvel **how I refrain from joining these men.** I scarcely ever see any of them but **my heart burns within me. I long to be with them,** and yet I am kept from them.

Thursday, May 7.—I reminded the United Society that many of our brethren and sisters had not needful food; many were destitute of convenient clothing; many were out of business, and that without their own fault; and many sick and ready to perish: that I had done what in me lay **to feed the hungry, to clothe the naked, to employ the poor, and to visit the sick**; but was not, alone, sufficient for these things; and therefore **desired all whose hearts were as my heart:"** [842]

Please take note how even such a highly anointed level in the Holy Spirit preacher (by God's Grace), John Wesley, writes in his own words above (in his journal) regarding the "unkind attitude of Whitefield", how he "longs" to be with "Bohler type Moravian Christian Universalists" despite the fact that he knows about it and is supposed to keep away? And how Wesley's thought

---

universalism may have played in the Moravians' 1740 schism with Whitefield". doi.org/10.5325/jmorahist.23.2.0129

[842] Wesley, John. ... *The Journal of John Wesley* ... 83.

next revolved around "Charity Doctrine" which was highly emphasized by the Moravians too.

So even the great faith of John Wesley had all these traits and best is, this is not an interpretation but his own words in his own journal. So, if we emulate Wesley's faith likewise and keep the weaker **Non Elect Salvation** as a *possibility*, it seems similar, isn't it?

> "**7Remember** those who rule over you, who have spoken the word of God to you, **whose faith follow**, considering the **outcome of their conduct**"[843]

27. Sadhu Sundar Singh (3 September 1889 – 1929), Christian missionary.

Dr. D.G.S. Dhinakaran (1 July 1935 – 20 February 2008) was Founder of Jesus Calls ministry and a famous evangelical preacher in India. Sadhu Sundar Singh (3 September 1889 – 1929) was a famous Christian in India who influenced the faith of many Indian Christians through his life and writings. Sundar Singh mysteriously disappeared into the Himalayas in 1929 never to be seen again. Sundar Singh claims that Christ appeared to him and caused his conversion after he had hated Christianity, burned a Bible and wanted to commit suicide on a railway line.[844] DGS Dhinakaran was Penteostal but **Sundar Singh was not Pentecostal.**[845]

Sundar Singh believed in **Non Elect Salvation** and claimed to have seen direct visions in the spirit world of it happening. Sadhu Sundar Singh said,

---

[843] Hebrews 13:7 (NKJV). biblehub.com/hebrews/13-7.htm

[844] Cyril J. Davey. *The Story of Sadhu Sundar Singh* (Chicago: Moody Press, 1963). Pages 32-33.

[845] The Methodist Church in Malaysia wrote, "INDIGENOUS CHRISTIANITY: Pentecostals and Charismatics emerged out of Christianity in the west, where for long periods Christianity neglected the importance of the gifts of the Holy Spirit in the life of the church. However, often when non-westerners were converted, many of them read about the work of the Holy Spirit in the Bible and begin to practice them naturally. Examples of this include **Sadhu Sundar Singh in India** and John Sung in China. They were **not Pentecostals or Charismatics** in the western sense, but they **freely exercised the Holy Spirit's gifts**. They are examples of **Indigenous Christianity,** i.e. forms of Christianity that emerged and grew under indigenous or local leadership in Asia, Africa and Latin America." (June 2007-The Holy Spirit and Revival. Approved By GCEC, 11-12 Aug 2006).

www.methodistchurch.org.my/newsmaster.cfm?&menuid=6&action=view&retrieveid=52

"I was also told that the **love of God operates even in Hell**. God does not shine in His full light, because those there could not bear it, but He gradually shows them more and more light, and by and by brings them on and moves their conscience towards something better, although they think that the desire is entirely their own. Thus God works on their minds from within, something in the same way, though in the opposite direction, as that in which Satan suggests temptation to us here. Thus, what with God's work within and the Light without, almost **all those in Hell will ultimately be brought to Christ's feet**. It will perhaps take millions of ages, but when it is attained they will be full of joy and thankfulness towards God ; though they will still be less happy than those who have accepted Christ on earth. …At least, **that is the case with the majority,** but there are some **few** personalities, Satan for instance, in regard to whom I was told, ` **Don't ask about them.**' And so I didn't like to ask, but I hoped that for them also there was some hope. " They also told me that the **Saints help in the work of saving souls in Hell**, because there can be no idleness in Heaven. Those in Hell will ultimately be brought to Heaven like the prodigal son, but with regard to the **ultimate fate of a certain number you must not ask**." [The Sadhu is inclined to think that perhaps these few will be annihilated]. " Once I said, 'So many people will be lost because they have not heard of Christ.' They said, `The contrary will be the case; **very few will be lost.**' There is a kind of heavenly joke -no, joke is not a good word for it. `**Very few will be lost but many will be saved.**"[846]

In one instance, Sundar Singh saw a relatively good atheist saved in the Spirit World after some judgment time. Sadhu Sundar Singh wrote (in Urdu),

"DEATH OF A PHILOSOPHER … The **soul of a German philosopher** entered into the **world of spirits** … . I asked one of the angels what the end of this man would be, and he replied "If this man's life had been altogether bad, then he would at once have joined the spirits of darkness, but he is **not without a moral sense**, so for a very long time **he will wander blindly round in the dim**

---

[846] Streeter, Burnett and A. J. Appasamy. *The Sadhu: a Study in Mysticism and Practical Religion*. London: Macmillan, 1923), Pages 100 – 102. Available online (pages 128 – 130 instead):

endtimemanna.org/magnusson/Data/Sundar/The_Sadhu-Streeter_and_Appasamy.pdf

light of the **lower parts of the intermediate state**, and keep on bumping his philosophical head, until tired of his foolishness, **he repents**. Then he will be ready to receive the necessary instruction from the angels appointed for that purpose, and, when instructed, will he be fit to **enter** into the **fuller light** of **God** in the **higher sphere.**" [847]

In another instance Sundar Singh saw a relatively good Hindu-idolater saved in the Spirit World too.

"THE MANIFESTATION OF CHRIST ... I saw in a vision the **spirit of an idolater** on reaching the world of spirits begin at once to search for his god. Then the saints said to him, "**There is no god here save the One True God, and Christ**, who is His **manifestation.**" At this, the man was a good deal astonished, but being a sincere seeker after truth, **he frankly admitted that he had been in error**. He eagerly sought to know the correct view of truth, and asked if he might see the Christ. Shortly after this Christ manifested Himself in a dim light to him, and to others who had newly arrived in the **world of spirits**, ... So, when these spirits saw Christ in this dim but attractive light, they were filled with a joy and peace ... **all their error was washed away**. Then with all their hearts, they **acknowledged Him as the Truth, and found healing**, and, bowing in lowly adoration before Him, thanked and praised Him. And the saints, who had been appointed for their instruction; also rejoiced over them."[848]

Despite all this, Dr. D.G.S. Dhinakaran claimed to have seen Sadhu Sundar Singh in heaven. Dr. D.G.S. Dhinakaran wrote,

"There were occasions when the Lord enabled me to have some time in the Second Heaven with **Sadhu Sundar Singh, the**

---

[847] Sadhu Sundar Singh. *Visions of the Spiritual World*. Translated by Rev. T. E. Riddle of the New Zealand Presbyterian Mission, Kharar, Punjab, from Urdu into English, Macmillan Co., 1926. Pages 4 – 5.

endtimemanna.org/magnusson/Data/Sundar/Visions_of_the_Spiritual_World_by_Sadhu_Sundar_Singh.pdf

[848] Sadhu Sundar Singh. *Visions of the Spiritual World*. Page 6.

great and acclaimed **Saint of India**. The divine joy that was reflected on his face is beyond any description"[849]

Now Sundar Singh claimed to have seen Swedenborg during his spirit world visions and they even spoke about some type of **Non Elect Salvation**. Sundar Singh wrote,

> "Yes, I have talked with the venerable **Swedenborg** and **some other saints** and angels about the **hells**, although I am unable to explain adequately all that they told me. But it is somewhat like this; No spirit can exist forever, if separated from God by sin or evil. It must either cease to exist or return to God who is the source of life. There is no spirit which will ever cease to exist ; therefore **every spirit finally must return to God**, even though it may be **after ages of ages**."[850]

Swedenborg (29 January 1688 – 29 March 1772) claimed to have seen St. Augustine of Hippo during his spirit world visits and believed in **Non Elect Salvation** even in his lifetime. Emanuel Swedenborg wrote,

> "I have several times talked with **Augustine**, who was **bishop of Hippo in Africa**, in the **third century**. He said that he is there at this time, inspiring them with the worship of the Lord, and that there is hope that this new gospel will be extended into the surrounding regions. I have heard the angels rejoicing over that revelation, because through it there is being opened to them a communication with the human rational, hitherto closed up by the universal dogma that the understanding must be kept in obedience to the faith of the ministers of the church."[851]

Emanuel Swedenborg also wrote,

> "The **Papists** in the **spiritual world** appear round about and **beneath the Protestants**, and separated from them by interspaces which they are forbidden to pass, although the monks by clandestine arts secure for themselves a way through, and also send

---

[849] Dhinakaran, D.G.S. *An Insight Into Heaven*. Jesus Calls or True Friend Management Support Service Pvt. Ltd. 2007. Page 101.

[850] Appasamy, A. J. *Sundar Singh*. Cambridge: Lutterworth, 1958. Page 216. archive.org/stream/in.ernet.dli.2015.51820/2015.51820.Sundar-Singh-A-Biography-1958_djvu.txt

[851] Swedenborg, Emanuel. *True Christian Religion*. [1771], tr. by John C. Ager [1906]). Section 840. sacred-texts.com/swd/tcr/tcr17.htm

out emissaries by hidden paths to make converts; but they are traced out, and after being punished, are either sent back to their companions or cast down. ... The **Mohammedans**, like **all nations who acknowledge one God, love justice and do good from religion**, have **their own heaven**, but it is **outside of the Christian heaven**. The Mohammedan heaven, however, is divided into two. In the lower they live uprightly with several wives; but only those who give up their concubines and acknowledge the Lord our Savior, and also His dominion over heaven and hell, are raised up from this into their higher heaven. I have heard that it is impossible for them to conceive of God the Father and our Lord as one, but that it is possible for them to believe that the Lord rules over the heavens and the hells because He is the Son of God the Father. It is because of their holding this belief that it is granted them by the Lord to ascend into the higher heaven."[852]

28. Watchman Nee (November 4, 1903 – May 30, 1972), Chinese Church leader.

Watchman Nee was a Protestant but **not a Pentecostal** either. He caused significant revival among Chinese Christians and was eventually martyred in prison in China. Some Pentecostal Christians tried to coerce him to *speak in tongues* but he didn't. He wrote,

> "Let us look at wonders. I personally am not antagonistic to them. I have seen with my own eyes cases of instantaneous divine healing. Some people profess they can heal diseases. We do not oppose healing, we only contend with erroneous ways of healing. **Some ask me if I oppose speaking in tongues. Certainly not, though I do question tongues which are obtained through faulty means.** As to visions and dreams**, I too have seen great light.** We acknowledge that there are such things in the Bible. But I do resist visions and dreams which are obtained through unlawful means. ... Let us talk about the **baptism in the Holy Spirit**. When I was in Shantung this time, I too told people to seek for it. Nevertheless, I do **not approve** of the shutting in of many people into a small room for several days' fasting, praying, and chorus singing. Should people do such a thing, it will not take too long for them to have their brain dazed, the will to be turned passive, and their lips to be **made to utter strange and incoherent sounds or**

---

[852] Swedenborg, Emanuel. *True Christian Religion*. [1771], tr. by John C. Ager [1906]). Sections 817 and 832. sacred-texts.com/swd/tcr/tcr17.htm

tongues. And in this way shall their latent power be released. In a meeting for seeking Spirit-baptism, people will keep shouting hallelujah for thousands of times. Eventually, their brain will grow dull, their mind becomes paralyzed, and they begin to see visions. How can you consider this as Spirit-baptism? It is but soul-baptism. **What they receive is not the power of the Holy Spirit; it is instead soul force**, the manifestation of the latent power of the soul."[853]

Regarding salvation, Watchman Nee first writes that *simply living a holy life* only merits a *small reward* if they never suffered nor stood up for say "doctrine":

"Now let us summarize what we have seen. The future of Christians is very simple. For a **saved Christian** the question of the **new heaven and new earth,** including all eternity, is solved. But the **age of the kingdom is controversial.** No one dares to say anything about what will happen. What we have to solve today is the problem of the kingdom. In the kingdom there are many ranks of Christians. Many will reign with Christ because they have worked faithfully and have undergone persecution, reproach, and suffering. **Some** may **not have undergone** persecution, reproach, and suffering, but they **do not have sins either.** They have lived **a clean life.** Although they have **done nothing that deserves special merit,** they have at least given a cup of water to a little one for the sake of the Lord's name (Matt. 10:42). They will also **receive a reward, but their reward will be very small.** In the age of the kingdom, some Christians will receive a reward in the kingdom. Some will receive a great reward; others will receive a small reward. ... There are still many things which we are not clear about concerning the future, but the Bible has shown us enough. Although there are details which we have not yet seen, we do know what the **children of God** will face. Some will receive a **reward**; some will go into **corruption.** Some will be put into **prison,** and still some will be **cast into the fire and be burned.**"[854]

---

[853] Watchman Nee. *The Latent Power of the Soul*. Christian Fellowship Publishers. 1972. ISBN 9780935008258. articles.ochristian.com/article1908.shtml

[854] Watchman Nee. *Collected Works of Watchman Nee*. Summary. The (Set 2) Vol. 29: The Gospel of God (2) (W. Nee). Living Stream Ministry. ISBN 9780870835902. 1934 – 1940. bibleread.online/all-books-by-Watchman-Nee-and-Witness-Lee/book-collected-works-of-watchman-nee-the-set-2-vol-29-the-gospel-of-god-2-Watchman-Nee-read-online/10/

Watchman Nee writes strangely in his quote above regarding some "Christians" not just receiving "no reward", but will also undergo "corruption", "prison" while others may be "cast into the fire and be burned". This is very similar to *my interpolations* using Bible verses such as 1 Corinthians 3:14 for "reward" case while 1 Corinthians 3:15's "saved by fire" with "till the last penny judgment verses in prison" or also Daniel 12:10's "purified" after judgments and Matthew 3:11 – 12's "Baptism by Fire" can be linked to his quote here.

Let's look at Watchman Nee's quote below next regarding those who will **not** receive any **reward** case:

> "Those who will **not receive a reward** are also divided into a **few categories**. One group will **not enter into the kingdom at all**. The Bible does not tell us where they will go. It only says that they will be **kept outside the kingdom** in the **outer darkness** (Matt. 8:12; 22:13; 25:30; Luke 13:28). They will be **left outside** the glory of God. Second, there will be many who, in addition to not having worked well, have specific sins not yet dealt with. **They are saved**, but when they die, they still have sins which they have not repented of and dealt with. They still have the problem of sin with them. These ones will be **temporarily put into the fire**. They will **come out only after they have paid all their debts**. This will **last at most until** the **end of the kingdom**. I do not know how long this period will actually be."[855]

One thing is clear though. Watchman Nee believed that the Bible teaches that *some* are *saved after some type of Spirit World Judgments*. Also, the *age of the kingdom* he speaks about is the 1000 years (Millennial) reign which matches the *Chiliasm* Prophecy Model timeline perfectly.

However, a key difference is he applies all these Bible verses to only fallen Christians but not non-Christians. If you look at the minimum thirtyfold reward level for Christian "good ground" (Matthew 13:8), since it is called "good" and is considered "reward" level (compare with Matthew 19:29's "hundredfold" reward level mentioned separately than "Eternal Life"), doesn't it seem that Watchman Nee's quotes for someone saved after

---

[855] Watchman Nee. *Collected Works of Watchman Nee*. Summary. The (Set 2) Vol. 29: The Gospel of God (2) (W. Nee). Living Stream Ministry. ISBN 9780870835902. 1934 – 1940. bibleread.online/all-books-by-Watchman-Nee-and-Witness-Lee/book-collected-works-of-watchman-nee-the-set-2-vol-29-the-gospel-of-god-2-Watchman-Nee-read-online/10/

Spirit World judgment seems more likely to match both a non-Christian and fallen Christian who do not enter heaven?

In short, I think Watchman Nee's quote above for the Bible verses he is thinking of for "those who will **not** receive any **reward** case" seem to match our **Non Elect Salvation** possibility rather than **Elect Salvation**.

29. Reverend Billy Graham (November 7, 1918 – February 21, 2018), Evangelist.

Reverend Billy Graham is probably America's No. 1 evangelist to date. He did not speak in tongues either but was neutral toward those who do (which is my stance too since I cannot determine whether it is real or not).

Billy Graham has even gone on TV to declare his belief regarding **Non Elect Salvation**.[856] Some erroneously quote the same video samples and *falsely claim* that he was a *universalist*. This is clearly not true since he did not say 'all men will be saved' but rather only 'relatively good *Non-Christians* may also be saved'. He did not detail out theologically how? but the *Chiliasm* Prophecy Model which I present here can answer that part (if true).

There is no need for Billy Graham to 'switch' into 'Non Elect Salvation' possibility due to any financial motivation nor because he wants to make himself popular simply because he is already renown and well to do by just preaching *Eternal Hell only for Non-Christians prior*! In fact, he lost some support from other Christians including his own personal supporters who claim that he is senile but you don't need to be a medical doctor to see that he is clearly speaking of his own will here rationally.

This does not prove *Non-Elect Salvation* but it shows that Billy Graham really had this conviction for such a belief in him for some time prior since no one just switches from one doctrinal possibility to the next like that especially when one is already at the pinnacle of success. Billy Graham's own words echo similarly with mine and I can resonate that he just wants to reveal a *possibility (not doctrine)* in regard to what he *hopes* could be true, which is just plain *honesty* and so likewise if he is not unsaved because of this, neither will I be unsaved due to to this either (if *Non Elect Salvation* turned out false), right? Let's look at some of his transcribed words for this:

"Quote 1—Are Muslims and Buddhists Saved? (an Interview with Robert Schuller)

---

[856] Billy Graham. Sample video evidence of believing in **Non Elect Salvation**. youtu.be/drt5VPfnnms

Schuller: Tell me, what do you think is the future of Christianity?

Graham: Well, Christianity and being a true believer, you know, **I think there's the body of Christ**, which comes from all the Christian groups around the world, or **outside the Christian groups**. I think everybody that **loves Christ, or knows Christ, whether they're conscious of it or not**, they're **members of the body of Christ**. And I don't think that we're going to see a great sweeping revival that will turn the whole world to Christ at any time. I think James answered that, the apostle James in the first council in Jerusalem, when he said that God's purpose for this age is to call out a people for His name. And that's what God is doing today, He's calling people out of the world for His name, whether they come from the **Muslim** world, or the **Buddhist** world, or the **Christian** world or the **nonbelieving** world, they are **members of the body of Christ** because they've been called by God. They may not even know the name of Jesus but they know in their hearts that they need something that they don't have, and they turn to the only light that they have, and **I think that they are saved, and that they're going to be with us in heaven**.

Schuller: What I hear you saying is that it's possible for Jesus Christ to come into human hearts and soul and life even if they've been born in darkness and **never had an exposure to the Bible**. Is that a correct interpretation of what you are saying?

Graham: Yes, it is because I believe that. I've met people in various parts of the world in tribal situations, that they have **never seen a Bible or heard about a Bible, and never heard of Jesus**, but **they've believed in their hearts that there was a God, and they've tried to live a life** that was quite **apart** from the surrounding community in which they lived.

Schuller: That's fantastic, I'm so thrilled to hear you say that, there's a wideness in God's mercy.

Graham: There is. There definitely is.

Quote 2—Salvation without Christ? (an Interview with McCall's Magazine)

I used to play God, but I can't do that anymore. I used to believe pagans in far-off countries were lost—were going to hell—if they did not have the Gospel of Jesus Christ preached to them. I no longer believe that. . . . I believe there are other ways of recognizing the existence of God—through nature, for instance—and plenty of other opportunities, therefore, of saying "yes" to God. (Graham later clarified what he meant here.)."[857]

Notice that Billy Graham's *unlearnt* case statement for those who "never heard the Gospel" *seems* **different** from the *body of Christ* which he mentions to consist also of those *conscious or not* (meaning they certainly include those who **heard of the Gospel**) since he uses also this phrase from the "**nonbelieving** world" [*where I add, someone can only be an "unbeliever" if he has heard the Gospel but did not believe, since others like this are the different unlearnt in comparison, right?*].

I am **not** encouraging people to remain *unbelieving* but rather am just stating what Billy Graham said here. Also, notice the criteria he attached to this possibility which is, such **Non Elect Salvation** ones are required to "**love Christ, or know Christ, whether they're conscious of it or not**", I think will be shown in their lifestyle where for example that they're kind to Christians and also do especially 6 of the last 10 Commandments relating to man which includes His *Charity Doctrine* Commands in some way.

I tell *unbelievers* to repent and believe in Christ and then intercede for *their unbelieving dead loved ones* (just try and let God decide). However, if you remain an *unbeliever*, then you are doing "no good" toward your *unbelieving dead loved one* either by simply blaming God or turning into an atheist. So, why not try this? as some of the *Non Elect Salvation* quotes from others which I have demonstrated seem to echo a hope likewise.

If *Non Elect Salvation* doesn't happen, remember also that it won't happen even if you remain an unbeliever and so, it's just a neutral attempt at it (deceiving no one).

Here's an important note while reading various Church Fathers' quotes regarding **Non Elect Salvation** *possibility* here: If any of these quotes turn out as false on Judgment Day, it's not my fault since I'm just doing an academic presentation of it and also the *Non Elect Salvation possibility* can be true even without the existence of one quote from this section either *if God Wills it*. Since I cannot conclusively determine the Will of God, I am just presenting the evidence for how the *Chiliasm* Prophecy Model can match even these quotes from some non-Chiliasm sources even for the area of *Non Elect Salvation possibility*. My point here is *honesty* because as you can read, these

---

[857] Viola, Frank. *ReGrace: What the Shocking Beliefs of the Great Christians Can Teach Us Today*. Baker Books. March 5, 2019. Note: The part I quote is *freely* available on a blog (written by Frank himself) and the earlier video and is not his personal interview with Billy Graham. www.patheos.com/blogs/frankviola/billygraham/

quotes exist and some are clearer than others, while some others seem to be a little vague or is *interpolated* by me as to how I think it can match the *Non Elect Salvation possibility*.

Does Romans 2 speak only of a hope for unlearnt case?

Notice that Romans 2:12 – 13[858] points not to the unlearnt case but learnt case since it reads "hearers of the Law (gospel)" can be "justified" if they "did the works of the Law (Gospel commands)" which could be the "saved by fire" case of 1 Corinthians 3:15. Also, if any person with faith in Christ must be able to get a minimum reward for faith which would assign him to 1 Corinthians 3:14's reward case for it is hard to conceive that a person with faith gets zero rewards and is saved by fire as mentioned in 1 Corinthians 3:15 since faith itself is a great thing, isn't it? Also, faith without works would be dead [859] meaning that any person with a living faith (hence a Christian) must be 1 Corinthians 3:14's honoured reward case, right?

I am writing this not to confuse you but to honestly present the deeper thoughts which arise when we map these verses to each other. Just like the unlearnt case requires such saved ones to see and believe in Lord Jesus Christ in the Spirit World, such "saved by fire" case ones of 1 Corinthians 3:15 also may refer to this class of "believing after seeing" case of John 6:29, 36, 40 where Christ was only angry with the Jews for not believing Him even after seeing Him and His miracles and other works.

Whether this is a misguided interpretation or accurate truth is open to debate and this particular topic of *non-elect salvation* is something I was attracted to from the writings of such earliest Church Fathers. How would it be fair to Christians then to believe here on earth and not in the Spirit World?

Many Pentecostals really believe in Dr. D.G.S. Dhinakaran's claim of going to heaven and seeing even Sadhu Sundar Singh. This means either Sundar Singh's *non-elect salvation* quotes are true or if wrong, they don't affect salvation at all (because quite a number of Christians and non-Christians have either believed or been affected by Sundar Singh's *non-elect salvation* quotes shown prior).

---

[858] Romans 2:12 – 13, "12For as many as have sinned without law will also perish without law, and as many as have **sinned in the law** will be judged by the law 13(for **not the hearers of the law** are just in the sight of God, but the **doers of the law will be justified;**" (NKJV). biblehub.com/nkjv/romans/2.htm

[859] James 2:26 "For as the body without the spirit is dead, so **faith without works** is dead also" (NKJV). biblehub.com/james/2-26.htm

As for me, though I present the evidence strongly and I hope that *non-elect salvation* possibility turns out to be true, but yet I can only stand neutral still in regard to things which I cannot know for sure until I die and meet the Lord. I often take this neutral stance on matters of prophecy but present the evidence for the side which I think is more probable so that I don't accidentally mislead anyone and have already told them all these facts in advance.

St. Justin of Rome has written that no Christian goes to heaven[860] until after the resurrection because we need that "change" from "human" to "no more flesh and blood" celestial body to be able to "enter the final heavens" which is the "change" from "natural body" to "spiritual body" [861] for the elect at the last trumpet. This is only understood accurately like this if we take all the *Chiliasm* church father quotes as a whole to understand what he failed to write explicitly. St. Justin is not denying that some can have heavenly visions if God permits it (2 Corinthians 12:2) but rather is writing against those who say they that there is no bodily resurrection (in flesh and blood first) and can live in the heavens permanently in a spirit state.

This is further substantiated by Lord Jesus Christ's own Resurrection where as a "Spirit" He did not go to "heaven"[862] yet and could only do so after "Bodily Resurrection"[863].

---

[860] St. Justin of Rome writes, "For if you have fallen in with some who are called Christians, but who do not admit this [truth], and venture to blaspheme the God of Abraham, and the God of Isaac, and the God of Jacob; who say there is **no resurrection of the dead**, and that **their souls**, when **they die**, are **taken to heaven**; do **not** imagine that they are Christians" (*Dialogue with Trypho*, Chapter 80)
www.newadvent.org/fathers/01286.htm

[861] 1 Corinthians 15:44, 46, 49, "44It is **sown a natural body**, it is **raised a spiritual body**. There is a natural body, and there is a spiritual body. 46However, the spiritual is not first, but the natural, and afterward the spiritual. 49And as we have borne the image of the man of dust, we shall also bear the **image** of the **heavenly Man**" (NKJV). biblehub.com/nkjv/1_corinthians/15.htm

[862] John 20:17, 'Jesus said to her, "Do not cling to Me, for I have **not yet ascended** to **My Father**; but go to My brethren and say to them, 'I am ascending to My Father and your Father, and to My God and your God.' " ' (NKJV). biblehub.com/john/20-17.htm

[863] Acts 1:9 – 11, "9Now when He had spoken these things, while they watched, He was taken up, and a cloud received Him out of their sight. 10And while they looked steadfastly toward heaven as He went up, behold, two men stood by them in white apparel, 11who also said, "Men of Galilee, why do you stand gazing up into **heaven**? This same **Jesus**, who was **taken up** from you **into heaven**, will so **come in like manner** as you **saw Him go into heaven**.' "(NKJV). biblehub.com/nkjv/acts/1.htm

Christ's Resurrection Body is not merely flesh and blood but beyond and when we rise from the dead, we are not immediately conformed to it yet until the marriage of the Lamb (that's one of the purpose for it) is complete after the 1000 years and our body sharing "one flesh" with Christ's is "transformed into some glory"[864] as per *Chiliasm* quotes shown earlier.

Roman Catholics like to quote both St. Irenaeus of Lyons[865] and Tertullian [866] for unity quotes and that they are the church with direct spiritual descent from the apostles themselves. The problem here is that the "Original Catholic Churches" at the time of their writing is quoted to believe even in *Chiliasm* quotes which they have written, right? So if even one quote of theirs is not believed or is different from what the Catholic church believes today, then doesn't that prove that either diversity was allowed and a tradition or an interpretation which prevailed has been dominant proving human free will? Isn't this same spiritual phenomena observable with the Jews themselves in that they had preserved Scripture, ensured the continuity and function of Levitical priesthood and converted many into Judaism for thousands of years but yet were wrong on many doctrinal points by the time of Christ, some even disbelieving Him?

---

[864] Philippians 3:21, "who will **transform** our **lowly body** that it may be **conformed** to **His glorious body**," (NKJV). biblehub.com/philippians/3-21.htm

[865] St. Irenaeus of Lyons writes, "1. Now all these [**heretics**] are of much later date than the **bishops** to whom the **apostles** committed the **Churches**; which fact I have in the third book taken all pains to demonstrate. It follows, then, as a matter of course, that these heretics aforementioned, since they are blind to the truth, and deviate from the [right] way, will walk in various roads; and therefore the footsteps of their doctrine are scattered here and there **without agreement** or **connection**. But the path of those belonging to the Church circumscribes the whole world, as possessing the **sure tradition** from the **apostles**, and gives unto us to see that the **faith** of all is **one** and the **same**," (*Against Heresies*, Book 5, Chapter 20, Point 1),

www.newadvent.org/fathers/0103520.htm

[866] Tertullian writes, "But if there be any (**heresies**) which are bold enough to plant themselves in the **midst** of the **apostolic age,** that they may thereby seem to have been **handed down** by the **apostles**, because they existed in the time of the apostles, we can say: Let them produce the original records of their churches; let them unfold the roll of their bishops, running down in due succession from the beginning in such a manner that [that first bishop of theirs] bishop shall be able to show for his ordainer and predecessor some one of the apostles or of apostolic men, — a man, moreover, who continued steadfast with the apostles. For this is the manner in which the apostolic churches transmit their registers: as the church of **Smyrna**, which records that **Polycarp** was placed therein by **John**; as also the church of **Rome**, which makes **Clement** to have been ordained in like manner by **Peter**." (*Prescription against Heretics*, Chapter 32), www.newadvent.org/fathers/0311.htm

My point is that majority in number of converts and prevalence of any doctrine or interpretation is not necessarily a sign of truth. For me, the earliest surviving writings of Christianity which mainly involves these *Chiliasm* church fathers, St. Irenaeus of Lyons, St. Justin of Rome and Tertullian seems to preserve the ancient faith most accurately and where they differ, these could be *possibilities* but I prefer St. Irenaeus and St. Justin over Tertullian since even the Roman Catholics have noticed some errors in Tertullian and so he is not sainted.

This same St. Clement of Rome (c. 35 AD – c. 99 AD) or Pope Clement I for Roman Catholics who is a direct disciple of apostle St. Peter himself has written a letter that is known as 1 Clement today which is considered Scripture in some early Christianity such as the 5th century Codex Alexandrinus[867] and is even mentioned by St. Irenaeus of Lyons as an authentic tradition from the apostles [868] that has a verse which almost sounds like a prophecy[869] and states that sometimes the person who leaves the church could be more accurate doctrinally despite the ruling of the majority. This is a clear proof of freewill practice which God has allowed even in the area of doctrinal accuracy in a Church.

In other words, St. Clement of Rome basically states that doctrinal accuracy may not always be found in the majority and a person who leaves a Church because of that will attain to great honour and glory in the Lord provided he turned out right[870]. So, knowing this should encourage each

---

[867] Aland, Kurt; Aland, Barbara. *The Text of the New Testament: An Introduction to the Critical Editions and to the Theory and Practice of Modern Textual Criticism*. Erroll F. Rhodes (trans.). Grand Rapids: William B. Eerdmans Publishing Company, ISBN 978-0-8028-4098-1, 1995) 107, 109.

[868] St. Irenaeus of Lyons writes, "for there were many still remaining who had received **instructions from the apostles. In** the time of this **Clement**, no small **dissension** having occurred among the brethren at Corinth, the Church in Rome dispatched a most **powerful letter** to the Corinthians, exhorting them to peace, **renewing their faith**, and **declaring the tradition** which it had lately **received** from the **apostles**," (*Against Heresies*, Book 3, Chapter 3, Point 3), www.newadvent.org/fathers/0103303.htm

[869] St. Clement of Rome writes, "Who then among you is noble-minded? Who compassionate? Who full of love? Let him declare, If on my account **sedition** and **disagreement** and **schisms** have arisen, I will depart, I will go away wherever ye desire, and **I will do whatever the majority commands**; only let the flock of Christ live on terms of peace with the presbyters set over it. He that acts thus shall procure to himself **great glory in the Lord**; and every place will welcome him. For the earth is the Lord's, and the fullness thereof. These things they who live a **godly life** that is **never** to be **repented of**, both have done and always will do." (*1 Clement*, Chapter 54), www.newadvent.org/fathers/1010.htm

[870] Luke 6:22 – 23, "22Blessed are you when men **hate you**, and when they **exclude you**, and **revile you**, and cast out **your name as evil**, for the **Son of Man's sake**. 23Rejoice

Christian to be more united and not worry about the approval of masses whenever they stand for some doctrinal accuracy be it in practice or in theory and especially in prophecy aspect too.

How does God's Will play a role in number of converts for a particular denomination then? Personally, I believe that God allows the leaders we deserve. I mean if more Christians are zealous for God in regards to accuracy and practice at St. Irenaeus of Lyons' level, then we will get a leader who believes the same as him and vice versa[871].

In fact, prophet Daniel has prophesied that though leading many to righteousness is a great thing but even that shines like the "stars" (lower level) whereas having doctrinal accuracy or "insight" say in prophecy too can result in that final resurrection body glory to inherit the glory like the "heavens" (higher level)[872]. Even St. Irenaeus of Lyons knew that Daniel 12:3 speaks of this glory relating to final resurrection body context[873] based on how much insight in prophecy and/or doctrinal accuracy a disciple of Christ has which remains forever and ever.

So, we as Christians should try our best to be accurate and let God decide who shines like heavens and who shine like stars in the end. God has warned through Prophet Jeremiah that in the context of prophecy/oracle, if one claims that it's one's own attempt, even if it turned out wrong it's okay since His Name was not taken in vain[874].

---

in that day and leap for joy! For indeed your **reward** is **great** in **heaven**, for in like manner their fathers did to the **prophets**" (NKJV). biblehub.com/nkjv/luke/6.htm

[871] Romans 10:2, "For I bear them witness that they have a **zeal for God**, but **not** according to **knowledge**" (NKJV). biblehub.com/romans/10-2.htm

[872] Daniel 12:3, "And those who have **insight** will **shine** like the glow of the expanse of **heaven**, and those who **lead the many** to righteousness, like the **stars** forever and ever" (NASB). biblehub.com/daniel/12-3.htm

[873] St. Irenaeus of Lyons writes, "**preaching** by anticipation the **inheritance** of the holy **Jerusalem**, and proclaiming beforehand that the man who **loves God** shall arrive at such excellency as even to see God, and **hear His word**, and from the **hearing** of His **discourse** be **glorified** to such an extent, that others cannot behold the **glory of his countenance**, as was said by Daniel: Those who do **understand**, shall **shine** as the **brightness** of the **firmament**, and **many** of the **righteous** as the **stars** for ever and ever. Daniel 12:3 Thus, then, I have shown it to be, **if any one read the Scriptures**." (*Against Heresies*, Book 4, Chapter 26, Point 1), www.newadvent.org/fathers/0103426.htm

[874] Jeremiah 23:36, "And the **oracle** of the LORD you shall **mention no more**. For **every man's word** will be **his oracle**, for you have perverted the words of the living God, the LORD of hosts, our God" (NKJV). biblehub.com/jeremiah/23-36.htm

However, if a prophet claims that "God told me so" but He didn't or that it turned out wrong, then such a person is liable to "eternal" shame or judgment of some sort (in fact, the Hebrew word *olam* which is translated as "everlasting and perpetual" here appears twice showing its seriousness)[875].

---

[875] Jeremiah 23:38 – 40, "38But since you say, 'The **oracle of the Lord!**' therefore thus says the Lord: 'Because you say this word, "The oracle of the Lord!" and I have sent to you, saying, "**Do not say,** 'The oracle of the Lord!' " 39therefore behold, I, even I, will utterly **forget** you and **forsake** you, and the city that I gave you and your fathers, and will **cast you out of My presence.** 40And I will bring an **everlasting** reproach upon you, and a **perpetual** shame, which shall **not be forgotten.**' '," (NKJV). biblehub.com/nkjv/jeremiah/23.htm

Jonathan Ramachandran

Essay 10: Baptism by Fire

St. Justin of Rome seems to see mankind classified into three categories (Christians or righteous, sinners and wicked) instead of two categories (righteous versus wicked) which agrees to some equally mysterious Bible verses[876] as well:

> "And, Be kind and merciful, as your Father also is kind and merciful, and makes His sun to rise on sinners, and the righteous, and the wicked.."[877]

As mentioned, maybe sinners are saved by fire and the ungodly (wicked) are unsaved while the righteous (Christians) are saved without judgment[878] (just a thought to match these 3 categories of men).

This is the Baptism of Fire's principal verse:

> "I indeed baptize you with water unto repentance, but He who is coming after me is mightier than I, whose sandals I am not worthy to carry. He will baptize you with the Holy Spirit and fire. 12His winnowing fan is in His hand, and He will thoroughly clean out His threshing floor, and gather His wheat into the barn; but He will burn up the chaff with unquenchable fire."[879]

Recall that St. Gregory's famous quote pointing to the context of 1 Corinthians 3:15's "saved by fire"[880] case is not for Christians but novation heretics who are not following Christ's way but their own way which is why I see it as a Non-Elect Salvation "possibility" below. St. Gregory writes,

> "Let these men then if they will, follow our way, which is Christ's way; but if they will not, let them go their own. Perhaps in

---

[876] Psalm 1:5 – 6 reads, "5Therefore the ungodly shall not stand in the judgment, Nor sinners in the congregation of the righteous. 6For the Lord knows the way of the righteous, But the way of the ungodly shall perish." (NKJV). biblehub.com/nkjv/psalms/1.htm

[877] St. Justin of Rome. First Apology. Chapter 15. What Christ himself taught. www.newadvent.org/fathers/0126.htm

[878] John 5:24 reads, "Most assuredly, I say to you, he who hears My word and believes in Him who sent Me has everlasting life, and shall not come into judgment, but has passed from death into life" (NKJV). biblehub.com/john/5-24.htm

[879] Matthew 3:11 – 12 (NKJV). biblehub.com/nkjv/matthew/3.htm

[880] 1 Corinthians 3:15, "If anyone's work is burned, he will suffer loss; but he himself will be saved, yet so as through fire" (NKJV).

it they will be baptized with Fire, in that last Baptism which is more painful and longer, which devours wood like grass, 1 Corinthians 3:12-19 and consumes the stubble of every evil."[881]

The above is probably St. Gregory's Non Elect Salvation quote here simply because he is quoting the context of 1 Corinthians 3's part which includes this saved by fire context and he is mentioning that fire as last Baptism where these Novation heretics (who follow their own way and not Christ's way) still get this chance to be baptized with Fire and saved by fire as this is intrinsically implied in the quoted Bible verses below:

> "If anyone's work is burned, he will suffer loss; but he himself will be saved, yet so as through fire"[882]

St. Gregory Nazianzus speaks of a Judgment Fire of God to have cleansing effect on some (causing them to be "saved") while another different "Judgment Fire" of God to have an 'eternal damnation' effect on others.

> "For I know a cleansing fire which Christ came to send upon the earth, and He Himself is analogically called a Fire. ... I know also a fire which is not cleansing, but avenging; either that fire of Sodom which He pours down on all sinners, mingled with brimstone and storms, or that which is prepared for the Devil and his Angels or that which proceeds from the face of the Lord, and shall burn up his enemies round about; and one even more fearful still than these, the unquenchable fire which is ranged with the worm that dieth not but is eternal for the wicked. For all these belong to the destroying power; though some may prefer even in this place to take a more merciful view of this fire, worthily of Him That chastises".[883]

St. Gregory's Possible Non-Elect Salvation quote here:

> "For I know a cleansing fire which Christ came to send upon the earth, and He Himself is analogically called a Fire. ... For all these belong to the destroying power; though some may prefer even in this place to take a more merciful view of this fire, worthily of Him That chastises".

---

[881] St. Gregory Nazianzus, Oration 39, Chapter XIX, Oration on the Holy Lights, www.newadvent.org/fathers/310239.htm

[882] 1 Corinthians 3:15 (NKJV). biblehub.com/1_corinthians/3-15.htm

[883] St. Gregory Nazianzus. Oration 40. Chapter 36.
www.ewtn.com/catholicism/library/select-orations-334-3741-11647

Notice that St. Gregory speaks of two different types of Fire.

St. Gregory's the Wicked being Damned quote here:

> "I know also a fire which is not cleansing, but avenging; either that fire of Sodom which He pours down on all sinners, mingled with brimstone and storms, or that which is prepared for the Devil and his Angels or that which proceeds from the face of the Lord, and shall burn up his enemies round about; and one even more fearful still than these, the unquenchable fire which is ranged with the worm that dieth not but is eternal for the wicked. For all these belong to the destroying power;"

Notice that he also acknowledges that some Christians even view the last fire to possibly have some cleansed through it where anyone cleansed from any Spirit World Judgment Fire like this is Non Elect Salvation possibility because he does not apply it to Christians but to heretics (who are considered same level or worse than non-Christians, right?) in his famous quote at the start toward Novations.

Now, let's look at the three Principal Chiliasm Church Father's quotes regarding the Context of Prophecy for Matthew 3:11 – 12's Judgment of Fire verse as follows:

Justin of Rome believes that "this Judgment of Fire" happens during the Second Coming of Christ.

> "And we know that this shall take place when our Lord Jesus Christ shall come in glory from heaven; whose first manifestation the Spirit of God who was in Elijah preceded as herald in [the person of] John, a prophet among your nation; after whom no other prophet appeared among you. He cried, as he sat by the river Jordan: 'I baptize you with water to repentance; but He that is stronger than I shall come, whose shoes I am not worthy to bear: He shall baptize you with the Holy Ghost and with fire: whose fan is in His hand, and He will thoroughly purge His floor, and will gather the wheat into the barn; but the chaff He will burn up with unquenchable fire.' Matthew 3:11-12"[884]

> "For the prophets have proclaimed two advents of His: the one, that which is already past, when He came as a dishonoured and suffering Man; but the second, when, according to prophecy,

---

[884] St. Justin of Rome. Dialogue with Trypho. Chapter 49. www.newadvent.org/fathers/01284.htm

> He shall come from heaven with glory, accompanied by His angelic host, when also He shall raise the bodies of all men who have lived, and shall clothe those of the worthy with immortality, and shall send those of the wicked, endued with eternal sensibility, into everlasting fire with the wicked devils. And that these things also have been foretold as yet to be, we will prove."[885]

Note: We know that the "Wicked" and "Devils" are sent into the Lake of Fire at the end of the Millennium as the above seems to be a summary as St. Justin's breakdown for this detail of 1000 years separation between the First Resurrection (only for Christians) and Second Resurrection (for the rest) is seen below (next). This can also imply that the context for Matthew 3:11 – 12 in St. Justin's first quote earlier refers to Judgment of Fire (cleansing for some while damnation for others) in the Spirit World Context as opposed to Final Judgment's Bodily Resurrection context which is at the end of this 1000 years meaning if anyone is saved during this period of Cleansing Fire (I interpolate based on other quotes later), then such ones could be Non Elect Salvation:

> "But I and others, who are right-minded Christians on all points, are assured that there will be a resurrection of the dead, and a thousand years in Jerusalem, which will then be built, adorned, and enlarged, [as] the prophets Ezekiel and Isaiah and others declare. … And further, there was a certain man with us, whose name was John, one of the apostles of Christ, who prophesied, by a revelation that was made to him, that those who believed in our Christ would dwell a thousand years in Jerusalem; and that thereafter the general, and, in short, the eternal resurrection and judgment of all men would likewise take place. Just as our Lord also said, 'They shall neither marry nor be given in marriage, but shall be equal to the angels, the children of the God of the resurrection.' Luke 20:35."[886]

St. Justin's quote below also affirms this timeline since it speaks of "Christians" being called as "gods" on Second Resurrection timeline since only then the judgment of all men likewise takes place and they're mentioned differently being transformed into "His Bride" (or no more flesh and blood into something angelic or heavenly being One Flesh with Christ as per

---

[885] St. Justin of Rome. The First Apology, Chapter 52.
www.newadvent.org/fathers/0126.htm
[886] St. Justin of Rome. Dialogue with Trypho. Chapters 80 – 81.
www.newadvent.org/fathers/01286.htm

Chiliasm prophecy for this part from other Church Father's quotes like Tertullian).

> "Listen, sirs, how the Holy Ghost speaks of this people, saying that they are all sons of the Highest; and how this very Christ will be present in their assembly, rendering judgment to all men. The words are spoken by David, and are, according to your version of them, thus: 'God stands in the congregation of gods; He judges among the gods.'"[887]

Tertullian clearly distinguishes that no Christian is baptized in Fire if his faith is real and only a person with pretended or weak faith gets baptized in Fire unto Judgment (which clearly links to his purgatorial quotes in hell shown next revealing Spirit World Judgment Context since a true and stable faith is already baptized in water unto salvation here on earth and so no further judgment is needed in the "Spirit World", right?):

> "John himself professes that the celestial things are not his, but Christ's, by saying, He who is from the earth speaks concerning the earth; He who comes from the realms above is above all; and again, by saying that he baptized in repentance only, but that One would shortly come who would baptize in the Spirit and fire; — of course because true and stable faith is baptized with water, unto salvation; pretended and weak faith is baptized with fire, unto judgment."[888]

My interpolation here is that those who get baptized in fire and are saved after any Spirit World judgment is possibly Non Elect Salvation since I don't think Christ would marry a Bride who has a weak or pretended faith and the Gospel's "good ground" harvest already specified that a minimum of thirtyfold level of faith is needed. Also, doesn't 'pretended' itself equals having 'no faith'? Hence this case could refer to even possibly non-Christians as well then to have a chance at this Baptism by Fire and be saved after Hell as Tertullian applies it to such weak or pretended faith Christian ones next [implied]):

> "before God the Judge (for in this light do we read of him, in another passage, as the accuser of the brethren, Revelation 12:10 or saints, where reference is made to the actual practice of legal prosecution); and lest this Judge deliver you over to the angel who

---

[887] St. Justin of Rome. Dialogue with Trypho. Chapter 124. www.newadvent.org/fathers/01288.htm
[888] Tertullian. On Baptism. Chapter 10. www.newadvent.org/fathers/0321.htm

is to execute the sentence, and he commit you to the prison of hell, out of which there will be no dismissal until the smallest even of your delinquencies be paid off in the period before the resurrection. What can be a more fitting sense than this? What a truer interpretation?"[889]

Notice that as opposed to St. Irenaeus of Lyons' quote for "last trumpet" verses (1 Corinthians 15:52) or even John 5:28 – 29's "hour is coming" timeline which could contain a Second badge of righteous to be raised during the Second resurrection as discussed in pages 28 – 29 in detail (compare with St. Irenaeus' quotes later in this essay too for the Purification Fire context for Matthew 3:11 – 12 of which, they may need to endure first), Tertullian doesn't face such a difficulty in his interpretations because he is the only Church Father who has this quote next describing that Christians themselves get raised at different times during the First Resurrection which spans 1000 years as follows:

> "Of the heavenly kingdom this is the process. After its thousand years are over, within which period is completed the resurrection of the saints, who rise sooner or later according to their deserts there will ensue the destruction of the world and the conflagration of all things at the judgment: ... when Abraham's seed, after the primal promise of being like the sand of the sea for multitude, is destined likewise to an equality with the stars of heaven — are not these the indications both of an earthly and a heavenly dispensation?"[890]

My point is that Tertullian can just take John 5:28 – 29 and read the part where the wicked rise simultaneously with the righteous literally (see his quote a bit later below for this part*:) and say that these must be the worst Christians since they rise last according to the "interpretation" he gives above. However, this causes problems such as these ones miss the "Wedding" of the Lamb which ends exactly after these 1000 years and also get immediately changed into 'no more flesh and blood' as his own quote rings (see page 68) or his direct quote below for those saved in Hades who also must undergo the change to angelic:

---

[889] Tertullian. A Treatise on the Soul. Chapter 35.
www.newadvent.org/fathers/0310.htm
[890] Tertullian, Against Marcion. Book 3. Chapter 25.
www.newadvent.org/fathers/03123.htm

"For who is there that will not desire, while he is in the flesh, to put on immortality, and to continue his life by a happy escape from death, through the transformation which must be experienced instead of it, without encountering too that Hades which will exact the very last farthing? Notwithstanding, he who has already traversed Hades is destined also to obtain the change after the resurrection. For from this circumstance it is that we definitively declare that the flesh will by all means rise again, and, from the change that is to come over it, will assume the condition of angels. Now, if it were merely in the case of those who shall be found in the flesh that the change must be undergone, in order that mortality may be swallowed up of life — in other words, that the flesh (be covered) with the heavenly and eternal raiment — it would either follow that those who shall be found in death would not obtain life, deprived as they would then be of the material and so to say the aliment of life, that is, the flesh; or else, these also must needs undergo the change, that in them too mortality may be swallowed up of life, since it is appointed that they too should obtain life."[891]

So if Tertullian is right in claiming that such righteous ones rising in John 5:28 – 29 includes also these just saved from Hades ones as well (as his other quotes here imply), these seem more to be "evidence" of Non Elect Salvation because apart from 'missing' out on the Wedding of the Lamb, don't these completely unworthy Christians since they only rise at the end of this 1000 years meaning they have no merit nor part to inherit the earthly 1000 years First Resurrection Millennium delights must match at least the minimum thirtyfold Gospel "good ground" level if they're "Elect", right? I mean how can they be "good ground" if they missed the entire millennium and only rise simultaneously with the wicked but inherit heaven being changed at this time? Also doesn't "good ground" (minimum "thirtyfold" level)[892] mean that they should not endure any type of Hades or Spirit World Judgment even?[893]

> "28Do not marvel at this; for the hour is coming in which all who are in the graves will hear His voice 29and come forth—those

---

[891] Tertullian. On the Resurrection of the Flesh. Chapter 42. www.newadvent.org/fathers/0316.htm

[892] Matthew 13:8, Matthew 19:29 calls hundredfold level as a final reward context.

[893] John 5:24, "Most assuredly, I say to you, he who hears My word and believes in Him who sent Me has everlasting life, and shall not come into judgment, but has passed from death into life" (NKJV). biblehub.com/john/5-24.htm

who have done good, to the resurrection of life, and those who have done evil, to the resurrection of condemnation."[894]

*Tertullian views Christ's John 5:28 – 29 literally and does not quote it as how some Christians do such as say that the Resurrection to Life part and Resurrection to Judgment part are separated by 1000 years for this verse which can only be seen via allegory, compare:

> "Then again, when He says, Marvel not at this: for the hour is coming, in which all that are in the graves shall hear the voice of the Son of God, and shall come forth; they that have done good, to the resurrection of life; and they that have done evil, unto the resurrection of damnation, John 5:28-29 — none will after such words be able to interpret the dead that are in the graves as any other than the bodies of the flesh, because the graves themselves are nothing but the resting-place of corpses: … For it is not the resurrection that is directly denied to flesh and blood, but the kingdom of God, which is incidental to the resurrection (for there is a resurrection of judgment also); and there is even a confirmation of the general resurrection of the flesh, whenever a special one is excepted. Now, when it is clearly stated what the condition is to which the resurrection does not lead, it is understood what that is to which it does lead; and, therefore, while it is in consideration of men's merits that a difference is made in their resurrection by their conduct in the flesh, and not by the substance thereof, it is evident even from this, that flesh and blood are excluded from the kingdom of God in respect of their sin, not of their substance; and although in respect of their natural condition they will rise again for the judgment, because they rise not for the kingdom. Again, I will say, Flesh and blood cannot inherit the kingdom of God; 1 Corinthians 15:50 and justly (does the apostle declare this of them, considered) alone and in themselves, in order to show that the Spirit is still needed (to qualify them) for the kingdom."[895]

Irenaeus of Lyons mentions only two advents of Christ (i.e. no secret coming as pre-tribulation rapture believers assert) in his quote next and that Matthew 3:11 – 12's context happens during the Second Coming of Christ

---

[894] John 5:28 – 29 (NKJV). biblehub.com/nkjv/john/5.htm
[895] Tertullian. On the Resurrection of the Flesh. Chapters 37 and 50. www.newadvent.org/fathers/0316.htm

where He "begins" to cleanse His Floor (so perhaps a "Judgment of Fire" in "Purification" context begins to eventually reveal the wheat?).

> "1. ... and do not recognise the advent of Christ, which He accomplished for the salvation of men, nor are willing to understand that all the prophets announced His two advents: the one, indeed, in which He became a man subject to stripes, and knowing what it is to bear infirmity, ... and remembered His own dead ones who had formerly fallen asleep, and came down to them that He might deliver them: but the second in which He will come on the clouds, Daniel 7:13 bringing on the day which burns as a furnace, Malachi 4:1 and smiting the earth with the word of His mouth, Isaiah 11:4 and slaying the impious with the breath of His lips, and having a fan in His hands, and cleansing His floor, and gathering the wheat indeed into His barn, but burning the chaff with unquenchable fire. Matthew 3:12; Luke 3:17"[896]

Christians are definitely wheat during "His Second Coming" and immediately participate in the First Resurrection after Christ destroys the Antichrist and ushers in the times of the kingdom (Sabbath or Millennium for 1000 years).

> "And they shall lay Babylon waste, and burn her with fire, and shall give their kingdom to the beast, and put the Church to flight. [22] ... so far useful and serviceable to the just, as stubble conduces towards the growth of the wheat, and its straw, by means of combustion, serves for working gold. And therefore, when in the end the Church shall be suddenly caught up from this, it is said, There shall be tribulation such as has not been since the beginning, neither shall be. Matthew 24:21 For this is the last contest of the righteous, in which, when they overcome they are crowned with incorruption."[897]

> "But when this Antichrist shall have devastated all things in this world, he will reign for three years and six months, and sit in the temple at Jerusalem; and then the Lord will come from heaven in the clouds, in the glory of the Father, sending this man and those who follow him into the lake of fire; but bringing in for the righteous the times of the kingdom, that is, the rest, the hallowed

---

[896] St. Irenaeus of Lyons. Against Heresies. Book 4. Chapter 33. Point 1. www.newadvent.org/fathers/0103433.htm

[897] St. Irenaeus of Lyons. Against Heresies. Book 5. Chapter 26. Point 1. www.newadvent.org/fathers/0103526.htm

seventh day; and restoring to Abraham the promised inheritance, in which kingdom the Lord declared, that many coming from the east and from the west should sit down with Abraham, Isaac, and Jacob. Matthew 8:11"[898]

Next, notice that St. Irenaeus of Lyons speaks of the "fashion of this world" passes away in the context of the current old earth and old heavens will eventually end in its current form after the times of the kingdom is accomplished first for the First Resurrection and speaks of its participants finally dwelling in the real heavenly city of God in the final new earth/heavens.

"Now this is what has been said by the apostle: For the fashion of this world passes away. 1 Corinthians 7:31 To the same purpose did the Lord also declare, Heaven and earth shall pass away. Matthew 24:35 When these things, therefore, pass away above the earth, John, the Lord's disciple, says that the new Jerusalem above shall [then] descend, as a bride adorned for her husband; and that this is the tabernacle of God, in which God will dwell with men. Of this Jerusalem the former one is an image — that Jerusalem of the former earth in which the righteous are disciplined beforehand for incorruption and prepared for salvation. And of this tabernacle Moses received the pattern in the mount; Exodus 25:40 and nothing is capable of being allegorized, but all things are steadfast, and true, and substantial, having been made by God for righteous men's enjoyment. For as it is God truly who raises up man, so also does man truly rise from the dead, and not allegorically, as I have shown repeatedly. And as he rises actually, so also shall he be actually disciplined beforehand for incorruption, and shall go forwards and flourish in the times of the kingdom, in order that he may be capable of receiving the glory of the Father. Then, when all things are made new, he shall truly dwell in the city of God. For it is said, He that sits on the throne said, Behold, I make all things new. And the Lord says, Write all this; for these words are faithful and true. And He said to me, They are done. Revelation 21:5-6 And this is the truth of the matter."[899]

---

[898] St. Irenaeus of Lyons. Against Heresies. Book 5. Chapter 29. Point 1. www.newadvent.org/fathers/0103529.htm

[899] St. Irenaeus of Lyons. Against Heresies. Book 5. Chapter 30. www.newadvent.org/fathers/0103530.htm

How does this quote affect our discussion? Notice that St. Irenaeus of Lyons' quote next uses the same phrase fashion of this world passes away or equivalent to "include the context of Matthew 3:11 – 12's Purification or Judgment Fire to imply the Millennium" timeline too.

> "3. But why do we speak of Jerusalem, since, indeed, the fashion of the whole world must also pass away, when the time of its disappearance has come, in order that the fruit indeed may be gathered into the garner, but the chaff, left behind, may be consumed by fire? For the day of the Lord comes as a burning furnace, and all sinners shall be stubble, they who do evil things, and the day shall burn them up. Malachi 4:1 Now, who this Lord is that brings such a day about, John the Baptist points out, when he says of Christ, He shall baptize you with the Holy Ghost and with fire, having His fan in His hand to cleanse His floor; and He will gather His fruit into the garner, but the chaff He will burn up with unquenchable fire. ... man, being endowed with reason, and in this respect like to God, having been made free in his will, and with power over himself, is himself the cause to himself, that sometimes he becomes wheat, and sometimes chaff."[900]

Also, doesn't St. Irenaeus of Lyons' quote above seems to reveal that this Matthew 3:11 – 12's Judgment of Fire context to cleanse His floor lasts this entire 1000 years Millennial Reign of Christ and so, an interesting interpolation is that some of the fruit that is gathered seems to be after this Judgment of Fire's Millenium or 1000 years timeline meaning it could be Non Elect Salvation for those saved by fire (perhaps these are the ones mentioned in 1 Corinthians 3:15 too) which seems to be different from those saved in the First Resurrection who are never hurt by the Second Death[901] and who in turn, could be calling these Non Elect Salvation ones as the thirsty in the "Final Scene" (Revelation 21:6, Revelation 22:17) to drink of the Water of Life since the "opposite" here regarding Fire could imply Thirst even "spiritually", right? Notice this is my personal possible interpolation in light of St. Irenaeus' quote above which also reveals that due to free will a man can be wheat or chaff and so maybe some repent, believe after seeing and are "saved by fire" then during this Last Day?

---

[900] St. Irenaeus of Lyons. Against Heresies. Book 5, Chapter 35. www.newadvent.org/fathers/0103535.htm

[901] Revelation 2:11, "He who has an ear, let him hear what the Spirit says to the churches. He who overcomes shall not be hurt by the second death" (NKJV). biblehub.com/revelation/2-11.htm

> "They also maintain that John indicated the same thing when he said, The fan is in His hand, and He will thoroughly purge the floor, and will gather the wheat into His garner; but the chaff He will burn with fire unquenchable. Luke 3:17 By this declaration He set forth the faculty of Horos. For that fan they explain to be the cross (Stauros), which consumes, no doubt, all material objects, as fire does chaff, but it purifies all those who are saved, as a fan does wheat."[902]

Possible Non Elect Salvation is mentioned here since notice that from St. Irenaeus own words from earlier parts regarding the context of this same verse (Matthew 3:11 – 12 or Luke 3:16 – 17), this is happening during the Second Coming of Christ timeline (not now, right?), where this Fire of Judgment that is revealed when He Returns causes the chaff to be unsaved but at the same time, it burns the wheat differently in that "it purifies all those who are saved, as a fan does wheat" as St. Irenaeus writes here.

I mean the general clause that this Fire purifies all who are meant to be saved seem to match St. Gregory Nazianzus' quote prior and more importantly, the 1 Corinthians 3:15's saved by fire case which could refer to someone who is possibly not even a "thirtyfold" (lowest Christian reward level for Gospel's "good ground" context) since such ones could be 1 Corinthians 3:14's those receiving "reward" case, right? In other words, if those purified and saved by this same Fire are called wheat which causes unquenchable fire to chaff at that future time when Christ Returns, then this could be Non Elect Salvation for some of them since such have "no reward" but are just saved by His Mercy, right? Difficult.

> "For we must all appear before the judgment seat of Christ, that each one may receive the things done in the body, according to what he has done, whether good or bad."[903]

> "29Jesus answered and said to them, "This is the work of God, that you believe in Him whom He sent." 35And Jesus said to them, "I am the bread of life. He who comes to Me shall never hunger, and he who believes in Me shall never thirst. 36But I said to you that you have seen Me and yet do not believe. 40And this is the will of Him who sent Me, that everyone who sees the Son and

---

[902] St. Irenaeus of Lyons. Against Heresies. Book 1. Chapter 3. Point 5. www.newadvent.org/fathers/0103103.htm

[903] 2 Corinthians 5:10 (NKJV). biblehub.com/2_corinthians/5-10.htm

believes in Him may have everlasting life; and I will raise him up at the last day"[904]

"If anyone's work is burned, he will suffer loss; but he himself will be saved, yet so as through fire"[905]

"And the Spirit and the bride say, "Come!" And let him who hears say, "Come!" And let him who thirsts come. Whoever desires, let him take the water of life freely".[906]

My further interpolation: Notice that this Last Day refers to this 1000 years Millennium First Resurrection timeline in Chiliasm context (e.g. see St. Irenaeus' quotes in pages 40, 131, 144, 236, 244 or 277 earlier) and so the believing after seeing case of John 6:29, 35, 36, 40 may apply (if God Wills) causing them to be raised at the last trumpet* as part of those who have done good (hence wheat) after being Judged in Fire (see St. Irenaeus' of Lyons quotes for this in page earlier) for their wrong works first as these quotes earlier describe especially the conclusion for purification of wheat part as being "saved by fire" in the end as St. Irenaeus wrote, "as fire does chaff, but it purifies all those who are saved, as a fan does wheat" earlier here.

Also notice that in the Final Scene, this same free will quote "Whoever desires" applies to "him who thirsts" and "the bride" or (Church/Christians/Elect Salvation) is mentioned differently and is even calling such ones to be saved here in Revelation 22:17 above. So the Chiliasm Model is consistent for Non-Elect Salvation possibility but whether this is true or not, I dare not say lest it be wrong and I add to Scripture or handle Scripture falsely and so I just leave it as it is honestly presenting it only. Also, do compare with 1 Corinthians 3:15's "saved by fire" argument given in page 115 right after St. Irenaeus of Lyons' mysterious let go phrases for Great White Throne Judgment Day context in pages 114 – 115.

My interpolations above are not entirely unique as the big picture part is similar to this quote below which has been attributed to St. Ambrose of Milan (c. 340 AD – c. 397 AD) as he describes some Non Elect Salvation (i.e. anyone saved from the Fire of Purification during the Millennium mirroring St. Justin and St. Irenaeus' timeline for Matthew 3:11 – 12 too) as follows:

---

[904] John 6:29, 35, 36, 40 (NKJV). biblehub.com/nkjv/john/6.htm
[905] 1 Corinthians 3:15 (NKJV). biblehub.com/1_corinthians/3-15.htm
[906] Revelation 22:17 (NKJV). biblehub.com/revelation/22-17.htm

> "Our Savior has appointed two kinds of resurrection in the Apocalypse. 'Blessed is he that hath part in the first resurrection,' for such come to grace without the judgment. As for those who do not come to the first, but are reserved unto the second resurrection, these shall be disciplined until their appointed times, between the first and the second resurrection."[907]

*For me, I think the earliest Church Fathers quoted have a higher chance of accuracy for this prophecy part since God Said prophecy is not of private interpretation.

> "1. Let our opponents — that is, they who speak against their own salvation— inform us [as to this point] ... This was symbolic of that man who had been bound in sins. And therefore the Lord said, Loose him, and let him depart. As, therefore, those who were healed were made whole in those members which had in times past been afflicted; and the dead rose in the identical bodies, their limbs and bodies receiving health, and that life which was granted by the Lord, who prefigures eternal things by temporal, and shows that it is He who is Himself able to extend both healing and life to His handiwork, that His words concerning its [future] resurrection may also be believed; so also at the end, when the Lord utters His voice by the last trumpet, 1 Corinthians 15:52 the dead shall be raised, as He Himself declares: The hour shall come, in which all the dead which are in the tombs shall hear the voice of the Son of man, and shall come forth; those that have done good to the resurrection of life, and those that have done evil to the resurrection of judgment. John 5:28"[908]

Notice that the only Bible verse containing this exact phrase "last trumpet" is 1 Corinthians 15:52. Now, if you compare these "last trumpet" quotes, which according to St. Victorinus of Pettau happens at the "end of 1000 years Millennial Reign" (see pages 19 – 20 with 85 – 106 for a thorough analysis for this part) where if combined with St. Irenaeus of Lyons' quote where he seems to imply a second badge of righteous saved in "identical human bodies" (so earthly/terrestrial resurrection glory)[909] meaning non-

---

[907] Source (no one seems to quote the original source but rather only this): www.tentmaker.org/Quotes/churchfathersquotes.htm

[908] St. Irenaeus of Lyons. Against Heresies. Book 5. Chapter 13. www.newadvent.org/fathers/0103513.htm

[909] Body with "glory" must be saved and there seems to be two types, 'earthly (terrestrial) vs heavenly (celestial)' in the resurrection context. 1 Corinthians 15:40 reads, "There are also

elect salvation even toward his "enemies/opponents" context above which could possibly be the surprised sheep of the nations who seem to not know the Lord but the Lord knows them[910] based on their Charity Doctrine good acts toward "His Brethren" (Christians).[911]

Please remember that under the Chiliasm Prophecy Timeline Christians are already saved for 1000 years participating in the first resurrection and now on Judgment Day, when the rest of the nations are judged, Christians are turned into no more flesh and blood being heavenly and so it seems hard to imagine these newly saved "surprised sheep" of the nations to be Christians because these are just saved now during this end of 1000 years!

Around this time, St. Clement of Alexandria (c. 150 AD – c. 215 AD) whose position of whether he is Chiliasm or non-Chiliasm is unknown since no direct quote of his exists for such comparison, writes the context of Matthew 3:11 – 12 as referring to some sheep who are saved after judgment in cleansing Fire at this time:

> "Sick, we truly stand in need of the Saviour; having wandered, of one to guide us; blind, of one to lead us to the light; thirsty, of the fountain of life, of which whosoever partakes, shall no longer thirst; John 4:13-14 dead, we need life; sheep, we need a shepherd; we who are children need a tutor, while universal humanity stands in need of Jesus; so that we may not continue intractable and sinners to the end, and thus fall into condemnation, but may be separated from the chaff, and stored up in the paternal garner. For the fan is in the Lord's hand, by which the chaff due to the fire is separated from the wheat. Matthew 3:12; Luke 3:17 You may learn, if you will, the crowning wisdom of the all-holy Shepherd and Instructor, of the omnipotent and paternal Word, when He figuratively represents Himself as the Shepherd of the sheep. And He is the Tutor of the children. He says therefore by Ezekiel, directing His discourse to the elders, and setting before them a

---

celestial bodies and terrestrial bodies; but the glory of the celestial is one, and the glory of the terrestrial is another" (NKJV).

[910] Matthew 25:37 – 40, "37"Then the righteous will answer Him, saying, 'Lord, when did we see You hungry and feed You, or thirsty and give You drink? 38When did we see You a stranger and take You in, or naked and clothe You? 39Or when did we see You sick, or in prison, and come to You?' 40And the King will answer and say to them, 'Assuredly, I say to you, inasmuch as you did it to one of the least of these My brethren, you did it to Me'." (NKJV).

[911] Matthew 12:50, "50For whoever does the will of My Father in heaven is My brother and sister and mother" (NKJV).

salutary description of His wise solicitude: And that which is lame I will bind up, and that which is sick I will heal, and that which has wandered I will turn back; and I will feed them on my holy mountain. Such are the promises of the good Shepherd. Feed us, the children, as sheep. Yea, Master, fill us with righteousness, Your own pasture; yea, O Instructor, feed us on Your holy mountain the Church, which towers aloft, which is above the clouds, which touches heaven."[912]

Notice that St. Clement of Alexandria writes in the above that the Elect Sheep is in heaven while the Fire of Judgment separates the chaff from the wheat:

"For the fan is in the Lord's hand, by which the chaff due to the fire is separated from the wheat. Matthew 3:12; Luke 3:17 … Feed us, the children, as sheep. Yea, Master, fill us with righteousness, Your own pasture; yea, O Instructor, feed us on Your holy mountain the Church, which towers aloft, which is above the clouds, which touches heaven."

There's more as his quote didn't end there. He writes that the context of Christ's Ransom for Many[913] (not few) seems to include some type of Non Elect Salvation as "chastisements of sinners" for some:

"because toiling for us, and promising to give His life a ransom for many. Matthew 20:28 For him alone who does so He owns to be the good shepherd. Generous, therefore, is He who gives for us the greatest of all gifts, His own life; and beneficent exceedingly, and loving to men, in that, when He might have been Lord, He wished to be a brother man; and so good was He that He died for us. Further, His righteousness cried, If you come straight to me, I also will come straight to you but if you walk crooked, I also will walk crooked, says the Lord of hosts; meaning by the crooked ways the chastisements of sinners. … For it were a legitimate inference to say, that rebuke and censure are suitable to men, since they say that all men are bad; but God alone is wise, from whom comes wisdom, and alone perfect, and therefore alone worthy of praise. But I do not employ such language. I say, then, that praise or blame, or whatever resembles praise or blame, are

---

[912] St. Clement of Alexandria. The Paedagogus. (The Instructor). Book 1. Chapter 9. www.newadvent.org/fathers/02091.htm

[913] Matthew 26:28 reads, "For this is My blood of the new covenant, which is shed for many for the remission of sins" (NKJV). biblehub.com/matthew/26-28.htm

medicines most essential of all to men. Some are ill to cure, and, like iron, are wrought into shape with fire, and hammer, and anvil, that is, with threatening, and reproof, and chastisement; while others, cleaving to faith itself, as self-taught, and as acting of their own free-will, grow by praise:—For virtue that is praised Grows like a tree."[914]

Notice carefully how St. Clement of Alexandria calls "those saved by faith with virtue" (i.e. Elect Salvation) as others in comparison to "those saved with Fire and Chastisement or Medicines" as someone different so "possibly" Non Elect Salvation as his other quote below seems to describe further that this Judgment of Fire happens in the Spirit World context, called the Sheep of other fold for those of weak faith to be assigned greatest torments meaning could some "unbelievers" (not all) get lesser torment for those assigned the same portion of Judgment be thus saved likewise[915] as he seems to link to the principle found in Luke 12:46 – 48? (I infer):

> "And other sheep there are also, says the Lord, which are not of this fold John 10:16 — deemed worthy of another fold and mansion, in proportion to their faith. ... but though he quit the flesh, he must put off the passions, so as to be capable of reaching his own mansion. ... he greatest torments, indeed, are assigned to the believer. For God's righteousness is good, and His goodness is righteous. And though the punishments cease in the course of the completion of the expiation and purification of each one, yet those have very great and permanent grief who are found worthy of the other fold, on account of not being along with those that have been glorified through righteousness."[916]

St. Clement of Alexandria calls the "sheep of other fold" to refer to some who undergo afterlife judgments which Catholics use in support of purgatory and these are placed in a more inferior final place. Notice also that

---

[914] St. Clement of Alexandria. The Paedagogus. (The Instructor). Book 1. Chapters 9, 10. www.newadvent.org/fathers/02091.htm

[915] Luke 12:46 – 48, "46the master of that servant will come on a day when he is not looking for him, and at an hour when he is not aware, and will cut him in two and appoint him his portion with the unbelievers. 47And that servant who knew his master's will, and did not prepare himself or do according to his will, shall be beaten with many stripes. 48But he who did not know, yet committed things deserving of stripes, shall be beaten with few. For everyone to whom much is given, from him much will be required; and to whom much has been committed, of him they will ask the more." (NKJV). biblehub.com/nkjv/luke/12.htm

[916] St. Clement of Alexandria. The Stromata. Book 6. Chapter 14. www.newadvent.org/fathers/02106.htm

the punishments and purifications described here are in Spirit World context as the phrase "he quit the flesh" means in the above. So, if non-elect salvation turns out to be true, then the "few" saved refers to Elect Salvation[917] who become His Bride[918] and enter heaven[919] while Christ's Ransom for "many"[920] includes those of non-elect salvation too who get the final abode on the final new earth only.[921]

In conclusion, we can boldly say that, in light of the evidence of these quotes by Chiliasm Church Fathers and some key almost contemporaries, the "Baptism by Fire" is applied to those whom the Lord will save after some type of Spirit World Judgment of Fire first be it in Hades now before the end of the 1000 years Millennium (e.g. Tertullian) or that it only starts when He Returns during His Second Coming but also lasts till the end of the 1000 years Millennial Reign of Christ (e.g. St. Justin of Rome, St. Irenaeus of Lyons, St. Ambrose of Milan) or whose timing part is not clearly specified as to when it occurs (e.g. St. Gregory Nazianzus, St. Clement of Alexandria).

I mean if for example, we say that St. Justin of Rome's quote is incomplete since it doesn't mention the "saved by fire" part when quoting this same verse Matthew 3:11 – 12, we have to conclude that he has taught either the same as St. Irenaeus of Lyons or Tertullian or St. Gregory Nazianzus or even as St. Clement of Alexandria or even St. Ambrose of Milan since these are the major ones in their timeline and if not, it also shows that such a doctrine is not unified across all Christianity even at that time due to some significant differences in quotes for these parts which can span the Salvation by Fire case to be applied from fallen Christians to possibly even Non Christians hence Non Elect Salvation (depending on which of the earlier quotes we are referring to).

---

[917] Matthew 7:14 reads, "Because narrow is the gate and difficult is the way which leads to life, and there are few who find it" (NKJV). biblehub.com/matthew/7-14.htm

[918] Revelation 21:9 – 10 reads partly, "Come, I will show you the bride, the Lamb's wife ... and showed me the [h]great city, the [i]holy Jerusalem, descending out of heaven from God" (NKJV). biblehub.com/nkjv/revelation/21.htm

[919] Matthew 7:21 reads, "21"Not everyone who says to Me, 'Lord, Lord,' shall enter the kingdom of heaven, but he who does the will of My Father in heaven" (NKJV). biblehub.com/matthew/7-21.htm

[920] Matthew 26:28 reads, "For this is My blood of the new covenant, which is shed for many for the remission of sins" (NKJV). biblehub.com/matthew/26-28.htm

[921] Revelation 21:24, 27 reads, "24And the nations of those who are saved shall walk in its light, and the kings of the earth bring their glory and honor into it. 27But there shall by no means enter it anything that defiles, or causes an abomination or a lie, but only those who are written in the Lamb's Book of Life" (NKJV).

Here's an Old Testament Verse describing the Millennial Reign (i.e. during the 1000 years, in that day) which describes a prison existing where at the end of it (i.e. after many days), they are visited (literal word) which can mean inspected to see if they can be released or not possibly which can refer to Non Elect Salvation too after such Baptism by Fire described earlier.

> "20The earth shall reel to and fro like a drunkard, and shall be removed like a cottage; and the transgression thereof shall be heavy upon it; and it shall fall, and not rise again. 21And it shall come to pass in that day, that the LORD shall punish the host of the high ones that are on high, and the kings of the earth upon the earth. 22And they shall be gathered together, as prisoners are gathered in the pit, and shall be shut up in the prison, and after many days shall they be visited. 23Then the moon shall be confounded, and the sun ashamed, when the LORD of hosts shall reign in mount Zion, and in Jerusalem, and before his ancients gloriously."[922]

We know this is describing the Millennial Reign timeline since this happens when the LORD has returned and literally punishes the kings of the earth (verse 21) and also verse 23 is a classical Chiliasm prophecy verse for this First Resurrection reigning on the old renewed earth context (verse 20 also) with earthly Jerusalem as the centre and in Mount Zion (old Heaven).

This cleansing fire existing in the Millennium also affects those who are alive at that time (but may not be limited to it as earlier quoted verses show that it seems to affect all mankind prior). Notice that some (two-thirds of all those literally alive in that land) seem to perish in this fire (as the LORD cleans the earth):

> "8And it shall come to pass in all the land," Says the Lord, "That two-thirds in it shall be cut off and die, But one-third shall be left in it:"[923]

While others (one-third of all those literally alive in that land) seem to be cleansed and saved in this same fire:

> "9I will bring the one-third through the fire, Will refine them as silver is refined, And test them as gold is tested. They will call

---

[922] Isaiah 24:20 – 23 (KJV). biblehub.com/kjv/isaiah/24.htm
[923] Zechariah 13:8 (NKJV). biblehub.com/zechariah/13-8.htm

on My name, And I will answer them. I will say, 'This is My people'; And each one will say, 'The Lord is my God.'"[924]

SUMMARY

Whenever I am not putting any Chiliasm Church Father quote when a Bible verse is listed for any of the discussion in the chapters presented, it is because I cannot find a direct quote from them. I always endeavour to show any Chiliasm Church Father quote for the Bible verse at hand to avoid doing any private interpretation of prophecy.[925]

I add my interpolations which could be new discoveries unless someone else has published in journals likewise with same words or equivalent meanings which in turn could be a nice coincidence since I did not plagiarize anyone nor copy but just did Original Research.

The other part of my discussions prior just involve well known facts from these same Church Fathers or in regard to Biblical interpretations for the parts which agrees to popular theology according to some denominations as well (e.g. post-tribulation rapture support arguments from the Reformed).

Some of these possible new discoveries via interpolation by myself could include:

Two types of final saved resurrection bodies with glory, one heavenly (Elect) and the other earthly (Non-Elect).[926]

Two water of life references or groups partaking of it are separated by 1000 years (i.e. the Elect at start of 1000 years while the Non Elect at end of this Millennial Reign of Christ Timeline which is the Last Day/Sabbath).[927] For example, could Isaiah 49:9 – 10 be referring to some of those in "darkness and prison" (indicating punished ones from the Spirit World first) be shown "Mercy" to have "limited access" on the final earth to "feed along the roads, And their pastures shall be on all desolate heights" who could be given the 'Water of Life' too[928] as they "shall neither hunger nor thirst" since

---

[924] Zechariah 13:9 (NKJV). biblehub.com/zechariah/13-9.htm
[925] 2 Peter 1:20, "knowing this first, that no prophecy of Scripture is of any private interpretation," (NKJV).
[926] Pages 16, 20, 27, 54, 76, 89, 148, 150, 177, 208, 387.
[927] Essay 3.
[928] Page 97.

by "springs of water He will guide them" indicating "Non Elect Salvation"? which are given at the end of this Millennial Reign of Christ?[929]

Parabolic view of John 5's keywords such as "hour now is" referring to "start of the Millennium" while "hour is coming" refers to "end of the Millennium" where the "Millennial Reign of Christ" lasts 1000 years and is called the "Last Day". The term "hour" refers to a subset of "day" and "now is" is "start" while "is coming" is "end".

Non-Elect Salvation possibility for those enduring Christ's "Judgment till the last penny Bible verses" since the Catholics themselves can demonstrate that many of the Church Fathers point to such verses as referring to someone saved rather than unsaved after some type of Spirit World Judgments which became the basis for their doctrine of purgatory. A key difference is I point for example that Matthew 18 calls such a person as "Wicked Servant" where the word wicked seems to contradict their position that this refers to those of 'lighter sins holy Catholics' type but Christ called such ones as "wicked". A "wicked servant" gets the same as an "unbeliever" according to Luke 12:46, right? So, the interpolation here is natural that some of the unbelievers too may likewise be saved after Spirit World Judgment if God Wills it. I even show the "Shadow of Death" Bible verses could refer to Non Elect Salvation for some in the "Spirit World".[930]

1 Thessalonians 4:17 ("Rapture verse") and 1 Corinthians 15:52 ("Twinkling of an Eye Bodily Change" Verse) are two separate events separated by 1000 years, the former at start of Millennium while the latter at end of Millennial Reign of Christ.[931]

Three categories of men (righteous, sinners and wicked) instead of two categories of men (righteous versus wicked) only implying possibly righteous to be saved in the final heavens zone as referring to any Christian who will be in the "Wedding" of the Lamb context, sinners being saved in the final new earth zone while the wicked unsaved in the Lake of Fire in comparison.

In light of Non-Elect Salvation possibility, I also present whether Christ's Reply in Matthew 19 can be viewed as presenting Elect vs Non-Elect

---

[929] Isaiah 49:9 – 10 reads, "9That You may say to the prisoners, 'Go forth,' To those who are in darkness, 'Show yourselves.' "They shall feed along the roads, And their pastures shall be on all desolate heights. 10They shall neither hunger nor thirst, Neither heat nor sun shall strike them; For He who has mercy on them will lead them, Even by the springs of water He will guide them" (NKJV).

[930] Essay 4.

[931] Essay 2.

Salvation.⁹³² The interpolation here is whether keeping the "last" 6 Commandments relating to man merits Non Elect Salvation while in addition to that, keeping the remaining "first" 4 Commandments (except Sabbath which is not necessary for Gentile believers either as shown in this book) will merit the fruit for Elect Salvation in comparison. In other Bible Verses where Christ quotes statements such as Love God and Love your neighbour as yourself, these could be referring exclusively for Elect Salvation only because the person is able to receive them or is "not far from the Kingdom of God (Heaven level)".⁹³³

I mean in Matthew 19, the rich man did walk away sorrowful since he couldn't obey Christ's "follow Me" part which involved "Charity Doctrine" as well so perhaps that's why Christ in His Foreknowledge gave a two-fold reply implying a Non-Elect Salvation requirement first before inviting that rich man to the higher Elect Salvation requirement for entrance into life. This is not salvation by works but the level and gradation of Salvation which is based on how much one could follow Christ's Commands here via believing after seeing possibility too as discussed in pages prior.

Book of 1Enoch's prophecy viewed as referring to Judgment Day instead of earlier scholars viewing it as some time of commencement of the Millenium context by arguing that the "change" prophecy also listed here in Chiliasm context happens at the end of the 1000 years instead of the start of it.

Also, sinners are only judged in bodily resurrection during the second resurrection timeline so this hope for Non Elect Salvation since it refers to a Salvation without honour (as Elect Salvation is with "glory" as compared in these verses itself) is evident clearly from this text (if preserved true).

Shepherd of Hermas possible Scripture writing viewed differently than traditional Catholic or Orthodox view especially in the context of Non Elect

---

⁹³² Essay 8.

⁹³³ Mark 12:29 – 34, "29Jesus answered him, "The [k]first of all the commandments is: 'Hear, O Israel, the Lord our God, the Lord is one. 30And you shall love the Lord your God with all your heart, with all your soul, with all your mind, and with all your strength.' [l]This is the first commandment. 31And the second, like it, is this: 'You shall love your neighbor as yourself.' There is no other commandment greater than these." 32So the scribe said to Him, "Well said, Teacher. You have spoken the truth, for there is one God, and there is no other but He. 33And to love Him with all the heart, with all the understanding, [m]with all the soul, and with all the strength, and to love one's neighbor as oneself, is more than all the whole burnt offerings and sacrifices." 34Now when Jesus saw that he answered wisely, He said to him, "You are not far from the kingdom of God." But after that no one dared question Him." (NKJV). biblehub.com/nkjv/mark/12.htm

Salvation to refer to a salvation outside the Tower meaning "outside heaven" so possibly on final New Earth and that it extends even to unbelievers since it includes those who have heard the Gospel and wish to be baptized but remain unbaptised and regress into their wicked sins (meaning this is not the unlearnt case or equivalent either).

A key point of argument is also Tertullian's reply to Bishop of Rome, Pope St. Callixtus I at that time where he affirms the Non Elect Salvation portion of the Shepherd of Hermas to be true since it favours adulterers and so it's difficult for any believer to digest (which is only implied in the aforementioned Shepherd of Hermas section for Non Elect Salvation for in other parts the judgment for Eternal Hell/Annihilation is clearly expressed) meaning this section must be preserved as it is since Tertullian's time as well.

1 Corinthians 3:15's "saved by fire" as possible Non Elect Salvation case argued differently from any previously known traditional way by doing "mapping" where this Verse is mapped to the three harvests of the Gospel in Matthew 13:8 (thirtyfold, sixtyfold or hundredfold) which are "reward" levels (e.g. Matthew 19:29 mentions definition for "hundredfold" reward) implying that any Christian who must be one of these three harvests are then referring to 1 Corinthians 3:14's reward case instead.

This opens the possibility that 1 Corinthians 3:15's "saved by fire" case as referring to someone with "no" reward at all hence cannot be even the lowest thirtyfold reward level of a Christian, right?[934] I also mapped these verses to Matthew 3:11 – 12's context with Chiliasm Church Father quotes to try study the accurate meaning of "Baptism by Fire".[935]

New way for viewing Revelation 21 (second last chapter in the Bible) as referring to Elect Salvation, Non-Elect Salvation and the Damned instead of the prevalent way of viewing it as only referring to Elect Salvation vs the Damned.

Similarly, a new way for viewing Revelation 22 (last chapter in the Bible, i.e. the "Final Scene") again as referring to Elect Salvation, Non-Elect Salvation and the Damned instead of the prevalent way of viewing it as only referring to Elect Salvation vs the Damned.[936]

New way of viewing the "Thirsty" who are given the "Water of Life" in the "Final Scene" even via the invitation of the "Bride" (Elect Salvation) at

---

[934] Essay 6
[935] Essay 10.
[936] Essay 3.

that time as referring to someone who could be 'believing a little but not strong enough to be considered faith level for then such a person would have been the Elect' and opposed to the "unbelieving" in the Lake of Fire who could be rejecting whatever Christ Said in comparison.

Sheep of the other fold to refer to those saved during second resurrection timeline. The Sheepfold1 (Elect Salvation) is saved during the First Resurrection at start of the Millennium while Sheepfold2 (Non Elect Salvation) is saved at the end of this same 1000 years during the Second Resurrection who rise simultaneously with the wicked and are only separated and saved on Judgment Day.

This is different from popular view within those who also believe in other types of Chiliasm where they claim that all those of second resurrection are unsaved.

"12Who can understand his errors? Cleanse me from secret faults."[937]

---

[937] Psalm 19:12 (NKJV). biblehub.com/psalms/19-12.htm

Jonathan Ramachandran

Appendix I: An Important Note on Methodology

If you notice, for these Chiliasm writings, I did not say that these are done by God's Grace because I am not sure how accurate they are. Suppose my interpolations presented here became wrong on Judgment Day, then how does it bring glory to God? Hence, I rather leave it as my attempt at prophecy which is allowed as discussed in earlier writings based on Jeremiah 23: 36 – 40.

If I turned out right on Judgment Day, then on that Day I will give all glory to God for His Mercy of revealing all these to me. My point is, I do not want to prematurely claim the truth of a prophecy which can neither be proven nor disproven conclusively before it comes to pass. All I am concerned is to present it rigorously with Chiliasm Church Father quotes so that I am honest even with the ambiguity which arises from such writings based on preserved Christian history. Hence, I rest my case.

These Non-Elect Salvation quotes from the Shepherd of Hermas which is said to be Scripture Level by St. Irenaeus of Lyons and Tertullian, both Chiliasm Church Fathers, are intriguing. Interestingly, for example, in the Non Elect Salvation submission pages 27 – 28, Tertullian himself had trouble with the Non Elect Salvation quotes of the Shepherd of Hermas (which proves this part is preserved authentically according to even Tertullian himself who is disagreeing or having trouble with its meaning) but yet please observe carefully Tertullian's wise and scholarly reply (no wonder Tertullian is the Father of Latin Christianity and Founder of Western Theological Scholarship) since he writes as follows,

"But I would yield my ground to you, if the scripture of the Shepherd, which is the only one which favours adulterers, had deserved to find a place in the Divine canon; if it had not been habitually judged by every council of Churches (even of your own) among apocryphal and false (writings); ... I, however, imbibe the Scriptures of that Shepherd who cannot be broken."

Basically, Tertullian in his discussion here (with Bishop of Rome, Pope Callixtus I at that time) is saying he has problem with the Shepherd of Hermas since it gives some type of Non Elect Salvation to "adulterers" (implied) and that's a reason for his hesitance that it has been included in the Divine Canon (e.g. Muratorian/Roman Canon which are first oldest known Bible Canon, etc.) but yet he says that he will "imbibe" (absorb) it since it is "Scripture which cannot be broken".

Ah, that's how we are supposed to do proper academic reporting and commenting honestly based on evidence like this regardless if we agree to the Shepherd of Hermas or not like how Tertullian did and that's exactly the methodology I followed.

Also, here is a set of Bible verses showing "sharp and no small debate" clearly between "Christian versus Christian" (both "believers with the Holy Spirit") but yet one of them can be wrong meaning God allows free will in doctrine and will reward those more accurate later and so we can likewise present both sides like this which is Biblical:

"1And certain men came down from Judea and taught the brethren, "Unless you are circumcised according to the custom of Moses, you cannot be saved." 2Therefore, when Paul and Barnabas had no small dissension and dispute with them, they determined that Paul and Barnabas and certain others of them should go up to Jerusalem, to the apostles and elders, about this question. ... 5But some of the sect of the Pharisees who believed rose up, saying, "It is necessary to circumcise them, and to command them to keep the law of Moses."

Remember, what's so "academic" if our beliefs turn out wrong not just on this topic of Non-Elect but also all other theological topics too as I demonstrated evidences of quotes from Chiliasm Church Fathers in this writing? Please don't misunderstand me as I am very aware that my interpretations and interpolations regarding Non-Elect Salvation could be wrong too and that's why I conclude this topic as a possibility only and not doctrine so that I don't accidentally mislead anyone.

Any reader can see that I have already revealed this side of the Non-Elect Salvation Possibility and hence it is their personal duty to check for arguments against it from other sides and either choose their belief or be neutral about it to be safe.

Also, using internet sources or hardcopies of books makes no difference here since these are all well known writings that are translated scholarly. I believe that the translations in English of the writings I used are universally accepted as accurate and since I cannot read the original language, this is the best I can do. Also, I doubt that by reading it in the original language would change any meaning of the translation in English unless someone from your side can show it. So, it's just whether we interpret the translation/original (just like the Bible) available for St. Irenaeus of Lyons or other Chiliasm

Church Fathers is accurate or not of which I sought to give my views (which could be wrong) but neither is your orthodox views on it is necessarily right either (but could be) and so, for that final word, we leave it to God.

For example, your orthodox view that St. Irenaeus of Lyons (or even St. Justin of Rome, Tertullian, St. Methodius of Olympus [no dubious writings which didn't exist during his lifetime period] or even St. Victorinus, i.e. all "Chiliasm" Church Fathers whom I quoted) which claims that all of them prayed to Virgin Mary has "not" even one quote in their "own writings" but I guess it's 'scholarly assumed with no proof in certain journals, and among their editors and others'.

Difference is, I did no such assumptions here and only interpolate based on some actual existing quotes. No personal insult meant but just stating that sometimes an academic journal claims "high level publication" just because they use the original languages or original manuscripts which are just as ambiguous with no proof of such quotes but are just "assumed" by certain journal readers and editors, sadly. This is what I mean as rigour, i.e. all claims and interpolations must be accompanied with some type of quotes or if not, just left it as it is for true academic scholarship, accuracy and honesty.

In another example, a Calvinism journal wrote:

"Thanks for your submission. I'll take a look at this submission and give you initial feedback by the end of October."

I responded in advance as follows (for constructive academia):

"I welcome your feedback. I may give mine too in response of yours should you rebut it so both sides can be well represented."

Regarding university supremacy, here are my comments: Actually, it's not about Harvard or any other universities but as I mentioned before, it's about number of new significant discoveries where the most important discoveries are theological since only these affect eternity which should be presented fairly and let God Decide which is right that day and reward with higher heavens level glory as Daniel 12:3 prophesies (so, there is no need to boycott or play racial games or religion games or even denominational games or even gender games or other nepotism since the real God doesn't play all these games, right? Shalom). However, it would be sad if "Non-Elect Salvation" possibility turns out to be not true on Judgment Day and so it is my sincere prayer and hope that as many readers of this book believe in Christ regardless of whether "Non-Elect Salvation" is true or not so that our faith is not conditional upon things which we are not sure. I mean we can hope for it but we cannot fixate upon it lest it becomes an idol (if wrong) but at the same time I am glad I revealed all these in detailed points so God can see that it is responsibly interpolated even if wrong and so He can have Mercy since it's so difficult to know for sure in light of all these evidences!

I believe that a Christian will believe in Christ regardless of whether Non Elect Salvation possibility is true or not and so only the reward level for this part can be affected and not our Salvation itself if viewed responsibly like this (being neutral). Last but not least, I do not see it as wrong even if I sell this writing as a book commercially since I see it as getting paid for the research work of presenting all these historical quotes and for my interpolation part, I consider giving it free of charge theoretically since I cannot be certain whether I am right or not.

Remember, if other authours can make money by selling "fiction or storybooks", then what is wrong even in selling some personal research on prophecy like this while discussing possibilities by quoting early Christian and Jewish writings? Yes, a prophecy book must quote many others so that it's not a "private interpretation" where even if wrong, at least God can see the honesty with evidence where I believe that God won't charge us for the wrong evidence since it's beyond our reach and we just made speculations or interpolations based on those writings. Maranatha! even so come Lord Jesus. Amen.

Thank you for reading this! Abbreviations: CPM = Chiliasm Prophecy Model while NESP = Non-Elect Salvation Possibility.

Appendix II: Author Photos

ESSAYS IN EARLY CHRISTIANITY

Appendix III: About the Author

JONATHAN RAMACHANDRAN
Theologian, Missionary, Engineer, Freelance Math Olympiad Coach & Musician

Jonathan Ramachandran is a self taught theological enthusiast who loves the Chiliasm Church Fathers and tries to understand Prophecy of the Bible with their writings. He has published with the Journal of Biblical Theology (JBT, 3 levels of peer reviews), the American Journal of Biblical Theology (AJBT, 2 levels of peer reviews) and also with Christian Publishing House (CPH, Cambridge, Ohio, USA). He runs his theology blog being a freelance missionary of tentmaker style at www.AnonymousChristian.org and lives in Malaysia where he is an operations manager for an engineering company.

Jon is a freelance preacher who is active both online and offline who has baptized some of his students into Christianity. His varied full time working experience includes working with Christian ministries dealing with charity, seismic engineering, educational centre management, teaching Math at schools (elementary and high school with a competition touch) and is one of Malaysia's International Mathematical Olympiad (IMO) coaches.

1) Books

Ramachandran, Jonathan. *HOPE BEYOND THE ELECT: Revisiting Early Christian Views on Prophecy and Salvation*. Cambridge, Ohio, USA: Christian Publishing House, 6 June 2025.

Link: https://www.amazon.com/dp/1949586405

Ramachandran, Jonathan. *ESSAYS IN EARLY CHRISTIANITY: Chiliasm Prophecy Model and Non-Elect Salvation Possibility*. Cambridge, Ohio, USA: Christian Publishing House, July 2025.

2) Journals

i) 1st Publication

Ramachandran, Jonathan. "Non Elect Salvation Possibility." *The American Journal of Biblical Theology* (AJBT) Vol 26, no. 6 (9 February 2025). www.biblicaltheology.com/Research/RamachandranJ01.pdf

ii) 2nd Publication

Ramachandran, Jonathan. "Thousand Year Gap for Prophecy in 1 Thessalonians 4:17 and 1 Corinthians 15:52 with Chiliasm Church Fathers." *The American Journal of Biblical Theology* (AJBT) Vol 26, no. 22 (1 June 2025). www.biblicaltheology.com/Research/RamachandranJ02.pdf

iii) 3rd Publication on a 3-level peer review as well

Ramachandran, Jonathan. "Thousand Year Gap for Prophecy in 1 Thessalonians 4:17 and 1 Corinthians 15:52 with Chiliasm Church Fathers." *Journal of Biblical Theology* (JBT) Vol 8, no. 3 (1 June 2025): 185-208. https://www.biblicaltheology.com/research.html

AWARDS

- Observer C for Malaysia at the International Math Olympiad (IMO 2020)
- Dean List (UKM, 2003)
- Bank Negara Scholarship (BNM Scholar) 2003 - 2006 for Bsc. Actuarial Science
- STPM Best Student (KHS, 2001 - 2002)
- One of the final six Math Olympians representing Malaysia to the International Mathematical Olympiad (IMO 2002, Glasgow, UK)
- Distinction in Senior Division Australian National Chemistry Quiz (2001)
- Bronze in National Physics Competition (2000) by IFM, Universiti Malaya
- Gates Medalist (Overall SPM best student at Kajang High School, KHS 2000)
- Malaysian National Math Olympiad - 2nd Place Silver (Sulong, Full Marks, Individual) OMK 2002 by PERSAMA

#My ORCID Link: https://orcid.org/0009-0008-4669-1077

#GoogleScholar Link:

https://scholar.google.com/citations?hl=en&user=Bv7IFrAAAAAJ

#Academia Link:

https://independent.academia.edu/RamachandranJonathan

Appendix IV: Why I wrote this Book

A chief reason why I wrote this book is to present my views and research regarding Christian philosophy, which if God judges as right, may indeed be doctrinal or prophetic accuracy. I leave it as a possibility since these cannot be confirmed with certainty as I have repeated this fact several times in this book itself to show both its importance (if right) and danger (if wrong).

Here's an example to illustrate this point: Worship or Doctrine?

In a Christian life, both are vital, but which is more significant, worship or doctrine? Christ stated that accuracy in doctrine/prophecy., is more significant than worship, thus we should aim for it to avoid making our worship in vain. Since He teaches that doctrine exposes more of the heart, which is closer to God than even worship or nice words, let's endeavour to follow Christ in this area as well. Scripture passage:

> "8'These people [c]draw near to Me with their mouth, And honour Me with their lips, But their heart is far from Me. 9And in **vain** they **worship** Me, teaching as **doctrines** the **commandments** of men.'" (Matthew 15:8 – 9, NKJV)

God determines who is more accurate, but we can strive for it by His grace. It should be emphasized that Christians typically have some degree of doctrine accuracy (thirtyfold vs. sixtyfold vs. hundredfold fruits/levels).

Frequently asked question (FAQ): What happens if your book's rank and sales decline on Amazon? Christian authors should focus on their contributions to theology, which is timeless if true (that God judges), rather than on sales. Being famous does not imply that it is true.

For instance, the Book of Revelation (or *Apocalypse*) and eschatology (*prophecy*) studies may not be popular, but they may hold important rewards in heaven if right (God decides). This is based on the insight of a prophet (Daniel 12:3), which states that prophecy gives greater glory than even converting many people to Christianity with less accuracy. Matthew 15:8–9 mentions that Christ emphasizes accurate doctrine as more important than worship, and 1 Timothy 5:17 mentions the apostle Paul's "double honour" reward is only for those who are more accurate in "word and doctrine" (implied). As usual, I'm not claiming to be the most correct or anything, but I'm urging all Christians to fairly consider their options and views so that we don't waste time on things that have no eternal worth.

Jonathan Ramachandran

Appendix V: My Stance Regarding the Pentecostal Claim of Speaking in Tongues

Rev. Billy Graham did not speak in tongues but was neutral regarding those who did (page 310). Personally, I know that both my parents use Pentecostal tongues. I don't since I tried praying at their church and didn't have the experiences that people who do say they had. I choose to remain neutral like Graham because I cannot delve into a Pentecostal's mind and see "how or why" they make the "non-human language sounds" because the Holy Spirit is a very sensitive topic in Scripture (for example, Christ makes it very clear that blasphemy against Him is not forgiven in this age or the next in Matthew 12:31–32).

I am well aware that, in contrast to Pentecostal Christians, who genuinely believe it is by heavenly force, many conservative and reformed Christians directly criticize this act as being only human-induced sounds. In light of the evidence of chiliasm and the entire church history prior to the 20th century, which had no such requirement for salvation or gifting—that is, God had saved Christians throughout those centuries without these "non-human language speaking in tongues claims"—I choose not to participate in it rather than take the risks involved. However, I offer the following sincere prayer for Pentecostals:

"Lord, if the Pentecostals were correct in producing those non-human sounds and calling in speaking in tongues, may they be rewarded in heaven for this additional gifting. However, if they were mistaken and simply conjured up these sounds in their own minds, thinking it was from the Holy Spirit when it wasn't, may your mercy forgive them and spare them from going to Hell because their pastors and leaders made the mistakes that led to this. Therefore, by your justice at most, may only their rewards be affected as lower to be fair to those who refrained and were correct if this occurs. If some of the Pentecostal church leaders I encountered disqualified me from ministry work simply because I don't speak in tongues, may they also be pardoned if they are wrong in this act. May the Body of Christ cease being divided on the basis of these criteria that You did not use to save Christians up until the 20th century. Amen."

Appendix VI: The Abrahamic Promise in Chiliasm Prophecy

St. Irenaeus' quote follows next, revealing that "abundant life" is not an "Abrahamic promise" on earth today, as prosperity gospel ideology or equivalents err, contradicting these quotes. Since most Christians missed all of these things, Irenaeus of Lyons makes it clear that the Lord taught—not his opinion—that material wealth is not a byproduct of any faith and that all Christians will fulfill the Abrahamic promise when they are repaid in bodily human resurrection for a thousand years, enjoying delicious meals and sinless pleasures of the restored earth after Christ returns and establishes his millennial reign. He writes:

> "For what are the **hundred-fold [rewards]** in this word, the entertainments given to the poor, and the suppers for which a return is made? These are [to take place] in the times of the kingdom, that is, upon the seventh day, which has been sanctified, in which God rested from all the works which He created, which is the true Sabbath of the righteous, which they shall not be engaged in any earthly occupation; but shall have a table at hand prepared for them by God, supplying them with all sorts of dishes. 3. The **blessing of Isaac** with which he blessed his younger son **Jacob** has the **same meaning**, when he says, Behold, the smell of my son is as the smell of a full field which the Lord has blessed. Genesis 27:27, etc. But the field is the world. Matthew 13:38 And therefore he added, God give to you of the dew of heaven, and of the fatness of the earth, plenty of grain and wine. And let the nations serve you, and kings bow down to you; and be lord over your brother, and your father's sons shall bow down to you: **cursed shall be he who shall curse you, and blessed shall be he who shall bless you**. Genesis 27:28-29 If any one, then, does **not accept these things as referring to the appointed kingdom**, he must fall into much contradiction and **contrariety**, as is the **case with the Jews**, who are involved in absolute **perplexity**. For not only did not the nations in this life serve this Jacob; but even after he had received the blessing, he himself going forth [from his home], served his uncle Laban the Syrian for twenty years; Genesis 31:41 and not only was he not made lord of his brother, but he did himself bow down before his brother Esau, upon his return from Mesopotamia to his father, and offered many gifts to him. Genesis 33:3 Moreover, in what way did he inherit much grain and

wine here, he who emigrated to Egypt because of the famine which possessed the land in which he was dwelling, and became subject to Pharaoh, who was then ruling over Egypt? ... The **predicted blessing**, therefore, belongs unquestionably to the **times of the kingdom**, when the **righteous** shall bear rule upon their **rising from the dead**; when also the creation, having been renovated and set free, shall fructify with an abundance of all kinds of food, from the dew of heaven, and from the fertility of the earth: as the elders who saw John, the disciple of the Lord, related that they had heard from him how the **Lord used to teach** in regard to these times, and say"[938]

The prophecies of prosperity gospel theology are predicated on the idea that the Abrahamic promise is fulfilled in this world as well. But according to the Chiliasm prophetic model based on Irenaeus's statement above, this Abrahamic Promise alludes to the Millennial reign following the First Resurrection, where Christians will receive compensation for all of their suffering in this world, rather than the present, which is also what the Jews believe and err. Irenaeus points that the Lord taught these things and it was not his opinion. So, this refutes any Christian claiming that them being rich on earth now proves that they are fulfilling the Abrahamic promise while discriminating those who are poor to feel lower in the Kingdom unnecessarily based on earthly blessings now which is by time and chance (Ecclesiastes 9:11).

Apart from that, the-Pentecostal movement's overall belief in fulfilling Abrahamic Promise on earth today when you are affluent as a show of large faith loses its sting and, worse, becomes perilous in light of the Chiliasm prophecy quotation by St. Irenaeus here, which contradicts all of that. I mean, if the Prosperity Gospel's claim to be fulfilling the Abrahamic Promise now in any small way is proven false and St. Irenaeus' quote here is correct, then their dominant prophets in that movement's claim to hear directly from the Holy Spirit while doing so becomes questionable and dangerous, because the Holy Spirit makes no prophecy mistakes. As I previously stated, a prophet, preacher, or Christian can err in prophecy, but when someone quotes the Holy Spirit to make a prophecy directly, he cannot err and incurs judgment, which God decides because the Holy Spirit does not err, as Scripture has warned about taking His Name in Vain (3rd of the 10 Commandments & see the related warning in this context of misusing God's Name in claiming "God told me so" in Jeremiah 23:36-40).

---

[938] Irenaeus of Lyons, *Against Heresies*, Book 5, Chapter 33, Points 2-3. www.newadvent.org/fathers/0103533.htm

Appendix VII: Garden of Eden in Chiliasm Framework

Many Christians today believe that the "Garden of Eden" (also known as Paradise) existed somewhere on earth. However, St. Irenaeus of Lyons informs us that this garden was located in the "heaven zone," which supports the Chiliasm quotations about tiers of heaven that we have seen previously.

In fact, according to Irenaeus, Adam, the first man, was born in Paradise and was only sent into "this world" (the present-day old earth) after he sinned. Such accuracy can help us understand the Chiliasm prophecy statements made by both St. Papias and St. Irenaeus' writing prior (pages 180–181), which indicate that "Paradise" spoken of in the final scene is not a region on the "final new earth" but a region of heavens distinct and separated from "this world" (the earths, whether old earth or final new earth). He writes:

> "For in Adam the hands of God had become accustomed to set in order, to rule, and to sustain His own workmanship, and to bring it and place it where they pleased. Where, then, was the **first man** placed? In **paradise** certainly, as the Scripture declares And God planted a **garden [paradisum]** eastward in **Eden**, and there He placed the man whom He had formed. Genesis 2:8 And then afterwards when [man] proved disobedient, he was **cast out** thence **into this world**. Wherefore also the **elders** who were **disciples** of the **apostles** tell us that those who were translated were transferred to that place (for **paradise** has been prepared for righteous men, such as **have the Spirit**; in which place also Paul the apostle, when he was caught up, heard words which are unspeakable as regards us in our present condition 2 Corinthians 12:4), and that there shall they who have been translated remain until the consummation [of all things], as a prelude to immortality."[939]

Interestingly, we also find the similar phrase "elders who were disciples of the apostles" used by St. Irenaeus here, which he also used while describing the earlier Chiliasm prophecy of the "thirtyfold, sixtyfold, and hundredfold reward levels" obtaining a final abode in the "heavens" zone, which are layered in increasing order as "the final New Jerusalem City, Paradise, and

---

[939] Irenaeus of Lyons, *Against Heresies*, Book 5, Chapter 5, Point 1. www.newadvent.org/fathers/0103505.htm

Heavens" respectively, implying that this was not his opinion but an interpretation with direct apostolic roots (pages 180–181).

It's also important to note that he states that "Paradise" is reserved for men who possess the "Holy Spirit" (i.e., only the elect, or transformed Christians at the final trumpet) who "don't go out from here" in the context of their final abode (Revelation 3:12). This allows for the possibility that some of the "nations saved on the final new earth" may not be elect and may not ascend to the heavens. Indeed, his earlier Chiliasm comment (which is also displayed below) that makes a distinction between "those worthy" and "those not worthy" to "enter the final heaven" based on the "final new earth context" after the end of the Millennium lends credence to this:

> "man has been renewed, ... [then] there shall be the new heaven and the **new earth, in which the new man shall remain [continually]**, always holding fresh converse with God. And since (or, that) these things shall ever continue **without end**, Isaiah declares, For as the new heavens and the new earth which I do make, continue in my sight, says the Lord, so shall your seed and your name remain. Isaiah 66:22 And as the **presbyters** say, Then those who are deemed **worthy** of an abode in heaven shall go there, others shall enjoy the delights of paradise, and others shall possess the splendour of the city; for everywhere the Saviour shall be seen according as they who see Him shall be worthy."[940]

Observe that "those deemed worthy of an abode in heaven" are accepted from the last new earth into the heavenly dominion (the elect), but the remainder of the "new man" will stay on the final new earth (non-elect). The rest may simply remain in human (terrestrial) sinless body on the final new earth supporting non-elect salvation possibility for these latter ones (1 Corinthians 15:40). This means that only a portion of the "new man" are "inherited by the Spirit" to "enter heaven" (the transformation from "flesh and blood" into celestial or angelic body as St. Irenaeus' other quote below uses the context of 1 Corinthians 15:50–52 for it at the last trumpet or end of these 1000 years). Compare:

> "But these are **inherited** by the Spirit when they are **translated** into the kingdom of **heaven**. ... and if you shall live frivolously and carelessly as if you were this only, viz., mere **flesh and blood**, you **cannot** inherit the kingdom of God." [941]

---

[940] Irenaeus of Lyons, *Against Heresies*, Book 5, Chapter 36, Point 1. www.newadvent.org/fathers/0103536.htm
[941] Irenaeus of Lyons, *Against Heresies*, Book 5, Chapter 9, Point 4.

Appendix VIII: Antichrist Prophecy in Chiliasm Model

Background: I spent a chapter of this book discussing the main feature of the pre-tribulation rapture idea, which is the "thief in night" phrase that is used to bolster the pre-tribulation rapture claim (essay 5). Based on this research, I demonstrate that the only rapture that appears more likely is the post-tribulation one, which would take place following the last great tribulation and at the conclusion of the Antichrist's last rule. In order for that to occur, the final Antichrist must rise, which will occur when he makes a pact with Israel to construct or continue the construction of the Temple in Jerusalem as the prophet Daniel predicted in the middle of the week (3.5 years later) (Daniel 9:27).

We shall be able to identify the Antichrist in this way. This son of perdition will be on the Jewish side as well (which is why many will be deceived by him until it is too late), but he will unleash his persecution on Christians and the world when he declares himself as "god" in the same "Temple at Jerusalem" as apostle Paul prophesied (2 Thessalonians 2:3-4). Many will follow the antichrist because he will perform a "resurrection type trick," but in reality, he was only wounded and healed by Satan's power, as the Bible predicts. He will then persecute everyone on the planet to convert and receive his mark (666, in this case symbolically) or be ruthlessly killed (Revelation 13:3–10).

Many people around the world will also be confused since their prophesies will not come to pass and the antichrist will kill them as well. Unfulfilled prophecies will also highlight the differences between the true and false prophets. So, by God's grace, let's be ready! The Antichrist will therefore remain unknown as long as Jerusalem's Jewish Temple is not constructed. However, when the temple is built, he will either be a part of it or appear and declare himself to be "god," as the Bible clearly states, and that is how you will know that the rapture will occur after this final persecution for about 3.5 years, and Christ will return like a "thief in the night," ending the "beast's reign," and sending him and those who follow him into the Lake of Fire.

www.newadvent.org/fathers/0103509.htm

Here are direct quotes from St. Irenaeus of Lyons and Bible scriptures that support the chronology of events mentioned above as part of the Chiliasm prophecy model timeline:

1) A seven-year Bible synopsis of the Antichrist chronology

"27Then he [Antichrist] shall confirm a [k]covenant with many for one week; But in the middle of the week He shall bring an end to sacrifice and offering. And on the wing of abominations shall be one who makes desolate, Even until the consummation, which is determined, Is poured out on the [l]desolate." (Daniel 9:27, NKJV)

2) First 3.5 years Bible summary for the Antichrist timeline

"3And I will give power to my two witnesses, and they will prophesy one thousand two hundred and sixty days, clothed in sackcloth." 4These are the two olive trees and the two lampstands standing before the [b]God of the earth. 5And if anyone wants to harm them, fire proceeds from their mouth and devours their enemies. And if anyone wants to harm them, he must be killed in this manner. 6These have power to shut heaven, so that no rain falls in the days of their prophecy; and they have power over waters to turn them to blood, and to strike the earth with all plagues, as often as they desire. 7When they finish their testimony, the beast that ascends out of the bottomless pit will make war against them, overcome them, and kill them. 8And their dead bodies will lie in the street of the great city which spiritually is called Sodom and Egypt, where also [c]our Lord was crucified." (Revelation 11:3 – 8, NKJV)

3) Last 3.5 years Bible summary for the Antichrist timeline

"9Then those from the peoples, tribes, tongues, and nations [d]will see their dead bodies three-and-a-half days, and not allow their dead bodies to be put into graves. 10And those who dwell on the earth will rejoice over them, make merry, and send gifts to one another, because these two prophets tormented those who dwell on the earth. 11Now after the three-and-a-half days the breath of life from God entered them, and they stood on their feet, and great fear fell on those who saw them. 12And [e]they heard a loud voice from heaven saying to them, "Come up here." And they ascended to heaven in a cloud, and their enemies saw them. 13In the same hour there was a great earthquake, and a tenth of the city fell. In the earthquake seven thousand people were killed, and the rest were afraid and gave glory to the God of heaven." (Revelation 11:9 – 13, NKJV)

and

"1Then [a]I stood on the sand of the sea. And I saw a beast rising up out of the sea, ... The dragon gave him his power, his throne, and great authority. 3And I saw one of his heads as if it had been mortally wounded, and his deadly wound was healed. And all the world marveled and followed the beast. 4So they worshiped the dragon who gave authority to the beast; and they worshiped the beast, saying, "Who is like the beast? Who is able to make war with him?" 5And he was given a mouth speaking great things and blasphemies, and he was given authority to [c]continue for forty-two months. 6Then he opened his mouth in blasphemy against God, to blaspheme His name, His tabernacle, and those who dwell in heaven. 7It was granted to him to make war with the saints and to overcome them. And authority was given him over every [d]tribe, tongue, and nation. 8All who dwell on the earth will worship him, whose names have not been written in the Book of Life of the Lamb slain from the foundation of the world. 9If anyone has an ear, let him hear. 10He who leads into captivity shall go into captivity; he who kills with the sword must be killed with the sword. Here is the [e]patience and the faith of the saints. ... 15He was granted power to give breath to the image of the beast, that the image of the beast should both speak and cause as many as would not worship the image of the beast to be killed. 16He causes all, both small and great, rich and poor, free and slave, to receive a mark on their right hand or on their foreheads, 17and that no one may buy or sell except one who has [g]the mark or the name of the beast, or the number of his name. 18Here is wisdom. Let him who has understanding calculate the number of the beast, for it is the number of a man: His number is 666." (Revelation 13:1, 3 – 10, 15 – 18, NKJV)

4) St. Irenaeus of Lyons writes,

4.1) The Antichrist (also known as the *Beast* in the Book of Revelation, the *Son of Lawlessness*, or the *Son of Perdition* in Apostle Paul's epistles) seeks to be adored as "god" after constructing the ultimate Temple in Jerusalem (deceiving both Jews and Christians).

"1. And not only by the particulars already mentioned, but also by means of the events which shall occur in the time of Antichrist is it shown that he, being an apostate and a robber, is anxious to be adored as God ... of whom the apostle thus speaks in the second Epistle to the Thessalonians: Unless there shall come a failing away first, and the man of sin shall be revealed, the son of perdition, who opposes and exalts himself above all that is called

God, or that is worshipped; so that he sits in the temple of God, showing himself as if he were God. The apostle therefore clearly points out his apostasy, and that he is lifted up above all that is called God, or that is worshipped — that is, above every idol — for these are indeed so called by men, but are not [really] gods; and that he will endeavour in a tyrannical manner to set himself forth as God. ... 2. Moreover, he (the apostle) has also pointed out this which I have shown in many ways, that the temple in Jerusalem was made by the direction of the true God. For the apostle himself, speaking in his own person, distinctly called it the temple of God. ..."[942]

4.2) When the Antichrist proclaims himself to be "god" halfway through his tenure, Christ foretells the "final Great Tribulation" and urges Christians to flee into seclusion since the beast would predominantly persecute and murder Christians for the next three and a half years.

"that no one is termed God by the apostles when speaking for themselves, except Him who truly is God, the Father of our Lord, by whose directions the temple which is at Jerusalem was constructed for those purposes which I have already mentioned; in which [temple] the enemy shall sit, endeavouring to show himself as Christ, as the Lord also declares: But when you shall see the abomination of desolation, which has been spoken of by Daniel the prophet, standing in the holy place (let him that reads understand), then let those who are in Judea flee into the mountains; and he who is upon the house-top, let him not come down to take anything out of his house: for there shall then be great hardship, such as has not been from the beginning of the world until now, nor ever shall be. ... and he shall speak words against the most high God, and wear out the saints of the most high God, and shall purpose to change times and laws; and [everything] shall be given into his hand until a time of times and a half time, Daniel 7:23, etc. that is, for three years and six months, during which time, when he comes, he shall reign over the earth. Of whom also the Apostle Paul again, speaking in the second [Epistle] to the Thessalonians, and at the same time proclaiming the cause of his advent, thus says: And then shall the wicked one be revealed, whom the Lord Jesus shall slay with the spirit of His mouth, and destroy by the presence of His coming; whose coming [i.e., the wicked one's] is after the working of Satan, in all power,

---

[942] Irenaeus of Lyons, *Against Heresies*, Book 5, Chapter 25, Points 1–2. www.newadvent.org/fathers/0103525.htm

and signs, and portents of lies, and with all deceivableness of wickedness for those who perish; because they did not receive the love of the truth, that they might be saved. And therefore God will send them the working of error, that they may believe a lie; that they all may be judged who did not believe the truth, but gave consent to iniquity, 2 Thessalonians 2:8. 4." [943]

4.3) St. Irenaeus reveals next that one of the key deceptions during these Antichrist times revolves around unbelieving Jews (or Israel that rejects Christ as Messiah and has not become Christians) enlisting the help and favour of this final Antichrist to construct the Temple of God in Jerusalem. This is very interesting because, in his previous quote above, Irenaeus mentions that the instructions for rebuilding the Temple are from the "true God of Israel," but in his next quote, he points out that the real God of Israel rejects helping Israel's Temple building efforts because they rejected Lord Jesus Christ as Messiah. As a result, the Antichrist (who is alienated from the Lord) provides practical assistance in the construction of this Temple of God throughout those times, but neither Israel nor *some* Christians are likely to understand this until the Beast declares himself as "god" in that same Temple!

> "The Lord also spoke as follows to those who did not believe in Him: I have come in my Father's name, and you have not received Me: when another shall come in his own name, him you will receive, John 5:43 calling Antichrist the other, because he is alienated from the Lord. This is also the unjust judge, whom the Lord mentioned as one who feared not God, neither regarded man, Luke 18:2, etc. to whom the widow fled in her forgetfulness of God — that is, the earthly Jerusalem, — to be avenged of her adversary. Which also he shall do in the time of his kingdom: he shall remove his kingdom into that [city], and shall sit in the temple of God, leading astray those who worship him, as if he were Christ. ... Daniel 8:12 And the angel Gabriel, when explaining his vision, states with regard to this person: And towards the end of their kingdom a king of a most fierce countenance shall arise, one understanding [dark] questions, and exceedingly powerful, full of wonders; and he shall corrupt, direct, influence (faciet), and put strong men down, the holy people likewise; and his yoke shall be directed as a wreath [round their neck]; deceit shall be in his hand, and he shall be lifted up in his heart: he shall also ruin many by deceit, and lead many to perdition, bruising them in his hand like eggs. Daniel 8:23, etc. And then he points out the time that his tyranny shall last, during which the

---

[943] Ibid., Points 2–3.

saints shall be put to flight, they who offer a pure sacrifice unto God: And in the midst of the week, he says, the sacrifice and the libation shall be taken away, and the abomination of desolation [shall be brought] into the temple: even unto the consummation of the time shall the desolation be complete. Daniel 9:27 Now three years and six months constitute the half-week."[944]

In another writing, St. Irenaeus re-confirms some of the previous points as follows:

4.4) The most deadly apostasy or error of all time, foretold in Holy Scripture, revolves around this prophecy of the Antichrist, who "dupes" everyone in order to build the Temple of the true God, where he would declare himself as the "christ and god"!

> "2. And for this reason the apostle says: Because they received not the love of God, that they might be saved, therefore God shall also send them the operation of error, that they may believe a lie, that they all may be judged who have not believed the truth, but consented to unrighteousness. 2 Thessalonians 2:10-12 For when he (Antichrist) has come, and of his own accord concentrates in his own person the apostasy, and accomplishes whatever he shall do according to his own will and choice, sitting also in the temple of God, so that his dupes may adore him as the Christ; wherefore also shall he deservedly be cast into the lake of fire: Revelation 19:20 [this will happen according to divine appointment], God by His prescience foreseeing all this, and at the proper time sending such a man, that they may believe a lie, that they all may be judged who did not believe the truth, but consented to unrighteousness;" [945]

4.5) Irenaeus connects the Antichrist prophesy to the Book of Revelation (known as the Apocalypse) here to explain the final great tribulation of the Antichrist's terror rule of 3.5 years! The peculiar prophecy found in the Bible is also highlighted here, in that the Antichrist will perform a "fake resurrection effect" because he did not truly die but was "healed by the workings of Satan" from a "mortal wound," which is when the deception reaches its peak, as many begin to wonder if this "beast is god" simply because he will use this to possibly claim that he has power over life and death:

---

[944] Ibid., Point 4.
[945] Irenaeus of Lyons, *Against Heresies*, Book 5, Chapter 28, Point 2. www.newadvent.org/fathers/0103528.htm

"whose coming John has thus described in the Apocalypse: And the beast which I had seen was like a leopard, and his feet as of a bear, and his mouth as the mouth of a lion; and the dragon conferred his own power upon him, and his throne, and great might. And one of his heads was as it were slain unto death; and his deadly wound was healed, and all the world wondered after the beast. And they worshipped the dragon because he gave power to the beast; and they worshipped the beast, saying, Who is like this beast, and who is able to make war with him? And there was given unto him a mouth speaking great things, and blasphemy and power was given to him during forty and two months."[946]

4.6) Christians become the major target for the Antichrist to pour his rage on, and he persecutes them viciously, mocking our True God in the process, while performing more deceptive magic-type marvels to entice the wicked:

"And he opened his mouth for blasphemy against God, to blaspheme His name and His tabernacle, and those who dwell in heaven. And power was given him over every tribe, and people, and tongue, and nation. And all who dwell upon the earth worshipped him, [every one] whose name was not written in the book of the Lamb slain from the foundation of the world. If any one have ears, let him hear. If any one shall lead into captivity, he shall go into captivity. If any shall slay with the sword, he must be slain with the sword. Here is the endurance and the faith of the saints. Revelation 13:2, etc. After this he likewise describes his armour-bearer, whom he also terms a false prophet: He spoke as a dragon, and exercised all the power of the first beast in his sight, and caused the earth, and those that dwell therein, to adore the first beast, whose deadly wound was healed. And he shall perform great wonders, so that he can even cause fire to descend from heaven upon the earth in the sight of men, and he shall lead the inhabitants of the earth astray. Revelation 13:11, etc. Let no one imagine that he performs these wonders by divine power, but by the working of magic."[947]

4.7) The Antichrist works through the combined power of Satan and his demons, and he uses this to convert them into 'his religion,' where anyone who does not convert is killed if caught, and an economic persecution decree

---

[946] Ibid., Point 2.
[947] Ibid.

is also issued, where those who do not have the mark of the beast (symbolically 666) will be unable to buy and sell:

> "And we must not be surprised if, since the demons and apostate spirits are at his service, he through their means performs wonders, by which he leads the inhabitants of the earth astray. John says further: And he shall order an image of the beast to be made, and he shall give breath to the image, so that the image shall speak; and he shall cause those to be slain who will not adore it. He says also: And he will cause a mark [to be put] in the forehead and in the right hand, that no one may be able to buy or sell, unless he who has the mark of the name of the beast or the number of his name; and the number is six hundred and sixty-six, Revelation 13:14, etc. that is, six times a hundred, six times ten, and six units." [948]

4.8) This number is also connected to the 6000-year creation model. Some critics of chiliasm argue that the literal 7000-year timeline for Earth's history appears incongruous with real factual assessments of human history. Yes, this difficulty emerges only if we read that the 7000 years would occur in successive order. However, this difficulty regarding the 7000 years in total time for the Scriptural reign of God toward the fulfillment of Scripture with particular highlight for the Jews in the world can be averted if seen in an analogous manner with prophet Daniel's famous 70 weeks prophecy, where 69 weeks were consecutive but the last 1 week is separated and distinct since this refers to the last 7 years of the Antichrist time, which is placed to happen at the end of this age as we have here likewise (pages 86, 112–113).

> "[He gives this] as a summing up of the whole of that apostasy which has taken place during six thousand years. 3. For in as many days as this world was made, in so many thousand years shall it be concluded. And for this reason the Scripture says: Thus the heaven and the earth were finished, and all their adornment. And God brought to a conclusion upon the sixth day the works that He had made; and God rested upon the seventh day from all His works. Genesis 2:2 This is an account of the things formerly created, as also it is a prophecy of what is to come. For the day of the Lord is as a thousand years; 2 Peter 3:8 and in six days created things were completed: it is evident, therefore, that they will come to an end at the sixth thousand year." [949]

---

[948] Ibid.
[949] Ibid., Points 2–3.

4.9) It is also worth noting that many similar Antichrists have arisen throughout history, but only the final Antichrist will be able to help in the rebuilding of the Temple in Jerusalem and declare himself as "god" there, while the rest can only achieve some measure of fulfilment of some of the Biblical traits for this son of perdition but are not able to attain this fullness, as Irenaeus clearly warns below (where misunderstanding this can cause doctrinal errors such as full Preterism):

> "But as for those who, for the sake of vainglory, lay it down for certain that names containing the spurious number are to be accepted, and affirm that this name, hit upon by themselves, is that of him who is to come; such persons shall not come forth without loss, because they have led into error both themselves and those who confided in them. Now, in the first place, it is loss to wander from the truth, and to imagine that as being the case which is not; then again, as there shall be no light punishment [inflicted] upon him who either adds or subtracts anything from the Scripture, Revelation 22:19 under that such a person must necessarily fall. Moreover, another danger, by no means trifling, shall overtake those who falsely presume that they know the name of Antichrist. For if these men assume one [number], when this [Antichrist] shall come having another, they will be easily led away by him, as supposing him not to be the expected one, who must be guarded against."[950]

4.10) Next, Irenaeus plainly provides examples of real-life persons who have fulfilled some of the Antichrist's prophetic qualities, including the well-known numerology calculations for the number 666. However, none of them are the final Antichrist since they are unable to announce themselves as "god" because none have yet completed the rebuilding of the Temple in Jerusalem.

> "3. It is therefore more certain, and less hazardous, to await the fulfilment of the prophecy, than to be making surmises, and casting about for any names that may present themselves, inasmuch as many names can be found possessing the number mentioned; and the same question will, after all, remain unsolved. For if there are many names found possessing this number, it will be asked which among them shall the coming man bear. It is not through a want of names containing the number of that name that I say this, but on account of the fear of God, and zeal for the truth: for the name Evanthas (ΕΥΑΝΘΑΣ) contains the required number, but I make no allegation regarding it. Then also

---

[950] Irenaeus of Lyons, *Against Heresies*, Book 5, Chapter 30, Point 1. www.newadvent.org/fathers/0103530.htm

Lateinos (ΛΑΤΕΙΝΟΣ) has the number six hundred and sixty-six; and it is a very probable [solution], this being the name of the last kingdom [of the four seen by Daniel]. For the Latins are they who at present bear rule: I will not, however, make any boast over this [coincidence]. Teitan too, (TEITAN, the first syllable being written with the two Greek vowels ε and ι, among all the names which are found among us, is rather worthy of credit. For it has in itself the predicted number, and is composed of six letters, each syllable containing three letters; and [the word itself] is ancient, and removed from ordinary use; for among our kings we find none bearing this name Titan, nor have any of the idols which are worshipped in public among the Greeks and barbarians this appellation. Among many persons, too, this name is accounted divine, so that even the sun is termed Titan by those who do now possess [the rule]. This word, too, contains a certain outward appearance of vengeance, and of one inflicting merited punishment because he (Antichrist) pretends that he vindicates the oppressed." [951]

4.11) Irenaeus explicitly states that the Holy Spirit will not reveal the name of the Antichrist before to his appearance, particularly because such a vile name is unworthy of His mention. People who try to do otherwise are being duped. He writes:

"We will not, however, incur the risk of pronouncing positively as to the name of Antichrist; for if it were necessary that his name should be distinctly revealed in this present time, it would have been announced by him who beheld the apocalyptic vision. For that was seen no very long time since, but almost in our day, towards the end of Domitian's reign. 4. But he indicates the number of the name now, that when this man comes we may avoid him, being aware who he is: the name, however, is suppressed, because it is not worthy of being proclaimed by the Holy Spirit. For if it had been declared by Him, he (Antichrist) might perhaps continue for a long period. But now as he was, and is not, and shall ascend out of the abyss, and goes into perdition, Revelation 17:8 as one who has no existence; so neither has his name been declared, for the name of that which does not exist is not proclaimed." [952]

4.12) The Chiliasm Millennial Reign and First Resurrection occur after all of these events, particularly after the culmination of the Antichrist's reign

---

[951] Ibid., Point 3.
[952] Ibid., Points 3–4.

in the final three and a half years, are fulfilled. The following is what Irenaeus says right away from the above:

> "But when this Antichrist shall have devastated all things in this world, he will reign for three years and six months, and sit in the temple at Jerusalem; and then the Lord will come from heaven in the clouds, in the glory of the Father, sending this man and those who follow him into the lake of fire; but bringing in for the righteous the times of the kingdom, that is, the rest, the hallowed seventh day; and restoring to Abraham the promised inheritance, in which kingdom the Lord declared, that many coming from the east and from the west should sit down with Abraham, Isaac, and Jacob. But when this Antichrist shall have devastated all things in this world, he will reign for three years and six months, and sit in the temple at Jerusalem; and then the Lord will come from heaven in the clouds, in the glory of the Father, sending this man and those who follow him into the lake of fire; but bringing in for the righteous the times of the kingdom, that is, the rest, the hallowed seventh day; and restoring to Abraham the promised inheritance, in which kingdom the Lord declared, that many coming from the east and from the west should sit down with Abraham, Isaac, and Jacob. Matthew 8:11" [953]

Indeed, the Bible warns against numerous Antichrists emerging before the ultimate one:

> "Little children, it is the last hour; and as you have heard that the Antichrist is coming, even now many antichrists have come, by which we know that it is the last hour." (1 John 2:18, NKJV)

---

[953] Ibid., Point 4.

Appendix IX: Chiliasm Description of the 1000 Years Wedding of the Lamb

All Christians become priests or kings if they take part in the First Resurrection, also known as Elect Salvation, which consists of the Lamb's marriage, which endures for a thousand years (page 112). As a result, anyone saved at the Second Resurrection who is not a king or a priest but is among the nations that are saved could be Non-Elect Salvation beneficiaries, supporting this possible assertion.

1) Tertullian and St. Irenaeus of Lyons both assert that the present old earth will be restored or healed so that Christians can enjoy it in accordance with God's Will in Genesis during the First Resurrection following the Second Coming of Christ (page 72).

2) The Bible scripture in Romans for this portion is:

> "18For I consider that the sufferings of this present time are not worthy to be compared with the glory which shall be revealed in us. 19For the earnest expectation of the creation eagerly waits for the revealing of the sons of God. 20For the creation was subjected to futility, not willingly, but because of Him who subjected it in hope; 21because the creation itself also will be delivered from the bondage of [f]corruption into the glorious liberty of the children of God. 22For we know that the whole creation groans and labors with birth pangs together until now. 23Not only that, but we also who have the firstfruits of the Spirit, even we ourselves groan within ourselves, eagerly waiting for the adoption, the redemption of our body." (Romans 8:18–23, NKJV).

How do we know that these verses refer to a renewed old earth?

    i. Continuing deeper from St. Irenaeus' quote earlier:

> "when they rise again to behold God in this creation which is renovated, ... It is fitting, therefore, that the **creation** itself, being **restored** to its **primeval condition**, should without restraint be under the dominion of the righteous; and the apostle has made this plain in the Epistle to the **Romans**, when he thus speaks: For the expectation of the creature waits for the manifestation of the sons of God. For the creature has been subjected to vanity, not willingly, but by reason of him who has subjected the same in hope; since the creature itself shall also

be delivered from the bondage of corruption into the glorious liberty of the sons of God. Romans 8:19, etc. ... 2. Thus, then, the promise of God, which He gave to **Abraham**, ... For all the earth which you see I will give to you and to your seed, even forever. ... But the Scripture, foreseeing that God would justify the heathen through faith, declared to Abraham beforehand, That in you shall all nations be blessed. ... Galatians 3:6, etc. Thus, then, they who are of **faith** shall be blessed with faithful Abraham, and these are the children of Abraham. Now God made promise of the earth to Abraham and his seed; yet **neither Abraham nor his seed**, that is, **those who are justified by faith, do now receive any inheritance in it**; but they shall **receive it at the resurrection of the just.** For God is true and faithful; and on this account He said, Blessed are the meek, for they shall inherit the earth. Matthew 5:5" [954]

Note how St. Irenaeus' comment here refutes the prosperity gospel argument that believing in Christ in this world now involves receiving the Abrahamic promise of wealth and health. In fact, Irenaeus makes it quite evident that the "Abrahamic blessing" promised to Abraham and his seed (those of faith) does not include the wealth of Abraham while he was alive (Genesis 13:2, 14:23); rather, it will only be given to us at the first resurrection of the righteous. Tertullian also says something similar, stating that the Lord does not promise reward on earth today based on faith and good works, but rather wants us to expect it in the resurrection. Compare:

> "What kind of persons does He bid should be invited to a dinner or a supper? Luke 14:12-14 Precisely such as he had pointed out by Isaiah: Deal your bread to the hungry man; and the beggars — even such as have no home — bring in to your house, Isaiah 58:7 because, no doubt, they are unable to recompense your act of humanity. Now, since **Christ forbids the recompense to be expected now, but promises it at the resurrection,** this is the very plan of the Creator, who **dislikes those who love gifts and follow after reward**. Consider also to which deity is better suited the parable of him who issued invitations: A certain man made a great supper, and bade many. Luke 14:16 The preparation for the supper is no doubt a figure of the abundant provision of eternal life. I first remark, that **strangers, and persons unconnected by ties of relationship, are not usually invited to a supper**; but that members of the household and family are more frequently the favoured guests.

---

[954] Irenaeus of Lyons, *Against Heresies*, Book 5, Chapter 32, Points 1–2. www.newadvent.org/fathers/0103532.htm

> ... If, however, he condemns them beforehand as about to reject his call, then beforehand he also predicts the election of the Gentiles in their stead. Certainly he means to come the second time for the very purpose of preaching to the heathen. But even if he does mean to come again, I imagine it will not be with the intention of any longer inviting guests, but of giving to them their places. Meanwhile, you who interpret the call to this supper as an invitation to a heavenly banquet of spiritual satiety and pleasure, must remember that the **earthly promises** also of wine and oil and grain, and even of the city, are equally employed by the Creator as figures of spiritual things." [955]

In the passage we just saw, Tertullian clearly interprets Luke 14:14 in an allegorical manner while cautioning that this compensation cannot be viewed solely in a "spiritual sense" but also in a "literal earthly one" in the context of resurrection [both of which are true]. He also notes that Charity Doctrine action has little to no value when done solely toward one's own family members.

ii. Tertullian describes the Millennial Reign of Christ timeline as having literal fulfilment of things like animals being harmonious with nature and being non-violent, and that during this same 1000 years the Devil is locked up in the bottomless pit, implying that it cannot be allegorically now because the animal part and all that are not fulfilled currently in parallel, as he says below:

> "But, as the argument now stands, since what is eternal can be deemed evil, the evil must prove to be invincible and insuperable, as being eternal; and in that case it will be in vain that we labour to put away evil from the midst of us; 1 Corinthians 5:13 in that case, moreover, God vainly gives us such a command and precept; nay more, in vain has God appointed any judgment at all, when He means, indeed, to inflict punishment with injustice. But if, on the other hand, there is to be an end of evil, when the chief thereof, the **devil**, shall go away into the fire which God has prepared for him and his angels Matthew 25:41 — having been first cast into the **bottomless pit**; Revelation 20:3 when likewise the manifestation of the children of God Romans 8:19 shall have delivered the **creature** Romans 8:21 from evil, which had been made subject to vanity; Romans 8:20 when the **cattle restored** in the **innocence** and integrity of their nature shall be at peace with the **beasts** of the field, when also little **children** shall play with **serpents**; Isaiah

---

[955] Tertullian, *Against Marcion*. Book 4. Chapter 31.
www.newadvent.org/fathers/03124.htm

11:6 when the Father shall have put beneath the feet of His Son His enemies, as being the workers of evil — if in this way an end is compatible with evil, it must follow of necessity that a beginning is also compatible with it; and Matter will turn out to have a beginning, by virtue of its having also an end." [956]

iii. According to St. Irenaeus, the Lord Himself taught all of these First Resurrection of the Just events pertaining to the promise of inheritance on the old earth:

> "3. John, therefore, did distinctly foresee the **first resurrection** of the just, Luke 14:14 and the inheritance in the kingdom of the earth; and what the prophets have prophesied concerning it harmonize [with his vision]. For the **Lord also taught these things,** when He promised that He would have the mixed cup new with His disciples in the kingdom. The apostle, too, has confessed that the **creation** shall be **free** from the bondage of corruption, [so as to pass] into the liberty of the sons of God. Romans 8:21 And in all these things, and by them all, the same God the Father is manifested, who fashioned man, and gave promise of the **inheritance of the earth** to the fathers, who brought it (the creature) forth [from bondage] at the resurrection of the just, and fulfils the promises for the kingdom of His Son; subsequently bestowing in a paternal manner those things which neither the eye has seen, nor the ear has heard, nor has [thought concerning them] arisen within the heart of man, 1 Corinthians 2:9; Isaiah 64:4 For there is the one Son, who accomplished His Father's will; and one human race also in which the mysteries of God are wrought, which the angels desire to look into; 1 Peter 1:12 and they are not able to search out the wisdom of God, by means of which His handiwork, confirmed and incorporated with His Son, is brought to perfection;" [957]

2) For this promised restored world Millennial Reign of Christ (i.e. in that Day), prophet Isaiah says:

> "6"The wolf also shall dwell with the lamb, The leopard shall lie down with the young goat, The calf and the young lion and

---

[956] Tertullian, *Against Hermogenes*. Chapter 11.
www.newadvent.org/fathers/0313.htm
[957] Irenaeus of Lyons, *Against Heresies*, Book 5, Chapter 36, Point 3.
www.newadvent.org/fathers/0103536.htm

> the fatling together; And a little child shall lead them. 7The cow and the bear shall graze; Their young ones shall lie down together; And the lion shall eat straw like the ox. 8The nursing child shall play by the cobra's hole, And the weaned child shall put his hand in the viper's den. 9They shall not hurt nor destroy in all My holy mountain, For the earth shall be full of the knowledge of the Lord as the waters cover the sea. 10'And **in that day** there shall be a Root of Jesse, Who shall stand as a banner to the people; For the Gentiles shall seek Him, And His resting place shall be glorious.'" (Isaiah 11:6–10, NKJV)

i. Tertullian strongly emphasizes that these passages have a literal fulfilment in the Millennium after the resurrection (implied) because these do not occur now, though their allegorical fulfilment can occur now in faith (both true; meaning the literal will happen as well!):

> "Happily the Creator has promised by **Isaiah** to give this power even to little children, of putting their hand in the cockatrice den and on the hole of **the young asps without at all receiving hurt**. Isaiah 11:8-9 And, indeed, we are aware (**without doing violence to the literal sense** of the passage, since even these noxious animals have actually been unable to do hurt where there has been faith) that under the figure of scorpions and serpents are portended evil spirits, whose very prince is described by the name of serpent, dragon, and every other most conspicuous beast in the power of the Creator. This power the Creator conferred first of all upon His Christ, even as the ninetieth Psalm says to Him: Upon the asp and the basilisk shall You tread; the lion and the dragon shall You trample under foot." [958]

ii. St. Irenaeus of Lyons mentions that the direct disciples of the Apostles such as St. Papias of Hierapolis taught a literal Chiliasm bodily resurrection for all Christians in a renewed old earth that produces various kinds of food, and that the animals cease to be carnivores in His Holy Mountain literally. Allegorical meanings of these passages can refer to the repentance and taming of the wild Gentile habits to be true simultaneously.

> "The predicted blessing, therefore, belongs unquestionably to the **times of the kingdom**, when the righteous shall bear rule upon their rising from the dead; when also the creation, having been

---

[958] Tertullian, *Against Marcion*. Book 4. Chapter 24. www.newadvent.org/fathers/03124.htm

renovated and set free, shall fructify with an abundance of all kinds of food, from the dew of heaven, and from the fertility of the earth: as the **elders** who saw **John**, the **disciple** of the Lord, related that they had heard from him how the **Lord used to teach** in regard to these times, and say: The days will come, in which vines shall grow, each having ten thousand branches, and in each branch ten thousand twigs, and in each true twig ten thousand shoots, and in each one of the shoots ten thousand clusters, and on every one of the clusters ten thousand grapes, and every grape when pressed will give five and twenty metretes of wine. And when any one of the saints shall lay hold of a cluster, another shall cry out, I am a better cluster, take me; bless the Lord through me. In like manner [the Lord declared] that a grain of wheat would produce ten thousand ears, and that every ear should have ten thousand grains, and every grain would yield ten pounds (quinque bilibres) of clear, pure, fine flour; and that all other fruit-bearing trees, and seeds and grass, would produce in similar proportions (secundum congruentiam iis consequentem); and that **all animals feeding [only] on the productions of the earth**, should [in those days] become peaceful and harmonious among each other, and be in perfect subjection to man.

4. And these things are borne witness to in writing by **Papias**, the hearer of John, and a companion of Polycarp, in his fourth book; for there were five books compiled (συντεταγμένα) by him. And he says in addition, Now these things are credible to believers. And he says that, when the traitor Judas did not give credit to them, and put the question, 'How then can things about to bring forth so abundantly be wrought by the Lord.' the Lord declared, 'They who shall come to these [times] shall see.' When prophesying of these times, therefore, Esaias says: The wolf also shall feed with the lamb, and the leopard shall take his rest with the kid; the calf also, and the bull, and the lion shall eat together; and a little boy shall lead them. The ox and the bear shall feed together, and their young ones shall agree together; and the lion shall eat straw as well as the ox. And the infant boy shall thrust his hand into the asp's den, into the nest also of the adder's brood; and they **shall do no harm**, nor have power to hurt anything in my holy mountain. And again he says, in recapitulation, Wolves and lambs shall then browse together, and the **lion shall eat straw like the ox**, and the serpent earth as if it were bread; and they shall neither hurt nor annoy anything in my holy mountain, says the Lord. Isaiah 40:6, etc. I am quite aware that some persons endeavour to refer these words to the case of savage

men, both of different nations and various habits, who come to believe, and when they have believed, act in harmony with the righteous. But although this is [true] now with regard to some men coming from various nations to the harmony of the faith, **nevertheless in the resurrection of the just [the words shall also apply] to those animals mentioned**. For God is rich in all things. And it is right that when the creation is restored, all the animals should obey and be in subjection to man, and revert to the food originally given by God (for they had been originally subjected in obedience to Adam), that is, the productions of the earth. But some other occasion, and not the present, is [to be sought] for showing that the lion shall [then] feed on straw. And this indicates the large size and rich quality of the fruits. For if that animal, the lion, feeds upon straw [at that period], of what a quality must the wheat itself be whose straw shall serve as suitable food for lions?"**959**

3) The promise for Christ's 1000-year Millennial Reign on a renewed old earth in Isaiah 65 is as follows:

"17"For behold, I create **new heavens and a new earth**; And the former shall not be remembered or [f]come to mind.18But be glad and rejoice forever in what I create; For behold, I create Jerusalem as a rejoicing, And her people a joy. 19I will rejoice in Jerusalem, And joy in My people; The voice of weeping shall no longer be heard in her, Nor the voice of crying. 20"No more shall an infant from there live but a few days, Nor an old man who has not fulfilled his days; For the child shall die one hundred years old, But the **sinner being one hundred years old shall be accursed**. 21They shall build houses and inhabit them; They shall plant vineyards and eat their fruit. 22They shall not build and another inhabit; They shall not plant and another eat; For as the days of a tree, so shall be the days of My people, And **My elect** shall long enjoy the work of their hands. 23They shall not labor in vain, Nor bring forth children for trouble; For they shall be the descendants of the blessed of the Lord, And their offspring with them. 24"It shall come to pass That before they call, I will answer; And while they are still speaking, I will hear. 25The wolf and the lamb shall feed together, The lion shall eat straw like the ox, And dust shall be the

---

[959] Irenaeus of Lyons, *Against Heresies*, Book 5, Chapter 33, Points 3–4. www.newadvent.org/fathers/0103533.htm

serpent's food. They shall not hurt nor destroy in all My holy mountain," Says the Lord." (Isaiah 65:17–25, NKJV)

Isaiah 65:17, 20 is an example verse that proves mortals (sinners) living alongside resurrected Christian immortals at that time, implying that this must only happen on the current "Old" earth because it can still be touched by those in sin, whereas the final "New" Earth cannot be touched by sin at all. But doesn't Isaiah 65:17 say that this will happen on "new earth/heavens" rather than "old earth/heavens"? This is because the context of the Isaiah prophecy is talking about a renewed old earth containing the old earthly Jerusalem as well as the final new earth/heavens (Revelation 21:1 - 3), as I learned from St. Justin of Rome who quotes Isaiah 65:17 in this way for the First Resurrection context, which lasts 1000 years here (page 95):

> "But I and others, who are right-minded Christians on all points, are assured that there will be **a resurrection of the dead**, and a **thousand years** in Jerusalem, which will then be built, adorned, and enlarged, the prophets Ezekiel and Isaiah and others declare. For **Isaiah** spake thus concerning this space of a **thousand years**: 'For there shall be the **new heaven and the new earth**, and the former shall not be remembered, or come into their heart; but they shall find joy and gladness in it, which things I create'. For, Behold, I make Jerusalem a rejoicing, and My people a joy; and I shall rejoice over Jerusalem, and be glad over My people. And the voice of weeping shall be no more heard in her, or the voice of crying. And there shall be no more there a person of immature years, or an old man who shall not fulfil his days. For the young man shall be an hundred years old; but the **sinner who dies an hundred years old, he shall be accursed**. And they shall build houses, and shall themselves inhabit them; and they shall plant vines, and shall themselves eat the produce of them, and drink the wine. They shall not build, and others inhabit; they shall not plant, and others eat. For according to the days of the tree of life shall be the days of my people; the works of their toil shall abound. Mine elect shall not toil fruitlessly, or beget children to be cursed; for they shall be a seed righteous and blessed by the Lord, and their offspring with them. And it shall come to pass, that before they call I will hear; while they are still speaking, I shall say, What is it? Then shall the **wolves and the lambs feed together**, and the **lion shall eat straw like the ox**; but the serpent [shall eat] earth as bread. They shall **not hurt or maltreat** each other on the holy mountain, says the Lord.

> Now we have understood that the expression used among these words, 'According to the days of the tree [of life] shall be the days of my people; the works of their toil shall abound' obscurely **predicts a thousand years**. For as Adam was told that in the day he ate of the tree he would die, we know that he did not complete a thousand years. We have perceived, moreover, that the expression, 'The **day of the Lord is as a thousand years**,' is connected with this subject. And further, there was a certain man with us, whose name was John, one of the apostles of Christ, who prophesied, by a revelation that was made to him, that **those who believed in our Christ would dwell a thousand years in Jerusalem**; and that thereafter the general, and, in short, the eternal resurrection and judgment of all men would likewise take place. Just as our Lord also said, 'They shall neither marry nor be given in marriage, but shall be **equal to the angels**, the children of the God of the **resurrection**.' Luke 20:35f." [960]

4) The presence of an actual moon and sun in Jerusalem can indicate whether Bible scriptures are referring to the old earth/old heavens context or the new earth/new heavens.

   i. In reference to the Millennium timeframe, the heavenly Jerusalem in Mount Zion is implied *in that day*, while the physical moon and sun have an impact on the old Jerusalem on old earth during this time.

> "21It shall come to pass **in that day**, That the Lord will punish on high the host of exalted ones, And on the **earth** the kings of the **earth**. 22They will be gathered together, As prisoners are gathered in the [f]pit, And will be shut up in the prison; After many days they will be punished. Then the **moon** will be disgraced And the **sun** ashamed; For the LORD of hosts will reign On **Mount Zion** and in **Jerusalem** And before His elders, gloriously." (Isaiah 24:21–23, NKJV)

Prophet Isaiah also states that the light from the sun and its reflection on the moon will be greater literally throughout the Millennium (1000 years), i.e. on that Day.

> "26Moreover the light of the **moon** will be as the light of the **sun**, And the light of the sun will be **sevenfold**, As the light of

---

[960] St. Justin of Rome (Justin Martyr), *Dialogue with Trypho*, Chapters 80–81. www.newadvent.org/fathers/01286.htm

seven days, **In the day** that the Lord binds up the bruise of His people And heals the stroke of their wound." (Isaiah 30:26, NKJV)

St. Irenaeus confirms that the context of these passages refers to the times of the kingdom or the First Resurrection in the renewed old earth context, and that his statements following are not allegorical regarding the sun/moon fulfilment.

> "2. That the **whole creation** shall, according to God's will, obtain a vast **increase**, that it may bring forth and sustain fruits such [as we have mentioned], Isaiah declares: And there shall be upon every high mountain, and upon every prominent hill, water running everywhere in that day, when many shall perish, when walls shall fall. And the light of the **moon** shall be as the light of the **sun, seven times** that of the day, when He shall heal the anguish of His people, and do away with the pain of His stroke. Isaiah 30:25-26 Now the pain of the stroke means that inflicted at the beginning upon disobedient man in Adam, that is, death; which [stroke] the Lord will heal when He **raises us from the dead**, and **restores the inheritance** of the fathers, as Isaiah again says: And you shall be confident in the Lord, and He will cause you to pass over the whole earth, and feed you with the inheritance of Jacob your father. Isaiah 58:14 This is what the Lord declared: Happy are **those servants whom the Lord when He comes shall find watching**. Verily I say unto you, that He shall gird Himself, and make them to sit down [to meat], and will come forth and serve them. And if **He shall come in the evening watch**, and find them so, blessed are they, because He shall make them sit down, and minister to them; or if this be in **the second, or it be in the third**, blessed are they. Luke 12:37-38 Again John also says the very same in the Apocalypse: Blessed and holy is he who has part in the **first resurrection**. Revelation 20:6" [961]

Notice an interesting point in the last sentences of St. Irenaeus' words above, where he quotes Luke 12:37 - 38 to refer to this 1000-year Millennial Reign for servants (mortals at the time, since some could be watching while others were not), which supports the Non-Elect Salvation for Israel's mortals at that time. This appears to be non-elect salvation because, as St. Irenaeus

---

[961] Irenaeus of Lyons, *Against Heresies*, Book 5, Chapter 34, Point 2. www.newadvent.org/fathers/0103534.htm

points out, Christians are raised from the dead and physically live as "human immortals" there.

The existence of slaves who "may not be watching" (i.e., sinners) during this chronology implies that this must be the restored old earth, as sin/sinners cannot touch the final new earth. Please take note of Christ's possible surprise visits to this old earth up to three times during the Millennium to check on these mortal slaves and reward or punish them. This is definitely not referring to "three Second Comings of Christ," as it would be if these lines were applied to any timeframe before His Glorious Second Coming.

Also, those saved during this period are mentioned as servants in Matthew 25:14-30 and appear to be distinct from those saved at the Lamb's wedding (Matthew 25:1-13), implying Non-Elect Salvation versus Elect Salvation by the rigorous approach of mapping these scriptures to each other.

Furthermore, these servants already see or know of Christ's Second Coming and can see the First Resurrection with Christians (along with Old Testament believers) as human immortals around them, so the element of faith (i.e. "believing without seeing") does not appear to apply, but rather a weaker "believing after seeing" is intrinsically implied here, making Non-Elect Salvation a possibility!

ii. In contrast, the heavenly new Jerusalem city cannot be impacted by physical moons or suns, even if they exist. This city connects to a sin-free new earth after 1000 years.

> "22But you have come to Mount Zion and to the city of the living God, the **heavenly Jerusalem,** to an innumerable company of angels, 23to the [j]**general assembly** and **church** of the firstborn who are registered in **heaven,** to God the Judge of all, to the spirits of just men made perfect, 24to Jesus the Mediator of the new covenant, and to the blood of sprinkling that speaks better things than that of Abel. (Hebrews 12:22–24, NKJV) ... 1Now I saw a **new heaven and a new earth,** for the **first heaven and the first earth had passed away.** Also there was **no more sea.** 2Then I, [a]John, saw the holy city, **New Jerusalem,** coming down out of heaven from God, prepared as a bride adorned for her husband. ... 6And He said to me, "It[c] is done! I am the Alpha and the Omega, the Beginning and the End. I will give of the fountain of the water of life freely to him who thirsts. 7He who overcomes [d]shall inherit all things, and I will be his God and he shall be My son. 8But the cowardly, [e]unbelieving, abominable, murderers, sexually immoral, sorcerers, idolaters, and all liars shall have their part in the lake which

burns with fire and brimstone, which is the second death." 9Then one of the seven angels who had the seven bowls filled with the seven last plagues came [f]to me and talked with me, saying, "Come, I will show you the [g]**bride, the Lamb's wife**." 10And he carried me away in the Spirit to a great and high mountain, and showed me the [h]great city, the [i]holy Jerusalem, descending out of heaven from God, ... 14Now the wall of the city had twelve foundations, and on them were the [j]names of the twelve apostles of the Lamb. ... 22But I saw **no temple** in it, for the Lord God Almighty and the Lamb are its temple. 23The city had **no need** of the **sun** or of the **moon** to shine [l]in it, for the [m]glory of God illuminated it. The Lamb is its light. 24And the **nations** [n]of **those who are saved** shall walk in its light, and the kings of the earth bring their glory and honor [o]into it. 25Its gates shall not be shut at all by day (there shall be **no night there**). 26And they shall bring the glory and the honor of the nations into [p]it. 27But there shall by no means enter it anything [q]that defiles, or causes an abomination or a lie, but only those who are written in the Lamb's Book of Life. ... (Revelation 21:1–2, 6–10, 14, 22–27, NKJV). 1And he showed me a [a]pure river of water of life, clear as crystal, proceeding from the throne of God and of the Lamb. 2In the middle of its street, and on either side of the river, was the tree of life, which bore twelve fruits, each tree yielding its fruit every month. The leaves of the tree were for the healing of the nations. 3And there shall be no more curse, but the throne of God and of the Lamb shall be in it, and **His servants** shall serve Him. 4They shall see His face, and His name shall be on their foreheads. 5There shall be **no night there**: They need no lamp nor light of the sun, for the Lord God gives them light. And they shall reign forever and ever. ... 17And the Spirit and the bride say, "Come!" And let him who hears say, "Come!" And let him who thirsts come. Whoever desires, let him take the water of life freely." (Revelation 22:1 – 5, 17, NKJV).

Notice that it is plainly stated that there will be no night, implying the possibility of "no moon" because a moon is required for the definition of night, correct? Also, no sunlight suggests that, even if the sun exists for the last new earth, it does not reach the final new Jerusalem heavenly city (Revelation 21:23, 25, Revelation 22:5).

This also exposes a deeper feature of Bible prophecy context: whether a verse refers to the Millennium or after the Millennium. As much as feasible, I try to uncover Chiliasm Church Fathers' quotes for those same scriptures, and if I can't find any, I do my interpolations or guesswork as shown here to provide a model of potential for truth in which only God decides whether it is correct or even how accurate it is.

For example, I cannot find any Chiliasm Church Fathers quoting the Bible verses below, but based on the equivalent phrases meaning no more sun nor moon's light are required, I believe these may refer to the final new earth context (*land*) after the Millennium, describing both Israel (Servants) and the final saved nations where all are called righteous (so no more sinners nor mortals are present here):

> "19"The sun shall no longer be your light by day, Nor for brightness shall the moon give light to you; But the Lord will be to you an everlasting light, And your God your glory. 20Your sun shall no longer go down, Nor shall your moon withdraw itself; For the Lord will be your everlasting light, And the days of your mourning shall be ended. 21Also your people shall all be righteous; They shall inherit the land forever, The branch of My planting, The work of My hands, That I may be glorified. 22A little one shall become a thousand, And a small one a strong nation. I, the Lord, will hasten it in its time." (Isaiah 60:19–22, NKJV)

Appendix X: Will all Christians be in the First Resurrection?

1) These First Resurrection Bible Verses highlight the Christians who died as martyrs at the hands of the Final Antichrist (as evidenced by not taking his mark on their hands or foreheads), proving that this occurs after Christ's Second Coming, which obliterates the Beast.

> "4And I saw thrones, and they sat on them, and judgment was committed to them. Then I saw the **souls** of those who had been beheaded for their witness to Jesus and for the word of God, who had **not** worshiped the **beast** or his image, and had **not** received his mark on their foreheads or on their hands. And they lived and reigned with Christ for [a]a **thousand years**. 5But the **rest of the dead** did **not** live again until the **thousand years** were finished. This is the **first resurrection**. 6Blessed and holy is he who has part in the first resurrection. Over such the second death has no power, but they shall be priests of God and of Christ, and shall reign with Him a thousand years." (Revelation 20:4–6, NKJV)

Notice that in the following Bible verses, we see all Christians participating in the same First Resurrection and 1000-year Millennial Reign of Christ, including those of that final great tribulation (remember the martyred/beheaded ones mentioned in verses prior?) who are specially highlighted but not limited to because a greater multitude of all nations, tribes, and languages are mentioned alongside them next during this same bodily resurrection time:

> "4And I heard the number of those who were sealed. **One hundred and forty-four thousand** of all the tribes of the children of Israel were sealed: ... 9After these things I looked, and behold, a **great multitude** which no one could number, of **all nations**, tribes, peoples, and tongues, standing before the throne and before the Lamb, clothed with white robes, with **palm branches in their hands**, 10and crying out with a loud voice, saying, "Salvation belongs to our God who sits on the throne, and to the Lamb!" 11All the angels stood around the throne and the elders and the four living creatures, and fell on their faces before the throne and worshiped God, ... 13Then one of the elders answered, saying to me, "Who are these arrayed in white robes, and where did they come from?"

14And I said to him, [b]"Sir, you know." So he said to me, 'These are the ones who come out of the **great tribulation**, and washed their robes and made them white in the blood of the Lamb. 15Therefore they are before the throne of God, and serve Him **day and night in His temple**. And He who sits on the throne will dwell among them. 16They shall neither hunger anymore nor thirst anymore; the sun shall not strike them, nor any heat; 17for the Lamb who is in the midst of the throne will shepherd them and lead them to [c]living fountains of waters. And God will wipe away every tear from their eyes.' " (Revelation 7:4, 9–11, 13–17, NKJV)

How do we know that Revelation 7 is a prophecy for the First Body Resurrection rather than a gathering of the spirits? In general, the phrase "palm branches in their hands" denotes corporeal resurrection because "palm" refers to an earthly plant or tree that is only palpable in a body context.

The word hands can also refer to bodily resurrection, while some claim that the spirit shares comparable characteristics. It's conclusively corporeal resurrection because they partake of the "[c]living fountains of waters" where footnote [c] itself here signifies other variant Manuscripts to have the equivalent phrase phrase "fountains of the waters of life," as evidenced in other translations, which render this passage as "springs of the water of life" (NASB). In what way does bodily resurrection follow from this fact?

The Tree of Life, as God forewarned in Genesis, can only be applied to a final, sinless resurrection body. This is implied because if a spirit or soul can partake of the Tree of Life, then there is no need for resurrection, and Scripture already states that even a sinful human body could partake of it but end up living in sin forever, indicating that it is a bodily context. Similarly, the "Water of Life" analogy can be drawn similarly as they are connected in the verses below:

> "Then the LORD God said, "Behold, the man has become like one of Us, to know good and evil. And now, lest he put out his hand and take also of the **tree of life**, and **eat**, and **live forever**" (Genesis 3:22, NKJV)

> "1And he showed me a [a]pure river of water of life, clear as crystal, proceeding from the throne of God and of the Lamb. 2In the middle of its street, and on either side of the river, was the **tree of life**, which bore twelve fruits, each tree yielding its fruit every month. The **leaves** of the tree were for the **healing of the nations**." (Revelation 22:1–2, NKJV)

I mean, asserting that either "water of life" or "tree of life" can be ingested in spirit (soul) form is not written in any Scripture. However, because both are linked in the *final scene* (Revelation 22), this implies that it is solely applicable to the sinless human bodily resurrection.

Words like "river," "water," and "tree" also denote "bodily" connected things, as we see certain shadows of perishable things on Earth currently having comparable forms. All of these data strongly supports the corporeal resurrection context, as opposed to any 'spiritual partaking', which is also not mentioned in any Bible verse, thus it is merely a speculation.

In Revelation 7, we are certain that this must be Elect Salvation with bodily resurrection rather than any sort of spiritual resurrection (an idea that is absent from Scripture because a person dwelling in the *spirit world* is referred to as a *spirit (soul)* and not as resurrected) since it incorporates the word "clothed with white robes" (e.g., Revelation 7:9), which can be contrasted to other Bible verses like follows, which contain comparable terminology for the Elect only:

> "After these things I looked, and behold, a great multitude which no one could number, of **all nations**, tribes, peoples, and tongues, standing before the throne and before the Lamb, **clothed with white robes**, with palm branches in their hands," (Revelation 7:9, NKJV)

> "4[c]You have a few names [d]even in Sardis who have not defiled **their garments**; and they shall walk with Me in **white**, for they are **worthy**. 5He who **overcomes** shall be clothed in **white garments**, and I will not blot out his name from the **Book of Life**; but I will confess his name before My Father and before His angels." (Revelation 3:4–5, NKJV)

> "Around the throne were twenty-four thrones, and on the thrones I saw twenty-four elders sitting, **clothed in white robes**; and they had crowns of gold on their heads." (Revelation 4:4, NKJV)

> "9When He opened the fifth seal, I saw under the altar the **souls** of those who had been slain for the word of God and for the testimony which they held. 10And they cried with a loud voice, saying, "How long, O Lord, holy and true, until You judge and avenge our blood on those who dwell on the earth?" Then **a white robe** was given to each of them; and it was said to them that they should rest a little while longer, until both the number of their fellow

servants and their brethren, who would be **killed** as they were, was completed." (Revelation 6:9–11, NKJV)

Consider how the Bible presents the Elect Salvation in Revelation 7, starting with "Israel's 144,000 first," then "all nations," including the 24 Elders, with particular emphasis on those of the "last great tribulation," as they represent the last of the Elect who attend the Wedding of the Lamb to become His "Bride" (implied) when viewed in conjunction with other verses.

In fact, "Israel's 144, 000 first" is stated separately (Revelation 7:4 - 8) because they indicate the holiest lot or firstfruits of salvation (sort of like "tithes" of salvation itself), which is defined elsewhere as follows: (Notice that while Revelation 7 accentuates their "race" as "Israelites" and compares it to the salvation of the rest of "all nations" in Revelation 7:9-10, the racial distinction here is literal, and "no spiritual Israel" designation is meant as some allegorists err. In fact, all the saved described in Revelation 7's Elect summation are "spiritual Israel" as a whole); see:

> "1Then I looked, and behold, a Lamb standing on Mount Zion, and with Him **one hundred and forty-four thousand**, having His Father's name written on their foreheads. 2And I heard a voice from heaven, like the voice of many waters, and like the voice of loud thunder. And I heard the sound of harpists playing their harps. 3They sang as it were a new song before the throne, before the four living creatures, and the elders; and no one could learn that song except the hundred and forty-four thousand who were redeemed from the earth. 4These are the ones who were **not defiled with women**, for they are **virgins**. These are the ones who follow the Lamb wherever He goes. These were redeemed from among men, being **firstfruits** to God and to the Lamb. 5And in their mouth was found **no deceit**, for they are **without fault** before the throne of God." (Revelation 14:1–5, NKJV)

As many church fathers have pointed out, the 144,000 are unmarried, and how many people in history who have converted many to Christianity were virgins and Jewish by descent? Is there a single example of such a person inside our own church or denomination? This, combined with the terms "no deceit" and "without fault," which are used in these verses to characterize them, shows that the quantity of converts in our church does not determine one's proximity to God, but rather accurate prophetic and doctrinal truth. This is because we can hardly think of anyone who converted many people to Christianity that fits this scriptural description. This is consistent with both the prophecy of St. Clement of Rome (page 11) and Daniel 12:3.

The definition of resurrection is spirit (soul) getting a physical body to live again, implying that there is no such thing as a "spiritual resurrection," as some allegorists mistakenly believe is happening now in their spirit (soul) condition. Compare:

I) According to St. Irenaeus of Lyons, the soul (spirit) of the righteous residing in the invisible place (also known as the spirit world) is not the same as resurrection. By using the example of the Lord Jesus Christ alone, who is perfect, Irenaeus makes it abundantly evident that resurrection is the moment when our souls receive the body later and ascend into the final heavens.

> "For as the Lord went away in the midst of the shadow of death, where the **souls of the dead** were, yet **afterwards arose** in the **body**, and **after the resurrection** was **taken up [into heaven]**, it is manifest that the **souls** of His **disciples** also, upon whose account the Lord underwent these things, shall go away into the invisible place allotted to them by God, and there remain until the resurrection, awaiting that event; then receiving their bodies, and rising in their entirety, that is bodily, just as the Lord arose, they shall come thus into the presence of God. For no disciple is above the Master, but every one that is perfect shall be as his Master. Luke 6:40 As our Master, therefore, did not at once depart, taking flight [to heaven], but awaited the time of His resurrection prescribed by the Father, which had been also shown forth through Jonas, and rising again after three days was taken up [to heaven]; so ought we also to **await the time of our resurrection** prescribed by God and foretold by the prophets, and so, **rising**, be **taken up**, as many as the Lord shall account worthy of this [privilege]." [962]

II) According to St. Justin of Rome, the term "resurrection" in Holy Scripture refers to a bodily resurrection, when a spirit with soul receives a flesh (body) to live again.

> "The **resurrection** is a **resurrection of the flesh which died**. For the spirit dies not; the soul is in the body, and without a soul it cannot live. The body, when the soul forsakes it, is not. For the body is the house of the soul; and the soul the house of the spirit. These three, in all those who cherish a sincere hope and unquestioning faith in God, will be saved." [963]

---

[962] St. Irenaeus of Lyons. *Against Heresies*. Book 5. Chapter 31. Point 2. www.newadvent.org/fathers/0103531.htm
[963] St. Justin of Rome (Justin Martyr). *On the Resurrection*. Chapter 10. www.newadvent.org/fathers/0131.htm

III) Tertullian states unequivocally that Christians do not use the term "spiritual resurrection" to refer to any other kind of bodily resurrection, such as in the spirit world or elsewhere, with the exception of sometimes using it allegorically to describe the life of a person who repents on earth while still alive (not to dead souls)!

> "It moreover follows, that the very maintenance of this spiritual resurrection amounts to a presumption in favour of the other bodily resurrection; for if none were announced for that time, there would be fair ground for asserting only this purely spiritual resurrection. Inasmuch, however, as (a **resurrection**) is proclaimed for the last time, it is proved to be a **bodily** one, because there is **no spiritual one** also then announced. For why make a second announcement of a resurrection of only one character, that is, the spiritual one, since this ought to be undergoing accomplishment either now, without any regard to different times, or else then, at the very conclusion of all the periods? It is therefore more competent for us even to maintain a **spiritual resurrection** at the **commencement of a life of faith**, who acknowledge the full completion thereof at the end of the world." [964]

IV) Tertullian makes it abundantly evident that whenever the Lord uses the term resurrection, it simply means bodily resurrection and that nothing of any allegory can ever be associated with it. Instead, he uses it to mean that a soul (spirit) getting literal flesh (body) and his usage in his writings means the same thing. The best part is that he applies the above specifically to the first resurrection of the just, which is Chiliasm timeline, and he claims that only a few comprehend these details below.

> "And again, It shall be recompensed to you at the **resurrection of the just.** Luke 14:14 Now, if the mention of these events (I mean the judgment-day, and the kingdom of God, and the resurrection) has a plain and absolute sense, so that **nothing about them can be pressed into an allegory**, neither should those statements be forced into parables which describe the arrangement, and the process, and the experience of the kingdom of God, and of the judgment, and of the resurrection. On the contrary, things which are destined for the body should be **carefully understood in a bodily sense — not in a spiritual sense**, as having nothing figurative in their nature. This is the reason why we have laid it down as a preliminary consideration, that the bodily substance both of the soul and of the flesh is liable to the

---

[964] Tertullian. *On the Resurrection of the Flesh*. Chapter 25. www.newadvent.org/fathers/0316.htm

recompense, which will have to be awarded in return for the co-operation of the two natures, that so the corporeality of the soul may not exclude the bodily nature of the flesh by suggesting a recourse to figurative descriptions, since both of them must needs be regarded as destined to take part in the kingdom, and the judgment, and the resurrection. And now we proceed to the special proof of this proposition, that the **bodily character of the flesh** is indicated by **our Lord whenever He mentions the resurrection**, at the same time without disparagement to the corporeal nature of the soul — a point which has been actually admitted but by a few." [965]

v) Tertullian affirms that the only definition of resurrection is the soul (spirit) receiving a body, even in the spiritual body setting specified in Scripture for resurrection.

"By what designation would they have it called, except that which it became through the soul, except that which it was not previous to the soul, except that which it can never be after the soul, but through its resurrection? For after it has recovered the soul, it once more becomes the natural (or animate) body, in order that it may become a **spiritual body**. For it only resumes in the **resurrection** the condition which it once had. There is therefore by no means the same good reason why the soul should be called the natural (or animate) body, which the flesh has for bearing that designation. The flesh, in fact, was a body before it was an animate body. When the flesh was joined by the soul, it then became the natural (or animate) body. ... As therefore the flesh was at first an animate (or natural) **body on receiving the soul**, so at last will it become a **spiritual body** when invested with the spirit." [966]

2) Here are statements from Chiliasm Church Fathers that agree that *all* Christians participate in the First Resurrection, which is the Marriage of the Lamb on this true Sabbath rest fulfillment of Scripture on the Seventh Day, which lasts 1000 years and is also known as Christ's Millennial Reign.

I) According to St. Justin of Rome, all Christians (i.e. "those who believed in our Christ") participate in physical bodily resurrection and first reside in earthly Jerusalem for 1000 years.

"there will be a **resurrection** of the dead, and a thousand years in Jerusalem, ... John, one of the apostles of Christ, who prophesied, by a revelation that was made to him, that **those who believed in our**

---

[965] Ibid., Chapter 33.
[966] Ibid., Chapter 53.

Christ would dwell a **thousand years in Jerusalem**; and that thereafter the general, and, in short, the eternal resurrection and judgment of all men would likewise take place."[967]

II) St. Polycarp, bishop of Smyrna and a direct follower of apostle St. John, who wrote the book of Revelation, states that all Christians will be part of the "world to come" and its "resurrection of the dead," referring to the Chiliasm's first resurrection here.

"If we please Him in this present world, we shall receive also the **future world**, according as He has promised to us that He will **raise us again from the dead**, and that if we live worthily of Him, we shall also reign together with Him, 2 Timothy 2:12 provided only we believe. In like manner, let the young men also be blameless in all things, being especially careful to preserve purity, and keeping themselves in, as with a bridle, from every kind of evil. For it is well that they should be cut off from the lusts that are in the world, since every lust wars against the spirit; 1 Peter 2:11 and neither fornicators, nor effeminate, nor abusers of themselves with mankind, **shall inherit the kingdom of God**, 1 Corinthians 6:9-10 nor those who do things inconsistent and unbecoming. Wherefore, it is needful to abstain from all these things, being subject to the presbyters and deacons, as unto God and Christ. The virgins also must walk in a blameless and pure conscience." [968]

It should be noted that the subjection to presbyters and deacons written here was directed at those who believed in Chiliasm, and that he did not have any prayers to the virgin Mary or saints, as that absent in Chiliasm church fathers' writings, and thus should not be claimed by any existing Christian unless they followed the same beliefs and rules as testified by Church History. St. Papias (page 27) and St. Irenaeus (pages 180–181) both use a similar statement to describe all Christians' participation in the "wedding" of the lamb and the first resurrection being either the thirtyfold, sixtyfold, or hundredfold fruit levels of the Gospel.

3) Since St. Irenaeus already quoted the context of new earth and new heavens based on Isaiah 66:22 (pages 81,95,180), let's look at these Bible verses first before comparing it with another of his statement soon.

---

[967] St. Justin of Rome (Justin Martyr). *Dialogue with Trypho*. Chapters 80–81. www.newadvent.org/fathers/01286.htm

[968] St. Polycarp of Smyrna. *Epistle of Polycarp to the Philippians*. Chapter 5. www.newadvent.org/fathers/0136.htm

"18"For I know their works and their thoughts. It shall be that I will gather **all nations** and tongues; and they shall come and see My glory. 19I will set a sign among them; and those among them who **escape** I will send to the nations: to Tarshish and [c]Pul and Lud, who draw the bow, and Tubal and Javan, to the coastlands afar off who have **not heard** My fame **nor seen** My glory. And they shall declare My glory among the Gentiles. … 24'And they shall go forth and look Upon the corpses of the men Who have transgressed against Me. For their worm does not die, And their fire is not quenched. They shall be an abhorrence to all flesh.'" (Isaiah 66:18 – 19, 24, NKJV)

"And this **gospel** of the kingdom will be **preached** in **all** the **world** as a witness to all the nations, and then the end will come." (Matthew 24:14, NKJV)

"6Then I saw another angel flying in the midst of heaven, having the **everlasting gospel to preach** to those who dwell on the earth— to every nation, tribe, tongue, and people— 7saying with a loud voice, "Fear God and give glory to Him, for the hour of His judgment has come; and worship Him who made heaven and earth, the sea and springs of water." (Revelation 14:6–7, NKJV)

Notice a few possibilities here:

First, because Isaiah 66:18-19, 24 verses earlier, establishes the context of some type of initial judgment for some of the wicked during the "start" of the Millennium, some of the wicked, such as those who took the mark of the beast (Antichrist) or worshipped his image, have no hope and are judged in that fire early on.[969] Another view is that since only the "corpses" (dead bodies with no souls) are mentioned to be burned in Isaiah 66:24 literally here, it shows that such ones miss the First Resurrection (having no bodies to resurrect with) and their souls (spirits) are judged elsewhere in the Spirit World first (implied) before the General Resurrection and Judgment at the end of this 1000 years because they too need to be raised bodily first before their final judgment sentence is pronounced.

---

[969] Revelation 14:9–11, "9Then a third angel followed them, saying with a loud voice, "If anyone worships the beast and his image, and receives his mark on his forehead or on his hand, 10he himself shall also drink of the wine of the wrath of God, which is poured out full strength into the cup of His indignation. He shall be tormented with fire and brimstone in the presence of the holy angels and in the presence of the Lamb. 11And the smoke of their torment ascends forever and ever; and they have no rest day or night, who worship the beast and his image, and whoever receives the mark of his name." (NKJV).

Regardless of which of these alternatives is correct, the key point is that this occurs during the Millennium, as St. Irenaeus' quotation already indicates (pages 81,95, and 180, previously). The Bible lines here in Isaiah 66:19 reference some of those who escape the judgment at the time when Christ Returns as missionaries to preach the Gospel (implied) to the nations, including those who have never heard of the Gospel or His Name.

But doesn't that "contradict" Matthew 24:14 and Revelation 14:6-7 (also referenced before), which imply that the Gospel must be spread to all nations before the end? The Great Commission verses speak of doing our part, but some parts of it may be fulfilled through the Chiliasm Prophecy's 1000-year Millennial Reign of Christ because some of those who have never heard the Gospel will finally hear it before the "end," which refers to the end of this Millennium and before the Great White Throne's Judgment Day, as Isaiah 66:18-19 points out.

St. Justin of Rome confirms that Isaiah 66:24 alludes to this Millennium setting (as those coming from the east and west shall join Abraham, Isaac, and Jacob at the "first resurrection" [implied]) and warns that the first resurrection cannot be asked on behalf of anyone, regardless of our level of righteousness, and that it is dependent only on each person's faith and works (individually) by God's Grace:

> "And Ezekiel: 'Even if Noah, and Jacob, and Daniel were to pray for sons or daughters, their request should not be granted.' 'But neither shall the father perish for the son, nor the son for the father; but every one for his own sin, and each shall be saved for his own righteousness.' Ezekiel 18:20 And again Isaiah says: 'They shall look on the **carcasses** of them that have transgressed: **their worm shall not cease, and their fire shall not be quenched**; and they shall be a spectacle to all flesh.' Isaiah 66:24 And our Lord, according to the will of Him that sent Him, who is the Father and Lord of all, would not have said, 'They shall come from the **east**, and from the **west**, and shall sit down with **Abraham**, and **Isaac**, and **Jacob** in the **kingdom of heaven**. But the children of the kingdom shall be cast out into outer darkness.' Furthermore, I have proved in what has preceded, that those who were foreknown to be unrighteous, whether men or angels, are not made wicked by God's fault, but each man by his own fault is what he will appear to be." [970]

---

[970] St. Justin of Rome. *Dialogue with Trypho*. Chapter 140. www.newadvent.org/fathers/01289.htm

Tertullian quotes Isaiah 66:24 (so same context for Isaiah 66:18-24 as a whole) to refer to the end of this 1000 years or Millennium (implied by his words next that these are fulfilled afterwards, which can agree with St. Justin's quote earlier because St. Justin quotes it to happen simultaneously when the "Kingdom of Heaven" [final new Heavens] is pronounced, which in Chiliasm timeline refers to the end of this 1000 years):

> "Isaiah 26:19 In another passage it is written: All flesh shall come to worship before me, says the Lord. Isaiah 66:23 **When?** When the **fashion of this world** shall begin to **pass away**. For He said before: As the **new heaven** and the **new earth**, which I make, remain before me, says the Lord, so shall your seed remain. Then also shall be **fulfilled what is written afterwards**: And they shall go forth (namely, from their graves), and shall see the **carcasses** of those who have transgressed: for their **worm shall never die, nor shall their fire be quenched;** and they shall be a spectacle to all flesh Isaiah 66:24 even to that which, being raised again from the dead and brought out from the grave, shall adore the Lord for this great grace." [971]

Those who escape during His Second Coming and live as mortals during the Millennium ("in that Day") can also be seen in these verses, as they are the Gentiles who seek Him and will no longer be enemies of Israel:

> "10"And **in that day** there shall be a Root of Jesse, Who shall stand as a banner to the people; For the Gentiles shall seek Him, And His resting place shall be glorious." 11It shall come to pass in that day That the Lord shall set His hand again the second time To recover the **remnant** of His people **who are left**," ... 12He will set up a banner for the nations, And will [e]assemble the outcasts of Israel, And gather together the dispersed of Judah From the four [f]corners of the earth. 13Also the envy of Ephraim shall depart, And the adversaries of Judah shall be cut off; Ephraim shall not envy Judah, And Judah shall not harass Ephraim. 14But they shall fly down upon the shoulder of the Philistines toward the west; Together they shall plunder the [g]people of the East; They shall lay their hand on Edom and Moab; And the people of Ammon shall obey them." (Isaiah 11:10–11, 12–14, NKJV)

---

[971] Tertullian. *On the Resurrection of the Flesh*. Chapter 31. www.newadvent.org/fathers/0316.htm

Jonathan Ramachandran

Appendix XI: Are All Christians Kings and Priests during the Millennium?

Let us return to Isaiah 66, which we have already seen is a prophecy for the Millennium.

> "20Then they shall bring all your brethren for an offering to the Lord out of **all nations**, on horses and in chariots and in litters, on mules and on camels, to My holy mountain Jerusalem," says the Lord, "as the children of Israel bring an offering in a clean vessel into the house of the Lord. 21And **I will also take some of them for priests and Levites**," says the Lord. 22"For as the new heavens and the new earth Which I will make shall remain before Me," says the Lord, "So shall your descendants and your name remain. 23And it shall come to pass That from one New Moon to another, And from one Sabbath to another, **All flesh shall come to worship before Me**," says the Lord." (Isaiah 66:20–23, NKJV)

In his comment below, St. Justin of Rome interprets the context of Isaiah 66:21 as referring to Christians, while certain mortals appear to be selected jointly to be priests and Levites in the Millennial Reign timeline. At this time, mortal priests may perform daily functions for the regular human beings who live on Earth alongside the resurrected Christian immortals.

> "Jesus the Son of God has promised again to deliver us, and **invest us with prepared garments**, if we do His commandments; and has undertaken to **provide an eternal kingdom [for us]**. For just as that Jesus (Joshua), called by the prophet a priest, evidently had on filthy garments because he is said to have taken a harlot for a wife, and is called a brand plucked out of the fire, because he had received remission of sins when the devil that resisted him was rebuked; even so we, who through the name of Jesus have believed as one man in God the Maker of all, have been stripped, through the name of His first-begotten Son, of the filthy garments, i.e., of our sins; and being vehemently inflamed by the word of His calling, we are the true high priestly race of God, as even God Himself bears witness, saying that in **every place** among the **Gentiles** sacrifices are

presented to Him well-pleasing and pure. Now God receives sacrifices from no one, **except through His priests."** **972**

St. Irenaeus of Lyons explicitly states that all disciples of the Lord become priests in His Kingdom (i.e., all Christians), implying that the Millennium banquet in the Kingdom of the Righteous will continue for 1000 years:

> "Now, in the preceding book I have shown that **all the disciples of the Lord are Levites and priests**, ... Promises of such a nature, therefore, do indicate in the clearest manner the feasting of that creation in the **kingdom of the righteous**, which God promises that He will Himself serve." **973**

Notice that in the Millennium context of Isaiah 66, only *some* (not all) become priests and Levites (Isaiah 66:21), allowing for non-elect salvation for those saved as non-priests in the final earth as well (Revelation 21:24), as these verses appear to extend into the final new earth and heavens as well (Isaiah 66:22).

St. Irenaeus of Lyons plainly indicates in another place that every righteous has a sacerdotal rank (some form of priesthood rank or level, implying gradations in His Kingdom for this). Additionally, he also points out that the higher levels, such as the apostles, do not own land or houses etc., (which, by modern adaptation, unless you have a church or support system, I believe you can will your money and property to charity, church or ministry via a will and live by these charity doctrine rules if you want to imitate this faith level):

> "justifying **His disciples** by the words of the law, and pointing out that it was lawful for the **priests to act freely**. For David had been appointed a priest by God, although Saul persecuted him. For **all the righteous** possess the **sacerdotal rank**. And **all** the **apostles** of the Lord are **priests**, who do **inherit** here **neither lands nor houses**, but serve God and the altar continually. Of whom Moses also says in Deuteronomy, when blessing Levi, Who said to his father and to his mother, I have not known you; neither did he acknowledge his brethren, and he disinherited his own sons: he kept Your commandments, and observed Your covenant. Deuteronomy

---

972 St. Justin of Rome (Justin Martyr). *Dialogue with Trypho*. Chapter 116. www.newadvent.org/fathers/01288.htm

973 St. Irenaeus of Lyons. *Against Heresies*. Book 5. Chapter 34. Point 3. www.newadvent.org/fathers/0103534.htm

33:9 But who are they that have left father and mother, and have said adieu to all their neighbours, on account of the word of God and His covenant, unless the disciples of the Lord? Of whom again **Moses** says, They shall have **no inheritance**, for the Lord Himself is their inheritance. Numbers 18:20 And again, The **priests** the **Levites** shall have **no part** in the whole tribe of Levi, **nor substance** with Israel; their substance is the offerings (fructifications) of the Lord: these shall they eat. Deuteronomy 18:1 Wherefore also Paul says, I do not seek after a gift, but I seek after fruit. Philippians 4:17 To **His disciples** He said, who had a **priesthood** of the Lord, to whom it was lawful when hungry to eat the ears of grain, For the workman is worthy of his meat. Matthew 10:10 And the **priests** in the temple **profaned the Sabbath**, and were **blameless**. Wherefore, then, were they blameless? Because when in the temple they were **not engaged in secular affairs**, but in the service of the Lord, fulfilling the law, but not going beyond it, as that man did, who of his own accord carried dry wood into the camp of God, and was justly stoned to death. Numbers 15:32, etc. For every tree that brings not forth good fruit shall be hewn down, and cast into the fire; Matthew 3:10 and whosoever shall defile the temple of God, him shall God defile. 1 Corinthians 3:17" [974]

Tertullian reveals that every Christian is a priest individually, but when gathered as a Church, some are laity (non-priests), while others are priests (but keep in mind that he is talking about priests who held to Chiliasm doctrines that agree with his writings here, not necessarily any modern Christianity pastor who does not follow it):

"Thence, therefore, among us the prescript is more fully and more carefully laid down, that they who are chosen into the **sacerdotal** order must be **men of one marriage**; which rule is so rigidly observed, that I remember some removed from their office for digamy. But you will say, Then all others may (marry more than once), whom he excepts. Vain shall we be if we think that what is not lawful for priests is lawful for laics. Are not even we **laics priests**? It is written: **A kingdom also, and priests to His God and Father, has He made us.** It is the authority of the Church, and the honour which has acquired sanctity through the joint session of the Order, which has established the difference between the Order

---

[974] St. Irenaeus of Lyons. *Against Heresies*. Book 4. Chapter 8. Point 3. www.newadvent.org/fathers/0103408.htm

and the laity. Accordingly, where there is **no joint session** of the ecclesiastical Order, you offer, and **baptize, and are priest**, alone for yourself. But where three are, a church is, albeit they be laics. For each individual lives by his own faith, nor is there exception of persons with God; since it is not hearers of the law who are justified by the Lord, but doers, according to what the apostle withal says. Therefore, if you have the right of a priest in your own person, in **cases of necessity**, it behooves you to have likewise the discipline of a **priest** whenever it may be **necessary to have the right of a priest**. If you are a digamist, do you baptize? If you are a digamist, do you offer? How much more capital (a crime) is it for a digamist laic to act as a priest, when the priest himself, if he turn digamist, is deprived of the power of acting the priest! But to necessity, you say, indulgence is granted. No necessity is excusable which is avoidable. In a word, shun to be found guilty of digamy, and you do not expose yourself to the necessity of administering what a digamist may not lawfully administer. God wills us all to be so conditioned, as to be ready at all times and places to undertake (the duties of) His sacraments. There is one God, **one faith**, one discipline too. So truly is this the case, that unless the laics as well observe the rules which are to guide the choice of presbyters, how will there be presbyters at all, who are chosen to that office from among the laics? Hence we are bound to contend that the command to abstain from second marriage relates first to the laic; so long as no other can be a presbyter than a laic, provided he have been once for all **a husband**." [975]

On a personal note, some pastors (but not all) have questioned the baptism I performed because I am not ordained. The main point is that Martin Luther (whom all protestants see as saved) was only baptized as a baby by a Roman Catholic priest and was never re-baptized. If that baptism is authentic, so are the ones I did via God's grace. Another example is Charles Spurgeon, known as the prince of preachers, who was never ordained and opposed the use of the title "reverend." The Great Commission commands us to both preach the gospel and baptize, and Tertullian wrote here that *any* Christian man can baptize, especially when necessary, as in my case, because these students refused to attend church despite believing in Christ due to a bad experience with certain Christians. I always recommend that they get baptized at a local church first.

---

[975] Tertullian. *On Exhortation to Chastity.* Chapter 7. www.newadvent.org/fathers/0405.htm

I recently emailed practically all significant denominations or Christian leaders in Malaysia, including bible schools, to request an ecumenical conversation to correct any issues on which they believe I am incorrect in a respectful, fair, and open forum, which may or may not take place at their discretion. So, if they are not keen on it, no one can be blamed for freedom. In these respects, because one denomination typically does not accept the baptism of another, we are equal. In another writing, Tertullian clearly points again that Christians are priests in the future resurrection context:

> "Us, moreover, Jesus, the Father's Highest and Great Priest, clothing us from His own store — inasmuch as they who are **baptized in Christ** have put on Christ — has made **priests to God** His Father, according to John. For the reason why He recalls that young man who was hastening to his father's obsequies, is that He may show that **we are called priests by Him**; (priests) whom the Law used to forbid to be present at the sepulture of parents: Over every dead soul, it says, the priest shall not enter, and over his own father and over his own mother he shall not be contaminated. Does it follow that we too are bound to observe this prohibition? No, of course. For our one Father, God, lives, and our mother, the Church; and neither are we dead who live to God, nor do we bury our dead, inasmuch as they too are living in Christ. At all events, **priests we are called by Christ**; debtors to monogamy, in accordance with the pristine Law of God, which **prophesied** at that time **of us in its own priests**." [976]

According to St. Victorinus of Pettau, Revelation 1:6 and 1 Peter 2:9 allude to the same context, implying that all Christians will be priests in the coming kingdom as the current kingdom of this world is being destroyed.

> "5. And from Jesus Christ, who is the faithful witness, the first-begotten of the dead. In taking upon Him manhood, He gave a testimony in the world, wherein also having suffered, He freed us by His blood from sin; and having vanquished hell, He was the first who rose from the dead, and death shall have no more dominion over Him, Romans 6:9 but by His own reign the kingdom of the world is destroyed. 6. And **He made us a kingdom and priests** unto God and His Father. That is to say, a **Church of all believers**;

---

[976] Tertullian. *On Monogamy*. Chapter 7.
www.newadvent.org/fathers/0406.htm

as also the Apostle Peter says: A holy nation, a **royal priesthood**. 1 Peter 2:9" [977]

The chiliasm church fathers never ordained any female priests or pastors because it is not mentioned in the New Testament. Faithful women will undoubtedly serve as priests in His Kingdom and after the resurrection, when gender is abolished. In the prior quotation, Tertullian solely addresses males (e.g., husband and those with one wife) seeking a priestly position on earth.

According to Tertullian, the context of Christ's casting of pearls to pigs includes heretics who reject the truth found in his writings (including parts of chiliasm) and those who appoint women priests in violation of New Testament verses. For this reason, I do not risk myself by allowing any female priests (pastors) to be ordained; instead, I let them be due to *free will* and let God demonstrate whether He truly permitted it on that particular day:

> "That which is **holy** they will cast to the **dogs**, and their **pearls**, although (to be sure) they are not real ones, they will fling to the **swine**. Simplicity they will have to consist in the overthrow of discipline, attention to which on our part they call brothelry. .... The **very women of these heretics**, how wanton they are! For they are **bold enough to teach, to dispute, to enact exorcisms, to undertake cures — it may be even to baptize**. Their ordinations, are carelessly administered, capricious, changeable. At one time they put novices in office; at another time, men who are bound to some secular employment; at another, persons who have apostatized from us, to bind them by vainglory, since they cannot by the truth. Nowhere is **promotion easier** than in the camp of **rebels**, where the mere fact of being there is a foremost service." [978]

In another text, Tertullian plainly emphasizes that these Bible precepts respecting women are applicable not only to married women but also to virgins, thus to all women:

> "Let us now see whether, as we have shown the arguments drawn from nature and the matter itself to be **applicable to the virgin** as well (as to **other females**), so likewise the precepts of **ecclesiastical discipline concerning women** have an eye to the virgin. It is **not permitted to a woman to speak in the church**; but neither (is it

---

[977] St. Victorinus of Pettau. *Commentary on the Apocalypse*. From the First Chapter. www.newadvent.org/fathers/0712.htm

[978] Tertullian. *Prescription against Heretics*. Chapter 41. www.newadvent.org/fathers/0311.htm

permitted her) **to teach, nor to baptize**, nor to offer, nor to claim to herself a lot in any manly function, not to say (in any) **sacerdotal office**." [979]

While St. Irenaeus of Lyons mentions some gnostic heretics with female priests, he does not mention any female pastors in his ancient Chiliasm Church, which was also a lineage of the Apostles.

"2Again, handing mixed cups to the **women**, he bids them consecrate these in his presence. When this has been done, he himself produces another cup of much larger size than that which the **deluded woman has consecrated**, ... Repeating certain other like words, and **thus goading on the wretched woman [to madness]**, he then appears a worker of wonders when the large cup is seen to have been filled out of the small one, so as even to overflow by what has been obtained from it. By accomplishing several other similar things, **he has completely deceived many**, and drawn them away after him." [980]

Interestingly, in this incident, St. Irenaeus of Lyons makes a perplexing claim: that this heretic who was ordaining women priests could also predict some things that came true, but only with the assistance of demons. Irenaeus then goes on to describe that this heretic runs some sort of "prophecy classes," encouraging these ladies to 'say something' in order to make them enthusiastic enough to believe they are now some sort of prophetess.

"3. It appears probable enough that **this man possesses a demon** as his familiar spirit, by means of whom he seems **able to prophesy**, and also enables as many as he counts worthy to be partakers of his Charis themselves to prophesy. **He devotes himself especially to women**, ... Behold Charis has descended upon you; **open your mouth and prophesy**. On the woman replying, I have never at any time prophesied, nor do I know how to prophesy; then engaging, for the second time, in certain invocations, so as to astound his deluded victim, he says to her, **Open your mouth, speak whatsoever occurs to you, and you shall prophesy**. She then, vainly puffed up and elated by these words, and greatly excited in soul by the expectation that it is herself who is to prophesy, her heart beating violently [from emotion], reaches the requisite pitch of audacity, and idly as well as impudently **utters**

---

[979] Tertullian. *On the Veiling of Virgins*. Chapter 9. www.newadvent.org/fathers/0403.htm

[980] St. Irenaeus of Lyons. *Against Heresies*. Book 1. Chapter 13. Point 2. www.newadvent.org/fathers/0103113.htm

some nonsense as it happens to occur to her, such as might be expected from one heated by an empty spirit." [981]

In contrast, Irenaeus' chiliasm church is likely the only place on credible record in early Christianity where the dead have been raised since the time of Christ and his apostles.

"Wherefore, also, those who are in truth His disciples, receiving grace from Him, do in His name perform [miracles], so as to promote the welfare of other men, according to the gift which each one has received from Him. For some do certainly and truly drive out devils, so that those who have thus been cleansed from evil spirits frequently both believe [in Christ], and join themselves to the Church. Others have foreknowledge of things to come: they see visions, and utter prophetic expressions. Others still, heal the sick by laying their hands upon them, and they are made whole. Yea, moreover, **as I have said, the dead even have been raised up, and remained among us for many years**. And what shall I more say? It is not possible to name the number of the gifts which the Church, [scattered] throughout the whole world, has received from God, in the name of Jesus Christ," [982]

Other church fathers have made statements against women priesthood [983], but I don't intend to include them here because I'm only interested in the chiliasm church fathers for the sake of doctrine accuracy. The reason certain church fathers haven't made statements about this topic—or really, about any topic—is that either they were unaware of such opposing practices or their writings on the subject may have been lost.

Here are some Bible scriptures that prove that all Christians are kings and priests, meaning that a non-king and non-priest in the final new earth setting could be a non-elect salvation option (assuming all these interpretations are correct).

"But you are a chosen generation, a royal **priesthood**, a holy nation, His own special people, that you may proclaim the praises of Him who called you out of darkness into His marvelous light;" (1 Peter 2:9, NKJV)

---

[981] Ibid., Point 3.
[982] St. Irenaeus of Lyons. *Against Heresies*. Book 2. Chapter 32. Point 4. www.newadvent.org/fathers/0103232.htm
[983] Catholic Source. *What the Early Church Believed: Women and the Priesthood*. www.catholic.com/tract/women-and-the-priesthood

> "5and from Jesus Christ, the faithful witness, the firstborn from the dead, and the ruler over the kings of the earth. To Him who [b]loved us and washed us from our sins in His own blood, 6and has **made us [c]kings and priests** to His God and Father, to Him be glory and dominion forever and ever. Amen." (Revelation 1:5–6, NKJV)

> "9And they sang a new song, saying: "You are worthy to take the scroll, And to open its seals; For You were slain, And have redeemed us to God by Your blood Out of every tribe and tongue and people and nation, 10And have **made [d]us kings[e] and priests** to our God; And [f]we shall reign on the earth." (Revelation 5:9–10, NKJV)

Note that all Christians are priests, which indicates that all Christians participate in Christ's first resurrection and his 1000-year Millennial Reign (Revelation 20:5-6, pages 83, 105). Lord Jesus Christ literally preached the 1000-year (Millennial) reign for the "age" to come (literally *Aeon* in Koine Greek or *Olam* in Hebrew, its equivalent) in these verses:

> "34Jesus answered and said to them, "The sons of this age marry and are given in marriage. 35But those who are counted **worthy to attain that age**, and the **resurrection from the dead**, neither marry nor are given in marriage; 36nor can they die anymore, for they are equal to the angels and are sons of God, being sons of the resurrection." (Luke 20:34–36, NKJV)

> "12Then He also said to him who invited Him, "When you give a dinner or a supper, do not ask your friends, your brothers, your relatives, nor rich neighbors, lest they also invite you back, and you be repaid. 13But when you give a feast, invite the poor, the [d]maimed, the lame, the blind. 14And you will be blessed, because they cannot repay you; for you shall be repaid at the **resurrection of the just**." (Luke 14:12–14, NKJV)

We know that the resurrection referred to here is the first resurrection context for Luke 14 because St. Irenaeus (pages 38, 372) and Tertullian (pages 370-371, 387) both mention it in this context.

Appendix XII: Chiliasm Prophecy Extension – An Example of My Interpolation

This chapter is describing Christ's Second Coming:

"4And in that day **His feet** will stand on the Mount of Olives, Which faces Jerusalem on the east. And the **Mount of Olives shall be split in two,** From east to west, Making a very large valley; Half of the mountain shall move toward the north And half of it toward the south." (Zechariah 14:4, NKJV) [984]

Christ's Second Coming marks the First Resurrection, as all saints (not just some) return with Him.

"5Then you shall flee through My mountain valley, For the mountain valley shall reach to Azal. Yes, you shall flee As you fled from the earthquake In the days of Uzziah king of Judah. Thus **the Lord my God will come,** And **all the saints with [c]You.**" (Zechariah 14:5, NKJV)

During the commencement of the Millennium, the renewed old earth and heavens exhibit some remarkable new physical changes as well.

"6It shall come to pass **in that day** That there will be no light; The [d]lights will diminish. 7It shall be one day Which is known to the Lord— Neither day nor night. But at evening time it shall happen That it will be light." (Zechariah 14:6–7, NKJV)

Christians are the only ones who can partake in the "living waters" (or "water of life"), as they are the only ones in the final sinless human resurrection body in the Chiliasm timeline now (compare with Revelation 7 in pages 382-385 earlier). However, an earthly allegorical water of life (not the real one) also forms for mortals during Christ's Millennial Reign (compare with Ezekiel verses in pages 103 & 105-106 prior). Also, the whole earth would physically know "who the real God is" (namely, Lord Jesus Christ),

---

[984] Compare: Acts 1:11–12, "11who also said, "Men of Galilee, why do you stand gazing up into heaven? This same Jesus, who was taken up from you into heaven, will so come in like manner as you saw Him go into heaven."12Then they returned to Jerusalem from the mount called Olivet, which is near Jerusalem, a Sabbath day's journey" (NKJV).

since His Second Coming recently occurred, followed by all these new physical restoration and renewal of the earth.

> "8And **in that day** it shall be That **living waters** shall flow from Jerusalem, Half of them toward [e]the eastern sea And half of them toward [f]the western sea; In both summer and winter it shall occur. 9And the **Lord shall be King over all the earth**. In that day it shall be— "The Lord is one," And His name one." (Zechariah 14:8–9, NKJV)

The interesting part is that mortals (sinners) exist in this timeline, proving conclusively that this is not the *Great White Throne Judgment Day* but rather a time before that, as sinful human beings coexist with the first resurrection Christian immortals (i.e. all saints mentioned in Zechariah 14:5 earlier) during this time. Even so, God punishes disobedient nations fairly and allows free will to exist for some of them who are allowed to live even when they do not submit to God, as prophet Zechariah describes next regarding those who are left of all the nations (some of whom even came up against Jerusalem but God has forgiven and let them live), indicating the clear existence of mortal/sinners as survivors, which also means that the *earth and its works burned up prophecy* (2 Peter 3:10, page 169) refers to selected judgment and physical renewal of earth whose "end result" is seen as follows:

> "16And it shall come to pass that everyone **who is left of all the nations which came against Jerusalem** shall go up from year to year to worship the King, the Lord of hosts, and to keep the Feast of Tabernacles. 17And it shall be that whichever of the families of the earth do not come up to Jerusalem to worship the King, the Lord of hosts, on them there will be no rain. 18If the family of Egypt will not come up and enter in, they shall have no rain; they shall receive the plague with which the Lord strikes the nations who do not come up to **keep the Feast of Tabernacles.** 19This shall be the [i]punishment of Egypt and the punishment of all the nations that do not come up to keep the Feast of Tabernacles." (Zechariah 14:16–19, NKJV)

In Chiliasm, the Feast of Tabernacles fulfillment happens in the coming millennium (e.g. see St. Methodius' quote in pages 70-71 & 112 earlier). The final part of Christ's 1000-year Millennial Reign is not written in Zechariah 14's prophecy above, but rather in the New Testament's Book of Revelation, as follows (which means we sometimes have to combine different parts of the Bible to get a better view of the prophecies because certain verses may be describing a specific aspect while others may be describing other details that are not mentioned in the earlier verses):

"2He laid hold of the dragon, that serpent of old, who is the Devil and Satan, and bound him for a thousand years; 3and he cast him into the bottomless pit, and shut him up, and set a seal on him, so that he should deceive the nations no more till the thousand years were finished. But after these things he must be released for a little while. ... 7Now when the thousand years have expired, Satan will be released from his prison 8and will go out to deceive the nations which are in the four corners of the earth, Gog and Magog, to gather them together to battle, whose number is as the sand of the sea. 9They went up on the breadth of the earth and surrounded the camp of the saints and the beloved city. And fire came down from God out of heaven and devoured them. 10The devil, who deceived them, was cast into the lake of fire and brimstone where[b] the beast and the false prophet are. And they will be tormented day and night forever and ever." (Revelation 20:2–3, 7–10, NKJV)

Notice that Satan did not deceive these nations (Revelation 20:3) throughout the Millennium. This implies that the earlier disobedience of some of these nations prophesied by prophet Zechariah was solely due to human free will. Also, by the time Satan did one last deception for these sinners (mortals) of the Millennial Reign (Revelation 20:7-9) and was tossed into the Lake of Fire (Revelation 20:10), both the beast and false prophet had already been burning for 1000 years since Christ's Second Coming. [985]

Take note that those of the First Resurrection, i.e. all saints (Revelation 20:9), are in the Millennium's earthly rebuilt Jerusalem. A conceivable rationale for how Revelation 20's last rebellion and deceit above occurs is with Satan as 'liberator', as I deduce from that Satan will be visible; otherwise, how will he deceive those nations at that time? Also, he will probably say something like, "He (Satan) is the real Christ because he resurrected or escaped the bottomless pit so is more powerful and was humbling himself to test and see who will remain loyal to him for 1000 years," and such a lie will easily be believed by those "sinners" among the "nations" who get jealous

---

[985] Revelation 19:11 – 13, 19 – 20, "11Now I saw heaven opened, and behold, a white horse. And He who sat on him was called Faithful and True, and in righteousness He judges and makes war. 12His eyes were like a flame of fire, and on His head were many crowns. He [e]had a name written that no one knew except Himself. 13He was clothed with a robe dipped in blood, and His name is called The Word of God. ... 19And I saw the beast, the kings of the earth, and their armies, gathered together to make war against Him who sat on the horse and against His army. 20Then the beast was captured, and with him the false prophet who worked signs in his presence, by which he deceived those who received the mark of the beast and those who worshiped his image. These two were cast alive into the lake of fire burning with brimstone." (NKJV).

with mortal Israel, the chosen ruling nation at that time during this 1000 years with Christian human immortals (who have perfect sinless bodies, possibly like Adam, the first man had 'before the fall' to fulfil God's Will for that "state of existence" during this Millennium) who participate in the First Resurrection (note that all of this occurs after Christ's Second Coming described in Revelation 19).

In the end, despite the "great numbers" these nations collect as a 'army' at that time to try encircle that earthly Jerusalem to destroy it, this deceit fails horribly, and God just sends "fire" from heaven and destroys them as a whole. Next, *Judgment Day* begins literally in chronological timeline order for these parts in the Book of Revelation like thus (note carefully that Judgment Day can only occur in a timeline where there are no more sinners or humans on the earth):

> "11Then I saw a great white throne and Him who sat on it, from whose face the earth and the heaven fled away. And there was found no place for them. 12And I saw the dead, small and great, standing before [c]God, and books were opened. And another book was opened, which is the Book of Life. And the dead were judged according to their works, by the things which were written in the books. 13The sea gave up the dead who were in it, and Death and Hades delivered up the dead who were in them. And they were judged, each one according to his works. 14Then Death and Hades were cast into the lake of fire. This is the second [d]death. 15And anyone not found written in the Book of Life was cast into the lake of fire." (Revelation 20:11–15, NKJV)

Here's a personal Chiliasm extension note regarding Tertullian: Tertullian's one major flaw that kept him from being sainted was that he followed Montanism. Since it was "new," as no other known Church Father had regarded Montanism as a possibility of truth, he dubbed it the "New Prophecy." In my view, Montanism is unquestionably incorrect. To clarify Tertullian's words, let us break them down:

To begin, here's the quote without *Montanism's New Prophecy* part:

> "But we do confess that a **kingdom is promised to us upon the earth, although before heaven**, only in **another state of existence**; inasmuch as it will be after the **resurrection** for a **thousand years** in the divinely-built city of Jerusalem, let down from heaven, Revelation 21:2 which the apostle also calls our mother from above; Galatians 4:26 and, while declaring that our πολίτευμα, or citizenship, is in heaven, he predicates of it that it is really a city in heaven. This both Ezekiel had knowledge of Ezekiel 48:30-35 and the Apostle John beheld. Revelation

> 21:10-23 ... We say that this city has been provided by God for receiving the saints on their resurrection, and refreshing them with the abundance of all really spiritual blessings, as a recompense for those which in the world we have either despised or lost; since it is both just and God-worthy that His servants should have their joy in the place where they have also suffered affliction for His name's sake. Of the **heavenly kingdom** this is the process." [986]

Tertullian plainly states that Christ's earthly Millennial Reign is literal and distinct from the heavenly kingdom, which will be established at the end of the 1000-year period, as detailed on Page 68.

Now, here is that *Montanism New Prophecy* part:

> "And the word of the **new prophecy** which is a part of our belief, attests how it foretold that there would be for a sign a picture of this very city exhibited to view previous to its manifestation. This prophecy, indeed, has been very lately fulfilled in an expedition to the East. For it is evident from the testimony of even heathen witnesses, that in Judæa there was suspended in the sky a city early every morning for forty days. As the day advanced, the entire figure of its walls would wane gradually, and sometimes it would vanish instantly." [987]

Here, Tertullian is undoubtedly paraphrasing Montanus or someone from Montanism who promised that this heavenly new Jerusalem city would be visible in the sky for forty days. It should be noted that although Tertullian has never personally witnessed that event, he references those who have, including pagan people, claimed to have "seen it." That's all. It's highly probably that these witnesses saw a scientific phenomenon known as *Fata Morgana* (mirage), which is a type of mirage that basically projects a distorted reflection of a real object even in the sky!

This is significant evidence from Tertullian himself that he was caught away by the *claim* of seeing the *heavenly new Jerusalem city* by others (not by himself) and believed it since it corresponded to established Christian prophesy that existed. As an analogy, if a Roman Catholic claims to have seen a vision of eternal torment as well as the virgin Mary, which agrees with the Roman Catholic belief today, they may believe the claim to be true.

---

[986] Tertullian. *Against Marcion*. Book 3. Chapter 25. www.newadvent.org/fathers/03123.htm
[987] Ibid.

Similarly, a Pentecostal may believe in a claim made by their "prophet" if he or she claims to have visited the spirit world and witnessed a vision of eternal torment, as well as pre-tribulation rapture events, because they generally agree with both of these viewpoints. Even if the "vision" proves to be "false," both the Roman Catholics and Pentecostals quoted in analogy here will continue to believe their core doctrines regardless, and likewise, Tertullian's *New Prophecy* error earlier does not diminish the other Chiliasm prophecy quotes that exist independently of it.

Notice also that this New Prophecy quote does not refer to anything other than the "existence" of the "New Jerusalem City," implying that the New Prophecy has "nothing" to do with, say, the Chiliasm prophecy of the change from human to angelic at the end of the Millennium, etc., because Tertullian does not quote nor link them at all.

Appendix XIII: Non-Elect Salvation Possibility for Servant Rank in Chiliasm

In his enigmatic contrast remark below, St. Justin of Rome might have taught non-elect salvation levels of servants as being distinct and considerably lower than sons, where the latter is solely for Christians now (together with Old Testament faithful):

> "Attend therefore to what I say. The marriages of Jacob were types of that which Christ was about to accomplish. For it was not lawful for Jacob to marry two sisters at once. And he serves Laban for [one of] the daughters; and being deceived in [the obtaining of] the younger, he again served seven years. Now Leah is your people and synagogue; but Rachel is our Church. And for these, and for the servants in both, Christ even now serves. For while Noah gave to the two sons the seed of the third as servants, now on the other hand Christ has come to restore both the free sons and the servants among them, conferring the same honour on all of them who keep His commandments; even as the children of the free women and the children of the bond women born to Jacob were all sons, and equal in dignity. And it was foretold what each should be according to rank and according to fore-knowledge. Jacob served Laban for speckled and many-spotted sheep; and Christ served, even to the slavery of the cross, for the various and many-formed races of mankind, acquiring them by the blood and mystery of the cross. Leah was weak-eyed; for the eyes of your souls are excessively weak. Rachel stole the gods of Laban, and has hid them to this day; and we have lost our paternal and material gods. Jacob was hated for all time by his brother; and we now, and our Lord Himself, are hated by you and by all men, though we are brothers by nature. Jacob was called Israel; and Israel has been demonstrated to be the Christ, who is, and is called, Jesus." [988]

Salvation rank of elect salvation here [interpolation mine]:

> "but **Rachel** is our **Church**. And for these [**Church**], ... Christ even now serves. For while Noah gave to the two **sons** ... now on the other hand Christ has come to restore both the **free sons** ..., conferring the same honour on all of them who keep His commandments; even as the

---

[988] St. Justin of Rome. *Dialogue with Trypho*. Chapter 134.
www.newadvent.org/fathers/01289.htm

children of the free women .... And it was foretold what each should be according to rank and according to fore-knowledge." [989]

If these lines are interpreted literally, the Church (Rachel or free women) has servants and sons level salvation ranks. This "level" is determined by their ability to "keep His Commandments". My interpolation here is that the servants' level could be non-elect salvation because they did not achieve the requisite thirtyfold level of obedience required to become part of "His bride (sons of God)," as just a *few* make it through this rigorous elect salvation in comparison.

Next, salvation rank of non-elect salvation here [interpolation mine]:

> "Now **Leah** is **your people** [unbelieving Jews] and **synagogue** [non-Christians]; ..., And for these [Church, implied in comparison of] and for the **servants in both** [Church and Synagogue], Christ even now serves. ... the seed of the third as **servants**, ... and the **servants** among them [among the Church and Synagogue], conferring the same honour on all of them who keep His commandments... and the children of the **bond women** born to Jacob were all sons, and equal in dignity. And it was foretold what each should be according to **rank** and according to fore-knowledge." [990]

Non-Elect Salvation appears to be a lesser rank for individuals who demonstrate servant-level obedience to His Commandments. To be ranked at the "His sons" level, one must unquestionably believe in Christ.

What is the "equality" meant here in regard to all being sons? [interpolation mine]

> "now on the other hand Christ has come to restore both the free sons [Elect Salvation] and the servants [Non Elect Salvation] among them, conferring the same honour on all of them who keep His commandments; even as the children of the free women [Elect Salvation] and the children of the bond women [Non Elect Salvation] born to Jacob were all sons [earthly context due to obeying God's Commands in some way], and equal in dignity [fair chance of being honoured by God]. And it was foretold what each should be according to rank [Elect vs Non Elect Salvation] and according to fore-knowledge [of God, His Predestination]." [991]

---

[989] Ibid.
[990] Ibid.
[991] Ibid.

St. Justin of Rome's classification of "sons versus servants" in salvation context mirrors that of St. Gregory Nazianzus, who also has this strange quote where he writes,

> "I know of three classes among the saved; the slaves, the hired servants, the sons."[992]

Now, since all those of elect salvation are "sons of God" and all Christians are saved in the marriage of the Lamb during the first resurrection in Chiliasm timeline, the hired servants could be Israel's non-elect salvation, while the slaves could be the gentiles' non-elect salvation as the 'surprised sheep' of the nations, if Matthew 25 is viewed as a judgment summary for this entire 1000-year (Millennial) reign of Christ. Christ also referred to Christians as servants at first, but as they obey His will, they get to know Him and are no longer servants, but friends.

> "14You are **My friends** if you do whatever I command you. **15No longer do I call you servants,** for a servant does not know what his master is doing; but I have called you friends, for all things that I heard from My Father I have made known to you." (John 15:14–15, NKJV)

This is consistent with Matthew 25:1-13's parable of the 5 wise and 5 foolish virgins because it is about the wedding of the Lamb and how real Christians become His bride and share one flesh with Him in some way (a great mystery, Ephesians 5:31-32). These interpolations are consistent with the final scene (Revelation 21 and 22, which are the "last chapters" of the Bible scriptures) which refers to the elect salvation as the *bride* exclusively.

However, keep in mind that, just as Matthew 25:14-46 refers to the salvation of the rest as servants or just righteous from the nations ("Gentiles"), the verse earlier in John 15:14-15 can mean that they are called such because they do not know His will (hence "servants", right?) which could imply that these are possibly "non-Christians" and this same label is carried forward in the final scene, likewise (neither called bride; see pages 96 and 182 prior).

My interpolations, along with St. Justin of Rome and St. Gregory Nazianzus' wordings, align with Galatians 4's Bible verses, which clearly distinguish between "slave" and "son" in the context of Salvation. Even non-Christians are referred to as "slaves" in this context. Galatians 4:1, 3 indicates a slave (servant) being under this world's elements and bondage, but when

---

[992] St. Gregory Nazianzus. *Oration 40*. Chapter 13. Point 13. www.newadvent.org/fathers/310240.htm

he trusts in Christ, he becomes a "son" (Christian, Galatians 4:4-7), where the former does not inherit the kingdom while the latter inherits it:

> "1Now I say that the **heir**, as long as he is a **child**, does not differ at all from a **slave**, though he is master of all, 2but is under guardians and stewards until the time appointed by the father. 3Even so we, when we were children, were in **bondage** under the elements of the world. 4But when the fullness of the time had come, God sent forth His Son, born[a] of a woman, born under the law, 5to redeem those who were under the law, that we might receive the **adoption as sons**. 6And because you are **sons**, God has sent forth the Spirit of His Son into your hearts, crying out, [b]"Abba, Father!" 7Therefore you are **no longer a slave but a son**, and if a son, then an heir [c]of God [d]through Christ." (Galatians 4:1–7, NKJV)

In light of Bible verses such as the one below (next), those "slaves" saved following the second resurrection mentioned below in Chiliasm chronology could thus be non-elect salvation since they govern the last new earth as the term city is specified here (which is more detailed than Matthew 25:31-46) where some could be saved as regulars or members of the nations of those who are saved, as we previously observed (meaning they are not kings and priests like Christians and, in general, cannot even enter heaven):

> "12Therefore He said: "A certain nobleman went into a far country to receive for himself a kingdom and to return. ... 15"And so it was that when he returned, having received the kingdom, he then commanded these **servants**, to whom he had given the money, to be called to him, that he might know how much every man had gained by trading. 16Then came the first, saying, 'Master, your mina has earned ten minas.' 17And he said to him, 'Well done, good servant; because you were faithful in a very little, have **authority over ten cities**.' 18And the second came, saying, 'Master, your mina has earned five minas.' 19Likewise he said to him, 'You also be over **five cities**.'" (Luke 19:12, 15–19, NKJV)

Example of more interpolations I made: The *far country* in Luke 19:12 above is the present-day Old Heavens, and it describes the Millennial Reign *kingdom* that Christ and His Bride (Christians) receive during the Marriage of the Lamb. After 1000 years, Christ returns and judges the servants (Israel) for how they ruled over the (old) earth nations, fulfilling all Old Testament Jewish prophecies relating to mortal earth and mortal man, and at the end, gives them a city to rule in that final new earth (so "possibly," these are part of the servant rankings both St. Justin of Rome and St. Gregory Nazianzus were discussing earlier).

Now, if they rule a city in that final new earth (as implied by the Chiliasm timeline), wouldn't there be a normal non-city-ruler, non-king, non-priest but saved person among those final "nations of those saved"? [ruled over by these faithful ones] as mentioned in Revelation 21:24-27 earlier who could be the even lower rank of this non-elect salvation. Matthew 25:31-46 relates to the same Judgment but for Gentiles ("nations") from all time during the second resurrection, in which some are saved and some are damned.

We must remember that different Bible scriptures may convey different sorts of final judgment, as we can see from Chiliasm church father quotes too, and so, we may attempt to interpolate a possible model like this. The only ones who be slaughtered at the end of this judgment timeline are those citizens who did not want Christ to rule over them (by their own free will choice), paralleling the last rebellion depicted in the Book of Revelation 20:7–9.

> "27But bring here those enemies of mine, who did not want me to reign over them, and slay them before me." (Luke 19:27, NKJV)

The passages in this Appendix, together with those by St. Justin of Rome and St. Gregory Nazianzus, may support a few types of non-elect salvation (see pages 31, 113, and 319-320).

Appendix XIV: Christian Apologetics Answers – Why believe in Christ?

"Lord, to whom shall we go? You have the words of eternal life…" (John 6:68, UASV Bible)

Question 1

Can someone who was never baptized be a Christian?

My Reply 1

If a person never had the opportunity of hearing the Gospel in their lifetime, they could be considered the "Elect" (or Christian) if they lived by a moral code which only God judges fairly. However, for those who heard the gospel and rejected it or never got baptized, I studied a different possible salvation for them called "Non Elect Salvation" which is discussed throughout this book and especially in chapter 1.

Question 2

What can we learn from Paul's sufferings?

My Reply 2

I think apostle Paul answered the question by himself when he wrote, "For I consider that the sufferings of this present time are not worthy to be compared with the glory which shall be revealed in us" (Romans 8:18, NKJV). The reason is that the more you suffer for Christ be it direct or indirect discriminations etc. by the enemies of the faith or even from envy of those within the faith, you stand to get greater final reward and resurrection body glory as this verse confirms likewise, "Others were tortured, not accepting deliverance, that they might obtain a better resurrection" (Hebrews 11:35, NKJV).

I expounded in detail some new research in this book regarding this aspect of resurrection body glory and gradation which may have been overlooked for centuries.

Question 3

Can Christians lose their salvation? If yes or no, what is the reason?

My Reply 3

Christ clearly denies some Christians in Matthew 7:21 - 23 despite their claims of "prophecy, miracles and wonders done in His Name". The reason He gives is "Lawlessness" and the remedy mentioned is immediately stated as "hear His Word and Obey it" (His Commands, in the immediate Matthew 7:24).

Question 4

If God is perfect, why did he create hell?

My Reply 4

Contrary to current prevailing popular views, there seems to be two ways Hell affects those Judged, one group unto purification and the other group unto everlasting destruction as the study in this book points. These are not for Christians. Christians escape the afterlife Judgment of Hell and come into the blessed comfort regions of the Spirit World (Hades) as the Story of the Rich Man and Lazarus by Lord Jesus Christ also prove.

Question 5

Is understanding Christian theology required to become a Christian?

Reply 5

Yes, because you cannot love God more without knowing more accurately about Him, which is what Theology aims to do. Some Christians reject theology and prefer worship etc. but Christ Himself clearly refuted this and said that accurate theology is more important than even worshipping God when He declared, "in vain they worship Me, Teaching as doctrines the commandments of men" (Mark 7:7, NKJV). Where the threshold is for our worship to be vain or still accepted but lesser in value, God alone knows.

We strive to increase in accuracy via studying the Bible with early Church Father's quotes especially in areas of prophecy since it is Written that, "For the testimony of Jesus is the spirit of prophecy." (Revelation 19:10, NKJV). Apart from that, accuracy in obeying which commands apply to Gentile believers under the New Testament and which does not also plays a role for "doctrine" part. I particularly discussed this in the chapter on 5 Wise and 5 Foolish virgins in this book.

Question 6

Can people leave hell and come to heaven if they are good?

My Reply 6

The problem is no one is good except God. If a person is good, they will have the ability to remain sinless. Since no human can remain sinless, they cannot be good. God in Flesh, Lord Jesus Christ alone walked the earth sinless as the Bible testifies. The level of human psychological deception increases in proportion to their innate assumption that "they are good".

In simple words, the more depraved and sinful a person is within, the reverse psychology often takes hold to pacify the natural conscience guilt God has given every man to realize this and they live in denial and find comfort in "assuming that they are good" to "feel better" and are locked in that sinful mindset. The only ones who can attain true goodness in some human measure are those who first acknowledge that they are sinners and rely on God's grace to do His commands. Yes, God gives grace to the humble and He works in them to do good works.

Now, for your question, no one can leave hell because no one is good there. Christ alone can decide this by His Mercy which I explored with early Christian orthodox quotes to view certain Bible verses differently in order to see if any could be saved from Hell and enter a lower grade salvation different from the Christian salvation.

Question 7

My 12-year-old son went to camp. Now he said we all need to receive Jesus or we will not be saved from hell. What do you think?

My Reply 7

Your 12 year old son is right. Similar claims are also made in other major religions apart from Christianity and if you can tolerate them, you can tolerate Christians too making this same claim. However, it's your personal choice to believe in Christ or in another religion which claims likewise. For me, believing in Christ alone leads to eternal life without any Spirit World Judgment, which is the Elect Salvation.

Regarding being saved from Hell post judgment for "some" (not all), I remain neutral since my recent research into this topic of Non-Elect Salvation Possibility with early authoritative writings from leaders of the Church just decades away from the apostles themselves seem to support this in various ways. This book details various aspects to bring such a matter to light. This, however, needs to be approached cautiously as a possibility and not doctrine since it cannot be confirmed with 100% certainty and so, that's honesty with evidence.

Question 8

Should Christians enforce their beliefs on others who don't share their beliefs?

My Reply 8

This is a popular misunderstanding. Every parent also enforces their beliefs upon a child who is born religion-less, right? I mean when a parent teaches their children their culture or language supremacy or race-bias claims etc., aren't they doing the same thing even if not in religion-context? Even an atheist when he teaches his children "his own ways" is enforcing it likewise on his children. My point is this: everybody is enforcing their own beliefs (be it religious or non-religious ones on others) knowingly or unknowingly via their opinions or practice on spiritual matters in daily life within family and without.

In light of this simple logical fact, all humans are thus equal in that part. However, one day, after we die, every man is going to give account to God. Now, please consider this for a moment: 'You meet God on Judgment Day. Now, imagine that His opening lines are, "why did you call that … as God?" You claim that you honestly assumed so and did not know who the real God was. God Replies, "If you really did not know who the real God was, then why did you assume so, even living a life of discrimination toward those who did?'

Conclusion here: It's okay to preach your religion where if you are right, you will rewarded by God and if you're wrong, likewise you will be judged by God for that part and also for the part where you discriminated those who were right. We will know this after we die and so, love one another since it covers a multitude of sins (1 Peter 4:8) even within same denomination instead of being dogmatic lest if we are wrong, we are condemned likewise or lose rewards for our actions. May God have Mercy on whomever He Wills.

Question 9

Do you believe that Jesus is coming back soon for Judgement Day?

My Reply 9

In the earliest testimony of Church Fathers on eschatology, we find the Chiliasm timeline clearly revealed. Lord Jesus' second coming occurs after the reign and tribulation enforced by the last Antichrist destroying him and after that, the 1000 years (millennial reign of Christ) follows. Christians will participate in the first resurrection (Revelation 20:1–6) together with some mortals until a final rebellion at the end of this millennium with Satan performing one last deception after being released from the bottomless pit but all those are destroyed with fire from heaven and Judgment Day begins only after all this as the Book of Revelation describes this chronologically in chapter 20. I have studied this Chiliasm prophecy model and even explored possibilities and interpolations together with it in my journal papers and more so in this book.

Question 10

Can people go to heaven if they follow the Ten Commandments but doesn't know Jesus?

My Reply 10

I devoted an entire chapter in this book (chapter 8) studying this Jewish possibility regarding the "righteous Gentiles" theory who also get a part of the world to come (Olam Ha-ba). I use Christ's reply in Matthew 19 to support this possibility. However, not all 10 commandments apply to Gentiles excluding the Sabbath as church fathers taught including protestant reformers. Also, only the commandments relating to man may qualify such ones to a lower grade salvation (details of proof quotes and sources for this interpolation together with further discussion points supporting it are found in chapter 8).

Question 11

Will children burn in hell forever?

My Reply 11

Children don't burn in hell forever. Unfortunately, such misunderstanding is found amongst some of the most famous preachers in both the protestant movements and in later church fathers. Consider this: Christ famously Said to some children (who were most likely unbaptized and were of a certain 'able to walk' age):

"Let the little children come to Me, and do not forbid them; for of such is the kingdom of heaven." (Matthew 19:14, NKJV).

So, where is the threshold age for someone to be considered a child or not? Only God knows but this passage demonstrates that He deals rightly even in this topic.

Notice that these children are said not to belong in "limbo" (an intermediate place between heaven and hell, i.e. purgatory type) but rather in "heaven" contradicting many Roman Catholic views on it too where they usually claim even babies only make it to limbo first and only later to heaven.

This means that the children may go to the blessed comfort regions of the spirit world (i.e. the heavenly regions) just like the elect upon their death with their spirit (soul) upon death but require the resurrection body in the first resurrection to enter into the final heavens or further into the heavens as Chiliasm prophecy quotes echo.

Question 12

Why didn't God make the punishment for atheism more severe during life, as that would have discouraged it effectively?

My Reply 12

God cannot be predicted and that's why He is God. Sometimes, God judges evil on this earth itself. However, at other times, we may see a man suffering the things which usually happens to a wicked as some call it 'karma' these days but in reality, that man could be the good guy relatively as opposed to the rich or not suffering man who could be the "real wicked", Bible verses (it takes a wisdom at the level of King Solomon to reveal this in God's Gift to him):

"that there are just men to whom it happens according to the work of the wicked; again, there are wicked men to whom it happens according to the work of the righteous." (Ecclesiastes 8:14, NKJV).

Why? For the righteous there is an eternal reward even if you suffer as a 'working-slave' unjustly due to biased human systems (e.g. Colossians 3:22 -24) while for the wicked, even if they were king-level prosperity on earth leading to a peaceful non-disease death, their end is still utter destruction with terrors in the Spirit World!, Bible verses:

"3For I was envious of the boastful,

When I saw the prosperity of the wicked.

4For there are no [a]pangs in their death,

But their strength is firm.

5They are not in trouble as other men,

Nor are they plagued like other men. ...

7Their [b]eyes bulge with abundance;

They have more than heart could wish.

12Behold, these are the ungodly,

Who are always at ease;

They increase in riches. ... 16When I thought how to understand this,

It was [e]too painful for me—

17Until I went into the sanctuary of God;

Then I understood their end.

18Surely You set them in slippery places;

You cast them down to destruction.

19Oh, how they are brought to desolation, as in a moment!

They are utterly consumed with terrors." (Psalm 73:3–5, 7, 12, 16 - 19, NKJV)

Conclusion here: You cannot judge anyone's spiritual state based on how much money they have in this life? or based on how healthy they are? either since these are not universal indicators according to Holy Scripture. Only God knows who is faithful and who is not. Indeed, for the New Testament, Christ also revealed that the "Sons of Light" are generally "less shrewd" when compared to the "sons of this world" when dealing with "money things" or just "secular matters in general" and so, the "prosperity gospel" claims are all false since some good Christians can be rich while others poor but none are promised either via some "faith or formula" but rather only "time and chance", Bible verses:

"And it is true that the children of this world are more shrewd in dealing with the world around them than are the children of the light." (Luke 16:8, NLT)

"I returned and saw under the sun that— The race is not to the swift, Nor the battle to the strong, Nor bread to the wise, Nor riches to men of understanding, Nor favor to men of skill; But time and chance happen to them all." (Ecclesiastes 9:11, NKJV)

Question 13

How can Christians explain a loving God that can allow the drowning of children and all other disasters? Not trying to be provocative, but truly cannot understand faith without reason.

My Reply 13

Firstly, how is it every time something wrong happens, it's the "Christian God's fault"? Ask yourself first: Were the children who died

Christians? If they were children of atheists or those of other religions, they still died in that natural disaster, right? I mean did becoming an atheist or changing into another religion or doing some protective charm via witchdoctors etc. protect those from their religion (adult or children) from this? Indeed, those from all religions also die globally due to such natural disasters, right? So, this proves that natural disasters and the like happens whether or not we are Christians and wisdom teaches us to try avoid being in the wrong place at the wrong time!

Further explanation: God allowed free will to humankind. Anything can happen to anyone on earth. God is not to be blamed since freewill is a complex web of game theory (a term from Mathematics to describe outcomes). For example, people in an area cut down trees which caused the flash floods and drowned those kids in the recent tragedy. So, aren't the action of those who cut down the trees or those who did not build a better irrigation system to blame? God did not instruct the cutting of trees, neither the birth of those children which is determined by parent's choices or the heavy rain which is also a product of nature as it is or due to increased weather changes attributed to human induced pollutions of some sort into our atmosphere. So, God did not do it!

Say a region on earth is prone to Tsunami or an earthquake or even a Tornado. So, if you build a house there and one day those natural disasters happen and kill your children, is God to blame for it too? In car accidents or machinery failures etc., these are human made machineries and so, human error or mechanical malfunction is always present too causing some to suffer injury or loss of life due to these as well.

Now, how about poverty? The Bible says, "Houses and riches *are* an inheritance from fathers," (Proverbs 19:14) and "A good *man* leaves an inheritance to his children's children" (Proverbs 13:22). So, if you follow the "Christian God's rule", you should only have children if you are able to provide both "houses and riches" to them. If you could not, maybe it was God's sign to "not marry" (which is just a choice). Some get lucky and become rich and are able to provide for their children in the future to this Biblical extent but most don't. In short, we cannot blame God for this hunger and poverty when it is a human decision of the parents who brought a child into the poverty especially when they're already poor and did it anyways. That's how freewill works. God judges at the end of time on Judgment Day. Look at the Jews. Even with the divinely promised child via Abraham, Isaac and Jacob, their population today is about the smallest meaning it's not about breeding recklessly and then blaming God when we find ourselves in poverty and increasing financial burdens due to our own decisions.

Before you ask, let me add one more famous difficulty: namely, how can God allow children and woman to be killed in ancient wars? The rule of judgment was "eye for an eye" where for example, it is written "8O daughter of Babylon, who are to be destroyed, Happy the one who repays you as you have served us! 9Happy the one who takes and dashes Your little ones against the rock!". In these verses, God allows only those who did that first to others to be judged in that way. No good people (be it children or woman) were simply allowed to be killed like that unless their own people had done it toward others first! Imagine if you knew a child in your hand today would one day smash one of your own children, would you rather kill it? This is called foreknowledge of God and sometimes He allowed judgment based on this especially in Israel's ancient wars. Don't rush to blame God for He will reveal all one day! It is to be noted that in the New Testament, Christ disallowed all this even allowing Christians to suffer in the hands of the wicked or enemies without retaliating teaching perfection! (in his famous sermon on the Mount, Matthew 5 to 7). This means a government authority can still bear sword against evil (Romans 13:4) but Christians also have a choice to refrain and suffer voluntarily against evil which will give them greater glory and final reward in heaven (Matthew 5:19).

Question 14

Is the Holy Spirit a person outside of God?

My Reply 14

The most Blessed Holy Spirit is the Third Person of the most Holy Trinity.

1) Christ clearly commanded Baptism to be done in the name of the Father, Son and Holy Spirit (Matthew 28:19). This is because we need to be baptized in the Name of God. We cannot be baptized in the name of a creation. Hence, the Father, Son and Holy Spirit make up One God in Three distinct Persons. That's how God is and we learn it from Scripture since He is not bound by our limitations of understanding what "one" is. However, there is not a fourth person etc. since Christ specifically revealed only three Names.

2) Another clear instance is seen in Christ's Own Baptism where Lord Jesus Christ was in Flesh, a voice from heaven Spoke and Said, "You are My beloved Son; in You I am well pleased" (Luke 3:22, NKJV) referencing God the Father and at the same time it is written that, " the Holy Spirit descended in bodily form like a dove upon Him" (Luke 3:22, NKJV) proving the distinction of the Three Persons of the Holy Trinity in One God.

3) Apostle Peter uses the name "God" directly to reference the Person of the "Holy Spirit" to whom Ananias lied to in his famous judgment verses in the Acts of Apostles, verses:

"But Peter said, "Ananias, why has Satan filled your heart to lie to the Holy Spirit and keep back part of the price of the land for yourself? ... You have not lied to men but to God." (Acts 5:3 - 4, NKJV)

4) How about the Verses which Describe Christ as "lower" than God the Father or angels or not knowing the Time of His Return?

It's to show that God Fulfills His Commands by Humility (Leadership by Perfect Example of Obedience), Verses:

"... You have heard Me say to you, 'I am going away and coming back to you.' If you loved Me, you would rejoice because I said, 'I am going to the Father,' for My Father is greater than I. ..." - The KING, Most Blessed Lord Jesus Christ (John 14:28, NKJV)

"... But of that day and hour no one knows, not even the angels of heaven, but My Father only. ..." - The KING, Most Blessed Lord Jesus Christ (Matthew 24:36, NKJV)

This being "lower" than angels also was only temporary for Christ as He became Man in Flesh:

"... For You have made him a little lower than the angels, And You have crowned him with glory and honor. ..." (Psalm 8:5, NKJV)

Christ was equal to God the Father but left His God-ship by Humility and made Himself lower than angels and that's why on earth, He Said that the Father was Greater than Him and He didn't know the Time of His Return to Fulfill All Righteousness:

"... 5Let this mind be in you which was also in Christ Jesus, 6who, being in the form of God, did not consider it [b]robbery to be equal with God, ... 11and that every tongue should confess that Jesus Christ is Lord, to the glory of God the Father. ..." (Philippians 2:5, 11, NKJV)

Note: The Equality Spoken of in Verses above is putting Lord Jesus Christ to be equal to God the Father. Can you see these words clearly written in Verse above?

Christ's Descent to be below God the Father was Temporary and His Ascent Eternal.

"... And now, O Father, glorify Me together with Yourself, with the glory which I had with You before the world was. ..."(John 17:5, NKJV)

Comment: Lord Jesus Christ is God in Flesh.

"... Jesus said to them, "Most assuredly, I say to you, before Abraham was, I AM." ..." (John 8:58, NKJV)

"... And God said to Moses, "I AM WHO I AM." And He said, "Thus you shall say to the children of Israel, 'I AM has sent me to you.' " ..." (Exodus 3:14, NKJV)

"... 3without father, without mother, without genealogy, having neither beginning of days nor end of life, but made like the Son of God, remains a priest continually. ..." (Hebrews 7:3, NKJV)

Notice that Hebrews 7:3 Speaks of Christ having even no father nor even beginning of days meaning He is co-Eternal with God the Father.

"... Jesus said to him, "Have I been with you so long, and yet you have not known Me, Philip? He who has seen Me has seen the Father; so how can you say, 'Show us the Father'? ..." (John 14:9, NKJV)

5) Trinity Doctrine in Isaiah 48:16 by God Directly

"... 16"Come near to Me, hear this:

I have not spoken in secret from the beginning;

From the time that it was, I was there.

And now the Lord God and His Spirit

[c]Have sent Me."

17Thus says the Lord, your Redeemer,

The Holy One of Israel:

"I am the Lord your God,

Who teaches you to profit,

Who leads you by the way you should go. ..." (Isaiah 48:16-17, NKJV)

Comments:

i) God the Father = "... And now the Lord God ..." (Isaiah 48:16)

ii) God the Holy Spirit = "... and His Spirit ..." (Isaiah 48:16)

iii) God the Son (Lord Jesus Christ) = "... Have sent Me." ..." (Isaiah 48:16)

iv) The 'First Person' identifying Himself as "Me" in Isaiah 48 is 'not an angel but God and so must be God the Son' in Retrospect of the New Testament Verses which is Identified throughout this Chapter too for example (in Isaiah 48:12), this 'First Person Speaking' Identifies Himself as the "First and Last" just like Christ Identifies Himself with Equivalent Terms, to quote:

"... 12"Listen to Me, O Jacob,

And Israel, My called:

I am He, I am the First,

I am also the Last. ..." (Isaiah 48:12, NKJV)

"... 12Hear me, O Jacob, and Israel whom I call; I am the first, and I endure for ever. ..." (Isaiah 48:12, LXX, Brenton Septuagint Translation)

Please compare with the words "first" and "last" in each of the verses below:

"... 12Then I turned to see the voice that spoke with me. And having turned I saw seven golden lampstands, 13and in the midst of the seven lampstands One like the Son of Man, clothed with a garment down to the feet and girded about the chest with a golden band. ... 17And when I saw Him, I fell at His feet as dead. But He laid His right hand on me, saying [i]to me, "Do not be afraid; I am the First and the Last. 18I am He who lives, and was dead, and behold, I am alive forevermore. Amen. And I have the keys of [j]Hades and of Death. ..." (Revelation 1:12-13, 17 - 18, NKJV)

"... 8"And to the [d]angel of the church in Smyrna write, 'These things says the First and the Last, who was dead, and came to life: 9"I know your works, tribulation, and poverty (but you are rich); and I know the blasphemy of those who say they are Jews and are not, but are a [e]synagogue of Satan. ..." (Revelation 2: 8-10, NKJV)

and

"... 12"And behold, I am coming quickly, and My reward is with Me, to give to every one according to his work. 13I am the Alpha and the Omega, the [f]Beginning and the End, the First and the Last." ... 16"I,

Jesus, have sent My angel to testify to you these things in the churches. I am the Root and the Offspring of David, the Bright and Morning Star." ..." (Revelation 22:14, 16, NKJV)

The "Septuagint" Reads Similarly as follows:

"...16Draw nigh to me, and hear ye these words; I have not spoken in secret from the beginning: when it took place, there was I, and now the Lord, even the Lord, and his Spirit, hath sent me. 17Thus saith the Lord that delivered thee, the Holy One of Israel; I am thy God, I have shewn thee how thou shouldest find the way wherein thou shouldest walk. ..." (Isaiah 48:16-17, LXX, Brenton Septuagint Translation)

Apostle Thomas declared the Risen Christ as both "Lord" and "God":

"And Thomas answered and said to Him, "My Lord and my God!" (John 20:28, NKJV)

Christ Declared Equality with the Father as One and Jews understood it literally that Christ is making Himself equal to God the Father which Christ did not deny:

"30I and My Father are one." 31Then the Jews took up stones again to stone Him. 32Jesus answered them, "Many good works I have shown you from My Father. For which of those works do you stone Me?" 33The Jews answered Him, saying, "For a good work we do not stone You, but for blasphemy, and because You, being a Man, make Yourself God." (John 10:30–33, NKJV)

Question 15

If hell is just the grave, why do so many Christian teachings focus on eternal fire and punishment?

My Reply 15

Hell is not just the grave. The word Hell in English is used to translate a whole bunch of words, which, in the original can mean a few things.

For example, Sheol (Hebrew) = Hades (Greek) = Hell (English). Some think that Sheol is just the grave but it carries another meaning deep into the Spirit World realm as Christ corrected this misunderstanding of some Jews in his famous story of the rich man and Lazarus.

Notice that in Christ's description of Hades (Sheol), He speaks of spirit (souls) being either consciously tormented (rich man) or comforted

(Abraham & poor Lazarus) even before the final bodily judgment. Hence the focus in Christian teachings is right and each man must decide his own fate by responding to the Christian message which they hear.

Whether there is hope or not for "some" (not all) to be purified and be saved after judgment via Hell, remains a mystery. My whole research in journals and a book reveals this as a possibility and not doctrine since we cannot be certain. I also have an academic version of the book coming up which is aimed presenting it in a scholarly manner (details on my profile - will be updated once that's done).

Question 16

What are the key elements of Christian eschatology, and do all Christian denominations believe in all those elements happening?

My Reply 16

My research points to the key Christian eschatology element to be Chiliasm prophecy timeline. Chiliasm refers to believing in a literal 1000 years reign of Christ on this earth following Christ's second coming and Christians' first resurrection.

To model this more accurately, I consulted the writings of three key Chiliasm church fathers namely, St. Irenaeus of Lyons, St. Justin of Rome (Justin Martyr) and Tertullian. I don't say that I have it all right but rather I encourage others to either support or contradict my research using these same writings so that we can better understand the study of prophecy in regard to the last things in Scripture.

Christian denominations differ in the areas of eschatology where for example using 1 Thessalonians 4:17, some believe in pre-tribulation rapture while some believe in mid-tribulation rapture as opposed to others believing in post-tribulation rapture. However, all of them still view 1 Corinthians 15:52 as referring to this same event only while recently (in year 2025), I have endeavored to show that 1 Corinthians 15:52 refers to something entirely different from the rapture event and this happens 1000 years later at the end of the millennial reign of Christ referring to something more remarkable which I published in the respected (3 level peer-reviewed) Journal of Biblical Theology (JBT, Vol 8, no. 3) where a more in depth analysis of it is found in my Christian eschatology book titled "Hope Beyond the Elect" with Christian Publishing House.

Question 17

Why didn't God use his power to get his people out of Egypt?

My Reply 17

If God used His Power in the way that it reflects supernatural interference, the element of faith diminishes. In fact, God did strike Egypt with some extraordinary plagues.

You must understand that if a person has seen more of God's Power, to be fair to all, the requirements of both faith and judgment increases for such persons since "more is given, more is required" (Luke 12:48) and "blessed are those who have not seen yet have believed" (John 20:29) meaning that such individuals are required to live in higher faith and are subject to stricter judgment.

God, in His Mercy, doesn't allow this arbitrarily to protect us unless we can rise to such levels of accountability to experience such level of His direct interference in our life. Even faith (or even "believing after seeing") may be measure in God's wisdom based on this principle as Christ replied, "But I said to you that you have seen Me and yet do not believe" (John 6:36, NKJV).

Note: each question in this Appendix was asked on Quora.com and the author has reproduced only his replies for edification to demonstrate real life apologetics.

May God bless you all with His salvation!

Appendix XV: Typos

Publisher's note: The author of *Hope Beyond the Elect* made a typo on pages 82 and 174 of his original work, which resulted in an unintended connotation that should have read as follows instead:

1) Page 82

i) Typo

He affirms that Christ descended *bodily* into the regions of the dead—"*the shadow of death*"—and will raise His disciples likewise:

ii) Correction

He affirms that Christ descended *in a spirit (soul) state* into the regions of the dead—"*the shadow of death*"—and will raise His disciples likewise:

iii) Explanation

Irenaeus affirms that Christ descended *spirit(soul)-state* into the regions of the dead—"*the shadow of death*"— but later rose *bodily* and only after that, our Lord could ascend into Heaven (i.e. after *bodily resurrection*); likewise, His disciples will undergo both these stages as well in its time.

2) Page 174

i) Typo

If even **wicked servants** and **unbelievers** (Luke 12:46–48) can be assigned different punishments, then some might be **saved by fire**, if God so wills.

ii) Correction

If even **wicked servants** and **unbelievers** (Luke 12:46–48) can be assigned same portion of punishments, then some might be **saved by fire**, if God so wills.

iii) Explanation

The word *different* is changed to *same portion of* in the above.

Bibliography

Ballard, Jordan P. *Defending the Doctrine of Hell. Eleutheria: John W. Rawlings School of Divinity Academic Journal* 8, no. 2 (2025).

Bible. Unless noted, all Scripture is taken from the *New King James Version (NKJV)*. Nashville: Thomas Nelson, 1996, c1982. Other translations used are from biblehub.com.

Borchert, G. L. "Matthew 5:48 – Perfection and the Sermon." *Review & Expositor* 89, no. 2 (1992): 265–269.

Calvin, John. *Institutes of the Christian Religion*. Edited by John T. McNeill. Louisville: Westminster John Knox Press, 1960.

Carter, John W. (Jack). "The Cost of Discipleship." *The American Journal of Biblical Theology* 26, no. 12 (March 3, 2025).

Chien, Dinh Van. "Humanistic Thought in Jesus' Sermon on the Eight Beatens." *Pakistan Journal of Life and Social Sciences* 22, no. 2 (2024): 15165–15170.

Chrysostom, John. *Homily 46 on Matthew*. Translated by George Prevost and revised by M. B. Riddle. In *Nicene and Post-Nicene Fathers*, First Series, Vol. 10. Edited by Philip Schaff. Buffalo, NY: Christian Literature Publishing Co., 1888.

Du Toit, Philip La Grange. "The Radical New Perspective on Paul, Messianic Judaism and Their Connection to Christian Zionism." *HTS Theological Studies* 73, no. 3 (2017): 1–8.

Earnhardt, Matthew P. "Exegetical Study of Matthew 19:16–26." *The American Journal of Biblical Theology* (March 10, 2023).

Feldmeier, R. "As Your Heavenly Father Is Perfect: The God of the Bible and Commandments in the Gospel." *Interpretation* 70, no. 4 (2016): 431–444.

Herberg, Will. "Judaism and Christianity: Their Unity and Difference. The Double Covenant in the Divine Economy of Salvation." *Journal of Bible and Religion* 21, no. 2 (1953): 67–78.

Inserra, Dean. *The Unsaved Christian: Reaching Cultural Christianity with the Gospel*. Chicago: Moody Publishers, 2019.

Irenaeus of Lyons. *Against Heresies*. Translated by Alexander Roberts and William Rambaut. In *Ante-Nicene Fathers*, Vol. 1. Edited by Alexander Roberts, James Donaldson, and A. Cleveland Coxe. Buffalo, NY: Christian Literature Publishing Co., 1885.

Justin of Rome (Justin Martyr). *Dialogue with Trypho*. Translated by Marcus Dods and George Reith. In *Ante-Nicene Fathers*, Vol. 1. Edited by Alexander Roberts, James Donaldson, and A. Cleveland Coxe. Buffalo, NY: Christian Literature Publishing Co., 1885.

———. *The First Apology*. Translated by Marcus Dods and George Reith. In *Ante-Nicene Fathers*, Vol. 1. Edited by Alexander Roberts, James Donaldson, and A. Cleveland Coxe. Buffalo, NY: Christian Literature Publishing Co., 1885.

Kolb, Robert, and Timothy J. Wengert, eds. *The Book of Concord: The Confessions of the Evangelical Lutheran Church*. Minneapolis: Fortress Press, 2000.

Koplitz, Michael. "Hebraic Analysis for Matthew 19:27–30" (2020).

Korver, Bill Fredric. "Biblical Use of Rewards as a Motivation for Christian Service." PhD diss., Liberty University, 2011.

Lactantius. *Divine Institutes*. Translated by William Fletcher. In *Ante-Nicene Fathers*, Vol. 7. Edited by Alexander Roberts, James Donaldson, and A. Cleveland Coxe. Buffalo, NY: Christian Literature Publishing Co., 1886.

MacArthur, John. *Hard to Believe: The High Cost and Infinite Value of Following Jesus*. Nashville, TN: Nelson, 2003.

O'Collins, G. "Difficult Texts: Being Made Perfect According to Matthew 5 and 19." *Theology* 124, no. 6 (2021): 404–409.

Ramachandran, Jonathan. "Non-Elect Salvation Possibility (NESP)." *The American Journal of Biblical Theology* 26, no. 6 (February 9, 2025).

Richardson, James. "Quotes from Early Church Fathers: The Sabbath, Lord's Day, and Worship – Apostles Creed." *Apostles Creed*, August 10, 2016.

Shepherd, Thomas R. "The Parable of the Rich Man and Lazarus: A Narrative-Exegetical Study of Its Relationship to the Afterlife, Wealth, and Poverty – Part 1: The Afterlife." *Journal of the Adventist Theological Society* 32, nos. 1–2 (2021): 171–189.

Stevenson, L. "On the Very Idea of Perfection." *International Journal of Philosophy and Theology* 85, nos. 3–4 (2024): 111–123.

Tanasyah, Yusak. "The Development of Hell from Jewish to Christian Theology: A Biblical Guide to Hell and Its Existence." *QUAERENS: Journal of Theology and Christianity Studies* 4, no. 1 (2022): 27–41.

Tertullian. *A Treatise on the Soul*. Translated by Peter Holmes. In *Ante-Nicene Fathers*, Vol. 3. Edited by Alexander Roberts, James Donaldson, and A. Cleveland Coxe. Buffalo, NY: Christian Literature Publishing Co., 1885.

———. *An Answer to the Jews*. Translated by S. Thelwall. In *Ante-Nicene Fathers*, Vol. 3. Edited by Alexander Roberts, James Donaldson, and A. Cleveland Coxe. Buffalo, NY: Christian Literature Publishing Co., 1885.

———. *On Fasting*. Translated by S. Thelwall. In *Ante-Nicene Fathers*, Vol. 4. Edited by Alexander Roberts, James Donaldson, and A. Cleveland Coxe. Buffalo, NY: Christian Literature Publishing Co., 1885.

Vacendak, Robert. "Is Assurance of Salvation of the Essence of Saving Faith in the Gospel of John?" PhD diss., Rawlings School of Divinity, Liberty University, 2023.

Vaught, Carl G. *The Sermon on the Mount: A Theological Interpretation*. Albany, NY: SUNY Press, 1986.

Vries, Simon John De. *From Old Revelation to New: A Tradition-Historical and Redaction-Critical Study of Temporal Transitions in Prophetic Prediction*. Grand Rapids: Wm. B. Eerdmans Publishing, 1995.

Wood, A. Skevington. "The Eschatology of Irenaeus." *The Evangelical Quarterly* 41, no. 1 (January–March 1969).

www.ingramcontent.com/pod-product-compliance
Lightning Source LLC
Chambersburg PA
CBHW050546160426
43199CB00015B/2560